D1261606

Guide to Financial Reporting and Analysis

Guide to Financial Reporting and Analysis

Eugene E. Comiskey
and
Charles W. Mulford

John Wiley & Sons, Inc.

New York • Chichester • Weinheim • Brisbane • Singapore • Toronto

This publication is designed to provide accurate and authoritative information in regard to the subject matter covered. It is sold with the understanding that the publisher is not engaged in rendering legal, accounting, or other professional services. If legal advice or other expert assistance is required, the services of a competent professional person should be sought.

Library of Congress Cataloging-in-Publication Data:

0471-35425-2

Printed in the United States of America.

10 9 8 7 6 5 4 3 2 1

To our children—Elizabeth, Paul, Patrick, and Mary Comiskey, and Mikey and Steven Mulford—for their good-natured support and tolerance over many years.

About the Authors

Eugene E. Comiskey is the Callaway Professor of Accounting and Charles W. Mulford is Professor of Accounting in the DuPree College of Management at the Georgia Institute of Technology in Atlanta. Both professors have doctorates in accounting and are professionally qualified as certified public accountants. In addition to their work at Georgia Tech, they actively consult with lenders at commercial banks in the United States and abroad. Professors Comiskey and Mulford have published articles on financial reporting and analysis issues in leading academic journals in the accounting and finance fields as well as in such widely read professional journals as the *Commercial Lending Review, Journal of Lending and Credit Risk Management,* and the *Financial Analysts' Journal.* Their first book, *Financial Warnings,* published in 1996, identifies warning signs of future corporate earnings difficulties.

Preface

The complexity of modern-day corporate annual reports has increased markedly in recent years. Over the past 20 years, we have seen significant increases in the absolute length of these documents and in the number of annual report pages devoted to an ever-expanding collection of required footnote disclosures. The growing complexity of annual reports is in large measure attributable to a rapidly changing business environment and the increased complexity of business itself. These changes have been met by a torrent of new financial accounting standards from the Financial Accounting Standards Board (FASB). In recent years, the FASB has issued numerous new standards with far-reaching accounting and disclosure-related consequences in such areas as pensions and postretirement benefits, taxes, investments, business segments, comprehensive income, financial derivatives, and proposals on accounting for mergers and acquisitions. Numerous other new standards are on the drawing board.

Financial analysts, both on the credit side and the equity side, as well as others responsible for evaluating financial performance and financial position, are on the front line and feel the brunt of this combination of a rapidly changing business environment and a dramatic increase in new accounting standards. Ultimately, their job is to determine corporate earning power. However, the financial statement guideposts they have for that purpose are ever changing, almost defying interpretation. For example, some analysts with whom we have worked have gone so far as to say that the approach they use with current income tax disclosures is often to simply skip them, hoping the accounts involved are not important. While we hope such an approach to analysis is the rare exception, we fear that it may not be.

It is in this atmosphere of rapid change and increasing complexity that *Guide to Financial Reporting and Analysis* was written. Our objective is to provide clarity and guidance—to help analysts navigate the maze of modern-day financial reports and enhance their ability to use financial statements effectively in formulating knowledgeable recommendations for action. Because the *Guide*'s focus is on financial analysis as well as financial reporting, the implications of financial reporting practices for analysis are considered to be of equal importance. Consistent with this emphasis, the book uses the assessment of financial quality, an approach to financial analysis whose value is widely recognized, as its organizing theme. In this way, the importance of reporting practices on financial analysis is continually highlighted.

In keeping with the financial quality theme, the financial analysis component of the book is integrated throughout the entire book, as well as emphasized in separate chapters devoted to the income statement, balance sheet, and cash flow statement. In the income statement chapter, net income is recalculated to derive a sustainable earnings base. In the chapter devoted to balance sheet analysis, reported balance sheet amounts are revised to more financially meaningful measures of assets, liabilities, and shareholders' equity. Finally, in the cash flow chapter, recommendations for identifying sustainable and recurring sources of cash flow are provided.

Guide to Financial Reporting and Analysis is anchored in the real world. It is written using examples drawn from hundreds of contemporary corporate annual reports. These are companies that informed readers will recognize. Our findings and recommendations, compiled from these examples, are supplemented with extant research findings drawn from the relevant literature.

We wrote *Guide to Financial Reporting and Analysis* for financial analysts. However, any reader of financial statements will find the book to be not only interesting and informative but also a helpful reference source for future use.

Contents

Chapter 1

Assessing Financial Quality: An Organizing Theme

Help, I am drowning in a sea of complexity!

Those words could be expressed today by any financial statement reader assigned the responsibility of formulating an opinion about a company's financial performance and position. Modern-day financial statements, including accompanying footnotes and supplementary materials, have become very complex. This complexity manifests itself in many ways, including the number of items reported in the financial statements themselves and the quantity and length of the footnotes accompanying them.

A HISTORICAL PERSPECTIVE

Consider, for example, the General Electric Company. A little over 20 years ago, in early 1978, the company published its annual report for the year ended December 31, 1977. That report was 48 pages in length, with four pages devoted to the financial statements themselves—the statement of earnings (income statement), the statement of financial position (balance sheet), the statement of changes in financial position, and the statement of changes in share owners' equity (statement of shareholders' equity)—and 9 pages used for 20 different accompanying footnotes.[1] The remaining sections of the report included such standard annual report enclosures as a letter to shareholders, information on company products and personnel, selected historical financial data, management's discussion and analysis of the company's results of operations and financial position, the independent auditors' report, and a letter from management on its financial responsibilities. In contrast, the company's 1998 annual report, the latest report available to us at the time of this writing, was 69 pages in length. Of these, six pages had now been devoted to the financial statements, not including a statement of shareowners' equity that had been relegated to a footnote. In addition, these financial statements were accompanied by 31 different footnotes consuming 21 pages of text.

Representative of the footnotes in General Electric's 1977 annual report were an accounting policy note; notes on income taxes and employee benefits; notes providing details of selected income statement accounts such as operating costs, other income, and interest expense; and notes providing details of selected balance sheet accounts such as receivables, inventories, investments, property, plant and equipment, other assets, short- and long-term borrowings, and share owners' equity. Also included within the notes was a summarized set of financial statements for General Electric Credit Corporation, which at the time was not consolidated but was accounted for as an investment.

The 1998 report included many of these same footnotes with notable changes and several additions. One key difference was that no longer were the financial statements of General Electric Credit reported in a footnote. Rather, that subsidiary was consolidated with the financial statements of General Electric and had been so since the release of Statement of Financial Accounting Standards (SFAS) No. 94, "Consolidation of All Majority-Owned Subsidiaries" in 1987.[2] Concern about how dissimilar the operations of this finance subsidiary were from those of the parent company led management to resort to an expanded set of financial statements. Such an expanded set was reported in the company's 1998 annual report, where the statement of earnings, statement of financial position, and the statement of cash flows all reported consolidated amounts for General Electric Company and consolidated affiliates and separate consolidating amounts for General Electric Company without the finance subsidiary and General Electric Capital Services.

There were many other differences in the footnotes included with the 1998 report. For example, there was an increase in the number of accounting principles disclosed in the accounting policy note to 14 from 7 in 1977. The employee benefits note was expanded to two separate notes, one on pension benefits and another on retiree health and life benefits.[3] The income tax note was also expanded to provide more detail on the provision for income taxes and on deferred income tax balances.[4] Also added was a separate note on supplemental cash flow information and much greater detail on the company's financial assets and liabilities, including book values, market values, terms, risks, and instruments used to hedge that risk.[5] These footnotes on financial assets and liabilities did much to increase the length and complexity of the company's annual report.

General Electric is certainly not alone among companies reporting financial results with significantly increased complexity. To demonstrate this point, for 10 large companies we compared the 1977 annual reports with their reports for the 1998 fiscal year. This comparison was performed on four measures of annual-report complexity—the total length of the annual report, the number of pages utilized by the primary financial statements, the number of footnotes, and the number of pages used by those footnotes. The results of this comparison are reported in Exhibit 1.1.

As can be seen in the exhibit, average annual report length for the companies surveyed has increased approximately 69 percent since 1977, to an average length of 66 pages from 39. All of these companies devoted more space to the softer side of their reports to shareholders, including more information and pictures focused on company products and services, personnel, and customers. Also growing sig-

Exhibit 1.1. Annual Reports, Then and Now

	Total Annual Report Length in Pages		Number of Financial Statement Pages		Number of Footnotes		Number of Footnote Pages	
	Then	Now	Then	Now	Then	Now	Then	Now
American Express Co.	49	61	4	4	14	18	9	20
AT&T Corp.	37	73	5	4	18	15	6	16
Coca-Cola Co.	24	65	4	5	11	17	5	15
Exxon Corp.	42	55	3	4	18	20[b]	8	11[b]
General Electric Co.	48	69	4	6	20	31	9	21
General Motors Corp.	29	93	3	7	15	24	6	26
IBM Corp.	37	93	4	5	10	25	5	22
Philip Morris Co., Inc.	51	61	5	5	17	17	9	17
Procter & Gamble Co.	27	37	4	5	9	12	4	10
Sears, Roebuck and Co.	45[a]	49	4	4	15	17	7	13
Averages	39	66	4	5	15	20	7	17

[a]Includes 12 pages of separate financial statements and footnotes for Allstate Insurance Co. that were not included in 1998.

[b]Excludes five pages of supplemental information on oil and gas exploration and production activities.

Source: Indicated company's annual report for 1977 (then) and 1998 (now). The number of footnotes and footnote pages include quarterly results and segment data. Multiyear financial statement summaries are excluded.

nificantly since 1977 was the amount of space consumed by accounting footnotes. During that time, the average number of footnotes accompanying the financial statements grew to 20 from 15, and the number of pages devoted to those footnotes more than doubled to 17 pages from 7. Little changed from 1977 was the number of pages utilized by the primary financial statements. This result was expected given that the number of required financial statements has not changed during the time frame under review. As this book is being written, companies have, for the first time, begun to fulfill a new financial statement reporting requirement—the disclosure of other comprehensive income. While one available option is to provide a new statement, the statement of comprehensive income, the 10 companies we surveyed opted to include the required information in their statements of shareholders' equity.

Two companies whose reports have changed significantly since 1977 are General Motors Corporation (GM) and International Business Machines Corporation (IBM). In the 1977 GM annual report, there were six pages of footnotes accompanying the company's financial statements. Among the notes were a statement of stockholders' equity, reported there as opposed to being reported as a stand-alone financial statement, and a condensed balance sheet for General Motors Acceptance Corporation. The other footnotes were not particularly noteworthy, including the required accounting policy note and notes on income taxes, an incentive program and pension plan, other miscellaneous income statement and balance sheet accounts, quarterly results, and segment data. Particularly noteworthy for its change in the 1998 report was the company's accounting policy footnote. In this note, a company reports significant accounting principles and procedures applied. In 1998, the GM accounting policy note had grown to 18 items consuming nearly two pages of small print, up from seven items and less than one page in 1977.[6] Also contributing to the significant increase in the number and length of footnotes in 1998 were expanded disclosures on income taxes, pensions and postretirement benefits, stock incentive plans, and new disclosures on financial instruments and derivatives.

The footnotes contained in the 1998 IBM annual report grew to 25 in number from 10 in 1977, covering 22 pages of text, up from 5. Here again, the accounting policy note grew to 2 pages with 15 items, from less than a single page and 10 items. Like GM, IBM's report included much expanded disclosures on taxes, pensions, stock options, and financial instruments and derivatives.

Certainly, the complexity of the businesses of the companies reviewed has increased in the period between 1977 and 1998, adding to the complexity of their financial statements. The companies are larger, with more assets, revenues, and earnings; they are involved in more intricate and involved transactions with more customers and, generally, they have increased the extent of their international reach. Increased size alone, however, does not explain the increase in length and complexity of these companies' financial statements. For example, owing to its break-up, AT&T is actually smaller today, when measured using total assets, than it was in 1977.[7] But beyond just the size factor, for the reasons noted, the businesses of these companies generally are more complex than they were in 1977.

While the increased complexity inherent in these companies' business operations could be expected to add somewhat to the length and difficulty of their annual reports, there is another factor at work—the increased number and complexity of the accounting rules or standards that guide their financial statements' preparation. In reviewing the annual reports for the 10 companies studied, the role played by this factor became evident in the number of footnotes and pages devoted to them and in the number of items reported in the accounting policy notes.

Contributions of the FASB

Over 20 years ago, around the early part of 1978 when the financial statements of the 10 companies reviewed had just been published, the Financial Accounting Standards Board (FASB), the chief accounting rule-making body in the United States, had issued 21 Statements of Financial Accounting Standards. Supplementing these accounting and reporting requirements were 22 Interpretations, an extant set of 31 Accounting Principles Board opinions, and a few remaining Accounting Research Bulletins issued by predecessor bodies. By 1998, however, that list of Statements of Financial Accounting Standards had grown to 137, and the number of Interpretations had increased to 42. In addition, by 1998, the FASB had issued 94 Technical Bulletins and 6 Statements of Financial Accounting Concepts. Moreover, this latter list does not even count the Statements of Position and industry audit and accounting guides issued by the American Institute of Certified Public Accountants (AICPA) or the consensus views of the FASB's Emerging Issues Task Force. While these industry audit and accounting guides, Statements of Position, and consensus views do not have the same status in the hierarchy of authoritative support as the FASB's Statements of Financial Accounting Standards, they nonetheless are generally viewed as being authoritative, requiring application in the preparation of financial statements. Also adding to the whole set of accounting and reporting requirements is an ever-growing list of Securities and Exchange Commission (SEC) reporting guidelines.

Their increasing numbers, as well as the topics dealt with in these accounting standards, attest to their increasing complexity. At the time, the standards written to address the topics of the 1970s often seemed intricate and difficult to apply. In hindsight, however, they seem almost quaint when compared with some of the more recently issued accounting standards. For example, in the 1970s, the FASB was dealing with such topics as accounting for research and development costs, reporting gains and losses from early extinguishment of debt, accounting for contingencies, and accounting for leases. During the 1990s, the FASB has issued standards on such complex topics as accounting for postretirement benefits, income taxes, derivative financial instruments, accounting for stock-based compensation, and a revision in the calculation of earnings per share. Also adding to today's complexity is the concept of comprehensive income, which is a broader definition of income than net income. It is disclosed, at a reporting company's option, on the income statement or the statement of shareholders' equity.

When learning of this latest requirement to disclose comprehensive income, Kenneth Johnson, vice president and controller of Motorola, Inc. asserted in a letter to the FASB's oversight body that the proposal for comprehensive income "will create a sixth bottom line for financial reports—as if we don't have enough today to confuse us."[8] Johnson is not alone in his expression of concerns about the added complexity of financial reports introduced by the FASB. William Stimart, vice president of Duke Power Company, expresses the concern that "the complexity and cost of the board's rules to businesses far outweigh any benefits, such as increased disclosure for investors."[9] Ray Groves, a former chairman of Ernst & Young, calculates that "if disclosure rules keep piling up over the next 20 years the way they have over the last 20, the typical big company's annual report will have grown by 234% in pages and 1,700% in footnotes."[10] Finally, John Reed, chairman of Citicorp, has stated, "Our only choice to rein in a runaway process may be to abolish FASB."[11]

Whether the FASB will be abolished or even changed significantly is open to a debate that will likely continue. In the interim, however, the FASB continues to work on new financial reporting and disclosure projects that promise to continue increasing financial statement complexity. For example, the FASB is currently working on new principles for business combinations that would potentially abolish the pooling-of-interests method and would provide new guidance on how purchased intangibles, including goodwill, should be accounted for. Also under consideration is a group of related projects on consolidations. These projects are intended to cover all aspects of accounting for affiliations between entities, including the definition of control, investments accounted for under the equity method, segment reporting, and joint ventures. Another significant project having a potentially pervasive effect on financial statements and footnotes is the FASB's ongoing consideration of accounting and reporting principles for financial instruments. This group of projects includes derivatives and hedging, measuring financial assets and liabilities at fair value, and accounting for instruments that have characteristics of both liabilities and equity. Other projects under deliberation include impaired assets scheduled for disposal, the use of present-value measurements, and a concerted effort to coordinate U.S. accounting principles with international accounting principles.[12]

Thus, it appears that the complexity of financial reports introduced by this standard-setting body is not likely to subside in the near term. When the ever-growing body of financial reporting rules is combined with the aforementioned increased complexity of business transactions, the implication is that the use of financial statements for purposes of analysis will continue to be a very complex and daunting task.

Other Sources of Complexity

Even without the complexities added by the FASB and more involved business transactions, just the nature of financial reporting itself, with many varied accounting and disclosure practices and differences in terminology, make financial statement analysis no place for the uninformed. Consider, for example, the January 1997 balance sheet of Autodesk, Inc. Among the company's current assets is the account "Deferred income taxes" reported in the amount of $35,616,000, up from $33,769,000 the previous year. Then, within noncurrent liabilities, the company also reports "Deferred income taxes" at $2,974,000, up from $1,912,000 in 1996.[13] The obvious question is, what are deferred income taxes and why are they being reported as both assets and liabilities? Moreover, what is the significance of the change in these accounts?

We ask these questions now not so much to provide answers, but rather to demonstrate how subtle complexities can make financial statement analysis difficult. Answers to the questions will be provided in subsequent chapters.

The responses of experienced financial analysts to our questions, asked in informal surveys, concerning companies' deferred income taxes are informative.

Exhibit 1.2. Disclosure of Excess of Current Cost of Inventory Over LIFO Valuation: J&L Specialty Steel, Inc., Inventory Footnote, Years Ending December 31, 1996–1997 (Thousands of Dollars)

	1996	1997
Raw materials	$14,567	$18,621
Work-in-process	104,512	107,572
Finished goods	39,448	40,270
Total inventories at current cost	158,527	166,463
Less allowance to reduce current cost value to LIFO basis	(14,951)	(15,348)
Total inventories	$143,576	$151,115

Source: J&L Specialty Steel, Inc., Form 10-K annual report to the Securities and Exchange Commission (December 1997), p. 11.

Their replies vary from the enlightened and informed to the uninformed and sometimes downright dangerous. More than one analyst has indicated that because of difficulties in understanding deferred income taxes, they were often simply ignored. Their position was just that they simply hoped the accounts were not important.

As another example of the complexities involved in analyzing modern financial reports, consider the different terminology used for a simple account item, revenue collected in advance, also known as deferred revenue. Various balance sheet titles used to describe this account include "Merchandise and other customer credits" (Tiffany & Co.), "Air traffic liability" (Delta Air Lines, Inc.), "Deferred income on shipments" (Intel Corp.), and "Billings in excess of costs and estimated profits on contracts in progress" (Avondale Industries, Inc.). A financial analyst can understand the concept of revenue collected in advance and its implications for current and future earnings and cash flow. However, with such varied terminology, it may not register with him or her that the identified accounts are in fact deferred revenue.

As a third example, consider inventory and the last-in, first-out (LIFO) method. Public companies are required to disclose the excess of the replacement cost, also known as current cost, of inventory over the LIFO valuation if that amount is material.[14] Various titles and descriptions are used to describe this difference. Some are very clear, such as the following textual disclosure reported in the inventory note of Interlake Corporation:

> The current cost of these inventories exceeded their valuation determined on a LIFO basis by $12,946,000 at December 29, 1996 and by $13,091,000 at December 31, 1997.[15]

Others, such as J&L Specialty Steel, Inc., use a tabular display (see Exhibit 1.2) to disclose the same information in a very clear and understandable manner.

Exhibit 1.3. Disclosure of Excess of Current Cost of Inventory Over LIFO
Valuation: Schawk, Inc., Inventory Footnote, Years Ending December 31,
1997–1998 (Thousands of Dollars)

	1997	1998
Raw materials	$1,239	$1,429
Work-in-process	4,130	5,706
	5,369	7,135
Less LIFO reserve	(905)	(1,187)
	$4,464	$5,948

Source: Schawk, Inc., Form 10-K annual report to the Securities and Exchange Commission (December 1998), p. 33.

As presented in Exhibit 1.2, at December 31, 1997, the company was carrying inventory at current cost in the amount of $166,463,000. At that time, the excess of current cost over LIFO cost was $15,348,000. Subtracting this amount from inventory at current cost yielded inventory at LIFO cost in the amount of $151,115,000. This latter amount was reported on the company's balance sheet.

Often, the disclosures provided of the excess of replacement cost over LIFO cost are less clear, as Exhibit 1.3, taken from the financial statements of Schawk, Inc., demonstrates.

What is unclear about the display presented in Exhibit 1.3 is what exactly is being reported. For example, what does the $7,135,000 in inventory at December 31, 1998, represent? Current cost? FIFO cost? Some other cost? Further, is the LIFO reserve the same thing as the excess of current cost over the LIFO amount? Is $5,948,000 the LIFO inventory? Also, the disclosed LIFO reserve increased from $905,000 in 1997 to $1,187,000 in 1998. What is the significance for analysis of that increase, and what would it mean if it were to decline?

As with the deferred income tax questions, we will answer these inventory questions in subsequent chapters. The point to be made is that differences in terminology and in financial accounting and disclosure practices add to the complexity of financial statement analysis. Without a carefully devised framework for understanding today's financial reports and the knowledge base necessary to apply it, financial statement analysis can be woefully deficient. It is a matter of determining what is and is not important and of developing the skills to deal with variations in terminology, presentation, and structure.

Guidance for Financial Statement Users

This book was written for two primary financial statement user groups: equity analysts and credit analysts. The ultimate objectives of the two groups are somewhat different. Equity analysts seek to facilitate share buy and sell decisions whereas credit analysts aim to assist in decisions on the possible extension of credit. To meet these objectives, however, both groups are interested in formulating expectations about future earnings and cash flows, about financial position and possible changes in that financial position. As a result, their information needs are very much the same. Financial statements have evolved to serve a significant part of those information needs.

Whether arising from the increased intricacies of contemporary business transactions, the numerous standards issued by the FASB, or the many and varied accounting and disclosure practices and differences in terminology employed by reporting companies, financial statement complexity can impede the work performed by equity and credit analysts. As a result, decisions reached using their analyses may be suboptimal.

Our objective is to provide clarity and guidance—to help analysts navigate the maze of modern-day financial reports and enhance their ability to use financial statements effectively in formulating knowledgeable recommendations for action.

ASSESSING FINANCIAL QUALITY: AN ORGANIZING THEME

To the novice analyst, the many different items reported in the financial statements and footnotes often appear to be unrelated. The deferred income tax accounts described earlier are a case in point. With no difference in description, the same account title appeared on the balance sheet as both a current asset and a noncurrent liability. In different situations, the accounts may appear as a noncurrent asset or a current liability. Moreover, though not discussed above, the change in the accounts' balances would affect the income tax provision reported on the income statement and the company's operating cash flow reported on the cash flow statement. Then, a complete analysis must incorporate the impact of these tax items with other, apparently unrelated financial statement accounts, such as deferred revenue and the LIFO reserve.

To effectively process the flood of information in financial reports, an organizing theme is needed. Such a theme should aid in relating how various, sometimes seemingly unrelated, accounts and account-balance changes are reported— making sense of the whole package—and should be consistent with the objectives of financial statement users. Assessing financial quality is such an organizing theme. It provides a thread that weaves through many seemingly unrelated financial reporting topics and shows how they are related to the overriding objective of effective financial statement analysis. In the process, this organizing theme affords a deeper, richer understanding of financial statements and how the accounts found in them and changes in these accounts are linked.

Consider the analysis of a company's financial statements for the first time. Even experienced analysts hesitate in the beginning. Where do I start? What is important? What can I ignore? Assessing financial quality provides a useful and efficient starting point.

What Is Financial Quality?

Ultimately, both equity analysts and credit analysts are interested in a company's ability to generate cash flow. For equity holders, cash flow can be used for reinvestment to produce capital gains, for dividends, and for stock buybacks. For credit holders, this cash can be used for the payment of interest and principal on loans. Through the liquidation of assets and expansion of liabilities, cash flow can be generated even in the absence of earnings. Without earnings, however, cash generation is a short-term phenomenon. Assets available for liquidation run short, and sources of credit dry up. For recurring production beyond the short-term, cash flow requires a renewable source, an engine of generation. Earnings provide that engine—a renewable source of cash flow.

All earnings, however, do not have the same cash flow implications. For example, some companies, often growth companies, report earnings for many years without producing any cash. This occurs as earnings are reinvested to maintain growth; increases in inventory and accounts receivable are good examples. The expectation of investors and creditors is that such companies will begin to generate cash flow as growth slows and the amount of new investment in these assets can be curtailed. This can take many years. Some companies never convert their growth-related investments to cash flow. The end result is a series of losses as prior-year investments are written off.

Thus, the interest of equity analysts and credit analysts in cash flow becomes one of an interest in earnings and earning power. They are interested in a company's ability to generate a sustainable, and likely growing, stream of earnings. Those earnings must eventually result in cash flow. Earnings without the prospect of cash flow are of no value to an equity or credit holder. Indeed, such earnings represent future losses. A company has earning power when it has the ability to generate a sustainable stream of earnings that provide cash flow. If that cash flow is not provided currently, it will be provided in subsequent years. Accordingly, we will not say that a company has earning power when it simply has the ability to generate earnings. Those earnings must also have cash flow prospects. Though given the heightened uncertainty that accompanies an extended time frame, the sooner that cash flow is generated, the better.

For equity analysts and credit analysts, assessing a company's earning power requires expectations about the future. For example, does the company have the ability to continue generating earnings? To what extent will those earnings result in cash flow? Their need for information to answer forward-looking questions such as these poses a problem because financial statement information is historical in nature. That is, analysts are expected to assess the ability of a company to generate a sustainable stream of earnings and cash flow using current financial statement information, which is a compilation of historical transactions.

Financial quality is a means of expressing, in terms of corporate earning power, the ability to generate sustainable earnings and cash flow—the implications of current financial statement information. A financial statement item is said to be of high financial quality when it sends a positive signal about corporate earning power. It is of low financial quality when it signals lower earning power. For example, in 1995, Tubby's, Inc. reported a $49,704 gain on the sale of fixed assets, which comprised 18 percent of pretax income for the year.[16] The gain stood out in terms of its magnitude, and was followed by a loss on the sale of fixed assets in 1996. The gain impaired financial quality in 1995. The company's true earning power was lower than reported income suggested. In contrast, in 1996, The Perkin-Elmer Corporation reported pretax earnings of $35,501,000 after recording a provision for restructured operations of $71,600,000.[17] The provision was nonrecurring and enhanced financial quality in 1996. The company's true earning power was actually higher than indicated by reported income.

It is more common to see references to the concept of earnings quality, or the quality of earnings, than it is to see references to more generic financial quality. For example, the financial publication *The Value Line Investment Survey* makes reference to the concept of the quality of earnings in its publications.[18] In two papers appearing in the *Financial Analysts Journal,* Bernstein and Siegel and Siegel also refer to the concept of earnings quality.[19] O'Glove's book is entitled *Quality of Earnings: The Investor's Guide to How Much Money a Company Is Really Making,* and he publishes a newsletter entitled *Quality of Earnings Report.*[20] This is an incomplete characterization as it seems to focus attention on the income statement while not emphasizing the other statements as well. In fact, these authors would no doubt agree that information found in all of the financial statements, as well as the footnotes and supplementary materials, can affect an analyst's assessment of earning power. For example, capitalized software costs carried on a balance sheet at an amount greater than can ultimately be realized will result in a loss when written down. This overvalued asset impairs financial quality and the company's earning power. Current earnings, which exclude the anticipated write-down, overstate the company's earning power. An overfunded pension plan can be terminated, resulting in a future gain. The existence of this off-balance-sheet asset enhances financial quality and the company's earning power. Even if the company elects not to terminate the pension plan, its overfunded status will allow the company to reap the gain indirectly as future pension expense and funding are curtailed. Thus, current earnings, which exclude the potential future benefit from the pension plan, understate the company's earning power. Neither the software nor the pension item is found on the income statement, but they nonetheless have significant implications for each company's earning power. By focusing our discussion on the broader-term financial quality, as opposed to the more narrow earnings quality, we can better present how various financial statement items impact corporate earning power.[21] This distinction is important as we set out to explain the intricacies of financial reporting and how they impact financial analysis.

A Closer Look at Financial Quality

We will look at financial quality from two points of view: earnings quality and position quality. In assessing earnings quality, we look to the income statement, the cash flow statement, and related footnotes to find items that affect earning power. With earnings quality, we are interested in how items that are either reported in income currently or are directly related to those items affect earning power. In assessing position quality, we look to the balance sheet and related footnotes. Here, too, we are interested in items that will affect earning power, though here the effects are more indirect and delayed because they have to work themselves through to the income statement before being reflected in earnings.

Earnings Quality

The nonrecurring gain on the sale of fixed assets by Tubby's, Inc. and Perkin-Elmer's nonrecurring provision for restructured operations are examples of earnings quality items. Tubby's gain impairs earnings quality, whereas Perkin-Elmer's provision enhances it. We must recall, however, that assessing earning power is more than simply judging whether a company can generate sustainable earnings. Assessing earning power also requires an evaluation of the company's cash-generating ability. Thus, as we look at various income statement items, we want to assess whether or not those items result in cash flow. Given the heightened uncertainty that naturally accompanies cash flow to be generated at some future date, we stress in our definition of earnings quality a preference for current cash flow.

This consideration of whether an income statement item results in cash flow opens yet another avenue for understanding earnings quality. Is the gain or loss cash flow backed? Tubby's sale of fixed assets was a cash sale, providing the company with more cash than just the amount of gain reported. From the viewpoint of cash flow, then, it was a positive event for the company. It was one step toward Tubby's collecting more cash flow for the year than the amount of net income reported. With increased collections, earning power, from the standpoint of cash flow, is improved. Thus, even though the transaction impaired earnings quality because it was a nonrecurring gain, it also enhanced earnings quality by providing cash flow. We will not try to say which—the nonrecurring gain or the cash flow—is more important to earnings quality. Rather, our objective is a complete understanding of the transaction—that it involves a nonrecurring gain and a heightened cash flow. To do this, we will identify the separate dimensions of the effects of the transaction on earnings quality. Specifically, Tubby's gain on sale of fixed assets impaired earnings quality on the *persistence* dimension. The fact that more cash was collected than the amount of gain reported enhanced earnings quality on the *cash* dimension. By carefully considering how transactions affect earnings quality on both the persistence and cash dimensions, analysts will be more focused on determining how those transactions affect earning power.

Perkin-Elmer's nonrecurring provision for restructured operations is a nonrecurring, noncash charge. The nonrecurring nature of the expense enhances earnings quality on the persistence dimension. The company's earning power is higher than reported income. Because the provision is noncash, it contributes toward net

Exhibit 1.4. Relationships between Income Statement Items and Earnings Quality on the Persistence and Cash Dimensions

Income Statement Item	Earnings Quality Dimension and Effect
Nonrecurring Revenue or Gain	Impairs earnings quality—persistence
Nonrecurring Expense or Loss	Enhances earnings quality—persistence
Cash Collected Exceeds Revenue or Gain	Enhances earnings quality—cash
Revenue or Gain Exceeds Cash Collected	Impairs earnings quality—cash
Cash Paid Exceeds Expense or Loss	Impairs earnings quality—cash
Expense or Loss Exceeds Cash Paid	Enhances earnings quality—cash

cash flow exceeding net income. As a result, it also enhances earnings quality on the cash dimension.

The cash dimension of earnings quality can also be related to recurring sources of income and expense, not simply nonrecurring gains and losses. For example, because it involves no cash payment but does reduce net income, deferred tax expense enhances earnings quality on the cash dimension. The company reports lower net income but not lower cash flow. In a similar way, because it results in cash flow exceeding net income, deferred revenue or revenue collected in advance enhances earnings quality on the cash dimension. The company reports a cash collection without accompanying income.

Note that the focus here is on current cash flows and not future cash flows. That is, although deferred tax expense involves no current cash payment, it will entail a cash payment when taxes deferred are ultimately paid. Similarly, as deferred revenue involves a current cash collection, cash will not be received when the revenue is finally earned. In both cases, this cash flow reversal may not occur for many years. Growth companies can experience increases in deferred tax liabilities and deferred revenue accounts indefinitely, boosting cash flow. This must be viewed as a positive development for corporate earning power. Analysts must be prepared for the possibility that these cash flows may reverse in the future, impairing earnings quality on the cash dimension.

The relationships that might arise between various income statement items, cash flow, and earnings quality on the persistence and cash dimensions are illustrated in Exhibit 1.4.

Two more examples will help demonstrate how different income statement items affect earnings quality. Dresser Industries, Inc. accounts for its investment in certain unconsolidated affiliates using the equity method. Under the equity method, the company records its share of the earnings of these affiliates. To avoid double counting, dividends—the cash received from the investments—are reported as a reduction in the investment account and are not included in income. During 1996, Dresser recorded $28,300,000 in equity-method income from its investments. However, the company received dividends from them of only

$8,200,000.[22] Here, earnings quality is impaired on the cash dimension—the income reported exceeded the cash collected. In terms of persistence, there was no information provided that would indicate that the equity-method income was derived from nonrecurring sources. That is, the earnings from the unconsolidated affiliates appear to be recurring in nature. Accordingly, reported income does not give a distorted picture of the company's earning power. For this item, from the standpoint of persistence, true earning power is neither higher nor lower than reported income. Earnings quality on the persistence dimension is neither impaired nor enhanced.

In 1995, Luxtec, Inc. reported a pretax loss of $6,127,000. In calculating the loss, the company included a charge for purchased research and development of $5,231,000.[23] Because the charge was nonrecurring, it enhanced earnings quality on the persistence dimension. The company's earning power was higher than the reported pretax loss would indicate. In terms of cash flow, the cash paid for this purchased research and development was only about 10 percent of the income statement charge. Thus, on the cash dimension, the noncash charge enhances earnings quality in terms of cash content.

Position Quality

The capitalized software costs and the overfunded pension plan mentioned earlier are examples of position quality items. As noted, the capitalized software costs were carried on a balance sheet at an amount greater than what could be ultimately realized, or their liquidation value.[24] The reporting of this overvalued asset impaired position quality. The company's balance sheet gave the impression of more assets and more equity than actually existed. This overvaluation of assets will find its way to the income statement as a loss when these capitalized costs are written down. Thus, the overvalued asset has negative implications for the company's earning power. To the extent that the loss from write-down is postponed and excluded from current earnings, those earnings overstate the company's earning power. As an aside, in a subsequent year when the capitalized costs are written down, earnings quality will be enhanced on the cash and persistence dimensions. The nonrecurring loss reported that year will serve to understate the company's earning power. After the write-down, position quality will no longer be impaired.

While the software costs are an example of the impact on position quality of an on-balance-sheet item, position quality is sometimes affected by off-balance-sheet assets and liabilities. The overfunded pension plan discussed above is just such an off-balance-sheet item. When the assets of a pension plan—the fair market value of its stocks and bonds—exceed its obligations to current and future retirees, the plan is overfunded. Current generally accepted accounting principles preclude recognition of that overfunding. Instead, the financial position of the pension plan is reported in a footnote to the financial statements. Companies are permitted by law to terminate such overfunded plans, and after the payment of income taxes and special franchise taxes, recover the amount of any overfunding for general

Exhibit 1.5.   Relationships between On-Balance-Sheet and Off-Balance-Sheet Items and Position Quality

Item	*Position Quality Effect*
On-Balance-Sheet	
Liquidation Value of Asset Exceeds Book Value	Enhances position quality
Book Value of Asset Exceeds Liquidation Value	Impairs position quality
Liquidation Value of Liability Exceeds Book Value	Impairs position quality
Book Value of Liability Exceeds Liquidation Value	Enhances position quality
Off-Balance-Sheet	
Off-Balance-Sheet Asset	Enhances position quality
Off-Balance-Sheet Liability	Impairs position quality

corporate use.[25] As noted, even without terminating the plan, companies can recover the overfunding indirectly by curtailing pension funding. This off-balance-sheet asset enhances position quality. The balance sheet is conservative; it understates the company's financial position. As the pension overfunding finds its way to the income statement, earnings will benefit. Thus, the off-balance-sheet asset has positive implications for the company's earning power. To the extent that income recognition of the pension gain is postponed, that income understates the company's earning power. In the year that a gain on pension termination is recognized, earnings quality will be impaired on the persistence dimension. The nonrecurring gain reported that year will overstate the company's earning power. After the gain is recognized, position quality will no longer be enhanced. From the standpoint of cash flow, because the amount of cash received will equal the gain recognized, earnings quality will be neither enhanced nor impaired.

The relationships that might arise between various on-balance-sheet and off-balance-sheet items and position quality are illustrated in Exhibit 1.5.

Additional examples will help demonstrate how on-balance-sheet and off-balance-sheet items impact position quality. At December 31, 1996, The Coca-Cola Company carried its investment in Coca-Cola Enterprises, Inc. on its balance sheet at $547 million. At that same time, the fair market value of the investment was $2.731 billion dollars.[26] Clearly, position quality was enhanced as the company could sell even a portion of the investment, generating a significant gain. Such an unrecognized gain lends support to the income statement and can be used to generate earnings in a future year.

In its 1996 annual report, Elsinore Corporation disclosed that during the year ended December 31, 1994, "$3 million of the original $60 million principal amount of First Mortgage Notes was repurchased by the Company and retired . . . The Company recorded an extraordinary gain of $735,000 as a result of this debt retirement."[27] Prior to the debt's repurchase, the market value of the debt was below book value. Such a condition might be caused by an increase in the level of interest rates generally, though a decline in Elsinore's credit quality would also produce the same result. The company's position quality was enhanced. It gave the company the opportunity to repurchase its debt at an amount less than book value. The difference, a gain, was reported as an extraordinary item on the company's income statement. In that year, the nonrecurring gain impaired earnings quality on the persistence dimension. Because it involved a cash payment, it also impaired earnings quality on the cash dimension.

Prab, Inc. provides an example counter to that of Elsinore. In a press release dated March 10, 1998, Prab disclosed the incurrence of an extraordinary loss:

> The extraordinary item in the first quarter of 1998 resulted from the company paying in full the 12 percent subordinated notes. The payoff amount exceeded the book carrying amount and resulted in a $77,512 decrease to income net of an income tax benefit of $39,931.[28]

Here, the liquidation value of the debt was more than book value impairing position quality.

In its October 31, 1997, annual report, Emergent Group, Inc. provides an example of what had been an off-balance-sheet liability. According to its annual report:

> The Company has accrued $51,000 for a former operating location to record the potential liability for environmental contamination at this site. The Company believes that the total cost for this environmental liability will not exceed the amount accrued.[29]

Prior to the recording of this accrual, the company had an off-balance-sheet liability. Position quality was impaired. The recording of the needed liability reduced reported earnings and brought the off-balance-sheet obligation onto the balance sheet. Now that the liability has been accrued, position quality is no longer impaired. However, if the amount accrued proves to be insufficient, the company will once again have impaired position quality until an additional amount is recorded.

Position Quality and Financial Flexibility

Up to this point, we have demonstrated a direct link between position quality and earning power. An undervalued asset, like Coca-Cola's investment in Coca-Cola Enterprises, can be sold at a substantial gain. Elsinore recorded an extraordinary gain and Prab an extraordinary loss when debt was retired early at amounts different from book value. Emergent's off-balance-sheet liability resulted in a charge to income. However, there can also be an indirect link between position quality and earning power that does not so clearly manifest itself in earnings. That indirect link involves the concept of financial flexibility.

Corporations are continually facing events that require corrective action in order to avoid significant financial setbacks. Financial flexibility gives them the wherewithal to deal with unexpected events as they occur, while sustaining earning power. As Kieso and Weygandt indicate:

> An enterprise with a high degree of financial flexibility is better able to survive bad times, to recover from unexpected setbacks, and to take advantage of profitable and unexpected investment opportunities. Generally, the greater the financial flexibility, the lower the risk of enterprise failure.[30]

Enhanced position quality is a source of financial flexibility. A firm with enhanced position quality has financial strength that is not indicated by a literal reading of its balance sheet. Similarly, the financial flexibility of a firm with impaired position quality is reduced. As this book is written, most business observers are contemplating with concern the extent to which a major financial crisis in Asia that began in 1997 might affect U.S. corporations. Although some companies will escape unharmed, many—especially those with major customers in Asia—will face declines in orders. Firms with enhanced position quality will be in better shape to weather this financial storm and sustain reported earnings until better times return.

Consider, for example, General Dynamics Corporation. At December 31, 1996, the company's balance sheet reported a postretirement benefit obligation of $261 million. At that same time, the actual underfunded status of that plan, the excess of the plan's liabilities over its assets was $425 million.[31] The balance sheet understated this obligation and position quality was impaired. Given the company's election to defer recognition, there is no requirement that the company record this obligation with a single charge to earnings. Rather, the company elected to amortize the obligation as a charge against earnings over future years. Eventually, the balance sheet will correctly reflect the financial position of the postretirement benefit plan.[32] Thus, there is no direct near-term, single-charge link between the off-balance-sheet liability and reported earnings as we saw in the position quality examples provided above. But the off-balance-sheet liability does in fact reduce the company's financial flexibility. It has an obligation to fund the postretirement liability. Funds that must be used for that funding cannot be earmarked for other purposes, whether for survival or to take advantage of investment opportunities that may arise.

Operating leases provide a similar example. At June 30, 1997, Delta Air Lines, Inc. reported operating lease commitments of over $14 billion.[33] These obligations are off-balance-sheet, being relegated to a footnote to the company's financial statements. Although not included with the company's liabilities, they are obligations that must be paid if the company is to continue operating. Because they are off-balance-sheet, the company has impaired position quality. There is no requirement that the obligation be brought onto the balance sheet. However, they do reduce the firm's financial flexibility and will hamper it, much like reported debt, in a business slowdown.

Other Position-Quality Factors

Beyond the obvious comparison of liquidation value with book value, there are other factors that affect the position quality of assets and liabilities. For example, the more marketable an asset, the higher its position quality. Thus, all else being equal, quoted investments in equity and debt securities imply somewhat higher position quality than undeveloped land. Also, the less specialized an asset, the higher its position quality. Clearly, in this regard, a used pickup truck has higher position quality than a used lion cage from the circus. And unencumbered assets, or assets that have not been pledged to secure financing, have higher position quality because management has more freedom to liquidate such assets and realize their appreciation.

Marketability is also an important factor in determining position quality for liabilities. Marketable debt can be more readily purchased and retired to capture book- versus market-value differences. Debt that is privately placed can be repaid early only with approval from the lender, and then a prepayment penalty may be assessed. In such a case, debt defeasance, in which discounted treasury securities earmarked for service of a company's debt offering are placed in an irrevocable trust, provides an alternative method of debt retirement.

Financial Quality as an Organizing Theme

As noted, equity analysts and credit analysts are interested in determining earning power—the ability to generate sustainable earnings that are backed by cash flow. Assessing financial quality (earnings quality and position quality) is consistent with the determination of earning power. By breaking down the concept of financial quality into its component dimensions, earnings-quality dimensions of persistence and cash, and position-quality dimensions of on-balance-sheet and off-balance-sheet assets and liabilities, we have an organizing framework for judging how various transactions, financial statement balances, and footnote disclosures affect earning power.

The assessment of financial quality as an organizing theme requires not only a deep understanding of financial reporting rules but also the ability to apply financial statement information to the analysis of earning power. Thus, rather than simply explaining how deferred taxes are accounted for and what the disclosure rules are, we can now relate the deferred tax accounts, whether found on the balance sheet, income statement, cash flow statement, or within the footnotes, to financial quality. Similarly, rather than a somewhat sterile depiction of LIFO accounting and the LIFO reserve, we can relate the account and changes in its balance to financial quality. In the process, analysts should be better served.

With financial quality as an organizing theme, the financial statements and footnotes no longer appear to be a disjointed, static collection of account balances. They can be tied together to assess earning power. Financial quality provides a common thread we can use to weave the accounts together, giving a clearer, more effective picture of corporate performance.

Exhibit 1.6. Fundamental Factors Examined for Value Relevance

Fundamental Factor	Factor Measurement
Inventory	Change in inventory less change in sales
Accounts receivable	Change in accounts receivable less change in sales
Capital expenditures	Change in industry capital expenditures less change in company capital expenditures
Research and development (R&D)	Change in industry less change in company R&D
Gross margin	Change in sales less change in gross profit
Sales and administrative (S&A) expenses	Change in S&A expenses less change in sales
Provision for doubtful receivables	Change in gross receivables less change in doubtful receivables
Effective tax rate	Change in effective tax rate: year t-1 minus year t
Order backlog	Change in sales less change in order backlog
Labor force	Change in sales per employee: year t-1 minus year t
LIFO earnings	0 for LIFO; 1 for FIFO
Audit qualification	1 for Qualified; 0 for Unqualified

Source: B. Lev and S. R. Thiagarajan, "Fundamental Information Analysis," *Journal of Accounting Research* (Autumn 1993), p. 193. All variables were measured using the percentage annual change from the average of the prior two years. Variables were defined such that negative coefficients or associations with stock market returns were expected.

Financial Quality as an Effective Analytical Tool

We were also drawn to financial quality as an organizing theme because research has shown that using financial quality as an analytical tool is an effective means of analyzing financial statements. For example, in an excellent study, Lev and Thiagarajan used a guided search procedure of the written pronouncements of financial analysts to identify fundamental factors traditionally associated with the quality of earnings.[34] Their list of 12 factors are depicted in Exhibit 1.6.

The authors' objective was to determine the extent to which these factors had relevance over earnings alone in explaining excess returns, or share price movements over and above amounts explained by the stock market generally.

The close relationship between these factors and financial quality can be seen readily. For example, due to the potential for write-down, earnings are less sustainable and are not backed by cash flow when accounts receivable and inventory are growing faster than sales. Earnings quality is impaired on the persistence and cash dimensions. Also, position quality is impaired as the collectibility of slow-turning accounts receivable and the marketability of slow-moving inventory is called into question. Similarly, earnings boosted by a cut in the effective tax rate or a reduction in the provision for doubtful accounts cannot be maintained. A decrease in capital expenditures and research and development (R&D) spending signals a concern about future cash flows. Declines in gross margin; increases in selling, general and administrative expenses as a percentage of sales; and reductions in sales per employee also provide warnings of future reductions in profitability.[35] While a reduction in order backlog warns of expected future declines in sales, the LIFO indicator identifies firms whose cost of goods sold are closer to replacement cost and, expectedly, their earnings are more sustainable. Finally, the audit qualification, denoting a qualified, disclaimed, or adverse audit opinion, indicates the auditors have problems with the financial statements, and this warning may be a precursor to future earnings difficulties.

Overall, the model constructed with these fundamental factors included explained significantly more of the cross-sectional variation in excess returns than did reported earnings alone. The variables having significant explanatory power in the expected direction, listed in order of declining statistical significance, were the gross margin, inventory, sales and administrative (S&A) expense and order backlog variables, the receivables variable, and capital expenditures.

In a follow-up test, the authors constructed an earnings-quality fundamental score for each firm. Excess share price returns for companies with high-quality fundamental scores were expected to be more highly correlated with unexpected earnings changes than for companies with low-quality fundamental scores. The authors obtained empirical results that supported their expectations. This test of the so-called earnings response coefficient showed that market participants paid more attention to, and valued more highly, earnings signals received from firms with high earnings quality.

A study by Elliott and Hanna is also relevant for earnings quality, especially on the persistence dimension.[36] The authors found that the earnings response coefficient—the ability of changes in earnings to explain changes in share prices—declined as the frequency of special nonrecurring charges increased. In this light, the inclusion of numerous special items reduced the quality of earnings.

In a follow-up study to Lev and Thiagarajan, Abarbanell and Bushee sought to determine the extent to which financial statement data were useful in predicting subsequent earnings changes.[37] Using the variables outlined in Exhibit 1.6, the authors found that changes in certain of these fundamental factors were useful in predicting one-year-ahead earnings and the long-term rate of growth in earnings. In a later study, these same authors showed that abnormal stock market returns could be earned on an investment strategy designed using these same fundamental variables.[38]

The studies performed by Lev and Thiagarajan, Elliott and Hanna, and Abarbanell and Bushee were more focused on earnings quality and its role in fundamental financial analysis than on position quality. Research has also looked at the value relevance of position quality. For example, a study by Barth, Beaver, and Landsman showed that fair value estimates of loans, securities, and long-term debt provided explanatory power for bank share prices beyond that provided by book values.[39] In an earlier work, Mulford showed that market values of debt were more important to market participants than book values in the assessment of systematic risk.[40] These studies looked at the relevance for valuation purposes of differences between book value and liquidation value for on-balance-sheet assets and liabilities. Research has also looked at the valuation role of off-balance-sheet items.

Comiskey, McEwen, and Mulford performed a *pro forma* consolidation of previously unconsolidated finance subsidiaries and recalculated leverage ratios.[41] The effect was to bring off-balance debt for these highly leveraged subsidiaries onto the balance sheet. The authors found that systematic risk was more highly correlated with these reconfigured leverage ratios than similar ratios calculated using reported debt levels. Ely found that market risk was more highly correlated with debt-to-equity ratios calculated using debt levels revised to include off-balance-sheet operating leases.[42] Barth and McNichols found that estimates of nonaccrued environmental liabilities, an off-balance-sheet obligation, provided explanatory power incremental to recognized assets and liabilities in explaining firms' market value of equity.[43] Although these studies do not address the credit side, they do indicate that in equity markets, participants are in fact incorporating off-balance-sheet items into their assessments of value and risk.

There are numerous studies, beyond those identified above, that have relevance for the usefulness of financial quality as a tool in analyzing financial statements. Many of them are very pointed in their focus and deal with individual account balances. For example, there are studies that have looked in-depth at the value relevance of the LIFO method of accounting for inventory and of LIFO liquidations.[44] Others have examined pension accounting.[45] Still others have studied accounting for deferred taxes.[46] It is well beyond the scope of this introductory chapter to review all such studies. Rather, as we cover various financial reporting and analysis topics throughout this book, we will review or reference some of the relevant research findings.

THE PLAN OF THIS BOOK

The chapter began with a cry for help from the ever-increasing complexity of modern-day corporate financial reports. This book is designed to be an aid, a guidebook, designed to help equity analysts and credit analysts use financial statements in a more efficient and effective way. The ultimate objective is to support their efforts to make more informed recommendations for action.

As a guidebook to financial reporting and analysis, the book needs an organizing theme. Assessing financial quality provides that theme. It provides a useful way to organize many seemingly unrelated accounting and reporting topics into a coherent approach to analysis. The plan of the book is to engage topics that have relevance to equity and credit decision making, but that have often proved to be confusing and difficult to understand. As such, it is a selective topical approach. We will not deal with all financial reporting topics, but only those we consider to be particularly relevant to analysis. Valid references for topics not covered can be found in good intermediate and advanced accounting textbooks. In the process, we will discuss and illustrate the key accounting and reporting issues related to the topics identified and demonstrate their relevance to financial quality. In the end, the reader will have a useful reference for better understanding how the financial reporting issues of the day impact on financial analysis.

In the next two chapters, we turn our attention to the income statement. We have already seen how nonrecurring items of income and expense can affect analysis. The objective of Chapters Two and Three is to arm the analyst to more effectively identify those nonrecurring items and remove them from reported results. This process begins with a thorough understanding of the income statement and how various items of income and expense, gain and loss, and other comprehensive income are reported. With a better understanding of the income statement, attention can then be turned to its revision. Using a specially designed worksheet, we demonstrate how analysts can adjust reported income to something we call a *sustainable earnings base*. Sustainable earnings base provides a more meaningful, sustainable measure of performance.

In Chapter Four, we examine some of the fundamental accounting principles and methods underlyling the preparation of financial statements. Included are topics of revenue recognition and matching, including inventory accounting and cost capitalization.

Chapter Five is the tax chapter. Here we look at reporting and analysis of the current and deferred components of the income tax provision and how they relate to the balance sheet and cash flow statement. Important topics here include a careful study of the differences resulting in deferred tax assets and liabilities; the valuation allowance, if any, credited against reported deferred tax assets; and the reconciliation of the statutory to the effective income tax rate.

We work with financial derivatives in Chapter Six and a related topic, foreign currency translation, in Chapter Seven. The popularity of financial derivatives has grown markedly in recent years. Many companies have reported significant losses as exotic trades that were not totally understood have moved against them. We seek to demystify the accounting and reporting guidelines for derivatives and show how the accounting rules for these specialty transactions are changing. Often, financial derivatives are used to hedge risk. Hedging foreign currency risk is one risk for which financial derivatives are useful. Thus, Chapter Six leads directly into Chapter Seven, the chapter on foreign currency translation. We start by outlining the two translation situations a company faces: the translation of foreign currency transaction balances and the translation of foreign currency financial statements. The former has immediate relevance for the income statement. The latter has income statement relevance but, arguably, can have a greater effect not on the income statement itself, but on comprehensive income. During the chapter's development, we relate in detail how financial derivatives and nonderivatives are used as foreign currency hedging vehicles.

Investments are taken up in Chapters Eight and Nine. We arrange the discussion around the various levels of ownership interest an investor might have in an investee. It begins with market-value accounting for investments not providing the investor with the ability to exert significant influence over the activities of the investee. The discussion proceeds to investment ownership positions permitting significant influence—typically one of 20 percent voting interest. Here, the equity method is applied as the investor records in income its share of the investee's earnings. The chapters are completed with a discussion of the reporting rules and relevance for analysis of full consolidation. Here, the ownership position is sufficient to confer control.

We work with leases in Chapter Ten. Here, we take the point of view of both the lessee and lessor and demonstrate accounting for both operating leases and capital leases. With the latter, lease accounting becomes more like one of ownership with a lease asset and liability recorded on the books. Also covered in the chapter are sale and leaseback transactions.

Continuing our look at liabilities, we address pensions and postretirement benefits in Chapter Eleven. These accounts have much relevance to analysis, particularly from the standpoint of potential off-balance-sheet assets in the case of pension plans, and potential off-balance-sheet liabilities, in the case of postretirement plans.

A series of sundry topics are covered in the final chapters of the book. In Chapter Twelve, we focus attention on the balance sheet. Our objective here is to pull the various topics together and demonstrate how they can be used to adjust reported shareholders' equity to a revised measure of equity that is more representative of effective owners' claims. We study the cash flow statement and point out potential problem areas for analysis in Chapter Thirteen. There is much talk today about earnings before interest, taxes, depreciation, and amortization (EBITDA), which is, in some sense, a measure of cash flow. In Chapter Thirteen, we look at EBITDA and other "new age" measures of cash flow and show what they mean when used in analysis.

FINANCIAL QUALITY EXAMPLES

We conclude this introductory chapter with a series of examples demonstrating how various financial statement balances affect financial quality. We point out whether the balances affect earnings quality, and if so, whether on the persistence or cash dimensions. We also provide examples of position-quality items and point out if the items are on-balance-sheet or off. For many readers, it will be premature to review these examples in detail now as their complete understanding requires a careful reading of the book. We encourage the reader to return to this section later. The financial quality examples are outlined in Exhibits 1.7 and 1.8. Exhibit 1.7 is devoted to earnings-quality examples, while position-quality examples are provided in Exhibit 1.8.

Exhibit 1.7. Earnings-Quality Examples

Revenues with high cash content (enhanced earnings quality on the cash dimension)

- Cost method for investments
- Completed contract method
- Installment sales method
- Service contracts—deferred revenue is growing

Revenues with low cash content (impaired earnings quality on the cash dimension)

- Equity method for investments—dividends less than earnings recognized
- Percentage-of-completion method—billings less than revenue recognized
- Sale and leaseback deferred gains—as amortized in years subsequent to year of sale

Expenses with low cash content (enhanced earnings quality on the cash dimension)

- Deferred income tax expense
- Warranty expense—liability balance is growing.
- Pension expense—when it exceeds pension funding

Expenses with high cash content (impaired earnings quality on the cash dimension)

- Net deferred tax benefit for the year
- Pension funding exceeds pension expense
- Capitalized interest—balance sheet account for capitalized interest is growing

Nonrecurring revenue or gain (impaired earnings quality on the persistence dimension)

- Asset sales (gain)
- Discontinued operations (gain)
- Early extinguishment of debt (gain)
- Net operating loss carryforward benefits not previously recognized
- Pension plan terminations with gains recognized
- LIFO liquidations—older costs below current levels
- Foreign currency gains
- Nonrecurring tax benefits
- Benefits from changes in accounting policy .

Nonrecurring expense or loss (enhanced earnings quality on the persistence dimension)

- Asset sales (loss)
- Discontinued operations (loss)
- Asset write-downs
- Provisions for expected losses
- LIFO liquidations—older costs above current levels
- Higher than normal loan-loss provisions.
- Inventory write-downs
- Investment write-downs
- Acquired research and development write-offs
- Unusually high warranty expense provisions
- Charges due to changes in accounting policy

Exhibit 1.8. Position-Quality Examples

Liquidation value of assets exceeds book value (enhances position quality)

- Appreciated fixed assets or investments
- Inventories at LIFO—current cost exceeds LIFO cost
- Separable intangibles—technology, trademarks, etc.— frequently shown at only nominal values
- Firm order and option positions—aircraft (aircraft in high demand and short supply)

Liquidation value of assets below book value (impairs position quality)

- Goodwill (troubled concern)
- Inventories at FIFO—relative to the LIFO alternative
- Deferred tax assets
- Deferred financing costs
- Leasehold improvements

Liquidation value of liabilities below book value (enhances position quality)

- Market yield on outstanding debt in excess of coupon rate—market value of debt is below book carrying value
- Deferred tax liabilities
- Overrecognition of postretirement benefit obligations

Liquidation value of liabilities greater than book value (impairs position quality)

- Underrecognition of postretirement benefit obligations
- Market yield on outstanding debt less than coupon rate—market value of debt exceeds book carrying value

Off-balance-sheet assets (enhances position quality)

- Pension plan assets exceed pension obligations
- Internally generated intangibles that are not on the books
- Fully reserved tax benefit carryforwards
- Landing slots—airlines
- Internally generated patents from R&D
- Acquired research and development write-offs

Off-balance-sheet liabilities (impairs position quality)

- Pension plan liabilities exceed pension assets
- Unrecorded deferred tax liabilities on permanently reinvested earnings of foreign subsidiaries
- Obligations under noncancelable operating leases
- Debt on the books of equity-accounted joint ventures or unconsolidated subsidiaries

---

SUMMARY

This chapter has characterized and documented the increasing complexity of current financial reporting. Further, a broad approach to financial analysis (i.e., the assessment of financial quality), which should help statement users cope with the challenge of these developments, has been outlined. Some of the key points raised in the chapter are:

- Using financial statements and associated notes and other disclosures has become a much greater challenge as the length and complexity of annual reports has steadily increased.

- Part, but clearly not all, of this challenge is the prodigious output of new accounting standards by the FASB. At 137 standards and counting as we move into a new century, the task of keeping up with the changing face of financial reporting has never been more daunting. A central goal of this book is to help statement users meet this challenge.

- To process the substantial body of financial statement information being provided by companies, the organizing theme of financial quality analysis is applied throughout the book. The two key dimensions of financial quality are (1) earnings quality and (2) position quality. Earnings quality has in turn two elements: the quality dimensions of persistence and cash content.

- The persistence dimension of earnings quality is enhanced if reported earnings are comprised principally of recurring revenues or gains. To the extent that earnings have benefited from nonrecurring revenues or gains, then the quality of earnings in terms of persistence is considered to be impaired. Alternatively, earnings quality is enhanced in terms of persistence if nonrecurring expenses or losses have been included in the determination of earnings. If, instead, the levels of expenses or losses are temporarily reduced, the quality of earnings in terms of persistence is seen to be impaired. The key to the analysis of the persistence dimension of earnings quality is the identification of nonrecurring items of revenues or gains and expenses or losses. Earnings quality is held to be impaired in terms of persistence if earnings are temporarily inflated but enhanced if temporarily depressed by nonrecurring items.

- Cash content is the other dimension of earnings quality. The cash quality of earnings is considered to be enhanced if current earnings have a high level of cash content. Alternatively, the cash quality of earnings is seen to be impaired if they are supported by more limited amounts of cash flow.

- The focus of position quality is on recognized versus unrecognized assets and liabilities as well as differences between the carrying amounts of assets and liabilities and their market or liquidation values. Position quality is considered to be enhanced if there is unrecognized financial strength and flexibility represented by off-balance-sheet assets. Moreover, position quality is also enhanced if (1) assets have market or liquidation values that are in excess of their book values or (2) liabilities have market or liquidation values that are below their book amounts. Alternatively, position quality is judged to be impaired if a firm has off-balance-sheet liabilities. Also, the presence of assets with market or liquidation values that are below book values and liabilities with market or liquidation values in excess of book values impairs position quality.

GLOSSARY

Book value   Balance sheet amount.

Cash dimension   A dimension of earnings quality that measures the extent to which a transaction is backed by cash flow.

Earning power   The ability to generate a sustainable stream of earnings that is backed by cash flow.

Earnings quality   One of two elements of financial quality that entails a measurement of the extent to which reported income is sustainable, termed the *persistence dimension* of earnings quality, and backed by cash flow, termed the *cash dimension* of earnings quality.

Financial Accounting Standards Board (FASB)   The chief accounting rule-making body in the United States. The organization is privately organized and funded. Its rules must be followed when filing with the Securities and Exchange Commission.

Financial flexibility   The financial ability to deal with unforeseen events as they occur, while sustaining earning power.

Financial quality   A means for expressing transactions in terms of corporate earning power, more specifically, in terms of their impact on a firm's ability to generate a sustainable stream of earnings that are backed by cash flow. Financial quality is comprised of two elements—earnings quality and position quality—both of which affect earning power.

Liquidation value   The amount that can ultimately be realized through sale or use of an asset or that will ultimately be paid to settle a liability in the normal course of operations.

Persistence dimension   A dimension of earnings quality that measures the extent to which a transaction affects the recurring nature of earnings.

Position quality   One of two elements of financial quality that entails a measurement of differences in liquidation values and book values for on-balance-sheet items and the amount of liquidation values for off-balance-sheet items.

NOTES

1. The statement of changes in financial position was replaced in 1987 with the statement of cash flows. Refer to Statement of Financial Accounting Standards (SFAS) No. 95, "Statement of Cash Flows" (Norwalk, CT: Financial Accounting Standards Board, November 1987).

2. SFAS No. 94, "Consolidation of All Majority-Owned Subsidiaries" (October 1987).

3. SFAS No. 87, "Employers' Accounting for Pensions" (December 1985) and SFAS No. 106, "Employers' Accounting for Postretirement Benefits Other Than Pensions" (December 1990).

4. SFAS No. 109, "Accounting for Income Taxes" (February 1992). While the standard increased the disclosure requirements for income taxes, it did not require more than one footnote to do so.

5. SFAS No. 105, "Disclosure of Information about Financial Instruments with Off-Balance Sheet Risk and Financial Instruments with Concentrations of Credit Risk" (March 1990), SFAS No. 115, "Accounting for Certain Investments in Debt and Equity Securities" (May 1993), and SFAS No. 119, "Disclosure about Derivative Financial Instruments and Fair Value of Financial Instruments" (October 1994).

6. For the 10 companies reviewed, the average number of items reported in the accounting policy notes increased to 14 in 1998 from 7 in 1977.

7. Total assets for AT&T were $94.0 billion in 1977 as compared with $59.6 billion at December 31, 1998. The company's revenues and earnings are somewhat higher, however. Revenues were $36.4 billion in 1977 compared with $53.2 billion in 1998 and net income was $4.5 billion in 1977 compared with $6.4 billion in 1998.

8. *The Wall Street Journal* (July 18, 1996), p. A9.

9. *Ibid.,* p. A9.

10. *The Wall Street Journal* (May 28, 1996), p. A19.

11. As recounted in the *Wall Street Journal* (March 21, 1996), p. C1.

12. FASB *Status Report* No. 181-B, January 14, 1998.

13. Autodesk, Inc., annual report, January 1997, p. 34.

14. Securities and Exchange Commission Regulation S-X, Rule 5-02.6.

15. Interlake Corp., annual report, December 1997. Information obtained from Disclosure, Inc. *Compact D/SEC: Corporate Information on Public Companies Filing with the SEC* (Bethesda, Maryland: Disclosure, Inc., March 1999).

16. Tubby's, Inc., Form 10-K annual report to the Securities and Exchange Commission (November 1996), p. 18.

17. The Perkin-Elmer Corp., Form 10-K annual report to the Securities and Exchange Commission (June 1997), p. 42.

18. "The Quality of Earnings," Selection and Opinion (New York: *The Value Line Investment Survey,* August 17, 1973), pp. 294–299, and "The Quality of Earnings II," Selection and Opinion (New York: *The Value Line Investment Survey,* October 5, 1973), pp. 266–268.

19. L. Bernstein and J. Siegel, "The Concept of Earnings Quality," *Financial Analysts Journal* (July/August 1979), pp. 72–75; and J. Siegel, "The 'Quality of Earnings' Concept—A Survey," *Financial Analysts Journal* (March/April 1982), pp. 60–68.

20. T. O'Glove, *Quality of Earnings: The Investor's Guide to How Much Money a Company Is Really Making* (New York: The Free Press, 1987).

21. Comiskey used the broader concept of financial quality as he demonstrated how to use the concept in credit analysis. Refer to E. E. Comiskey, "Assessing Financial Quality: An Organizing Theme for Credit Analysis," *Journal of Commercial Bank Lending* (December 1982), pp. 32–47.

22. Dresser Industries, Inc., Form 10-K annual report to the Securities and Exchange Commission (October 1997), p. 32.

23. Luxtec, Inc., Form 10-K annual report to the Securities and Exchange Commission (October 1997), p. 21.

24. We are not referring to liquidation value in a forced liquidation scenario, but rather through an organized plan of sale, or through use.

25. More specifics on how pension plan termination works and the tax rates involved are provided in Chapter Eleven.

26. The Coca-Cola Co., annual report, December 1996, pp. 50, 56.

27. Elsinore Corp., annual report, December 1996. Information obtained from Disclosure, Inc. *Compact D/SEC: Corporate Information on Public Companies Filing with the SEC* (Bethesda, Maryland: Disclosure, Inc., December 1997).

28. Prab, Inc., press release, March 10, 1998.

29. Emergent Corp., annual report, October 1997. Information obtained from Disclosure, Inc. *Compact D/SEC: Corporate Information on Public Companies Filing with the SEC* (Bethesda, Maryland: Disclosure, Inc., December 1997).

30. D. E. Kieso and J. J. Weygandt, *Intermediate Accounting*, 9th ed. (New York: Wiley, 1998), p. 205.

31. General Dynamics Corp., annual report, December 1996. Information obtained from Disclosure, Inc. *Compact D/SEC: Corporate Information on Public Companies Filing with the SEC* (Bethesda, Maryland: Disclosure, Inc., December 1997).

32. SFAS No. 106, "Employers' Accounting for Postretirement Benefits Other Than Pensions" (Norwalk, CT: Financial Accounting Standards Board, December 1990).

33. Delta Air Lines, Inc., annual report, June 1997. Information obtained from Disclosure, Inc. *Compact D/SEC: Corporate Information on Public Companies Filing with the SEC* (Bethesda, Maryland: Disclosure, Inc., December 1997).

34. B. Lev and S. R. Thiagarajan, "Fundamental Information Analysis," *Journal of Accounting Research* (Autumn 1993), pp. 190–215.

35. In our book, *Financial Warnings* (New York: John Wiley & Sons, Inc., 1996), declines in gross margin and increases in selling, general and administrative expense as a percentage of sales were key factors found to precede significant earnings declines.

36. J. A. Elliott and J. D. Hanna, "Repeated Accounting Write-Offs and the Information Content of Earnings," *Journal of Accounting Research* (Supplement 1996), pp. 135–155.

37. J. S. Abarbanell and B. J. Bushee, "Fundamental Analysis, Future Earnings, and Stock Prices," *Journal of Accounting Research* (Spring 1997), pp. 1–24.

38. J. S. Abarbanell and J. D. Hanna, "Abnormal Returns to a Fundamental Analysis Strategy," *The Accounting Review* (January 1998), pp. 19–45.

39. M. E. Barth, W. H. Beaver, and W. R. Landsman, "Value-Relevance of Banks' Fair Value Disclosures under SFAS No. 107," *The Accounting Review* (October 1996), pp. 513–537.

40. C. W. Mulford, "The Importance of a Market Value Measurement of Debt in Leverage Ratios—Replication and Extensions," *Journal of Accounting Research* (Autumn 1985), pp. 897–906.

41. E. E. Comiskey, R. A. McEwen, and C. W. Mulford, "A Test of Pro Forma Consolidation of Finance Subsidiaries," *Financial Management* (Autumn 1987), pp. 45–50.

42. K. Ely, "Operating Lease Accounting and the Market's Assessment of Equity Risk," *Journal of Accounting Research* (Autumn 1995), pp. 397–415.

43. M. E. Barth and M. F. McNichols, "Estimation and Market Valuation of Environmental Liabilities Relating to Superfund Sites," *Journal of Accounting Research* (Supplement 1994), pp. 177–209.

44. For example, refer to R. Jennings, P. J. Simko, and R. B. Thompson, "Does LIFO Inventory Accounting Improve the Income Statement at the Expense of the Balance Sheet?" *Journal of Accounting Research* (Spring 1996), pp. 85–109; and H. Z. Davis, N. Kahn, and E. Rozen, "LIFO Inventory Liquidations: An Empirical Study," *Journal of Accounting Research* (Autumn 1984), pp. 480–496.

45. D. S. Dhaliwal, "Measurement of Financial Leverage in the Presence of Unfunded Pension Obligations," *The Accounting Review* (October 1986), pp. 651–661.

46. D. Givoly and C. Hayn, "The Valuation of the Deferred Tax Liability: Evidence from the Stock Market," *The Accounting Review* (April 1992), pp. 394–410.

Chapter 2

Analyzing Business Earnings I: The Income Statement

> Every company I follow has a write-off. No one has any idea of what anyone is earning.[1]

That lament, expressed by a Wall Street analyst, captures well the impact that special charges have on the interpretation and analysis of business results. Special charges, which may include not only write-offs, but also such items as provisions for restructurings, severance pay, and plant closings tend to be nonrecurring in nature. As such, they cloud the identification of sustainable earnings and make the determination of earning power more difficult.

Consider, for example, the Eastman Kodak Company. In 1994, the company recorded a restructuring charge in the amount of $340 million, or about 25 percent of pretax income before the special charge, for ". . . severance and other termination benefits and exit costs related to the realignment of the company's world-wide manufacturing, marketing, administrative and photofinishing operations." Interestingly, the company also applied to the restructuring $50 million in reserves previously provided in another restructuring undertaken in 1993. Then, in 1996, the company recorded another restructuring charge, this time for $358 million or 19 percent of pretax income before the charge, to ". . . eliminate infrastructure and operational inefficiencies and redundancies." Once again, a portion of reserves set up as part of the 1993 restructuring were used for actions associated with the 1996 event. Then again in 1997, the company recorded yet another restructuring charge, this time for $1.5 billion or 96 percent of pretax income before the charge, for ". . . severance and other termination benefits and exit costs related to the realignment of the company's worldwide manufacturing sales and marketing, research and development (R&D), and administrative operations."[2] Including 1993, the company recorded significant special charges for restructuring in four out of five years. However, with similar charges in 1989, 1991, and 1992, the company was recording regular restructuring charges well before 1993. With so many charges, it is certainly difficult to determine what the company's historical earning power has been.

As part of a financial analysis of Kodak, there is no quick resolution of what to do with so many special charges. As a first step, they should be removed. While they have been occurring with a certain regularity, they cannot be viewed as an integral component of the company's recurring operations. The charges did occur, however, and cannot be ignored. They are part of the company's effort to transition to a changing and more competitive economic environment. They entail a cost to gain competitive advantage and to some extent to adjust for prior-year investment mistakes. To this end, in determining the company's earning power in recent years, the average of these charges should be spread over the past several years. Because the problems causing the charges likely predate the 1989 fiscal year, they should be spread back even further. The exact year would require a careful examination of the industry, the company's position in it, and a clearer understanding of when the firm's competitiveness began to suffer.

Unfortunately, when it comes to the active recording of special charges, Kodak is not alone. Although they make financial analysis more difficult, the frequency of such special charges has increased markedly in recent years. For example, in a study on accounting write-offs and earnings, researchers Elliott and Hanna found that in 1975 approximately five percent of public companies reported a material asset write-off.[3] That percentage increased to 14 percent in 1985 and to 23 percent in 1993—a 360 percent increase in frequency in 18 years. That is nearly one firm in four with a special charge, all playing havoc with the determination of earning power.

Although their frequency is not as great as with special charges, there are also a number of firms reporting special credits or nonrecurring increases to earnings. Using additional data provided by Elliott and Hanna, approximately six percent of public firms reported special credits in 1993, up from about two percent in 1975. These credits most often consist of a gain on the sale of an asset, but might also include an insurance or litigation settlement, a gain on the sale of a business, or the reversal of a portion of a prior-year restructuring charge.

The lower frequency of special credits when compared with special charges is not surprising considering the nature of historical-cost accounting and conservatism. In fact, accounting standards require the accrual of all potential losses where it is probable that they have been incurred and for which an amount of loss can be reasonably estimated. In contrast, the accrual of a contingent gain must await realization.[4] Also helping to increase the number of special charges in recent years has been Statement of Financial Accounting Standards (SFAS) No. 121, "Accounting for the Impairment of Long-Lived Assets."[5] That standard, issued in 1995, forced many companies to record impairment losses where asset book values exceeded their expected future net cash flows.

While special credits do not appear as frequently as special charges, they nonetheless do appear with sufficient frequency that they must be considered when analyzing financial statements. For example, the results of the Coca-Cola Company frequently include gains on the sale of stakes in certain of the company's bottlers. Those gains added $508 million or nine percent to pretax income in 1997. The company has recorded similar gains in previous years. Are the gains recurring? Should they be included or taken out when measuring earning power? According to Coca-Cola, such gains from sales "are an integral part of the soft-drink business." The investment community does not have a consensus on this view, however. Some analysts leave the gain in as though it were a recurring source of operating profit. For example, according to one analyst, "Of course [the gain] is nonrecurring. But if Coca-Cola can deliver such feats each year, his report suggests, who cares?" Says another who includes the gain, "It's controversial, . . . it's an issue we have been struggling with." Other analysts are not so sure. Says one about the gain on sale of a bottler, "that doesn't get valued like selling a case of Coke, . . . In a sense, it's a discontinued operation."[6]

The importance of properly dealing with these investment gains when calculating earning power cannot be overemphasized. They have added several percentage points to Coke's earnings growth rate in recent years. We tend to side with analysts who would remove the gains in calculating recurring earnings. The increases in the market values of these bottling operations occur over many years, not in a single year, and not in the year in which the gains are recognized. We liken them more to investment gains, the recurrence of which cannot be counted on like the sale of products or the provision of services. Moreover, the values of these investments have been aided in recent years by a general rise in equity prices that can be reversed at any time. Further, the company does not have the same control over the growth of these gains like it does the growth in its concentrate sales. However, we would not discount the cumulative impact of these gains entirely. Unrealized and unrecognized gains on these investments do enhance position quality giving the company financial flexibility and a pool of resources on which to draw when needed. The amounts of these unrecognized gains are substantial. Coke reports that for those bottlers for which the company has a sufficient ownership interest to exert significant influence, the excess of the market values of shares owned exceeded reported book values by approximately $8 billion.[7] That is a sizable sum and offers the company much unrecognized financial flexibility.

From the examples provided, it should be apparent that special charges and credits cloud investment analysis. They are nonrecurring items and should be removed from income in a first step toward analyzing business earnings. To do so, however, requires that these nonrecurring items be identified. This chapter is designed to help in locating such nonrecurring items. In Chapter Three, we demonstrate a systematic method to adjust for them.

NONRECURRING ITEMS AND INVESTMENT ANALYSIS: RESEARCH RESULTS

Research results provide support for the view that market participants appreciate the value of identifying the recurring and nonrecurring components of earnings. For example, in his study, Lipe found that a higher proportion of stock market returns were explained by a model that explicitly includes six commonly disclosed components of earnings than a model that included earnings only.[8] Those six components—gross profit, general and administrative expense, depreciation expense, interest expense, income taxes, and other items—provide investors with information that enables them to identify the extent to which earnings are derived from recurring sources. In another study, Ali, Klein, and Rosenfeld found that financial analysts were aware of and employed transitory and permanent components of earnings in their analyses.[9] They found that analysts rely more on the permanent components of earnings in devising their forecasts. In the academic literature, a nonrecurring item is referred to as a transitory component of earnings. Sustainable earnings, or earnings that have been adjusted to exclude such transitory components, are referred to as permanent components of earnings. In another study, Elliott and Hanna removed nonrecurring items from reported earnings for a selected sample of firms.[10] They found that the association between movements in share prices and earnings improved when earnings were adjusted to remove nonrecurring items. According to the authors, this result was consistent with the nonrecurring or transitory component of earnings having less information that is relevant for estimating future firm performance than does the recurring or permanent component. The implication is that there is value in identifying nonrecurring items and adjusting earnings to remove them.

NONRECURRING ITEMS AND EARNINGS QUALITY

Before proceeding to locate nonrecurring items, it is important, in keeping with the theme of this book, to comment on the earnings quality impact of the Kodak restructuring charges and the Coca-Cola bottling gains. On the persistence dimension, Kodak's restructuring charges enhance earnings quality. The company's earning power is greater than reported earnings would indicate. It is for this reason that we advocate an adjustment, in whole or part, to remove the charges from income in analyzing earnings. On the cash dimension, earnings quality is also enhanced as the cash payments accompanying these charges are exceeded by the charges themselves. This too is consistent with an adjustment to remove the charges from reported income. However, the purpose of the adjustment process is to identify sustainable earnings—earnings devoid of nonrecurring items—without an explicit consideration of cash flow. We will look at cash flow analysis and consider more carefully the cash flow aspects of various transactions in Chapter Thirteen.

The gains from selling bottling companies, as reported by Coca-Cola, impair earnings quality on the persistence dimension. Although, as noted, there is some disagreement on this, we view the gains as nonrecurring and advocate their removal from income. The bottling company sales do, however, provide more cash flow than their reported gains. Thus, on the cash dimension, earnings quality is enhanced. When, as is the case here, the two earnings-quality dimensions—persistence and cash—diverge, it is natural to seek an identification of which is more important. As noted in Chapter One, our objective is a complete understanding of the transaction and its earnings and cash flow effects on the company. From this point of view, we hesitate to stress one earnings-quality dimension over the other. We will, however, make the point that while cash flow is of great importance to both equity analysts and credit analysts, sustainable cash flow is paramount. Without the support of sustainable earnings, positive cash flow cannot be maintained. From this point of view, we would side with the persistence dimension, stressing the importance of identifying a sustainable earnings stream. What we would then recommend is a separate analysis to take a careful look at the extent to which those earnings are cash flow backed. By understanding each transaction and the extent to which it impacts earnings quality on the persistence and cash dimensions, the determination of sustainable earnings and the analysis of cash flow will be facilitated.

LOCATING NONRECURRING ITEMS

Although one might expect that most nonrecurring items would be located by a careful review of the income statement, that is not the case. In fact, research indicates that less than a quarter of nonrecurring items are disclosed on the income statement itself.[11]

Material nonrecurring items can be located in the most efficient way by following the search sequence outlined in Exhibit 2.1. In fact, nearly 60 percent of all nonrecurring items can be located by following the first five steps in the search sequence—namely, the income statement, the operating section of the cash flow statement, the inventory note for last-in, first-out (LIFO) firms, the income tax note, and the other income and expense note.[12] Moreover, that 60 percent reading can be increased if the focus is on material nonrecurring items only. Proceeding to steps six through seven in Exhibit 2.1 will yield details on the remaining nonrecurring items, though in these locations, the number of nonrecurring items disclosed is far fewer and the amounts are less likely to be material.

This chapter is organized around Exhibit 2.1. It illustrates how nonrecurring items can be identified in the various locations of a company's annual report using the preferred search sequence. At each step along the way, background is provided, as needed, on the structure of the financial statements being examined.

NONRECURRING ITEMS IN THE INCOME STATEMENT

Although only about 25 percent of nonrecurring items can be located on the income statement, it is still the most fruitful place to look and an excellent place to start. Many nonrecurring items are displayed here as separate line items, both before and after tax, and can be quickly identified. Often, items reported as "other income (expense)" are detailed in a footnote reference for efficient identification of additional nonrecurring items. This is actually step 5 in the search sequence.

Exhibit 2.1.   Efficient Search Sequence for Nonrecurring Items

Step and Search Location

1. Income statement
2. Statement of cash flows—operating activities section only
3. Inventory note—assuming that significant inventories exist and that the firm employs the LIFO method
4. Income tax note
5. "Other income and expense" note in cases in which this balance is not detailed on the face of the income statement
6. Management's Discussion and Analysis of Financial Condition and Results of Operations—a Securities and Exchange Commission requirement and, therefore, available only for public companies
7. Other notes that occasionally reveal nonrecurring items:

Note	*Nonrecurring Item Revealed*
Property and equipment	Gains and losses on asset sales
Long-term debt	Foreign currency and debt retirement gains and losses
Foreign currency	Foreign currency gains and losses
Restructuring	Current and prospective impact of restructuring activities
Contingencies	Potential revenue or expense items
Quarterly financial data	Nonrecurring items in quarterly results

Those footnotes should be reviewed carefully because significant components of other income or expense often consist of recurring items such as interest income and interest expense.

Income Statement Formats

To better understand where to look on the income statement for nonrecurring items and whether those items are being reported before or after income tax, it is important to have a complete understanding of a modern-day income statement. Under generally accepted accounting principles (GAAP), there are two principal income statement formats currently being employed—single-step and multistep. Carter-Wallace, Inc. uses the single-step format. An example is presented in Exhibit 2.2. In contrast, Herman Miller, Inc. uses the multistep format. An example is presented in Exhibit 2.3.

   An annual survey of financial statements conducted by the American Institute of Certified Public Accountants (AICPA) reveals that about one-third of the 600 companies in its survey use the single-step format and the other two-thirds use the multistep format.[13] The distinguishing feature of the multistep statement is that it provides an intermediate earnings subtotal designed to reflect pretax operating

Exhibit 2.2.   Single-Step Income Statement: Carter-Wallace, Inc., Consolidated Statements of Earnings, Years Ending March 31, 1995–1997 (Thousands Except Per-Share Data)

	1995	1996	1997
Revenues:			
Net sales	$663,642	$658,940	$648,755
Interest income	3,574	5,128	4,226
Royalty and other income	2,762	3,409	3,200
	669,978	667,477	656,181
Cost and expenses:			
Cost of goods sold	240,318	246,220	243,657
Advertising and promotion	125,450	123,573	122,407
Marketing and other selling	127,152	124,765	127,444
Research and development	41,315	26,494	27,284
General and administrative	81,321	78,634	79,440
Provision for restructuring of operations and facilities	74,060	16,500	—
Provision for plant closing	—	23,100	—
Provision for loss on Felbatol	37,780	8,200	—
Provision for loss on discontinuance of the Organidin (iodinated glycerol) product line	17,500	(5,800)	—
Interest	2,512	3,889	4,186
Other	9,600	9,105	6,414
	757,008	654,680	610,832
Earnings (loss) before taxes on income	(87,030)	12,797	45,349
Provision (benefit) for taxes on income	(30,762)	5,247	18,593
Net earnings (loss)	$(56,268)	$7,550	$26,756
Net earnings (loss) per average share of common stock	($1.22)	$.16	$.58

Source: Carter-Wallace, Inc., Form 10-K annual report to the Securities and Exchange Commission (March 1997), p. 13.

performance. In principle, this operating income or operating profit should be composed almost entirely of recurring items of revenue and expense that result from the main operating activities of the firm. In practice, it is common for numerous material nonrecurring items to be included in operating income. For example, where present, "restructuring charges," one of the most popular nonrecurring items of the 1990s, is virtually always included in operating income. Other nonrecurring items included in operating income are provisions for environmental costs, asset write-downs, acquired in-process research and development (R&D),

Exhibit 2.3. Multistep Income Statement: Herman Miller, Inc., Consolidated Statements of Earnings, Years Ending June 3, 1995, June 1, 1996, and May 31, 1997 (Thousands Except Per-Share Data)

	1995	1996	1997
Net sales	$1,083,050	$1,283,931	$1,495,885
Cost of sales	704,781	848,985	961,961
Gross margin	378,269	434,946	533,924
Operating expenses:			
Selling, general and administrative	303,621	316,024	359,601
Design and research	33,682	27,472	29,140
Patent litigation settlement	—	16,515	—
Loss on divestiture/restructuring charges	31,900	—	14,500
Total operating expenses	369,203	360,011	403,241
Operating income	9,066	74,935	130,683
Other expenses:			
Interest expense	6,299	7,910	8,843
Interest income	(6,154)	(6,804)	(8,926)
Loss on foreign exchange	3,067	1,614	1,687
Other, net	1,815	2,119	3,196
Net other expenses	5,027	4,839	4,800
Income before income taxes	4,039	70,096	125,883
Income taxes	(300)	24,150	51,485
Net income	$4,339	$45,946	$74,398
Net income per share	$.09	$.91	$1.55

Source: Herman Miller, Inc., Form 10-K annual report to the Securities and Exchange Commission (March 1997), p. 23.

and merger-related expenses. With so many special items included in operating profit, one must question the extent to which operating profit is truly operating.

Another popular subtotal for multistep income statements is gross profit or gross margin. This measure of income is calculated by subtracting cost of goods sold from total revenues. Approximately one-half of firms employing the multistep format report gross profit on their income statements.[14] Interestingly, while cost of goods sold would be expected to be a recurring source of expense, it often includes nonrecurring elements. Identification of these items requires a careful review of the footnotes and emphasizes once again how the income statement cannot be used alone to identify nonrecurring items. Consider the following footnote provided by the Eastman Kodak Company:

In December 1997, the Company committed to implement a restructuring program and recorded a pre-tax provision of $1,455 million for severance and other termination benefits and exit costs related to the realignment of the Company's worldwide manufacturing, sales and marketing, research and development (R&D), and administrative operations. The Company recorded $165 million of the $1,455 million provision as cost of goods sold. The remaining $1,290 million includes $862 million of restructuring costs and $428 million of asset impairments.[15]

Here, the company has included $165 million of its restructuring charge, a nonrecurring item, in cost of goods sold.

The Herman Miller, Inc. multistep income statement presented in Exhibit 2.3 reports both the gross margin and operating income subtotals. In contrast, the Carter-Wallace, Inc. single-step income statement presented in Exhibit 2.2 does not partition income into such intermediate subtotals. Instead, all revenues and expenses are separately totaled and "earnings (loss) before taxes on income" is computed in a single step, as total expenses are simply deducted from total revenues.

Nonrecurring Items Located in Income from Continuing Operations

Whether a single-step or multistep format is used, the composition of income from continuing operations is the same. It includes all items of revenue or gain and expense or loss with the exception of those (1) identified with discontinued operations, (2) meeting the definition of extraordinary items, and (3) resulting from the cumulative effect of changes in accounting principles. Because all expenses and losses associated with continuing operations have been subtracted, income from continuing operations is an after-tax measure. While referred to by analysts as income from continuing operations, that title is not used on an income statement unless the reporting firm has discontinued operations. Then, it would report separately income from continuing operations and income from discontinued operations. If there are no discontinued operations, extraordinary items, or changes in accounting principle reported on the income statement, the likely title for income from continuing operations would be net income or net earnings. For firms with an extraordinary item or a change in accounting principle, a likely title for income from continuing operations would be income before extraordinary item or income before cumulative effect of change in accounting principle.

Income from continuing operations can, as noted, include many nonrecurring items. On a single-step income statement, nonrecurring items are listed with other revenues and gains or expenses and losses. For example, the Carter-Wallace single-step income statement in Exhibit 2.2 lists among its costs and expenses "provision for restructuring of operations and facilities," "provision for plant closing," "provision for loss on Felbatol," and "Provision for loss on discontinuance of the Organidin (iodinated glycerol) product line." These expense items would clearly qualify as nonrecurring in nature.

Some examples of other nonrecurring items reported by companies employing a single-step format income statement are presented in Exhibit 2.4. Care should be taken in reviewing the income statement for items such as these as they might be identified clearly on the income statement or included with "other income (expense)," where positive identification can be made only by reviewing a relevant footnote.

Companies using the multistep income statement format will often include nonrecurring items within operating profit—clearly a component of income from continuing operations. Nonrecurring items will also appear outside of operating income, but they are still part of income from continuing operations. For example, Herman Miller reports a "patent litigation settlement" and a "loss on divestiture/restructuring charges" within operating income. Also, among its "other expenses," outside of operating income but within income from continuing operations, the firm lists a "loss on foreign exchange." We would judge all three items to be nonrecurring, including the foreign exchange item, even though those losses have repeated for three years. One cannot expect the foreign currencies in which the company does business to continue moving in the same direction indefinitely. As such, foreign exchange gains are also likely to occur. Foreign currency will be discussed further in Chapter Seven.

Nonrecurring Items Included in Operating Income

A sampling of nonrecurring items included in the operating income subtotal of multistep income statements is provided in Exhibit 2.5. It was noted earlier that under current GAAP it is more likely to see instances of nonrecurring expense or loss than of nonrecurring revenue or gain. That was our experience as we collected examples of nonrecurring items.

The nonrecurring items presented in Exhibit 2.5 are many and varied. On the expense or loss side, restructuring charges and asset write-downs are very common. Also appearing on the list are the effects of severance packages, acquired in-process R&D, and costs associated with the clean-up of an environmental contamination. On the revenue or gain side are the reversal of restructuring charges, litigation settlements, and gains from asset sales.

The nonrecurring items found in Exhibit 2.5 can generally be linked with core operations as implied by the title operating income, though at times that link is stretched, as in the case of the merger-related expenses of Steris Corp or National Semiconductor's gain on sale of a company. A review of the list reveals that the subtotal operating income cannot be viewed generally as a sustainable source of profit.

Nonrecurring Items Excluded from Operating Income

Nonrecurring items excluded from operating income are typically reported in a separate section of "other income (expense)." These items are usually less closely associated with the basic operating activities of the firm. A sampling of nonrecurring items reported outside the operating income subtotal of multistep income statements is provided in Exhibit 2.6.

Exhibit 2.4. Nonrecurring Items of Revenue or Gain and Expense or Loss Reported on Single-Step Format Income Statements

Company	Nonrecurring Item
Expense or Loss	
American Airlines, Inc. (1996)	Write-down in value of aircraft interiors
Campbell Soup Co. (1996)	Restructuring program
Chart House Enterprises, Inc. (1996)	Write-down of note receivable and investment
Kellwood Company (1999)	Cost of Koret merger
Crompton & Knowles Corp. (1996)	Environmental costs
Detroit Diesel Corp. (1996)	Write-down of investment in Mexico
Ekco Group, Inc. (1996)	Write-down of goodwill
Foster Wheeler Corp. (1996)	Asbestos claims
Horizon CMS Healthcare Corp. (1997)	Lease exit costs
Rockwell International Corp. (1997)	Purchased in-process R&D
Revenue or Gain	
Arvin Industries, Inc. (1996)	Gain on sale of affiliate
Titanium Metals Corp. (1995)	Restructuring credit
Wells Gardner Electronics Corp. (1995)	Gain on sale of fixed assets

Sources: Companies' annual reports. The year following each company name designates the annual report from which each example was drawn.

Litigation settlements dominate the list of nonrecurring expense or loss items reported outside of operating income. These items did not appear on the list of expense or loss items reported in operating income. There were, however, cases of similar nonrecurring expense or loss items reported both within operating income and outside operating income by different firms. For example, environmental costs and in at least one instance, the write-down of assets, can be found both within and outside of operating income.

On the revenue or gain side, the list of nonrecurring items reported outside of operating income are clearly dominated by asset sales—securities, businesses, and fixed assets. There are also gains from legal judgments on the list as well as one reversal of an accrual related to a store closure. There does not appear to be much difference between the nonrecurring revenue or gain items reported outside of operating profit from those reported within operating profit. All of the items listed, however, whether included within operating income or excluded from it, are inherently nonrecurring, and care should be taken to note that in doing an analysis of earnings.

Exhibit 2.5. Nonrecurring Items of Revenue or Gain and Expense or Loss Included in Operating Income—Multistep Format Income Statements

Company	Nonrecurring Item
Expense or Loss	
Aerovox, Inc. (1996)	Provision for environmental costs
Allergan, Inc. (1996)	Restructuring and asset write-offs
Armor All Products Corp. (1996)	Correction of aerosol packaging
Barra, Inc. (1999)	Write-off of capitalized software costs
C. Brewer Homes, Inc. (1997)	Asset impairment loss
Cascade Corp. (1996)	Environmental expenses
Dean Foods Company (1999)	Plant closure costs
Donnelley Enterprise Solutions, Inc. (1996)	Severance agreement
First Aviation Services, Inc. (1999)	Nonrecurring charges
Integrated Circuit Systems, Inc. (1997)	Acquired in-process R&D
Interlinq Software Corp. (1996)	Write-off of capitalized software costs
IVI Publishing, Inc. (1997)	Impairment loss on leasehold improvements
Microware Systems Corp. (1997)	Employee severance
National Semiconductor Corp. (1997)	Write-down of fixed assets
Polaroid Corp. (1996)	Write-offs of fixed assets
Prosource, Inc. (1997)	Restructuring charge
Railtex, Inc. (1995)	Write-down of leasehold improvements
Steris Corp. (1997)	Merger-related expenses
Sun Television and Appliances, Inc. (1997)	Restructuring charge
Uno Restaurant Corp. (1997)	Asset impairment charge
Yellow Corp. (1996)	Write-down of nonoperating real estate
Revenue or Gain	
Adolph Coors Co. (1996)	Arbitration ruling
Alliant Techsystems, Inc. (1999)	Change in environmental liability estimate
Datascope Corp. (1996)	Settlement of litigation
Engelhard Corp. (1994)	Reversal of restructuring reserves
H. J. Heinz Co. (1995)	Gain on sale of confectionery business
Life Technologies, Inc. (1996)	Gain on product line disposal
National Semiconductor Corp. (1997)	Gain on sale of Fairchild Semiconductor

Sources: Companies' annual reports. The year following each company name designates the annual report from which each example was drawn.

Exhibit 2.6. Nonrecurring Items of Revenue or Gain and Expense or Loss Excluded from Operating Income—Multistep Format Income Statements

Company	Nonrecurring Item
Expense or Loss	
Adaptec, Inc. (1994)	Settlement of shareholder class action suit
Applied Extrusion Technologies, Inc. (1995)	Litigation settlement
Baltek Corp. (1995)	Foreign currency loss
Centocor, Inc. (1995)	Litigation settlement
Champion Enterprises, Inc. (1995)	Environmental reserve
Cryomedical Sciences, Inc. (1995)	Settlement of shareholder class action suit
Gibson Greetings, Inc. (1995)	Loss on derivative transactions
Imperial Holly Corporation (1994)	Workforce reduction charge
International Thunderbird Gaming Corp. (1997)	Write-down of California assets
Revenue or Gain	
Artistic Greetings, Inc. (1995)	Unrealized gain on trading securities
Atwood Oceanics, Inc. (1996)	Realized gain on sale of securities
Baltek Corp. (1998)	Foreign currency gains
Calloways Nursery, Inc. (1995)	Reversal of accruals related to store closure
CommNet Cellular, Inc. (1995)	Gain from legal judgment
Meredith Corp. (1994)	Sale of broadcast stations
New England Business Services, Inc. (1996)	Gain on sale of product line
Pollo Tropical (1995)	Business interruption insurance recovery
Tech Data, Corp. (1999)	Gain on sale of Macroton AG
United Dominion Industries, Ltd. (1996)	Gain on sale of businesses
VideoLabs, Inc. (1996)	Gain on sale of fixed assets

Sources: Companies' annual reports. The year following each company name designates the annual report from which each example was drawn.

Nonrecurring Items Located below Income from Continuing Operations

The area of the income statement below "Income from continuing operations" has a standard organization that is the same for both single-step and multistep income statements. The format is outlined in Exhibit 2.7. The income statement of The Interlake Corp., shown in Exhibit 2.8, illustrates this format. The company's income from continuing operations line item is titled "income from continuing operations before extraordinary loss and accounting change." It is positioned after

Exhibit 2.7.   Standard Income Statement Format below Income
from Continuing Operations

Income from continuing operations	$000
Discontinued operations	000
Extraordinary items	000
Cumulative effect of changes in accounting principles	000
Net income	$000

"minority interest," a recurring charge that attributes to minority or outside shareholders their share of the earnings of a less than 100 percent owned and consolidated subsidiary. Following the company's income from continuing operations
are, in order, and net of any related income tax effects, a gain from discontinued
operations, an extraordinary loss on early extinguishment of debt, and a cumulative-effect gain on a change in accounting principle. Each of these special line
items—discontinued operations, extraordinary items, and changes in accounting
principles—are, by nature, nonrecurring. They are discussed, along with illustra-
tive examples, in the sections that follow.

Discontinued Operations

The Interlake income statement reports an apparent gain from discontinued operations in each year presented. There was, however, a discontinued operation in only
one of the three years. The company sold its packaging business, viewed as a
separate business segment, in 1996. Income from operations of that segment together with the gain on disposal of the business was reported as income from
discontinued operations in 1996. The company's income statement for 1995 was
then restated to present income from operations of that segment as income from
discontinued operations. For 1997, the company received additional proceeds
from the sale and reported those amounts as income from discontinued operations
for that year.

    Thus, the discontinued operations section includes two sources of income or
loss reported net of income taxes: (1) income from operations of the discontinued
segment for all periods presented prior to the date on which a disposal decision
is definitively reached and (2) any gain or loss on disposal. In addition to the
results of the actual sale, the gain or loss on disposal would include income from
operations of the discontinued segment from the time the decision is reached to
dispose of the segment until the sale is consummated.[16]

    A discontinued operation refers only to the disposal of an entire line of busi-
ness or business segment and not simply to the disposal of a product line. For
example, a decision by Philip Morris Companies, Inc. to dispose of its foods
division—a business segment—would be reported as a discontinued operation.

Exhibit 2.8. Disclosure of Discontinued Operations, Extraordinary Loss, and Cumulative Effect of Change in Accounting Principle: The Interlake Corp., Consolidated Statement of Operations, December 31, 1995, December 29, 1996, and December 28, 1997 (Thousands of Dollars)

	1995	1996	1997
Net sales from continuing operations	$689,913	$709,585	$725,591
Cost of products sold	530,465	546,151	574,338
Selling and administrative expense	101,844	99,739	97,755
Gain on sale of foreign handling businesses*	—	—	35,613
Operating Profit	57,604	63,695	89,111
Interest expense	47,486	48,297	45,220
Interest income	(1,780)	(2,413)	(2,770)
Nonoperating (income) expense*	(1,043)	(2,088)	(9,360)
Income from continuing operations before taxes, minority interest, extraordinary loss, and accounting change	12,941	19,899	37,301
Provision for income taxes*	7,415	8,481	16,400
Income from continuing operations before minority interest, extraordinary loss, and accounting change	5,526	11,418	20,901
Minority interest	4,533	3,893	4,531
Income from continuing operations before extraordinary loss and accounting change	993	7,525	16,370
Income from discontinued operations, net of applicable income taxes*	3,220	46,376	1,833
Extraordinary loss on early extinguishments of debt, net of applicable income taxes	(3,448)	(267)	(1,482)
Cumulative effect of change in accounting principle*	—	1,610	—
Net income	$765	$55,244	$16,721

*The original report made reference to notes, which are not included here.

Source: The Interlake Corp., Form 10-K annual report to the Securities and Exchange Commission (December 1997), p. 20.

However, a decision by General Motors Corporation to sell its Oldsmobile division would not. Any gain or loss on the sale of Oldsmobile, a product line within a business segment, would likely be reported as other income within income from continuing operations.

The separation of discontinued operations from continuing operations is designed to enhance the interpretive value of the income statement. In so doing, the

Exhibit 2.9. Discontinued Operations

Company	Principal Businesses	Discontinued Operation
Alexander & Baldwin (1996)	Food, transportation, and property development	Container leasing
Alliant Techsystems (1997)	Aerospace and defense technologies	Marine systems
Aeroflex, Inc. (1997)	Electronics and isolator products	Envelopes
Ball Corporation (1996)	Packaging, aerospace, and technologies	Glass containers
Black and Decker (1996)	Consumer and home-improvement products	Information technology and services
Dean Foods Co. (1999)	Food processor	Vegetables segment
Gleason Corporation (1995)	Gear machinery and equipment	Metal stamping and fabricating
Maxco, Inc. (1996)	Manufacturing, distribution, and real estate	Automotive refinishing products
TRW, Inc. (1996)	Advanced technology products	Information systems and services
Worthington Industries, Inc. (1999)	Steel pressure cylinders	Custom and cast products

Sources: Companies' annual reports. The year following each company name designates the annual report from which each example was drawn.

reader is informed of the components of earnings that can more reasonably be expected to continue. Examples of discontinued operations are provided in Exhibit 2.9.

Extraordinary Items

Referring again to Exhibit 2.8, Interlake reported an extraordinary loss on early extinguishment of debt in all three years presented. The company repurchased senior debt and repaid certain outstanding bank loans. The amounts reported as extraordinary losses are premiums incurred in repurchasing and repaying debt amounts and unamortized debt issuance costs related to the previously outstanding debt balances. They are reported net of applicable income taxes.

Income statement items are considered extraordinary if they are *both* (1) unusual in nature and (2) infrequent in occurrence.[17] Items are considered unusual if they are not related to the company's typical activities or operations while giving consideration to its industry, location, and environment. For example, flood damage would not be considered unusual for a firm located in a floodplain, nor would

Exhibit 2.10. Extraordinary Items

	1994	1995	1996	1997
Debt extinguishments	59	53	60	62
Other	—	3	5	3
Total extraordinary items	59	56	65	65
Presenting extraordinary items	59	55	63	64
Not presenting extraordinary items	541	545	537	536
Total companies	600	600	600	600

Source: American Institute of Certified Public Accountants, *Accounting Trends and Techniques* (1998), p. 397.

hurricane damage for a firm located on the coast in southern Florida. Similarly, a loss arising from a change in government regulation would not be considered unusual for a regulated entity. In most instances, fire damage would appear to qualify as an unusual event. Infrequency of occurrence implies that the item is not expected to recur in the foreseeable future. It may have happened once, but is not expected to occur again.

The requirements of "unusual and nonrecurring" would appear to exclude Interlake's losses on early extinguishment of debt. However, generally accepted accounting principles do require that gains and losses associated with selected transactions be classified as extraordinary without reference to whether the items are unusual and nonrecurring. Two transactions that are common and are always classified as extraordinary are: (1) gains and losses from the extinguishment of debt[18] and (2) gains and losses resulting from "troubled debt restructurings."[19] Thus, Interlake's transactions are afforded extraordinary item treatment.

The requirements for extraordinary item treatment are stringent, and few items qualify. This is made apparent in Exhibit 2.10, in which a tabulation of extraordinary items, based on an annual survey of 600 companies conducted by the AICPA is provided. Not surprisingly, debt extinguishments constitute the largest single category of extraordinary item. The treatment of operating loss carryforwards as extraordinary was discontinued under SFAS No. 109, "Accounting for Income Taxes."[20] This leaves very few *judgmental* extraordinary items among the 600 companies surveyed.

The use of judgment by reporting companies in deciding whether gains and losses are extraordinary is clearly evident by the examples provided in Exhibit 2.11. The exhibit presents a variety of items and events, some of which are reported as extraordinary and some of which are not. The items reported in the extraordinary item group would, for the most part, appear to fulfill the requirements of unusual and nonrecurring. For example, Avoca reports as extraordinary the insurance proceeds received resulting from destruction of a building by fire, Farm Family Mutual includes costs incurred related to demutualization, and Noble

Exhibit 2.11.   Extraordinary Item Classification Decisions

Item or Event	*Company*
Reported as Extraordinary	
Write-off of deferred financing costs	Aavid Thermal Technologies, Inc. (1996)
Discontinuance of regulatory accounting practices	Aliant Communications Co. (1995)
Gain from early extinguishment of debt	Alpine Lace Brands, Inc. (1995)
Gain on insurance settlement due to damage to its building from the San Francisco earthquake	American Building Maintenance, Inc. (1989)
Insurance proceeds resulting from destruction of a building by fire	Avoca, Inc. (1995)
Costs of canceled business acquisition agreement	Bria Communications Corp. (1996)
Partial asset distribution from an unaffiliated trust	Danielson Holding Corp. (1994)
Partial recovery of Iraqi receivables	Dimon, Inc. (1996)
Costs incurred related to demutualization	Farm Family Mutual Insurance Co. (1996)
Gain on sale of residential mortgage loan servicing operations	KeyCorp. (1995)
Gain on downward revision of obligation to United Mine Workers of America Combined Benefit Fund	NACCO Industries, Inc. (1995)
Insurance settlement due to deprivation of use of logistics and drilling equipment abandoned in Somalia due to civil unrest	Noble Drilling Corp. (1991)
Gain from settlement with the government of Iran over the expropriation of Phillips' oil production interests	Phillips Petroleum Co. (1990)
Settlement of class action litigation	Raychem Corp. (1992)
Write-off of unamortized balance of intrastate operating rights	Schwerman Trucking Co. (1995)
Not Reported as Extraordinary	
Flood costs	Argosy Gaming Co. (1993)
Damage caused by Hurricane Andrew	BellSouth Corp. (1992)
Loss provision for costs associated with cleanup of oil spill in Valdez Alaska	Exxon Corp. (1989)
Insurance proceeds resulting from a headquarters building fire	Norwest Corp. (1983)
Insurance claim settlement (airplane crash)	On The Border Cafes, Inc. (1994)

(continued)

Exhibit 2.11.   (Continued) Extraordinary Item Classification Decisions

Item or Event	Company
Gain from insurance settlement as a result of the loss of Rowan Gorilla I jack-up drilling rig, which capsized and sank while being towed to the North Sea	Rowan Companies, Inc. (1988)
Settlement of securities class action litigation	Scientific-Atlanta, Inc. (1994)
Gain from a settlement with the government of Iran over the expropriation of Sun oil production interests	Sun Company, Inc. (1992)

Sources: Companies' annual reports. The year following each company name designates the annual report from which each example was drawn.

Drilling reports an insurance settlement from deprivation of use of logistics and drilling equipment abandoned in Somalia due to civil unrest. Similarly, the non-extraordinary items include gains and losses that would not appear to be unusual and nonrecurring. In this group, BellSouth reports the damage caused in South Florida by Hurricane Andrew, Rowan Companies report a gain from insurance settlement as a result of the loss of a drilling rig that capsized and sank while being towed to the North Sea, and Exxon reports a loss provision for costs associated with the cleanup of the oil spill in Valdez, Alaska.

There are exceptions, however, in which judgment gives some surprising results. For example, while Avoca viewed its fire as an extraordinary event, Norwest did not consider the destruction of its headquarters building to be extraordinary. The company included the gain, totaling approximately 10 percent of net income, with other noninterest income. And while Philips Petroleum reported as an extraordinary gain its settlement with the government of Iran over the expropriation of the company's oil production interests, Sun Company considered a similar settlement not to be extraordinary. Further, Raychem considered the settlement of its class action securities litigation extraordinary, but Scientific-Atlanta did not.

These exceptions, in which seemingly similar items are reported by some companies as extraordinary and by others as nonextraordinary, highlight the need for caution when examining financial statements for nonrecurring items. While the presence of extraordinary items provides help in identifying nonrecurring items, their lack does not provide assurances that nonrecurring items are not present. The underlying nature of all sources of income and gain, expense and loss must be considered carefully in the search for nonrecurring items.

Changes in Accounting Principles

In Exhibit 2.8, Interlake reports a "cumulative effect of change in accounting principle" in 1996. That year, the company changed its method of amortizing unrecognized actuarial gains and losses with respect to its postretirement benefits plan. As a change in accounting principle, the company recorded the cumulative effect of the change—the cumulative impact of the change for all years prior to 1996, the current year—net of income taxes, as a separate line item on the income statement. Not disclosed on the income statement, but provided in a footnote, would be the impact of the change on current-year earnings.

A change in accounting principle entails a switch from one GAAP or method to another. For example, a change from an accelerated method of depreciation to straight-line or from the first-in, first-out (FIFO) method of inventory costing to the weighted average method represents a change in accounting principle. Such changes may be needed to conform with a newly issued accounting standard or to provide for a continued fair presentation of financial results and position over time as companies, circumstances, and industries change.

The cumulative-effect approach employed by Interlake is the most common form of accounting treatment for changes in accounting principle. A less common form of treatment is the retroactive-effect approach in which the cumulative income effect of the change is adjusted to retained earnings and is not reported as a component of net income. The financial statements of all years presented are then restated on the new accounting basis. This accounting method is reserved for only a select few instances in which an accounting change would have a very pervasive, material effect on the financial statements taken as a whole. Examples include a change from the last-in, first-out (LIFO) method of inventory costing to another method, a change between the percentage-of-completion and completed-contract methods for long-term contracts, or a change in reporting entity. The retroactive approach is also called for, in some instances, by new accounting standards. A recent accounting standard requiring retroactive treatment is SFAS No. 128, "Earnings per Share."[21] While not entailing a prior-year income effect, adoption of this standard did require firms to restate earnings per share amounts for all prior years to conform with its newly mandated calculations for basic and diluted earnings per share.

Coachman Industries, Inc. provides an example of an application of the cumulative-effect approach for a change in accounting principle. In 1996, the company changed its method of accounting for its investments in life insurance contracts. That year, the company provided in its annual report a description of the new accounting method, the reason for the change (the new method was the preferred method under GAAP), and the following disclosure of the cumulative and current-year income effects of the change:

> On January 1, 1996, the Company recorded a $2.3 million noncash credit for the cumulative effect of this accounting change ($.15 per share for both basic and diluted earnings per share). This change in accounting method also increased income before cumulative effect of accounting change and net income for the year ended December 31, 1996 by $1,087,678 or $.07 per share for both basic and diluted earnings per share. If the cash surrender value method had been applied during 1995, pro forma net income would have been $18,292,792 and pro forma net income per share would have been $1.23—basic and $1.22—diluted.[22]

According to the note, the company recorded a $2.3 million cumulative effect gain on its 1996 income statement. In addition, though not reported separately on the income statement, the company recorded an increase to income from continuing operations of $1,087,678.

Clearly, from this disclosure, the cumulative effect amount is a nonrecurring item. It represents the effect of the accounting change on several years and appears only in one year's income statement. However, as the current-year effect will be continuing into future years, it is not a nonrecurring item, though for a comparison of results for 1996 with earlier years, it should be considered nonrecurring.

Changes in Estimates

Changes in estimates involve revisions in accounting measurements based on new events, additional experience, or improved judgment. For example, changes in the useful lives of equipment, their residual values, the uncollectible portion of accounts receivable, or the interim effects of price changes on LIFO inventory accounts would entail changes in estimates. Such changes are handled prospectively. That is, the income effects of the changes are accounted for over current and future reporting periods.

An example of a change in estimate is provided in the following footnote taken from the annual report of Blowout Entertainment, Inc.:

> Videocassette rental inventory purchased for base stock is stated at cost and amortized, beginning on the date the videocassettes are placed into service, to a salvage value of $6 per videocassette over an estimated useful life of 36 months. All copies of new release videocassettes are amortized on an accelerated basis during their first four months to an average net book value of $22 and then on a straight-line basis to their salvage value of $6 over the next 32 months.

> As of January 1, 1997, the Company changed the estimates used to amortize rental inventory. Prior to January 1, 1997, the Company amortized new release videocassettes purchased for more than $20 to a value of $15 over the first four months, then to a $6 salvage value over the next 32 months. New-release videocassettes purchased for less than $20 were depreciated to $8 over the first four months, then to a $6 salvage value over the next 32 months. The overall effect of this change in estimate for the year ended December 31, 1997 was to reduce the net loss by approximately $1,470,000.[23]

The company has altered the residual values used in the calculation of amortization expense for new-release videos. Note that the company refers to the change as a change in estimate and does not give reference to a cumulative-effect adjustment. Instead, only the current year's effect of the change is disclosed. Because this new amortization amount will be maintained for future periods, it cannot be viewed as a nonrecurring item. However, for comparison of results in 1997 with earlier years, the $1,470,000 gain in 1997 should be considered nonrecurring.

Exhibit 2.12.   Summary of Accounting Changes

Subject of the Change	Number of Companies			
	1994	*1995*	*1996*	*1997*
Impairment of long-lived assets (SFAS 121)	3	87	134	39
Business process reengineering (Emerging Issues Task Force 97-13)	—	—	—	28
Environmental remediation liabilities (Statement of Position 96-1)	—	—	6	21
Transfer of financial assets (SFAS 125)	—	—	—	19
Reporting period for subsidiaries	1	3	4	5
Inventories	5	3	5	4
Depreciation method	—	3	4	3
Depreciable lives	6	2	3	3
Reporting entity	1	6	1	1
Investments (SFAS 115)	108	47	1	—
Postretirement benefits (SFAS 106)	44	1	1	—
Postemployment benefits (SFAS 112)	80	18	—	—
Impairment of loans (SFAS 114)	1	6	—	—
Reinsurance contracts	2	—	—	—
Income taxes (SFAS 109)	89	—	—	—
Other	23	18	11	10

Source: American Institute of Certified Public Accountants, *Accounting Trends and Techniques* (1998), p. 53.

A survey of changes in accounting principles and estimates is provided in Exhibit 2.12. As can be seen in the exhibit, accounting changes in recent years have been dominated by the effects of new accounting pronouncements for long-lived assets, investments, postretirement and postemployment benefits, impairment of loans, and income taxes. These would all be considered changes in accounting principle, as would the changes in accounting methods for depreciation and inventories and the changes in reporting entity. The changes for depreciable lives and, most likely, environmental remediation costs, entail changes in accounting estimates.

New Developments in the Measurement of Income

With the issuance of SFAS No. 130, "Reporting Comprehensive Income," the Financial Accounting Standards Board (FASB) defined a new, more inclusive measure of income that goes beyond traditional net income. That new income measure, comprehensive income, includes all changes in shareholders' equity except those resulting from investments by owners and distributions to owners. Thus,

Exhibit 2.13. Statement of Income and Comprehensive Income: Example Format (Hypothetical Amounts)

Revenues		$200,000
Operating expenses		(95,000)
Other gains and losses		15,000
Gain on sale of securities		5,000
Pretax income		125,000
Income tax expense		(50,000)
Net income		75,000
Other comprehensive income, net of tax:		
Foreign currency translation adjustments		8,000
Unrealized gains on securities:		
Unrealized holding gains arising during the period	$13,000	
Less: reclassification adjustment for gains included in net income	(1,500)	11,500
Minimum pension liability adjustment		(2,500)
Other comprehensive income		17,000
Comprehensive income		$92,000

it includes net income plus other items, such as adjustments for underfunded pension plans, unrealized gains and losses on available-for-sale investments in debt and equity securities, and cumulative foreign currency translation adjustments, which historically have been reported directly in shareholders' equity.

The FASB offers much flexibility in reporting comprehensive income under SFAS No. 130. However, the standard does recommend a reporting format that extends the income statement to include disclosure of comprehensive income. An example of that format is provided in Exhibit 2.13. As shown in the exhibit, the recommended format reports traditional net income and proceeds with a presentation of other comprehensive income. Net income and other comprehensive income are then summed to derive comprehensive income.

Other permitted formats for disclosing comprehensive income include the use of a separate income statement and statement of comprehensive income and the disclosure of comprehensive income within the traditional statement of shareholder's equity. As this latter format deemphasizes comprehensive income as a measure of income, it is proving to be the most popular reporting format.

As presented in Exhibit 2.14, Lubrizol Corporation used its statement of shareholders' equity to disclose comprehensive income. Then accompanying the statement of shareholders' equity was a footnote describing the components of other comprehensive income. In that note, the company disclosed that other com-

Exhibit 2.14. Consolidated Statements of Shareholders' Equity: Lubrizol Corp., for the Year Ended December 31, 1997 (Thousands of Dollars)

	Number of Shares Outstanding	Common Shares	Retained Earnings	AOCI*	Total
Bal., Dec. 31, 1996	58,522,676	$78,534	$744,310	$(3,468)	$819,376
Comprehensive income:					
Net income 1997			154,869		154,869
Other comprehensive income (loss)				(36,937)	(36,937)
Comprehensive income					117,932
Cash dividends			(58,469)		(58,469)
Common shares—treasury:					
Shares purchased	(1,812,841)	(2,538)	(67,526)		(70,064)
Shares issued upon option exercise	257,059	6,673			6,673
Bal., December 31, 1997	56,966,894	$82,669	$773,184	$(40,405)	$815,448

*Accumulated other comprehensive income.

Source: Lubrizol Corp. Form 10-K annual report to the Securities and Exchange Commission (December 1997), p. 25.

prehensive income for 1997 consisted of foreign currency translation adjustments. The company's income statement was presented in a traditional single-step format. On its balance sheet, the company reported a line item within shareholders' equity titled "accumulated other comprehensive income."

It was noted earlier that in addition to net income, comprehensive income includes all changes in shareholders' equity except those resulting from investments by owners and distributions to owners. The question that arises is whether such items now included in comprehensive income such as adjustments for underfunded pension plans, unrealized gains and losses on available-for-sale investments, and cumulative foreign currency translation adjustments, should be considered as nonrecurring. We think they should. These items are not related to operations and are not generated by a recurring source.

NONRECURRING ITEMS IN THE STATEMENT OF CASH FLOWS

After the income statement, the operating activities section of the statement of cash flows is an excellent secondary source of disclosure of nonrecurring items. Two factors contribute to the statement's usefulness in earnings analysis. First, gains and losses arising from investing and financing activities must be removed from net income in arriving at cash flow provided by operating activities. On the investing side, this includes gains and losses on the sale of investments and property, plant, and equipment. On the financing side, examples include gains and losses on early debt retirement and recognized gains on sale/leaseback transactions. Gains and losses on early debt retirement are classified as extraordinary and are identified clearly on the income statement. However, gains and losses from the sale of investments and property, plant, and equipment and from sale/leaseback transactions are not extraordinary items. Often, these items are not identified separately on the income statement, leaving the operating activities section of the cash flow statement as the primary or only source of information for their identification. Second, noncash items of revenue or gain and expense or loss must be removed from net income in calculating cash provided by operating activities. Many nonrecurring expenses or losses do not involve a current-period cash outflow. As a result, such items must be adjusted out of net income in arriving at cash flow provided by operating activities. Examples include such nonrecurring items as asset write-downs, special liability accruals, and restructuring charges. When these special charges are not highlighted on the income statement, the cash flow statement provides an effective means of identification.

The partial statement of cash flows of Advanced Micro Devices, Inc., as presented in Exhibit 2.15, illustrates the disclosure of nonrecurring items in the operating activities section of the statement of cash flows. The nonrecurring items would appear to include (1) "Accrual for litigation settlement," (2) "Net loss on sale of property, plant, and equipment," (3) "Write-down of property, plant, and equipment," and (4) "Net gain realized on sale of available-for-sale securities." "Compensation recognized under employee stock plans" and the "Undistributed (income) loss of joint venture" are noncash items but do not appear to be nonrecurring. The only nonrecurring item disclosed on the company's income statement for the periods presented was the litigation accrual. Thus, the operating activities section of the statement of cash flows provided a very effective source for identifying several other nonrecurring items.

Frequently, nonrecurring items appear in both the income statement and the statement of cash flows. There are exceptions, however, as seen with Advanced Micro Devices. Other examples, in which the statement of cash flows surfaced nonrecurring items that were not disclosed on the income statement, are presented in Exhibit 2.16. The exhibit demonstrates the importance of examining the statement of cash flow carefully in completing an earnings analysis.

NONRECURRING ITEMS IN THE INVENTORY DISCLOSURES OF LIFO FIRMS

The carrying values of inventories maintained under the LIFO method are often significantly understated in relationship to replacement cost. For public companies, the difference between the LIFO carrying value and replacement cost (frequently approximated by FIFO) is a required disclosure under Securities and Ex-

Exhibit 2.15. Nonrecurring Items Disclosure in the Statement of Cash Flows: Advanced Micro Devices, Inc. Consolidated Statements of Cash Flow, Operating Section Only, for the Years Ended December 25, 1994, December 31, 1995, and December 29, 1996 (Thousands of Dollars)

	1994	1995	1996
Cash flow from operating activities:			
Net income (loss)	$270,942	$216,326	$(68,950)
Adjustment to reconcile net income (loss) to net cash provided by operating activities:			
Depreciation and amortization	217,665	264,675	332,640
Accrual for litigation settlement	58,000	—	—
Net loss on sale of property, plant, and equipment	276	2,152	11,953
Write-down of property, plant, and equipment	2,230	611	1,081
Net gain realized on sale of available-for-sale securities	—	(2,707)	(41,022)
Compensation recognized under employee stock plans	1,971	2,483	24
Undistributed (income) loss of joint venture	10,585	(34,926)	(54,798)
Changes in operating assets and liabilities:			
Net (increase) decrease in receivables, inventories, prepaid expenses, and other assets	(128,914)	19,548	28,096
Payment of litigation settlement	—	(58,000)	—
Net (increase) decrease in deferred income taxes	(32,543)	(925)	17,134
Increase (decrease) in tax refund receivable and income tax payable	61,910	11,772	(110,058)
Net increase (decrease) in payables and accrued liabilities	63,737	124,058	(42,863)
Net cash provided by operating activities	$525,859	$545,067	$73,237

Source: Advanced Micro Devices, Inc., annual report, December 1996, p. 21.

change Commission (SEC) regulations.[24] An example of a substantial difference between LIFO and current replacement value is found in a summary of the precious metals inventory disclosures of Handy and Harman in Exhibit 2.17. As seen in the exhibit, the replacement cost of the company's precious metals inventories is about five times their LIFO valuation.

Under normal circumstances, where inventory quantities are stable or increasing, the use of LIFO does not result in nonrecurring items. However, when a LIFO firm reduces inventory quantities, a nonrecurring gain or a loss can result. A reduction in the physical inventory quantities of a LIFO inventory is called a LIFO liquidation. Inventory quantities purchased at older inventory costs are charged to cost of goods sold. In a rising price environment, these older inventory costs will be lower than current replacement costs. The result is a nonrecurring reduction in

Exhibit 2.16.   Nonrecurring Items in the Operating Activities Section
of the Statement of Cash Flows but Not in the Income Statement

Company	Nonrecurring Item
Apogee Enterprises, Inc. (1996)	Gain on sale of a business
Arvin Industries, Inc. (1994)	Goodwill impairment
Ben & Jerry's Homemade, Inc. (1995)	Loss on disposition of assets
Biomet, Inc. (1996)	Gain on sale of securities
Black Box Corp. (1995)	Gain on sale of subsidiary
Crawford & Co. (1996)	Loss on disposal of risk control unit
Cleveland-Cliffs, Inc. (1997)	Increase to environmental reserve
CytRx Corp. (1997)	Charge for beneficial conversion feature of convertible debentures
Equity Corp. International (1996)	Gain on sale of assets
Homestake Mining Co. (1996)	Write-downs of investments in mining securities
Mail Boxes Etc. (1996)	Loss on retirement of fixed assets
Sun Television & Appliances, Inc. (1997)	Impairment of long-lived assets
Tyco International Ltd. (1996)	Provisions for losses on accounts receivable
VideoLabs, Inc. (1995)	Provision for losses on accounts receivable and inventory write-downs

Sources: Companies' annual reports. The year following each company name designates the annual report from which each example was drawn.

Exhibit 2.17.   LIFO Inventory Valuation Differences: Handy and Harman
Inventory Footnote, December 31, 1996 and 1997 (Thousands of Dollars)

	1996	1997
Precious metals stated at LIFO cost	$24,763	$20,960
LIFO inventory—excess of year-end market value over LIFO cost	$97,996	$106,201

Source: Data obtained from Disclosure, Inc., *Compact D/SEC: Corporate Information on Public Companies Filing with the SEC* (Bethesda, Maryland: Disclosure, Inc., June 1998).

cost of goods sold and an increase in gross profit. When older inventory costs are higher than current replacement costs, a nonrecurring increase in cost of goods sold and reduction in gross profit results. Both effects are nonrecurring because once inventories purchased at older costs are depleted, cost of goods sold will return to current amounts paid for replacement items.

While it is possible for a LIFO liquidation to result in either a nonrecurring increase in gross profit or decrease in gross profit, it is more likely, due to a general rise in the inventory costs for LIFO firms, that a LIFO liquidation will result in the former. An example of a LIFO liquidation for Handy and Harman is provided below:

> Included in continuing operations for 1996 and 1997 are profits before taxes of $33,630,000 and $6,408,000, respectively, resulting from reduction in the quantities of precious metal inventories valued under the LIFO method. The after-tax effect on continuing operations for 1996 and 1997 amounted to $19,260,000 ($1.40 per basic share) and $3,717,000 ($.31 per basic share), respectively.[25]

This disclosure of the earnings effect of the LIFO liquidation is also an SEC requirement.[26] Note that the LIFO liquidation added $19,260,000 and $3,717,000, respectively, in 1996 and 1997 to after-tax income from continuing operations. In 1996 and 1997, the company reported after-tax income from continuing operations, including the LIFO liquidation effects, of $33,773,000 and $20,910,000, respectively. Thus, the LIFO liquidations added significantly to the company's reported results for those years. Moreover, it should be remembered that the effects of a LIFO liquidation are not reported on the income statement. Their effects are buried within cost of goods sold. Equity analysts and credit analysts must search the inventory note to identify this nonrecurring earnings impact.

The analyst cannot rely on the disclosure requirements of the SEC when reviewing the statements of nonpublic companies, especially where the outside accountant's association with the statements takes the form of either a review or a compilation.[27] However, one can infer the possibility of a LIFO liquidation through the combination of a decline in the dollar amount of inventory and an otherwise unexplainable improvement in gross margin. A preliminary estimate of the pretax effect of a LIFO liquidation can be developed by multiplying sales times the increase in the gross margin percentage for the year of the liquidation. Details on the existence and impact of a LIFO liquidation should then be a subject for discussion with management.

NONRECURRING ITEMS IN THE INCOME TAX NOTE

The income tax provision is a major component of total corporate expenses, consuming up to 40 percent or more of income before tax. Interestingly, the tax provision itself is a likely source of covert nonrecurring items. Consider, for ex-

Exhibit 2.18.   Income Statement Excerpts: Biogen, Inc., for the Years Ended December 31, 1995, 1996, and 1997 (Thousands of Dollars)

	1995	*1996*	*1997*
Income before income taxes	$7,445	$40,829	$148,968
Income taxes	1,785	299	59,801
Net income	$5,660	$40,530	$89,167

Source: Biogen, Inc., Form 10-K annual report to the Securities and Exchange Commission (December 1997), Exhibit 13.

ample, the income statement for Biogen, Inc., excerpts of which are presented in Exhibit 2.18.

The company had a good year in 1997, with income before income taxes rising 265 percent from 1996. That same year, net income also increased significantly, approximately 120 percent. Although that increase in net income was noteworthy, it was much less in percentage terms than the increase in income before income taxes. The reason was the marked increase in income tax expense. It increased to $59,801,000 or 40.1 percent of income before income taxes, termed the *effective tax rate,* in 1997 from $299,000 or .7 percent in 1996. Clearly, something changed between 1996 and 1997 in the manner in which the tax provision was calculated. Information found in the income tax footnote, in particular, the reconciliation of the federal statutory income tax expense with reported income tax expense, explains why the tax provision changed.

The reconciliation of the statutory to reported income tax expense, a required disclosure under GAAP, is the key source of information in the income tax note for identifying nonrecurring items. That disclosure for Biogen is provided in Exhibit 2.19.

The reconciliation presented in Exhibit 2.19 begins with income tax expense calculated using the statutory federal income tax rate. In 1996 and 1997, that rate was 35 percent. Added to the statutory federal tax are state income taxes net of a federal income tax benefit for the tax deductibility of those state taxes. State taxes are a recurring tax expense. Also added are foreign rate differentials. This line incorporates the effects of foreign subsidiaries whose earnings are taxed at rates different than in the United States. Since these foreign earnings are taxed at rates in existence in those foreign countries, this too is a recurring component of income tax expense. A key nonrecurring item that surfaces in the reconciliation is actually the combination of three items: (1) the current utilization of net operating loss carryforwards, (2) reversal of valuation allowance, and (3) investment tax and research and development credits. The effects of these items on the tax provision were most pronounced in 1996.

Current U.S. tax law permits net operating losses to first be carried back, providing a refund of prior taxes, for two years and then, if not fully utilized, to

Exhibit 2.19.   Income Tax Footnote Excerpts, Reconciliation of Statutory
Income Tax Expense with Reported Income Tax Expense: Biogen, Inc.,
for the Years Ended December 31, 1995, 1996, and 1997 (Thousands of Dollars)

	1995	1996	1997
Income tax expense at statutory rates	$2,606	$14,350	$52,115
States taxes, net of federal income tax benefit	138	509	4,090
Foreign rate differential	7,812	8,887	9,394
Current utilization of net operating loss carryforwards, reversal of valuation allowance, investment tax, and research and development credits	(9,485)	(23,000)	(5,700)
Other, net	714	(447)	(98)
Reported income tax expense	$1,785	$299	$59,801

Source: Biogen, Inc., Form 10-K annual report to the Securities and Exchange Commission (December 1997), Exhibit 13.

be carried forward for 20 years, providing a shield against future tax payments. This is a recent change from a three-year carry back and 15-year carryforward arrangement. When a current-year loss generates a loss carryforward, the future tax savings associated with that carryforward may be recognized in the loss year. The reporting company records that future tax savings as an asset, termed a *deferred tax asset,* and as a credit to income tax expense, termed a *deferred tax benefit.* If the reporting company determines that it is more likely than not that some portion of that carryforward will not be realized, that is, that it will not be utilized before the carryforward period expires, then the amounts of the deferred tax asset and benefit are reduced, with a valuation allowance for the portion of the future tax savings that is called into question. Here, recognition of all or a part of the tax savings associated with the net operating loss carryforward is postponed until the loss carryforward is realized, or until the company reverses itself and determines that it is now more likely than not that the portion of the carryforward in question will ultimately be realized. Tax credits, such as research and development credits and other such targeted credits, have one-year carryback and twenty-year carryfoward provisions and are accounted for like net operating losses.

At December 31, 1995, Biogen reported net operating loss and tax credit carryforwards of $84 million and $15 million, respectively. The company reported that these carryforwards expired at various dates through 2010. At that time, the company reported deferred tax assets for loss carryfowards of $30.6 million and $20.6 million for the tax credit carryforwards. These deferred tax credits were fully reserved with a valuation allowance, which was described by the company as follows:

The Company has concluded, based on the standard set forth in Statement of Financial Accounting Standards (SFAS) No. 109, "Accounting for Income Taxes," that it is more likely than not that the Company will not realize any benefits from its net deferred tax asset. Realization of the net deferred tax asset and future reversals of the valuation allowance depend on the Company's ability to achieve future profitability through earnings from existing sources and from sales of AVONEX℠ or other proprietary products. The timing and amount of future earnings will depend on the Company's success in obtaining approval for and in marketing and selling AVONEX℠, as well as the results of development, clinical trials and commercialization of other products under development. The Company will assess the need for the valuation allowance at each balance sheet date based on all available evidence.[28]

Thus, the company was not recognizing the tax benefits of the loss and tax credit carryforwards until they were realized. A portion was realized and thus recognized in 1995, as the company made money that year. However, in 1996, the company's fortunes and expectations about the future began to improve markedly. Thus, that year, the company recognized a tax benefit for the reversal of the valuation allowance set up in previous years. The net effect was the significant, nonrecurring tax benefit and reduction in the tax expense reported for the year. As the company described in a footnote in 1996:

During the third quarter of 1996, the Company determined that it was more likely than not that it would realize the benefits of its net deferred tax assets and therefore released the related valuation allowance. The reversal of the valuation allowance resulted in a realization of income tax benefits of approximately $23 million. The income tax benefit represented the balance of tax-loss carryforwards and tax credits that had not been recognized through the third quarter in 1996 and tax credits generated during the quarter.[29]

There was no additional reduction of the deferred tax asset valuation allowance to be recognized in 1997. The tax benefit reported that year was likely for new tax credits earned and recognized that year. Because such credits require continued eligibility on the part of the company and continued favorable treatment in the tax code, they too should be viewed as nonrecurring items.

A strong indicator of nonrecurring tax benefits is an unusually low effective tax rate. This condition should first be noticed upon initial review of the income statement. Biogen's effective income tax rate, or income tax expense divided by pretax income, increased to 40.1 percent in 1997 from .7 percent in 1996. The effective tax rate in 1995 was 24 percent. Such a low effective tax rate as the one seen in 1996 provides an important reason to examine the tax note carefully to determine if the unusually low rate can be sustained.

Another source of nonrecurring tax benefits are tax reductions, sometimes called *tax holidays,* offered by foreign governments to encourage investment and increase employment in their countries. The tax reconciliation schedule of C. R. Bard, Inc., presented in Exhibit 2.20, provides an example.

Bard is enjoying a substantial reduction in its effective tax rate, ranging from 8 percent to 13 percent of pretax income for the three years presented, as a result

Exhibit 2.20.   Effective Tax Rate Reduced by Operations in Ireland and Puerto Rico: C. R. Bard, Inc., for the Years Ended December 31, 1996, 1997, and 1998

	1996	*1997*	*1998*
U.S. federal statutory rate	35%	35%	35%
State income taxes net of federal income tax benefits	3	3	3
Foreign operations taxed at less than the U.S. statutory rate, primarily Ireland and Puerto Rico	(13)	(10)	(8)
Reversal of tax reserve	(15)	—	—
Other, net	—	3	5
Effective tax rate	10%	31%	35%

Source: C. R. Bard, Inc., annual report, December 1998. Information obtained from Disclosure, Inc., *Compact D/SEC: Corporate Information on Public Companies Filing with the SEC* (Bethesda, Maryland: Disclosure, Inc., June 1999).

of a lower tax rate on the earnings of its foreign operations located primarily in Ireland and Puerto Rico. These effective tax rate reductions will be maintained only if Bard continues to conduct operations in Ireland and Puerto Rico, if the associated laws remain in effect, and if Bard's eligibility for these tax benefits continues. Typically, such eligibility expires after completion of a preset time limit. This series of "ifs" means that an important element of Bard's future net income is subject to an additional element of uncertainty. As a result, in most instances, such tax benefits should be viewed as nonrecurring.

In summary, income tax items of expense or benefit that should be considered nonrecurring, including those reviewed in the preceding paragraphs and some additional items, include the following:

• Tax decreases from foreign and domestic loss carryforwards and various tax credits and tax credit carryforwards such as net operating loss carryforwards, capital loss carryforwards, research and development and other targeted tax credits, alternative minimum tax credits, and foreign tax credits.

• Tax decreases due to temporary foreign tax reductions and tax holidays.

• Tax increases or decreases resulting from revaluations of deferred tax assets and liabilities as a result of changes in income tax rates.

• Tax increases or decreases resulting from the resolution of prior-year disputes with tax authorities.

• Tax increases or decreases attributable to changes in the deferred tax valuation allowance based on (a) realization of previously unrecognized deferred tax benefits or (b) revised estimations of the likelihood of realization of deferred tax assets.

NONRECURRING ITEMS IN THE "OTHER INCOME (EXPENSE)" NOTE

An "other income (expense)—net," or equivalent title, line item or section is commonly found in both the single- and multistep income statements. In the case of the multistep format, the composition of other income and expenses is sometimes detailed on the face of the income statement. In both the multistep and single-step formats, the most typical presentation is a single line item with a supporting note, if the items included in the total are material. Even though a note detailing the contents of other income and expense may exist, guidance is typically not provided as to its location. That is, the reader is seldom told to see note number 5, or note K. A note often exists even in the absence of a specific note reference. Where present, other income and expense notes tend to be listed close to last among the notes to the financial statements.

Small Net Balances May Obscure the Presence of Large Nonrecurring Items

Even if their net amount is small, the composition of other income and expense balances should be explored. Consider, for example, Calgon Carbon Corporation. In its 1997 annual report, the company's income statement reported other (expense) net in the amount of ($2,041,000), ($742,000), and ($1,440,000), respectively, for the years ended December 31, 1995, 1996, and 1997.[30] The footnotes to the income statement provided the following description of other (expense) net:

> Other (expense)—net includes net foreign currency transaction losses of ($358,000) and ($238,000) for the years ended December 31, 1995 and 1997, respectively, and gains of $1,002,000 for the year ended December 31, 1996. Also included are taxes other than on income of ($1,161,000), ($1,152,000), and ($691,000) for the years ended December 31, 1995, 1996 and 1997, respectively.[31]

Two distinct items are disclosed in the note. The first, foreign currency transaction gains and losses, is a nonrecurring item. The second, taxes other than on income, is a recurring expense. In 1996, according to the note, the company reported a foreign currency transaction gain of $1,002,000. That nonrecurring gain offset the recurring taxes other than on income in the amount of ($1,152,000) that same year, netting to an expense of ($150,000). The company did not disclose the remaining difference between the identified net expense of ($150,000) and the reported other expense of ($742,000). Presumably, it consisted of other immaterial items. Failure to investigate the company's other (expense) note would have resulted in the failure to detect the $1,002,000 foreign exchange gain.

Exhibit 2.21.   Revenues Section of Statements of Consolidated Operations:
Homestake Mining Company, for the Years Ended December 31, 1995, 1996,
and 1997 (Thousands of Dollars)

	1995	1996	1997
Revenues			
Gold and ore sales	$871,959	$921,685	$863,628
Sulfur and oil sales	40,620	30,749	26,821
Interest income	19,152	20,392	17,320
Gain on termination of Santa Fe merger*			62,925
Other income (note 5)	17,520	25,620	721
	$949,251	$998,446	$971,415

*The original report made reference to a note, which is not included here.
Source: Homestake Mining Company, annual report, December 1997, p. 38.

A Careful Examination of "Other Income (Expense)" Notes Is Necessary to Determine Recurring and Nonrecurring Components

The revenues section of the Statements of Consolidated Operations of Homestake
Mining Company for the years ended December 31, 1995, 1996, and 1997 includes revenues and gains of many origins, some recurring, some nonrecurring.
That section of the statement of operations—the income statement—is reproduced
in Exhibit 2.21.

From the income statement excerpts presented in Exhibit 2.21, it is unclear
whether "other income" is recurring. Given that the item is included with revenues,
a renewable, recurring source of income, a recurring source of origin for other
income is implied. However, a gain on the termination of a merger, clearly a
nonrecurring item, is also included with revenues. Thus, it is very possible that
other income includes nonrecurring items as well. The reader is referred to footnote five, where a detailed description of other income is provided. The footnote
is reproduced in Exhibit 2.22.

In reviewing the contents of footnote five to the Homestake Mining annual
report, presented in Exhibit 2.22, it is clear that notwithstanding the fact that the
company has reported other income as a component of revenues, it is made up
mostly of nonrecurring items. In fact, the royalty income is the only part of other
income that can be considered to be recurring. The other items, including gains
on asset disposals, foreign currency gains and losses, a pension curtailment gain
and a gain on sale of an option, are nonrecurring. In 1995 and 1996, royalty income
is a very small part of total other income. Only in 1997, a year when nonrecurring
items have provided offsets to each other, does royalty income comprise the bulk
of other income reported on the income statement. When provided, the other

Exhibit 2.22.   Note 5, Other Income: Homestake Mining Company, for the Years Ended December 31, 1995, 1996, and 1997 (Thousands of Dollars)

	1995	1996	1997
Gains on asset disposals	$5,575	$12,305	$16,926
Royalty income	2,252	2,888	2,425
Foreign currency contract gains (losses)	(151)	1,632	(28,453)
Foreign currency exchange losses on intercompany advances	(883)	(8,943)	(5,657)
Pension curtailment gain		1,868	
Gain on sale of Great Central Option*		4,699	10,419
Other	10,727	11,171	5,061
	$17,520	$25,620	$721

*The original report made reference to a note, which is not included here.
Source: Homestake Mining Company, annual report, December 1997, p. 46.

income (expense) note is a valuable source of information for detecting nonrecurring items.

NONRECURRING ITEMS IN MANAGEMENT'S DISCUSSION AND ANALYSIS

Management's discussion and analysis of financial condition and results of operations (MD&A) is both an annual and a quarterly SEC reporting requirement. Provisions of this regulation have a direct bearing on our goal of locating nonrecurring items. As part of MD&A, the SEC requires registrants to:

> Describe any unusual or infrequent events or transactions or any significant economic changes that materially affected the amount of reported income from continuing operations and, in each case, indicate the extent to which income was so affected. In addition, describe any other significant components of revenues and expenses that, in the registrant's judgment, should be described in order to understand the registrant's results of operations.[32]

Responding to the above charge requires firms to identify and discuss many of the items that will already have been located in the first five steps of the Exhibit 2.1 search sequence. In reviewing MD&A with a view to locating nonrecurring items, attention should be focused on the section dealing with the "results of operations." Here, a comparison of results over the most recent three years will be presented, with the standard pattern involving discussion of, for example, 1997 with 1996 and 1996 with 1995.

The location of nonrecurring items in MD&A is somewhat more difficult than in steps one through five of the search-sequence in Exhibit 2.1. Typically, the nonrecurring items in MD&A are included in textual discussion and are not set out in more user-friendly schedules or statements. As a result, their discovery becomes somewhat more problematic and less efficient. Moreover, most nonrecurring items discussed in the MD&A will already have been discovered earlier in the search process. This is, however, not always the case, arguing for a very careful review of MD&A in the search for nonrecurring items.

Consider Diplomat Corporation as an example. In the company's 1997 annual report, the MD&A provided a comparison of its results for 1996 with the same period in 1995. Among the comparisons provided was the following for cost of sales:

> Consolidated cost of sales were 69% of net sales in 1996 and 52% in 1995. Cost of sales of Diplomat increased 32% primarily from a writedown of inventory from its restructuring.[33]

In another footnote, the company provided the following detail of its restructuring:

> During the quarter ended September 30, 1996, management instituted various actions designed to significantly cut costs in the Company's manufacturing operation located in Stony Point, New York, and to refocus the operation on its most profitable product lines and channels of distribution. . . . As a result of the actions taken, the Company incurred restructuring charges of approximately $1,738,975. The restructuring charges include approximately $568,000 primarily for write-offs and other costs associated with the discontinuance of various products and $771,000 for severance pay and professional and consulting fees payable in connection with the restructuring plan.[34]

In agreement with the note, the company's income statement for 1996 reported a restructuring charge in the amount of $1,738,975. The inventory write-down, discussed in MD&A and included in cost of sales, was not part of the restructuring charge reported on the income statement. There were no other disclosures provided concerning the inventory write-down. Thus, the only way to ascertain its existence and amount, estimated to be approximately $3.2 million based on the information provided, was to examine MD&A carefully.

A small subset of firms do summarize nonrecurring items in schedules within MD&A. The information on nonrecurring items in Exhibit 2.23 is from the 1997 Annual Report of Unocal Corporation. This schedule summarizes, in a single location, the after-tax impact of the listed nonrecurring items on Unocal's results for 1995, 1996, and 1997. Most of these items would have been located in steps one through five of the search sequence outlined in Exhibit 2.1. Items not located in these five steps would have been the impairment of long-lived assets item, disclosed in a note titled "Impairment of assets" and the environmental and litigation provisions, disclosed in a note titled "Accrued abandonment, restoration and environmental liabilities."

The presentation within MD&A of information on nonrecurring items in schedules is still a fairly limited practice but may be on the rise. Though helpful

Exhibit 2.23. Management's Discussion and Analysis: Unocal Corp., for the Years Ended December 31, 1995, 1996, and 1997 (Millions of Dollars)

	1995	1996	1997
Reported after-tax earnings from continuing operations	$249	$456	$669
Special items:			
Deferred tax adjustments	—	—	207
Impairment of long-lived assets	(65)	(46)	(43)
Environmental and litigation provisions	(63)	(123)	(84)
Asset sales	70	70	43
Other	20	(7)	31
Total special items	(38)	(106)	154
Adjusted after-tax earnings from continuing operations	287	562	515
After-tax earnings (loss) from discontinued operations	11	(420)	(50)
Special item: discontinued operations	(1)	486	50
Adjusted after-tax earnings from discontinued operations	10	66	—
Extraordinary item—early extinguishment of debt	—	—	(38)
Special item: extraordinary item—early extinguishment of debt	—	—	38
Adjusted after-tax extraordinary item	—	—	—
Adjusted after-tax earnings	$297	$628	$515

Source: Unocal Corp., Form 10-K annual report to the Securities and Exchange Commission (December 1997), p. 19.

for the task of locating nonrecurring items, such schedules must be viewed as useful complements to, but not substitutes for, a complete search process. A review of the scope of items presented in such schedules reveals that the displays are sometimes limited to only a subset of nonrecurring items, reflecting issues of materiality as well as the judgmental aspect of the nonrecurring designation.

NONRECURRING ITEMS IN OTHER SELECTED NOTES

The above discussion has illustrated locating nonrecurring items through steps one through five of the search sequence outlined in Exhibit 2.1. Typically, a large percentage of the material nonrecurring items is discovered by proceeding through these first five steps. However, additional nonrecurring items are sometimes located in the other notes. Some nonrecurring items may have been present but simply missed in steps one through five. These nonrecurring items may be discovered through examination of other notes. For example, in the case of Unocal Corporation presented in Exhibit 2.23, the special charges for the impairment of long-lived assets and for environmental and litigation problems first surfaced in MD&A, step six. Had these nonrecurring items been missed at that stage, they could have been picked up later in special, dedicated footnotes. It is possible for nonrecurring items to surface in virtually any note to the financial statements. Three selected notes, which frequently contain other nonrecurring items, are discussed below: foreign exchange, restructuring, and quarterly and segment financial data.

Foreign Exchange Notes

Foreign exchange gains and losses can result from both transaction (e.g., accounts receivable or payable denominated in foreign currencies) and translation exposure from foreign subsidiaries. They can also result from the use of various currency contracts such as forwards, futures, options, and swaps used for purposes of both hedging and speculation. It is not uncommon to observe foreign exchange gains and losses year after year in a company's income statement. However, it is also the case that the amount and nature, a gain versus loss, of these items will typically be very irregular. It is because of this irregular nature, due to the fact that currencies move both up and down, that foreign exchange gains and losses should be considered nonrecurring items.

For example, in a note titled "foreign currency translation," Crown Cork & Seal Company, Inc. described its income statement exposure to foreign currency movements as follows:

> For non-U.S. subsidiaries that operate in U.S. dollars (functional currency) or whose economic environment is highly inflationary, local currency inventories and plant and other property are translated into U.S. dollars at approximate rates prevailing when acquired; all other assets and liabilities are translated at year-end exchange rates. Inventories charged to cost of sales and depreciation are remeasured at historical rates; all other income and expense items are translated at average exchange rates prevailing during the year. Gains and losses that result from remeasurement are included in earnings.[35]

Showing the irregular nature of foreign currency gains and losses, the company reported,

> Unfavorable foreign exchange adjustments of $7,900,000 in 1997 resulted primarily from the remeasurement of the Company's operations in highly inflationary economies. Favorable foreign exchange adjustments of $36,500,000 and $1,100,000 were recorded in 1996 and 1995, respectively.[36]

After a minor foreign exchange gain of $1.1 million in 1995, the company reported a significant foreign exchange gain (8.5 percent of pretax income) in 1996. These gains were followed by a foreign exchange loss of $7.9 million in 1997.

Concord Camera Corporation provides another example that demonstrates the irregular nature of foreign exchange gains and losses. In a foreign exchange note, the company provided the following disclosure:

Exhibit 2.24. Excerpts from Footnote 4, Restructuring Charge: America Online, Inc., June 30, 1997 (Thousands of Dollars)

In connection with a restructuring plan adopted in the second quarter of fiscal 1997, the Company recorded a $48,627,000 restructuring charge associated with the Company's change in business model, the reorganization of the Company into three operating units, the termination of approximately 300 employees, and the shutdown of certain operating divisions and subsidiaries.

The components of the restructuring charge are as follows:

Write-off of impaired assets and discontinued businesses	$31,215
Severance and personnel related	8,734
Other expenses	8,678
Total restructuring charge	$48,627

Source: America Online, Inc., Form 10-K annual report to the Securities and Exchange Commission (June 1997), p. F-9.

Gains or losses resulting from foreign currency transactions are included in "Other (income) expense, net" in the Consolidated Statements of Operations. For the Fiscal years ended June 30, 1997, 1996 and 1995, consolidated other (income) expense, net includes approximately $192,000, ($103,000) and $57,000, respectively, of net foreign-currency (gains) losses.

Running at 109 percent, 19 percent, and 72 percent of pretax income before the foreign exchange items for the years 1995, 1996, and 1997, respectively, those foreign exchange items were material to the company's results of operations. Other sources of disclosure in the company's annual report were the other income (expense) note and MD&A, steps five and six, respectively, in the search sequence. If the search sequence failed to identify these items, then an examination of the foreign exchange note would provide a useful backup procedure to ensure that this important foreign exchange information is taken into consideration.

Restructuring Notes

The 1990s were dominated with companies taking special charges. Their purpose was to facilitate a streamlining or restructuring of operations, a redeployment of assets, and a rightsizing of employment levels to boost profitability.

Notes on restructuring charges are among the most common of the transaction-specific notes. Although some companies record them with disarming regularity, they are not part of ordinary operations and should be considered nonrecurring in nature.

During 1997, America Online, Inc. undertook a significant restructuring. The company described the activity in a restructuring footnote as seen in Exhibit 2.24.

Exhibit 2.25. Footnote 6, Write-Downs and Other Unusual Charges: Homestake Mining Co., Annual Report, June 30, 1996 and 1997 (Thousands of Dollars)

	1996	1997
Write-down of Homestake's investment in the Main Pass 299 sulfur mine*		$107,761
Reduction in the carrying values of resource assets*		84,655
Increase in the estimated accrual for future reclamation expenditures*		29,156
Write-downs of noncurrent investments*	$8,983	47,932
Other*		15,811
	$8,983	$285,315

*The original report made reference to a note that is not included here.
Source: Homestake Mining Company, annual report, December 1997, p. 46.

That charge of $48,627,000 comprised approximately 11 percent of the company's 1997 loss from operations before the charge. As might be expected, this targeted footnote disclosure of the restructuring event was not the only place in the company's annual report where the nonrecurring item was disclosed. Using the search sequence described in this chapter, the restructuring charge would have been identified in step one, the income statement; step two, the cash flow statement (for the noncash component of the charge only); and step six, MD&A.

Closely related to the restructuring note is a targeted note describing other special charges, including asset write-downs and special liability accruals. Like restructuring charges, these charges are also nonrecurring. Homestake Mining Company provides an example.

In its 1997 annual report, Homestake Mining provided a note titled, "Write-downs and Other Unusual Charges." The note, presented in Exhibit 2.25, was in addition to its other income note presented in Exhibit 2.22.

The note describes several nonrecurring items, including writedowns of investments and resource assets and an increase in a special liability accrual for future reclamation expenditures. The total charge, which pushed a pretax profit of $39,260,000 in 1997 into a pretax loss of $246,055,000, was also disclosed in the income statement, the statement of cash flows, and MD&A.

As an interesting aside, Francis, Hanna, and Vincent researched the market's reaction to restructurings and discretionary asset write-offs.[37] More specifically, how did the market price of a company's stock react to such events? They found that the market reacted positively to restructuring charges. Market participants were presumably pricing the anticipated cash flow effects of the restructuring event. The authors found a negative price reaction to inventory write-downs. The issue is one of impairment and suggests that future earnings will be impacted by problems with the company's product line. There was no price reaction noted for write-offs of goodwill and property, plant, and equipment.

Quarterly and Segmental Financial Data

Quarterly and segment financial disclosures frequently provide information on nonrecurring items. In the case of segment disclosures, the goal is to aid in the evaluation of profitability trends by segments. For example, in its 1997 report, Philip Morris Companies, Inc. disclosed the impact of a special charge taken against operating profit in its domestic tobacco segment of $1,457,000,000 for settlement of certain domestic tobacco litigation.[38] The charge was also reported on the income statement, disclosed in a note on contingencies, and discussed in MD&A.

In its 1997 report, General Electric Company provided the following information on a nonrecurring item in its fourth quarter results, "Fourth-quarter gross profit from sales in 1997 was reduced by restructuring and other special charges. Such charges, including amounts shown in "Other costs and expenses," were $2,322 million before tax."[39] The item was also discussed in MD&A.

SUMMARY

This chapter opened with a quotation, "Every company I follow has a write-off. No one has any idea of what anyone is earning."[40] It is hard to argue against the point of view that reported earnings today often include many contaminants. These contaminants affect the usefulness of reported earnings and diminish their value in anticipating future results. The identification and removal of nonrecurring items is strongly advocated. The result is a sustainable measure of performance, a measure of earnings that is more likely to continue into the future.

The most efficient and effective way to identify nonrecurring items is to review the annual report in a systematic way. An efficient approach to reviewing the annual report in search of nonrecurring items is to follow these steps:

1. Begin with the income statement. It provides reported earnings and often highlights numerous nonrecurring items.
2. The statement of cash flow is an important second step, in which certain gains and losses and noncash charges that are often not disclosed on the income statement are identified.
3. From here, certain selected footnotes should be studied. In particular, the inventory note for LIFO firms, the income tax note, and the other income (expense) note.
4. Management's Discussion and Analysis should be next. Managements will often discuss nonrecurring items here. Sometimes those items are not disclosed elsewhere in the financial statements or footnotes.

5. Finally, other footnotes should be reviewed, including such notes as the foreign currency note, a restructuring note, and notes on quarterly and segmental financial data.

The topic of analyzing business earnings is continued in Chapter 3. There the process of identifying and adjusting for nonrecurring items is demonstrated for a sample firm.

GLOSSARY

Change in estimate   A revision in an accounting measurement based on new events, additional experience, or improved judgment.

Comprehensive income   A measure of income that includes all changes in shareholders' equity except those resulting from investments by owners and distributions to owners. In addition to items traditionally included in net income, comprehensive income includes items that have historically been reported directly in shareholders' equity. Such items include adjustments for underfunded pension plans, unrealized gains and losses on available-for-sale investments in debt and equity securities, and cumulative foreign currency translation adjustments.

Cumulative effect of change in accounting principle   The cumulative prior-year income effect of a change from one generally accepted accounting principle to another.

Discontinued operations   Operating income and the gain or loss on disposal of a discontinued business segment.

Extraordinary item   Gain or loss that is unusual and infrequent in occurrence.

Generally accepted accounting principles (GAAP)   The conventions, rules, and procedures necessary to define accepted accounting practice at a particular time. It includes not only broad guidelines of general application, but also detailed practices and procedures.

Income from continuing operations   After-tax income excluding the effects of discontinued operations, extraordinary items, and the cumulative effect of changes in accounting principle.

Multistep income statement   An income statement format that provides an intermediate earnings subtotal that reflects pretax operating income.

Other comprehensive income   Changes in shareholders' equity except those resulting from investments by owners and distributions to owners, and excluding net income as traditionally measured. Includes adjustments for underfunded pension plans, unrealized gains and losses on available-for-sale investments in debt and equity securities, and cumulative foreign currency translation adjustments.

Permanent component   A component of earnings that is recurring or sustainable.

Single-step income statement   An income statement format that provides no intermediate earnings subtotal to reflect pretax operating income.

Transitory component   A component of earnings that is nonrecurring or non-sustainable.

NOTES

1. *The Wall Street Journal* (February 15, 1996), p. C1.

2. Eastman Kodak Co., annual report, December 1996, pp. 34 and 44 and Form 10-K annual report to the Securities and Exchange Commission (December 1997), pp. 21 and 38.

3. J. Elliott and J. Hanna, "Repeated Accounting Write-Offs and the Information Content of Earnings," *Journal of Accounting Research,* (Supplement 1996) pp. 135–155. The authors used Standard & Poor's *Compustat* database (Englewood, Colorado: Standard & Poor's Corp., 1996), as their universe of public companies. While the authors referred to their special charges as write-offs, they included items typical of special charges, including not only write-offs but also expense accruals. They defined a material charge as one comprising at least one percent of total assets.

4. Statement of Financial Accounting Standards (SFAS) No. 5, "Accounting for Contingencies" (Norwalk, CT: Financial Accounting Standards Board, March 1975).

5. SFAS No. 121, "Accounting for the Impairment of Long-Lived Assets" (Norwalk, CT: Financial Accounting Standards Board, March 1995).

6. Quotations taken from *The Wall Street Journal* (May 1, 1997), p. C1.

7. The Coca-Cola Co., Form 10-K annual report to the Securities and Exchange Commission (December 1977), p. 33.

8. R. Lipe, "The Information Contained in the Components of Earnings." *Journal of Accounting Research,* (Supplement 1986), pp. 37–64.

9. A. Ali, A. Klein, and J. Rosenfeld, "Analysts' Use of Information about Permanent and Transitory Earnings Components in Forecasting Annual EPS," *The Accounting Review* (January 1992), pp. 183–198.

10. J. Elliott and J. Hanna, "Repeated Accounting Write-Offs and the Information Content of Earnings," *Journal of Accounting Research* (Supplement 1996), pp. 135–155.

11. H. Choi, "Analysis and Valuation Implications of Persistence and Cash-Content Dimensions of Earnings Components Based on Extent of Analyst Following." Unpublished Ph.D. thesis, Georgia Institute of Technology (October 1994), p. 80.

12. Ibid. The authors of this book served on Dr. Choi's thesis advisory committee.

13. *Accounting Trends and Techniques: Annual Survey of Accounting Practices Followed in 600 Stockholders' Reports,* 51st ed. (New York: American Institute of Certified Public Accountants, 1997), p. 281.

14. *Ibid.*

15. Eastman Kodak Co., Form 10-K annual report to the Securities and Exchange Commission (December 1997), p. 38.

16. Accounting Principles Board Opinion No. 30, "Reporting the Results of Operations" (NY: Accounting Principles Board, July 1973).

17. *Ibid.*

18. SFAS No. 4, "Reporting Gains and Losses from the Extinguishment of Debt" (Norwalk, CT: Financial Accounting Standards Board, March 1975).

19. SFAS No. 15, "Accounting by Debtors and Creditors for Troubled Debt Restructurings" (Norwalk, CT: Financial Accounting Standards Board, June 1977).

20. SFAS No. 109, "Accounting for Income Taxes" (Norwalk, CT: Financial Accounting Standards Board, February 1992).

21. SFAS No. 128, "Earnings Per Share" (Norwalk, CT: Financial Accounting Standards Board, February 1997).

22. Coachmen Industries, Inc., annual report, December 1996. Information obtained from Disclosure, Inc., *Compact D/SEC: Corporate Information on Public Companies Filing with the SEC* (Bethesda, Maryland: Disclosure, Inc., June 1998).

23. Blowout Entertainment, Inc., annual report, December 1997. Information obtained from Disclosure, Inc. *Compact D/SEC: Corporate Information on Public Companies Filing with the SEC* (Bethesda, Maryland: Disclosure, Inc., June 1998).

24. Securities and Exchange Commission Regulation S-X, Rule 5–02.6.

25. Handy and Harman, annual report, December 1997. Information obtained from Disclosure, Inc. *Compact D/SEC: Corporate Information on Public Companies Filing with the SEC* (Bethesda, Maryland: Disclosure, Inc., June 1998).

26. Securities and Exchange Commission, *Staff Accounting Bulletin No. 40.*

27. Reviews and compilations represent a level of service below that of an audit. With compilations, it is typical that only an income statement and balance sheet are provided. Neither notes nor a statement of cash flows are part of the disclosures.

28. Biogen, Inc., Form 10-K annual report to the Securities and Exchange Commission (December 1995), Exhibit 13.

29. *Ibid.,* December 1996, Exhibit 13.

30. Calgon Carbon Corp., Form 10-K annual report to the Securities and Exchange Commission (December 1997), p. 21.

31. *Ibid.,* p. 36.

32. Securities and Exchange Commission, *Regulation S-K*, Subpart 229.300, Item 303(a)(3)(i).

33. Diplomat Corp., Form 10-K annual report to the Securities and Exchange Commission (September 1997), p. 16.

34. *Ibid.,* p. F-11.

35. Crown Cork & Seal Co., Inc., annual report, December 1997. Information obtained from Disclosure, Inc. *Compact D/SEC: Corporate Information on Public Companies Filing with the SEC* (Bethesda, Maryland: Disclosure, Inc., June 1998).

36. *Ibid.*

37. J. Francis, D. Hanna, and L. Vincent, "Causes and Effects of Discretionary Asset Write-Offs," *Journal of Accounting Research* (Supplement 1996), pp. 117–134.

38. Philip Morris Companies, Inc., annual report, December 1997, p. 48.

39. General Electric Company, Inc., annual report, December 1997, p. 66.

40. *The Wall Street Journal* (February 15, 1996), p. C1.

Chapter 3

Analyzing Business Earnings II: Calculating Sustainable Earnings Base

"Your future profit is linked to the past."[1]

That message, that future profit is linked to the past, implies that future profits are, at least in part, based on or extrapolated from past profits. Not all financial statement users, however, would agree with the view that historical earnings are useful in predicting future earnings. For example, in Standard & Poor's publication on debt ratings, *S&P's Corporate Finance Criteria*, it is noted, "In the analytical experience, we are constantly reminded that the past is less and less prologue to the future."[2] Such a statement is an accurate observation to the extent that past earnings are contaminated by nonrecurring items. Indeed, it is an alternative expression of the analyst's lament from Chapter Two, "Every company I follow has a write-off. No one has any idea of what anyone is earning."[3]

To be useful as a starting point for developing an earnings forecast, past earnings must be cleared of nonrecurring items, or noise, in the derivation of a more reliable, sustainable earnings base. A study by a committee of the American Institute of Certified Public Accountants (AICPA) makes a similar point, "Users want information about the portion of a company's reported earnings that is stable or recurring and that provides a basis for estimating sustainable earnings."[4]

In this chapter, we demonstrate a systematic method for removing nonrecurring items from reported earnings. The nonrecurring items removed will be those identified in Chapter Two. To facilitate the adjustment process, a worksheet is provided that is designed to summarize information on nonrecurring items. A case study is employed to illustrate use of the worksheet. In addition, various examples of sustainable earnings presentations, provided by companies themselves, are analyzed. Finally, the treatment of income taxes in the preparation of the worksheet is discussed.

SUSTAINABLE EARNINGS BASE WORKSHEET

The sustainable earnings worksheet is presented as Exhibit 3.1.[5] Instructions for completion of the sustainable earnings base (SEB) worksheet follow:

Exhibit 3.1.   Adjustment Worksheet for Sustainable Earnings Base

	Year	*Year*	*Year*
Reported net income or (loss)	___	___	___
Add			
Pretax LIFO liquidation losses	___	___	___
Losses on sales of fixed assets	___	___	___
Losses on sales of investments	___	___	___
Losses on sales of "other" assets	___	___	___
Restructuring charges	___	___	___
Investment writedowns	___	___	___
Inventory writedowns	___	___	___
Other asset writedowns	___	___	___
Foreign currency losses	___	___	___
Litigation charges	___	___	___
Losses on patent infringement suits	___	___	___
Exceptional bad debt provisions	___	___	___
Temporary expense increases	___	___	___
Temporary revenue reductions	___	___	___
Other	___	___	___
Other	___	___	___
Other	___	___	___
Subtotal	___	___	___
Multiply by			
(1-combined federal and state tax rates)	___	___	___
Tax-adjusted additions	___	___	___
Add			
After-tax LIFO liquidation losses	___	___	___
Increases in deferred tax valuation allowances	___	___	___
Other nonrecurring tax charges	___	___	___
Losses on discontinued operations	___	___	___
Extraordinary losses	___	___	___
Losses/cumulative-effect accounting changes	___	___	___
Other	___	___	___
Other	___	___	___

(continued)

Exhibit 3.1.   (Continued) Adjustment Worksheet for Sustainable Earnings Base

	Year	*Year*	*Year*
Other	____	____	____
Subtotal	____	____	____
Total additions	____	____	____
Deduct			
Pretax LIFO liquidation gains	____	____	____
Gains on sales of fixed assets	____	____	____
Gains on sales of investments	____	____	____
Gains on sales of other assets	____	____	____
Reversals of restructuring charges	____	____	____
Investment write-ups (trading account)	____	____	____
Foreign currency gains	____	____	____
Litigation revenues	____	____	____
Gains on patent infringement suits	____	____	____
Temporary expense decreases	____	____	____
Temporary revenue increases	____	____	____
Reversals of bad debt allowances	____	____	____
Other	____	____	____
Other	____	____	____
Other	____	____	____
Subtotal	____	____	____
Multiply by			
(1-combined federal and state tax rate)	____	____	____
Tax-adjusted deductions	____	____	____
Deduct			
After-tax LIFO liquidation gains	____	____	____
Reductions in deferred tax valuation allowances	____	____	____
Loss carryforward benefits	____	____	____
Other nonrecurring tax benefits	____	____	____
Gains on discontinued operations	____	____	____
Extraordinary gains	____	____	____
Gains/cumulative-effect accounting changes	____	____	____

(continued)

Exhibit 3.1. (Continued) Adjustment Worksheet for Sustainable Earnings
Base

	Year	*Year*	*Year*
Other	____	____	____
Other	____	____	____
Other	____	____	____
Subtotal	____	____	____
Total deductions	____	____	____
Sustainable earnings base	____	____	____

1. Net income or loss is recorded on the top line of the SEB worksheet.

2. All identified items of nonrecurring expense or loss, which were included in the income statement on a pretax basis, are recorded on the "add" lines provided. Where a prelabeled line is not listed, then a descriptive title should be recorded on one of the "Other" lines and the amounts recorded there. In practice, the process of locating nonrecurring items and recording them on the SEB worksheet would take place at the same time. However, effective use of the SEB worksheet calls for the background provided in the previous chapter. This explains the separation of these steps in this book.

3. When all pretax, nonrecurring expenses and losses have been recorded, subtotals should be computed. These subtotals are then multiplied by 1 minus a representative combined federal and state income tax rate. This puts these items on an after-tax basis so that they are stated on the same basis as net income or net loss.

4. The results from step 3 should be recorded on the line titled "tax-adjusted additions."

5. All tax-adjusted nonrecurring expenses or losses, or comparable items, are next recorded in the section headed "tax-adjusted additions." These items will typically be either tax items or special income statement items that are disclosed on an after-tax basis under GAAP (e.g., discontinued operations, extraordinary items, or the cumulative effect of accounting changes). The effects of last-in, first-out (LIFO) liquidations are sometimes presented pretax and in other cases after tax. Note that a line item is provided for the effect of LIFO liquidations in both the pretax additions and tax-adjusted additions sections of the SEB worksheet.

6. Changes in deferred-tax valuation allowances are recorded in the tax-adjusted additions (or deductions) section only if such changes affected net income or net loss for the period. Evidence of an income statement impact will usually

take the form of an entry in the income tax rate reconciliation schedule. More background on this matter is provided later in this chapter.

7. The next step is to subtotal the tax-adjusted additions entries and then combine this subtotal with that for the pretax additions above (step six) and then record the result on the "Total additions" line at the bottom of the first page of the worksheet.

8. Completion of page 2 of the SEB worksheet, for nonrecurring revenues and gains, follows exactly the same steps as those outlined for nonrecurring expenses and losses.

9. With the completion of page 2, the sustainable earnings base for each year is computed by adding the total additions line item to net income or loss and then deducting the total deductions line item.

ROLE OF THE SUSTAINABLE EARNINGS BASE

The SEB provides profitability information from which the distorting effects of nonrecurring items have been removed. Some analysts refer to such revised numbers as representing "core" earnings. The SEB is history analyzed, as opposed to history simply revealed. The SEB provides a profit series that is a more reliable depiction of the past, and more worthy of the message, expressed earlier, that future profit is linked to the past.

"Sustainable" is used in the sense that earnings devoid of nonrecurring items of revenue or gain and expense or loss are much more likely to be maintained in the future if previous operating conditions persist. "Base," as in foundation, implies that the sustainable earnings base provides the most reliable starting point for projections of future results. The more reliable such forecasts become, the less the likelihood that frequent earnings surprises will result. Chevron Corporation captures the essence of nonrecurring items in the following:

> Transactions not considered representative of the company's ongoing operations. These transactions, as defined by management, can obscure the underlying results of operations and affect comparability between years.[6]

APPLICATION OF THE SUSTAINABLE EARNINGS BASE WORKSHEET: BAKER HUGHES, INC.

A case illustration using the SEB worksheet employs the 1997 annual report of Baker Hughes, Inc. and its results for 1995 to 1997. To provide a realistic illustration of the process of comprehensive identification of nonrecurring items and the completion of the SEB worksheet, the income statement, statement of cash flows, management's discussion and analysis of financial condition and results of operations (MD&A), and selected notes disclosing nonrecurring items are provided in Exhibits 3.2 through 3.9. Further, to reinforce the objective of efficiency in financial analysis, the search sequence outlined in Exhibit 2.1 from the previous chapter is followed.

COMMENTS ON THE BAKER HUGHES WORKSHEET

An enumeration of the nonrecurring items located in the Baker Hughes, Inc. annual report is provided in the completed SEB worksheet found in Exhibit 3.10. Each of the nonrecurring items is recorded on the SEB worksheet. When an item is disclosed for the first, second, third, or fourth time, it is designated by a corresponding superscript in a summary of the search process provided in Exhibit 3.11. For purposes of illustration, all nonrecurring items have been recorded on the SEB worksheet without regard to their materiality. We believe this to be the best procedure to follow. A materiality threshold could exclude a series of either immaterial gains or losses that, in combination, could distort a firm's apparent profitability. An effort is made to consider the possible effects of materiality in a report on the efficiency of the search process presented in Exhibit 3.12.

The tax rate assumed in the analysis in the Baker Hughes's worksheet was a combined 42 percent. This is the three-year average effective tax rate for the company once nonrecurring tax items were removed from the tax provision. One nonrecurring tax item that stands out is the lack of tax deductibility for $118 million of acquired in-process research and development in 1997. The tax effect of this item, $41.3 million, pushed the effective rate up to an unsustainably high 49 percent for that one year. The tax item is disclosed in Exhibit 3.4. This lack of tax deductibility for the acquired in-process research and development led us to record the $118 million of acquired in-process research and development on the SEB worksheet on an after-tax basis. And because the item was added back to net income on an after-tax basis, no additional adjustment was needed for the $41.3 million tax item itself. More discussion of income taxes and the worksheet is provided later in this chapter.

Without adjustment, Baker Hughes's income statement reports net income of $105.4 million, $176.4 million, and $97 million in 1995, 1996, and 1997, respectively. The impression obtained is a company with a volatile earnings stream and no apparent growth. However, the complete restatement represented by the worksheet conveys quite a different message. With restated, sustainable earnings reported at $97.4 million, $158.6 million, and $241.3 million in 1995, 1996, and 1997, respectively, the company is enjoying a remarkable growth period, though acquisitions have contributed to it. With these changes in mind, it is clear that the number and magnitude of nonrecurring items identified in the Baker Hughes's annual report suggest a lack of reliability of the unanalyzed earnings data. Without the comprehensive identification of nonrecurring items accounted for in the worksheet, the company's three-year operating performance is difficult to discern.

Exhibit 3.2. Baker Hughes, Inc., Consolidated Statements of Operations, Years Ending September 30, 1995, 1996, and 1997 (Millions of Dollars)

	1995	1996	1997
Revenues:			
Sales	$1,805.1	$2,046.8	$2,466.7
Services and rentals	832.4	980.9	1,218.7
Total	2,637.5	3,027.7	3,685.4
Costs and expenses:			
Costs of sales	1,133.6	1,278.1	1,573.3
Costs of services and rentals	475.1	559.5	682.9
Selling, general and administrative	743.0	814.2	966.9
Amortization of goodwill and other intangibles	29.9	29.6	32.3
Unusual charge		39.6	52.1
Acquired in-process research and development			118.0
Total	2,381.6	2,721.0	3,425.5
Operating income	255.9	306.7	259.9
Interest expense	(55.6)	(55.5)	(48.6)
Interest income	4.8	3.4	1.8
Gain on sale of Varco stock		44.3	
Income before income taxes and cumulative			
effect of accounting changes	205.1	298.9	213.1
Income taxes	(85.1)	(122.5)	(104.0)
Income before cumulative effect of accounting changes	120.0	176.4	109.1
Cumulative effect of accounting changes:			
Impairment of long-lived assets to be disposed of			
(net of $6.0 income tax benefit)			(12.1)
Postemployment benefits (net of $7.9			
income tax benefit)	(14.6)		
Net income	$105.4	$176.4	$97.0

Source: Baker Hughes, Inc., annual report, September 1997, p. 37.

An efficient search sequence for identifying nonrecurring items was outlined in Exhibit 2.1 of Chapter Two. This search sequence was based on the experience of the authors supported by a large-scale study of nonrecurring items by Choi.[7] While the recommended search sequence may not be equally effective in all cases, Exhibit 3.11 demonstrates that most of Baker Hughes's nonrecurring items could be located by only employing steps 1 through 5, a sequence that is very cost effective. That is, the items located in these steps require reading very little text, plus the nonrecurring items are generally set out prominently in either statements or schedules.

Exhibit 3.3. Baker Hughes, Inc., Consolidated Statements of Cash Flows
(Operating Activities Only), Years Ending September 30, 1995, 1996, and 1997
(Millions of Dollars)

	1995	1996	1997
Cash flows from operating activities:			
Net income	$105.4	$176.4	$97.0
Adjustments to reconcile net income to net cash flows from operating activities:			
Depreciation and amortization of:			
Property	114.2	115.9	143.9
Other assets and debt discount	40.4	39.9	42.1
Deferred income taxes	44.8	30.2	(6.8)
Noncash portion of unusual charge		25.3	32.7
Acquired in-process research and development			118.0
Gain on sale of Varco stock		(44.3)	
Gain on disposal of assets	(18.3)	(31.7)	(18.4)
Foreign currency translation (gain)/loss-net	1.9	8.9	(6.1)
Cumulative effect of accounting changes	14.6		12.1
Change in receivables	(94.7)	(84.1)	(129.8)
Change in inventories	(79.9)	(73.8)	(114.9)
Change in accounts payable	51.7	22.6	65.3
Changes in other assets and liabilities	(52.9)	9.4	(35.6)
Net cash flows from operating activities	127.2	194.7	199.5

Source: Baker Hughes, Inc., annual report, September 1997, p. 40.

Exhibit 3.12 presents information on the efficiency of the search process. The meaning of each column in the exhibit is as follows:

Column 1 The number of nonrecurring items located at each step in the search process. This is based on all 17 nonrecurring items without regard to their materiality.

Column 2 The cumulative percentage of all nonrecurring items located through each step of the search process. Ninety-four percent of the total nonrecurring items were located through the first 5 steps of the search process. All nonrecurring items were located by step 6.

Column 3 Same as column 1 except that only material nonrecurring items, those items, once tax adjusted, exceeding five percent of net income, were considered.

Column 4 Same as column 2 except that only material nonrecurring items were considered.

Exhibit 3.4. Baker Hughes, Inc., Income Tax Note, 1995–1997 (Millions of Dollars)

NOTE 9 Income Taxes

The geographical sources of income before income taxes and cumulative effect of accounting changes are as follows:

	1995	1996	1997
United States	$128.3	$116.4	$20.6
Foreign	76.8	182.5	192.5
Total	$205.1	$298.9	$213.1

The provision for income taxes is as follows:

Current:			
United States	$3.7	$40.1	$46.5
Foreign	36.6	52.2	64.3
Total current	40.3	92.3	110.8
Deferred:			
United States	42.1	20.7	(.2)
Foreign	2.7	9.5	(6.6)
Total deferred	44.8	30.2	(6.8)
Provision for income taxes	$85.1	$122.5	$104.0

The provision for income taxes differs from the amount computed by applying the U.S. statutory income tax rate to income before income taxes and cumulative effect of accounting changes for the reasons set forth below:

Statutory income tax	$71.8	$104.6	$74.6
Nondeductible acquired in-process research and development charge			41.3
Incremental effect of foreign operations	24.8	12.5	(6.5)
1992 and 1993 IRS audit agreement			(11.4)
Nondeductible goodwill amortization	4.2	5.4	4.5
State income taxes—net of U.S. tax benefit	1.0	2.1	2.9
Operating loss and credit carryforwards	(13.1)	(3.3)	(4.2)
Other—net	(3.6)	1.2	2.8
Provision for income taxes	$85.1	$122.5	$104.0

Deferred income taxes reflect the net tax effects of temporary differences between the carrying amounts of assets and liabilities for financial reporting purposes and the amounts used for income tax purposes, and operating loss and tax credit carryforwards. The tax effects of the Company's temporary differences and carryforwards are as follows:

(continued)

Exhibit 3.4. (Continued) Baker Hughes, Inc., Income Tax Note, 1995–1997 (Millions of Dollars)

	1996	1997
Deferred tax liabilities:		
Property	$62.3	$90.6
Other assets	57.7	147.5
Excess costs arising from acquisitions	64.0	67.6
Undistributed earnings of foreign subsidiaries	41.3	41.3
Other	37.4	36.5
Total	262.7	383.5
Deferred tax assets:		
Receivables	4.1	2.8
Inventory	72.4	72.4
Employee benefits	44.0	21.5
Other accrued expenses	20.2	40.6
Operating loss carryforwards	16.6	9.0
Tax credit carryforwards	30.8	15.9
Other	15.9	34.9
Subtotal	204.0	197.1
Valuation allowance	(13.1)	(5.7)
Total	190.9	191.4
Net deferred tax liability	$71.8	$192.1

A valuation allowance is recorded when it is more likely than not that some portion or all of the deferred tax assets will not be realized. The ultimate realization of the deferred tax assets depends on the ability to generate sufficient taxable income of the appropriate character in the future. The Company has reserved the operating loss carryforwards in certain non-U.S. jurisdictions where its operations have decreased, currently ceased or the Company has withdrawn entirely.

Provision has been made for U.S. and additional foreign taxes for the anticipated repatriation of certain earnings of foreign subsidiaries of the Company. The Company considers the undistributed earnings of its foreign subsidiaries above the amounts already provided for to be permanently reinvested. These additional foreign earnings could become subject to additional tax if remitted, or deemed remitted, as a dividend; however, the additional amount of taxes payable is not practicable to estimate.

At September 30, 1997, the Company had approximately $15.9 million of foreign tax credits expiring in varying amounts between 1998 and 2001 available to offset future payments of U.S. federal income taxes.

Source: Baker Hughes, Inc., annual report, September 1997, pp. 48–49.

Exhibit 3.5. Baker Hughes, Inc., Management's Discussion and Analysis (Excerpts from Results of Operations Section), 1995–1997

Revenues
1997 vs. 1996
Consolidated revenues for 1997 were $3,685.4 million, an increase of 22% over 1996 revenues of $3,027.7 million. Sales revenues were up $419.9 million, an increase of 21%, and services and rentals revenues were up $237.8 million, an increase of 24%. Approximately 64% of the Company's 1997 consolidated revenues were derived from international activities. The three 1997 acquisitions contributed $192.1 million of the revenue improvement.

Oilfield Operations 1997 revenues were $2,862.6 million, an increase of 19.4% over 1996 revenues of $2,397.9 million. Excluding the Drilex acquisition, which accounted for $70.5 million of the revenue improvement, the revenue growth of 16.4% outpaced the 14.4% increase in the worldwide rig count. In particular, revenues in Venezuela increased 37.6%, or $58.6 million, as that country continues to work towards its stated goal of significantly increasing oil production.

Chemical revenues were $417.2 million in 1997, an increase of 68.5% over 1996 revenues of $247.6 million. The Petrolite acquisition was responsible for $91.6 million of the improvement. Revenue growth excluding the acquisition was 31.5% driven by the strong oilfield market and the impact of acquiring the remaining portion of a Venezuelan joint venture in 1997. This investment was accounted for on the equity method in 1996.

Process Equipment revenues for 1997 were $386.1 million, an increase of 9.4% over 1996 revenues of $352.8 million. Excluding revenues from 1997 acquisitions of $32.7 million, revenues were flat compared to the prior year due to weakness in the pulp and paper industry combined with delays in customers' capital spending.

1996 vs. 1995
Consolidated revenues for 1996 increased $390.2 million, or 14.8%, over 1995. Sales revenues were up 13.4% and services and rentals revenues were up 17.8%. International revenues accounted for approximately 65% of 1996 consolidated revenues.

Oilfield Operations revenues increased $325.7 million or 15.7% over 1995 revenues of $2,072.2 million. Activity was particularly strong in several key oilfield regions of the world including the North Sea, Gulf of Mexico and Nigeria where revenues were up $93.4 million, $56.8 million and $30.1 million, respectively. Strong drilling activity drove a $35.5 million increase in Venezuelan revenues.

Chemical revenues rose $23.9 million, or 10.7% over 1995 revenues as its oilfield business benefited from increased production levels in the U.S.

Process Equipment revenues for 1996 increased 10.4% over 1995 revenues of $319.6 million. Excluding revenues from 1996 acquisitions of $21.5 million, revenues increased 3.7%. The growth in the minerals processing and pulp and paper industry slowed from the prior year.

(continued)

Exhibit 3.5.   (Continued) Baker Hughes, Inc., Management's Discussion and Analysis (Excerpts from Results of Operations Section), 1995–1997

Costs and Expenses Applicable to Revenues

Costs of sales and costs of services and rentals have increased in 1997 and 1996 from the prior years in line with the related revenue increases. Gross margin percentages, excluding the effect of a nonrecurring item in 1997, have increased from 39.0% in 1995 to 39.3% in 1996 and 39.4% in 1997. The nonrecurring item relates to finished goods inventory acquired in the Petrolite acquisition that was increased by $21.9 million to its estimated selling price. The Company sold the inventory in the fourth quarter of 1997 and, as such, the $21.9 million is included in cost of sales in 1997.

Selling, General and Administrative

Selling, general and administrative (SG&A) expense increased $152.7 million in 1997 from 1996 and $71.2 million in 1996 from 1995. The three 1997 acquisitions were responsible for $54.3 million of the 1997 increase. As a percent of consolidated revenues, SG&A was 26.2%, 26.9% and 28.2% in 1997, 1996 and 1995, respectively.

Excluding the impact of acquisitions, the Company added approximately 2,500 employees during 1997 to keep pace with the increased activity levels. As a result, employee training and development efforts increased in 1997 as compared to the previous two years. These increases were partially offset by $4.1 million of foreign exchange gains in 1997 compared to foreign exchange losses of $11.4 million in 1996 due to the devaluation of the Venezuelan Bolivar.

The three-year cumulative rate of inflation in Mexico exceeded 100% for the year ended December 31, 1996; therefore, Mexico is considered to be a highly inflationary economy. Effective December 31, 1996, the functional currency for the Company's investments in Mexico was changed from the Mexican Peso to the U.S. Dollar.

Amortization Expense

Amortization expense in 1997 increased $2.7 million from 1996 due to the Petrolite acquisition. Amortization expense in 1996 remained comparable to 1995 as no significant acquisitions or dispositions were made during those two years.

Unusual Charge

1997: During the fourth quarter of 1997, the Company recorded an unusual charge of $52.1 million. In connection with the acquisitions of Petrolite, accounted for as a purchase, and Drilex, accounted for as a pooling of interests, the Company recorded unusual charges of $35.5 million and $7.1 million, respectively, to combine the acquired operations with those of the Company. The charges include the cost of closing redundant facilities, eliminating or relocating personnel and equipment and rationalizing inventories that require disposal at amounts less than their cost. A $9.5 million charge was also recorded as a result of the decision to discontinue a low margin, oilfield product line in Latin America and to sell the Tracor Europa subsidiary, a computer peripherals operations, which resulted in a write-down of the investment to its net realizable value. Cash provisions of the unusual charge totaled $19.4 million. The Company spent $5.5 million in 1997 and expects to spend substantially all of the remaining $13.9 million in 1998. Such expenditures relate to specific plans and clearly defined actions and will be funded from operations and available credit facilities.

(continued)

Exhibit 3.5. (Continued) Baker Hughes, Inc., Management's Discussion and Analysis (Excerpts from Results of Operations Section), 1995–1997

1996: During the third quarter of 1996, the Company recorded an unusual charge of $39.6 million. The charge consisted primarily of the write-off of $8.5 million of Oilfield Operations patents that no longer protected commercially significant technology, a $5.0 million impairment of a Latin America joint venture due to changing market conditions in the region in which it operates and restructuring charges totaling $24.1 million. The restructuring charges include the downsizing of Baker Hughes INTEQ's Singapore and Paris operations, a reorganization of EIMCO Process Equipment's Italian operations and the consolidation of certain Baker Oil Tools manufacturing operations. Noncash provisions of the charge totaled $25.3 million and consist primarily of the write-down of assets to net realizable value. The remaining $14.3 million of the charge represents future cash expenditures related to severance under existing benefit arrangements, the relocation of people and equipment and abandoned leases. The Company spent $4.2 million of the cash during 1996, $6.3 million in 1997 and expects to spend the remaining $3.8 million in 1998.

Acquired In-Process Research and Development
In the Petrolite acquisition, the Company allocated $118.0 million of the purchase price to in-process research and development. In accordance with generally accepted accounting principles, the Company recorded the acquired in-process research and development as a charge to expense because its technological feasibility had not been established and it had no alternative future use at the date of acquisition.

Interest Expense
Interest expense in 1997 decreased $6.9 million from 1996 due to lower average debt levels, primarily as a result of the maturity of the 4.125% Swiss Franc Bonds in June 1996. Interest expense in 1996 remained comparable to 1995 as slightly higher average debt balances were offset by a slightly lower weighted average interest rate.

Gain on Sale of Varco Stock
In May 1996, the Company sold 6.3 million shares of Varco International, Inc. ("Varco") common stock, representing its entire investment in Varco. The Company received net proceeds of $95.5 million and recognized a pretax gain of $44.3 million. The Company's investment in Varco was accounted for using the equity method. Equity income included in the Consolidated Statements of Operations for 1996 and 1995 was $1.8 million and $3.2 million, respectively.

Income Taxes
During 1997, the Company reached an agreement with the Internal Revenue Service ("IRS") regarding the audit of its 1992 and 1993 U.S. consolidated income tax returns. The principal issue in the examination related to inter-company pricing on the transfer of goods and services between U.S. and non-U.S. subsidiary companies. As a result of the agreement, the Company recognized a tax benefit through the reversal of deferred income taxes previously provided of $11.4 million ($.08 per share) in the quarter ended June 30, 1997.

(continued)

Exhibit 3.5.   (Continued) Baker Hughes, Inc., Management's Discussion and Analysis (Excerpts from Results of Operations Section), 1995–1997

The effective income tax rate for 1997 was 48.8% as compared to 41.0% in 1996 and 41.5% in 1995. The increase in the rate for 1997 is due in large part to the nondeductible charge for the acquired in-process research and development related to the Petrolite acquisition offset by the IRS agreement as explained above. The effective rates differ from the federal statutory rate in all years due primarily to taxes on foreign operations and nondeductible goodwill amortization. The Company expects the effective income tax rate in 1998 to be between 38% and 39%.

Source: Baker Hughes, Inc., annual report, September 1997, pp. 30–32.

For the case of Baker Hughes, Exhibit 3.12 reveals that 92 percent of all *material* nonrecurring items were located through the first four steps of the search sequence. This result is achieved very efficiently because most of the nonrecurring items are located in either statements or schedules, with little requirement to read more time-consuming text. Further, locating nonrecurring items in text is subject to a greater risk that a nonrecurring item will simply be overlooked.

SUSTAINABLE EARNINGS BASE ANALYSIS IN COMPANY ANNUAL REPORTS

Our review of hundreds of annual reports revealed only a small number of company-prepared sustainable earnings analyses. Several of these were provided by petroleum companies, possibly attesting to the existence of a higher number of nonrecurring items for that industry. One excellent example of a sustainable earnings calculation, provided in the annual report of a petroleum company, is the schedule provided by Unocal Corp. That schedule was presented earlier in Exhibit 2.23. In addition to the petroleum companies, other industries were represented with sustainable earnings calculations, including specialty chemicals, building materials, and food processing.

While the degree of completeness of the company-provided sustainable earnings analyses varies, the information and insight they provide is very useful. They help establish what managements consider to be nonrecurring income and expense, providing some external confirmation to our views. For example, some analysts argue that foreign currency gains and losses are not nonrecurring because they are the direct result of doing business in foreign countries. Such gains and losses should be expected. We consider them to be nonrecurring as such gains and losses do not continue as gains or as losses indefinitely, but change course with changes in currency direction. In agreement with this view, Phillips Petroleum Company included "Foreign currency gains (losses)" in its list of what were termed *special items.*[8] Similarly, Chevron included "Environmental Remediation

Exhibit 3.6. Baker Hughes, Inc., Summary of Significant Accounting Policies Note (Partial), 1995–1997

NOTE 1
Summary of Significant Accounting Policies

Impairment of assets: The Company adopted Statement of Financial Accounting Standards (SFAS) No. 121, Accounting for the Impairment of Long-Lived Assets and for Long-Lived Assets to be Disposed Of, effective October 1, 1996. The statement sets forth guidance as to when to recognize an impairment of long-lived assets, including goodwill, and how to measure such an impairment. The methodology set forth in SFAS No. 121 is not significantly different from the Company's prior policy and, therefore, the adoption of SFAS No. 121 did not have a significant impact on the consolidated financial statements as it relates to impairment of long-lived assets used in operations. However, SFAS No. 121 also addresses the accounting for long-lived assets to be disposed of and requires these assets to be carried at the lower of cost or fair market value, rather than the lower of cost or net realizable value, the method that was previously used by the Company. The Company recognized a charge to income of $12.1 million ($.08 per share), net of a tax benefit of $6.0 million, as the cumulative effect of a change in accounting in the first quarter of 1997.

Source: Baker Hughes, Inc., annual report, September 1997, p. 41.

Provisions" and "Restructurings and Reorganization" in its list of special items even though these items were reported in each year, 1995 through 1997.[9]

This section summarizes the items that selected companies identified as being nonrecurring and reports how those companies presented that information. The purpose is to broaden and enrich the discussion of what constitutes nonrecurring income and expense.

Hercules, Inc.

In its 1997 annual report, Hercules, Inc. provided an extensive textual discussion of sources of nonrecurring income and expense. The discussion was followed with a table that reported the components of operating profit, adjusted to exclude the nonrecurring items. Among the nonrecurring items identified were the operating results of divested business segments, the effects of "asset rationalizations and impairment, severance, benefits and other adjustments," "probable environmental recoveries, a . . . favorable settlement of an environmental remediation claim," a portion of selling, general and administrative expenses, from the "early vesting of the . . . long-term incentive compensation programs and the grant of stock awards to all Hercules employees," and certain "environmental charges." At the conclusion of the textual discussion, the company provided its table of adjusted operating earnings comparisons, and noted that it "should make it easier to compare year-over-year operating results."[10] That table is reproduced in Exhibit 3.13. As a point of comparison, the company's actual operating earnings for 1995, 1996, and 1997,

Exhibit 3.7. Baker Hughes, Inc., Acquisitions and Dispositions Note, 1995–1997

NOTE 4

Acquisitions and Dispositions

1997

Petrolite

In July 1997, the Company acquired Petrolite Corporation ("Petrolite") and Wm. S. Barnickel & Company ("Barnickel"), the holder of 47.1% of Petrolite's common stock, for 19.3 million shares of the Company's common stock having a value of $730.2 million in a three-way business combination accounted for using the purchase method of accounting. Additionally, the Company assumed Petrolite's outstanding vested and unvested employee stock options which were converted into the right to acquire 1.0 million shares of the Company's common stock. Such assumption of Petrolite options by the Company had a fair market value of $21.0 million resulting in total consideration in the acquisitions of $751.2 million. Petrolite, previously a publicly held company, is a manufacturer and marketer of specialty chemicals used in the petroleum and process industries. Barnickel was a privately held company that owned marketable securities, which were sold after the acquisition, in addition to its investment in Petrolite.

The purchase price has been allocated to the assets purchased and the liabilities assumed based on their estimated fair market values at the date of acquisition as follows (millions of dollars):

Working capital	$64.5
Property	170.1
Prepaid pension cost	80.3
Intangible assets	126.0
Other assets	89.6
In-process research and development	118.0
Goodwill	263.7
Debt	(31.7)
Deferred income taxes	(106.7)
Other liabilities	(22.6)
Total	$751.2

In accordance with generally accepted accounting principles, the amount allocated to in-process research and development, which was determined by an independent valuation, has been recorded as a charge to expense in the fourth quarter of 1997 because its technological feasibility had not been established and it had no alternative future use at the date of acquisition.

(continued)

Exhibit 3.7. (Continued) Baker Hughes, Inc., Acquisitions and Dispositions Note, 1995–1997

The Company incurred certain liabilities as part of the plan to combine the operations of Petrolite with those of the Company. These liabilities relate to the Petrolite operations and include severance of $13.8 million for redundant marketing, manufacturing and administrative personnel, relocation of $5.8 million for moving equipment and transferring marketing and technology personnel, primarily from St. Louis to Houston, and environmental remediation of $16.5 million for redundant properties and facilities that will be sold. Cash spent during the fourth quarter of 1997 totaled $7.7 million. The Company anticipates completing these activities in 1998, except for some environmental remediation that will occur in 1998 and 1999.

The operating results of Petrolite and Barnickel are included in the 1997 consolidated statement of operations from the acquisition date, July 2, 1997. The following unaudited pro forma information combines the results of operations of the Company, Petrolite and Barnickel assuming the acquisitions had occurred at the beginning of the periods presented. The pro forma summary does not necessarily reflect the results that would have occurred had the acquisitions been completed for the periods presented, nor do they purport to be indicative of the results that will be obtained in the future, and excludes certain nonrecurring charges related to the acquisition which have an after tax impact of $155.2 million.

(Millions of dollars, except per share amounts)	1996	1997
Revenues	$3,388.4	$3,944.0
Income before accounting change	189.3	283.9
Income per share before accounting change	1.16	1.69

In connection with the acquisition of Petrolite, the Company recorded an unusual charge of $35.5 million. See Note 5 of Notes to Consolidated Financial Statements.

Environmental Technology Division of Deutz AG

In July 1997, the Company acquired the Environmental Technology Division, a decanter centrifuge and dryer business, of Deutz AG ("ETD") for $53.0 million, subject to certain post-closing adjustments. This acquisition is now part of Bird Machine Company and has been accounted for using the purchase method of accounting. Accordingly, the cost of the acquisition has been allocated to assets acquired and liabilities assumed based on their estimated fair market values at the date of acquisition, July 7, 1997. The operating results of ETD are included in the 1997 consolidated statement of operations from the acquisition date. Pro forma results of the acquisition have not been presented as the pro forma revenue, income before accounting change and earnings per share would not be materially different from the Company's actual results. For its most recent fiscal year ended December 31, 1996, ETD had revenues of $103.0 million.

(continued)

Exhibit 3.7. (Continued) Baker Hughes, Inc., Acquisitions and Dispositions
Note, 1995–1997

Drilex

In July 1997, the Company acquired Drilex International Inc. ("Drilex") a provider of
products and services used in the directional and horizontal drilling and workover of oil
and gas wells for 2.7 million shares of the Company's common stock. The acquisition was
accounted for using the pooling of interests method of accounting. Under this method of
accounting, the historical cost basis of the assets and liabilities of the Company and Drilex
are combined at recorded amounts and the results of operations of the combined companies
for 1997 are included in the 1997 consolidated statement of operations. The historical
results of the separate companies for years prior to 1997 are not combined because the
retained earnings and results of operations of Drilex are not material to the consolidated
financial statements of the Company. In connection with the acquisition of Drilex, the
Company recorded an unusual charge of $7.1 million for transaction and other one time
costs associated with the acquisition. See Note 5 of Notes to Consolidated Financial Statements. For its fiscal year ended December 31, 1996 and 1995, Drilex had revenues of $76.1
million and $57.5 million, respectively.

1996

In April 1996, the Company purchased the assets and stock of a business operating as
Vortoil Separation Systems, and certain related oil/water separation technology, for $18.8
million. In June 1996, the Company purchased the stock of KTM Process Equipment, Inc.,
a centrifuge company, for $14.1 million. These acquisitions are part of Baker Hughes
Process Equipment Company and have been accounted for using the purchase method of
accounting. Accordingly, the costs of the acquisitions have been allocated to assets acquired
and liabilities assumed based on their estimated fair market values at the dates of acquisition. The operating results are included in the consolidated statements of operations from
the respective acquisition dates.

In April 1996, the Company exchanged the 100,000 shares of Tuboscope Inc. ("Tuboscope") Series A convertible preferred stock held by the Company since October 1991, for
1.5 million shares of Tuboscope common stock and a warrant to purchase 1.25 million
shares of Tuboscope common stock. The warrants are exercisable at $10 per share and
expire on December 31, 2000.

In May 1996, the Company sold 6.3 million shares of Varco International, Inc. ("Varco")
common stock, representing its entire investment in Varco. The Company received net
proceeds of $95.5 million and recognized a pretax gain of $44.3 million. The Company's
investment in Varco was accounted for using the equity method. Equity income included
in the consolidated statements of operations for 1996 and 1995 was $1.8 million and $3.2
million, respectively.

Source: Baker Hughes, Inc., annual report, September 1997, pp. 43–45.

Exhibit 3.8.   Baker Hughes, Inc., Unusual Charge Note, 1995–1997 (Millions of Dollars)

NOTE 5
Unusual Charge

1997

During the fourth quarter of 1997, the Company recognized a $52.1 million unusual charge consisting of the following (millions of dollars):

Baker Petrolite:

Severance for 140 employees	$2.2
Relocation of people and equipment	3.4
Environmental	5.0
Abandoned leases	1.5
Integration costs	2.8
Inventory write-down	11.3
Write-down of other assets	9.3

Drilex:

Write-down of property and other assets	4.1
Banking and legal fees	3.0

Discontinued product lines:

Severance for 50 employees	1.5
Write-down of inventory, property and other assets	8.0
Total	$52.1

In connection with the acquisitions of Petrolite and Drilex, the Company recorded unusual charges of $35.5 million and $7.1 million, respectively, to combine the acquired operations with those of the Company. The charges include the cost of closing redundant facilities, eliminating or relocating personnel and equipment and rationalizing inventories that require disposal at amounts less than their cost. A $9.5 million charge was recorded as a result of the decision to discontinue a low margin, oilfield product line in Latin America and to sell the Tracor Europa subsidiary, a computer peripherals operation, which resulted in a write-down of the investment to net realizable value. Cash provisions of the unusual charge totaled $19.4 million. The Company spent $5.5 million in 1997 and expects to spend substantially all of the remaining $13.9 million in 1998.

1996

During the third quarter of 1996, the Company recognized a $39.6 million unusual charge consisting of the following (millions of dollars):

Patent write-off	$8.5
Impairment of joint venture	5.0

Restructurings:

Severance for 360 employees	7.1
Relocation of people and equipment	2.3

(continued)

Exhibit 3.8.   (Continued) Baker Hughes, Inc., Unusual Charge Note, 1995–
1997 (Millions of Dollars)

Abandoned leases	2.8
Inventory write-down	1.5
Write-down of assets	10.4
Other	2.0
Total	$39.6

The Company has certain oilfield operations patents that no longer protect commercially
significant technology resulting in the write-off of $8.5 million. A $5.0 million impairment
of a Latin America joint venture was recorded due to changing market conditions in the
region in which it operates. The Company recorded a $24.1 million restructuring charge
including the downsizing of Baker Hughes INTEQ's Singapore and Paris operations, a
reorganization of EIMCO Process Equipment's Italian operations and the consolidation of
certain Baker Oil Tools manufacturing operations. Cash provisions of the charge totaled
$14.3 million. The Company spent $4.2 million in 1996, $6.3 million in 1997 and expects
to spend the remaining $3.8 million in 1998.

Source: Baker Hughes, Inc., annual report, September 1997, p. 45.

without adjustment, were $363 million, $441 million, and $228 million, respec-
tively. Clearly, the adjustments had the greatest positive benefit for the most recent
year, 1997, in which adjusted operating profit came in at $386 million, 69 percent
above the unadjusted figure.

Armstrong World Industries, Inc.

Armstrong World Industries did not provide a recalculated sustainable earnings
number. The company did, however, provide a useful summary of restructuring
charges and other nonrecurring items included in operating income. The company's disclosures are provided in Exhibit 3.14. Adjusting for the reported nonrecurring items resulted in revised operating profit amounts of $358.7 million,
$329.8 million, and $381.4 million, in 1995, 1996, and 1997, respectively. Reported operating profit numbers were $286.9 million, $283.3 million, and $351.7
million, respectively, for those same years.

Quaker Oats Company

Quaker Oats devoted a footnote on restructuring charges to identify several nonrecurring items. The items, consisting of severance and termination benefits, asset
write-offs, losses on contract and lease cancellations, and losses due to reductions
in manufacturing capacity, were discussed in textual form and presented in a table.
Following that table was another that reported a revised operating income measure

Exhibit 3.9. Baker Hughes, Inc., Segment and Related Information Note, 1995–1997

NOTE 10

Segment and Related Information

The Company adopted SFAS No. 131, Disclosures About Segments of an Enterprise and Related Information, in 1997 which changes the way the Company reports information about its operating segments. The information for 1996 and 1995 has been restated from the prior year's presentation in order to conform to the 1997 presentation.

The Company's nine business units have separate management teams and infrastructures that offer different products and services. The business units have been aggregated into three reportable segments (oilfield, chemicals and process equipment) since the long-term financial performance of these reportable segments is affected by similar economic conditions.

Oilfield: This segment consists of five business units—Baker Hughes INTEQ, Baker Oil Tools, Baker Hughes Solutions, Centrilift and Hughes Christensen—that manufacture and sell equipment and provide services and solutions used in the drilling, completion, production and maintenance of oil and gas wells. The principle markets for this segment include all major oil and gas producing regions of the world including North America, Latin America, Europe, Africa and the Far East. Customers include major multinational, independent and national or state-owned oil companies.

Chemicals: Baker Petrolite is the sole business unit reported in this segment. They manufacture specialty chemicals for inclusion in the sale of integrated chemical technology solutions for petroleum production, transportation and refining. The principle geographic markets for this segment include all major oil and gas producing regions of the world. This segment also provides chemical technology solutions to other industrial markets throughout the world including petrochemicals, steel, fuel additives, plastics, imaging and adhesives. Customers include major multi-national, independent and national or state-owned oil companies as well as other industrial manufacturers.

Process Equipment: This segment consists of three business units—EIMCO Process Equipment, Bird Machine Company and Baker Hughes Process Systems—that manufacture and sell process equipment for separating solids from liquids and liquids from liquids through filtration, sedimentation, centrifugation and floatation processes. The principle markets for this segment include all regions of the world where there are significant industrial and municipal wastewater applications and base metals activity. Customers include municipalities, contractors, engineering companies and pulp and paper, minerals, industrial and oil and gas producers.

The accounting policies of the reportable segments are the same as those described in Note 1 of Notes to Consolidated Financial Statements. The Company evaluates the performance of its operating segments based on income before income taxes, accounting changes, nonrecurring items and interest income and expense. Intersegment sales and transfers are not significant.

(continued)

Exhibit 3.9.   (Continued) Baker Hughes, Inc., Segment and Related
Information Note, 1995–1997

Summarized financial information concerning the Company's reportable segments is
shown in the following table. The "Other" column includes corporate related items, results
of insignificant operations and, as it relates to segment profit (loss), income and expense
not allocated to reportable segments (millions of dollars).

1997	*Oilfield*	*Chemicals*	*Process Equipment*	*Other*	*Total*
Revenues	$2,862.6	$417.2	$386.1	$19.5	$3,685.4
Segment profit (loss)	416.8	41.9	36.3	(281.9)	213.1
Total assets	3,014.3	1,009.5	363.7	368.8	4,756.3
Capital expenditures	289.7	24.8	6.4	21.8	342.7
Depreciation and amortization	143.2	20.5	8.4	4.1	176.2
1996					
Revenues	$2,397.9	$247.6	$352.8	$29.4	$3,027.7
Segment profit (loss)	329.1	23.3	31.2	(84.7)	298.9
Total assets	2,464.6	270.3	258.9	303.6	3,297.4
Capital expenditures	157.5	16.6	6.6	1.5	182.2
Depreciation and amortization	123.6	12.2	6.7	3.0	145.5
1995					
Revenues	$2,072.2	$223.7	$319.6	$22.0	$2,637.5
Segment profit (loss)	249.6	17.8	29.7	(92.0)	205.1
Total assets	2,423.7	259.8	187.3	295.8	3,166.6
Capital expenditures	119.1	11.0	5.0	3.8	138.9
Depreciation and amortization	123.9	12.4	5.4	2.4	144.1

The following table presents the details of "Other" segment profit (loss).

	1995	*1996*	*1997*
Corporate expenses	$(39.7)	$(40.2)	$(44.3)
Interest expense—net	(50.8)	(52.1)	(46.8)
Unusual charge		(39.6)	(52.1)
Acquired in-process research and development			(118.0)
Nonrecurring charge to cost of sales for Petrolite inventories			(21.9)
Gain on sale of Varco stock		44.3	
Other	(1.5)	2.9	1.2
Total	$(92.0)	$(84.7)	$(281.9)

(continued)

Exhibit 3.9. (Continued) Baker Hughes, Inc., Segment and Related
Information Note, 1995–1997

The following table presents revenues by country based on the location of the use of the
product or service.

	1995	1996	1997
United States	$972.9	$1,047.2	$1,319.7
United Kingdom	207.6	277.9	288.0
Venezuela	122.7	160.0	244.2
Canada	157.5	165.1	204.5
Norway	104.2	145.6	175.0
Indonesia	54.5	92.7	128.0
Nigeria	33.5	64.1	83.5
Oman	45.7	56.8	77.2
Other (approximately 60 countries)	938.9	1,018.3	1,165.3
Total	$2,637.5	$3,027.7	$3,685.4

The following table presents property by country based on the location of the asset.

	1995	1996	1997
United States	$353.0	$359.9	$593.3
United Kingdom	67.6	77.7	145.3
Venezuela	19.0	25.1	33.3
Germany	18.4	19.3	21.4
Norway	11.3	10.9	20.0
Canada	8.0	9.1	16.9
Singapore	25.0	17.7	11.7
Other countries	72.8	79.3	141.0
Total	$575.1	$599.0	$982.9

Source: Baker Hughes, Inc., annual report, September 1997, pp. 49–51.

calculated to exclude the nonrecurring items. The company's disclosures are presented in Exhibit 3.15. Quaker's revised operating income measures were $409
million, $535 million, and $577.1 million in 1995, 1996, and 1997, respectively.
These profit measures compare with unadjusted amounts of $300.8 million, $410.5
million, and $511.9 million, respectively, for those same years.

Phillips Petroleum Company

Phillips Petroleum provided a detailed schedule of nonrecurring items, supplemented with a disclosure of revised net operating income that was calculated to
exclude those items. Among the nonrecurring items identified by the company

Exhibit 3.10. Adjustment Worksheet for Sustainable Earnings Base: Baker Hughes, Inc., 1995–1997 (Millions of Dollars)

	1995	1996	1997
Reported net income or (loss)	$105.4	$176.4	$97.0
Add			
Pretax LIFO liquidation losses			
Losses on sales of fixed assets			
Losses on sales of investments			
Losses on sales of "other" assets			
Restructuring charges (Unusual charge)		39.6	52.1
Investment write-downs			
Inventory write-downs (Included in cost of sales)			21.9
Other asset write-downs			
Foreign currency losses	1.9	11.4	
Litigation charges			
Losses on patent infringement suits			
Exceptional bad debt provisions			
Temporary expense increases			
Temporary revenue reductions			
Other			
Other			
Other			
Subtotal	$1.9	$51.0	$74.0
Multiply by			
(1-combined federal and state tax rates)	58%	58%	58%
Tax-adjusted additions	$1.1	$29.6	$42.9
Add			
After-tax LIFO liquidation losses			
Increases in deferred tax valuation allowances			
Other nonrecurring tax charges			
Losses on discontinued operations			
Extraordinary losses			
Losses/cumulative-effect accounting changes	14.6		12.1
Other (Acquired in-process R&D)			118.0

(continued)

Exhibit 3.10. (Continued) Adjustment Worksheet for Sustainable Earnings Base: Baker Hughes, Inc., 1995–1997 (Millions of Dollars)

	1995	*1996*	*1997*
Other	___	___	___
Other	___	___	___
Subtotal	$14.6	___	$130.1
Total additions	$15.7	$29.6	$173.0
Deduct			
Pretax LIFO liquidation gains	___	___	___
Gains on sales of fixed assets (disposal of assets)	18.3	31.7	18.4
Gains on sales of investments (Varco stock)	___	44.3	___
Gains on sales of other assets	___	___	___
Reversals of restructuring charges	___	___	___
Investment write-ups (trading account)	___	___	___
Foreign currency gains	___	___	4.1
Litigation revenues	___	___	___
Gains on patent infringement suits	___	___	___
Temporary expense decreases	___	___	___
Temporary revenue increases	___	___	___
Reversals of bad debt allowances	___	___	___
Other	___	___	___
Other	___	___	___
Other	___	___	___
Subtotal	$18.3	$76.0	$22.5
Multiply by			
(1-combined federal and state tax rate)	58%	58%	58%
Tax-adjusted deductions	$10.6	$44.1	$13.1
Deduct			
After-tax LIFO liquidation gains	___	___	___
Reductions in deferred tax valuation allowances	___	___	___
Loss carryforward benefits—from prior periods	13.1	3.3	4.2
Other nonrecurring tax benefits (IRS audit agreement)	___	___	11.4
Gains on discontinued operations	___	___	___
Extraordinary gains	___	___	___
Gains/cumulative-effect accounting changes	___	___	___

(*continued*)

Exhibit 3.10. (Continued) Adjustment Worksheet for Sustainable Earnings Base: Baker Hughes, Inc., 1995–1997 (Millions of Dollars)

	1995	1996	1997
Other	——	——	——
Other	——	——	——
Other	——	——	——
Subtotal	$13.1	$3.3	$15.6
Total deductions	$23.7	$47.4	$28.7
Sustainable earnings base	$97.4	$158.6	$241.3

were a tax settlement, property impairments, net gains on asset sales and a subsidiary stock transaction, capital loss carryforwards, workforce reduction charges, foreign currency gains and losses, and pending claims and settlements. The company's schedule of the nonrecurring items is presented in Exhibit 3.16.

Chevron Corporation

Chevron provided a tabular summary of special items affecting net income. The items, reported on an after-tax basis, consisted of asset write-offs and revaluations, implementation of Statement of Financial Accounting Standards (SFAS) No. 121, asset disposition gains, prior-year tax adjustments, environmental remediation provisions, restructurings and reorganizations, and LIFO inventory gains and losses. The company described its special items as follows:

> SPECIAL ITEMS. Net income is affected by transactions that are unrelated to, or are not necessarily representative of, the company's ongoing operations for the periods presented. These transactions, defined by management and designated "special items," can obscure the underlying results of operations for a year, as well as affect comparability between years. Following is a table that summarizes the gains or (losses), on an after-tax basis, from special items included in the company's reported net income.[11]

Chevron reported net income of $930 million, $2,607 million, and $3,256 million in 1995, 1996, and 1997, respectively. Once adjusted for the special items reported below, net income is $1,962 million, $2,651 million, and $3,180 million, respectively, for those same years. The company's schedule of special items is presented in Exhibit 3.17.

Summary of Nonrecurring Items

A summary of nonrecurring or special items disclosed in the annual reports reviewed here is presented in Exhibit 3.18. Also included are the items reported in

Exhibit 3.11.   Summary of Nonrecurring Items Search Process: Baker
Hughes, Inc.

Step and Search Location	Nonrecurring Item Revealed
1. Income statement	Unusual charge (1996–1997)[1]
	Acquired in-process research and development (1997)[1]
	Gain on sale of Varco stock (1996)[1]
	Cumulative effect of accounting changes (1995, 1997)[1]
2. Statement of cash flows	Acquired in-process research and development (1997)[2]
	Gain on sale of Varco stock (1996)[2]
	Gain on disposal of assets (1995–1997)[1]
	Foreign currency translation (gain)/loss-net (1995–1997)[1]
	Cumulative effect of accounting changes (1995, 1997)[2]
3. Inventory note (LIFO firm)	Not a LIFO firm
4. Income tax note	1992 and 1993 IRS audit agreement (1997)[1]
	Operating loss and credit carryforwards (1995–1997)[1]
5. Other income (expense) note	No note provided
6. MD&A	Petrolite inventory writedown in cost of sales (1997)[1]
	Unusual charge (1996–1997)[2]
	Acquired in-process research and development (1997)[3]
	Gain on sale of Varco stock (1996)[3]
	1992 and 1993 IRS audit agreement (1997)[2]
7. Other notes revealing nonrecurring items:	
a. Significant accounting policies	Cumulative effect of accounting changes (1995, 1997)[3]
b. Acquisitions and dispositions	Acquired in-process research and development (1997)[4]
	Unusual charge (1996–1997)[3]
	Gain on sale of Varco stock (1996)[4]
c. Unusual charge	Unusual charge (1996–1997)[4]

(continued)

Exhibit 3.11. (Continued) Summary of Nonrecurring Items Search Process: Baker Hughes, Inc.

Step and Search Location	Nonrecurring Item Revealed
d. Segment and related information	Unusual charge (1996–1997)[5]
	Acquired in-process research and development (1997)[5]
	Petrolite inventory writedown included in cost of sales (1997)[2]
	Gain on sale of Varco stock (1996)[5]

Note: The superscripts 1, 2, 3 indicate in how many search locations the nonrecurring item was found. For instance, "Gain on sale of Varco stock" was found in the income statement (first location); in the statement of cash flows (second location); in MD&A (third location); in "Acquisitions and dispositions" note (fourth location); and "Segment and related information" note (fifth location).

Exhibit 3.12. Efficiency of Nonrecurring Items Search Process: Baker Hughes, Inc.

	Incremental Nonrecurring Items Discovered			
	(1)	(2)	(3)	(4)
	All	Cumulative	All	Cumulative
	Nonrecurring	%	Material*	%
Step and Search Location	Items	Located	Items	Located
1. Income statement	6	35%	6	50%
2. Statement of cash flows	6	71	3	75
3. Inventory note	0	71	0	75
4. Income tax note	4	94	2	92
5. Other income (expense) note	0	94	0	92
6. MD&A	1	100	1	100
7a. Significant accounting policies note	0	100	0	100
7b. Acquisitions and dispositions note	0	100	0	100
7c. Unusual charge note	0	100	0	100
7d. Segment and related information note	0	100	0	100
Total nonrecurring items	17	100%	12	100%

*Five percent or more of the amount of the net income or net loss, on a tax-adjusted basis.

Exhibit 3.13. Operating Profit Adjusted for Nonrecurring Items: Hercules, Inc., Years Ending December 31, 1995, 1996, and 1997 (Millions of Dollars)

	1995	1996	1997
Net sales	$1,840	$1,774	$1,782
Cost of sales	1,175	1,095	1,101
Selling, general and administrative expenses	254	234	243
Research and development	49	50	52
Other operating expenses (income)—net	19	(3)	—
Profit from operations	$343	$398	$386

Source: Hercules, Inc., annual report, December 1997, p. 17.

the sustainable earnings calculations of Unocal Corporation presented in Chapter Two. Exhibit 3.18 provides no surprises. Most of the items appeared in the discussion of nonrecurring items in Chapter Two or in the sustainable earnings calculations in this chapter.

INCOME TAXES AND SUSTAINABLE EARNINGS BASE ANALYSIS

Selection of an Average Effective Tax Rate

Step 3 of the instructions for completion of the sustainable earnings base worksheet calls for recording of all pretax, nonrecurring expenses and losses. To put these items on an after-tax basis, their subtotal is multiplied by 1 minus a representative combined federal and state income tax rate. A similar approach is followed for all pretax, nonrecurring income and gains.

Selection of a representative combined federal and state income tax rate requires care and attention to detail. Where there is no state income tax, an appropriate rate should approximate the current federal statutory rate of 35 percent. With a state rate, the combined rate will generally range between 38 and 42 percent, depending on the effects of differences between pretax income for financial statement purposes and taxable income for tax purposes and the effects of taxes on foreign subsidiaries. More is said about these topics in Chapter Five. A useful approach for determining an appropriate tax rate is to use the average effective tax rate for the most recent three years, adjusted for any nonrecurring tax items. This was the method employed earlier in the Baker Hughes, Inc. example.

Information on a company's tax rates is found in the required schedule that reconciles statutory, or expected, to effective, or actual, tax rates or amounts.[12] An example reconciliation of the statutory with the effective tax rates for TRW, Inc. is provided in Exhibit 3.19. In 1997, TRW reported earnings from continuing

Exhibit 3.14.   Footnote Excerpts Disclosing Nonrecurring Items: Armstrong World Industries, Inc., Years Ending December 31, 1995, 1996, and 1997 (Millions of Dollars)

Note 1

Restructuring Charges in Operating Income	1995	1996	1997
Floor coverings	$25.0	$14.5	$—
Building products	6.3	8.3	—
Industry products	31.4	4.0	—
Unallocated corporate expense	9.1	19.7	—
Total restructuring charges in operating income	$71.8	$46.5	$—

Note 2

1997 operating income includes a $29.7 million loss as a result of charges incurred by Dal-Tile International Inc. for uncollectible receivables, overstocked inventories and other asset revaluations.

Source: Armstrong World Industries, Inc., annual report, December 1997. Information obtained from Disclosure, Inc. *Compact D/SEC: Corporate Information on Public Companies Filing with the SEC* (Bethesda, Maryland: Disclosure, Inc., June 1998).

operations before income taxes of $240 million. That same year, the company's income tax provision was $289 million, or 120.3 percent of pretax income, obviously an unsustainably high rate of tax. The statutory to effective tax rate reconciliation indicates why.

The nonrecurring tax items found in Exhibit 3.19 consist of "Prior-year adjustments" and "Purchased in-process research and development." Adjusting the effective tax rate for these items in each year results in adjusted effective tax rates of 39.8 percent, 41.5 percent, and 43.8 percent, respectively, in 1995, 1996, and 1997. An average adjusted effective tax rate for the three years is 41.7 percent. Forty-two percent would appear to be an appropriate rate to use in a sustainable earnings base calculation.

Dealing with Changes in Deferred Tax Valuation Allowances

The sustainable earnings base worksheet indicates that increases in deferred tax valuation allowances should be added back to net income and decreases subtracted. The deferred tax valuation allowance is required in cases in which the realization of deferred tax assets is unlikely.[13] It is used as a contra account to or reduction from deferred tax assets, much like the allowance for doubtful accounts is used to reduce accounts receivable to amounts ultimately expected to be collected. Changes in the allowance are recorded as changes occur in the likelihood of realization. These changes also, in most instances, affect income tax expense

Exhibit 3.15. Footnote Disclosing Nonrecurring Items and Sustainable Operating Income: Quaker Oats Co., Years Ending December 31, 1995, 1996, and 1997 (Millions of Dollars)

Note 3 Restructuring Charges

During 1997, the Company recorded pretax restructuring charges totaling $65.9 million. In the U.S. and Canadian Foods business restructuring charges of $44.3 million were recorded for various plant consolidations, including $30.7 million for the closing of a rice cakes plant in Gridley, California, $5.9 million for the closing of a Near East plant in Leominster, Massachusetts, and $3.6 million and $4.1 million for manufacturing consolidations in the food service and hot cereals businesses, respectively. A Brazilian pasta plant consolidation in the International Foods business resulted in restructuring charges of $10.7 million. In Worldwide Beverages, restructuring charges of $3.1 million and $1.1 million were recorded to reconfigure U.S. Gatorade manufacturing lines and to close an office in Singapore, respectively. The Company also recorded $4.9 million and $1.8 million of restructuring charges related to staffing reductions in the U.S. and Canadian Foods and Beverages businesses, respectively. The restructuring charges are comprised of asset write-offs, loss on leases, severance and termination benefits and other shut down costs. Savings from these actions substantially began in 1997 and are estimated to be about $29 million annually, with approximately 90 percent in cash. While the restructuring actions taken during the current year are expected to result in the elimination of much of the overhead costs previously allocated to the Snapple beverages business, certain costs will remain. These costs have been reallocated to the ongoing businesses and represent resources for future growth.

In 1996, the Company recorded restructuring charges of $23.0 million. These charges included $16.6 million to change how the Company sold Snapple beverages in certain Texas markets and $6.4 million for plant consolidations in the U.S. and Canadian Foods business. Savings realized from these restructuring actions have been in line with expectations.

In December 1995, the Company recorded restructuring charges of $40.8 million. These charges included $24.4 million to reduce the amount of contract manufacturing capacity for Snapple beverages and $16.4 million to realign the European beverage and Asia/Pacific grain-based food businesses. The realignment in Europe and Asia/Pacific resulted in the elimination of about 80 positions and allowed the Company to focus on more attractive growth areas in Southern Europe for beverages and China for foods. In June 1995, the Company recorded restructuring charges of $76.5 million for cost-reduction and realignment activities in order to address the changes in its business portfolio and to allow it to more quickly and effectively respond to the needs of trade customers and consumers. These changes resulted in the elimination of approximately 850 positions and primarily included the realignment of the corporate, U.S. shared services and business unit structures, the European cereal business and the U.S. distribution center network. Savings realized from these restructuring activities have been in line with expectations.

(continued)

Exhibit 3.15.   (Continued) Footnote Disclosing Nonrecurring Items and
Sustainable Operating Income: Quaker Oats Co., Years Ending December
31, 1995, 1996, and 1997 (Millions of Dollars)

With the 1997 divestiture of the Snapple beverages business, there are no remaining reserves and no recurring savings to be realized from the restructuring activities related to
that business. Restructuring provisions were determined based on estimates prepared at the
time the restructuring actions were approved by management and the Board of Directors.
The 1997 and 1996 restructuring reserve balances are considered adequate to cover committed restructuring actions.

The restructuring charges and utilization to date were as follows:

As of December 31, 1997

Dollars in Millions	Cash	Amounts Charged Noncash	Total	Amounts Utilized	Remaining Reserve
1997					
Severance and termination benefits	$12.6	$—	$12.6	$4.0	$8.6
Asset write-offs	—	49.1	49.1	35.9	13.2
Loss on lease and other	4.2	—	4.2	0.9	3.3
Subtotal	16.8	49.1	65.9	40.8	25.1
1996					
Severance and termination benefits	1.4	—	1.4	1.2	0.2
Asset write-offs	—	18.9	18.9	18.2	0.7
Loss on lease and other	2.6	0.1	2.7	2.5	0.2
Subtotal	4.0	19.0	23.0	21.9	1.1
1995					
Severance and termination benefits	48.8	—	48.8	48.8	—
Loss on reduction of contract manufacturing capacity	22.5	1.9	24.4	24.4	—
Asset write-offs	0.1	22.8	22.9	22.9	—
Contract cancellation fees, loss on leases and other	21.2	—	21.2	14.4	6.8
Subtotal	92.6	24.7	117.3	110.5	6.8
Total	$113.4	$92.8	$206.2	$173.2	$33.0

(*continued*)

Exhibit 3.15. (Continued) Footnote Disclosing Nonrecurring Items and Sustainable Operating Income: Quaker Oats Co., Years Ending December 31, 1995, 1996, and 1997 (Millions of Dollars)

Operating income excluding restructuring charges, losses and gains on divestitures and divested businesses in all periods was as follows:

Dollars in Millions	1995	1996	1997
Operating (loss) income as reported	$1,415.0	$565.9	$(924.3)
Restructuring charges:			
Foods	70.4	6.4	59.9
Beverages	22.5	—	6.0
Ongoing businesses	92.9	6.4	65.9
Divested businesses	24.4	16.6	—
Subtotal	117.3	23.0	65.9
Losses (gains) on divestitures	(1,170.8)	(136.4)	1,420.4
Operating loss from divested businesses	47.5	82.5	15.1
Subtotal	(1,123.3)	(53.9)	1,435.5
Operating income excluding restructuring charges, losses, gains and divested businesses	$409.0	$535.0	$577.1

Source: Quaker Oats Co., annual report, December 1997, pp. 48–50.

Exhibit 3.16. Footnote Disclosing Nonrecurring Items and Sustainable Net Operating Income: Phillips Petroleum Co., Years Ending December 31, 1995, 1996, and 1997 (Millions of Dollars)

Earnings for the three years included the following special items on an after-tax basis:

	1994	1995	1996
Kenai liquefied natural gas (LNG) tax settlement	$—	$—	$565
Property impairments	—	(51)	(183)
Net gains on asset sales	13	—	14
Gain on subsidiary stock transaction	20	—	—
Capital loss carryforwards	50	—	—
Workforce reduction charges	(36)	(31)	(2)
Foreign currency gains (losses)	3	(3)	41
Pending claims and settlements	17	(12)	(18)
Other items	10	(14)	(5)
Total special items	$77	$(111)	$412

Net operating income, which excludes the above items, was $407 million in 1994, $580 million in 1995, and $891 million in 1996.

Source: Phillips Petroleum Co., annual report, December 1996, p. 33.

Exhibit 3.17. Footnote Disclosing Special Items: Chevron Corp., Years
Ending December 31, 1995, 1996, and 1997 (Millions of Dollars)

	1995	*1996*	*1997*
Asset write-offs and revaluations	$(304)	$(337)	$(86)
Initial implementation of SFAS No. 121	(659)	—	—
Asset dispositions	7	391	183
Prior-year tax adjustments	(22)	52	152
Environmental remediation provisions	(90)	(54)	(35)
Restructurings and reorganizations	(50)	(14)	(60)
LIFO inventory gains (losses)	2	(4)	5
Other	84	(78)	(83)
Total special items	$(1,032)	$(44)	$76

Source: Chevron Corp., Form 10-K annual report to the Securities and Exchange Commission (December 1997), pp. FS-5–FS-6.

and, accordingly, alter the effective income tax rate. More is said about this topic
in Chapter Five.

Consider the case of Pharmaceutical Formulations, Inc. The company's reconciliation of the statutory to its effective income tax, presented in dollars and not
percentages, is presented in Exhibit 3.20. As the tax amounts are presented in
dollars, amounts reported need to be divided by pretax income to derive tax rates.
In 1995, the company reported an effective income tax benefit of $517,000, even
though income before income taxes was $1,529,000. That year, the effective tax
rate was a *negative* 33.8 percent. The primary reason for the negative effective
tax rate was the reduction in the deferred tax valuation allowance account in the
amount of $1 million. The company noted that this reduction in the valuation
allowance resulted from, "changes in management's estimates of the utilization
of such temporary differences caused primarily by the Company's improved operating results."[14] The $1 million reduction in the valuation allowance would need
to be recorded on the sustainable earnings base worksheet as a reduction in net
income. Note that the company increased the valuation allowance again in 1996
and 1997 as new questions arose about realization of its deferred tax assets. These
increases would be added to net income on the sustainable earnings base worksheet.

One additional example is provided in Exhibit 3.21. During fiscal 1998, Standard Commercial Corporation increased its deferred tax valuation allowance by
$1,548,000, from $5,503,000 to $7,051,000 because of "tax-loss carryforwards
for which no benefit had been recognized."[15] During that same year, the company's
deferred tax asset associated with the net operating loss carryforward increased
by approximately the same amount. In effect, the company was fully reserving
the increase in the deferred tax asset derived from the increase in the net operating

Exhibit 3.18.   Summary of Nonrecurring Items and Sustainable Earnings Base Information Provided by Selected Companies

---

Armstrong World Industries, Inc. (1997)
Restructuring charges
Charge for uncollectible receivables
Charge of overstocked inventories
Charge for other asset revaluations

Chevron Corp. (1997)
Asset write-offs and revaluations
Initial implementation of SFAS No. 121
Asset dispositions
Prior-year tax adjustment
Environmental remediation provisions
Restructurings and reorganizations
LIFO inventory gains (losses)

Hercules, Inc. (1997)
Discontinued operations
Operating results of divested business
    segments
Asset rationalizations and impairment
Severance pay
Benefits
Probable environmental recoveries
Favorable settlement of an environmental
    remediation claim
Portion of SG&A from early vesting of
    long-term incentive compensation and
    grant of stock awards
Environmental charges

Phillips Petroleum Co. (1996)
Tax settlement
Property impairments
Net gains on asset sales
Gain on subsidiary stock transaction
Capital loss carryforwards
Workforce reduction charges
Foreign currency gains (losses)
Pending claims and settlements

Quaker Oats Company (1997)
Severance and termination benefits
Asset write-offs
Losses on contract and lease cancellations
Losses due to reduction in manufacturing
    capacity

Unocal Corp. (1997)
Deferred tax adjustments
Impairment of long-lived assets
Environmental and litigation provisions
Asset sales
Early extinguishment of debt

Sources: Companies' annual reports.

loss carryforward. As a result, the company did not include the tax benefit associated with the additional loss carryforward in 1998, the year in which it arose. The company's effective tax rate was increased accordingly.

In completing the sustainable earnings base worksheet, changes in the deferred tax valuation allowance are included only when those changes alter the effective income tax rate. That was the case in both instances above, namely, Pharmaceutical Formulations and Standard Commercial. Occasionally, a change in the valuation allowance account is not accompanied with a change in the effective tax rate. For example, in an acquisition, the acquiring company consolidates all acquired account balances, including deferred tax assets and related valu-

Exhibit 3.19. Reconciliation of Statutory with Effective Income Tax Rates: TRW, Inc., Years Ending December 31, 1995, 1996, and 1997

	1995	1996	1997
U.S. statutory income tax rate	35.0%	35.0%	35.0%
Nondeductible expenses	1.3	2.4	2.7
U.S. state and local income taxes net of U.S. federal tax benefit	3.8	3.0	7.6
Non-U.S. tax rate variances net of foreign tax credits	(.1)	3.4	(2.2)
Prior-year adjustments	(3.0)	(1.9)	(3.5)
Purchased in-process research and development	—	—	80.0
Other	(.2)	(2.3)	.7
	36.8%	39.6%	120.3%

Source: TRW, Inc., annual report, December 1997, p. 43.

Exhibit 3.20. Reconciliation of Statutory with Effective Income Taxes: Pharmaceutical Formulations, Inc., Years Ending December 31, 1995, 1996, and 1997

	1995	1996	1997
Statutory U.S. tax	$520,000	$(1,488,000)	$753,000
Increase (decrease) resulting from:			
Utilization of federal net operating loss carryforwards	(56,000)	—	—
Net change in valuation account	(1,000,000)	681,000	30,000
Other	19,000	(104,000)	99,000
Effective income taxes (benefit)	$(517,000)	$(911,000)	$882,000

Source: Pharmaceutical Formulations, Inc., annual report, June 1997, p. 30.

ation allowance accounts. In such cases, the increase in the valuation allowance would not be accompanied with an increase in income tax expense and would not alter the effective tax rate. As a result, the increase in the valuation allowance would not be recorded on the sustainable earnings base worksheet. A similar result occurs when a valuation allowance is recorded against a deferred tax asset arising from the decline in market value of available-for-sale investment securities. Here again, the change in the valuation allowance would not affect income tax expense and would not appear on the tax rate reconciliation schedule. More is said about taxes and the investment's topic in Chapters Eight and Nine. Generally, when deciding whether to include a change in the deferred tax asset valuation allowance on the sustainable earnings base worksheet, look to the tax rate reconciliation schedule. If the change in the valuation account appears there, altering the effective tax rate, include it in calculating sustainable earnings.

Exhibit 3.21. Reconciliation of Statutory with Effective Income Taxes: Standard Commercial Corp., Years Ending March 31, 1996, 1997, and 1998 (Millions of Dollars)

	1996	1997	1998
Expense (benefit) at U.S. federal statutory tax rate	$768	$11,286	$12,601
Foreign tax losses for which there is no relief available	4,359	321	1,585
U.S. tax on foreign income	200	500	400
Different tax rates in foreign subsidiaries	(177)	680	(207)
Elimination of deferred tax liabilities due to a change in foreign law	—	—	(6,864)
Change in valuation allowance	2,350	(1,518)	1,548
Other—net	(664)	1,513	(294)
	$6,836	$12,782	$ 8,769

Source: Standard Commercial Corp., annual report, March 1998, p. 24.

SUMMARY

This chapter demonstrated how the sustainable earnings base worksheet is completed. Key points raised in the chapter are:

• The purpose of the sustainable earnings worksheet is to remove all nonrecurring items from reported net income in the derivation of a more meaningful and reliable measure of performance results. The calculation of sustainable earnings is an important first step toward forecasting future earnings.

• The case study company examined in the chapter, Baker Hughes, Inc., disclosed numerous nonrecurring items in their financial statements, footnotes, and management's discussion and analysis.

• The systematic approach to identification of nonrecurring items, introduced in Exhibit 2.1 in Chapter Two, was applied. The vast majority of nonrecurring items, certainly of material nonrecurring items, were located by step 5, before a careful reading of textual material was needed.

• The annual reports of several companies providing their own analysis of sustainable earnings provided examples of what their managements considered to be nonrecurring or special items of income and expense.

• A summary of these nonrecurring items was provided in the chapter. The items identified provided no surprises and were consistent with the nonrecurring items discussed in Chapter Two and identified in the examples presented in this chapter.

• Because the sustainable earnings base worksheet requires entry of certain income and expense amounts on a pretax basis, the selection of an appropriate tax rate becomes very important. The chapter presented a careful summary of how to calculate such a rate along with other specialized tax topics.

NOTES

1. Fortune cookie message received in a Chinese-food restaurant in Chicago, October 1997.

2. Standard & Poor's Corp., *S&P's Corporate Finance Criteria* (New York: Standard & Poor's Corp., 1991), inside cover.

3. *The Wall Street Journal,* February 15, 1996, p. C1.

4. American Institute of Certified Public Accountants, *Improving Business Reporting—A Customer Focus* (New York: American Institute of Certified Public Accountants Special Committee on Financial Reporting, 1993), p. 4.

5. Earlier versions of this sustainable earnings worksheet were published by E. Comiskey, C. Mulford, and H. Choi, "Analyzing the Persistence of Earnings: A Lender's Guide," *The Commercial Lending Review* (Winter 1994–95), pp. 4–23; C. Mulford and E. Comiskey, *Financial Warnings* (New York: Wiley, 1996), pp. 121–122; and E. Comiskey and C. Mulford, "Analyzing Business Earnings," *The Portable MBA in Finance and Accounting* (New York: Wiley, 1997), pp. 27–78.

6. Chevron Corporation annual report, December 1994, p. 24. The quotation cited here appeared in Chevron's Glossary of Energy and Financial Terms. The description is actually for the term *special items.* However, it is clear that the term is being used to describe nonrecurring items as the term is used in this book.

7. H. Choi, *Analysis and Valuation Implications of Persistence and Cash-Content Dimensions of Earnings Components Based upon Extent of Analyst Following,* unpublished PhD thesis (Atlanta: Georgia Institute of Technology, October 1994), Chapters Five and Six.

8. Phillips Petroleum Co., annual report, December 1996, p. 33.

9. Chevron Corp., Form 10-K annual report to the Securities and Exchange Commission (December 1997), p. FS-5.

10. Hercules, Inc., annual report, December 1997, p. 17.

11. Chevron Corp., Form 10-K annual report to the Securities and Exchange Commission (December 1997), p. FS-5.

12. SFAS No. 109, "Accounting for Income Taxes" (Norwalk, CT: Financial Accounting Standards Board, February 1992), para. 47.

13. *Ibid.,* para. 17.

14. Pharmaceutical Formulations, Inc., annual report, June 1995, p. 17.

15. Standard Commercial Corp., annual report, March 1998, p. 23.

Chapter 4

Topics in Revenue Recognition and Matching

> "KnowledgeWare booked sales for software even after telling customers they weren't obligated to pay for it and could return it at any time or they didn't have to pay until they resold the software," the SEC said.[1]

The early development of financial reporting was characterized by a balance sheet orientation. In more recent decades, an income statement focus, with its attendant emphasis on revenue recognition and matching, displaced this balance sheet emphasis. Currently, a focus on comprehensive income, with income measurement based on changes in net assets, represents a partial movement back toward a balance sheet orientation.[2] Under the net assets approach, the emphasis is placed on the inclusive recording of all assets and liabilities. Income is derived from "the change in equity, i.e., net assets, of a business enterprise during a period from transactions and other events and circumstances from non-owner sources."[3]

This changes-in-net-assets approach is illustrated by the recognition in other comprehensive income of changes in the current valuation of selected investment securities under Statement of Financial Standards (SFAS) No. 115, "Accounting for Certain Investments in Debt and Equity Securities."[4] Also, the recent mandate under SFAS No. 133, "Accounting for Derivative Instruments and Hedging Activities," to value all derivatives at fair value is further evidence of some shift to the net-assets approach.[5] However, in spite of this trend, there remains a strong income statement emphasis in financial reporting along with an attendant focus on the matching of revenues and expenses.

This chapter explores several important revenue recognition and matching topics as a means of illustrating both the financial reporting and analysis issues that may raise. Primary attention will be given to the topics of contracts, inventory, and interest capitalization. However, the chapter opens with a wide-ranging review of revenue recognition and matching examples based on an extensive review of financial statement disclosures. Following this, a more detailed consideration of the selected topics is provided.

FOUNDATIONS OF REVENUE RECOGNITION AND MATCHING

Key revenue recognition and matching policies of firms are usually disclosed in the initial notes to financial statements. Accounting Principles Board (APB) Opinion No. 22, "Disclosure of Accounting Policies," mandates these disclosures.[6] Under APB 22, these disclosures must, ". . . identify and describe the accounting principles followed by the reporting entity and the methods of applying those principles that materially affect the determination of financial position, cash flows, or results of operations."[7] The APB, the predecessor body to the Financial Accounting Standards Board (FASB), expressed its preference for a separate disclosure of a "Summary of Significant Accounting Policies," to appear as the initial note to the financial statements.

The accounting policies presented below are selected to illustrate how firms implement revenue recognition and matching concepts in specific application areas. For convenience, revenue and expense policies are presented separately.

Revenue Recognition Policies

The revenue recognition policy for the most typical sales transactions is very standard. The policy simply calls for the recognition of sales revenue when the shipment of product is made to the customer. However, in an increasingly complex business world, there are growing numbers of revenue transactions that do not fit this simple model. A sampling of revenue recognition policies is presented in Exhibit 4.1. The policies are discussed in the order in which they appear in the exhibit.

Key recognition and matching themes are evident in the policies in Exhibit 4.1. Gleason Corporation ensures that revenues are not overstated by reducing current sales by estimated returns and allowances. Johnston Industries, Inc. deviates from the standard ship-and-recognize standard for sales recognition. However, its sales recognition based on bill-and-hold is a common practice in the textile industry, and Johnston states that title and risks of ownership are transferred to the customer.[8]

Unitrode Corporation reports that it accounts for shipments to distributors as sales. However, it does reduce sales by a reserve for estimated returns. Some firms delay revenue recognition until products have been sold by their distributors to third parties. For example, this is the policy of Advanced Micro Devices, Inc.:

> We recognize revenue from product sales direct to customers when shipped. In addition, we sell to distributors under terms allowing the distributors certain rights of return and price protection on unsold merchandise they hold. The distributor agreements, which may be canceled by either party upon specified notice, generally contain a provision for the return of our products in the event that the agreement with the distributor is terminated. Accordingly, we defer recognition of revenue and related gross profits from sales to distributors with agreements that have the aforementioned terms until the merchandise is resold by the distributors.[9]

Meredith Corporation's deferral of recognition until magazines have actually been delivered is a classic example of delaying revenue recognition until the firm has performed (i.e., produced and delivered the magazine in this case). Matching is achieved because revenue is recognized in the same period as the costs of magazine production and distribution. The treatment of ticket sales by Delta Air Lines, Inc. is a similar example. The proceeds of advance ticket sales are not recognized in revenues until the customer has actually taken the flight. Until then, Delta classifies the ticket proceeds as a liability on its balance sheet. Norfolk Southern Company, as a shipper, recognizes revenue during transport as opposed to either at the point of shipment or upon delivery. This is somewhat analogous to the percentage-of-completion method that is typically applied to the accounting for long-term contracts.

With much diversity found in practice, Statement of Position (SOP) No. 97–2, "Software Revenue Recognition," was issued to bring greater consistency to the recognition of revenue in this important area.[10] The policy statement of Infinium, Inc. identifies the key revenue recognition criteria: evidence of an agreement, shipment of product, fixed or determinable fees, and probable collection.

The warranty revenue case of Xeta Corporation is often handled in a different manner. That is, Xeta defers a portion of sales revenue and then recognizes this revenue over the warranty period. Alternatively, as in the case of automobile warranties, the estimated expenses of providing the warranty service are typically accrued on a current basis. The associated revenue is also recognized currently because the warranty revenue is part of the basic sales price of the vehicle. Matching is therefore achieved.[11]

Compass Bancshares, Inc. terminates income recognition when the likelihood of collection falls, based on a measure of the number of days that a loan is past due.

The income recognition policies of New Mexico and Arizona Land Company reflect the increased levels of uncertainty often associated with sales of property. In the 1960s, there were some spectacular cases of land company failures. Dramatic growth in profits was fueled by sales transactions in which customers made little or no down payment and later simply walked away from the deals. The FASB responded by issuing SFAS No. 66, "Accounting for Sales of Real Estate," which among other requirements calls for minimum initial investments before a sale can be recorded.[12] This requirement for minimum investments by the purchaser before income may be recognized is specifically designed to address problems underlying the earlier debacles. Requiring a minimum investment by the purchaser before a sale may be recognized reduces the likelihood that they will at some point simply walk away from the transaction.

Expense Recognition Policies

Disclosures of expense recognition policies tend to be more numerous than policies dealing with revenue recognition. A sampling of expense recognition policies

Exhibit 4.1.   Selected Revenue Recognition Policies

Gleason Corporation: Sales Recognition (1998)
Sales are generally recognized by the company when products are shipped or services have been provided. Sales are reported net of returns and allowances.

Johnston Industries, Inc.: Bill-and-Hold Sales Recognized (1998)
Revenue is generally recognized as products are shipped to customers. When customers, under the terms of specific orders, request that the Company manufacture and invoice goods on a bill-and-hold basis, the Company recognizes revenue based on the completion date required in the order and actual completion of the manufacturing process, because at that time, the customer is invoiced and title and risks of ownership are transferred to the customer pursuant to the terms of the sales contract.

Unitrode Corporation: Distributor Sales (1998)
A portion of the Company's sales are made to certain distributors which provide for price protection and certain rights of return on products unsold by the distributors. The Company records a distributor liability reserve for price adjustments and estimated returns.

Meredith Corporation: Subscriptions (1998)
Revenues from magazine subscriptions are deferred and recognized proportionately as products are delivered to subscribers. Revenues from newsstand magazines and books are recognized at shipment, net of provisions for returns.

Norfolk Southern Corporation: Freight Revenue (1998)
Revenue is recognized proportionally as a shipment moves from origin to destination.

Delta Air Lines, Inc.: Passenger Tickets (1998)
Passenger ticket sales are recorded as air traffic liability in the Company's consolidated balance sheets. Passenger and cargo revenues are recognized when the transportation is provided, reducing the air traffic liability, as applicable.

Infinium Software, Inc.: Software and Related Revenue (1998)
The Company recognizes revenue in accordance with the provisions of Statement of Position 97–2, "Software Revenue Recognition." Revenue from software license fees is recognized when there is evidence of an arrangement, the product has been shipped, fees are fixed and determinable, and collection of the related receivable is probable. Revenue from sales through distributors is recorded net of distributor commissions. Maintenance revenue, including those bundled with the initial license fee, are deferred and recognized ratably over the service period. Consulting and training service revenue is recognized as the services are performed.

Xeta Corporation: Warranty Revenue (1997)
The Company defers a portion of each system sale to be recognized as service revenue during the warranty period. The amount deferred is generally equal to the sales price of a maintenance contract for the type of system under warranty and length of the warranty period.

(continued)

Exhibit 4.1.   (Continued) Selected Revenue Recognition Policies

---

Compass Bancshares, Inc.: Interest Income (1998)

It is the general policy of the Company to stop accruing interest income and place the recognition of interest on a cash basis when any commercial, industrial or real estate loan is 90 days or more past due.

New Mexico and Arizona Land Company: Property and Installment Sales (1998)

Profits on property sales are recognized, subject to the assessment of collectibility of the related receivables, when the buyer's initial and required continuing investment amounts to at least 20% of the sales price when development is to commence within a two-year period, or 25% of the sales price on all other sales other than retail land sales . . . Profits on sales that do not meet these requirements and profits from retail land sales are recognized on the installment basis provided minimum payments are received.

Sources: Companies' annual reports. The year following each company name designates the annual report from which each example was drawn.

is provided in Exhibit 4.2. The policies are discussed in the order in which they appear in the exhibit.

The amortization of subscription acquisition costs by Meredith Corporation achieves matching because the amortization is over the same period as that used to amortize subscription revenue.

The benefits of the debt issuance costs, incurred and capitalized by American Standard Company, Inc., are presumably realized over the same period that the related debt is outstanding. Use of the effective-yield amortization method amortizes a larger portion of the cost in the early years when the debt outstanding is greater.

Matching of revenues and expenses is the basis for capitalization and amortization of clinic agreement costs by PHYCOR, Inc.

WHX Corporation's accounting policy for environmental remediation costs draws on the requirements of SFAS No. 5, "Accounting for Contingencies."[13] The key requirements for recognition of the expense and associated obligation are that the contingency be probable and that its amount be estimable.

The drydocking costs of Pool Energy Services are capitalized on the basis that the required drydocking and inspection costs produce future benefits. Notice that the amortization period is two and one-half years, consistent with the requirement for two drydockings over a five-year period.

Illinois Tool Works, Inc. reports the immediate expensing of research and development costs. This treatment is required by SFAS No. 2, "Accounting for Research and Development Costs."[14] Research expenditures are clearly made with the expectation of future benefits. Hence, the FASB requirement to expense such costs as incurred may seem surprising. However, SFAS No. 2 was the first substantive standard issued by the then new standard-setting body (i.e., the FASB). There was a clear sense that reducing the range of choice in accounting was a top

Exhibit 4.2.   Selected Expense Recognition Policies

Meredith Corporation: Subscription Acquisition Costs (1998)
Subscription acquisition costs primarily represent direct-mail agency commissions. These costs are deferred and amortized over the related subscription term, typically two years.

American Standard Companies, Inc.: Debt Issuance Costs (1998)
The costs related to the issuance of debt are capitalized and amortized to interest expense using the effective interest method over the lives of the related debt.

PHYCOR, Inc.: Clinic Service Agreement Costs (1998)
Costs of obtaining clinic service agreements are amortized using the straight-line method over the periods during which the agreements are effective, up to a maximum of 25 years.

WHX Corporation: Environmental Remediation Costs (1998)
The Company accrues for losses associated with environmental remediation obligations when such losses are probable and reasonably estimable.

Pool Energy Services Company: Drydocking Costs (1998)
Deferred costs consist primarily of drydocking costs incurred in conjunction with marine inspections of offshore support vessels and debt financing costs. Under applicable maritime regulations, vessels must be drydocked twice in a five-year period for inspection. Drydocking costs are deferred and amortized on a straight-line basis over a period normally not to exceed 30 months.

Illinois Tool Works, Inc.: Research and Development Costs (1998)
Research and development costs are recorded as expense in the year incurred.

Hasbro, Inc.: Advertising Costs (1998)
Production costs of commercials and programming are charged to operations in the fiscal year during which the production is first aired. The costs of other advertising and marketing programs are charged to operations in the fiscal year incurred.

Alaska Air Group: Frequent-Flyer Award Costs (1998)
The estimated incremental cost of providing free travel is recognized as an expense and accrued as a liability as miles are accumulated. Alaska Air Group also defers recognition of income on a portion of the payments it receives from travel partners associated with its frequent-flyer program. The frequent-flyer award liability is relieved as travel awards are issued.

AirTran Holdings, Inc.: Aircraft and Engine Maintenance Costs (1998)
The Company accounts for airframe and engine overhaul costs using the direct expensing method. Overhauls are preformed on a continuous basis and the cost of overhauls and routine maintenance costs for airframe and engine maintenance are charged to maintenance expense as incurred.

Vulcan Materials Company: Repair, Maintenance, Renewal, and Betterment Costs (1998)
Repairs and maintenance are charged to costs and operating expenses. Renewals and betterments that add materially to the utility or useful lives of property, plant and equipment are capitalized.

Exhibit 4.2.   (Continued) Selected Expense Recognition Policies

---

Amerihost Properties, Inc.: Cost of Management Contracts Acquired and Preopening Costs (1998)

The costs of management contracts acquired included amounts paid to acquire hotel management contracts. Preopening cost includes hiring, training, and other costs incurred in connection with new hotel openings and new management contracts. These amounts were being amortized by use of the straight-line method over periods ranging from two to five years. These costs were expensed in 1998 pursuant to the adoption of Statement of Position (SOP) No. 98–5, "Reporting on the Costs of Start-Up Activities," which requires these costs to be expensed as incurred.

Sources: Companies' annual reports. The year following each company name designates the annual report from which each example was drawn.

priority of the FASB. Mandating a single policy for all firms to use in accounting for research expenditures was consistent with this priority. However, an additional key consideration was the difficulty of establishing predictable relationships between research spending and the likelihood and duration of future benefits.

Available research indicates that the stock market values research spending even though, as a result of the expensing requirement of SFAS No. 2, these costs are left off the balance sheet.[15] Moreover, in contrast to the expensing requirement of SFAS No. 2, the FASB has reported that "The Board has concluded that all purchased in-process research and development should be recognized as an asset and amortized over its useful economic life."[16] Currently, portions of a purchase price attributed to acquired in-process research and development are written off immediately. However, the FASB has also reported that it will delay for now any movement toward a new standard in this area.

Hasbro capitalizes some advertising-related costs and expenses others as incurred. Immediate expensing is the typical treatment for most advertising costs. An American Institute of Certified Public Accountants (AICPA) SOP, No. 93–7, "Reporting on Advertising Costs," permits the capitalization of direct-response advertising costs.[17] The capitalization requirements of SOP No. 93–7 are as follows:

(a) The primary purpose of the advertising is to elicit sales to customers who could be shown to have responded specifically to the advertising, and

(b) The direct-response advertising results in probable future benefits.[18]

Examples of two advertising cost disclosures, one involving capitalization of direct-response costs and one involving direct expensing, are provided below.

1. *Blackrock Golf Corp.: Direct-response advertising costs not capitalized.* The Company follows the AICPA's Statement of Position 93–7, "Reporting Advertising Costs." The Company expenses the cost of television airtime as it is

incurred. The cost of producing an infomercial is considered to be direct-response advertising. However, the Company's infomercial development costs do not meet the SOP's criteria for capitalization that the direct-response advertising would result in probable future benefits, and therefore are expensed at the time of the first airing.[19]

2. *Blue Fish Clothing, Inc.: Direct-response advertising costs are capitalized.* The Company capitalizes and amortizes the costs associated with direct-response advertising over its expected period of future benefit. Direct-response advertising consists primarily of seasonal catalogs. The capitalized costs of the advertising are amortized throughout the sales season associated with the catalog.[20]

Blackrock Golf may have found it difficult to establish the period over which the benefits of the advertising could be expected to last. Hence, no reasonable amortization period could be established. Blue Fish, however, could more readily establish the likelihood of benefits and the period over which they would persist (i.e., the sales season of the catalog).

Accounting for the cost of frequent-flyer awards by Alaska Air is the industry standard. Because there is no separate revenue associated with the frequent-flyer award, the expense of the award (i.e., cost of providing the free flight) is matched against current ticket revenues.[21]

The accounting treatment used by AirTran Holdings for aircraft and engine maintenance costs is not used by all firms in the industry. Some of the alternative treatments are given below:

1. *Hawaiian Airlines, Inc.: Engine overhaul costs expensed in the year engines are overhauled.* Costs of overhauling engines are charged to operations in the year the engines are removed for overhaul, and scheduled heavy airframe overhauls on DC-9 aircraft are recorded under the deferral method, whereby the cost of overhaul is capitalized and amortized over the shorter of the period benefited or the lease term (1997, p. 24).

2. *Southwest Airlines, Inc.: Engine overhauls expensed but airframe overhauls capitalized.* The cost of engine overhauls and routine maintenance costs for aircraft and engines are charged to maintenance expense as incurred. Scheduled airframe overhaul costs are capitalized and amortized over the estimated period benefited, presently ten years (1997, p. 10).

The policy covering repairs, maintenance, renewal, and betterments of Vulcan Materials is standard. Amerihost Properties reports the adoption of SOP No. 98–5, "Reporting on the Costs of Start-Up Activities."[22] Previously, Amerihost had capitalized its start-up costs and amortized them on a straight-line basis over two to five years. Under SOP No. 98–5, start-up activities are defined broadly as:

Those one-time activities related to opening a new facility, introducing a new product or service, conducting business in a new territory, conducting business with a new class of customer or beneficiary, initiating a new process in an existing facility, or commencing some new operation.[23]

All start-up costs are to be expensed as incurred under SOP No. 98–5. The term *start-up costs* includes the costs of activities that are sometimes referred to as preopening costs, preoperating costs, organization costs, or start-up costs.[24]

The motivation for this SOP appears to be the variation of previous practice in defining start-up costs as well as the wide range of differences in the periods selected for their amortization. Over a quarter of a century ago, a similar motivation influenced adoption of the expensing treatment for all research and development costs by the FASB.[25]

Recap of Revenue and Expense Recognition Policies

The revenue and expense recognition policies presented in Exhibits 4.1 and 4.2 illustrate current practice and also highlight key factors that guide these policies. The themes of matching and accrual accounting are evident in virtually all of the disclosed policies. Accounting alternatives are selected so that, to the extent possible, expenses are matched to associated revenues. This matching is not always possible, and this inability explains the expensing as incurred of most selling and administrative (S&A) costs as well the current expensing requirement for research and development.

Accrual accounting calls for the recognition of revenues only when earned and of expenses as they are incurred. The shipment of product is the revenue recognition test in most cases; however, this test is not applicable to many other firms. This is the case where there is the delivery of a service over a period of time. Revenue recognition may also be delayed in cases in which there is greater than normal uncertainty of collection.

In addition to the above themes, it is also evident that revenue and expense recognition often calls for the exercise of substantial judgment. It is not uncommon to find quite different recognition policies being employed in what appear to be very similar circumstances.

Beyond GAAP: Fraudulent Revenue and Expense Recognition

In recent years, the timing of revenue and expense recognition has been heavily represented in enforcement actions by the Securities and Exchange Commission (SEC). The quotation that opens this chapter suggests an activity that is alive and well as we move into the twenty-first century. A study of SEC enforcement actions taken during the decade from 1988 to 1998 revealed that 50 percent of the 204 companies that used fraudulent financial reporting employed improper revenue recognition practices.[26] This 50% was broken down as follows:

Improper revenue recognition:

Recording fictitious revenues	26%
Recording revenues prematurely	24
No description—overstated	16
	66%*

*The failure to total to 50 percent results from the fact that some firms employed more than one of the listed tactics.

The specific improper revenue recognition actions included the following:

- Sham sales—goods shipped to another company location
- Premature revenue recognition before all the terms of sale were completed
- Conditional sales
- Improper cutoff of sales—sales recognized on goods shipped after the end of the period
- Improper use of the percentage-of-completion method
- Unauthorized shipments—shipped goods that had not been ordered
- Consignment sales—booking consigned goods as having been sold[27]

Fifty percent of the 204 companies in the study also engaged in asset overstatement. Included in the asset overstatement category was the improper capitalization of items that should have been expensed. Eighteen percent of the sample firms engaged in direct understatement of expenses, a separate category in the study.

The extent to which judgment is involved in the selection and implementation of revenue and expense recognition policies makes them a natural avenue for use in earning's management.[28] Beyond this, it is important to note the dominance of revenue and expense recognition issues when management activities transcend earnings management and move into the area of fraudulent financial reporting.[29]

With the foundation provided by this general review of revenue recognition and matching, attention now turns to a more detailed examination of several important application areas: contracts, inventories, and interest capitalization.

CONTRACT REPORTING AND ANALYSIS

The central reporting issue in contract reporting is the measurement and timing of the recognition of contract earnings. Key generally accepted accounting principles (GAAP) guidance in this area is provided by SOP 81–1, "Accounting for the Performance of Construction-Type and Certain Production-Type Contracts."[30] Contracts differ from other purchase and sale relationships in that performance "specifications are provided by the customer for the construction of facilities or the production of goods or for the provision of related services."[31] References to contract reporting normally invoke the image of construction contractors. However, contract reporting applies to a far broader range of firms.

Exhibit 4.3 provides a sampling of firms that disclosed the use of contract reporting.[32] Construction, production, and services are all represented among the listed companies. The exhibit shows that contract reporting is not simply a matter of concern to construction contractors or to those who use their financial statements.

While "long-term" is the common prefix employed with contract reporting, SOP 81–1 notes that "The term long-term is not used as an identifying characteristic because other characteristics are considered more relevant for identifying the types of contracts covered."[33] SOP 81–1 does explain that the completed contract method might be used if mainly short-term contracts are involved, and the results would not differ materially if the percentage-of-completion method were employed. The example of a small plumbing contractor is cited.[34] Under the income tax law, a long-term contract "is a building, installation, construction or manufacturing contract that is not completed within the tax year in which it is entered into."[35]

Basic Contract Reporting Methods

The two principal contract reporting methods involve recognition of revenue either as progress is achieved or upon contract completion. These two methods are referred to as percentage-of-completion (POC) and completed contract (CC), respectively. Units-of-delivery is a common variation on the POC method. Under units-of-delivery, revenue is recognized as units are delivered, costs of units delivered are charged against the revenue recognized, and the costs of undelivered units are carried in inventory.

Relative Use of Alternative Contract Reporting Methods

POC is by far the dominant method used. SOP 81–1 calls for the use of POC in cases in which firms have the ability to make reasonably dependable estimates of progress toward completion, contract revenues, and contract costs.[36] A sampling of the use of alternative contract reporting methods is provided in Exhibit 4.4. Prior to the issuance of SOP 81–1, the POC method was not as dominant. In the 1976 survey results (units of production data were not provided), the ratio of CC to POC was 12 to 75, against 2 to 69 for 1997.[37]

Advantage and Disadvantages of the Methods

The principal advantage of the POC method is that it recognizes results in the income statement as progress is made on a contract. This is consistent with the central concept of accrual accounting. However, achieving this reporting advan-

Exhibit 4.3. Firms Disclosing the Use of Contract Reporting

Company	Business
ABC Railroad Products Corp.	Railway signal construction and maintenance
Avondale Industries, Inc.	Shipbuilding and repairs
Daktronics, Inc.	Manufacture and installation of information display systems for scoring statistics, animation displays for sports facilities
DSC Communications Corp.	Development and customization of software
Gundle Environmental Systems, Inc.	Environmental installation of polyolefin lining systems
Kaman Corporation	Helicopter manufacture
LaFarge Corp.	Road construction
Lynch Corp.	Production of glass-forming machines
Showscan Entertainment, Inc.	Sale and installation of projectors, screens, sound systems, and other equipment used to exhibit Showscan films
Stewart & Stevenson Services, Inc.	Manufacture of medium tactical vehicles for the Defense Department
Tyco International, US, Inc.	Fire protection systems and other construction-related projects

Sources: Principally 1998 annual reports to shareholders.

Exhibit 4.4. The Relative Use of Alternative Contract Reporting Methods

	Number of Companies		
	1995	*1996*	*1997*
Percentage-of-completion	80	70	69
Units-of-delivery	28	33	26
Completed contract	4	3	2

Source: American Institute of Certified Public Accountants (AICPA), *Accounting Trends and Techniques,* 52nd ed., 1998, p. 389. These data are based on an annual survey conducted by the AICPA of 600 companies. The companies span a wide range of industries, but are confined principally to commercial and industrial firms.

tage calls for the use of estimates of progress achieved and the eventual total revenue from the contract. To the extent that either progress or eventual revenue is misjudged, it will mean subsequent revisions of earnings.

The principal advantage of the CC method is that results are recognized in the income statement only upon completion of the contract. Profits are not included in the income statement until all costs and revenues are known. Unlike the

POC method, there is less likelihood of a need for subsequent profit revisions. However, under the CC method results are not reported in the income statement as progress is made. Reported profitability is simply determined by the contracts that are completed during the year.[38]

Because of the dominance of POC, the remaining discussion will focus mainly on this method. A range of technical issues associated with POC will be presented and implications for financial analysis identified.

Percentage-of-Completion: Implementation and Analysis

Although a general characterization of POC might suggest a relatively simple procedure, there are a number of important issues associated with its implementation. The following are considered in this section:

- Alternative approaches to gauging stage of completion
- Immediate versus delayed start-up of percentage of completion
- Alternative thresholds for booking claims
- Balance sheet classification of contract-related balances
- Nature and disclosure of retainage
- Loss recognition on contracts

Alternative Approaches to Gauging Stage of Completion

Cost-to-cost is the most common method used to estimate stage of completion. Consider a contract with a fixed price of $1 million and estimated total costs of $600,000. Also assume that the costs and revenue estimates are exact, and that the costs are incurred in a pattern of $300,000, $200,000, and $100,000, in years one through three, respectively. In this case, the income statement effects will be as presented in Exhibit 4.5.

Revenues are recognized in Exhibit 4.5 based on the incremental stage of completion achieved in each year. In year one, the contract is considered to be 50 percent complete at year-end. Costs incurred of $300,000 are 50 percent of total expected contract costs of $600,000. Cumulative completion at the end of year two is $83\frac{1}{3}$ percent. However, only the $33\frac{1}{3}$ percent of incremental progress ($83\frac{1}{3}$ percent minus 50 percent) is attributed to year two. Hence, the revenue already recognized in year one, $500,000, is subtracted from the cumulative revenue earned to date, $833,333, to arrive at the incremental revenue earned in year two of $333,333.

Contract profits are arrived at by simply deducting the contract costs incurred for each year from the recognized contact revenues.

In addition to total contract costs, cost-to-cost POC is sometimes implemented with a measure that is less inclusive, such as labor costs.[39] Some other approaches to estimating stage of completion are presented in Exhibit 4.6.

Exhibit 4.5. Profit Measurement Under Cost-to-Cost Percentage-of-
Completion

	Year 1	Year 2	Year 3
Contract revenues	$500,000	$333,333	$166,667
Contract costs	300,000	200,000	100,000
Gross contract profits	$200,000	$133,333	$66,667

Stage of completion and revenue earned each year:
Year 1: $300,000/$600,000 x $1,000,000 = $500,000
Year 2: $500,000/$600,000 x $1,000,000 = $833,333 − $500,000 =   333,333
Year 3: $600,000/$600,000 x $1,000,000 = $1,000,000 − $833,333 =   166,667
    Total revenue $1,000,000

Notice in Exhibit 4.6 that Gundle Environmental Systems switched from a measure of progress based on yards of liner deployed to total contract cost. Total cost generally represents a more inclusive measure of progress. Todd Shipyards uses labor hours, which could be seen as a rather narrow basis for judging progress.

Immediate versus Delayed Start-Up of POC

Most firms start the application of the POC method as soon as the project has begun and contract costs are incurred. However, some firms delay application of POC until progress has reached a point where the ultimate outcome is clearer. Some examples of these policies are provided in Exhibit 4.7. Several other firms with delayed-start policies were also identified. It is of note that, with the exception of Avondale Industries, a shipbuilding and repair company, each of the delayed-start firms is a construction contractor. The dominance of construction contractors among firms with delayed-start policies may suggest that the level of uncertainty of their contracts is much higher than it is for other types of firms that employ the POC method. In addition, a higher percentage of fixed-price contracts may also add to the uncertainty of the eventual amount of contract profits.[40] This would appear to add to the appeal of the delayed-start procedure.

Some additional information on the application of POC is available in an annual survey of the construction industry, which is published by the Construction Financial Management (CFM) Association. The 1997 edition of this survey discloses information on when construction firms commence application of the POC method. The 1997 edition was based on survey responses from 935 companies. The percentage distribution by commencement alternatives is as follows[41]:

Exhibit 4.6. Alternative Approaches to Estimating Stage of Completion

Company	Measure of Stage of Completion
California Microwave, Inc. (1996)	Sales on certain long-term, small quantity, high unit-value contracts are recognized at the completion of significant milestones.
Daktronics, Inc. (1998)	Earnings on long-term contracts are recognized on the percentage-of-completion method, measured by the percentage of costs incurred to date to estimated total costs for each contract.
GenCorp, Inc. (1998)	Sales and income under most government fixed-price and fixed-price-incentive production type contracts are recorded as deliveries are made. For contracts where relatively few deliverable units are produced over a period of more than two years, revenue and income are recognized at the completion of measurable tasks rather than upon delivery of the individual units.
Gundle SLT Environmental, Inc. (1995)	During fiscal 1995, Gundle changed its method of determining percentage of completion from the units installed method—units of lining material deployed—to the cost-to-cost method. The Company believes that the change to the cost-to-cost method results in a better measurement of the overall economic performance through its installation contracts.
Todd Shipyards Corp. (1999)	Profits on major contracts, those in excess of $3 million or six months' duration, are recorded on the percentage-of-completion method (determined based on direct labor hours).

Sources: Companies' annual reports. The year following each company name designates the annual report from which each example was drawn.

1. Recognize profit as soon as costs are charged to the job   58%

2. Recognize profit as soon as work begins   19

3. Defer profit recognition until a base level of completion has been reached   16

4. Defer profit recognition until ultimate profitability can be reasonably estimated   7
                                                                    100%

Alternative Thresholds for Booking Claims

Disputes with respect to contract pricing are common. Contract changes are often requested by the customer, but the changes are not priced until a later date. These

Exhibit 4.7. Delayed-Start Policies for Percentage-of-Completion

Company	Delayed Start Policy
Avondale Industries, Inc. (1998)	Profits on long-term contracts are recorded on the basis of the Company's estimates of the percentage of completion of individual contracts, commencing when progress reaches a point where contract performance is sufficient to estimate final results with reasonable accuracy.
Granite Construction Co. (1998)	Revenue in an amount equal to cost incurred is recognized prior to contracts reaching 25% completion. The related earnings are not recognized until the period in which such percentage completion is attained.
Kasler Holding Co. (1996)	Profit recognition on certain contracts is deferred until progress reaches a level of completion sufficient to establish the probable outcome. The company generally begins to recognize profit on these contracts under percentage-of-completion accounting when the project is 20% complete.
Morrison-Knudsen Corp. (1998)	Recognition of earnings on certain long-term construction contracts is deferred until progress reaches a level of completion sufficient to reasonably estimate the probable outcome.

Sources: Companies' annual reports. The year following each company name designates the annual report from which each example was drawn.

unpriced change orders may become the source of subsequent disputes between contractor and customer. Disputes over delays may also raise questions about who should bear their cost.

Uncertainty associated with the ultimate outcome of these disputes results in different thresholds being used by contractors in deciding when to record disputed amounts as assets and associated revenues. In the case of loss contingencies, GAAP calls for losses to be recorded if they are both probable and estimable.[42] SOP 81–1 employs comparable criteria.[43] However, SOP 81–1 calls for recording revenue from the claim "only to the extent that contract costs relating to the claim have been incurred."[44]

A sampling of alternative policies for recognizing claims is provided in Exhibit 4.8. There is a degree of variability in recognition standards in the policies in Exhibit 4.8. The benchmarks of probable and estimable from SOP 81–1, are present. However, some policies appear to be more conservative. For example, Guy F. Atkinson, Halliburton, Johnson Controls, and Kasler Holdings[45] do not recognize revenue until the claims are resolved. Granite Construction recognizes revenue only to the extent of costs incurred.

Exhibit 4.8. Alternative Recognition Policies for Claims

Company	Claims Policy
Alliant TechSystems (1998)	Estimated amounts for contract changes and claims are included in contract sales only when realization is probable.
Granite Construction, Inc. (1998)	Claims for additional contract revenue are recognized to the extent of costs incurred if it is probable that the claim will result in additional revenue and the amount can be reliably estimated.
Guy F. Atkinson Co. (1998)	Revenue from claims by the Company for additional contract compensation is recorded when agreed to by the owner.
Halliburton Co. (1998)	Claims for additional compensation are recognized during the period such claims are resolved.
Johnson Controls, Inc. (1998)	Claims against customers are recognized as revenue upon settlement.
Kasler Holdings Co. (1996)	Revenues from claims for additional compensation are not recorded until settled. All costs related to work for which a claim has been made are expensed as incurred.
Morrison Knudsen Co. (1998)	Revenue from claims are recorded, to the extent that contract costs have been incurred, when it is probable that the claim will result in additional contract revenue and it can be reliably estimated.

Sources: Companies' annual reports. The year following each company name designates the annual report from which each example was drawn.

Kasler Holdings expenses all costs that are related to work for which a claim has been made. While conservative, the Kasler policy may result in later earnings amounts that are not sustainable. For example, Granite Construction explained a decrease in 1995 gross profit as follows: "The decrease primarily reflected the 1994 recovery of significant claims revenue without the associated costs that were recognized in years prior to 1994."[46] Granite's profitability was boosted in 1994 because it had recognized claims revenue with no offsetting costs. However, this earnings increase was not sustained into 1995. In terms of earnings quality, Granite Construction's earnings quality was impaired in terms of persistence in 1994 as a result of nonrecurring revenues from the claim settlement.

Survey results from the CFM Association Survey revealed the following dominant claim recognition policy from its survey of construction firms,

> Consistent with the prior year, the highest percentage (47 percent) of respondents recognize contract claim revenue when settlement is probable and amounts can be reasonably estimated, rather than when the claim is settled or paid.[47]

In addition to data on revenue recognition on unpriced change orders, the CFM survey documents the use of different policies in accounting for the costs of unpriced change orders. The alternative policies and their relative use are summarized below:

- Cost associated with an unpriced change order is deferred until the change order is priced or revenue equal to the unpriced change order is recognized: 23 percent.
- Estimated cost and revenue of an unpriced change order is recognized in the current accounting period: 36 percent.
- Estimated cost of an unpriced change order is recognized, but not revenues: 30 percent.[48]

Balance Sheet Classification of Contract Balances and Retainage

Traditional measures of liquidity and balance sheet classification must be used with care in the case of firms using contract reporting. This is because of contract retainages and the use of an expanded concept of current assets in the classification of contract balances. Retainages represent amounts billed on contracts in which collection is delayed until after contract completion.

Classification of Contract Balances
It is standard practice to classify all contract-related balances as either current assets or current liabilities. This is based on the traditional practice of classifying balances based on a firm's operating cycle, that is, the time period spanned in starting with cash and moving through the production and sale cycle and returning to cash. For many contracts, the operating cycle spans more than a single year. As a result, all contract-related balances are generally classified as current.

Abrams Industries provides an example of a contract classification policy based on the operating cycle:

> Assets and liabilities related to contracts in progress are included in current assets and liabilities as they will be liquidated in the normal course of contract completion, although this may require more than one year.[49]

The usual interpretation of the relationship between current assets and liabilities as an indicator of liquidity must be modified in the case of balance sheets with material amounts of contract-related balances. Amounts listed as accounts receivable may in some cases not be collected for several years. A working capital ratio that might appear to be exceptionally strong by traditional standards may be marginal for a firm with all contract-related balances classified as current.

Retainage Balances
The presence of retainage balances must also be considered in using current asset and current liability relationships to evaluate liquidity. As previously noted, re-

tainage is a unique feature of contract reporting. It represents a portion of billed accounts receivable that will not be collected until a contract is either completed or other specified contract conditions are met. Retentions are governed by contract provisions and are typically a fixed percentage (e.g., 5 percent or 10 percent) of each billing.[50]

Although retainage balances may be collected over several years, the entire balance will typically be classified within the current asset section of the balance sheet. SEC requirements call for the disclosure of retainage balances and also encourage the provision of information on estimated collections by year, if this can be done with reasonable accuracy.[51]

An example of the disclosure of retainage balances is provided below:

Note three: Accounts Receivable (thousands of dollars)
Accounts receivable include retained percentages of $31,044 and $13,336 at December 31, 1996 and 1995, respectively. The amount for 1996 is expected to be collected as follows: $23,559 in 1997, $7,145 in 1998 and $340 in 2000 and later years.[52]

Loss Recognition on Contracts

Losses on contracts must be recognized as soon as they become evident. Losses may not simply be recorded as excess costs are actually incurred. Most firms with significant contracts disclose their loss recognition policy. For example, the contract loss recognition policy of General Dynamics is as follows: "Any anticipated losses on contracts or programs are charged to earnings when identified. Such losses encompass all costs, including general and administrative expenses, allocable to the contracts."[53]

The fiscal 1997 disclosure by Todd Shipyards provides an example of a loss recognition policy in operation.

Based upon its reviews initiated in conjunction with the fiscal year-end, the Company estimates that it will incur contracts costs of approximately $11.5 in excess of contract prices for the three-ship Mark II Ferry program, resulting in the fourth quarter 1997 reversal of previously recognized program profit of $2.4 million and the establishment of a program loss reserve of $11.5 million.[54]

While firms uniformly declare that they monitor the recovery of contract costs, there may be an understandable reluctance to write off costs that may not be recoverable.

A Set of Contract Reporting Disclosures

To both apply and expand on the preceding discussion of contract reporting, a representative set of contract disclosures is provided in Exhibits 4.9 and 4.10. The following discussion will both highlight the effects of the contract reporting on the Stewart & Stevenson Services, Inc. financials and also consider issues related to financial analysis of this information.

Exhibit 4.9.   Contract Accounting Policy: Stewart & Stevenson Services, Inc.

Revenues relating to contracts or contract changes that have not been completely priced, negotiated, documented, or funded are not recognized unless realization is considered probable. Generally, revenue is recognized when a product is shipped or accepted by the customer, except for certain Petroleum Equipment products, where revenue is recognized using the percentage-of-completion method. The revenues of the Tactical Vehicle Systems segment are generally recognized under the units-of-production method, whereby sales and estimated average cost of the units to be produced under the Family of Medium Tactical Vehicle (FMTV) contracts are recognized as units are substantially completed. Profits expected to be realized on contracts are based on the Company's estimates of total revenue value and costs. Changes in estimates for revenues, costs, and profits are recognized in the period in which they are determinable using the cumulative catch-up method of accounting. In certain cases, the estimated revenue values included amounts expected to be realized from contract adjustments when recovery of such amounts is probable. Any anticipated losses on contracts are charged in full to operations in the period in which they are determinable.

Source: Stewart & Stevenson Services, Inc., annual report, January 31, 1999, p. 25.

Stewart & Stevenson Services, Inc.

The accounting policy note of Stewart & Stevenson Services, Inc. (S&S), Exhibit 4.9, includes a typical claims recognition policy that turns on the threshold of "probable" realization. The POC method is used in accounting for certain petroleum equipment products. The units-of-production method, a variation on POC, is used for tactical vehicle systems.

    S&S reports use of the "cumulative catch-up method" of accounting for changes in estimates of revenues, costs, and profits. Under this approach, the current-period profits will reflect a combination of adjustments: (1) a restatement of prior-year results and (2) the effect on current-year contract performance of the updated estimates for revenues, costs, and profits.[55]

    As is typical, S&S declares its intent to record anticipated losses on contracts when they are determinable.

    The S&S contracts-in-process note, Exhibit 4.10, sets out the cost and accrued profits of the contracts in process at the end of 1997 and 1998. These disclosures reveal a sharp decline in the rate of profitability on contracts in process: accrued profits of $19,440,000 divided by cumulative contract revenues of $1,156,660,000 equals a profit rate of 1.70 percent in 1997 versus $8,655,000 divided by $1,476,612,000 or 0.60 percent in 1998.

    Although not labeled as such by S&S, the sum of accrued profits and costs incurred on uncompleted contracts represents the cumulative revenue recognized to date on the contracts in process. Hence, accrued profits divided by the sum of accrued profits and contract costs yields the gross profit rate on the contracts.

    In other notes, S&S did disclose a number of special charges in 1998 that may explain this decline in profitabilty. Estimated costs associated with a government directive amounted to $40 million, and a charge related to a series of claims totaled $36.8 million. There was also a charge for a change in estimated profit upon contract completion of $9.7 million.[56] These charges indicate that the decline in the rate of profitability may be nonrecurring. To this extent, the 1998 earnings quality of S&S, in terms of persistence, is somewhat enhanced.

Again, the combination of costs incurred on uncompleted contracts and accrued profits represents the cumulative revenue recognized to date on the contracts still in process. The excess of revenues recognized over progress payments represents the net unbilled accounts receivable—$98,873,000 at the end of 1998. Standard disclosure practice calls for grouping contracts by billing status (i.e., under- or overbilled). Underbilled amounts are listed in the balance sheet as current assets and overbilled amounts as current liabilities. This breakdown is shown for 1998, in which the underbilled amount is $99,097,000 and the overbilled amount is $224,000.

While S&S uses the caption "Customer progress payments" in Exhibit 4.10, it is likely that some portion of this balance actually represents billed amounts that have not yet been collected.

The caption "Recoverable costs and accrued profits not yet billed" is often replaced by the shorter "Unbilled accounts receivable." "Cost and estimated earnings in excess of estimated earnings" is the most common label. This balance indicates that revenues have been recognized that could not have been collected yet because they have not been billed. The 1998 decline of $39,111,000 in this asset balance appears in the 1998 S&S statement of cash flows as an addition to earnings in arriving at cash from operating activities. Although not disclosed separately because of its size, the $216,000 increase in the liability balance, "Billings on uncompleted contracts in excess of incurred cost and accrued profits," would also be added to net income in arriving at cash flows from operating activities.[57]

The 1998 reduction in "Recoverable costs and accrued profits not yet billed," net of the decrease in "Billings on uncompleted contracts in excess of incurred costs and accrued profits," increased cash flow from operating activities. However, on a cumulative basis the contracts are still underbilled by a net amount of about $98,873,000 at the end of 1998. Revenues have been recognized that have not been billed and, as a result, not yet collected.

From a strictly cash flow perspective, an overbilled position, assuming that collection has also taken place, results in a stronger cash flow position than the underbilled position. However, analysts sometimes express concern about overbilled positions if the cash that has been collected in advance cannot be found on the balance sheet in some relatively liquid form. Their concern is that the cash may be used on a contract whose costs have exceeded those projected. That is, Peter is being robbed to pay Paul. Also, some analysts see significant underbilled positions as possibly a reflection of overly optimistic assessments of progress made to date.

Exhibit 4.10. Contracts-in-Process: Stewart & Stevenson Services, Inc., January 31, 1998 and 1999 (Thousands of Dollars)

Amounts included in the financial statements which related to recoverable costs and accrued profits not yet billed on contracts in process are classified as current assets, and billings on uncompleted contracts in excess of incurred costs and accrued profits are classified as current liabilities. Summarized below are components of the amounts:

	1997	1998
Costs incurred on uncompleted contracts	$1,137,220	$1,467,957
Accrued profits	19,440	8,655
	1,156,660	1,476,612
Less: Customer progress payments	(1,018,892)	(1,377,739)
	$137,768	$98,873
Included in the statements of financial position:		
Recoverable costs and accrued profits not yet billed	$138,208	$99,097
Billings on uncompleted contracts in excess of incurred costs and accrued profits	(440)	(224)
	$137,768	$98,873

Recoverable costs and accrued profits related to the Tactical Vehicle Systems segment include direct costs of manufacturing and engineering and allocable costs. Generally, overhead costs include general and administrative expenses allowable in accordance with the United States Government contract cost principles and are charged to cost of sales at the time revenue is recognized. General and administrative costs remaining in recoverable costs and accrued profits not yet billed amounted to $0 and $13,993 at January 31, 1999 and 1998, respectively. The Company's total general and administrative expenses incurred, including amounts capitalized and charged to cost of sales under the FMTV contract, totaled $83,092, $88,235 and $105,887 in Fiscal 1996, 1997 and 1998, respectively.

Source: Stewart & Stevenson Services, Inc., annual report, January 31, 1999, p. 29.

Finally, it should be noted that S&S treats a portion of its general and administrative costs as contract costs. This is due to the governmental character of this work and the ability to recover these costs under government costing standards. These costs are not treated as contract costs in the case of commercial contracts.

With this review of the S&S disclosures, as well as the earlier discussions, a summary of some of the implications of contract reporting for financial analysis is provided.

Contract Reporting: Financial Analysis Guidance

- There is more than the normal degree of uncertainty associated with contract reporting profits, especially when fixed-price contracts dominate a firm's business.
- Care should be taken in evaluating the earnings of firms whose profits have been the subject of frequent revisions in the past: The past may be prologue. Earnings quality in terms of persistence may be impaired.
- Cash flow is increased by growth in net overbilled contract balances and by decreases in net underbilled positions. Alternatively, cash flow is reduced by reductions in net overbilled positions and increases in net underbilled positions.
- Whereas a net overbilled (and collected) position increases cash flow, it carries with it a responsibility on the part of the contractor to employ most of this cash on the customer's behalf. A substantial overbilled position, with no liquid resources on hand, could be a source of concern. Has the cash been used on other projects?
- Underbilled contract positions may be seen as positive because they indicate that work has been done and that, when billing does occur, cash will be collected. However, in the face of significant underbilled amounts, some analysts become concerned that overly optimistic estimates of contract progress may have been made.
- Some firms commence application of POC immediately and others employ a specified delay. A delay in starting POC, especially for firms in similar lines of business and with comparable contracts, should reduce the likelihood of unfavorable profit revisions in the future. That is, earnings quality in terms of persistence may be enhanced by this practice.
- For firms with retainage balances, it is important to examine note disclosures to determine when the amounts are likely to be collected.
- All contract-related balances are typically classified as current. This may result in an overstatement of a firm's liquidity position.
- Amounts included in accounts receivable for claims are subject to varying degrees of uncertainty. The policy followed by firms in booking claims should be examined; some are less conservative than others, and for these the likelihood of subsequent charges against earnings may be higher.
- Firms with a concentration of fixed-price contracts bear the risk of costs exceeding original estimates.[58] A greater potential for future charges against earnings should be expected. Earning quality in terms of persistence may be impaired in these cases.

INVENTORY REPORTING AND ANALYSIS

Inventory accounting alternatives have the potential to create major differences in reported earnings and financial position. The treatment of inventory in this chapter focuses mainly on the influence of different inventory cost flow assumptions (i.e., last-in, first-out (LIFO), first-in, first-out (FIFO), etc.) on financial performance and position. Purely technical aspects related to inventory accounting such as periodic versus perpetual systems, specific identification, retail method, and so forth are not explored.[59] Emphasis is placed on aspects of the topic that have important implications for the analysis of financial performance and position.

Alternative Inventory Methods

Alternative inventory methods can have a major influence on results and position. The major methods (i.e., cost flow assumptions) include LIFO, FIFO, and average cost. The specific identification method involves no cost flow assumption, but rather assigns the identifiable cost of units sold to cost of sales.

Relative Use of Alternative Inventory Methods

Explosive increases in prices around 1974 produced a significant growth in the number of firms using the LIFO method. Over 400 firms listed on the New York and American Stock Exchanges adopted LIFO between the period June 1974 to May 1975.[60] LIFO results in a much higher cost of sales when prices are rapidly rising, reducing taxable earnings and with it tax payments. However, if prices are relatively flat, then cost of sales will be approximately the same under each of the major inventory alternatives.

Information on the use of alternative inventory methods is available from an annual survey of 600 companies conducted by the AICPA. A summary of this AICPA data for 1995 through 1997 is provided in Exhibit 4.11.

In addition to information on overall use of inventory alternatives, the AICPA survey also details the use of LIFO by industry. A summary of this information is provided in Exhibit 4.12.

Grocery stores lead the list in Exhibit 4.12 for the use of LIFO. However, it is unlikely that each of the grocery stores in the sample used LIFO for all of their inventories. For example, for the complete 600-company AICPA sample, only 17 reported using LIFO for all of their inventories. To illustrate, although not in the 600-company sample, Kroger reports that it used LIFO for approximately 90 percent of its inventories in 1997. The remainder of Kroger's inventory is on FIFO.[61]

Not surprisingly, the leading LIFO users are in industries in which inventory is a very major asset. In addition, at least over long periods of time, they are in industries that have experienced significant inflation in the replacement cost of inventories. This difference is apparent in the contrast of food retailing as the

Exhibit 4.11.   Inventory Cost Determination

	\multicolumn{3}{c}{*Number of Companies*}		
Methods	*1995*	*1996*	*1997*
First-in, first-out (FIFO)	411*	417	415
Last-in, first-out (LIFO)	347	332	326
Average cost	185	181	188
Others	40	37	32

*Columns total more than 600 because most firms report the use of more than one inventory method.
Source: American Institute of Certified Public Accountants, *Accounting Trends and Techniques,* 52nd ed., 1998, p. 178.

Exhibit 4.12.   The Relative Use of LIFO by Industry

Highest Rates of Use		*Lowest Rates of Use*	
Retailing—grocery stores	100%	Computers, office equipment	10%
Forest and paper products	89	Electronics, electrical equipment	25
Chemicals	88	Engineering, construction	25
Petroleum—refining	87	Entertainment	33
Textiles	80	Photographic and control equipment	32

Source: American Institute of Certified Public Accountants, *Accounting Trends and Techniques,* 52nd ed., 1998, p. 179.

leading LIFO user, with computers and office equipment at the bottom. Consider the cost of a box of breakfast cereal and a personal computer today and a decade ago. In terms of functionality, the computer has a lower price today than a decade ago. The same can probably not be said for the box of breakfast cereal or a loaf of bread.

Why Firms Use LIFO: Advantages and Disadvantages

Differences in the rate of use of inventory alternatives raise questions about the advantages that accrue to the use of these different methods. This issue is reviewed by considering the apparent advantages and disadvantages of LIFO. The implicit contrasting methods are FIFO and average cost. A summary is provided in Exhibit 4.13.

Cash Flow Improvement

It seems clear that firms use LIFO mainly to reduce taxable earnings and, with it, tax payments. Balanced against this positive is the reduction in book earnings that typically goes hand in hand with the use of LIFO for tax purposes. The LIFO

Exhibit 4.13. Potential Advantages and Disadvantages of LIFO

Advantages of LIFO
- Improves cash flow by reducing taxable income, and with it cash tax payments
- Provides an improved measure of net income by matching current costs against current revenues
- Smoothes earnings
- Provides earnings management potential

Disadvantages of LIFO
- Reduces reported earnings
- Understates inventory and, with it, working capital ratios
- Reduces shareholders' equity and, as a result, increases leverage ratios
- Employs a cost flow assumption that is typically at odds with actual physical flow of inventory

conformity requirement calls for firms that elect LIFO for income tax purposes to also use LIFO in the financial statements provided to shareholders and creditors. Some firms no doubt believe that the valuation of their shares will be reduced as a result of the reduction in earnings associated with the use of LIFO. Thus, the reduction in earnings that typically results from LIFO could be seen as both an advantage and disadvantage. LIFO reduces earnings and as a result cash tax payments. However, some believe that the reduced profits will lead to lower share prices.

Improved Matching
Improved matching is virtually always invoked as one of the main reasons for the initial adoption of LIFO. However, matching is not used in this case in the traditional fashion. Matching normally refers to setting expenses off against related revenues or recording revenues or expenses in the correct period. In the case of LIFO, the emphasis is on matching a LIFO cost that approximates current replacement costs against current sales prices of items sold.

Income Smoothing Potential
There is a potential smoothing feature inherent in the operation of LIFO. As business expands and prices rise, the growth of earnings is restrained because sales revenue bears the burden of the most recent, highest costs under LIFO. Similarly, in periods of declining business and prices, the reduction in earnings is mitigated by the fact that declining inventory costs are charged against declining sales revenues. Smoothing may not result if there is a lack of harmony in the changes in product prices and costs. Moreover, the effects of LIFO liquidation may introduce a significant degree of volatility to earnings.[62]

Earnings Management Potential

If queried, our experience is that analysts will usually indicate that they have encountered companies that have adjusted inventory levels in order to achieve a particular earnings result. LIFO has earnings management potential not found in other inventory methods. To achieve an increase in earnings, a firm may permit inventory levels to decline. This brings typically older and lower LIFO costs into cost of sales and results in an increase in earnings. Alternatively, some firms facing reductions (LIFO liquidations) in LIFO inventories may wish to avoid the increase in earnings and the associated increase in tax payments.[63] This is achieved by restoring inventory levels prior to year-end.[64]

Whereas the earnings management potential of LIFO could be seen as an advantage for the LIFO firm, it might be viewed as a disadvantage by a statement user if the result were to obscure actual trends in operating performance.[65]

Inventory Undervaluation and Reduction in Working Capital Ratios

LIFO almost always results in an understatement of inventory value in relationship to current replacement cost. This undervaluation causes working capital or current ratios to appear weaker than they would under either FIFO or average cost. To deal with this issue, some LIFO firms provide working capital ratios computed on a FIFO basis. Others simply highlight this asset understatement. Chevron Corporation provides an example of the latter disclosure:

> Two items negatively affected Chevron's current ratio but in the company's opinion do not affect its liquidity. Current assets in all years included inventories valued on a LIFO basis, which at year-end 1998 were lower than current costs by $584 million.[66]

Reduction in Shareholders' Equity and Increase in Leverage Ratios

The understatement of current assets also results in an offsetting understatement of shareholders' equity. This in turn causes the ratio of debt to equity to be higher than it would be if either the FIFO or average-cost methods were used.

Disparity between LIFO Cost Flow Assumption and Physical Flow Goods

Finally, some find it objectionable when the LIFO cost flow assumption is not the same as the actual physical movement of inventory. The authors are aware of a chief financial officer (CFO) of a public company who objected to the use of LIFO for product that was imported. The shipping terms were free-on-board shipping point, meaning that title transferred when the goods were shipped. His position was that LIFO costs were being assigned to cost of sales for merchandise that could not have been sold because it was not yet in the country. Without regard to the merits of this position, the CFO did switch the firm back to FIFO. Information on switches from LIFO or declared reasons for not adopting LIFO can provide further insight into the perceived advantages and disadvantages of LIFO.

Reasons for Switches from LIFO and for Not Adopting LIFO

A study by Johnson and Dhaliwal provides valuable information about why firms abandon LIFO.[67] The key circumstances associated with firms that abandoned LIFO were:

• Declining earnings and share price declines
• Earnings and share price declines that were greater than for firms that retained LIFO
• Greater financial leverage
• Closer to the violation of working capital covenants in credit agreements
• Larger operating loss carryforwards than firms retaining LIFO

Johnson and Dhaliwal summarize their findings by noting that:

> The general conclusion suggested by the data is that LIFO abandonments are concentrated in industries experiencing adverse economic conditions and involve firms that are particularly sensitive to those adversities.[68]

There have been well-known examples of firms abandoning LIFO when they fell on hard times. Westinghouse (now CBS) and Chrysler Corporation are prominent examples. Firms in a loss carryforward position need future profits in order to realize the tax benefits of these losses. Using LIFO, with its typically depressing influence on profitablility, could make it more difficult to utilize such carryforwards. In a more recent example, Cross Continent Auto Retailers changed its tax basis of accounting for inventories in 1996 from LIFO to FIFO and specific identification. Consistent with the above discussion, at the end of 1996, Cross Continent had a $3.2 million tax loss carryforward.[69]

There is some research available on why firms choose not to adopt LIFO. Results from a survey by Granof and Short are summarized in Exhibit 4.14. The role of income tax benefits in LIFO adoption decisions is highlighted by the absence of expected tax benefits (159 out of 251 responses, or 63 percent, in Exhibit 4.14) as a reason not to adopt LIFO.

An example of rapid turnover, as a tax-related disincentive for LIFO adoption, is reinforced by the disclosure below from the annual report of Dean Foods Company:

> Dairy inventory turnover is at a high rate, whereas inventories of the Vegetables, Pickles and Specialty segments have lower turnover rates. A large portion of the Vegetables, Pickles and Specialty inventories are valued on the LIFO inventory valuation method, which enhances the Company's cash flow.[70]

The majority of Vegetables and Pickles, the lower turnover inventories, are valued on the LIFO method, whereas the majority of high turnover Dairy and certain

Exhibit 4.14. Reasons for Not Adopting LIFO

Reasons for Rejecting LIFO	Number	Percentage of Total
No expected tax benefit:		
No required tax payment	34*	16%
Declining prices	31	15
Rapid inventory turnover	30	14
Immaterial inventory	26	12
Miscellaneous tax related	38	17
	159	74
Excessive cost:		
High administrative costs	29	14
LIFO liquidation—related costs	12	6
	41	20
Regulatory and other restrictions	26	12
Other adverse consequences:		
Lower reported earnings	18	8
Bad accounting	7	3
	25	11%

*Percentages do not add to 100% because of more than one explanation for not adopting LIFO by some firms.
Source: M. Granof and D. Short, "Why Do Companies Reject LIFO," Journal of Accounting, Auditing, and Finance" (Summer 1984), p. 327.

Specialty inventories are valued on the FIFO method.[71] Lower inventory turnover provides a greater opportunity for significant differences to develop between LIFO cost and current replacement costs of inventories. The greater the excess of replacement value over LIFO cost, the greater the tax savings potential of the LIFO method.

The above discussion provides a general overview of issues related to the adoption of inventory alternatives. The discussion that follows focuses on the application of these alternatives and continues to highlight their implications for financial analysis.

Reporting and Analysis under the LIFO Method

It is important to understand how the use of different inventory methods creates differences in both earnings and financial position. This section illustrates the emergence of LIFO versus FIFO differences, the effects of LIFO liquidations on earnings, the nature and role of the LIFO reserve, the restatement of financial statements from LIFO to FIFO, and the nature and interpretation of standard LIFO inventory disclosures.

The Emergence of LIFO/FIFO Differences and Their Implications for Financial Analysis

Exhibit 4.15 provides an example of how differences between LIFO and FIFO inventory values and cost-of-sales amounts, and with it differences in earnings and shareholders' equity, are created. As only cost of sales is considered in the example below, gross profit is the relevant measure of earnings.

Between the beginning and end of the year, an excess of FIFO over LIFO inventory value of $60 emerged. In subsequent examples, this inventory valuation difference is referred to as the LIFO reserve. It is an SEC requirement that public companies using LIFO disclose the excess of replacement cost, generally approximated by FIFO, over the LIFO inventory-carrying value.[72] The SEC obviously believes that this valuation difference is relevant to statement users.

Because the purchases for the period exactly met sales requirements, the LIFO cost of sales in this case is simply equal to the purchases, the last goods in, for the period. However, FIFO cost of sales is made up of the cost of the six units from the opening inventory, the first in, plus the cost of four units from the purchases made during the period. The cost-of-sales calculation, on a more direct basis from that illustrated in Exhibit 4.15, follows:

LIFO cost of sales:

10 units at $15 equals	$150

FIFO cost of sales:

6 units at $5 equals	$30
4 units at $15 equals	60
	$90

Note that the LIFO reserve at the beginning of the period was zero because the LIFO and FIFO inventories were both $30. However, across the period the LIFO reserve, the difference between the LIFO and FIFO inventory value, grew to $60. Further note that this increase in the inventory valuation difference (i.e., the LIFO reserve) is exactly equal to the difference in cost of sales between LIFO and FIFO.

The excess of LIFO over FIFO cost of sales in this example is due to the sharp increase in inventory replacement costs. With more moderate price increases, the cost of sales and ending inventory differences would be less. Moreover, if replacement costs of inventory had declined, then cost of sales under LIFO would have been lower than under FIFO. The relatively modest inflation of recent years has caused the year-to-year effects of LIFO on cost of sales to be smaller.

Exhibit 4.15. Illustration of the Emergence of LIFO/FIFO Differences

Data: Initial inventory: 6 units @ a cost of $5.00 each		$30.00
Purchases: 10 units @ a cost of $15.00 each		$150.00
Sales: 10 units @ a sales price of $30 each		$300.00
Sales	$300.00	$300.00

Cost of sales computation:	**LIFO**	**FIFO**
Beginning inventory	$30.00	$30.00
Purchases	150.00	150.00
Goods available for sale	180.00	180.00
Less ending inventories:		
LIFO: 6 units @ $5.00	30.00	
FIFO: 6 units @ $15.00		90.00
Cost of sales	150.00	90.00
Gross profit	$30.00	$90.00

However, the cumulative effect of the use of LIFO still results in substantial inventory undervaluations for many firms.

Without considering tax effects or any other expenses, assets (inventory) at the end of the period are $60 lower under LIFO, and stockholders' equity (retained earnings) is likewise $60 lower because earnings are $60 less under LIFO than under FIFO. With current assets lower by $60 under LIFO, the LIFO current ratio is lower than it would be if FIFO were used. As assets are undervalued by $60 in relationship to the current replacement cost (FIFO cost of $90 minus LIFO cost of $30), there is unrecognized strength in the balance sheet. Position quality is enhanced by this favorable valuation difference. Cash flow is also increased due to the tax savings resulting from the use of LIFO. Assuming a combined 40 percent tax rate, the cash tax savings would be 40 percent times the $60 by which LIFO earnings are below those under FIFO, or $24.

To round out the LIFO/FIFO comparison above, inventory and cost of sales under the average cost method are summarized Exhibit 4.16.

Under the average cost method the values for both the cost of sales and ending inventory fall between the LIFO and FIFO amounts. This is the typical result when the average cost method is compared to LIFO and FIFO.

LIFO Liquidations

For a firm using LIFO, a reduction in inventory quantities is termed a LIFO liquidation. That is, current period purchases or production of inventory items do not keep pace with sales. If the older LIFO costs are lower than current purchase

Exhibit 4.16. Inventory and Cost of Sales under the Average Cost Method

Cost of goods available for sale	$180.00
Divided by number of units available for sale	16
Equals average cost per unit of	$11.25
Cost of sales and ending inventory would in turn be:	
Cost of sales: $11.25 × 10 units	$112.50
Ending inventory: $11.25 × 6 units	67.50

Exhibit 4.17. The Effects on Earnings of a LIFO Liquidation

Data: Opening inventory: 2 units @ a cost of $5.00 each		$10.00
Purchases: 10 units @ a cost of $20.00 each in the case of no liquidation		$200.00
9 units @ $20.00 each in the liquidation case		$180.00
Sales: 10 units @ $35.00 each		$350.00

	LIFO Liquidation	
	No	Yes
Sales	$350.00	$350.00
Cost of sales computation:		
Beginning inventory	$10.00	$10.00
Purchases	200.00	180.00
Goods available for sale	210.00	190.00
Less ending inventories:		
No liquidation: 2 units @ $5.00	10.00	
Liquidation: 1 unit @ $5.00		5.00
Cost of sales	200.00	185.00
Gross profit	$150.00	$165.00

prices or production costs of inventory, then the LIFO liquidation will increase earnings. If older costs are higher than current inventory replacement costs, an unusual condition, then the LIFO liquidation will reduce earnings. The example in Exhibit 4.17 highlights the effects of a LIFO liquidation by presenting parallel results, with and without a LIFO liquidation.

In the absence of the LIFO liquidation, cost of sales is simply the 10 units purchased at the price of $20, or $200. With the one-unit liquidation, cost of sales is the purchase of nine units at $20 plus one unit from the opening inventory at $5, or $185. The $15 reduction in cost of sales from the liquidation increases gross profit by the same amount. Note that the reduction in cost-of-sales, and increase in profit, is equal to the difference between the current inventory cost of one unit of inventory of $20 and the LIFO cost of the single liquidated unit of $5.

In terms of financial analysis, the LIFO liquidation benefit should be treated as nonrecurring. It is analogous to realizing a gain from selling an undervalued asset. In recognition of its nonrecurring character, there is an SEC requirement that firms disclose material benefits from LIFO liquidations.[73] Because of their nonrecurring status, the presence of material LIFO liquidation gains should be seen as reducing earnings quality in terms of persistence.

There is some variation in the disclosure of the effects of LIFO liquidations. These effects are disclosed either in terms of pretax earnings or net income, but in some cases both are provided. Also, in some cases the effect of the LIFO liquidation on cost of sales is provided, which is the equivalent of the effect on pretax earnings. It is important to examine these disclosures carefully to be certain of the form of disclosure. Listed below are three examples of these alternative disclosures:

1. For the year ended December 26, 1998, the liquidation of LIFO inventories *decreased cost of sales* by approximately $1.4 million (Golden Books Family Entertainment, Inc., 1998 annual report).

2. LIFO inventory quantities were reduced. In 1996, this resulted in an *increase in income before taxes* of $2,518,000 or $.44 per share after applicable income taxes of $856,000 (Monarch Machine Tool Company, 1998 annual report).

3. The *effect of LIFO liquidations on net income* was $0.6 million, $5.4 million, and $2.9 million for 1998, 1997, and 1996, respectively (Steelcase, Inc., 1998 annual report).

Nature and Operation of the LIFO Reserve

In the discussion surrounding the example in Exhibit 4.15, the difference between inventory valued at LIFO and FIFO is referred to as the LIFO reserve. The typical excess of the current replacement cost of inventory—usually approximated by FIFO—over inventory valued at LIFO is a valuation difference that enhances the quality of financial position.

The operation of the LIFO reserve is outlined with the example in Exhibit 4.18.

The LIFO reserve is almost always a contra-asset account.[74] Notice that it is deducted from the FIFO inventory to arrive at the LIFO valuation in Exhibit 4.18. In cases where the inventory valued at LIFO exceeds FIFO cost, then the LIFO reserve is positive (i.e., an adjunct account), and the balance is added to the FIFO inventory value to arrive at LIFO.[75]

The change in the LIFO reserve across a period represents the adjustment required to FIFO cost of sales in order to arrive at LIFO cost of sales. In the case

Exhibit 4.18.   The Operation of the LIFO Reserve

	FIFO	LIFO Reserve	LIFO
Beginning inventory	$100	$(50)	$50
Purchases	1,000		1,000
Goods available for sale	1,100		1,050
Ending inventory	200	(100)	100
Change in LIFO reserve		50	
Cost of sales	$900		$950
Difference in cost of sales		$50	
Cost of sales determined under FIFO			$900
Add: LIFO charge (increase in LIFO reserve)			50
LIFO cost of sales			$950

in Exhibit 4.18, the LIFO reserve increased by $50 and the addition of this amount to the FIFO cost of sales produces LIFO cost of sales. If the LIFO reserve had instead declined, then the dollar amount of the decrease would be subtracted from the FIFO cost of sales to arrive at LIFO cost of sales.

While seldom detailed as such, the change in the LIFO reserve represents the effects of changes in both inventory prices and quantities.

LIFO Reserve Disclosures

While analysts commonly use the expression "LIFO reserve," this is not the most common label attached to differences between inventory valued at FIFO versus LIFO. An example of an inventory disclosure that uses the LIFO reserve label is provided in Exhibit 4.19. While unlabeled, the sum of the balances for raw materials and supplies, work-in-process and finished goods represents the FIFO valuation of the Thomaston Mills' inventories in Exhibit 4.19. The LIFO inventory value is produced when the LIFO reserve is deducted from the FIFO balances. Notice that the disclosures equate current costs with the FIFO inventory valuation.

The Thomaston Mills' disclosures also indicate what the loss would have been if FIFO had been used. Under LIFO, Thomaston Mills reported a net loss in 1998 of $11,529,000. However, the disclosures indicate that under FIFO the loss would have been even greater (i.e., $13,520,000). This larger loss under FIFO is consistent with the LIFO reserve balance decreasing, as it did between 1997 and 1998. Where the LIFO reserve balance decreases, cost of sales under FIFO will be greater than under LIFO. With a larger cost of sales, FIFO produces a larger loss than LIFO. Alternatively, if the LIFO reserve had increased, then the loss under FIFO would have been less than under LIFO.

Using Thomaston's effective tax rate in 1998 of about 35.4 percent, the FIFO net loss disclosed in Exhibit 4.19 can be reconstructed:

Exhibit 4.19.   LIFO Disclosures and the LIFO Reserve: Thomaston Mills, Inc., Years Ending June 28 and 27, 1997 and 1998, Respectively (Thousands of Dollars)

Inventories consisted of the following:

	1997	1998
Raw materials and supplies	$9,197	$7,569
Work-in-process	32,012	29,525
Finished goods	22,242	21,631
LIFO reserve	(15,222)	(12,140)
	$48,229	$46,585

The Company uses the LIFO method of inventory valuation because it results in a better matching of current costs and revenues. Some of the Company's competitors use the FIFO method of inventory valuation. Had the Company reported its LIFO inventories at values approximating current cost, as would have resulted from using the FIFO method, and had applicable tax rates in 1998 and 1997 been applied to changes in operations resulting therefrom, and had no other assumptions been made as to changes in operations, net income (loss) would have been approximately $(13,520,000) in 1998 and $(6,326,000) in 1997.

Source: Thomaston Mills, Inc., annual report, June 1998, p. 18.

Net loss under LIFO		$11,529,000
Plus		
1997 LIFO reserve	$15,222,000	
Minus 1998 LIFO reserve	12,140,000	
LIFO reserve increase	3,082,000	
Times (1 minus the 1998 effective tax rate of .354)	.646	1,991,000
Equals net loss for 1998 assuming the FIFO inventory method		$13,520,000

It is important to be able to recognize disclosures of LIFO reserves, even when they appear under a variety of different labels and are sometimes embedded in text and in other cases disclosed in a tabular format. The size of the LIFO reserve determines the extent of the undervaluation of LIFO inventories. Moreover, the change in the LIFO reserve across the year determines the difference between earnings or losses under LIFO versus FIFO. Some examples of the range of titles used for the excess of current or FIFO cost over LIFO cost are presented in Exhibit 4.20.

In addition to the variation in labels found in Exhibit 4.20, it is common for the disclosures of LIFO reserves not to be in a schedule format, such as that in Exhibit 4.19. Instead, the cost information is often simply included in textual

Exhibit 4.20.   LIFO Reserves: Alternative Terminology

Firm	*Alternative LIFO Reserve Term*
Amcast Industrial Corporation (1998)	Amount to reduce inventories to LIFO value
Baldor Electric Company (1998)	LIFO valuation deduction
Florida Rock Industries, Inc. (1998)	Excess of current cost over LIFO stated values
Gorman-Rupp Company (1998)	Excess of replacement cost over LIFO cost
Graco, Inc. (1998)	Reduction to LIFO cost
Robert Mondavi Corporation (1998)	Reserve for LIFO valuation method
OroAmerica, Inc. (1998)	LIFO cost less than FIFO cost
The Sherwin-Williams Company (1998)	Excess of FIFO and average cost over LIFO

Sources: Companies' annual reports. The year following each company name designates the annual report from which each example was drawn.

Exhibit 4.21.   Significant LIFO Reserve Balances

Firm	*Industry*	*LIFO Reserve Percentage of Shareholders' Equity*
Graco, Inc. (1998)	Fluid handling products	400*
Handy & Harman (1996)	Manufacturing of metals products	95
Caterpillar, Inc. (1998)	Construction equipment	39
Deere & Company (1998)	Agricultural equipment	26
The Gorman-Rupp Company (1998)	Pumps and related equipment	26
Gleason Corporation (1998)	Gear manufacturing machines	20
Allegheny Teledyne, Inc. (1998)	Steel and speciality metals	15
Winn Dixie Stores, Inc. (1998)	Food retailer	15
Thomaston Mills, Inc. (1998)	Textiles and home furnishings	14
The Robert Mondavi Corporation (1998)	Winery	12

*Graco's shareholders' equity dropped dramatically in 1998 due to share repurchases. In 1997, the LIFO reserve percentage was 23% of shareholders' equity. Robert Mondavi switched back to FIFO for the year ending June 30, 1999.

Sources: Companies' annual reports. The year following each company name designates the annual report from which each example was drawn.

inventory disclosures. Care must be exercised in reading inventory notes to ensure that LIFO reserves are identified.

The Magnitude of LIFO Reserves

The relative significance of LIFO reserve balances varies considerably, and industry category is a key factor. Although not presented as representative, a range of larger LIFO reserve balances is provided in Exhibit 4.21. Heavy industrial companies appear in general to have the larger LIFO reserve balances. Whereas petroleum companies previously had large LIFO reserves, the sharp decline in oil prices in the late 1990s has reduced their balances. As a result of the decline in petroleum prices, the LIFO reserve of Phillips Petroleum Company declined from $457 million to $258 million during 1998, even in the face of modest increases in LIFO inventories.[76]

These oil price reversals have also resulted in some write-downs of LIFO inventories. The write-down of LIFO inventories to the lower of cost or market is fairly unusual because LIFO costs are normally well below inventory replacement values (i.e., market). Nevertheless, Valero Energy Corporation reported an inventory writedown in 1998 as follows:

> Due to a significant decline in feedstock and refined product prices during 1998, the Company reduced the carrying amount of its refinery inventories to market value, resulting in a $170.9 million pre-tax charge to earnings.[77]

Restatement of Financial Statements Using LIFO Reserve Balances

LIFO reserve disclosures make it possible to recast key financial statement totals from LIFO to FIFO. No similar disclosures are available that would permit recasting from FIFO to LIFO. The inventory disclosures and other financial information of The Robert Mondavi Corporation are provided in Exhibit 4.22 and are used to illustrate the restatements of earnings and other balances from LIFO to FIFO. The reasons offered for restatement are usually to either (1) produce financial information that can be compared to other firms in an industry that use FIFO, or (2) measure financial position based on more realistic inventory valuations. Mondavi cites the issue of comparability but not that of attempting to present more realistic inventory valuations.

The Mondavi annual report includes comments on one of the reasons for the magnitude of its LIFO reserve as follows:

> In the premium wine business, the difference between LIFO and FIFO inventory costs can be significant due to the extended period of time that wines remain in inventory, typically from one to three years or longer depending on the style and variety of wine.[78]

The very slow turnover of the Mondavi inventory contrasts with the earlier example of the high turnover dairy products of Dean Foods Company. Mondavi's

Exhibit 4.22. Selected Inventory and Other Financial Information: Robert Mondavi Corporation, Years Ending June 30, 1997–1998 (thousands of dollars)

	1997	1998
Wine in production	$127,922	$170,708
Bottled wine	53,734	70,572
Crop costs and supplies	14,793	15,490
Inventories stated at FIFO cost	196,449	256,770
Reserve for LIFO valuation method	(28,754)	(30,629)
LIFO inventory	$167,695	$226,141

Wine inventory costs are determined using the LIFO method, which attempts to match the most current inventory cost with sales for the period. Information related to the FIFO method may be useful in comparing operating results to those of companies not on LIFO. If inventories valued at LIFO cost had been valued at FIFO cost, net income would have increased by approximately $1,144 and $9,899, respectively, for the year ended June 30, 1998 and 1997, and decreased by approximately $329 for the year ended June 30, 1996.

Other data at June 30, 1998:

Total current assets	$307,846
Total current liabilities	$50,171
Total liabilities	$294,025
Total shareholders' equity	$253,083
Net income	$29,015
Total tax provision	$18,554

Source: Robert Mondavi Corporation, annual report, June 30, 1999, pp. 32–33, 40.

cost of sales for 1998 was about $176 million, but its average inventory (i.e., the simple average of 1997 and 1998 ending inventories) was about $197 million. Although probably not uncommon in the wine business, Mondavi's average inventory turned less than one time in 1998: cost of sales of $176 million divided by average inventory of $197 equals about .9/1. An inventory of dairy products obviously turns over many times during the year.

Restatement of Mondavi's Earnings to FIFO
The restatement of Robert Mondavi's LIFO 1998 net income to a FIFO basis requires only the change in the LIFO reserve and an effective tax rate. The Mondavi LIFO reserve increased by $1,875,000 during fiscal 1998, in contrast to the decline in the LIFO reserve of Thomaston Mills in Exhibit 4.19. To produce the correct LIFO cost of sales, the LIFO reserve increase is added to FIFO cost of sales. Because LIFO cost of sales is greater than FIFO, pretax LIFO earnings will less than those under FIFO by the LIFO reserve increase of $1,875,000.

The Mondavi effective tax rate was a very stable 39 percent over the three-year period of 1996 to 1998. This rate was made up of a 35 percent federal rate and a 4 percent state rate, net of the federal tax benefit. The 1998 effective rate is the total provision of $18,554,000 divided by 1998 pretax income. Net income of $29,015,000 plus the tax provision of $18,554,000 yields pretax income of $47,569,000. The tax provision of $18,554,000 divided by pretax income of $47,569,000 equals the 1998 effective tax rate of 39 percent. With this effective tax rate and the 1998 increase in the LIFO reserve, Mondavi's LIFO earnings can be restated to their FIFO amount as follows:

Restatement of Mondavi's LIFO Earnings to FIFO

Net income under LIFO method for fiscal 1998		$29,015,000
Deduct the tax adjusted LIFO reserve increase during 1998:		
Pretax LIFO reserve increase	$1,875,000	
Times (1 minus 1998 effective tax rate of 39%)	.61	1,143,750
Net income on a FIFO basis for fiscal 1998		$27,871,250

Multiplying the LIFO reserve increase by one minus the effective tax rate results in the after-tax effect on net income of the pretax LIFO reserve increase.

Notice that the above increase in net income conforms to this same difference in net income disclosed in the text of the Mondavi inventory note in Exhibit 4.22. While the 1998 excess of FIFO over LIFO net income amounts to only about 4 percent, notice that Mondavi also discloses, in the text of Exhibit 4.22, that FIFO net income would have exceeded LIFO net income by $9,899,000 in 1997. This amounts to 35 percent of 1997's LIFO net income of $28,225,000. There was obviously a much larger increase in the LIFO reserve in 1997 than in 1998.

Restatement of Mondavi's Balance Sheet Ratios to FIFO

Because income statements and balance sheets are articulated statements, LIFO cannot affect net income without also affecting balance sheet amounts. An earlier reference to Chevron Corporation illustrated a firm emphasizing that its working capital ratio was stronger than it appeared to be because of the undervaluation of its LIFO inventories.[79] In addition, measures of financial leverage are also affected by the use of LIFO. Measures of financial leverage are increased under LIFO because the typically lower amounts of net income result in lower retained earnings.

It is common for analysts to compute revised working capital and leverage ratios on the basis of the selective restatement, from LIFO to FIFO, of key balance sheet totals.[80] These restatements are usually designed to achieve more realistic measures of current balance sheet strength in the face of significant undervaluations of LIFO inventories.

On occasion, pressure for restatements also comes from bank borrowers. They may request credit for the undervaluation of their LIFO inventories in the measurement of both working capital and leverage-related ratios. Financial covenants that employ these ratios are a common feature of bank credit agreements. Re-

Exhibit 4.23.   Restated Working Capital and Leverage Ratios: The Robert
Mondavi Corporation, June 30, 1998 (Thousands of Dollars)

Restated Ratio	No Tax Adjustment	Tax Adjusted
Working Capital Ratio		
As-reported current assets	$307,846	$307,846
Plus the LIFO reserve	30,629	
Plus the LIFO reserve times (1–.39)		18,684
Restated current assets	338,475	326,530
Divide by current liabilities	50,171	50,171
Restated working capital ratios	6.75/1	6.51/1
Leverage ratio		
Total liabilities	$294,025	$294,025
Divide by restated shareholders equity:		
As-reported shareholders' equity	$253,083	$253,083
Plus the LIFO reserve	30,629	
Plus the LIFO reserve times (1–.39)		18,684
Restated shareholders' equity	283,712	271,767
Restated leverage ratios	1.04/1	1.08/1

Source: Based on the data in Exhibit 4.22 from the 1998 annual report of The Robert Mondavi
Corporation.

ceiving credit for LIFO inventory undervaluations results in stronger measures of
the borrower's working capital and leverage positions.

Mondavi's working capital and leverage ratios are restated using the information in Exhibit 4.22. Mondavi's working capital ratio based on its as-reported
current assets and current liabilities is: current assets of $307,846,000 divided by
current liabilities of $50,171,000 or 6.14/1.[81] A measure of its leverage, based
simply on its reported total liabilities and total shareholders' equity is: total liabilities of $294,025,000 divided by total shareholders' equity of $253,083,000
equals 1.16/1. Mondavi's restated ratios are presented in Exhibit 4.23.

Each of the restated ratios is marginally stronger than the ratios based on the
as-reported LIFO data. The restated ratios are presented both without and with
tax adjustments. Practice varies somewhat on whether tax adjustments are made
in developing revised balance sheet ratios. For example, in an article by Erik Day,
no tax adjustments are made in computing a working capital ratio; the entire LIFO
reserve is added to as-reported current assets. However, tax adjustments, such as
those outlined in Exhibit 4.23, are made by Day in developing adjusted leverage
ratios. He does comment that "Although adding back 100% of the LIFO reserves
creates an unbalanced ratio calculation, it gives a more accurate depiction of liquidity."[82]

Not making a tax adjustment would seem to be appropriate if, as implied above by Day, the focus of the revised working capital ratio is simply to gauge the additional strength added to the liquidity position by the undervalued inventory. However, tax adjustments would be in order if restatement were designed to show how the financials would appear if FIFO had been applied.

If FIFO had been in use, then cumulative pretax earnings would initially be higher by the amount of the end-of-period LIFO reserve.[83] However, there would also have been additional taxes charged against these higher earnings. The tax adjustment could take the form of either a reduction in current assets or an increase in tax liabilities. However, the addition to retained earnings is the end-of-period LIFO reserve times one minus the effective tax rate.

In outlining his proposed revised leverage ratio, Day defines a debt to tangible net worth ratio as follows:

Debt to tangible net worth = [Total Liabilities – Subordinated Debt + 40% of LIFO Reserves] divided by [Tangible Net Worth + Subordinated Debt + 60% of LIFO Reserves].[84]

The 40 percent of LIFO reserves, which is added to the numerator above, is the tax on the unrecognized inventory undervaluation (i.e., the LIFO reserve). The 60 percent of LIFO reserves added to the denominator is the cumulative after-tax increase in net income that would result from a taxable realization of the LIFO reserves.

The absence of a tax adjustment in computing the revised working capital ratio is supported by the objective of simply achieving a more accurate depiction of liquidity. However, applying a tax rate in revising the leverage ratio would imply that a tax charge might actually be incurred. This would be the case if in the longer term the additional value represented by the LIFO reserve were realized. This could take place in part as a result of LIFO liquidations. It might also be incurred if the firm were sold or liquidated. Therefore, a realization of the LIFO reserve is implicit in Day's application of a tax adjustment in computing the revised leverage ratio.[85]

Based on the preceding treatment of inventory reporting and analysis, a summary of financial analysis guidance is provided below.

Inventory Reporting: Financial Analysis Guidance

- Additional balance sheet strength is represented by the LIFO reserve and the inventory undervaluation that it typically represents. The larger the LIFO reserve, the greater the strengthening of position quality.
- The additional balance sheet strength represented by the LIFO reserve can be recognized by adding the reserve to current assets. This results in a stronger working capital ratio and a more realistic representation of liquidity. Where the focus is simply on the extra liquidity represented by the LIFO reserve, no tax adjustment needs to be made.

- The unrecognized value represented by the LIFO reserve may also be added to shareholders' equity so that the effect of the LIFO inventory undervaluation can be reflected in stronger and more realistic measures of financial leverage. In such a restatement, the deduction of a tax effect would be appropriate.

- Increases and decreases in LIFO reserves cause net income on a LIFO basis to be less than or greater than, respectively, net income on a FIFO basis.

- Reductions in the levels of LIFO inventories will normally result in nonrecurring income. These increases in net income reduce the quality of earnings in terms of persistence. In addition, they result in additional cash outflows for income taxes.

- The presence of large LIFO reserves places a potential earnings management tool in the hands of management. Inventory disclosures should be carefully examined to identify the effects of any LIFO liquidations on earnings.

- In the absence of disclosures on the effects of LIFO liquidations, their presence could be inferred from the combination of: (a) the firm is using the LIFO method; (b) there is an otherwise unexplained increase in gross-margin percentages; and (c) there is a reduction in inventory levels. The pretax effect of the LIFO liquidation on earnings can be approximated by multiplying the improvement in the gross-margin percentage times total sales.

- The adoption of the LIFO inventory method might be viewed as a signal of positive future prospects for net income. Alternatively, the change from LIFO to some other method may imply a decline in current and/or future profit prospects.

INTEREST CAPITALIZATION

The dominant cost-based approach to the accounting for assets always raises issues regarding the inclusiveness of the measure of cost for any particular asset. Traditionally, expenditures that could not be associated with the emergence of a particular asset were simply recorded as expenses.

From a tax perspective, it is appealing to define asset-related expenditures narrowly so as to minimize taxable earnings. However, with the passage of the Tax Reform Act of 1986, the tax law reduced the range of outlays that could be expensed immediately. Examples included such items as costs associated with the acquisition of inventory, package design costs, and interest costs associated with the construction of fixed assets.[86] This movement also delayed the recognition of bad debt expenses, reduced the availability of the installment sales method, and the completed contract method of accounting for long-term contracts. In general, the tax law further embraced the accrual method of accounting and reduced the availability of the cash basis.

Under GAAP, the traditional treatment of interest was to deduct it as it was incurred. This was true even in cases in which interest was associated with money borrowed and used for the construction or development of specific assets. However, for decades interest has been capitalized on borrowings associated with the construction of assets in regulated industries, such as electric utilities. In fact, this capitalization includes interest on debt and an opportunity cost of equity funds. For example, in describing the cost of its utility plant, Maine Public Service Company explains that it includes "allowances for the cost of equity and borrowed funds used during construction (AFUDC)."[87]

Interest capitalization by regulated firms increases the cost of its revenue-producing assets. The cost of these fixed assets is in turn a key determinant of the rates that can be charged for the utility's product. Therefore, capitalizing funding costs during the period of construction helps make possible the recovery these costs in the rates established by the regulatory bodies.

The capitalization of interest was expanded beyond regulated firms with the issuance of SFAS No. 34, "Capitalization of Interest Cost."[88] Again, the capitalization of interest means that interest is added to the carrying value of the related asset. This distinction is important because the same term is sometimes used to refer to interest that has accrued on a loan but, instead of being paid, is simply added (i.e., capitalized) to the loan balance.

Overview of SFAS No. 34: Capitalization of Interest

In issuing a standard on interest capitalization, the FASB adopted the position that, in some cases, interest should be considered part of the cost of an asset. This Statement provides only general characterizations and limited enumeration of the assets for which capitalization is required:

> To qualify for interest capitalization, assets must require a period of time to get them ready for their intended use. Examples are assets that an enterprise constructs for its own use (such as facilities) and assets intended for sale or lease that are constructed as discrete projects (such as ships or real estate projects).[89]

The interest to be capitalized is intended to represent the interest that could have been avoided if the asset were not constructed (i.e., avoidable interest). When a specific borrowing is identified with and used on a particular project, then interest on the portion of the funding that is used on the project is capitalized. If this specific borrowing does not cover the entire funding requirements of the project, then interest from other borrowings of the firm is capitalized. The interest capitalized is based on the average accumulated construction expenditures for each period.[90]

Interest capitalization ceases when assets are ready for sale or use.[91] In addition, if construction activity ceases for a period of time, then capitalization ceases and is continued when construction activity begins again. However, SFAS No. 34 includes the following guidance on interruptions: "However, brief interruptions in activities, interruptions that are externally imposed, and delays that are inherent in the asset acquisition process shall not require cessation of interest capitalization."[92]

When an asset is developed for sale, then previously capitalized interest is recognized in determining earnings when the asset is sold. In most cases, this previously capitalized interest is included in cost of sales. Where an asset is held for use, then the previously capitalized interest is included in the annual depreciation expense.

GAAP versus Tax Law Interest Capitalization Requirements

The tax law requirements for interest capitalization are based on the same underlying logic as the GAAP requirements. However, the tax law provides more detailed guidance than GAAP. Fewer items would appear to require interest capitalization under the specific guidance of the tax law than is true under the more conceptual GAAP guidance. This results on occasion in temporary differences and the disclosure of associated deferred taxes.

A sampling of company tax disclosures reveals that both deferred tax assets and liabilities are disclosed on interest capitalization temporary differences. However, deferred tax liabilities appear to be more common. This is consistent with the somewhat broader scope for interest capitalization under the GAAP requirements than those under the tax law. That is, more items satisfy the capitalization requirements of SFAS No. 34 than satisfy the tax law requirements outlined below. This will cause pretax financial income to exceed that in the tax return and, as a result, call for the recording of deferred tax liabilities.

Current tax law requires interest capitalization in the three circumstances listed below:

1. The property has a long, useful life, which is defined as either real property or property with a class life of 20 years or more.
2. The property has an estimated production period exceeding two years.
3. The property has an estimated production period exceeding one year and a cost exceeding $1 million.[93]

An Illustration of Interest Capitalization

An illustration of the interest capitalization process is provided in Exhibit 4.24. The interest capitalized totals $430,000 out of the total interest incurred of $700,000. All of the interest incurred could have been capitalized if the average accumulated expenditures of $5 million had instead been equal to or greater than the total borrowings of $8 million.

The current and future effects on the income statement and balance sheet of interest capitalization in this case are as follows:

• The construction-in-process balance is increased by the $430,000 of capitalized interest.
• The net interest expense balance is only $270,000, even though the interest incurred amounted to $700,000.

Exhibit 4.24.   An Illustration of Interest Capitalization

Data:
- The average of the accumulated construction expenditures for the year is $5,000,000
- Interest is $160,000 for the year on a $2,000,000 specific project borrowing, all of which is used during the year on the project
- Total interest for the year on $6,000,000 of other borrowings is $540,000, or a weighted average interest rate of 9%: $540,000 divided by $6,000,000 = 9%.

Capitalized interest computation:

	Amount Capitalized	
Total interest incurred [$160,000 plus $540,000]		$700,000
Interest capitalized:		
Interest on the $2,000,000 specific borrowing	$160,000	
Average accumulated expenditures	$5,000,000	
Expenditures covered by a specific borrowing	2,000,000	
Expenditures funded by remaining borrowings	3,000,000	
Multiply by average interest rate on other borrowings	.09	
Other interest capitalized	270,000	
Total interest capitalized	$430,000	430,000
Total interest expensed		270,000
Total interest incurred		$700,000

- Assuming that all incurred interest is paid during the year, there is a cash outlay of $700,000.
- Future earnings will be affected when the completed asset is depreciated and the previously capitalized interest is deducted as part of depreciation expense in arriving at earnings.
- Future earnings could also be reduced if the level of construction in progress declines but there is no pay-down of outstanding debt.

With this overview of interest capitalization, the next section provides actual examples of interest capitalization and related disclosures. The final section will discuss issues of financial analysis that result from interest capitalization.

Interest Capitalization Subjects and Associated Disclosures

As noted above, SFAS No. 34 provides only limited examples of assets on which interest might properly be capitalized. The most common subjects of interest capitalization are major fixed assets, mainly structures, constructed either for sale or

Exhibit 4.25. Example of the Subjects of Interest Capitalization

Company	*Subject of Interest Capitalization*
AMFAC JMB Hawaii, Inc. (1998)	Acquisition, development and construction of real estate projects
Brown Forman (1998)	Barreled whiskey
Comair Holdings, Inc. (1999)	Advance payments on aircraft purchase contracts
D. H. Horton, Inc. (1998)	Residential homebuilding, development and construction
Huntway Refining Company (1998)	Wastewater treatment facility
Private firm	Chickens raised for egg production, with capitalization only up to the point of initial egg production—about 5 months
Scheid Vineyards (1998)	The development of vineyards
Smithfield Foods, Inc. (1999)	Capital projects
Standard Commercial Corporation (1996)	Tobacco inventories

Sources: Companies' annual reports. The year following each company name designates the annual report from which each example was drawn.

use. Some examples of these and other capitalization targets are provided in Exhibit 4.25.

Each of the above items shares the characteristic of having an extended period of development before being ready for sale or use. This is especially true if compared to the routine production of manufactured products. The example of chickens raised for egg production is particularly instructive. However, interest is not capitalized in the case of broiler chickens. The period of time required for them to be ready for market is only about 8 to 10 weeks. Alternatively, chickens raised for egg production do not begin to lay eggs until they are about 5 months old.

Capitalization of interest in the case of the broiler chickens would appear to be precluded by the following provision of SFAS No. 34:

> However, interest cost shall not be capitalized for inventories that are routinely manufactured or otherwise produced in larger quantities on a repetitive basis because, in the Board's judgment, the informational benefit does not justify the cost of so doing.[94]

Disclosures of Capitalized Interest

It is common for firms to make brief references to interest capitalization in the notes to their financial statements. More extensive disclosures are usually found only where the amounts capitalized are quite material. Homebuilders have the most detailed disclosures because it is common for them to capitalize all of their incurred interest.

Extensive Disclosures of Capitalized Interest: Beazer Homes, Inc.

Beazer Homes, a residential homebuilder, has capitalized all of its interest in recent years. The income statements and schedule of capitalized interest of Beazer Homes, Inc. are provided in Exhibits 4.26 and 4.27, respectively. Consistent with capitalization of all of its interest, Exhibit 4.27 shows that the amounts of interest incurred and interest capitalized are equal. Also, increasing end-of-year balances of homes under construction—not disclosed in the exhibits—explain the growth in the end-of-year capitalized interest balances in each year from 1996 to 1998.

The Beazer Homes' income statement in Exhibit 4.26 includes all interest deducted during the year on the line item labeled "Amortization of previously capitalized interest." As all the interest is capitalized, interest is included in its income statement only when homes are sold. A common alternative treatment is to simply include the previously capitalized interest in cost of sales when homes are sold. Later discussion of interest capitalization and interest coverage ratios will highlight the usefulness of Beazer's style of interest disclosure.

Limited Disclosure of Capitalized Interest: Cyprus Amax Minerals Company

The capitalized interest disclosures of Beazer Homes in Exhibits 4.26 and 4.27 have a separate schedule devoted to capitalized and amortized interest—Exhibit 4.27. These disclosures are more extensive than those typically encountered. The disclosures of Cyprus Amax Minerals, provided in Exhibit 4.28, are typical for firms with capitalized interest amounts that are not consistently material. Cyprus Amax Minerals discloses capitalized interest only on the face of the income statement and in the investing activities section of its statement of cash flows. There is no separate schedule on capitalized interest such as Beazer Homes provided in Exhibit 4.27.

The treatment of capitalized interest in the Cyprus Amax income statement is consistent with its classification in the statement of cash flows. Interest is capitalized, instead of being immediately expensed, because it is viewed as part of the cost of producing a fixed asset. Consistent with this treatment, the capitalized interest is classified as an investing, and not an operating, cash outflow.

The line item in Exhibit 4.28, "Pretax income (loss), net of nonrecurring items," is provided in order to highlight the influence of the decline in capitalized interest on results for 1997. If capitalized interest in 1997 had been at the same level as 1996, then Cyprus Amax would have reported pretax results, exclusive of nonrecurring items, of \$188 million [\$115 + (83 − 10) = \$188], instead of only \$115 million. The income statement display by Cyprus Amax helps statement users to quickly determine the effect of a change, a decline in the present case, in the amount of capitalized interest upon earnings. More on the effect of interest capitalization on earnings is provided with some additional analysis of the interest capitalization of Beazer Homes.

Exhibit 4.26.   Beazer Home Income Statements: Years Ending September 30, 1996–1998 (Thousands of Dollars)

	1996	1997	1998
Total revenue	$866,627	$852,110	$977,409
Costs and expenses:			
Home construction and land sales	732,395	721,184	811,203
Amortization of previously capitalized interest	15,134	14,857	19,031
Selling, general and administrative	88,976	92,087	110,259
Write-down of inventory	—	6,326	—
	836,505	834,454	940,493
Operating income	30,122	17,656	36,916
Other income	71	538	578
Income before income taxes	30,193	18,194	37,494
Provision for income taxes	11,927	7,005	14,293
Net income	$18,266	$11,189	$23,201

Source: Beazer Homes, Inc., Form 10-K annual report to the Securities and Exchange Commission (December 1998), p. 30. Preferred dividend requirements and earnings-per-share information were provided in the income statements of Beazer Homes but are not reproduced above.

Exhibit 4.27.   Detailed Interest Capitalization Schedule: Beazer Homes, Inc., Years Ending September 30, 1996–1998 (Thousands of Dollars)

	1996	1997	1998
Capitalized interest in inventory, beginning of the year	$6,511	$5,553	$6,855
Interest incurred and capitalized	14,176	16,159	21,259
Capitalized interest amortized to cost of sales	(15,134)	(14,857)	(19,031)
Capitalized interest in inventory, end of the year	$5,553	$6,855	$9,083

Source: Beazer Homes, Inc., Form 10-K annual report to the Securities and Exchange Commission (December 1998), p. 37.

Impact of Interest Capitalization on Current Earnings

The increases in the end-of-year capitalized interest balances (Exhibit 4.27) represent the amounts by which Beazer's income before taxes are higher in 1997 and 1998 as a result of interest capitalization. This is illustrated below for 1998:

Exhibit 4.28. Capitalized Interest Disclosures: Cyprus Amax Minerals Company, Years Ended December 31, 1996–98 (Millions of Dollars)

	1996	*1997*	*1998*
Capitalized Interest as Disclosed in the Income Statement			
Interest expense	$(189)	$(208)	$(168)
Capitalized interest	83	10	5
Other Information Developed from the Income Statement Disclosures			
Pretax income (loss), net of nonrecurring items	152	115	(82)
Capitalized Interest Disclosure in the Investing Activities' Section of the Statement of Cash Flows			
Capitalized interest (outflow)	(83)	(10)	(5)

Source: Cyprus Amax Minerals Company, annual report, December 31, 1998, pp. 32, 34.

Total interest expense in the absence of interest capitalization—simply the total interest incurred in 1998	$21,259,000
Less total interest deducted with interest capitalization—the capitalized interest amortized to cost of sales	19,031,000
Excess interest expense in the absence of capitalization	$2,228,000

In 1998, Beazer Homes' pretax income is higher by $2,228,000 because it capitalizes interest. This same result can be obtained by simply computing the change in the capitalized interest balance (Exhibit 4.27) across 1998: ending balance of $9,083,000 minus beginning balance of $6,855,000 equals $2,228,000. As long as the capitalized interest balance increases for the year, then pretax profits will be higher with interest capitalization than in the absence of capitalization. The opposite results if the capitalized interest balance declines across the year.

Effect of Interest Capitalization on Future Earnings

As can be seen from the above illustration, earnings will be increased by interest capitalization as long as the capitalized interest balance increases each year. However, if Beazer's homebuilding activity were to be reduced, and inventories were drawn down, then earnings might decline. This results because the reduction in homebuilding may mean that some of the current interest is not capitalized. In addition, the reduction in inventories puts additional interest carried forward from previous periods into the current income statement.

The reduction in earnings from a decline in new home construction, as well as in inventories, will either lower the absolute amount of earnings or cause their growth to be reduced. However, unless both of these dimensions—construction activity reduction and inventory declines—were quite dramatic, then the drop in earnings would probably be modest.

However, the profit reduction from the completion of a large expansion project by an industrial company could sharply reduce earnings. For example, TJ International disclosed no interest expense in 1994, and only $631,000 in 1995.[95] TJ International completed two new plants in the third and fourth quarters of 1995. This resulted in a substantial decline in interest capitalization in 1996 and interest expense increased in 1996 to $6,328,000.

As is common in such cases, TJ International did not pay down its debt once the new plants were completed. The interest capitalized in 1995 was about $6.5 million and amounted to 42 percent of income from continuing operations before taxes. In the absence of its otherwise strong profit performance in 1996, TJ International would probably have suffered a sharp decline in earnings by the inability to capitalize significant interest in 1996.[96]

Recall that the example of Cyprus Amax Minerals Company, in Exhibit 4.28, also provided an additional example of the potential influence of interest capitalization on future earnings.

Interest Capitalization and Financial Analysis

Some of the implications for financial analysis of interest capitalization were raised above with the discussion of the potential effects of capitalization on future earnings. Analysts should be alert to the potential contraction of earnings that can result when a major capital project is completed, as in the case of TJ International.

An earnings reduction from the completion of a major capital project should not be seen by equity analysts as having a negative implication for share valuation or by credit analysts as reducing a firm's debt service capacity. Rather, the completion by TJ International of new plant facilities should have a positive effect on future earnings and cash flows.

In addition to effects on future earnings, interest capitalization can affect fixed-charge coverage ratios as well as the key dimensions of financial quality.

Interest Capitalization and Fixed-Charge Coverage Ratios

Most firms that capitalize interest simply report a net interest expense line item in the income statement. That is, interest expense is the interest incurred minus the interest capitalized. For example, M.D.C. Holdings, Inc. disclosed the following interest expense line item in its income statements for 1995 to 1998.[97]

(Thousands of Dollars)	1995	1996	1997	1998
Corporate and homebuilding interest	$7,773	$3,773	$761	0

Information about M.D.C. Holdings' interest is found in its schedule of Corporate and Homebuilding Interest Activity in Exhibit 4.29. Focusing on 1997, the

Exhibit 4.29. Corporate and Homebuilding Interest Activity: M.D.C. Holdings, Inc., Years Ended December 31, 1996–1998 (Millions of Dollars)

	1996	1997	1998
Interest capitalized in homebuilding inventory, beginning of year	$40,217	$40,745	$37,991
Interest incurred	30,296	26,368	22,525
Interest expensed	(3,773)	(761)	—
Previously capitalized interest included in cost of sales	(25,995)	(28,361)	(34,184)
Interest capitalized in homebuilding inventory, end of year	$40,745	$37,991	$26,332

Source: M.D.C. Holdings, annual report, December 1998, p. 32.

Exhibit 4.30. Interest Capitalization and Alternative Fixed-Charge Coverage Ratios: M.D.C. Holdings, Inc., Year Ending December 31, 1997 (Thousands of Dollars)

	Basis: Net Interest	Basis: Total Interest Incurred
Earnings before interest and taxes (EBIT)	$40,088,000	$68,449,000
Interest	$761,000	$26,368,000
Coverage	52.7 times	2.6 times

Source: M.D.C. Holdings, Inc., annual report, December 1998, p. 11.

actual corporate and homebuilding interest incurred by M.D.C. Holdings was $26,368,000. Previously capitalized interest included in 1997 cost of sales was $28,361,000, and interest incurred but not capitalized was $761,000. Therefore, interest deducted in the 1997 income statement totaled $29,122,000: $28,361,000 + $761,000 = $29,122,000.

Interest coverage would be vastly overstated if the interest expense line item in the M.D.C. Holdings' income statement were taken to represent the fixed charge for interest. The fixed charge coverage, if only the $761,000 of 1997 interest expense is used as opposed to the actual interest incurred of $26,368,000, is outlined in Exhibit 4.30.

Earnings before interest and taxes (EBIT) is a common index of a firm's ability to service interest and other fixed-charge requirements. EBIT is computed in the "Net interest" column of Exhibit 4.30 by simply adding back the disclosed interest expense of $761,000 to income before taxes of $39,327,000. However, in the "Total interest incurred" column, the total interest, which was deducted in arriving at 1997 net income, of $29,122,000 (the $761,000 of interest not capitalized plus the $28,361,000 of previously capitalized interest included in cost of sales), is added back to income before taxes.

The coverage of M.D.C. Holdings is dramatically overstated if the as-reported interest data are used. The distortion of EBIT coverage is so great that it would cause most analysts to investigate the reasons for this condition. However, it is important to be alert to this issue in cases in which the effects of capitalization may be significant, but not so much so that it would be obvious. It would also be important to ensure that fixed-charge coverage ratios in credit agreements and bond indentures be defined to include all interest incurred and not simply the interest that was not capitalized.

If an EBITDA (earnings before interest, taxes, depreciation, and amortization) coverage statistic is used, it is also important to ensure that all interest deducted in computing net income is added back to earnings. This is facilitated by the practice of some firms to disclose an income statement line item that includes both interest that was not capitalized during the year as well as all previously capitalized interest included in cost of sales.

This practice is followed by Beazer Homes in the income statements provided in Exhibit 4.26. The relevant line item lists only the "Amortization of previously capitalized interest." However, recall that Beazer Homes has capitalized all of its interest in recent years. Hovnanian Enterprises, Inc. follows a similar practice. It lists all of the interest deducted for the year—interest not capitalized and previously capitalized interest now amortized—on a single line item labeled "Interest" in its income statements.[98] Neither Hovnanian Enterprises nor Beazer Homes bury the capitalized interest being charged-off in cost-of-sales.

Some commercial cash flow software products are designed to handle capitalized interest along the lines outlined above. A common treatment is to add interest capitalized during the period back to the interest line item in the cash flows statement, and to remove it in turn from capital expenditures. Specialized contractor versions of these products, which would be applied to the financial statements of homebuilders, also return capitalized interest to the interest line item and back out the capitalized amounts from cost of sales and inventory totals. Whereas these products will handle capitalized interest appropriately, this is true only if the capitalized amounts are located and incorporated at the data-inputting stage of the process.

In practice, an alternative view is sometimes encountered about handling capitalized interest in coverage calculations. A distinction is made between capital projects, on which interest is being capitalized, that represent expansion of scale and capacity versus those that simply maintain the current capacity levels of the firm.

This view is that current earnings and cash flows should not be expected to cover the interest requirements of an expansion project during the period of construction and development. Therefore, interest capitalized on such an activity would not be added back to interest in computing coverage. Only interest capitalized on "maintenance" level projects would be added to the interest line item in gauging coverage.

This different perspective is sometimes supported by the claim that financing during the period of construction and development is designed to be sufficient to handle the interest payments as well as the construction costs.

Interest Capitalization and Financial Quality

Interest capitalization has the potential to affect both the quality of earnings as well as the quality of financial position. When interest is capitalized, the income statement line item for interest expense will fall short of the actual cash outlay for interest. In principle, this reduces the cash quality of earnings.

The earlier example of TJ International highlighted the fact that the capitalization of interest on major capital projects can result in sharp reductions in earnings when these projects are completed. Hence, significant interest capitalization also has the potential to reduce the quality of earnings in terms of persistence.

Finally, care must be taken that the capitalization of interest does not result in an asset overvaluation, that is, an asset carrying value that is unlikely to be recovered from future net revenues. SFAS No. 34, "Capitalization of Interest Cost," maintains that since "Capitalization of material, labor, and overhead costs does not end when a net realizable value limit is reached; interest cost should be treated no differently."[99] However, if interest capitalization results in an asset being carried at an amount greater than its value, position quality would be diminished.

However, if the net realizable value of an asset held for sale falls below its cost, then it should be written down to net realizable value. If an asset is instead held for use, the need for a write-down will be determined by the provisions of SFAS No. 121, "Accounting for the Impairment of Long-Lived Assets and for Long-Lived Assets to be Disposed Of".[100] In each case, if a write-down is required for an asset on which interest has been capitalized, some of the write-down will be of previously capitalized interest.

Interest Capitalization: Financial Analysis Guidance

- Interest capitalization may reduce the cash quality of earnings because it is common for the actual cash outlay for interest to exceed the interest expense deduction in the income statement.

- Earnings quality in terms of persistence may be diminished in cases where major capital projects result in a substantial portion of a firm's interest expense being capitalized. Upon completion of such a project, and in the absence of a substantial reduction in debt levels, there may be a sharp reduction in earnings as a result of an increase in interest expense.

- Position quality may be diminished if interest capitalization raises an asset's carrying value above the level of its net realizable value, if the asset is held for sale, or of its fair value if the asset is held for use.

- Interest coverage ratios, such as EBIT or EBITDA, may be substantially over-stated unless the amounts of interest capitalized for each period are added to the amounts of any uncapitalized interest in order to arrive at actual interest incurred. EBIT and EBITDA coverage ratios should typically be computed with total interest incurred in the denominator of the ratio.

- A case can be made for dividing either EBIT or EBITDA by interest incurred minus interest capitalized on major expansion capital projects. The logic is that current earnings and cash flow should not be expected to cover the interest requirements of expansion capital projects.

SUMMARY

The following are key points for the reader to consider. Given the structure of this chapter, with summary points for financial analysis provided after each of the three major topical sections, the summary points here will be principally confined to GAAP issues.

- The matching of revenues and expenses, under the accrual accounting principle, remains the dominant method of measuring earnings and judging the periodic performance of firms. Although accrual-based earnings have significant com-petition from a variety of cash flow and related measures, market reactions to deviations from expectations for accrual earnings provide daily demonstrations of their stature and relevance.

- The traditional emphasis on matching of revenues and expenses has been aug-mented in recent years by new accounting standards that are based on a changes-in-net-assets metric. These new standards, in such areas as investments and derivative instruments, place heavy reliance on either the availability of market prices or on the ability to develop reasonable estimates of value. This require-ment will no doubt place severe limitations on the continued expansion of the changes-in-net-assets approach to income measurement. Therefore, accrual ac-counting, with its emphasis on the matching of revenues and expenses, will continue to play a key role in income measurement.

- Implementation of accrual accounting requires the exercise of a great deal of judgment, and it also calls for significant reliance on numerous estimates. There is the potential that firms will use these requirements to manage their earnings, especially in an environment that strips away market value for the smallest of deviations from earnings expectations. Recent activity by the SEC, in bringing numerous actions against firms for improper financial reporting, provides ample documentation of just such behavior.

- While measures of accrual earnings and cash flows are often pitted against each other, they should instead be seen as complementary. Accrual earnings are designed to provide a somewhat longer-term perspective on firm performance. A firm that in the long run provides a service or sells a product at a price that fails to cover all associated costs will not survive. However, projections of the amount, timing, and uncertainty of future cash flows are also critical to the management of the firm. Both accrual measures of earnings and various measures of cash flow are essential to both the internal management and outside assessment of the firm.

• The coverage of the long-term contracts topic reveals an area that involves a great deal of judgment and much reliance on estimates. As a result, there may be a greater degree of uncertainty surrounding the earnings of firms whose business is done under contracts. This uncertainty is increased when fixed-price contracts dominate the business, as is the case with construction contractors.

• Some of the key contract reporting issues involved: (a) the alternative methods of gauging contract progress, (b) the different thresholds for commencing the application of POC accounting, (c) the different thresholds used to book revenues in the case of contract disputes, and (d) the classification as current of contract-related assets whose conversion to cash may take years.

• The inventory topic focused on the influence of different inventory cost flow assumptions on measures of earnings and financial position. The selection of LIFO was seen to be motivated principally by the tax savings that it can produce, especially for firms experiencing substantial inflation in the replacement cost of their inventories. However, the use of LIFO often results in a substantial understatement of balance sheet strength. The LIFO reserve measures this undervaluation as the difference between the replacement cost of inventory—usually approximated by FIFO—and its LIFO cost. Changes in the LIFO reserve drive the differences in earnings under LIFO versus FIFO, with LIFO reserve increases causing LIFO earnings to be less than FIFO earnings, and decreases in the LIFO reserve producing the opposite result. LIFO liquidations produce nonrecurring income, which should be seen as reducing the quality of earnings in terms of persistence.

• Interest capitalization, the final special topic, calls in some cases for the inclusion of interest within the scope of an asset's historical cost. The key requirement for interest capitalization is that an extended period of construction or development be required before an asset is ready for sale or use. Interest is capitalized only during the period of construction and development. Interest capitalization ceases when the asset is ready for sale or use. Interest on direct borrowings for a project may be capitalized, as well as interest on other borrowings. All of a firm's interest may be capitalized in cases where total accumulated construction or development costs equal or exceed the total borrowings of the firm. Care must be taken in developing measures of interest coverage in cases in which firms capitalize significant portions of their interest.

GLOSSARY

Accrual accounting   The income measurement process that recognizes revenues as earned and expenses as incurred, without regard to the timing of associated cash inflows or outflows.

Advance billings   Billings made on contracts that exceed revenues earned to date. Also see "billings in excess of cost and estimated earnings" below.

Amortization of capitalized interest   The process of including previously capitalized interest in a cost or expense account (e.g., cost of sales or depreciation expense).

Average cost method   An inventory method that determines cost of sales by using an average unit cost based on the combination of the opening inventory cost and purchases divided by total units available for sale.

Avoidable interest   Interest that, in principle, could have been avoided if a project had not been under development. In concept, avoidable interest is the interest that should be capitalized for the period.

Billings in excess of cost and estimated earnings   Billings in excess of revenue recognized to date. This balance is analogous to unearned income and is usually classified among the current liabilities.

Cash-basis accounting   The income measurement process that recognizes both revenue and expense when cash is either received or disbursed.

Capitalized or to capitalize   The recording of an expenditure on the balance sheet as an asset as opposed to deducting it currently as an expense.

Capitalized interest   Interest considered to be avoidable and therefore added into the carrying value of the asset under development (e.g., new plant, new home).

Completed contract method   A contract reporting method that recognizes contract revenue only when the contract is completed. All contract costs are accumulated and deducted when the contract revenue is recognized.

Contract claims   "Amounts in excess of the agreed contract price (or amounts not included in the original contract price) that a contractor seeks to collect from customers or others for customer-caused delays, errors in specifications and designs, contract terminations, change orders in dispute or unapproved as to both scope and price, or other causes of unanticipated additional costs."[101]

Contractor   An entity that enters into contracts to construct facilities, produce goods, or render services to the specifications of a buyer either as a general or prime contractor, as a subcontractor to a general contractor, or as a construction manager.[102]

Cost-to-cost method   A method of estimating stage of completion for the purpose of applying the percentage-of-completion method. Cumulative completion to date is approximated by dividing cost incurred to date by total expected contract cost.

Contract cost   Typically includes all direct costs such as labor and materials as well as portions of contract-related indirect costs.

Cost and estimated earnings   For contracts in process, this balance represents the cumulative revenue recognized to date on these contracts.

Cost and estimated earnings in excess of billings   Revenue recognized to date in excess of billings. The short title for this item is simply unbilled accounts receivable. This balance is normally included with the current assets of the contractor.

Cost-plus contract   A contract whose ultimate revenue is based on the contract costs incurred plus an additional amount, with such amount being either a percentage of costs incurred or a fixed amount.

Delayed start percentage-of-completion   Commencing revenue recognition only after the project has progressed to some minimum threshold (e.g., 15 to 25 percent). On occasion, the threshold is simply judgmental and is characterized as a point at which the ultimate outcome is reasonably assured.

Direct-response advertising   Advertising that is designed to elicit sales from customers who could be shown to have responded directly to the advertising.

Dollar-value LIFO   Increases and decreases in inventory are determined with the use of dollar-value estimates of inventory as opposed to changes in physical quantities. Price indexes are normally employed in determining the inventory dollar values.

EBIT (earnings before interest and taxes)   A measure of a firm's ability to meet its interest and other fixed charges.

EBITDA (earnings before interest, taxes, depreciation, and amortization)   A measure of both firm performance as well as an indicator of a firm's ability to meet its interest and other fixed-charge requirements. In practice, it is also common to adjust EBITDA for selected nonrecurring items of gain or loss and other noncash items.

Expenses   Resources consumed in the production of revenues.

FIFO (first-in, first-out)   The inventory cost flow assumption that assigns the earliest inventory acquisition costs to cost of sales.

Fixed-price contract   A contract whose price is fixed and is not adjusted for cost performance that is either better or worse than originally expected.

Inventory turnover   Measure of the number of times that average inventory is used up during a period. Typically measured as cost of sales divided by average (finished costs) inventory.

LIFO (last-in, first out)   The inventory cost flow assumption that assigns the most recent inventory acquisition costs to cost of sales.

LIFO conformity requirement   Calls for the use of the LIFO method for shareholder reporting and credit purposes when LIFO has been adopted for income tax purposes.

LIFO liquidation   A reduction in the physical quantity of an inventory that is accounted for using the LIFO inventory method.

LIFO liquidation effect   The increase, typically, in income resulting from the inclusion in cost of sales of older and lower costs associated with the liquidated inventory quantities.

LIFO pool   A grouping of similar units for purposes of applying the LIFO method.

LIFO reserve   A term commonly used to identify the difference between the current replacement cost (typically approximated with a FIFO valuation) of a LIFO inventory and its LIFO carrying value. The LIFO reserve is almost always a contra-asset balance; that is, it is deducted from the current cost or FIFO inventory value to arrive at LIFO cost.

Lower of cost or market   An inventory valuation procedure that calls for reducing the carrying value of inventory when replacement cost (i.e., market) falls below cost. In application, market is limited to an amount that is no greater than net realizable value nor lower than net realizable value minus a normal profit margin.

Matching   The process of charging costs incurred against the recognized revenues associated with or produced by these same costs. Where no identifiable association exists between the incurrence of a cost and the revenues of a firm, then the item is either recognized as an expense immediately (advertising) or written off using an allocation rule (depreciation).

Net realizable value   The sales value of an asset, minus any costs to complete and sell the item.

Percentage-of-completion (POC) method   A revenue recognition method that records revenues based on the stage of contract completion.

Probable   A probability threshold that supports the recognition of, for example, a contingent liability, assuming that the obligation is also subject to reasonable estimation. The "probable" threshold is also used in recognizing claims-related income by contractors.

Realization   The process of converting noncash resources or rights into money.

Recognition   The process of formally recording or incorporating an item into the financial statements of an entity as an asset, liability, revenue, or expense.[103]

Requests for equitable adjustments   Claims by contractors for additional payments, typically in the case of governmental contracts.

Retainage   Billed amounts that are withheld from the contractor by the customer to ensure performance. Such amounts are usually remitted after the project or product has been accepted by the customer.

Revenues   Asset inflows or liability reductions resulting from the production or delivery of goods or services.

Revenue recognition criteria   (1) Completion of principal revenue-producing activities, (2) the incurrence, or reasonable ability to estimate, all associated costs, (3) the inflow or a valid asset or reduction of a liability, and (4) transfer of risks and rewards of ownership to the customer.

Unbilled accounts receivable   A current asset balance representing the excess of revenues recognized on contacts over billings to date.

Unit-of-delivery method A contract revenue recognition method that records revenues and associated cost of sales as units are delivered under the contract.

Unpriced change orders Changes in a contract for which there has been no agreement between the contractor and the customer regarding the additional revenue to be received by the contractor.

NOTES

1. M. Schroeder and E. MacDonald, "SEC Enforcement Actions Target 68, Including Former NFL Star," *The Wall Street Journal,* September 29, 1999, p. A4.

2. SFAS No. 130, "Reporting Comprehensive Income" (Norwalk, CT: Financial Accounting Standards Board, June 1997).

3. Statement of Financial Accounting Concepts (SFAC) No. 6, "Elements of Financial Statements" (Stamford, CT: Financial Accounting Standards Board, December 1985), para. 70.

4. SFAS No. 115, "Accounting for Certain Investments in Debt and Equity Securities" (Norwalk, CT: Financial Accounting Standards Board, May 1993).

5. SFAS No. 133, "Accounting for Derivative Instruments and Hedging Activities" (Norwalk, CT: Financial Accounting Standards Board, June 1998).

6. APB Opinion No. 22, "Disclosure of Accounting Policies" (New York: American Institute of Certified Public Accountants, April 1972).

7. *Ibid.,* para. 12.

8. In most cases, recording revenue on the basis of bill-and-hold arrangements is something that should be investigated to ensure that revenue recognition is in fact appropriate. Bill-and-hold practices have been associated with improper revenue recognition practices in some SEC enforcement actions.

9. Advanced Micro Devices, Inc., annual report, December 1998, p. 28.

10. Accounting Standards Executive Committee, SOP No. 97–2: "Software Revenue Recognition" (New York: American Institute of Certified Public Accountants, October 27, 1997).

11. FASB Technical Bulletin No. 90–1, "Accounting for Separately Priced Extended Warranty and Product Maintenance Contracts" (Stamford, CT: Financial Accounting Standards Board, December 1990), deals with warranties that are not included in the original price of the product. This Bulletin generally requires that revenue on separately priced contracts be deferred and recognized evenly over the contract period (para. 9).

12. SFAS No. 66, "Accounting for Sales of Real Estate" (Stamford, CT: Financial Accounting Standards Board, October 1982).

13. SFAS No. 5, "Accounting for Contingencies" (Stamford, CT: Financial Accounting Standards Board, May, 1975). Other guidance in this area is found in Accounting Standards Executive Committee, SOP 96–1, "Accounting for Environmental Remediation Liabilities" (New York: Accounting Standards Division, American Institute of CPAs, October 1996).

14. SFAS No. 2, "Accounting for Research and Development Costs" (Stamford, CT: Financial Accounting Standards Board, October 1974).

15. B. Lev and T. Sougiannis, "The Capitalization, Amortization, and Value-Relevance of R&D," *Journal of Accounting and Economics* (February 1996), pp. 107–138.

16. Financial Accounting Series: "Status Reports" (Norwalk, CT: Financial Accounting Standards Board, No. 195-C/March 30, 1999). The Board has decided to delay taking any final action on the current accounting for acquired research and development.

17. Accounting Standards Executive Committee, SOP 93-7, "Reporting on Advertising Costs" (New York: American Institute of Certified Public Accountants, December 1993), pp. 17–22.

18. *Ibid.,* p. 17.

19. Blackrock Golf Corp., annual report on Form 10-K to the Securities and Exchange Commission (December 1997), p. F-8.

20. Blue Fish Clothing, Inc., annual report on Form 10-K to the Securities and Exchange Commission (December 1998), p. F-7.

21. We are aware of one airline that uses $20 as the estimate of the incremental costs of a frequent-flyer award. However, this same airline uses $200 as a measure of the opportunity cost of the award for its planning and scheduling purposes.

22. Accounting Standards Executive Committee, SOP No. 98–5, "Reporting on the Costs of Start-Up Activities" (New York: American Institute of Certified Public Accountants, April 3, 1998).

23. *Ibid.,* pp. 7–8.

24. Accounting Standards Executive Committee, SOP No. 98–5, "Reporting on the Costs of Start-Up Activities" (New York: American Institute of Certified Public Accountants, April 3, 1998), p. 8.

25. SFAS No. 2, "Accounting for Research and Development Costs" (Stamford, CT: Financial Accounting Standards Board, October 1974).

26. M. Beasley, J. Carcello, and D. Hermanson, *Fraudulent Financial Reporting: 1987–1997—An Analysis of U.S. Public Companies,* Commissioned by the Committee of Sponsoring Organizations of the Treadway Commission, 1999. *Note:* This report is available through the AICPA.

27. *Ibid.,* pp. 24–25.

28. For further discussion of the subject of earnings management, see C. Mulford and E. Comiskey, *Financial Warnings* (New York: Wiley, 1996), Chapter Twelve.

29. For additional background, see C. Mulford and E. Comiskey, *Financial Warnings* (New York: Wiley, 1996), Chapters Eight to Eleven.

30. Accounting Standards Executive Committee, American Institute of Certified Public Accountants, SOP 81–1, "Accounting for Performance of Construction-Type and Certain Production-Type Contracts" (July 15, 1981).

31. *Ibid.,* para. 1.

32. For a more extensive listing, see E. Comiskey and C. Mulford, "Contract Reporting and Analysis: Some Guidance for Lenders," *Commercial Lending Review* (Winter 1998–99), pp. 30–47.

33. Accounting Standards Executive Committee, American Institute of Certified Public Accountants, SOP 81–1, "Accounting for Performance of Construction-Type and Certain Production-Type Contracts" (July 15, 1981), para. 11.

34. *Ibid.,* para. 31.

35. Internal Revenue Code Regulations, Section 1.451–3(B).

36. Accounting Standards Executive Committee, SOP 81–1, "Accounting for Performance of Construction-Type and Certain Production-Type Contracts" (New York: American Institute of Certified Public Accountants, July 1981), para. 23.

37. American Institute of Certified Public Accountants, *Accounting Trends and Techniques* (1977).

38. If a firm has a large number of contracts of relatively short duration, then the use of POC versus CC may not result in substantial differences in profits.

39. As an example, Avondale Industries, Inc. uses direct labor charges to estimate stage of completion.

40. *1997 Construction Industry Annual Financial Survey* (Princeton, NJ: Construction Financial Management Association, 1997), p. 45. This annual survey reports that 57 percent of annual contractor revenues were under fixed-price contracts. In its 1998 annual report, Morrison Knudsen makes the following statement on contract risk: "Both anticipated income and economic risk are greater under fixed-price and unit-price contracts than under cost-type contracts."

41. *Ibid.*, p. 42.

42. SFAS No. 5, "Accounting for Contingencies" (Stamford, CT: Financial Accounting Standards Board, May 1975), para. 8.

43. Accounting Standards Executive Committee, SOP 81–1, "Accounting for Performance of Construction-Type and Certain Production-Type Contracts" (New York: American Institute of Certified Public Accountants, July 1981), paras. 65–67.

44. *Ibid.*, para. 65.

45. Kasler Holdings is now Morrison Knudsen Corporation.

46. Granite Construction Corporation, annual report, December 1995, p. 18.

47. *1997 Construction Industry Annual Financial Survey* (Princeton, NJ: Construction Financial Management Association, 1997), p. 43.

48. *Ibid.*, p. 43. Failure of the numbers to total 100 percent is due to rounding.

49. Abrams Industries, Inc., annual report, April 1998, p. 24.

50. Audit and Accounting Guide, *Construction Contractors* (New York: American Institute of Certified Public Accountants, May 1996), para. 8.18.

51. *SEC Handbook* (Chicago: CCH Incorporated, November 1995), para. 206.02.

52. Guy F. Atkinson Company, annual report, December 1997. Information obtained from Disclosure, Inc. *Compact D/SEC: Corporate Information on Public Companies Filing with the SEC* (Bethesda, MD: Disclosure, Inc., June 1999).

53. General Dynamics, annual report, December 1998, p. 30. Notice that the disclosure includes general and administrative costs within the scope of contract costs. This in not uncommon in the case of contracts with the U.S. government, where explicit recovery of these costs is allowed.

54. Todd Shipyards, Inc., annual report on Form 10-K to the Securities and Exchange Commission (June 1997), no page number available. This loss accrual on a fixed-price contract illustrates the risk associated with these arrangements.

55. For a complete numerical example of the cumulative catch-up adjustment, refer to E. Comiskey and C. Mulford, "Contract Reporting and Analysis: Some Guidance for Lenders," *Commercial Lending Review* (Winter 1998–99), pp. 41–42.

56. Stewart & Stevenson Services, Inc., annual report, January 1999, p. 10.

57. The standard metric is: increases in assets and decreases in liabilities are deducted from earnings to arrive at cash from operating activities and decreases in assets and increases in liabilities are added.

58. This risk associated with fixed-price contracts is highlighted by Newport News Shipbuilding, Inc.: "Nearly half of the Company's principal U.S. Navy business is currently being performed under firm fixed price or fixed price incentive contracts, which wholly or

partially cause the risk of construction costs that exceed the contract target cost to be borne by the Company." Newport News Shipbuilding, Inc., annual report, December 1998, p. 21.

59. Any standard intermediate financial accounting text will cover these technical matters in detail.

60. G. Biddle and W. Ricks, "Analyst Forecast Errors and Stock Price Behavior Near the Earning Announcement Dates of LIFO Adopters," *Journal of Accounting Research* (Autumn 1988), p. 169.

61. Kroger Company, annual report, December 1997. Information obtained from Disclosure, Inc. *Compact D/SEC: Corporate Information on Public Companies Filing with the SEC* (Bethesda, MD: Disclosure, Inc., September 1998).

62. Interestingly, The Robert Mondavi Corporation takes a contrary view on smoothing: "The use of the LIFO method has led, and will continue to lead, to volatility in quarterly and annual financial results" (annual report, June 1998, p. 27). It may be that there is little harmony between the movement in grape prices and the market price of wine. Interestingly, Robert Mondavi changed to FIFO in fiscal 1999.

63. Available research suggests that LIFO liquidations tend to be related to industry classification, with a large portion of liquidations concentrated in two cyclical industries: primary metals and rubber and plastics. See P. Cottell, "LIFO Layer Liquidations: Some Empirical Evidence," *Journal of Accounting Auditing and Finance* (Winter 1986), pp. 30–45. This research also reports on the factors considered in the decision of whether or not to replace liquidated inventory.

64. In a recent airplane conversation, one of the authors queried the owner of some large auto dealerships about his use of LIFO. The owner indicated that he received intense pressure each year from his accountant to make certain that new-car shipments were received prior to year-end, in order to avoid an LIFO liquidation, and along with it a growth in taxable profits and tax payments. There have been some cases where tax authorities overturned such year-end inventory replacements on the grounds that they were primarily motivated by the desire to avoid the payment of income taxes.

65. Available research suggests the absence of a positive security return response associated with the earnings increase that results from the LIFO liquidation. For example, see T. Stober, "The Incremental Information Content of Financial Statement Disclosures: The Case of LIFO Inventory Liquidations," *Journal of Accounting Research* (Supplement 1996), pp. 138–160.

66. Chevron Corporation, annual report, December 1998, p. 33. The second item affecting Chevron's current ratio was $2.1 billion of commercial paper classified as a current liability, even though Chevron believes that it will be outstanding indefinitely.

67. W. Johnson and D. Dhaliwal, "LIFO Abandonment," *Journal of Accounting Research* (Autumn 1988), pp. 236–272.

68. *Ibid.,* p. 271.

69. There may well be other factors at work in the case of public auto retailers. Several auto dealerships have changed from LIFO to FIFO or specific identification upon going public. Whereas the action of Cross Continent is consistent with their inability to realize the tax benefits of LIFO while in a loss carryforward position, there may also be other considerations. Previously private companies may place a higher priority on their reported profit performance and financial position as they go public. Switching to FIFO has the potential to improve both measures.

70. Dean Foods Company, annual report, December 1997, p. 20

71. *Ibid.,* p. 29.

72. Securities and Exchange Commission, Regulation S-X, Rule 5-02.6.

73. Securities and Exchange Commission, Staff Accounting Bulletin No. 40.

74. If the LIFO reserve is not a contra-asset balance, then it is added to the FIFO valuation in arriving at the LIFO inventory value. Cases like this, where old costs exceed current costs, are usually only observed in industries that have experienced sustained declines in prices. When Steel went through a long period of decline, there were cases where the LIFO reserve was an adjunct balance (i.e., added to the related asset) instead of a contra-balance.

75. Recent examples of positive LIFO reserves include Bayou Steel Corporation (1998) and Encore Wire Corporation (1997).

76. Phillips Petroleum Company, annual report, December 1998, p. 56.

77. Valero Energy Corporation, annual report, December 1998, p. 46.

78. The Robert Mondavi Corporation, annual report, June 1998, p. 27.

79. Chevron Corporation, annual report, December 1998, p. 37.

80. E. Day, "Get in the Driver's Seat of Lending to Automobile Dealerships," *The Journal of Lending and Credit Risk Management* (November 1998), pp. 42–51. This recent article includes discussion of LIFO adjustments made to both working capital and leverage ratios for LIFO valuation differences (i.e., for LIFO reserves). The focus is on auto dealerships where LIFO has been the dominant inventory method and where LIFO reserve balances have been exceptionally large.

81. Mondavi's current ratio appears very high if compared to other commercial and industrial firms. This is due to the size of its inventories and the fact that they are all classified as current assets, even though it may be years in some cases before the wine is sold. The same issue of judging liquidity from current ratios, when somewhat illiquid assets are classified as current, was raised in the earlier case of contract reporting.

82. *Ibid.,* pp. 50–51.

83. A higher ending inventory under FIFO would result in lower cost of sales and, therefore, higher income.

84. E. Day, "Get in the Driver's Seat of Lending to Automobile Dealerships," *The Journal of Lending and Credit Risk Management* (November 1998), pp. 50–51.

85. The general motivation behind this tax adjustments in the case of revised leverage ratios, but not in the case of revised working capital ratios, was confirmed in correspondence by the authors with Mr. Day. We are grateful to Mr. Day for responding to our request for clarification on this point.

86. This area of the tax law is referred to as the Uniform Cost Capitalization (UNICAP) rules.

87. Maine Public Service Company, annual report, December 1998, p. 22.

88. SFAS No. 34, "Capitalization of Interest" (Stamford, CT: Financial Accounting Standards Board, December 1979). Interest was capitalized prior to the issuance of SFAS No. 34. However, practice varied a great deal and the FASB felt the need to regularize and guide practice.

89. *Ibid.,* from the Summary of SFAS No. 34.

90. SFAS No. 34, "Capitalization of Interest" (Stamford, CT: Financial Accounting Standards Board, December 1979) paras. 12–16.

91. It is common for smaller homebuilders to continue to capitalize interest even after a home is placed on the market. This is obviously not consistent with SFAS No. 34. However, their position is that continued capitalization of interest helps them to judge whether a real gain is ultimately earned on the home. In their view, this requires a charge

for the carrying cost of the investment in the home during the period that it is on the market. This is achieved by the continuing capitalization of interest until the home is sold.

92. SFAS No. 34, "Capitalization of Interest" (Stamford, CT: Financial Accounting Standards Board, December 1979), para. 17.

93. Internal Revenue Code, Section 263(A)f.

94. SFAS No. 34: "Capitalization of Interest" (Stamford, CT: Financial Accounting Standards Board, December 1979), para. 10.

95. TJ International, annual report, December 1995, pp. 10, 14, 24.

96. In a case very similar to TJ International, Union Camp Corporation had an almost $50 million reduction in capitalized interest in 1992 as the result of the completion of a major new paper mill. Two-thirds of Union Camp's 1993 decline in earnings was attributed to this reduction in capitalized interest.

97. M.D.C. Holdings, annual report, December 1998, p. 11.

98. Hovnanian Enterprises, Inc., October 1998. Information obtained from Disclosure, Inc., *Compact D/SEC: Corporate Information on Public Companies Filing with the SEC* (Bethesda, MD: Disclosure, Inc., June 1999).

99. SFAS No. 34, "Capitalization of Interest" (Stamford, CT: Financial Accounting Standards Board, December 1979), para. 62.

100. SFAS No. 121, "Accounting for the Impairment of Long-Lived Assets and for Long-Lived Assets to be Disposed Of" (Norwalk, CT: Financial Accounting Standards Board, March 1995).

101. Accounting Standards Executive Committee, SOP 81–1, "Accounting for Performance of Construction-Type and Certain Production-Type Contracts" (New York: American Institute of Certified Public Accountants, July 1981), para. 65.

102. *Ibid.,* para. 16.

103. SFAC No. 5, "Recognition and Measurement in Financial Statements of Business Enterprises" (Stamford, CT: Financial Accounting Standards Board, December 1984), para. 6.

Chapter 5

Income Tax Reporting and Analysis

But in this world nothing can be said to be certain, except death and taxes.[1]

Income taxes represent one of the more challenging areas of financial reporting and analysis. Whereas some accounting topics have a relatively narrow scope, income taxes have a pervasive effect on business decisions, financial statements, and associated disclosures. All dimensions of financial quality are affected by income taxes. Further, income taxes are usually material items in the balance sheet, income statement, and statement of cash flows. Finally, in spite of their pervasiveness and importance, taxes are typically not well understood by important users of financial statements.

SOME KEY FOUNDATIONS

Several important matters must be kept firmly in mind as the subject of income tax reporting and analysis is considered:

- *Profits in the shareholder income statement and tax return are usually different.* It is typical for pretax financial income in the shareholder income statement to differ significantly from the taxable income reported in the tax return. These differences reflect the fact that, while generally accepted accounting principles (GAAP) guide the reporting to shareholders, the income tax law determines the results reported in the tax return. Although not common, Delta Air Lines, Inc., disclosed its pretax financial and taxable income in its 1997 annual report to shareholders. Delta's disclosure is provided in Exhibit 5.1.

  Notice that Delta's pretax financial income was almost twice the level of its taxable income in 1995. However, in the next year, 1996, taxable income was almost three times the level of pretax financial income.

- *The income tax provision expense or benefit is based on shareholder income.* The income tax provision or benefit included in the shareholder income statement is based on the pretax financial income or loss reported in that statement, and not simply on the taxable income or loss reported in the income tax return.[2]

Exhibit 5.1.   Disclosure of Both Pretax Financial and Taxable Income: Delta Air Lines, Years Ended June 30, 1995–1997 (Millions of Dollars)

	1995	*1996*	*1997*
Pretax financial income (books)	$494	$276	$1,415
Taxable income (tax return)	282	635	1,246
Total tax provision (books)	200	120	561
Tax payments	25	192	336

Source: Delta Air Lines, Inc., Form 10-K annual report to the Securities and Exchange Commission (June 1997), p. 24.

- *Tax payments are based on tax return and not shareholder results.* While the income tax provision or benefit is based on the pretax financial income or loss reported in the shareholder income statement, the actual tax payment, or recovery in the event of losses, is based on the taxable income or loss reported in the income tax return. Exhibit 5.1 reveals how the tax payments of Delta Air Lines followed taxable income more closely than pretax financial income. Tax payments rose in 1996 as taxable income likewise increased. However, pretax financial income fell sharply in 1996. Tax payments in 1996 exceeded the total tax provision, which is based only on pretax financial income. In 1997, pretax financial income was greater than taxable income and now tax payments fall below the tax provision. Tax payments, as suggested, are more closely tied to taxable income than to pretax financial income.

    For both shareholder and tax return reporting, there are varying degrees of choice that may be exercised in arriving at pretax results. Moreover, tax law varies from GAAP in its inclusion of some items of revenue or gain and expense or loss in the determination of taxable income. These differences in treatment, whether a matter of choice or a result of deviations between the tax law and GAAP, create much of the complexity associated with the reporting and analysis of income taxes.

SHAREHOLDER AND TAX RETURN PROFIT DIFFERENCES

As noted above, disparities between shareholder and tax return profits result from differences between accounting policies used to arrive at pretax financial income versus those used to arrive at taxable income. In addition, differences in the items that are considered revenues or gains and expenses or losses for purposes of determining pretax financial income and taxable income also contribute to this gap.

Statement of Financial Accounting Standards (SFAS) No. 109, "Accounting for Income Taxes," refers to pretax shareholder results as "pretax financial income" and tax return results as "taxable income."[3] For consistency, this convention is generally followed in subsequent discussion. However, it is also common for statement users to refer to "book" or "shareholder" and "tax" or "tax return" earnings. These references are to pretax financial income and taxable income, respectively. These terms will be used occasionally as alternative characterizations of pretax financial income and taxable income, respectively.

Differences between pretax financial income (shareholder results) and taxable income (tax return results) are classified as either (1) temporary differences or (2) permanent differences. Each category is defined and discussed below. After these overviews, the implications of both the temporary and permanent differences for tax reporting and analysis are extensively discussed and illustrated in subsequent sections.

Temporary Differences

Temporary differences result principally from the adoption of different accounting policies for the determination of pretax financial income and taxable income.[4] These policy differences cause the amounts of revenues or gains and expenses or losses to differ on a year-by-year basis in the determination of pretax financial versus taxable income. Or, as explained in SFAS No. 109, they result from "differences between the years in which transactions affect taxable income and the years in which they enter into the determination of pretax financial income."[5] Eventually, however, the total of these items is the same in each income calculation; hence, the differences are termed *temporary*.

Upon their origination, temporary differences result in the recording of deferred income tax provisions or benefits and associated deferred tax liabilities or assets, respectively. The tax consequences of temporary differences for both financial reporting and analysis are discussed and illustrated in the following sections.

Temporary Differences and the Basis of Assets and Liabilities

SFAS No. 109 sometimes refers to temporary differences in terms of their effects on the basis or carrying value of assets and liabilities. For example, consider a $1 million write-down of an asset for purposes of computing pretax financial income. Also, assume that prior to the write-down the asset had a cost or carrying value of $5 million for both shareholder reporting and income tax purposes.

A write-down will typically not give rise to a deductible item in the tax return until the asset is sold. Therefore, after the write-down, the basis or carrying value of the asset is $4 million for shareholder reporting purposes, but it is still $5 million for income tax purposes. No write-down has been taken for tax purposes, and the tax basis of the asset is therefore unchanged. This temporary difference, a loss recognized now in computing pretax financial income but only later in determining taxable income, creates an asset "basis" difference.

Alternatively, consider the accrual of a $1 million expense and associated liability for postretirement benefits that is deducted currently in computing pretax financial income. This expense accrual will normally be deductible in computing taxable income only when it is paid. A liability is recorded currently for shareholder reporting but none exists for income tax purposes. This temporary difference creates a liability basis difference of $1 million. The liability is on the shareholder books at $1 million, but has no current recognized value or basis for income tax purposes. The cumulative amounts of deferred tax assets and liabilities are determined by these cumulative basis differences.

Temporary Differences and Deferred Tax Assets and Liabilities

In each of the two temporary difference examples above, a deferred tax asset and associated deferred tax benefit would be recorded in the shareholder books. The deferred tax asset represents a future tax benefit that will be realized when the expense deduction, included earlier in the computation of pretax financial income, is deducted in the determination of taxable income. Assuming a combined income tax rate of 40 percent, a deferred tax asset of $400,000 (the $1 million temporary difference times 40 percent) is recorded along with a deferred tax benefit of $400,000.

The logic of the deferred tax asset, or future tax benefit, is that the accrual of a $1 million expense in measuring pretax financial income carries with it a future tax savings of $400,000. Under GAAP, this future tax savings is considered to be an asset and hence must be recorded when the loss or expense deduction is taken in computing pretax financial income. By recognizing the deferred tax asset and associated deferred tax benefit in the same period as the loss and expense accruals, the net burden on earnings for the current period is only $600,000—$1,000,000 asset write-down or expense accrual minus a $400,000 deferred tax benefit. If the deferred tax asset and associated deferred tax benefit were not recorded, then current net income would be understated by $400,000. However, future pretax financial income would also be overstated by $400,000.[6]

Both the asset write-down and expense accrual result in the recording of deferred tax assets. However, a deferred tax liability would be recorded if, for example, a temporary difference involved the inclusion of revenue in pretax financial income that was not yet included in taxable income. Assume that land with a cost of $100,000 is sold on an installment basis for $500,000. For income tax purposes, the gain of $400,000 may be included in taxable income as and when the installments are collected. Since the gain is equal to 80 percent of the selling price ($500,000 − $100,000 / $500,000 = 80 percent), gain equal to 80 percent of the installments will be recognized in the tax return as they are collected. However, the entire gain is normally included in pretax financial income in the year of sale.

Assuming a 40 percent tax rate, a deferred tax provision and associated deferred tax liability of $160,000 would be recorded in the year of sale—$400,000 total gain × 40 percent = $160,000. The matching logic discussed above applies here as well. Failure to accrue a deferred tax provision in the year of sale would overstate net income for the period. Recognition of the full gain of $400,000 carries with it an obligation for future taxes of $160,000—a deferred tax liability. This tax will be paid in the future as the gain is included in taxable income as and when installment payments are received.

Failure to accrue the deferred tax provision would also result in an under-statement of future net income. In this case, taxes would be deducted in arriving at net income as the installments are collected in future periods and taxes are paid on the profits included in the tax return. However, the gain giving rise to these taxes was all included in pretax financial income in the year of the sale. A clear mismatching of the gain and its associated tax consequences results unless the entire tax on the gain is recorded in the same period (i.e., the period in which the sale took place).

The recording of deferred tax provisions or benefits as temporary differences originate produces a proper matching of revenues and expenses and also ensures that the balance sheet includes all deferred tax assets and liabilities.

Income Statement versus Balance Sheet Orientation to Deferred Taxes

The traditional focus on temporary differences has been on their period-to-period effects on pretax financial income and deferred taxes. When accumulated, these annual income effects determine the cumulative differences in the carrying amounts, or bases, of assets or liabilities. The changes in cumulative temporary differences in a single period result in the recording of associated deferred tax provisions and benefits. Cumulative deferred taxes assets and liabilities represent the tax effects of cumulative basis differences.

Because contemporary financial analysis places an emphasis on earnings anal-ysis, the presentation in this chapter will stress the annual effects of temporary differences on the income tax provision. However, where the analysis of financial position is the primary focus, the tax effects of the cumulative temporary differ-ences will be emphasized.

Permanent Differences

Differences between pretax financial income and taxable income are referred to as *permanent* when an item of revenue or gain and expense or loss is included in the computation of either pretax financial income or taxable income, but not both. Permanent differences cause a firm's effective income tax rate, that is, the total tax provision divided by pretax financial income, to be either higher or lower than the amount expected based on statutory income tax rates.

Some common examples of permanent differences would be nondeductible meal and entertainment expenses and nontaxable life insurance proceeds. In gen-eral, 50 percent of meal and entertainment expenses are disallowed as a deduction in computing taxable income.[7] However, 100 percent of the expense is deducted

Exhibit 5.2. The Influence of Permanent Differences on Effective Tax Rates: Case 1

Pretax financial income before permanent differences; also taxable income	$1,000
Add nontaxable life insurance proceeds	400
Deduct nondeductible meal and entertainment expenses	(200)
Pretax financial income	$1,200
Tax provision	(400)
Net income	$800
Computation of tax provision:	
Pretax financial income before permanent differences; also taxable income	$1,000
Times income tax rate	.40
Tax provision	$400
Effective income tax rate:	
Tax provision	$400
Divide by pretax financial income	$1,200
Equals effective tax rate	33%

in arriving at pretax financial income. Life insurance proceeds received by companies from policies held on employees are included in pretax financial income, but are not included in taxable income.[8]

Each of the above items—one an expense and the other income—represent permanent differences because they are included in only one of the two income calculations, that is, pretax financial and not taxable income in the present example. Again, they are distinguished from temporary differences that *are* eventually included in each income calculation. As illustrated earlier, temporary differences give rise to deferred tax assets and liabilities, whereas permanent differences simply cause effective tax rates to differ from expected statutory levels. Unlike temporary differences, permanent differences do not give rise to deferred taxes.

Permanent Differences and Effective Tax Rates

Assume, case 1, that a company's pretax financial and taxable income are each $1,000, prior to inclusion of nondeductible meal and entertainment expenses of $200 and life insurance proceeds of $400. For simplicity, a flat combined income tax rate of 40 percent is assumed.[9] The tax provision and effective tax rate for this case are summarized in Exhibit 5.2.

Note that the nondeductible meal and entertainment expense is deducted and the nontaxable life insurance proceeds are added in arriving at pretax financial income. However, they are not included in the determination of taxable income, which remains at $1,000. They will never be included in the computation of taxable income—they are permanent differences.

The effective tax rate is reduced below the 40 percent combined (federal and state) statutory rate to 33 percent. The effective rate is reduced because nontaxable income of $400 exceeded the nondeductible expense of $200. Notice that the total tax provision is based on the taxable portion of pretax financial income only (i.e., $1,000).

A second case is added in Exhibit 5.3 to contrast with case one in Exhibit 5.2. With case two, pretax financial income remains at $1,000, but the nondeductible meal and entertainment expenses and nontaxable insurance proceeds are now $400 and $200, respectively. The total tax provision remains $400: 40 percent times the pretax financial income *exclusive of the permanent differences* or $1,000. (*Note*: In this simplified example, pretax financial income, exclusive of the two permanent differences, is equal to taxable income. This would not be the case if there were also temporary differences.) As shown below, pretax financial income *with the permanent differences included* is now only $800. Dividing the tax provision of $400 by pretax financial income of $800 results in a new effective tax rate of 50 percent.

The increase in the effective tax rate results because nondeductible expenses now exceed nontaxable income by $200, the opposite of the relationship in case 1.

In addition to permanent differences, a variety of other factors can cause effective tax rates to differ from statutory rates: research and development (R&D) tax credits, net operating loss carryforwards, rate reductions from operations in lower-tax-rate countries, resolution of disputes with tax authorities, and so on. A key issue in judging the potential effects of rate differences on earnings quality is the likelihood that they will continue in the future. This issue will be discussed and illustrated in a subsequent discussion.

With the preceding overview of some of the key foundations of income tax reporting, the balance of this chapter is devoted to expanding on this background. This involves further review of tax-related GAAP, an examination of examples of company tax disclosures, and a careful consideration of the implications of taxes for the quality of both a firm's earnings and financial position. This initial expanded discussion will be divided by temporary and permanent differences. This will be followed by a comprehensive example of GAAP requirements for tax reporting. Finally, focused attention will be given to the implications of income taxes for financial analysis.

TEMPORARY DIFFERENCES AND INCOME TAX REPORTING

There are many areas in which firms choose different accounting methods for the determination of pretax financial versus taxable income. For example, a study of the 100 largest U.S. banking companies revealed 33 specific areas in which temporary differences were present.[10] For firms in general, the single most common source of temporary differences results from the selection of different depreciation methods for use in the determination of pretax financial versus taxable income.

Exhibit 5.3. Permanent Differences and Decreases and Increases in Effective Tax Rates: Cases 1 and 2 Compared

	Case 1	*Case 2*
A. Total tax provision		
Total tax provision: .40 x $1,000	$400	$400
B. Pretax financial income		
Pretax financial income before permanent differences	$1,000	$1,000
Deduct nondeductible meal and entertainment expenses	(200)	(400)
Add nontaxable insurance proceeds	400	200
Pretax financial income	$1,200	$800
C. Effective tax rates		
A divided by B in each case	33%	50%
D. Explanation of effective rate differences		
Statutory tax rate	40%	40%
Tax rate changes from permanent differences:		
Nontaxable insurance proceeds	$(400)	$(200)
Nondeductible meals and entertainment expenses	200	400
Net nontaxable (income) or nondeductible expense	(200)	200
Times combined tax rate	40%	40%
Tax (decrease) increase	(80)	80
Divided by pretax financial income	$1,200	$800
(Reduction) or increase in effective tax rate	(7)%	10%
Effective tax rate	33%	50%

The 1998 annual report of Archer Daniels Midland Company declares that "The Company generally uses the straight-line method in computing depreciation for financial reporting purposes and generally uses accelerated methods for income tax purposes."[11]

Temporary Differences and Deferred Tax Assets and Liabilities

In a consideration of temporary differences, it is important to remember that they result mainly from differences in the timing of the recognition of revenues or gains and expenses or losses in the shareholder books versus the tax return, that is, in the determination of pretax financial and taxable income, respectively. Further, upon origination, a temporary difference results in pretax financial income being either higher or lower than taxable income.[12] In turn, these income differences require the recording of deferred tax assets or liabilities.

A Classification of Temporary Differences

Exhibit 5.4 provides a classification of selected temporary differences resulting from both accounting policy choices and the presence of variations in accounting treatments available under GAAP and the income tax law.[13]

A Sampling of Deferred Tax Assets and Liabilities

To appreciate the substantial range of temporary differences, a sampling is provided in Exhibit 5.5. The temporary differences are divided into those resulting in deferred tax assets versus deferred tax liabilities. Most of the listed deferred tax assets arose as a result of the recognition of expenses or losses in the determination of pretax financial income before they could be included in the determination of taxable income.

Again, deferred tax assets represent future tax benefits, that is, reductions in net tax payments that will be realized when an expense or loss deduction taken earlier in computing pretax financial income is deducted in computing future taxable income. Many deferred tax liabilities result from the recognition of expenses sooner in the determination of taxable income than in pretax financial income. Some also result from the recognition of revenues or gains in pretax financial income sooner than in taxable income. Deferred tax liabilities represent future tax payments that will occur when (1) the level of expense recognized in the tax return falls below that in the books or (2) the level of income recognized in the tax return rises above that in the books. In each case, an increase in taxable income and tax payments will result.

Each item in Exhibit 5.5 represents the tax effect, either a deferred tax asset or liability, of a revenue or gain and expense or loss that is included in a different year in the determination of pretax financial versus taxable income. These assets and liabilities represent the cumulative tax effects of their underlying temporary differences. That is, they result from cumulative basis differences of associated assets and liabilities.

The disclosures of deferred tax assets and liabilities are seldom explicit about the exact nature of the difference in accounting policies employed. For example, Books-A-Million, Inc. simply uses the word "Depreciation" as a label for a deferred tax liability. However, Furon Company uses a more descriptive label—"Tax over book depreciation." This usually implies that accelerated depreciation is being used in the tax return while straight-line is being used in the books. Con Agra identifies "Accrued expenses" as the source of one of its deferred tax assets. Again, in the typical case this would imply the accrual of expenses on the books before they are available as a deduction in the tax return. The reference to "Accrued expenses not currently deductible" by SCI Systems means that the expenses are deducted currently on the books but only later, when paid, in the tax return.

Exhibit 5.4.   Classification of Selected Temporary Differences

Item	Book Treatment	Tax Return Treatment
(A) Revenue or gains recognized in the books in advance of in the tax return		
Long-term contracts	Percentage of completion	Completed contract (contractors with receipts less than $10 million)
Installment sales	Accrual	Installment method
Foreign exchange gains	Recognized as accrued	Recognized as realized
Equity earnings	Recognized as earned by the investor company	Recognized as dividends are received by the investor
(B) Revenue or gain recognized in the tax return in advance of the books		
Rent received in advance	Recognized over the term of the prepayment	Recognized when the cash is received
Sale and lease-back gain	Recognized over the lease-back term	Recognized at the date of the sale
Loan origination fees	Recognized over the term of the loan	Recognized in the period cash is received
(C) Expense or loss recognized in the books in advance of recognition in the tax return		
Investment write-down	Recognized in the period of the write-down	Recognized upon sale of the investment
Warranty expense	Recognized on an estimated basis in the year of sale of the item under warranty	Recognized when the warranty service is provided
Bad debts	Recognized on an estimated basis	Recognized when the asset is actually charged off
Charitable contributions in excess of annual limitation	Full contribution recognized currently	Excess contributions recognized in future years
(D) Expense recognized in the tax return in advance of the books		
Depreciation	Straight-line	Accelerated
Software development costs	Capitalized when incurred beyond the point technological feasibility is established	Expensed as incurred
Construction interest	Capitalized and amortized	Expensed as incurred*

*There are also tax law requirements to capitalize interest in certain cases: *Internal Revenue Code,* §263A(F)(1)(B). However, the tax law requirements generally result in fewer cases of interest capitalization than do the GAAP requirements, which are found in SFAS No. 34, "Capitalization of Interest Costs" (Stamford, CT: Financial Accounting Standards Board, October 1979) para. 9–11.

Exhibit 5.5.   Temporary Differences and Deferred Tax Assets and Liabilities

Company	Temporary Difference
Deferred Tax Assets	
ABIOMED, Inc. (1998)	Nondeductible reserves
Advanced Micro Devices, Inc. (1997)	Deferred distributor income
Alaska Air Group, Inc. (1997)	Frequent flyer program costs
Alaska Air Group, Inc. (1997)	Capital leases
Alliant Techsystems (1999)	Reserves for employee benefits
BARRA, Inc. (1999)	Capitalized research and development
Bowlin Outdoor Advertising (1999)	Compensated absences
Claire's Stores, Inc. (1998)	Deferred rent
Comair Holdings, Inc. (1999)	Gains on sale and leasebacks
Con Agra, Inc. (1998)	Accrued expenses
Fleetwood Enterprises, Inc. (1999)	Product warranty reserves
Gerber Scientific (1998)	Foreign exchange losses
Gleason Corporation (1997)	Restructuring accruals
H. J. Heinz Company (1999)	Provision for estimated expenses
Johns Manville Corporation (1997)	Provision for furnace rebuilds
Mentor Corporation (1998)	Litigation obligation
The Robert Mondavi Corporation (1998)	Deferred compensation
Parker Hannifin Corporation (1998)	Long-term contracts
Paychex Corporation (1998)	Accrual for future medical claims
Petroleum Helicopters (1998)	Vacation accrual
Spiegel, Inc. (1997)	Capitalized overhead in inventory
Sunoco Products Company (1997)	Asset impairment
Techne Corporation (1998)	Inventory costs capitalized
Techne Corporation (1998)	Unrealized intercompany sales profit
Worthington Industries, Inc. (1999)	Allowance for doubtful accounts
Xeta Corporation (1997)	Prepaid service contracts
Deferred Tax Liabilities	
Aegis Consumer Funding Group, Inc. (1997)	Securitization transactions
Alexander & Baldwin, Inc. (1997)	Tax deferred gains on real estate
Archer Daniels Midland Company (1998)	Unrealized gain on marketable securities
Bluegreen Corporation (1999)	Installment sale
Books-A-Million, Inc. (1999)	Depreciation
Brown-Forman Corporation (1999)	Intercompany transactions
Comair Holdings, Inc. (1999)	Major engine-inspection costs
Dean Foods Company (1998)	Self-insurance reserves
Dura Automotive Systems (1997)	Deferred design costs
Furon Company (1998)	Tax over book depreciation

(continued)

Exhibit 5.5.   Temporary Differences and Deferred Tax Assets and Liabilities

Company	*Temporary Difference*
Gerber Scientific (1998)	Foreign exchange gains
Gottschalks, Inc. (1997)	LIFO inventory reserve
Gottschalks, Inc. (1997)	Supplies inventory
Holly Corporation (1998)	Deferred turnaround costs
Pall Corporation (1998)	Pension assets
Smithfield Foods, Inc. (1999)	Investments in subsidiaries
Spiegel, Inc. (1997)	Earned but unbilled finance charges
Spiegel, Inc. (1997)	Prepaid and deferred expenses
Tech Data Corporation (1999)	Capitalized advertising costs
Universal American Financial Corp. (1997)	Deferred policy acquisition costs
Western Digital Corporation (1998)	Unremitted income of foreign subsidiaries
Xeta Corporation (1997)	Unamortized software development costs
Xoma Corporation (1997)	Capitalized R&D Expense

Sources: Companies' annual reports to shareholders. The year following each company name designates the annual report from which the example was drawn.

A key to understanding the treatment used in the books versus the tax return hinges on whether a deferred tax asset or liability is recorded on the temporary difference. If a deferred tax asset is recorded, the temporary difference initially (i.e., upon origination) results in a reduction in pretax financial income in relationship to taxable income. The deferred tax asset represents the future tax savings that will be realized when, upon reversal of the temporary difference, taxable income is reduced below pretax financial income. Almost all of the deferred tax assets in Exhibit 5.5 arise from the same source, expenses accrued on the books before they are deductible in the tax return.

For a deferred tax liability, the temporary difference initially (i.e., upon origination) results in an excess of pretax financial income over taxable income. The deferred tax liability represents the additional tax payment that will result when, upon reversal of the temporary difference, taxable income increases in relationship to the level of pretax financial income.

Origination and Reversal of a Temporary Difference

As discussed above, deferred tax assets and liabilities are initially recorded when a temporary difference originates. Origination refers to the initial creation of a temporary difference between pretax financial and taxable income. At some later date or dates, the relationship between pretax financial and taxable income upon origination of the temporary must be reversed. If this were not the case, then the income difference could not be considered temporary.[14]

Exhibit 5.6.   Origination and Reversal of a Depreciation-Related Temporary Difference

Data: A machine with a cost of $100,000 is depreciated straight-line assuming a useful life of five years on the books. Depreciation for tax purposes uses the 200% declining balance method. A zero salvage value is assumed and a half-year of depreciation is taken in the year of acquisition and disposition. The depreciation tables for tax purposes include a switch to a straight-line computation when it yields a larger amount of depreciation.*

	Depreciation		Asset Carrying Value		Cumulative Temporary
Year	*Books*	*Tax Return*	*Books*	*Tax Return*	*Difference*
1	$10,000	$20,000	90,000	80,000	10,000
2	20,000	32,000	70,000	48,000	22,000
3	20,000	19,200	50,000	28,800	21,200
4	20,000	11,520	30,000	17,280	12,720
5	20,000	11,520	10,000	5,760	4,240
6	10,000	5,760	0	0	0
	$100,000	$100,000			

*Tables are found in the Internal Revenue Service, "Revenue Procedure 87–57."

An example of a temporary difference originating and then reversing is provided in Exhibit 5.6. The computation of depreciation for tax purposes employs the tables included in the tax law for assets placed in service after December 31, 1986. These tables provide for a switching to straight-line depreciation when straight-line provides a larger depreciation amount.

Exhibit 5.6 reveals originating temporary differences in years 1 and 2. The sum of the temporary differences in years 1 and 2 is $22,000 ($10,000 in year 1 and $12,000 in year 2). Notice that $22,000, the sum of the year 1 and 2 originating temporary differences, represents the asset basis difference at the end of year 2—book basis of $70,000 minus tax basis of $48,000. At this point, the cumulative deferred tax liability, assuming a 40 percent tax rate, would be $8,800.

With the data in Exhibit 5.6, the temporary difference originations and reversals, along with the increases and decreases in the deferred tax liability, are shown in Exhibit 5.7.

In years 1 and 2, taxable temporary differences originate and deferred tax liabilities are recorded. The increases in deferred tax liabilities in years 1 and 2 are matched by the recording of deferred income tax provisions. These provisions are required because pretax financial income exceeds taxable income. The deferred tax provision is a tax accrual on these taxable temporary differences.

The deferred tax provisions are noncash expenses. They are offset by an increase in deferred tax liabilities and not by an outflow of cash. The result is an

Exhibit 5.7.   Temporary Differences and Deferred Tax Liabilities
and Provisions (Benefits)

Year	Temporary Difference		Deferred Tax Liability	
	Originating	Reversing	Increasing	Decreasing
1	$10,000		$4,000	
2	12,000		4,800	
3		$800		$320
4		8,480		3,392
5		8,480		3,392
6		4,240		1,696
Totals	$22,000	$22,000	$8,800	$8,800

increase in the cash quality of earnings for each of the first two years. Consistent with their noncash status, the deferred tax provisions of $4,000 in year 1 and $4,800 in year 2 would be added back to net income in arriving at cash flow from operating activities.

In years 3 through 6, the taxable temporary differences reverse and the deferred tax liabilities are reduced. The reduction in the deferred tax liabilities is matched by reductions in the deferred tax provision. These benefits are matched by a reduction in the deferred tax liability and not an inflow of cash. That is, the deferred tax benefits, when viewed separately, increase net income but are noncash, and therefore they impair the cash quality of earnings.

However, the reduction in the deferred tax provision is matched by an increase in the current tax provision. The reversal of the temporary difference increases taxable income and with it the current tax provision. The offsetting increases and decreases in the current and deferred tax provisions, respectively, mean that there is not a final increase in net income as a result of the reversal of this temporary difference.

It is important to note that the examples of the origination and reversal of the temporary differences in Exhibits 5.6 and 5.7 simply illustrate the pattern for a single asset. It does not represent a typical pattern of origination and reversal at the level of the firm. At the firm level, it is common for deferred tax liability positions to grow for decades. Individual assets do move thorough the cycle of origination and reversal illustrated in Exhibits 5.6 and 5.7. However, continued replacement of depreciated assets and overall growth in depreciable assets usually results in either relatively stable or growing deferred tax liabilities.

Although not illustrated here, the preceding pattern is exactly reversed in the case of deductible temporary differences—temporary differences that, upon reversal, put additional deductions as opposed to additional income into the determination of taxable income. Also, upon origination, these deductible differences call for the recording of deferred tax assets.

With this additional background on temporary differences, the next section will provide additional development on the nature and tax effects of permanent differences. As with temporary differences, some of the implications of permanent differences for financial analysis and the assessment of financial quality will also be identified.

PERMANENT DIFFERENCES AND INCOME TAX REPORTING

Permanent differences are classified in Exhibit 5.8 in much the same way as the temporary differences are in Exhibit 5.4. This exhibit includes only items of revenue or gain and expense or loss that are included in the books or the tax return, but not both. The presence of permanent differences will cause effective tax rates to deviate from statutory levels. However, the effective tax rate can also be affected by various tax credits, changes in tax rates, resolutions of tax disputes, and a variety of other items. These other items will also be explored later in this chapter.

A summary of the effects of permanent differences on effective tax rates is provided in Exhibit 5.9. An important issue in subsequent discussion is the extent to which either increases or decreases in effective tax rates are likely to be sustained. To the extent that increases or decreases in effective tax rates are nonrecurring, then projections of future net income should not employ these temporarily higher or lower rates.

A reduction in the effective tax rate resulting from nontaxable interest income will be sustained if the firm maintains a comparable ongoing investment in tax-exempt investments. However, a rate reduction from the receipt of nontaxable proceeds from a life insurance policy will not be sustained.

Permanent differences are not the only items that can cause the effective tax rate to deviate from statutory levels. Nonrecurring tax increases or decreases from the resolution of disputes with tax authorities are a common source of increases or decreases in effective tax rates. Other items include various tax credits, loss carryovers, higher or lower foreign tax rates, and so forth. More detailed attention is directed to the implications of effective tax rates for financial analysis later in this chapter.

As with the temporary differences, a sampling of disclosed permanent differences from a range of recent annual reports is provided in Exhibit 5.10.

The preceding sections have provided an overview of tax reporting and the roles played by both temporary and permanent differences. Some implications for financial analysis have been identified. To move forward to more detailed and comprehensive analysis of company tax disclosures, it is essential to have further background on their development. This is the primary role of the next section, which is organized around a comprehensive tax accounting example. However, this example will also be used both as a vehicle to reinforce previous discussion and as a device for outlining the value of these disclosures to financial analysis. In the final section of this chapter, application of the financial reporting founda-

Exhibit 5.8. Classification of Permanent Differences

Item	Book Treatment	Tax Treatment
(A) Revenue or gains included in book but not in the tax return		
Municipal bond interest income	Included in book income	Exempt from taxation
Dividends received	Included in book income	Wholly or partially exempt from taxation[a]
Life insurance proceeds, company is the beneficiary	Included in book income	Generally exempt from taxation
(B) Revenue or gains included in the tax return but not in book income		
Dividends received on equity-accounted investments	Treated as an investment reduction	Subject to only partial taxation when received
(C) Expenses or losses deductible in the books but not in the tax return		
Goodwill amortization	Deducted in arriving at book income	Often not deductible in the tax return
Interest expense on money borrowed to invest in tax-exempt securities	Deducted fully in arriving at book income	Not deductible
Fines and penalties payable to a government	Deducted fully in arriving at book income	Not deductible
Life insurance premiums for employee policies on which the company is the beneficiary	Deducted in part in arriving at book income[b]	Not deductible
(D) Expenses or losses deductible in the tax return but not in the books		
Compensation expense from early disposition of stock acquired under incentive stock option plans	Not deducted in arriving at book income	Fully deductible[c]
Percentage depletion in excess of cost depletion	Not deducted in arriving at book income	Fully deductible
Excess of fair value over cost or basis in assets contributed to selected charities	An amount equal to cost is deduced in arriving at pretax financial income	Fair value of the contributed asset is deducted

[a]Corporations that own less than 20% of the shares of a company paying a dividend can effectively exclude 70% of the dividends received. This exclusion rises to 80% when ownership ranges from 20% to less than 80%. This feature of the tax law is referred to as the "dividends received deduction." The nontaxable portion of the dividends received is included as part of "Special deductions" on line 29 of the U.S. Corporation Income Tax Return, Form 1120. See Internal Revenue Code, §243(a) and (c) for details.

[b]The deduction on the books is normally only the excess of the insurance premium over the growth in the cash surrender value of the policy each year.

[c]While this is a permanent difference, the effective tax rate is not affected. Rather, the tax benefit from this expense, deductible only in the tax return, is recorded in shareholders' equity and not in the income statement.

Exhibit 5.9.   Permanent Differences and Effective Tax Rates

Nature of the Permanent Difference	*Effective Tax Rate Effect*
Revenue or gain in the books but not in the tax return	Decreased
Revenue or gain in the tax return but not in the books	Increased
Expense or loss in the books but not in the tax return	Increased
Expense or loss in the tax return but not in the books	Decreased

tions of income taxes to the financial analysis of company tax disclosures will be undertaken.

TAX REPORTING AND DISCLOSURE REQUIREMENTS: A COMPLETE ILLUSTRATION

The principal source of income tax reporting and disclosure requirements is SFAS No. 109, "Accounting for Income Taxes."[15] The accounting and disclosure requirements of SFAS No. 109 are illustrated with the information in Exhibit 5.11.

Computation and Disclosure of the Tax Provisions

SFAS No. 109 outlines the basic requirements for measuring the total tax provision and related assets and liabilities.[16] Beyond this, SFAS No. 109 includes requirements to partition the total tax provision into two different elements: current and deferred tax provisions. As we will illustrate, this partition recognizes the strong interest on the part of statement users in the cash content of the total provision.

Computation of the Total Tax Provision

The total tax provision, before tax credits, is based on pretax financial income, after adjustment for the effects of permanent differences. Therefore, the nondeductible goodwill amortization of $50,000 must be added back to pretax financial income and the $100,000 of tax-exempt interest income must be deducted from pretax financial income before the tax rate is applied. Determination of the taxable portion of pretax financial income and computation of the total tax provision are both illustrated in Exhibit 5.12.

The adjustments made in Exhibit 5.12 do not change the amount of pretax financial income reported in the shareholder income statement of the firm. However, because the tax-exempt interest is never subject to taxation, it would be improper to accrue a tax on this portion of pretax financial income. Likewise, the goodwill amortization is never deductible in the tax return. Therefore, the nontaxable interest income is deducted from and the nondeductible goodwill amor-

Exhibit 5.10. A Sampling of Permanent Differences from Company Reports

Company	Permanent Difference
Alexander & Baldwin, Inc. (1997)	Fair market value over cost of donations
Archer Daniels Midland Company (1998)	Litigation settlements and fines
BARRA, Inc. (1999)	Nondeductible acquisition charges
Claire's Stores, Inc. (1998)	Stock options
Con Agra, Inc. (1999)	Nondeductible goodwill amortization
Delta Airlines (1998)	Nondeductible meals and entertainment
Fleetwood Enterprises, Inc. (1999)	Tax-exempt income
Gerber Scientific, Inc. (1998)	Life insurance benefits
Pall Corporation (1998)	Acquired in-process R&D
Parker Hannifin Corp. (1998)	Foreign sales corporation income
Pennzoil (1997)	Dividends received deduction
Newmont Mining Corporation (1997)	Excess percentage depletion
Smithfield Foods, Inc. (1999)	Nondeductible settlements
United Retail Group, Inc. (1997)	Charitable contribution benefit
Valley National Bancorp (1997)	Interest incurred to carry tax-exempts

Sources: Companies' annual reports to shareholders. The year following each company name designates the annual report from which the example was drawn.

Exhibit 5.11. Data for Comprehensive Illustration of Tax Reporting and Disclosure

Pretax financial income for 2001	$1,000,000
Taxable income in the 2001 tax return	800,000
Additional depreciation deducted in the tax return beyond the amount deducted in arriving at pretax financial income	350,000
Additional warranty expense accrual recorded in arriving at pretax financial income in excess of the tax return deduction	200,000
Nondeductible goodwill amortization included in arriving at pretax financial income	50,000
Tax-exempt interest income included in pretax financial income	100,000
Research and experimentation tax credit earned for the year	80,000
Combined income tax rate	40%

tization is added back to pretax financial income before the tax rate is applied.[17] As with all tax credits, the research credit of $80,000 reduces the tax provision on a dollar-for-dollar basis.

The remaining items in Exhibit 5.11 are temporary differences, and they are considered in computing the deferred tax portion of the total tax provision and in developing a schedule of deferred tax assets and liabilities.

Exhibit 5.12. Computation of Taxable Financial Income and the Total
Tax Provision

Pretax financial income	$1,000,000
Add nondeductible goodwill amortization	50,000
Deduct tax-exempt interest income	(100,000)
Taxable portion of pretax financial income	950,000
Multiply by the combined income tax rate	40%
Total tax provision (before research tax credit)	380,000
Deduct research tax credit	(80,000)
Total tax provision after research tax credit	$300,000

Exhibit 5.13. Computation of the Current Tax Provision

Taxable (tax return) income	$800,000
Tax rate	.40
Current tax provision (pretax credit)	320,000
Deduct research tax credit	(80,000)
Current tax provision	$240,000

Computation of the Current Tax Provision

In the presence of temporary differences, the total income tax provision of
$300,000 in Exhibit 5.12 is made up of both current and deferred components.
The current component is based on taxable income for the year—$800,000 per
Exhibit 5.11. The deferred component is based on the originating temporary differences for the year.[18] Computation of the current provision is outlined in Exhibit
5.13.

    The total tax provision is based on the portion ($950,000) of pretax financial
income that is subject to taxation, either currently or in the future. However, the
current provision is determined by the taxable income of $800,000. The deferred
tax provision is the tax effect of the $150,000 excess of the taxable portion of the
pretax financial, $950,000, over the taxable income of $800,000.

Direct Computation of the Deferred Tax Provision

The deferred tax provision above can be computed directly by multiplying the
two originating temporary differences times the tax rate of 40 percent. The accrual
of a deferred tax on each temporary difference is mandated by SFAS No. 109,
"Accounting for Income Taxes." This method of accounting for income taxes is
referred to as *comprehensive* income tax allocation. The direct computation of the
deferred tax provision is provided below:

Direct Computation of the Deferred Tax Provision

Due to the depreciation temporary difference	$350,000	× (40%)	=	$140,000
Due to the warranty temporary difference	$200,000	× (40%)	=	(80,000)
Deferred tax provision				$60,000

The deferred tax resulting from the $350,000 depreciation temporary difference is a positive provision. Pretax financial income is higher than taxable income by $350,000 because book depreciation is lower than tax depreciation by this amount. An additional tax provision must be accrued on this additional book income in the period in which it is included in pretax financial income. Because there is no current cash outflow for this deferred tax provision, an offsetting deferred tax liability is recorded. The cash quality of earnings is enhanced.

Unlike the depreciation temporary difference above, the warranty temporary difference results in a negative deferred tax provision, or deferred tax benefit, and is normally distinguished from a positive deferred tax provision by parentheses. Although the depreciation-related temporary difference results in an excess of pretax financial income over taxable income, the warranty temporary difference produces the opposite result. The tax benefit created by the $200,000 of additional warranty expense is recognized through the recording of a deferred tax asset and an associated deferred tax benefit. The $80,000 deferred tax asset will be realized in the future when the additional $200,000 warranty expense deduction is taken in the tax return. This will lower taxable income in relationship to pretax financial income and produce a tax savings of $80,000.[19]

Indirect Computation of the Deferred Tax Provision

The total tax provision is made up of only two elements. Therefore, the net deferred tax provision can be determined by deducting the current tax provision from the total tax provision:

Total tax provision	$300,000
Minus the current tax provision	240,000
Net deferred tax provision	$60,000

Disclosure of the Current and Deferred Tax Provisions

The requirements of SFAS No. 109 call for the separate disclosure of the current and deferred components of the total tax provision.[20] This may be done either in the body of the income statement or in the income tax note. The breakdown for the current example is given below:

Total tax provision	
Current tax provision	$240,000
Deferred tax provision	60,000
	$300,000

Exhibit 5.14. Disclosure of Deferred Tax Assets and Liabilities
by Temporary Difference

Temporary Difference	Deferred Tax Asset (Liability)
Excess of book warranty expense accrual over tax return amount	$80,000
Excess of tax return over book depreciation	(140,000)
Net deferred tax liability	$(60,000)

Deferred Tax Provision and the Cash Quality of Earnings

Corporations pay their taxes in installments, and the above $240,000 current pro-vision requires a cash outlay across the year.[21] However, the above net deferred provision of $60,000 is offset in the balance sheet by the combination of a $140,000 increase in a deferred tax liability and an $80,000 increase in a deferred tax asset. The balance sheet change, a net liability increase of $60,000, requires no current cash outlay. The cash quality of results is enhanced by this $60,000 net noncash deferred tax provision. Consistent with its noncash character and cash quality effect, the deferred tax provision of $60,000 would be added back to net income in arriving at cash flow from operating activities.

Calculation and Disclosure of Deferred Tax Assets and Liabilities

In addition to the preceding breakdown of the total income tax provision into current and deferred components, SFAS No. 109 also requires public firms to "disclose the approximate tax effect of each temporary difference . . . that gives rise to a significant portion of deferred tax liabilities and deferred tax assets."[22] There are two temporary differences in this example that originate in 2001. The tax rate used is based on enacted tax law and does not attempt to anticipate changes in tax rates. If rates do change in the future, then the deferred tax assets and liabilities are remeasured at the new rates. The effect of the rate change on the tax provision is disclosed in the income tax notes and is included in income from continuing operations.[23]

Exhibit 5.14 presents the schedule of deferred tax assets and liabilities, by type of temporary difference, as required by SFAS No. 109.

Reversal of Temporary Differences and Elimination of Deferred Tax Assets and Liabilities

The deferred tax asset and liability balances in Exhibit 5.14 result from the orig-ination of temporary differences. When temporary differences reverse, the asso-ciated deferred tax assets or liabilities are removed from the balance sheet. In

Exhibit 5.15. Effects of the Origination and Reversal
of a Taxable Temporary Difference

	Origination	*Reversal*
Increase in deferred tax provision	X	
Increase in deferred tax liability	X	
Cash tax payment is less than the total tax provision	X	
Cash quality of earnings is enhanced	X	
Decrease in deferred tax provision		X
Decrease in deferred tax liability		X
Cash tax payment exceeds the total tax provision		X
Cash quality of earnings is impaired		X

addition, a deferred tax provision or benefit, which is the opposite of that recorded upon origination of the temporary difference, is recorded.

Summary of the Cash Quality Effects of Originations and Reversals of Temporary Differences

The financial statement effects on both origination and reversal of taxable temporary difference are summarized in Exhibit 5.15.

Upon origination of a taxable temporary difference, cash tax payments are less than the total tax provision. This results in an increase in the cash quality of earnings. Alternatively, cash tax payments exceed the total tax provision when this temporary differences reverses. Cash quality is diminished in this case.

An increase in the current tax provision upon reversal of the temporary difference results from the associated growth in taxable income. Temporary differences that increase taxable income upon their reversal are referred to as "taxable" temporary differences in SFAS No. 109.[24] Deferred tax liabilities are recorded upon the origination of taxable temporary differences.

The deferred tax provision recorded upon origination of the temporary difference is added to net income in arriving at cash from operating activities, and, upon reversal, the deferred tax benefit is deducted from net income in the cash flow statement.

Although not a part of the deferred tax accounting summarized in Exhibit 5.15, upon reversal of the temporary difference, the current tax provision increases. This results from the increase in taxable income upon the reversal of the taxable temporary difference. However, this increase in the current provision is exactly offset by the deferred tax benefit shown in Exhibit 5.15. Net income is therefore not affected when the cash tax payments exceed the total tax provision upon reversal of the temporary difference. This additional tax payment was provided for upon origination of the temporary when the deferred tax liability was recorded. Therefore, subsequent payment of the deferred tax does not affect net income.

Exhibit 5.16. Effects of Origination and Reversal of a Deductible
Temporary Difference

	Origination	*Reversal*
Decrease in deferred tax provision—a benefit	X	
Increase in deferred tax asset	X	
Cash tax payment exceeds the total tax provision	X	
Cash quality of earnings is impaired	X	
Increase in deferred tax provision		X
Decrease in deferred tax asset		X
Cash tax payment is less than the total tax provision		X
Cash quality of earnings is enhanced		X

Where a deferred tax asset is involved, the outcomes are exactly the opposite of the case of the deferred tax liability in Exhibit 5.15. This case is summarized in Exhibit 5.16. Upon origination of a deductible temporary difference, cash tax payments are greater than the total tax provision. In a sense, taxes have been prepaid. The result is a decrease in the cash quality of earnings. Alternatively, cash tax payments are less than the total tax provision when this temporary differences reverses. In this case cash quality is enhanced. The deferred tax provision recorded upon reversal of the temporary difference results from the amortization of the related deferred tax asset.

The deferred tax benefit recorded upon origination of the temporary difference is deducted from net income in arriving at cash from operating activities and, upon reversal, the deferred tax provision is added to net income.

Temporary differences that give rise to deferred tax assets result in a reduction in pretax financial income in relationship to taxable income when they originate. Upon reversal, an expense deduction is taken in the tax return that was earlier deducted in the determination of pretax financial income statement. Temporary differences of this type are referred to in SFAS No. 109 as "deductible" temporary differences.[25]

Just as in the case of the taxable temporary difference in Exhibit 5.15, accounting for the reversal of the deductible temporary difference has no effect on net income. The reduction in the current tax provision is offset by the amortization of the deferred tax asset in the same amount.

Reconciliation of Statutory and Actual Tax Provision

The final tax disclosure required under SFAS No. 109 is a schedule that reconciles the expected or statutory rate tax provision with the actual or effective tax provision or tax rate. Each of the first two required disclosures—(1) a breakdown of the total tax provision into current and deferred components, and (2) a schedule

Exhibit 5.17.   Reconciliation of Expected with Actual Taxes

Statutory (expected) income tax	40.0%	$400,000
Nondeductible goodwill amortization	2.0	20,000
Tax-exempt interest income	(4.0)	(40,000)
Research and experimental tax credit	(8.0)	(80,000)
Effective taxes	30.0%	$300,000

of deferred tax assets and liabilities by temporary difference—deal only with the effects of temporary differences. This third required disclosure outlines why the reported tax provision differs from the one that would result from simply multiplying the statutory tax rate times pretax financial income. This requirement is outlined in SFAS No. 109 as follows:

> A public enterprise shall disclose a reconciliation using percentages or dollar amounts of (a) the reported amount of income tax expense attributable to continuing operations for the year to (b) the amount of income tax expense that would result from applying domestic statutory tax rates to pretax income from continuing operations.

Exhibit 5.17 illustrates this disclosure for the continuing example above. The statutory or expected tax is computed by simply multiplying the statutory tax rate times pretax financial income: 40 percent × $1,000,000 = $400,000. This is a hypothetical tax that is used as a benchmark for explaining the differences between this amount, $400,000, and the actual tax provision of $300,000 or 30 percent of pretax financial income.

Recall that the $1 million of pretax financial income includes the effects of the nondeductible goodwill of $50,000 and the tax-exempt interest income of $100,000. The $400,000 would represent the actual tax provision only if the full $1 million of pretax book income were subject to tax at the assumed statutory rate of 40 percent, and if, in addition, there were no tax credits.

As illustrated in Exhibit 5.17, the actual tax provision is increased by $20,000 or two percentage points because the $50,000 of goodwill amortization, deducted in arriving at pretax financial income, is not deductible for tax purposes: $50,000 × 40 percent = $20,000. The increase in the effective tax rate from this item is derived by dividing the dollar increase in tax of $20,000 by pretax financial income of $1 million: $20,000 / $1,000,000 = 2 percent.

The tax-exempt interest income is likewise included in pretax book income, but it is not subject to tax. The tax saving is $100,000 × 40 percent, or $40,000. This $40,000 tax saving amounts to a reduction in the effective tax rate of 4 percent: $40,000 / $1,000,000 = 4 percent. The research and experimentation tax credit reduces the tax provision on a dollar-for-dollar basis. The credit reduces the provision by the full $80,000 and the effective tax rate by eight percentage points: $80,000 / $1,000,000 = 8 percent.

It is important to notice that the above schedule includes only the permanent differences and the tax credit. *The effective tax rate is not affected by the temporary differences.* The temporary differences determine the size and nature of only the deferred tax provision or benefit. On a cumulative basis, the temporary differences determine the amounts and the mix of the deferred tax assets and liabilities. However, *the permanent differences influence only the level of the tax provision in relation to pretax financial income.*

The tax reconciliation schedule in Exhibit 5.17 includes one item that is not a permanent difference. The tax credit does not create a permanent difference between pretax financial and taxable income. However, the credit does reduce the effective tax rate by eight percentage points and the amount of taxes by $80,000. If this benefit level cannot be maintained in the future, then the research and experimentation tax credit takes on the character of a nonrecurring benefit. Therefore, presence of material research credits should be seen as reducing earnings quality in terms of persistence.

The research and experimentation tax credit is a vulnerable source of earnings. Although it has existed for many years, it is not a permanent feature of the tax law and each year there is spirited debate in Congress over its renewal. However, in 1999 Congress renewed this credit for five years. Further, earning this credit is tied to incurring research expenditures above base amounts. It may not be in a firm's interests to spend additional amounts on research simply to earn the credit.[27]

A broader range of nonrecurring tax items will be reviewed in the tax reconciliation schedules of companies in the last section of this chapter.

Tax reporting and analysis is a rich topical area with many unique reporting procedures and a substantial body of specialized terminology. Tax disclosures can also be quite involved, and discerning the implications for financial analysis is a challenge. The implications of tax reporting and associated disclosures for financial analysis have been engaged to some extent in the preceding sections. We continue to engage the implications of income taxes for financial analysis in this last section of the chapter. However, here the focus is primarily on the review of tax disclosures of individual firms.

TAX DISCLOSURES AND FINANCIAL ANALYSIS

The focus of the chapter to this point has been to outline the foundations of income tax reporting and analysis. Now, the emphasis can evolve to a more exclusive focus on issues of financial analysis, drawing on actual company tax disclosures. We continue to employ the framework of financial quality assessment. The company examples provide an opportunity to both expand the analytical focus as well as to reinforce our treatment of GAAP financial reporting and disclosure requirements.

Exhibit 5.18. Current and Deferred Tax Provision's: Pre-Paid Legal Services, Inc., Years Ended December 31, 1996–1998 (Thousands of Dollars)

The provision for income taxes consists of the following:

	1996	1997	1998
Current	$—	$88	$—
Deferred	5,857	12,293	11,122
Total provision for income taxes	$5,857	$12,381	$11,122

Source: Pre-Paid Legal Services, Inc., annual report, December 1998, p. 42

Deferred Taxes and Financial Quality: Pre-Paid Legal Services, Inc.

Pre-Paid Legal Services Corporation (PPL) offers insurance that covers the provision of legal services. Their insurance policies are sold through a substantial network of associates. The business is described in its 1998 annual report as:

> Pre-Paid Legal Services, Inc. (the "Company") underwrites and markets legal service plans (referred to as "Memberships") which provide for or reimburse a portion of legal fees incurred by members in connection with specified matters. Contracts are generally guaranteed renewable and are marketed primarily in 26 states by an independent sales force referred to as "Associates." Membership premiums are principally collected on a monthly basis.[28]

The typical policy remains in force for several years, and premiums are collected from policyholders over this time period. The commissions earned by associates are advanced to them by PPL when the policies are sold. Because the commissions are a cost associated with an insurance policy that benefits the earnings of PPL over several years, the commission advances are capitalized on the books of PPL and amortized over the expected term of the policy.

Portions of PPL's income tax disclosures and other financial information are provided in Exhibits 5.18 through 5.20.

Cash Quality of Pre-Paid Legal's Earnings

Note in Exhibit 5.18 that virtually all of PPL's tax provisions from 1996 to 1998 are deferred. Given the absence of a current provision, it is not surprising that PPL disclosed no tax payments.[29] The cash quality of PPL's earnings is significantly enhanced by its large noncash deferred tax provisions. In spite of its strong earnings growth, however, operating cash flow is rather modest. The typical cash demands of a growing business, coupled with the practice of advancing commissions when premiums have not yet been collected, appear to explain cash flow's trailing earnings.

Consistent with the noncash nature of deferred taxes in the total tax provision, PPL's cash flow statement in Exhibit 5.19 reveals that the deferred tax provision

Exhibit 5.19. Deferred Taxes and Cash Flow from Operating Activities:
Pre-Paid Legal Services, Inc., Years Ended December 31, 1996–1998
(Thousands of Dollars)

Pre-Paid Legal Services, Inc., Consolidated Statements of Cash Flows

	1996	1997	1998
Cash flows from operating activities:			
Net income	$10,263	$17,523	$30,210
Adjustments to reconcile net income to net cash provided by operating activities:			
Provision for associate stock options	1,122	644	—
Provision for deferred income taxes	5,857	12,293	11,122
Depreciation and amortization	533	2,026	2,944
Increase in accrued membership income	(672)	(689)	(1,196)
Increase in commission advances	(18,381)	(22,891)	(28,142)
Increase in other assets	(1,360)	(678)	(304)
Increase in inventories	(1,270)	(489)	(472)
Decrease (increase) in prepaid product commissions	(622)	(513)	752
(Decrease) increase in deferred revenue	1,390	771	(805)
Increase in membership benefits	315	787	1,159
Increase (decrease) in accounts payable and accrued expenses	1,914	5,688	(5,373)
Net cash provided by operating activities	(911)	14,472	9,895

Source: Pre-Paid Legal Services, Inc., annual report, December 1998, p. 32.

is added back to net income in arriving at cash flows from operating activities.
Beyond simply noting the contribution of tax deferrals to PPL's cash flow, an
analyst should be interested in the reason(s) for this unusually strong tax deferral
position. This is the key first step in judging the likelihood that this favorable cash
flow condition might be maintained in the future.

Source of Pre-Paid Legal's Tax Deferral Capacity

PPL's schedule of its deferred tax assets and liabilities (Exhibit 5.20) reveals the
source of its major tax deferrals. The schedule shows that almost all of the growth
in its net deferred tax liability position (i.e., excess of deferred tax liabilities over
deferred tax assets) was related to its accounting for "Commissions advanced."
Because these temporary differences resulted in deferred tax liabilities, it follows
that PPL's accounting caused book earnings to exceed those in the tax return.
This suggests that PPL capitalized these outlays on its books but deducted them
immediately in its tax returns. At the end of 1998, almost $29 million of deferred
tax liabilities resulted from this temporary difference.

Exhibit 5.20. Schedule of Deferred Tax Assets and Liabilities: Pre-Paid Legal Services, Inc., Years Ended December 31, 1997 and 1998 (Thousands of Dollars)

	1997	*1998*
Deferred tax liabilities:		
Commissions advanced	$18,784	$28,650
Unrealized investment gains (net)	—	467
Depreciation	—	224
Total deferred tax liabilities	18,784	29,341
Deferred tax assets:		
Expenses not yet deducted for tax purposes	445	449
Depreciation	14	—
Net operating loss carryforward	5,099	1,053
Premerger net operating loss carryforward	—	1,980
General business credit carryforward	325	325
Alternative minimum tax credit carryforward	366	366
Total deferred tax assets	6,249	4,173
Valuation allowance for deferred tax assets	(3,936)	(1,980)
Total net deferred tax assets	2,313	2,193
Net deferred liability	$(16,471)	$(27,148)

Source: Pre-Paid Legal Services, Inc., annual report, December 1998, p. 42.

At the end of 1998, PPL also had about $82 million of commission advances on its balance sheet—$21 million classified with current assets and $61 million classified as long term. Assuming that the entire $82 million of commission advances has been written off in the tax return, then the $82 million should represent the cumulative taxable temporary difference. Multiplying the commission advances of $82 million by the statutory tax rate of 35 percent results in a deferred tax liability of about $29 million. This is, of course, the amount that PPL discloses as due to this temporary difference.

Capitalization and amortization of commission advances seems reasonable because the associated polices have an average life of several years. Therefore, these advances take on the character of investment outlays.

Pre-Paid Legal's Tax Deferrals: Will the Good Times Last?

For PPL to continue to defer a substantial portion of its total tax provision, it will need continued growth and, along with it, continued growth in its deferred commission advances. Should PPL's business plateau or decline, it would reach a point where its taxable income would equal or exceed its pretax financial income.

If taxable income exceeds pretax financial income (i.e., the taxable temporary differences reverse), then the deferred tax liabilities would be paid down. Cash outlays for taxes will exceed the total book tax provision and the cash quality of its earnings would be impaired.

The pattern of origination and reversal of PPL's temporary differences, along with the associated increases and decreases in the deferred tax liabilities that result from its accounting for commission advances, are presented graphically in Exhibit 5.21.

The graphs in Exhibit 5.21 are intended to represent the firm as a whole and not simply a single transaction over its life cycle. As long as PPL stays in a growth mode, or at least does not have a decline in business, then it should remain in the "origination" state and its deferred tax liability balance should grow or at least not decline. Cash quality will continue to be enhanced. However, the degree of strengthening of cash quality will depend on the rate of growth in business.

If business declines, then PPL will move into the "reversal" state and its deferred tax liability will start to decline. This will result in a reduction in the cash quality of earnings because the cash outlay for taxes will exceed the total tax provision.

As noted, the graphical presentation in Exhibit 5.21 is intended as a representation of the firm as a whole over time. The presentation in Exhibit 5.22 represents the accounting life cycle of a single commission advance. The temporary difference originates when the membership (insurance coverage) is provided and the commission advanced. The temporary difference then reverses as the expense deduction, already taken in the tax return, is amortized to expense in computing pretax financial income. This pattern is illustrated in Exhibit 5.22.

It is unusual for a firm to be in a position of 100 percent tax deferral for an extended period of time. At some point, a slowdown in PPL's growth will reduce the deferred tax provision and the current tax provision will grow. There will probably continue to be some positive deferred tax provision, but it will become only a portion and not all of the total tax provision.

Examples of deferred tax liabilities being paid down are not currently very numerous because of the long period of prosperity in the U.S. economy. However, some examples known to the authors include: (1) a defense contractor's having a sudden reversal of deferred tax liabilities associated with long-term contract reporting; (2) a cement company's having a reversal of depreciation-related deferred tax liabilities due to a slowdown in construction activity and an associated decline in the replacement of cement trucks; and (3) a regional airline's having a depreciation-related deferred tax liability reversal as a result of aging fleet of aircraft.

Taxes and the Persistence Dimension of Pre-Paid Legal's Earnings

PPL's tax reconciliation schedule (Exhibit 5.23) shows an effective tax rate that is close to statutory levels in 1996 but above them in 1997 and below them in 1998. A small permanent difference associated with tax-exempt interest income

Exhibit 5.21. Origination and Reversal of Commissions-Related Deferred
Tax Liabilities

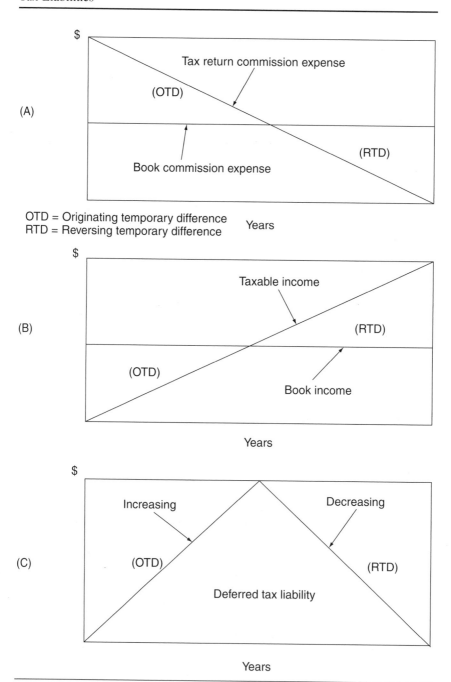

(A)

Tax return commission expense

(OTD)

Book commission expense

(RTD)

OTD = Originating temporary difference
RTD = Reversing temporary difference

Years

(B)

Taxable income

(RTD)

(OTD)

Book income

Years

(C)

Increasing

Decreasing

(OTD)

(RTD)

Deferred tax liability

Years

Exhibit 5.22. Individual Temporary Difference Originating and Reversing: PPL

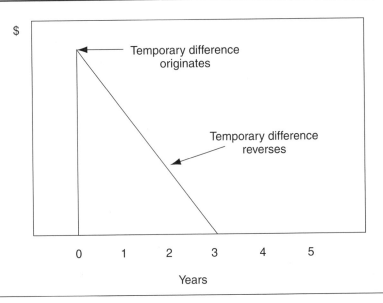

Exhibit 5.23. Tax Reconciliation Schedule of Pre-Paid Legal Services, Inc., Years Ended December 31, 1996–1998

A reconciliation of the statutory federal income tax rate to the effective income tax rate is as follows:

	1996	*1997*	*1998*
Statutory federal income tax rate	34.0%	34.0%	34.0%
Change in valuation allowance	2.9	6.4	(8.2)
Tax-exempt interest	(.2)	(.2)	(.1)
State income taxes and other	(.4)	1.2	1.2
Effective income tax rate	36.3.%	41.4%	26.9%

Source: Pre-Paid Legal Services, Inc., annual report, December 1998, p. 42.

lowered the tax rate slightly in each year. As is typical of these schedules, state income taxes are omitted from the initial statutory tax rate line. As a result, there is typically a tax increase for state income taxes in moving from the statutory federal to the overall effective tax rate.

Changes in the "valuation allowance" are the primary cause of the increased 1997 effective tax rate and reduced 1998 effective tax rate. The valuation allowance is a contra-asset account and it is adjusted from time to time as prospects for the realization of the deferred tax assets changes (see Exhibit 5.20 for disclosure of PPL's valuation allowance).

Changes in the valuation allowance should typically be viewed as creating nonrecurring increases and decreases in earnings. The sustainable earnings worksheet in Chapter Three includes line items to adjust for these changes in developing the sustainable earnings base (SEB). Moreover, there is discussion of changes in the valuation allowance in Chapter Three in connection with the completion of the SEB worksheet.

In conjunction with the valuation allowance changes, PPL disclosed in its management's discussion and analysis of financial condition and results of operations (MD&A) a tax decrease in 1998 of $3.5 million and a tax increase of $1.9 million in 1997.[30] The 1998 benefit contributed 28% of PPL's $12.7 million net income increase for the year. The PPL earnings quality should be considered enhanced in terms of persistence in 1997 but impaired in 1998.

Significant increases or decreases in effective tax rates above or below expected statutory levels are fairly common. From an analyst's perspective, the key is to distinguish between continuing and nonrecurring increases and decreases. Some additional examples, which provide a contrast to the case of PPL, are presented later in this chapter.

Pre-Paid Legal's Deferred Tax Liabilities and Its Position Quality

For several decades, it has been common for companies to contend, especially with lenders, that analysts should not worry about deferred tax liabilities because "they will never have to be paid."[31] If this is the case, then deferred tax liabilities could represent (1) quasi-equity, (2) a contingent liability, or (3) an overstated liability. In each of these cases, it would be fair to characterize position quality as enhanced.

At the end of 1998, PPL's net deferred tax liability (deferred tax liabilities minus net deferred tax assets) totaled $27 million, or about 27 percent of its shareholders' equity. Many would argue that a deferred tax liability balance that simply grows year after year is much less of a liability than, for example, an equivalent amount of bank debt. Bank debt requires interest payments to service, and it typically has scheduled repayments that are known with reasonable certainty. Analysts and company management will argue that, in some circumstances, deferred tax liabilities should be considered as "quasi-equity" and that they should be added to shareholders' equity in evaluating financial leverage.

Growth in the net deferred tax liabilities of PPL has been driven by the underlying growth in its business and its tax return versus book treatment of commission advances. PPL's total revenues increased by about 550 percent during the five-year period from 1994 through 1998. It will obviously be difficult to maintain this rate of growth and associated increases in the net deferred tax liability. At some point, one should expect that PPL would produce taxable income, incur a current tax provision, and begin to pay some income taxes. In the meantime, however, PPL's tax deferrals improve its cash flow and, arguably, its financial position quality.

Deferred Income Taxes and Position Quality: Further Case Examples

The tax disclosures of Pre-Paid Legal were used to consider the interactions between income tax accounting and the full range of financial quality dimensions, earnings quality in terms of both cash content and persistence, and the quality of financial position. Here, the focus is principally on position quality. However, there remains a relationship between the cash quality of earnings and position quality. For example, the cash quality of earnings will be enhanced if a major source of taxable temporary differences, which give rise to deferred tax liabilities, is likely to continue to exist or grow. Moreover, in this circumstance, position quality would also be considered enhanced.

The Deferred Tax Liability as Quasi-Equity: Pilgrim's Pride Corporation

Pilgrim's Pride Corporation represents a case in which a deferred tax liability appeared to be economically equivalent to shareholders' equity, that is, quasi-equity, or perhaps simply a contingent obligation. A change in the tax law, implemented in 1988, required that Pilgrim's Pride switch, for tax purposes, from the cash to accrual basis of accounting.[32] The Company had already been using the accrual method on its books, and a deferred tax liability had been recorded for the cumulative excess of pretax financial income, under the accrual method, versus taxable income under the cash basis.

This mandated change would normally have required that previously deferred taxes be paid over a relatively limited number of years. However, the new tax law made it possible to avoid payment, on a relatively permanent basis, if certain requirements related to the level of continued family ownership were satisfied. But the 1987 law was changed again in 1997. This change called for the deferred liability to be paid down on a scheduled basis.[33]

Prior to the enactment of the 1997 Act, some analysts took the position that the deferred tax liability associated with the earlier use of cash basis accounting should be considered to be "quasi"-equity. Deferral was essentially permanent if requirements calling for ownership continuity were satisfied. However, the new rules introduced by the Taxpayer Relief Act of 1997 called for the previously deferred amounts to now be taken into income over 20 years, beginning in fiscal 1998.[34] The deferred tax liability that must now be paid down is listed in Exhibit 5.24 as "Prior use of cash accounting." The decline between 1997 and 1998 reflects the initial amortization of the deferred income into taxable earnings and the associated reversal of a portion of the deferred tax liability.

In the absence of the second change in the tax law (i.e., the Taxpayer Relief Act of 1997), the remote likelihood of repayment of this deferred tax liability meant that position quality of Pilgrim's Pride was enhanced. Even now, while the liability must be paid over a period of 20 years, the deferred tax liability should still be viewed as overstated, compared to other liabilities on the balance sheet. Because there is no current requirement for deferred tax liabilities to be carried at their "present value," their current burden is overstated.

To approximate the initial overstatement of the Pilgrim's Pride deferred tax liability from the prior use of cash accounting, consider the balance at the end of fiscal 1997 that is to be paid over the following 20 years. Assuming a level year-end annual payment of $1.7 million ($34 million / 20 years), finding the present value of this stream at 8 percent yields a liability of about $17 million. This indicates a liability overstatement of 100 percent; that is, the balance sheet liability is $34 million but a reasonable approximation of its present value is only $17 million. This is a favorable valuation difference that enhances the quality of the financial position of Pilgrim's Pride.

The pre-1997 circumstances of Pilgrim's Pride (i.e., payment of the deferred tax liability could be avoided on a relatively permanent basis) provided a compelling case for viewing their deferred tax liability as quasi-equity. Most cases are far less clear cut. Currently, some of the more compelling cases are found in capital-intensive industries in which substantial deferred tax liabilities have accumulated over many years. Firms in service industries, financial firms, exclusive of lessors, technology firms, and retailers generally have relatively limited amounts of either deferred tax assets or liabilities.

Deferred Tax Liabilities and Capital-Intensive versus Non–Capital-Intensive Firms

Depreciation is by far the most common and the most material of temporary differences. It should generally follow that the most significant deferred tax liability positions would be found in the disclosures of firms in capital-intensive industries. Exhibit 5.25 provides examples of capital-intensive firms with significant net deferred tax liability positions. Notice that "net" deferred tax liabilities are presented; deferred tax assets have been subtracted from the deferred tax liabilities. Some capital-intensive firms that have significant deferred tax liabilities also have very substantial deferred tax assets.

For example, in its fiscal 1998 annual report, Delta Air Lines disclosed deferred tax liabilities of $1.8 billion, but it had an overall net deferred tax asset position because of offsetting deferred tax assets of $2.0 billion. Although very capital intensive, Hertz disclosed a net deferred tax liability that is less than one might have expected. However, a review of the useful lives for its depreciable assets, especially rental cars, reveals very short lives. As a result, there is less capacity to produce substantial temporary differences due to differences between book and tax return depreciation.

If the likelihood of repayment is sufficiently remote, then treating net deferred tax liabilities as quasi-equity may be in order. Recasting the ratio of liabilities-to-equity can capture the significance of this alternative view of deferred tax liabilities. In Exhibit 5.26, the liabilities-to-equity ratio of Anadarko Petroleum is com-

Exhibit 5.24.   Deferred Tax Liabilities and Assets: Pilgrim's Pride Corporation, Years Ended September 27, 1997, and September 26, 1998 (Thousands of Dollars)

Significant components of the Company's deferred tax liabilities and assets are as follows:

	1997	*1998*
Deferred tax liabilities:		
Tax over book depreciation	$24,584	$25,303
Prior use of cash accounting	34,223	32,905
Other	823	1,059
Total deferred tax liabilities	59,630	59,267
Deferred tax assets:		
Alternative minimum tax credit carryforward	3,518	234
Expenses deductible in different years	6,692	7,643
Total deferred tax asset	10,210	7,877
Net deferred tax liabilities	$49,420	$51,390

Source: Pilgrim's Pride Corporation, Form 10-K annual report to the Securities and Exchange Commission (September 1998), p. 47.

Exhibit 5.25.   Deferred Tax Liabilities and Capital Intensive Firms (Millions of Dollars except percentages)

Company	*Business*	*Net Deferred Tax Liability*	*Percentage of Shareholders' Equity*
CSX Transportation Corp. (1998)	Transportation	$3,045	52
Anadarko Petroleum Corp. (1998)	Petroleum	$523	42
Norfolk Southern Corp. (1998)	Transportation	$2,404	41
Galey & Lord, Inc. (1998)	Textiles	$50	39
Westvaco Corp. (1998)	Paper	$728	32
Southwest Airlines Co. (1998)	Transportation	$528	22
The Hertz Corp. (1997)	Vehicle rental	$166	15

Sources: Companies' annual reports. The year following each company name designates the annual report from which the example was drawn.

Exhibit 5.26. Liability-to-Equity Ratios with Net Deferred Tax Liabilities
as Quasi-Equity: Anadarko Petroleum Company, December 31, 1998 (Millions
of Dollars, except Ratios)

As-Reported Basis		
Liabilities	$2,373	1.88/1
Shareholders' equity	$1,259	
Revised Basis		
Liabilities	$1,850	1.04/1
Shareholders' equity	$1,782	

Source: Anadarko Petroleum Company, annual report, December 1998. Information obtained from
Disclosure, Inc., Compact/D/SEC: Corporate Information on Companies Filing with the SEC (Bethesda, MD: Disclosure, Inc., June 1999).

Exhibit 5.27. Net Deferred Tax Positions: Non–Capital-Intensive Firms
(Millions of Dollars, except Percentages)

Company	Business	Net Deferred Tax (Asset) Liability	Percentage of Shareholders' Equity
Books a Million, Inc. (1999)	Book retailer	$(3)	3
Chico's FAS, Inc. (1999)	Clothing retailer	$(2)	6
Claire's Stores, Inc. (1998)	Clothing retailer	$(7)	2
Gerber Scientific, Inc. (1998)	Technology	$1	0
Paychex, Inc. (1998)	Business services	$2	1
Techne Corp. (1998)	Biotechnology	$3	5

Sources: Companies' annual reports. The year following each company name designates the annual
report from which the example was drawn.

puted on an as-reported basis and then with the net deferred tax liability balance
deducted from liabilities and added back to shareholders' equity.

This alternative view of the nature of net deferred tax liabilities results in a
very substantial reduction in Anadarko's financial leverage as represented by the
relationship of its total liabilities to shareholders' equity. Anadarko Petroleum is
much less highly leveraged if its net deferred tax liability position is treated as
quasi-equity.

To provide a contrast to the more capital-intensive industries, the net deferred
tax positions of less capital-intensive firms are provided in Exhibit 5.27. With
these firms, it is common to observe net deferred tax asset and not net liability
positions. Removing the liability-producing feature of depreciation temporary differences results in the deferred tax asset being dominant.

The net positions in Exhibit 5.27 present an equal mix of net asset and net liability positions. It is common for the non–capital-intensive firms to be in net deferred tax asset positions. First, their depreciation-related temporary differences will be smaller than the capital-intensive firms. Second, the combination of changes in tax law, new accounting standards, restructurings, reorganizations, downsizing, and the like have tipped temporary differences into the direction of "deductible" as opposed to "taxable" temporary differences.

Deferred Taxes and Changes in the Tax Law and in GAAP

The Tax Reform Act of 1986 removed a number of common sources of temporary differences. Most were taxable temporary differences that called for recording deferred tax liabilities. Eliminated, or simply available on a more restrictive basis, were such treatments as:

1. The installment method of accounting for installment sales
2. The completed contract method of accounting for long-term contracts
3. The current expensing of acquisition-related inventory costs
4. The cash basis of accounting
5. The reserve method of accounting for bad debts

In some cases these changes reduced deferred tax liabilities (1, 2, and 4), and in others they created new sources of deferred tax assets (3 and 5).

The combination of existing tax law and new Financial Accounting Standards Board (FASB) statements has also created additional temporary differences over the past 15 years. Several of the more significant standards almost always create deferred tax assets—for example, SFAS No. 106, "Employers' Accounting for Postretirement Benefits,"; SFAS No. 112, "Employers' Accounting for Postemployment Benefits,"; and SFAS No. 121, "Accounting for Impairment of Long-Lived Assets"—while SFAS No. 115, "Accounting for Certain Investments in Debt and Equity Securities," creates deferred tax assets or liabilities depending on whether unrealized investment losses or gains are recognized.[35]

The pace of change over the past decade has resulted in substantial corporate restructurings. Asset write-downs and liability accruals are always associated with these activities. The associated charges are, in whole or in part, recorded as expenses in computing pretax financial income before they can be deducted in the determination of taxable income. The resulting deductible temporary differences require the recording of deferred tax assets.

Financial Quality and the Reversal of Temporary Differences

The focus of much of the discussion to this point in the chapter has been on the prospect of deferred tax liabilities simply continuing to grow. However, should the level of business decline or the depreciable assets of a firm age, then a reversal of temporary differences and the reduction of deferred tax liabilities may result. Exhibit 5.28 provides a graphical presentation of both the origination and reversal of depreciation-related temporary differences. This is similar to the graphical treatment provided in Exhibit 5.21 for the commission advances of Pre-Paid Legal Services. It is provided here as a convenient reference for the discussion that follows.

As long as a firm is, on balance, originating taxable temporary differences—new originating differences exceed reversing temporary differences—then deferred tax liabilities should continue to rise. The firm occupies the originating temporary difference (OTD) regions of Exhibit 5.28. However, when temporary differences begin to reverse, the firm then occupies the reversing temporary differences (RTD) region, part A of Exhibit 5.28. Taxable income will exceed pretax financial income, the RTD region of part B, and the deferred tax liabilities are drawn down, the RTD region of part C. Upon reversal, cash outlays for taxes will exceed the total tax provision and the cash quality of earnings will be impaired.

Whereas individual assets move through a cycle of origination and reversal of temporary differences, the reversing temporary differences are often more than offset by new originating temporary differences. However, for the going and growing firm, it has been relatively uncommon to observe overall declines in deferred tax liabilities. This is especially true if, as is typically the case, the primary source of deferred tax liabilities has been depreciation temporary differences.

A Case of Reversing Temporary Differences: ASA Holdings, Inc.

The net deferred tax liability of ASA Holdings, Inc., a regional airline headquartered in Atlanta, had been increasing from the time of its founding in 1979. Through the end of 1996, ASA Holdings had consistently originated depreciation-related temporary differences. This resulted in positive deferred tax provisions, growth in its deferred tax liabilities, and an excess of its total tax provision over cash tax payments; the cash quality of ASA's earnings was enhanced. However, with an aging fleet, and prior to placing a new generation of aircraft into service, ASA's depreciation-related temporary differences began to reverse.

A 1997 decline in the deferred tax liability related to "Tax over book depreciation" of $3,166,568 is disclosed in Exhibit 5.29. This is the portion of the deferred tax benefit that resulted from the reversal of depreciation-related temporary differences. The remainder of the deferred tax benefit of $2,248,729 (total benefit of $5,415,297 minus the portion related to depreciation of $3,166,568) resulted mainly from originating deductible temporary differences that gave rise to increases in deferred tax assets. Additional insight into the financial effects of reversing temporary differences can be gained by reviewing portions of the financial statements and tax disclosures of ASA Holdings provided in Exhibits 5.29 and 5.30.

In 1997, a deferred tax benefit of $5,415,297 (federal, $4,927,897, and state, $487,400) is disclosed by ASA (Exhibit 5.29). This benefit also appears in the

Exhibit 5.28. Origination and Reversal of Depreciation-Related Deferred
Tax Liabilities

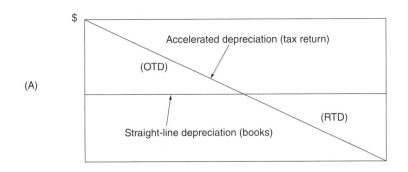

(A)

OTD = Originating temporary difference
RTD = Reversing temporary difference

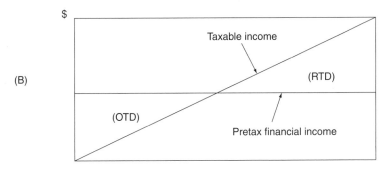

(B)

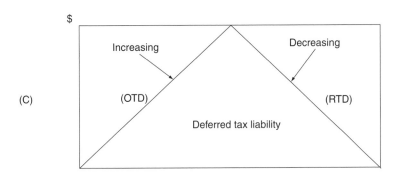

(C)

Exhibit 5.29.   Selected Tax Disclosures: ASA Holdings, Inc., Years Ended
December 31, 1995–1997

NOTE F—INCOME TAXES

Deferred income taxes reflect the net tax effect of temporary differences between the carrying amounts of assets and liabilities for financial reporting purposes and the amounts used for income tax purposes. Significant components of the Company's deferred income tax liabilities and assets as of December 31, 1996 and 1997 are as follows:

	1996	*1997*
Deferred income tax liabilities:		
Tax over book depreciation	$72,736,336	$69,569,768
Other	110,225	737,973
Total deferred income tax liabilities	72,846,561	70,307,741
Deferred income tax assets:		
Accounts receivable and inventory reserves	749,755	1,156,869
Other	2,462,033	4,931,396
Total deferred income tax assets	3,211,788	6,088,265
Net deferred income tax liabilities	$69,634,773	$64,219,476

For financial reporting purposes, the provision for income taxes includes the following components for the years ended December 31, 1995, 1996, and 1997:

	1995	*1996*	*1997*
Federal:			
Current	$23,397,695	$30,993,254	$34,347,947
Deferred	2,978,705	396,046	(4,927,897)
	26,376,400	31,389,300	29,420,050
State:			
Current	2,891,900	3,065,300	3,397,050
Deferred	368,100	39,200	(487,400)
	3,260,000	3,104,500	2,909,650
	$29,636,400	$34,493,800	$32,329,700

Source: ASA Holdings, Inc., annual report, December 1997. Information obtained from Disclosure, Inc., *Compact/D/SEC: Corporate Information on Companies Filing with the SEC* (Bethesda, MD: Disclosure, Inc., September 1998).

Exhibit 5.30. Partial Statements of Cash Flows: ASA Holdings, Inc., Years
Ended December 31, 1995–1997

ASA Holdings, Inc.
Partial Consolidated Statement of Cash Flows

	1995	1996	1997
Operating Activities			
Net Income	$51,137,417	$56,612,720	$54,511,615
Adjustments to reconcile net income to			
net cash provided by operating activities:			
Depreciation	26,794,942	26,518,027	27,351,713
Amortization and provision for			
obsolescence	900,393	1,016,030	1,334,551
Amortization of engine overhauls	7,710,438	6,656,680	7,381,705
Deferred income taxes	3,346,805	435,246	(5,415,297)
Other	(174,173)	(107,722)	2,051,505
Changes in operating assets and liabilities:			
Receivables	(5,014,461)	5,187,991	(229,971)
Expendable parts	640,194	(1,859,712)	863,596
Other assets	(3,147,901)	742,274	(5,517,143)
Accrued compensation and related			
expenses	3,014,807	983,488	4,330,204
Accrued interest payable	(195,201)	(1,622,461)	(261,030)
Other liabilities	10,971,435	(1,213,312)	4,515,089
Income taxes payable	(1,243,399)	—	6,395,077
Net cash provided by operating activities	94,741,296	93,349,249	97,311,614
Investing Activities			
Purchase of marketable securities	(198,048,934)	(189,882,992)	(167,840,499)
Proceeds from sale of marketable			
securities	210,597,389	258,806,167	149,001,159
Purchases of property and equipment			
including advance payments	(13,851,990)	(15,321,851)	(46,188,478)
Purchase of investments	—	—	(11,777,109)
Other	5,329,796	5,699,260	698,075
Net cash provided by (used in)			
investing activities	4,026,261	59,300,584	(76,106,852)

Source: ASA Holdings, Inc., annual report, December 1997. Information obtained from Disclosure, Inc., *Compact/D/SEC: Corporate Information on Companies Filing with the SEC* (Bethesda, MD: Disclosure, Inc., September 1998).

statement of cash flows (Exhibit 5.30), where it is deducted from net income in arriving at cash from operating activities. The tax effects of reversing temporary differences are recorded by reducing the deferred tax liabilities and offsetting this change with a deferred tax benefit. There is no current cash inflow associated with this recorded tax benefit. Rather, the cash benefit was realized when the temporary difference originated.

Upon origination, tax return depreciation exceeded that in the book income statement, thereby reducing taxable income and tax payments. Upon reversal, tax return depreciation is less than book depreciation, thereby increasing taxable income and tax payments.

Viewed separately, the deferred tax benefit does reduce the total tax provision, but it does not increase net income. This is because it is offset in turn by the increase in the current tax provision. The current provision increases upon reversal of a taxable temporary difference because taxable income is increased above the level of pretax financial income. Again, reference to Exhibit 5.28, section B, shows that the reversal of a taxable temporary difference increases taxable income in relationship to pretax financial income.

The recognition of "deferred" tax benefits, whether by reducing deferred tax liabilities or increasing deferred tax assets, involves no cash inflow. Cash outflows and inflows are represented only by the presence of a "current" tax provision or "current" tax benefit. This follows from the fact that (1) the current tax provision or benefit is based on results in the tax return, and (2) income taxes are paid or recovered only on the basis of tax return results.

A review of the partial cash flow statement in Exhibit 5.30 helps to understand the reason for the partial reversal of ASA's depreciation-related temporary differences. Observe, in the operating activities section of the cash flow statement, that in the years 1995 and 1996 depreciation expense exceeded new purchases of "Property and equipment including advance payments," found in the investing activities section of the cash flow statement, by almost two times. This resulted in a decline in net property and equipment in the balance sheet of ASA Holdings. This decline in property and equipment, the underlying source of almost all of the company's deferred tax liabilities, led to the 1997 reversal of the depreciation-related temporary differences.

While net property and equipment including advance payments declined in 1995 and 1996, this balance increased in 1997. Expenditures on property and equipment, including advances, amounted to $46 million and were offset by only $27 million of depreciation. However, the majority of the $46 million outlay was for advances related to future aircraft acquisitions. That is, there was little or no increase in depreciable property and equipment.

A return to a condition where depreciation-related temporary differences are originating would call for a rebuilding of the company's depreciable assets. This had not yet happened by the end of 1998. ASA's depreciation-related deferred tax liability declined by a further $2.7 million in 1998, and ASA once again reported a deferred tax benefit of about $3.0 million.

ASA has an active aircraft acquisition and fleet expansion program underway. Therefore, it would seem likely that this should return the firm to originating depreciation-related temporary differences. This will result in turn in the deferral of taxes and enhancement of the cash quality of its earnings.

In the past, however, ASA has placed heavy reliance on financing aircraft acquisitions through leases. Leased aircraft will not result in the increase in depreciation expense that would be required to once again produce tax deferrals. Though, acquisition of new aircraft through leasing does present separate tax advantages.

Ownership of aircraft, and the use of accelerated depreciation methods in the tax return, raises the possibility that ASA would be required to pay the alternative minimum tax (AMT). The excess of accelerated depreciation, over the amount permitted under the AMT, is normally treated as a tax preference and added back to regular taxable income in arriving at AMT income. There are also other adjustments and exemptions.[36] Ownership of new aircraft presents an opportunity for ASA to return to a tax deferral position. However, ownership also may result in a tax disadvantage by moving ASA into an AMT position. ASA no doubt evaluates these trade-offs as it decides on the optimal mix of ownership and leasing for its new aircraft acquisitions.

Taxes and Earnings Quality: Case Examples

Illustrations of the substantial effect that income taxes can have on the quality of financial position have been provided above. In addition, the effects on financial quality of temporary-difference reversals have been examined. Here, some additional examples of the effects of income taxes on earnings quality are provided.

Taxes and the Cash Quality of Earnings

On a year-to-year basis, the effects of income taxes on the cash quality of earnings can be judged from the combination of the signs and the amounts of current and deferred tax provisions. The possible combinations of the signs of current and deferred tax provisions, and their implications for the cash quality of earnings, are summarized in Exhibit 5.31.

Notice that the cash quality of earnings is enhanced in cases 1 and 3 in Exhibit 5.31 in which the deferred tax provision is positive. A positive deferred provision means that a portion of the total tax provision does not require a cash outlay. In both cases 1 and 3, the deferred tax provision will be added back to net income in the statement of cash flows. The extent of the strengthening of cash quality depends on the size of the deferred provision in relationship to the total tax provision as well as the likelihood that the deferral will persist. The negative current provision in case 3 means that taxes are being refunded to the company. This would normally be the result of a loss or tax credit carryback.[37]

Cash quality is impaired in cases 2 and 4 because the deferred tax provisions are negative (i.e., benefits). However, with a deferred tax benefit there is no as-

Exhibit 5.31. Current and Deferred Provisions and the Cash Quality of Earnings

	Case 1	Case 2	Case 3	Case 4
Current tax provision	+	+	—	—
Deferred tax provision	+	—	+	—
Tax provision to payments (refunds) relationships	Prov. > Pmt.	Prov. < Pmt.	Prov. > Ref.	Ref. < Prov.
Cash quality of earnings	Enhanced	Impaired	Enhanced	Impaired

Prov., tax provision; Pmt., tax payment; Ref., tax refund.

sociated cash inflow. There will be a cash inflow in case 4 from the "current" tax benefit. However, cash quality is still diminished because the total benefit, current plus deferred, exceeds the amount of the tax recovery, which is equal only to the "current" benefit. This interpretation would be reinforced by a statement of cash flows in which the deferred benefit would be deducted from net income in arriving at cash flows from operating activities.

Examples from practice, which illustrate the four cases in Exhibit 5.31, are provided in Exhibit 5.32.

Norfolk and Southern's deferred tax provision is positive each year and its cash quality is strengthened. The Kellwood Company situation is the exact opposite; its deferred tax provision is negative, a benefit, each year and its cash quality is impaired. The 1996 current and deferred tax combination of the Fairchild Corporation conforms to case 3 of Exhibit 5.31. Because the current benefit of $39,723,000 exceeded the total benefits recognized of $26,230,000 in 1996, cash quality is enhanced. The cash recovered from previously paid taxes is greater than the total tax benefit recognized. The year 1999 of First Aviation Services conforms to case 4 of Exhibit 5.31. A total tax benefit of $699 is recognized, but only $422 would represent a refund of taxes. Cash quality is somewhat impaired.

Taxes and the Persistence Dimension of Earnings Quality

The tax rate reconciliation schedule is key to the analysis of taxes and the persistence dimension of earnings quality. The focus of analysis should be the identification of increases or decreases in the effective tax rate that are unlikely to be recurring. Some examples are presented and discussed below.

Reduced Foreign Tax Rates and Tax Liability Reversals: C. R. Bard, Inc.

The case of C. R. Bard presents some tax rate reductions that appear to be recurring and some that do not. Bard's tax rate reconciliation schedule is presented in Exhibit 5.33. The persistence of Bard's tax benefits from its foreign operations hinges on (1) the continued availability of the benefits in the tax law, and (2) Bard's capacity to continue to operate in such a way that it earns such benefits. These

Exhibit 5.32.   Taxes and Cash Quality: Case Examples (Thousands of Dollars)

Case 1, Cash quality enhanced: Norfolk Southern (1998)

	1996	1997	1998
Current income taxes	$321,000	$224,000	$101,000
Deferred income taxes	92,000	75,000	114,000
Total income tax provision	$413,000	$299,000	$215,000

Case 2, Cash quality diminished: Kellwood Company (1999)

	1997	1998	1999
Current income taxes	$34,613	$39,531	$11,057
Deferred income taxes	(7,446)	(2,031)	(5,531)
Total income tax provision	$27,167	$37,500	$ 5,526

Case 3, Cash quality enhanced (in 1996): The Fairchild Corporation (1997)

	1995	1996	1997
Current income taxes	$(6,700)	$(39,723)	$7,295
Deferred income taxes	(26,806)	13,403	(12,495)
Total income tax provision	$(33,506)	$(26,230)	$(5,200)

Case 4, Cash quality diminished: First Aviation Services, Inc. (1999)

	1997	1998	1999
Current income taxes	$—	$2,257	$(442)
Deferred income taxes	—	(757)	(257)
Total income tax provision	$—	$1,500	$(699)

Sources: Companies' annual reports. The year following each company name designates the annual report from which the example was drawn.

two requirements mean that there is some uncertainty about being able to produce these benefits at their 1996–1998 levels. The continuation of any element of income is subject to varying degrees of uncertainty. However, in addition to normal operational uncertainties, maintenance of these tax benefits hinges on the continuation of the relevant tax law. While no precise level of uncertainty can be specified in the present case, Bard's earnings quality is somewhat impaired in terms of persistence as a result of the Irish and Puerto Rican tax benefits. In recent years, there has been some reduction in the tax benefits available to operations located in Puerto Rico, and this may explain some of the reduction in these benefits over the 1996–1998 interval.

The 15 percent point reduction in the effective tax rate in 1996 is nonrecurring. It resulted from the removal of a tax liability accrued in an earlier period that was no longer deemed to be necessary. Earnings are temporarily elevated by this benefit and earnings quality is thus impaired in terms of persistence. This is

Exhibit 5.33.   Recurring and Nonrecurring Tax Rate Reductions: C. R. Bard, Inc., Years Ended December 31, 1996–1998

	1996	*1997*	*1998*
U.S. federal statutory rate	35%	35%	35%
State income taxes, net of federal income tax benefits	3	3	3
Foreign operations taxed at less than the U.S. statutory rate, primarily Ireland and Puerto Rico	(13)	(10)	(8)
Reversal of tax reserve	(15)	—	—
Other, net	—	3	5
Effective tax rate	10%	31%	35%

Source: C. R. Bard, Inc., annual report, December 1998. Information obtained from Disclosure, Inc., *Compact/D/SEC: Corporate Information on Companies Filing with the SEC* (Bethesda, MD: Disclosure, Inc., June 1999).

apparent from the effective rate increase of from 10 percent in 1996 up to 31 percent in 1997.

The remaining rate increases of 3 percent and 5 percent are not explained in Bard's disclosures. An inquiry of management would be necessary to assess their influence on the sustainability of these increases.[38]

Foreign Sales Corporations, Litigation, and Fines: Archer Daniels Midland Company

The tax rate reconciliation schedule of Archer Daniels Midland (ADM) Company is presented in Exhibit 5.34. Favorable tax treatment of the earnings of foreign sales corporations (FSCs) has reduced its effective tax rate in each of the last three years.[39] The percentage benefit fluctuates because of both changes in pretax financial income as well as the absolute dollar amount of the benefit. The absolute dollar benefits amounted to approximately $25 million, $22 million, and $28 million, respectively, for 1996, 1997, and 1998. These benefits appear to be recurring in nature, but analysts must remember that the degree of control over these benefits is generally less than comparable elements of profits produced from core operating activities.

The increases in the effective tax rates, 1997 and 1998, from the effects of the nondeductibility of litigation settlements and fines are nonrecurring. However, the actual nonrecurring items are the dollar amounts of the litigation settlements and fines. Because they are nondeductible (i.e., permanent differences), a restatement of earnings to remove the effects of nonrecurring items would simply add these nondeductible amounts back to net income. That is, their pretax and after-tax amounts are the same.

In completing the sustainable earnings worksheet of Chapter Three, the amounts of the litigation settlements and fines would simply be added back to net income as part of tax items and other items that are already tax-adjusted (e.g.,

Exhibit 5.34. Nonrecurring Tax-Rate Increases: Archer Daniels Midland, Years Ended June 30, 1996–1998

A reconciliation of the federal statutory tax rate to the Company's effective tax rate follows:

	1996	1997	1998
Federal statutory tax rate	35.0%	35.0%	35.0%
Foreign sales corporation	(2.4)	(3.4)	(4.7)
State income taxes, net of federal benefit	2.2	2.7	2.4
Litigation settlement and fines	—	7.5	1.4
Other	(0.8)	(0.4)	(0.3)
	33.8%	41.4%	33.8%

Source: Archer Daniels Midland Company annual report, June 1998, p. 32.

Exhibit 5.35. Foreign Sales Corporations and Research Tax Credits: Gerber Scientific, Inc., Years Ended April 30, 1996–1998

	1996	1997	1998
Federal income taxes at statutory rate	35.0%	35.0%	35.0%
State income taxes, net of federal benefit	0.9	0.7	(0.4)
Foreign tax rate differences	—	0.8	3.8
Life insurance benefits	—	(1.6)	—
Tax-exempt interest income	(3.8)	(3.4)	(4.6)
Foreign Sales Corporation	(2.4)	(2.2)	(10.9)
R&D tax credits	(0.2)	(3.2)	(5.2)
Goodwill amortization	0.9	1.2	4.7
Other, net	1.7	0.6	2.9
Provision for income taxes	35.3%	27.9%	25.3%

Source: Gerber Scientific, Inc., annual report, April 1998, p. 45.

extraordinary items, losses on discontinued operations). These adjustments are made in the second section of the sustainable earnings worksheet.

Gerber Scientific, Inc.: Foreign Sales Corporations and Research Tax Credits

Gerber Scientific has a number of items that cause its effective tax rate to either exceed or fall short of the statutory federal rate. In gauging the potential effects of these items on the persistence dimension of earnings quality, the key is to distinguish between those sources of increases or decreases that are likely to continue versus those that appear to be nonrecurring. As in much of financial analysis, items will frequently not fall neatly into one or the other of these two categories.

Three of the reconciling items represent the tax effects of permanent differences, life insurance benefits, tax-exempt interest income, and goodwill amortization. The entries for these items simply represent the tax reduction for the nontaxable items of income (i.e., life insurance benefits and tax-exempt interest income), and the tax increase due to nondeductible goodwill amortization. Only the underlying life insurance benefits should be considered to be nonrecurring. In completing the sustainable earnings worksheet presented in Chapter Three, the life insurance benefits would be deducted from net income, along with tax items and items already presented in the income statement on an after-tax basis. Given their nontaxable status, the pretax and after-tax amounts of the insurance benefits are the same.

The R&D tax credits could represent a continuing benefit. However, as discussed earlier in this chapter, continuation of these benefits requires Congress to periodically renew the benefit. Further, Gerber must normally make incremental R&D expenditures to earn further benefits. Given the level of uncertainty associated with continuation of these benefits, these benefits should be considered nonrecurring.

ASSESSING THE REALIZABILITY OF DEFERRED TAX ASSETS

SFAS No. 109 introduced a unique new requirement that called for an assessment for the likelihood that deferred tax assets, once recorded, would be realized. The form that "realization" takes depends on whether the deferred tax asset results from a loss carryforward, or deductible temporary difference. The key to realization is that sufficient taxable income be earned within the carryforward period. Moreover, in the case of capital loss carryforwards, capital gains must be produced during the carryforward period. Further, in the case of state, federal, and foreign carryforwards, taxable income must be produced in the appropriate taxing jurisdictions in order to serve as a basis for realization of deferred tax assets.

The mandate to assess the realizability of deferred tax assets was outlined as follows in SFAS No. 109:

> Reduce deferred tax assets by a **valuation allowance** if, based on the weight of available evidence, *it is more likely than not* (a likelihood of more than 50 percent) that some or all of the deferred tax assets will not be realized. The valuation allowance should be sufficient to reduce the deferred tax asset to the amount that is more likely than not to be realized.[40]

The "valuation allowance," referred to above, is a contra-asset account and is analagous to an allowance for doubtful accounts. It represents that portion of the deferred tax assets that is not expected to be realized. Significant judgment is required in arriving at the proper contra-asset balance in the case of both accounts receivable and deferred tax assets. However, unlike accounts receivable, SFAS 109 introduced a specific probability threshold to employ in estimating the like-

Exhibit 5.36.   Positive and Negative Evidence and Deferred-Tax-Asset
Realization

Positive evidence
- Existing contracts or firm sales backlog that will produce more than enough taxable income to realize the deferred tax asset based on existing sales prices and cost structures.
- An excess of appreciated asset value over the tax basis of the entity's assets in an amount sufficient to realize the deferred tax asset.
- A strong earnings history exclusive of the loss that created the future deductible amount . . . with evidence indicating the loss (for example, an unusual, infrequent, or extraordinary item) is an aberration rather than a continuing condition.

Negative evidence
- A history of operating-loss or tax-credit carryforwards expiring unused.
- Losses expected in early future years (by a presently profitable entity).
- Unsettled circumstances that, if unfavorably resolved, would adversely affect future operations and profit levels on a continuing basis in future years.
- A carryback or carryforward period that is so brief that it would limit relization of tax benefits if (1) a significant deductible temporary difference is expected to reverse in a single year or (2) the enterprise operates in a traditionally cyclical business.

Source: SFAS No. 109, *Accounting for Income Taxes* (Norwalk, CT: Financial Accounting Standards Board, February 1992, para. 23–24).

lihood of realization of deferred tax assets. Beyond this realization threshold, the Statement includes other specific guidance for judging the likelihood of realization.

GAAP Guidance on Assessing Realization

In assessing the likelihood of realizing deferred tax assets, SFAS 109 calls for the consideration of all relevant positive and negative evidence.[41] Examples of positive and negative evidence provided in SFAS 109 are summarized in Exhibit 5.36. This listing is brief and does not exhaust the factors that might be relevant in assessing the likelihood of realization. The objective of the assessment process is to identify any facts, conditions, or circumstances that help to judge the timing and amounts of future taxable income. Again, future taxable income is the key to realization.

SFAS 109 also provides additional guidance by suggesting four possible sources of future taxable income that might be available to realize a tax benefit for deductible temporary differences and carryforwards.[42] These sources are listed in Exhibit 5.37.

With respect to item one in Exhibit 5.37, a review of panel B of Exhibit 5.28 highlights how the reversal of a "taxable" temporary difference increases the level of taxable income in relationship to pretax financial income. Again, realization of

Exhibit 5.37.   Realization of Deferred Tax Assets: Possible Sources
of Taxable Income

1. Future reversals of existing taxable temporary differences
2. Future taxable income exclusive of reversing temporary differences
3. Taxable income in prior carryback (years) if carryback is permitted under the tax law
4. Tax planning strategies that would, if necessary, be implemented to, for example:
   a. Accelerate taxable amounts to utilize expiring carryforwards
   • Structure a sale so as to avoid installment-sale treatment and make possible imme-
     diate recognition of the entire gain on the sale
   • Sell installment receivables to accelerate the reversal of the associated taxable tem-
     porary difference for the gains on installment sales
   b. Change the character of taxable or deductible amounts from ordinary income or loss
      to capital gain or loss
   c. Switch from tax-exempt to taxable investments
   d. Accelerate the reversal of deductible temporary differences so as to offset taxable
      income expected in early future years
   • Dispose of inventory already carried at net realizable value on the books to accelerate
     a tax deduction in the tax return
   • Sell loans carried net of an allowance for bad debt to accelerate tax deduction of the
     allowance for bad debts

Source: Adapted from SFAS No. 109, *Accounting for Income Taxes* (Norwalk, CT: Financial Accounting Standards Baord, February 1992, para. 21 and pp. 246–248).

Exhibit 5.38.   Valuation Allowance Target: Analog Devices, Inc., Years
Ended November 30, 1995–1997 (Thousands of Dollars)

	1995	*1996*	*1997*
Deferred tax assets:			
Inventory reserves	$18,309	$20,061	$21,734
Capital loss carryover	8,513	7,394	5,559
	—	—	—
	—	—	—
Total gross deferred tax assets	54,478	55,523	66,113
Valuation allowance for deferred tax assets	(10,035)	(7,394)	(5,559)
Total deferred tax assets	$44,443	$48,129	$60,554

Source: Analog Devices, Inc., annual report, November 1997. Information obtained from Disclosure,
Inc., *Compact D/SEC: Corporate Information on Public Companies Filing with the SEC* (Bethesda,
MD: Disclosure, Inc., September 1998).

deferred tax assets hinges on the production of sufficient future taxable income in the right periods. Reversing taxable temporary differences can be a source of such income.

Some available research highlights the importance of a firm's overall position with respect to taxable temporary differences when it comes to assessing the likelihood of realizing deferred tax assets. The presence of a net deferred-tax-liability position, as opposed to a net deferred-tax-asset position, appears to represent positive evidence. That is, the need for a valuation allowance is diminished when a firm is in a net deferred tax liability position. From a sample of 100 firms with both net deferred tax asset and liability positions, only 43 percent of the firms with net deferred tax liability positions recorded valuation allowances against 72 percent of those firms with net deferred tax asset positions.[43]

The logic of this finding is that the presence of a net deferred tax liability means that, upon reversal, more taxable income will be created than deductible expenses. If the reversals occur in the appropriate periods, then realization of the deferred tax assets is reasonably assured.

The Composition of Deferred-Tax-Asset Valuation Allowances

Once established, firms seldom enumerate the composition of the valuation allowance. That is, the specific deferred tax assets for which the valuation allowance is established are not identified. Such enumeration would give analysts an opportunity to perform their own assessment of the deferred tax assets that management views as unlikely to be realized. However, in some cases, the subject of the valuation allowance is clear because the valuation allowance is equal to the amount of a disclosed deferred tax asset balance.

For example, a partial display of the deferred tax assets and valuation allowances of Analog Devices, Inc. (Exhibit 5.38) makes it clear that deferred tax assets associated with capital loss carryovers are the target of the valuation allowances in 1996 and 1997. The valuation allowances are equal to the deferred tax assets associated with the capital loss carryovers.

Analog Devices and the Earnings Management Potential of the Valuation Allowance

It is interesting to note that Analog Devices used up the last of its capital loss carryover in 1998. Both the $5,559,000 deferred tax asset and the associated valuation disappeared from the 1998 fiscal year-end balances. Moreover, the $5,559,000 reduction in the valuation allowance also appeared in the tax-reconciliation schedule. The realized benefit from the capital loss carryover reduced the 1998 tax provision by $5,559,000 and increased net income by the same amount.

Over a several year period, Analog Devices managed to steadily use up its capital loss carryforward. Yet, over the period from 1995 to 1997, the associated deferred tax assets were fully reserved by the valuation allowance.[44] The simultaneous realization and recognition into earnings of the capital loss carryforwards injected a steady earnings boost each year for several years.[45] A firm interested in producing a somewhat smoother earnings stream might fully reserve (record a 100 percent valuation allowance) the tax-saving potential of a loss carryover upon its origination. Then, by timing the realization of capital gains, it could realize this tax benefit over several future years. This is not to suggest that Analog Devices was in fact motivated by a degree of earnings management in its treatment of its capital loss carryforwards and its realized capital gains.

SOME RELEVANT RESEARCH FINDINGS

There is some available research that bears on the tax reporting and analysis issues discussed above. This work breaks down quite neatly into the topical areas of temporary differences and effective tax rates.

Research Bearing on Decisions Creating Temporary Differences

This work studies the relationship between tax advice dealing with the conformity of treatments for book and tax return purposes.[46] In particular, the work suggests that decisions about book and tax-return treatments are not independent, as apparently has been a traditional view. Rather, the research concludes that:

> When the treatment of a transaction is ambiguous, tax preparers' recommendations regarding the tax treatment are influenced by the corresponding financial accounting treatment. Specifically, without conformity of tax and financial accounting treatments, subjects estimated the probability of an IRS audit as being greater and the probability of successfully defending aggressive tax positions as lower. In turn, the strength with which tax-preparer subjects recommended aggressive tax return positions was significantly greater in the presence of financial accounting conformity than in its absence.[47]

Temporary differences are sometimes inevitable because GAAP and tax law requirements are simply different. For example, a sale-leaseback transaction may require that a gain be deferred for book purposes, while the tax law calls for its immediate inclusion in taxable income. However, in other cases temporary differences simply result from an accounting policy "choice" made by a firm. An example of an "aggressive" choice could be the decision of Pre-Paid Legal Services, discussed earlier in this chapter, to capitalize and amortize commission advances for book purposes but to expense them immediately in the tax return. The above research suggests that the lack of conformity between the book and tax return treatment of item of revenue and gain or expense and loss may increase the possibility of an Internal Revenue Service (IRS) audit.

Research Bearing on Effective Tax Rates

Prior to the enactment of the Tax Reform Act of 1986, there was a growing sense that some large and profitable firms were failing to pay their fair share of taxes, or in some cases not paying any taxes at all. This view provided the foundation for the introduction of the AMT, discussed earlier in this chapter. The research cited here considered whether there was evidence that firms took discretionary actions designed to increase their effective tax rates.[48] The presumption is that a higher effective tax rate reduces the likelihood of being accused of not paying one's fair share of taxes.

For the purposes of this study, the effective rate was defined as the current tax provision divided by pretax accounting income. This study tested, among others, the proposition that firms with low effective tax rates might attempt to increase these rates by using discretionary accounting accruals that would reduce book income without affecting taxable income. If book income were decreased, with no offsetting effect on the current tax provision, then the effective tax rate would be increased.

Elsewhere in this chapter, the deferred tax provision is part of the computation of the effective tax rate. However, here the effective tax rate is simply the current tax provision divided by pretax financial income. A decrease in pretax financial income, with no offsetting change in the current provision, results in an increase in the effective tax rate.

The results of this research were generally consistent with expectations. That is, the sample firms did appear to engage in discretionary accounting accruals to increase their effective tax rates.

SUMMARY

The purpose of this chapter has been to (1) outline and illustrate the foundations of accounting and reporting for income taxes along with the associated disclosures required under GAAP, and (2) to identify and illustrate the implications of income taxes and associated disclosures for financial analysis. The analytical framework of "financial quality assessment" has been applied in linking tax reporting and associated disclosures with their implications for financial analysis.

The key points made in this chapter are:

- Pretax financial (shareholder) income and taxable (tax return) income are usually different. Whereas the total tax provision or benefit is based on pretax financial income or loss, income taxes are always paid, or recovered in the case of losses, based on taxable income or loss.
- Disparities between pretax financial and taxable income result from both temporary and permanent differences. Temporary differences result mainly from inclusion of revenues or gains and expenses or losses in the determination of pretax financial income in different periods than in the determination of taxable income.
- Upon origination, taxable temporary differences initially cause pretax financial income to exceed taxable income, and they give rise to deferred tax liabilities.

Upon reversal, taxable temporary differences result in an excess of taxable income over pretax financial income.

- Upon origination, deductible temporary differences cause pretax financial income to be less than taxable income and they give rise to deferred tax assets. Upon reversal, deductible temporary differences result in an excess of pretax financial income over taxable income.

- The tax provision is deducted from pretax financial income in arriving at net income, while a tax benefit is deducted from a pretax financial loss in arriving at a net loss. The total income tax provision is based on the taxable portion of pretax financial income or loss (i.e., pretax financial income or loss with permanent differences excluded). The total provision may also be either increased or decreased by other tax credits or charges. The total tax provision or benefit is made up of current and deferred elements and GAAP requires that this breakdown be disclosed.

- If the total tax provision includes a positive deferred tax provision, then the cash quality of results is enhanced. That is, cash tax payments are less than the tax provision. However, if the tax provision includes a deferred tax benefit, then the cash quality of results is impaired. Here, cash tax payments exceed the tax provision. Deferred tax provisions and benefits are usually distinguished by the presence of parentheses in cases of tax benefits and the absence of parentheses in cases of deferred tax provisions.

- The quality of financial position may be enhanced by the presence of relatively stable or growing net deferred tax liabilities. Stable or growing deferred tax liabilities are typically associated with depreciation-related temporary differences. As long as the level of fixed assets is maintained or increased, the deferred tax liability will be stable or growing. In such cases, the deferred tax liability may be considered a form of quasi-equity. A review of the schedule of deferred tax assets and liabilities will reveal the sources of a net deferred tax liability position and help the analyst to judge, from its sources, the likelihood of its continuation.

- The presence of a significant net deferred tax asset position may reduce position quality. Deferred tax assets share many of the characteristics of goodwill, an asset that is often dismissed in the evaluation of financial position. Deferred tax assets are intangible and they have no separable value, unlike some intangible assets (e.g., a patent). Further, deferred tax assets can be only be realized if the firm produces sufficient taxable income in the future and produces such income in the appropriate periods.

- Both deferred tax assets and liabilities should be considered overstated because of the failure of current GAAP to require that they be stated at their present value. From this perspective alone, this means that a firm's liabilities are overstated if it has a net deferred tax liability position. Similarly, a firm's assets are overstated if it has a net deferred tax asset position.

- Increases and decreases in effective tax rates that come from nonrecurring sources result in increases and decreases in earnings quality, respectively, in terms of persistence. Examples of nonrecurring decreases in effective rates in-clude the favorable resolution of disputes with tax authorities, research and experimentation tax credits, and the realization of previously unrecognized net operating loss carryforward benefits. Nonrecurring increases in effective rates are less common. However, an example could be a nonrecurring addition to taxes from an unfavorable resolution of a tax dispute that was either not pre-viously recognized in the tax provision or not adequately recognized. The tax rate reconciliation schedule is the key source of information on the reasons for increases and decreases in effective tax rates.

- Deferred tax assets must be recorded on all deductible temporary differences as well as loss and tax-credit carryforwards. Once recorded, the prospects of these assets being realized must be assessed. If the prospect of their not being realized, in whole or in part, is over 50 percent, then a valuation allowance must be set off against the portion that is unlikely to be realized. It is common for deferred tax asset to be recognized and then immediately fully reserved through the valuation allowance. That is, the deferred tax asset remains but it is fully offset by the valuation allowance, a contra-asset account.

- In cases where maintaining the assumption of a going concern becomes more tenuous, then a less positive view should be taken of reserved deferred tax assets. The realization of deferred tax assets ultimately hinges on the production of taxable income. If this does not take place, then the deferred tax assets have little or no liquidation value. In a sense, they share some of the same charac-teristics of goodwill. The defrred tax assets are both (1) intangible, and (2) not separable assets. However, even in this case, there is some possibility that the tax attributes that underlie deferred tax assets (e.g., loss or tax-credit carryovers) could be utilized by another firm through a properly structured acquisition.

- The flexibility and complexity associated with the deferred-tax-asset valuation allowance makes it a potentially powerful earnings-management tool. Analysts need to make some effort to assess the valuation-allowance decisions of com-panies in conducting their own financial analysis. An impression that a company employs valuation-allowance adjustments to smooth earnings or to hit earnings targets, should raise some concern about similar activity in other areas.

GLOSSARY

Alternative minimum tax (AMT)   The AMT is a tax beyond that computed under the regular tax system. The AMT calculation starts with taxable income and then makes a number of required adjustments to arrive at alternative minimum taxable income. The AMT tax is computed as 20 percent of AMT income. If the AMT tax is greater than the tax under the regular tax system, then this additional amount must be paid, together with the regular tax. How-ever, the amount of tax paid in excess of the regular tax can then be carried forward indefinitely. The carryover amount can be used in years when the regular tax amount exceeds the AMT.

Alternative minimum tax system   A tax system designed to ensure that all taxpayers with substantial economic income pay some tax. This is achieved by adding back to regular taxable income a number of exclusions and deductions.

Basis   A term that generally refers to the cost or carrying value of an asset or liability for income tax purposes.

Basis differences   Differences between the cost or carrying value of assets and liabilities for shareholder reporting versus income tax purposes. Basis differences are the source of deferred tax assets and liabilities. Deferred tax assets and liabilities represent the tax effects of cumulative annual temporary differences (i.e., basis differences).

Capital loss carryback and carryforward   For U.S. Federal income tax purposes, any excess of current-period capital losses over current-period capital gains may be carried back for three years and forward for five years. Corporations can only realize the tax-saving potential of net capital losses by setting them off against past or future capital gains.

Capitalize or capitalized   The recording of an expenditure on the balance sheet as an asset instead of in the income statement as an expense. If an outlay is capitalized in the shareholder books, but is expensed in the tax return, a temporary difference results and an associated deferred tax liability must be recorded.

Carrybacks   Losses or tax credits that can be used to recompute either taxable income (loss carrybacks) or the current tax provisions (tax credit carrybacks) of previous years. Tax refunds result only from carrybacks.

Carryforwards   Losses or tax credits that exceed those that can be utilized through carryback provisions of the tax law. Loss carryforwards are realized by setting them off against future taxable income, and tax credit carryforwards are realized by setting them off against future current tax provisions.

Cash tax rate   The current tax provision divided by pretax financial income before discontinued operations, extraordinary items, and the cumulative effect of accounting changes.

Charge   A term commonly used to refer to the recording of expenses and losses.

Combined tax rate   An income tax rate that combines both federal and state taxes.

Credit   A term commonly used to refer to the recording of revenues and gains.

Current income tax provision (expense)   That portion of the total tax provision that is based on taxable income.

Deductible temporary differences   A temporary difference that, upon origination, causes pretax financial income to be reduced below the level of taxable income. Upon origination, deductible temporary differences give rise to deferred tax assets. Upon reversal, deductible temporary differences cause taxable income to be reduced below the level of pretax financial income. That is, upon reversal an additional expense deduction is available in the tax return.

Deferred tax assets   Future tax benefits that result from (1) the origination of a deductible temporary difference or (2) a loss, credit, or other carryover. These future tax benefits are realized upon either the reversal of deductible temporary differences or the offsetting of a loss carryforward against taxable income or a tax-credit carryforward against the current tax provision. Also see "deductible temporary differences."

Deferred income tax benefit   A portion of the total tax provision that either reduces a pretax loss or increases net income. It is essentially a negative expense, and it therefore improves results for the period. This label is also used on occasion for deferred tax assets.

Deferred tax liabilities   Future tax obligations that result from the origination of taxable temporary differences. Upon origination, these temporary differences cause pretax financial income to exceed taxable income. Also see "taxable temporary differences."

Deferred tax provision   That portion of the total tax provision that is the result of current period originations and reversals of temporary differences. Equivalently, the tax provision that results from current period changes in cumulative asset and liability basis differences.

Earnings management   The selective recognition of revenues or gains and expenses or losses so as to achieve a target earnings objective. The methods employed should fall within the boundaries of choice and flexibility that are part of the application of generally accepted accounting principles. If carried too far, earnings management turns into fraudulent financial reporting. There is the same tension here as in the distinction between tax avoidance (is to be expected) and tax evasion (may get you put in jail).

Effective tax rate   The total tax provision divided by pretax financial income before discontinued operations, extraordinary items and the cumulative effect of accounting changes.

Income tax expense   The total income tax expense is the deduction made from pretax financial income for both current and deferred taxes. Where a benefit is disclosed, its absolute value is either added to pretax financial income or deducted from a pretax loss. The terms income tax expense and income tax provision are often used interchangeably.

Income tax provision   Same as income tax expense. See "income tax expense."

More likely than not   The threshold, a probability level of over 50 percent, used to judge whether it is more likely than not that some or all of a firm's deferred tax assets will never be realized.

Net operating loss carrybacks and carryforwards   Operating losses represent an excess of corporate deductions over gross income. For U.S. federal tax purposes, they may be carried back for two years and then forward for 20 years. Corporations may also elect to forgo the carryback and only carry the loss forward for 20 years.

Negative evidence   Information that increases the likelihood of a need for a valuation allowance against deferred tax assets. A history of operating losses expiring unused is an example of negative evidence that would bear on the realizability of a deferred tax asset associated with a net operating loss carryforward.

Originating temporary difference   The initial creation of a difference between pretax financial and taxable income. Applies only to temporary and not permanent differences.

Permanent differences   A difference between pretax financial income and taxable income that results from the recognition of revenues or gains and expenses or losses in the determination of pretax financial income or taxable income, but never in both. Permanent differences cause effective tax rates to deviate from expected statutory tax rate levels.

Positive evidence   Information that decreases the likelihood that a valuation allowance against deferred tax assets will be required. *Example:* The presence of appreciated assets that could be sold to produce a capital gain is an example of positive evidence that could bear on the realizability of a deferred tax asset associated with a capital loss carryforward.

Reserving   When used with respect to accounting for deferred tax assets, reserving refers to the act of setting up a valuation allowance against deferred tax assets because it is judged to be over 50 percent that some or all of these assets will not be realized.

Reversing temporary differences   The inclusion of items of revenue or gain and expense or loss in the computation of pretax financial income where recognition has taken place earlier in the determination of taxable income. Also, the recognition of items of revenue or gain and expense or loss in the computation of *taxable income* where recognition has taken place earlier in the determination of pretax financial income.

Schedule of deferred tax assets and liabilities   A schedule, required by SFAS No. 109, "Accounting for Income Taxes," that lists deferred tax assets and liabilities by their associated temporary differences, loss, and tax credit carryforwards. This schedule usually lists only the tax effects of these items and not, additionally, the amounts of the temporary differences.

Statutory income tax rates   These are the income tax rates that are stated in income tax law. They are applied to taxable income reported in income tax returns. The U.S. federal statutory income tax rates start out at 15 percent for taxable income up to $50,000 and top out at 35 percent on taxable income in excess of about $18 million.

Tax planning strategies   Actions that a firm might not otherwise take but would take to ensure the realization of deferred tax assets. The ultimate realization of deferred tax assets calls for taxable income of sufficient amount in the right periods. Tax planning strategies are actions that are capable of producing taxable income. Examples of strategies that firms have disclosed include changes from the LIFO to FIFO inventory method, the sale of appreciated assets and the execution of sale and leaseback transactions.

Tax preferences   Additions to regular taxable income as part of the process of arriving at alternative minimum taxable income (AMTI). Excess depletion is an example of a tax preference. Excess depletion represents the excess of depletion for the year over adjusted basis (original cost minus accumulated depletion) at year-end of the asset being depleted. That is, excess depletion is that amount that exceeds the actual cost or basis of the asset. Even though such excess depletion is permitted in computing regular taxable income, it is added back to taxable income as part of the process of determining AMTI.[49]

Tax reconciliation schedule   A schedule, required by SFAS No. 109, "Accounting for Income Taxes," that explains the differences between the actual total tax provision and the provision that would be expected if all pretax financial income were simply taxed at statutory rates. The primary reconciling items are permanent differences plus loss and tax credit carryforwards.

Taxable temporary differences   A temporary difference that upon its reversal will cause taxable income to be increased above the level of pretax financial income. Upon origination, taxable temporary differences give rise to deferred tax liabilities.

Temporary difference   A difference between pretax financial income and taxable income that results from the recognition of revenues or gains and expenses or losses in different periods in the determination of pretax financial and taxable income. Temporary differences give rise to either deferred tax assets or liabilities.

Valuation allowance   A contra-asset account to deferred tax assets. The valuation allowance represents that portion of total deferred tax assets that the firm judges is unlikely to be realized. The probability threshold applied in evaluating realization is 50 percent. That is, if it is over 50 percent likely that some or all of a deferred tax asset will not be realized, then a valuation allowance must be set off against part or all of the deferred tax asset.

NOTES

1. A widely cited statement by Benjamin Franklin in a letter to Jean-Baptiste Leroy, November 13, 1789.

2. In computing the total tax provision, income tax rates are applied to pretax financial income only after adjustments have been made to remove any nontaxable income and nondeductible expenses that may have been included in the determination of pretax financial income.

3. SFAS No. 109, "Accounting for Income Taxes" (Norwalk, CT: Financial Accounting Standards Board, February 1992).

4. Temporary differences may also result from business combinations. Deferred taxes are recorded on differences between the tax and book basis of acquired assets and liabilities.

5. SFAS No. 109, "Accounting for Income Taxes" (Norwalk, CT: Financial Accounting Standards Board, February 1992), from the summary, no page number.

6. Failure to recognize the deferred tax benefit in the year that the expense is recognized in the determination of pretax financial income results in the benefit being recognized in the future periods in which the loss or expense deduction is included in computing taxable income. This results in a matching failure.

7. Internal Revenue Code, §274(n).

8. Internal Revenue Code, §101. While the insurance proceeds are not taxable, the associated insurance premiums are likewise not deductible.

9. The combined rate includes both federal and state income taxes. By combining federal and state taxes, the implicit assumption is that the tax treatment of meal and entertainment expenses and life insurance proceeds is the same under both federal and state tax law. This may or may not be the case on a state-by-state basis.

10. E. Comiskey, C. Mulford, and H. Choi, "Deferred-Tax-Asset Valuation Allowances: A Survey of Large Banks' Allowance Decisions," *Commercial Lending Review* (Spring 1995), pp. 4–23. The set of 33 different sources of temporary differences represents only those that were sufficiently material to be disclosed separately.

11. Archer Daniels Midland Company, annual report, June 1998, p. 24.

12. Under SFAS No. 130, "Reporting Comprehensive Income" (Norwalk, CT: Financial Accounting Standards Board, June 1997), it remains possible for certain temporary differences (i.e., unrealized gains and losses on selected investments, foreign currency translation adjustments, and adjustments for underfunded pensions) to be disclosed directly in shareholders' equity. The associated deferred tax effects of these items are also reported directly in shareholders' equity.

13. A version of this classification scheme was earlier used in E. Comiskey and C. Mulford, "Income Tax Disclosures: Their Role in Credit Analysis," *Commercial Lending Review* (Winter 1992), pp. 15–31.

14. It is not uncommon for a firm to be in an originating position for many years, even decades. This is especially true for depreciation-related temporary differences. As a result, a firm could establish a deferred tax liability that continues to grow. Such a condition has implications for financial quality and will be discussed later in this chapter.

15. SFAS No. 109, "Accounting for Income Taxes" (Norwalk, CT: Financial Accounting Standards Board, February 1992).

16. SFAS No. 109, paras. 6–16.

17. Some goodwill is now deductible as a result of changes in the tax law that became effective in 1993. See Internal Revenue Code, §197 for details. Where deductible for income tax purposes, goodwill is amortized on a straight-line basis over 15 years. To the extent that a longer amortization period is used for book purposes, a temporary difference will result.

18. In most cases, the originating temporary differences will also be equal to the changes in the cumulative basis differences, books versus tax return, of the firm's assets and liabilities.

19. If the warranty expense were deducted in a year in which a loss was incurred, then its realization could be achieved on a current basis through carryback of the loss or in the future as part of a loss carryforward.

20. SFAS No. 109, "Accounting for Income Taxes" (Norwalk, CT: Financial Accounting Standards Board, February 1992).

21. SFAS No. 109 requires disclosure of the total income taxes paid during the year. See SFAS No. 109, para. 92 and 121.

22. SFAS No. 109, para. 43.

23. SFAS No. 109, paras. 8 and 27.

24. SFAS No. 109, para. 13.

25. There are cases where the temporary differences associated with the accounting for revenues or gains create a deferred tax asset. Such a case, involving the accounting for a gain on a sale and leaseback transaction, is found in Chapter Ten.

26. SFAS No. 109, "Accounting for Income Taxes" (Norwalk, CT: Financial Accounting Standards Board, February 1992), para. 47.

27. For details on this complex feature of the tax law, see the Internal Revenue Code, §44.

28. Pre-Paid Legal Services, Inc., annual report, December 1998, p. 35.

29. Pre-Paid Legal's statement of cash flows disclosed no tax payments for the period 1996 to 1998.

30. Pre-Paid Legal Services, Inc., annual report, December 1998, p. 22.

31. Over the past 25 years, in their work with bankers, the authors have observed firms taking this position on numerous occasions.

32. Omnibus Budget Reconciliation Act of 1987. This provision applied to family-owned farms. Continued deferral of the tax obligation required that certain family ownership levels be maintained.

33. The Taxpayer Relief Act of 1997.

34. Pilgrim's Pride Corporation, annual report on form 10-K to the Securities and Exchange Commission (September 1998), p. 29.

35. SFAS No. 106, "Employers' Accounting for Postretirement Benefits Other Than Pensions" (Norwalk, CT: Financial Accounting Standards Board, December 1990); SFAS No. 112, "Employers' Accounting for Postemployment Benefits" (Norwalk, CT: Financial Accounting Standards Board, November 1992); SFAS No. 115, "Accounting for Certain Investments in Debt and Equity Securities" (Norwalk, CT: Financial Accounting Standards Board, May 1993); and SFAS No. 121, "Accounting for the Impairment of Long-Lived Assets" (Norwalk, CT: Financial Accounting Standards Board, May 1995).

36. See §§55 to 59 of the Internal Revenue Code for complete information on the alternative minimum tax system.

37. The carry forward of a loss improves cash flow by reducing tax payments.

38. Directing inquiries to Investor Relations is usually the most efficient and productive way to go about seeking explanations of financial statement data. This assumes that there is no existing direct line of communication with the company of interest.

39. The requirements to achieve the favorable tax treatment of a Foreign Sales Corporation are found in Internal Revenue Services Regulations, §1.921–2.

40. SFAS No. 109, paras. 17–26.

41. SFAS No. 109, para. 20.

42. SFAS No. 109, para. 21.

43. E. Comiskey and C. Mulford, "Evaluating Deferred Tax Assets: Some Guidance for Lenders," *Commercial Lending Review* (Summer 1994), pp. 12–25.

44. We cannot make this statement with certainty for 1995 because the valuation allowance is not equal to the deferred tax assets identified as associated with the capital loss carryovers. However, it seems very likely to be true.

45. The capital loss carryovers of Analog Devices are realized by producing capital gains in its tax returns. Upon the use in 1998 of the last of the capital loss carryover, Analog Devices simply removed the valuation allowance of $5,559,000 and the associated deferred tax asset of the same amount. Finally, net income is increased by the utilization of the capital loss carryover and the consequent reduction in the current tax provision.

46. C. Cloyd, "The Effects of Financial Accounting Conformity on Recommendations of Tax Preparers," *The Journal of the American Tax Association* (Fall 1995), pp. 50–70.

47. *Ibid.,* p. 67

48. W. Northcut and C. Vines, "Earnings Management in Response to Political Scrutiny of Effective Tax Rates," *The Journal of the American Tax Association* (Fall 1998), pp. 22–36.

49. See §57 of the Internal Revenue Code for details.

Chapter 6

Financial Derivatives

> History teaches that in the financial markets there will come a day
> unlike any other day. The leverage that once multiplied income will
> now devastate principal.[1]

From rudimentary beginnings in commodity and foreign currency forward contracts, the market for financial derivatives has grown in recent years to a multi-trillion-dollar industry. With mind-numbing frequency, new derivatives are being invented to respond to perceived market needs. These new financial derivative instruments add to an ever-growing body of existing contracts to create an endless array of financial possibilities where market participants can take long or short positions and use their potential payoffs for hedging or speculative purposes.

Accounting standard setters have had difficulty keeping up with the explosion of these new financial agreements. Over the past several years, several standards have been issued, creating a patchwork quilt of regulations for accounting and disclosure. As a result, reporting companies have had several places to turn to for direction, including Statement of Financial Accounting Standards (SFAS) No. 52, "Foreign Currency Translation"; SFAS No. 80, "Accounting for Futures Contracts"; SFAS No. 105, "Disclosure of Information about Financial Concentrations of Credit Risk"; SFAS No. 107, "Disclosures about Fair Value of Financial Instruments"; and SFAS No. 119, "Disclosure about Derivative Financial Instruments and Fair Value of Financial Instruments."[2] Unfortunately, the direction this hodgepodge of regulations provided was focused more on disclosure and less on the actual accounting for financial derivatives, leaving companies to fend for themselves when dealing with this important component of financial reporting. As a result, companies went in many directions causing a general lack of consistent accounting treatment.

In 1998, the Financial Accounting Standards Board (FASB) took an important step to clean up and standardize the accounting and disclosure guidelines for financial derivatives. SFAS No. 133, "Accounting for Derivative Instruments and Hedging Activities," was issued in June 1998.[3] The new standard superseded SFAS No. 80, SFAS No. 105, and SFAS No. 119. It left in place SFAS No. 52, though it added accounting guidance for foreign currency hedges. The new standard also left in place SFAS No. 107, though amended it to include disclosure provisions about concentrations of credit risk.

In this chapter, we look at extant accounting and disclosure guidelines for financial derivatives. We examine how these financial contracts can be used to reduce risk and earnings volatility and, importantly, how they are sometimes employed to increase risk and earnings volatility in a quest for speculative gain. Our focus will be an improved understanding of the significance to financial analysis of derivatives-related disclosures.

UNDERSTANDING FINANCIAL DERIVATIVES

Financial derivatives are financial instruments that derive their value from the price or rate of an underlying financial contract or index. The price or rate of an underlying contract or index, which is typically referred to simply as the underlying, can be a specified security price, foreign exchange rate, commodity price, interest rate, or an index of prices or rates. For example, the price of a share of stock in Dell Computer Corporation, the value of the British pound expressed in dollars, the price of heating oil, and the London Interbank Offered Rate (LIBOR) are all underlyings. While an underlying may be the price or rate of an asset or liability, the underlying is not itself an asset or liability.

Settlement of financial derivatives can be effected through the receipt or payment of cash outside the contract or through delivery of another asset. For example, settlement of a short position in a put option on Dell Computer stock would be handled through purchase of the underlying stock, or through expiration of the option. Settlement of a forward exchange contract for the purchase of British pounds would be effected through a payment of dollars and receipt of British pounds. Settlement of a short position in a futures contract on heating oil or a receive-fixed, pay-variable position in an interest rate swap, based on three-month dollar LIBOR as the variable rate, would be settled through payment or receipt of cash and ultimate expiration of the derivatives contracts.

The terms of settlement are calculated using a notional amount—a number of shares for the put option, a number of currency units for the foreign currency forward contract, a number of gallons for the futures contract on heating oil, or the principal amount covered by the swap agreement. Settlement of a derivative instrument is determined by relating, through a formula, the notional amount to the underlying. In some instances, financial derivatives do not require settlement, providing instead for worthless expiration, as was the case with the put option.

The acquisition of financial derivatives requires either no initial net investment or an initial net investment that is smaller than the notional amount or an amount determined by applying the notional amount to the underlying. For example, the premium on the put option is less than the market value of the stock covered by the option, while the foreign currency forward contract, the futures contract on heating oil, and the interest rate swap agreement require either no or minimal initial net investments.

Examples of Financial Derivatives

In understanding financial derivatives, it is helpful to refer to examples. The paragraphs that follow provide an elaboration of the examples identified above. With each example, the economic objective of the derivative is provided together with additional clarification of the underlying, the notional amount, the net investment, and the means of settlement.

Common Stock Put Option

A put option giving its holder the right but not the obligation to sell 100 shares of Dell Computer Corporation through January 2001 at $30 per share is a financial derivative. At the close of trading on June 11, 1999, when Dell Computer was quoted at $34.1875, the put option in question was quoted at $6.25. That is, a purchaser of this option would pay $625 (100 shares × $6.25 each), plus commissions and fees, to have the right to sell 100 shares of Dell Computer at $30 per share through January 2001. The option here is said to be out of the money; that is, it gives the holder the right to sell Dell stock at $30, a price lower than its current price. Such an out-of-the-money option has no intrinsic value, but does have a time value, as demonstrated by the quoted $6.25 for the right to sell stock at a price that is lower than currently quoted.

In this example, the $30 exercise price for sale of the common stock of Dell Computer is the underlying and the 100 shares is the notional amount. The initial net investment for this contract, $625, is less than the notional amount of 100 shares times the $30 underlying. Settlement of the option can be effected through exercise and use of the option to sell the 100 shares of stock and receive $30 per share in the process, through sale of the option, or by simply letting the option expire worthless.

A buyer of the put option that has no investment position in Dell Computer stock is speculating that Dell's share price will decrease below $30 by the time the option expires. That buyer will realize an overall gain on the transaction if Dell's price is less than $23.75 at the time the option expires, consisting of the $30 received per share from selling the stock less the $6.25 paid for each put option.

A holder of 100 shares of stock in Dell Computer might buy the put option as a way to hedge the value of his or her investment. In buying the put option, the seller pays the $625 option premium, plus commissions and fees. That option provides the holder with protection against decline in Dell Computer's stock price below $30. If Dell's price closes below $30 when the option expires, the option holder is assured of receiving $30 per share for the Dell stock.

A speculative investor may decide to sell short the put option on Dell stock. Here, the seller receives the $625 option premium on a bet that Dell's share price will not fall below the $30 exercise price before the option's expiration. If the stock price were to stay above $30, the option will expire worthless and the option seller will have no additional obligation under the contract. If the stock price were to fall below $30, the option seller must be prepared to either buy the stock from the option holder at $30 per share or buy back the option. Ignoring commissions and fees, the option seller will have a gain on the transaction provided Dell is not trading below $23.75 when the option seller buys the stock at $30 or buys back the option. In buying the stock, the option seller will pay $30 per share for the Dell shares delivered, which, when netted with the $6.25 per-share premium received earlier, equals $23.75 per share. Any amount below $23.75 at which the stock is trading at the expiration date of the option will be a loss to the option seller.

If the option seller decides instead to purchase the put option that was sold earlier, any resulting gain or loss will depend on the price paid for the option. That price will reflect a time value that depends on the amount of time remaining until the option expires, and an intrinsic value, representing any excess of the $30 exercise price over Dell's per-share market price.

Foreign Currency Forward Exchange Contract

A foreign currency forward exchange contract is a privately negotiated agreement to buy or sell a foreign currency at a specified future date and a specified exchange rate. The specified future date is typically within 12 months of the agreement's signing. On that settlement date, the currencies covered by the contract are exchanged. The agreed-to exchange rate, known as the *forward rate,* might be slightly above or below the existing spot rate of exchange for the currencies in question due primarily to differences in interest rates obtainable on the currencies in international money markets for the duration of the contract.

For example, assume that in June 1999, a U.S. company incurred an obligation of 100,000 British pounds payable on September 1, 1999. The company was concerned about fluctuations in the value of the British pound relative to the U.S. dollar before settlement of the obligation. In particular, the company was concerned about a loss it would incur if the value of the British pound were to rise. To hedge that risk, the company entered into a forward exchange contract to purchase 100,000 British pounds for delivery on September 1, 1999.

On June 11, 1999, a day when the spot rate for the British pound was 1.61 U.S. dollars, a valid forward exchange rate for settlement on September 1, 1999, would be approximately 1.62 U.S. dollars.[4] In entering into such an agreement, the U.S. company would be agreeing to deliver $162,000 (100,000 British pounds × 1.62 U.S. dollars). In return, the U.S. company would receive 100,000 British pounds. The difference between the 100,000 British pounds translated at the spot rate (1.61 U.S. dollars) and forward rate (1.62 U.S. dollars) would represent a financing cost. That cost, $1,000 in this example (100,000 British pounds × .01 U.S. dollars), the U.S. company has incurred to eliminate the foreign currency risk from its British pound obligation.

The counterparty to the U.S. company in this example, likely a commercial bank, may have British pound–denominated financial assets and use this forward exchange contract as a way to hedge its own risk. That is, at settlement, the bank will receive U.S. dollars translated at the agreed-to forward rate and deliver 100,000 British pounds. Alternatively, the bank may speculate that the value of the British pound will decline in value relative to the U.S. dollar over the life of the forward exchange contract. In such a setting, the bank would not carry British pound–denominated financial assets, but rather plan on buying the needed currency at the spot rate at settlement to effect delivery of the agreed British pounds. If the spot rate were to fall below the 1.62 U.S. dollar forward rate, the bank would gain. It would lose if the spot rate would rise above the 1.62 U.S. dollar forward rate.

An investor, other than the U.S. company with a British pound obligation, might speculate that the British pound will increase in value relative to the dollar in the near future. Such an investor could enter into a forward exchange contract to purchase British pounds for future delivery. Using the forward exchange rate of 1.62 U.S. dollars per British pound expressed earlier, the investor will gain if the spot rate on the day of settlement of the forward exchange contract is greater than the 1.62 U.S. dollar agreed to forward rate.

The forward exchange contract to purchase British pounds described here is a financial derivative. The underlying is the forward exchange rate, 1.62 U.S. dollars per British pound. The notional amount is the 100,000 British pounds covered by the contract. There is no net investment in the forward exchange contract. No moneys are exchanged when the parties enter into the agreement. Finally, settlement is effected by delivery and exchange of the agreed currencies.

A Commodity Futures Contract

A futures contract is an agreement to purchase or sell a commodity or financial instrument for future delivery. Unlike a forward contract that is privately negotiated and includes tailored terms and size to fit individual needs, a futures contract is a standardized agreement, leaving variable only the price and the month of settlement.

Futures contracts trade actively on contract markets and commodity exchanges. While futures contracts specify a settlement date, their active trading on organized markets permits cash settlement on a daily basis. The purchase of a futures contract entails deposit of a margin balance to a commodity trading account. The margin balance is typically set at around 10 percent of the total contract amount, though it will vary, depending on the commodity and whether or not the futures contract is being used as a hedging instrument. Each day as the underlying commodity price changes, changing the value of the total contract amount, any resulting gain or loss will be added to or subtracted from the commodity trading account. The minimum margin balance will also be adjusted, keeping it in line with the changing total contract amount.

The ultimate expiration and settlement of commodity futures contracts is typically handled by offset with cash prior to delivery. That is, a long position is closed by sale and a short position is closed by purchase. However, certain commodity futures contracts can settle through delivery of the underlying commodity if the parties so choose. The focus here will be on cash settlement as opposed to settlement through delivery.

Assume, for example, that in June 1999, a company concerned about a possible decline in the price of heating oil before its sale in December 1999, seeks to hedge the value of its heating oil inventory. The company sells short a futures contract covering 42,000 gallons of heating oil, the standard contract size, at the futures price of $.4812 per gallon. Ignoring commission and fees, the total contract amount is $20,210.40 (42,000 gallons × $.4812 per gallon). In effect, the company has sold 42,000 gallons of heating oil for delivery in December 1999 at $.4812. As it has a guaranteed price, the company need no longer be concerned about changes in the price of oil during the contract term.

The company would deposit a minimum of approximately $2,021 into its commodity trading account. If the next day heating oil were quoted at $.50 per gallon, the total contract would be valued at $21,000. Since the company had sold short the heating oil futures contract, the resulting loss of $789.60 ($20,210.40 − $21,000) would be subtracted from its commodity trading account. If the resulting balance is below a new minimum margin amount, the company would need to add cash margin to its commodity trading account.

With a futures contract there is no known counterparty as there was with the foreign currency forward exchange contract. With futures contracts, a separate organization—a clearinghouse—stands between the long and short trading positions.

During the December 1999 heating season, the company sells its heating oil inventory at going market prices. The company closes its futures contract position by buying back the futures contract that it had sold short in June. As the contract had settled on a daily basis, the only remaining gain or loss on the contract would be for any price change during the last day of trading prior to closing the short position.

An investor without heating oil inventory might use a futures contract to speculate on changes in the price of heating oil. If the investor believed the price would decline, he or she would take a short position in a futures contract. The mechanics of the investment would be handled just as they were for the company hedging its heating oil inventory. If the investor believed that the price would rise, then a long position in the futures contract would be appropriate. In fact, such an investor might be the offsetting position to the company with heating oil inventory that sold short the futures contract.

The futures contract on heating oil is a financial derivative. The underlying is the futures price for heating oil, $.4812, at the time the futures contract was sold short by the heating oil company. The notional amount is the 42,000 gallons covered by the contract. There is no net investment in the futures contract, though a party to the contract must maintain a minimum margin deposit in its commodity trading account. Settlement of the futures contract was handled by offset. The company purchased the futures contract that had been sold short. An investor who had a long position in the heating oil contract sold the position to settle it.

Interest Rate Swap

An interest rate swap provides the means for a company to alter the sensitivity of its earnings to changes in interest rates. Specifically, a company can use swaps to change the nature of its interest payments, changing them from fixed to variable, or variable to fixed. A company with fixed-rate debt might enter into an interest rate swap to receive a fixed amount from a counterparty to the agreement in exchange for a variable payment. In the process, the company has converted its fixed-rate debt into a variable-rate obligation. Similarly, a company with variable-rate debt might enter into an interest rate swap to receive a variable amount from a counterparty to the agreement in exchange for a fixed payment. Here, the company has converted variable-rate debt into a fixed-rate obligation.

An interest rate swap agreement will specify a borrowing date, the date on which the contract begins, a maturity date, the notional amount, or the amount of principal covered by the agreement, the fixed interest rate, the variable interest rate, dates on which the variable rate is reset, and interest payment dates. Note that like the foreign currency forward contract, the terms of the agreement are privately negotiated and the counterparties to the agreement are identified.

Assume that in June 1999, a company sought to convert to a variable rate its $1 million principal of outstanding 7 percent fixed-rate debt, payable quarterly, set to mature in June 2001. The company entered into a two-year receive-fixed, pay-variable interest rate swap. During the two-year term of the swap agreement, the company will receive payments of 7 percent of the $1,000,000 principal balance. These receipts will exactly offset the interest payments the company is making to its lender. The company will pay a variable interest amount to its swap counterparty based on the three-month LIBOR as applied to the same $1,000,000 principal balance. That rate will reset at the end of each three-month period. At the time the agreement is signed, LIBOR is 6 percent.

As a result of this interest rate swap agreement, the company has converted its fixed-rate debt into a variable-rate obligation. The company will receive an amount equal to the fixed rate it is paying on its debt and pay a variable amount on that same debt. For example, during the first three-month period, the company will receive $17,500 (7 percent × $1,000,000 divided by 4), an amount equal to the interest it pays its lender on that debt. However, the company will pay $15,000 (6 percent × $1 million divided by 4) to its counterparty.[5] During subsequent three-month periods, the company will continue receiving $17,500, but the amount it pays will vary depending on the three-month LIBOR.

At maturity of the interest rate swap agreement, the company and its counterparty make their last cross-payments for interest differences and the contract expires. The company with fixed-rate debt will pay the principal on its debt, settling its obligation to its lender.

As interest rates change, so does the value of interest rate swap agreements. Using the example above, if interest rates were to rise, the counterparty that has swapped into the receive-variable, pay-fixed position will see the value of its agreement increase. Similarly, the company that has swapped into the receive-fixed, pay-variable position will see the value of its agreement decline. Confirmation of this change in value will appear if one or both of the counterparties to the agreement seek premature settlement of their positions.

These value changes in interest rate swap agreements provide the potential for gains and losses to speculative swap investors. A commercial bank may decide to assume for itself the offsetting position to the above company's receive-fixed, pay-variable interest rate swap. The bank would thus be expected to assume a receive-variable, pay-fixed position. If interest rates were to rise, the bank would gain. With little invested in the contract, its potential return on investment could be quite large. However, a drop in interest rates would result in a significant loss.[6]

An interest rate swap is also a financial derivative. The underlying is the difference between the fixed and variable interest rates—1 percent at the time the agreement is reached. The notional amount is the $1 million principal amount covered by the agreement. There is no net investment in the interest rate swap, though the receive-variable, pay-fixed counterparty would be paying an interest premium on each interest payment date. Settlement of the agreement was handled through maturity of the swap and a discontinuation of interest cross-payments. However, the two counterparties could also settle their agreement through an agreed-upon cash receipt or payment.

Financial Derivatives as Vehicles for Hedging Risk

Financial derivatives were developed to fulfill a need to manage risk. From the farmer concerned about the price he will receive for his corn crop at harvest to the small business borrower with variable-rate debt concerned about being able to make her loan payment if interest rates were to rise, to the toy wholesaler with manufacturing operations in Taiwan concerned about the effects of a rising Taiwanese dollar, businesses are faced with many risks that increase the volatility of their earnings streams. Financial derivatives offer a means for hedging or managing risk exposure—replacing one risk with another, reducing risk to a lower level, or in some instances, eliminating risk altogether.

Types of Risk

Risk is uncertainty or potential variability of financial outcomes. Companies clearly face a host of different risks of varying nature that can affect financial results. Consider the following statement from Advanced Energy Industries:

> The Company continues to be subject to certain risks similar to other companies in its industry. These risks include the volatility of the semiconductor industry, customer concentration within the industry, technological changes, dependence on the Japanese market, foreign currency risk and competition. A significant change in any of these risk factors could have a material impact on the Company's business.[7]

The company identifies many of the risks faced by all firms. Most of these risks cannot be managed with financial derivatives. For example, derivatives do not currently exist that would enable the company to hedge its customer concentration or its competition. Financial derivatives would permit the company to hedge its foreign currency risk and potentially, the volatility in prices of its semiconductors.

In the examples dealt with here, there are four kinds of risk being addressed. These four risks represent four primary types of risk for which financial derivatives have been designed to manage.

The first kind of risk is commodity price risk. In response to market forces, the prices of commodities—oil and natural gas; coal; industrial metals such as iron, steel, aluminum, and copper; precious metals such as gold and silver; and agricultural commodities such as cotton, coffee, and sugar—are constantly changing. These price changes add significant risk and volatility to the earnings of the companies that produce them. Aware of the effects that commodity price risk can have on its operations, Belco Oil and Gas Corporation made the following statement in its annual report:

> Belco engages in a wide variety of commodity price risk management transactions with the objective of achieving more predictable revenues and cash flows and reducing its exposure to fluctuations in natural gas and oil prices.[8]

A second kind of risk is foreign currency risk—the risk of changes in foreign currency exchange rates that affects all firms that operate in currencies that span national borders. This risk affects companies that buy from vendors or sell to customers for which the transaction is denominated in a foreign currency, that have investments or subsidiaries located in foreign countries, or that have foreign-denominated borrowings. Representative of companies with foreign currency risk is Walsh International, Inc.:

> The reported net income (loss) of foreign subsidiaries will be affected by changes in the exchange rates of foreign currencies against the U.S. dollar. Approximately 89% of the Company's revenues for fiscal 1997 were generated outside the United States in local currencies.[9]

A third risk type is interest rate risk. When a debt obligation is denominated in a variable interest rate, changes in rates will alter the cash amounts paid for interest. Such changes in interest payments create volatility for both the issuing firm and the investor in the debt obligation. Changes in interest rates also pose a risk to issuers and investors in fixed-rate debt. When interest rates are fixed, changes in market rates of interest will alter the market value of the outstanding debt obligation or debt investment. The earnings of commercial banks are affected directly by interest rate risk, as the following statement by PNC Bank Corporation makes evident:

> Interest rate risk arises primarily through the Corporation's core business activities of extending loans and taking deposits. Many factors, including economic and financial

conditions, movements in market interest rates and consumer preferences, affect the spread between interest earned on assets and interest paid on liabilities. In managing interest rate risk, the Corporation seeks to minimize its reliance on a particular interest rate scenario as a source of earnings, while maximizing net interest income and net interest margin.[10]

A fourth type of risk is the risk of changes in market value or fair value.[11] The risk of changes in market value of an equity investment is described by Baker Hughes, Inc. as follows:

> The Company's investment in common stock and common stock warrants of Tuboscope, Inc. ("Tuboscope") is subject to equity price risk as the common stock of Tuboscope is traded on the New York Stock Exchange. Warrants to buy shares of Tuboscope common stock derive their value, in part, from the market value of Tuboscope common stock. This investment is classified as available for sale and, consequently, is reflected in the consolidated statement of financial position at fair value with unrealized gains and losses reported as a separate component of stockholders' equity. At September 30, 1997, the fair value of the Company's investment in common stock and common stock warrants of Tuboscope was $120.5 million. The Tuboscope common stock was valued at the closing price reported on the New York Stock Exchange, and the warrants were valued using the Black-Scholes option-pricing model. No actions have been taken by the Company to hedge this market risk exposure. A 20% decline in the market price of the Tuboscope common stock would cause the fair value of the investment in common stock and common stock warrants of Tuboscope to decrease $26.1 million.[12]

The risk of changes in market value is a broader, more encompassing concept than the other types of risk described here. For example, changes in market value can be caused by changes in commodity price risk, foreign currency risk, or interest rate risk. Changes in market value can also be caused by other factors. A change in the market value of a share of stock can occur in the absence of changes in commodity prices, foreign currencies, and interest rates. As will be seen later, careful identification of the expected cause of changes in market value is important in accounting for financial derivatives as hedges because accounting guidelines require an accurate assessment of hedge effectiveness. Hedge effectiveness cannot be accurately measured unless the risk factors potentially causing changes in market value are anticipated. A company might attempt to hedge changes in the market value of a common stock investment with a short position in a treasury bond futures contract. To the extent that changes in interest rates affect both instruments, the hedge might work. But so many other factors affect the market value of a common stock investment that the hedge is unlikely to be considered effective.

Earlier in the chapter, examples of four different financial derivatives were provided. Each derivative instrument was used to hedge one of the four types of risk described here. For example, the holder of common stock in Dell Computer used a put option to reduce the risk of declines in the market value of the stock—a market-value hedge. Although the put option eliminated the risk of the stock falling, it did so at a cost (the option premium), and in the process reduced the investment's potential. The U.S. company with the British pound obligation used a foreign currency forward exchange contract to eliminate its risk of changes in foreign currency exchange rates—a foreign currency hedge. The heating oil company used a short position in a commodity futures contract to lock in the price it will receive for a portion of its heating oil inventory when it is sold months in the future—a commodity price hedge. Finally, the borrower with $1 million of fixed-rate debt outstanding used an interest rate swap to effectively convert its debt to a variable-rate obligation. Such a move would increase the volatility of its interest payment stream, and may increase the company's risk. However, it would also reduce or eliminate changes in the market value of that debt, providing an effective hedge of the market value of a balance sheet item. The company has replaced one risk, variability in the market value of the company's debt, with another, volatility in the company's interest payment stream. This is a hedge of changes in the market value of the debt obligation. Such changes can be caused by factors other than changes in interest rates. For example, a change in the creditworthiness of the issuer will affect the debt's market value. To the extent the company has designated the hedge against changes in market value caused by changes in interest rates, it is an interest rate–type hedge.

Other Company Examples

Financial statements are replete with examples of companies using financial derivatives to hedge commodity price risk, foreign currency risk, interest rate risk, and the risk of changes in market value. For example, Anderson's, Inc., an operator of grain elevators and distributor of farm-related products, uses commodity futures and options to hedge commodity price risk. Note that the company is careful to point out that to contain risk, it limits its unhedged gain positions:

> For the purpose of hedging its market price risk exposure on grain owned and related forward grain purchase and sale contracts, the Company holds regulated commodity contracts in the form of futures and options contracts for corn, soybeans and wheat. The Company accounts for all commodity contracts using a daily mark-to-the-market method; the same method it uses to value grain inventory and forward purchase and sale contracts. Company policy limits the Company's unhedged grain position.[13]

Century Aluminum Company uses commodity forward contracts to hedge its commodity price risk. The company describes its hedging program as follows:

> The Company enters into forward primary aluminum contracts, principally with the Glencore Group, to hedge fixed-price purchase and sale commitments and inventory positions ("specific contracts") and to cover expected future sales and to otherwise manage the Company's exposure to changing prices ("general contracts").[14]

One company that has been particularly successful in hedging commodity price risk in the face of chronically declining prices is Barrick Gold Corporation. As the company notes:

Over the past ten years, Barrick's hedge program has demonstrated that it can both maximize revenue and minimize the gold price risk. This is especially important given that in early 1998, gold prices declined to an 18-year low of approximately $280 per ounce. Under the Company's 10-million-ounce hedge position, 100% of 1998 and 1999 gold production is hedged at a minimum price of $400 per ounce. This represents a $100 per ounce premium over the current spot price, or more than $650 million in additional revenue over the two-year period.[15]

To hedge its foreign currency risk, UAL Corporation uses foreign currency forward contracts and currency options. The company describes its foreign currency risk and steps taken to hedge it as follows:

United has established a foreign currency hedging program using currency forwards and currency options (purchasing put options or selling call options) to hedge exposure to the Japanese yen and Hong Kong dollar. The goal of the hedging program is to effectively manage risk associated with fluctuations in the value of the foreign currency, thereby making financial results more stable and predictable. United does not use currency forwards or currency options for trading purposes.[16]

In its disclosure of its hedging program, UAL is careful to point out that it is not trading in financial derivatives. Trading in financial derivatives adds a new dimension of risk to a company's financial performance. Another firm that is careful to point out that it does not trade in financial derivatives is Data General Corporation. The company provides the following description of its foreign currency risk and the hedging practices used to mitigate that risk:

Because a substantial portion of the Company's operations and revenue occurs outside of the United States, the Company's results can be significantly impacted by changes in foreign currency exchange rates. The Company manages its foreign currency risk through the use of forward foreign currency contracts. The Company does not hold or enter into derivative financial instruments for trading purposes.[17]

Two companies that provide detailed descriptions of the interest rate risks they face and the steps taken to mitigate that risk are Cendant Corporation and Chevron Corporation. Both companies use interest rate swaps to hedge their interest rate risk. As disclosed by Cendant Corporation:

If the interest characteristics of the funding mechanism that the Company uses does not match the interest characteristics of the assets being funded, the Company enters into interest rate swap agreements to offset the interest rate risk associated with such funding. The swap agreements correlate the terms of the assets to the maturity and rollover of the debt by effectively matching a fixed or floating interest rate with the stipulated revenue stream generated from the portfolio of assets being funded. Amounts to be paid or received under interest rate swap agreements are accrued as interest rates change and are recognized over the life of the swap agreements as an adjustment to interest expense.[18]

Chevron Corporation provides the following disclosure:

The company enters into interest rate swaps as part of its overall strategy to manage the interest rate risk on its debt. Under the terms of the swaps, net cash settlements, based on the difference between fixed-rate and floating-rate interest amounts calculated by reference to agreed notional principal amounts, are made either semiannually or annually, and are recorded monthly as "Interest and debt expense." At December 31, 1997, there were four outstanding contracts, with remaining terms of between 11 months and eight years.[19]

Mellon Bank Corporation hedges market value risk by addressing a key cause of changes in the market value of financial assets and liabilities—interest rate risk. The company provides the following disclosure:

The Corporation enters into interest rate swaps, interest rate caps and floors, financial futures and financial options primarily to manage its sensitivity to interest rate risk. This is accomplished by using these instruments to offset the inherent price or interest rate risk of specific on-balance-sheet assets or liabilities. The Corporation uses interest rate floor contracts and interest rate swap contracts to hedge against value impairment . . . resulting from a decrease in interest rates. The Corporation also uses total return swaps to offset the inherent market value risk of investments in startup mutual funds.[20]

Natural Hedges

Some companies use natural hedges to manage one or more of the risk types described here. With natural hedges, the company is not using financial derivatives to manage risk, but rather existing or newly created offsetting financial instruments. Such natural hedges are not financial derivatives because they require initial net investments that are not less than the notional amounts of the financial positions they seek to hedge. For example, a company might offset Canadian dollar–denominated accounts receivable with a similarly denominated borrowing. Similarly, an individual investor with significant short-term capital gains in a common stock holding, who is concerned about a decline in the share's price before completion of the one-year holding period for long-term capital gain treatment, could sell short the same number of shares. Neither of these offsetting positions, a Canadian dollar borrowing or a common stock short sale would be considered a financial derivative.

Belden, Inc. seeks to hedge cash flows from foreign operations that are denominated in foreign currencies. As described in the following note, the company hedges these cash flows using borrowings denominated in the same currency:

As a result of having various foreign operations, the Company is exposed to the effect of exchange rate movements on the U.S. dollar value of anticipated cash flows of its foreign operations, which will be remitted to the U.S. The Company sometimes utilizes a natural hedge to mitigate this exposure by denominating a portion of the Company's borrowing in the same currency as the currency of the anticipated cash flow of its foreign operations. The foreign currency denominated cash flow from the foreign operation, when remitted, can be used to reduce the foreign currency borrowing.[21]

To manage interest rate risk, First Virginia Banks, Inc. ladders the maturities of the securities in its fixed-income investment portfolio. As such, equal amounts mature each month to fund the company's loan growth and to mitigate the effects of changing interest rates on the market value of the company's portfolio. The company describes the process as follows:

> The average outstanding investment portfolio decreased 8.6% to $1.825 billion after increasing nominally in 1996. This decline in the investment portfolio was used to fund loan growth. The corporation has constructed its portfolio in a "laddered" approach so an approximately equal amount matures each month. This supplies liquidity to fund loan growth and provides for a natural hedge against changes in interest rates.[22]

Financial Derivatives as Vehicles for Speculative Gain

In his article, "The Dangers of Derivatives," from which the opening quote to this chapter was drawn, Martin Mayer stresses the inherent level of risk that exists in open or unhedged positions in financial derivatives. According to Mr. Mayer:

> Unfortunately, these "over the counter" derivatives—created, sold and serviced behind closed doors by consenting adults who do not tell anybody what they are doing—are also a major source of the almost unlimited leverage that brought the world financial system to the brink of disaster last fall. These instruments are creations of mathematics, and within its premises mathematics yields certainty. But in real life, as Justice Oliver Wendell Homes wrote, "certainty generally is an illusion."[23]

The opportunity for significant gain and loss from financial derivatives is clear from the examples provided earlier in this chapter. A buyer of the put option on Dell Computer stock could lose 100 percent of the investment made in a matter of months. Theoretically, the losses are unlimited for a seller of that same option. A buyer of the forward exchange contract on the British pound could gain significantly if the British pound were to rise in value, though losses would accrue to a decline in that currency's value. Similarly, an uncovered long or short position in the futures contract on heating oil could produce dramatic gains or losses depending on price changes in the underlying commodity. Given that a margin deposit of only about 10 percent of the total contract amount is required to enter into the contract, the resulting gains or losses are magnified many times over. The interest rate swap noted earlier is also a source of speculative gains or losses.

Some companies note explicitly that they do not trade or speculate in financial derivatives. Data General and UAL Corporation from above are cases in point. Nextel Communications, Inc. is also in this category, as described in the following note:

> The Company does not use financial instruments for trading or other speculative purposes, nor is it a party to any leveraged derivative instrument. The use of derivative financial instruments is monitored through regular communication with senior management.[24]

The managements of other companies believe that the prospects of reward outweigh the risks, motivating them to make risky trades. Their speculation does serve a useful purpose by increasing the liquidity of the derivatives markets and providing a ready market for others wishing to use them as hedges. Unfortunately, there is a significant downside. Numerous examples can be cited where companies have ventured into such risky investments, resulting in substantial losses when underlying fundamentals moved in unexpected directions.

During 1994, significant, unexpected increases in interest rates led to substantial losses at many companies that had made speculative investments in financial derivatives. The following excerpt from a story about Dell Computer Corporation appeared during 1994:

> Dell Computer Corp.'s stock tumbled 12% after the company estimated it would incur losses from derivatives for the quarter ending May 1. The projected paper loss, which some analysts pegged at between $5 million and $15 million, comes amid a string of derivatives-related hits in recent weeks.[25]

During that same year, Procter & Gamble Company made a similar disclosure about its speculative investments in financial derivatives:

> The option portions of the two out-of-policy leveraged interest rate swaps entered into during 1994 were closed in the January–March quarter. The related $157 million charge in the quarter to close these options is reflected in other income/expense, net. Leveraged options can magnify the effect of interest rate changes. At June 30, 1994, no such instruments were in our portfolio and it is the company's intent not to enter such leveraged contracts in the future.[26]

The company was very clear in noting that the speculative investments were made outside of company policy and would not happen again. Concern about continued investor fallout from the surprisingly large loss led the company to provide the following "statement of financing philosophy" in its annual report:

> The derivative's write-off, which results in a $102 million charge [after-tax] to third-quarter earnings, warrants special comment to our shareholders.
>
> Procter & Gamble is in the business of developing and marketing consumer products of superior value in a broad range of categories. The financing objective is in support of this business. Our philosophy about the use of financial instruments is to manage risk and cost. Our policy on derivatives is not to engage in speculative leveraged transactions.
>
> The company has taken steps to substantially increase the oversight of the company's financial activities, including the formation of a Risk Management Council.
>
> The council's role is to insure that the policies and procedures approved by the Board of Directors are being followed within approved limits, that transactions are properly analyzed prior to implementation, and that they are regularly monitored once implemented.
>
> The Risk Management Council goes well beyond normal corporate operating controls. With these new procedures in place, the shareholders of the corporation can be assured that the company's management has taken the appropriate steps so that the situation that led to the third-quarter write-off will not happen again.[27]

The early 1990s was a difficult period for companies that speculated in financial derivatives. Other companies incurring derivatives-related losses during that time were Air Products and Chemicals, Inc., which lost $113 million pretax on leveraged interest rate and currency swaps, Gibson Greetings, Inc., which lost $20 million pretax on leveraged interest rate swaps, and Mead, Inc., which lost $12 million, also on leveraged interest rate swaps. These unexpected losses were instrumental in pushing the FASB to tighten the disclosure requirements for financial instruments, including financial derivatives. Those disclosure requirements are described in the next section.

The year 1994 did not end the parade of derivatives-related losses. While the number of companies incurring such losses has declined in recent years, there continue to be noteworthy examples, including Long Term Capital Management, LP and BankAmerica Corporation. In 1998, BankAmerica incurred significant losses when a speculative joint venture to which it had made sizable loans began incurring derivatives-related losses. As reported at the time:

> BankAmerica Corp., the giant bank formed by last month's merger of NationsBank Corp. and the former BankAmerica, reported an unexpectedly steep 78% plunge in third-quarter earnings, with most of the damage coming from volatile global markets and a surprisingly large loss tied to a securities-trading account shared with a New York investment firm . . . The Shaw loss occurred in a trading account set up with an unsecured $1.4 billion loan from the former BankAmerica. Shaw managed the account, doing sophisticated fixed-income and equity trades tied to spreads between different securities, including the Treasury market, according to a bank spokesman. Under the terms of the account, both the bank and Shaw shared in the profits or losses from the trades. According to people familiar with the situation, the account collapsed in late September when yields on U.S. Treasuries fell sharply.[28]

ACCOUNTING REQUIREMENTS FOR FINANCIAL DERIVATIVES

After years of deliberation, in June 1998 the FASB released SFAS No. 133, "Accounting for Derivative Instruments and Hedging Activities."[29] The effects of the new standard are far reaching, embracing fair-value accounting and incorporating into the financial statements financial instruments that had traditionally been excluded. In fact, the provisions of the new standard were considered to be so sweeping that in order to give reporting companies and their auditors more time to study, understand, and implement them, the effective date was delayed and made effective for fiscal years beginning after June 15, 2000. As a result, companies reporting on a calendar-year basis will not fall under the accounting and disclosure provisions of SFAS No. 133 until 2001.

SFAS No. 133 requires that companies recognize financial derivatives as either assets or liabilities in the balance sheet and recognize those financial instruments at fair value. This requirement encompasses all financial derivatives, including those that have traditionally been considered to be off balance sheet.

For example, an open position in a receive-fixed, pay-variable interest rate swap would become an asset if interest rates were to decline. While a decline in rates would leave fixed the company's interest receipts, the amount of interest the company pays would decrease. The present value of that new interest differential, discounted over the term of the swap agreement, would represent the swap's fair value. Prior to SFAS No. 133, that fair value would have been disclosed in a footnote, but it probably would not have been recognized. Rather it would have been carried at cost, an amount that in all probability, would have been zero. Under SFAS No. 133, the fair value of the swap agreement would be reported as an asset in the balance sheet. Similarly, using the same example, if rates were to increase, the swap would be reported at fair value as a liability.

Generally, changes in the fair value of financial derivatives—gains and losses—are to be included in realized net income. Thus, the increase in the fair value of the swap agreement mentioned above would be reported as an income statement gain. A decline in its fair value would be reported as a loss. However, depending on whether or not a position in a financial derivative is considered to be an effective hedge of an existing risk, and on the nature of the risk being hedged, gains and losses resulting from changes in the fair value of financial derivatives might be excluded temporarily from net income and reported with the other comprehensive income component of shareholders' equity. Much of the text of the new standard is focused on helping users determine whether or not financial derivatives are effective hedges and the nature of the risk being hedged. In fact, without the hedging component, SFAS No. 133 would be fairly simple and straightforward: Measure financial derivatives at fair value and recognize gains and losses in income.

Hedge Accounting under SFAS No. 133

The standard identifies the following hedging situations:

- A hedge of the exposure to changes in the fair value of a recognized asset or liability or an unrecognized firm commitment (fair value hedge)
- A hedge of the exposure to variable cash flows of a forecasted transaction (cash flow hedge)
- A hedge of the foreign currency exposure of a net investment in a foreign operation, or an unrecognized foreign currency–denominated firm commitment, available-for-sale security, or forecasted transaction (foreign currency hedge)

All of the risks described earlier that companies may seek to hedge—the risk of changes in commodity prices, foreign currencies, interest rates, and market values—can be classified into one or more of these three risk situations.

The accounting requirements for each of the three hedging situations are provided in the paragraphs that follow. To facilitate the discussion, each of the examples of financial derivatives provided above—the common stock put option, the foreign currency forward exchange contract, the commodity futures contract, and the interest rate swap—are used, where appropriate, to describe hedge accounting.

Fair Value Hedges

In a fair value hedge, a company designates a financial derivative as hedging its exposure to changes in the fair value of all or part of a recognized asset or liability or of an unrecognized firm commitment. To qualify a recognized asset or liability or unrecognized firm commitment and a financial derivative for hedge accounting, several criteria must be met. The following six points summarize these criteria:

1. There must be a formal documentation of the hedging relationship and the entity's risk management objective and strategy for undertaking the hedge, including identification of the hedging instrument, the hedged item, the nature of the risk being hedged, and how the hedging instrument's effectiveness in offsetting the exposure to changes in the hedged item's fair value attributable to the hedged risk will be measured.

2. Both at inception of the hedge and on an ongoing basis, the hedging relationship is expected to be highly effective. An assessment of effectiveness is required whenever financial statements or earnings are reported, and at least every three months.

3. The hedged item must be specifically identified. It may be either all or a specific portion of a recognized asset or liability or of an unrecognized firm commitment.

4. The hedged item may be a portfolio of similar assets or liabilities that share the risk exposure for which they are being hedged. If a portfolio approach is used, individual items must be expected to respond proportionately with overall changes in the fair value of the portfolio.

5. The hedged item presents an exposure to changes in fair value attributable to the hedged risk that could affect reported earnings.

6. A nonderivative instrument, such as a Treasury note, may not be designated as a hedging instrument of a fair value hedge, except in a hedge of a foreign currency–denominated firm commitment or of foreign currency exposure to a net investment in a foreign operation.

When the criteria for hedge accounting are met, gains and losses on the qualifying fair value hedge are accounted for as follows:

• The gain or loss on the hedging instrument is recognized currently in earnings.
• The gain or loss, that is, the change in fair value, on the hedged item attributable to the hedged risk is recognized currently in earnings.

If the fair value hedge is fully effective, the gain or loss on the hedging instrument will exactly offset the loss or gain on the hedge item attributable to the hedged risk. Any difference between the two that arises would be due to hedge ineffectiveness and would be recognized currently in earnings. Even changes in the fair value of hedged items that are otherwise measured at fair value but for which changes in fair value are normally reported in the other comprehensive income component of shareholders' equity, such as available-for-sale investments, would be included currently in earnings. A series of examples are provided to demonstrate the application of hedge accounting to fair value hedges.

Fair Value Hedge of Investments in Equity Securities

The purchase of a put option, described earlier, to hedge the risk of changes in the market value of the investment in stock of Dell Computer could qualify for hedge accounting. Whether hedge accounting would be appropriate would depend on whether the put option was expected to be effective in hedging the risk of changes in market value of the investment.

An effective put option strategy would require more than a single option contract. The company undertaking the hedge would need to monitor its position, buying and selling contracts as needed, in order to ensure that changes in the fair value of the options could be expected to offset changes in the market value of the stock investment. Under these conditions, and assuming the hedging company designated the put options as a hedge of the fair value of the common stock investment and continually monitored the hedge's effectiveness, then hedge accounting would be appropriate.

Under hedge accounting, the investment in common stock of Dell Computer would be carried at market value with resulting gains and losses reported in income. Those gains and losses would be reported in income even if the investment is considered to be available for sale. Similarly, the put option contracts would be carried at market value with resulting gains and losses also reported in income. The gains and losses on the put option contracts would be used to offset losses and gains on the common stock investment. Any net difference between the two would be due to hedge ineffectiveness and would be included in income.

Fair Value Hedge of Heating Oil Inventory

Earlier, a company used a short position in a futures contract to hedge the fair value of its heating oil inventory. This is a hedge of commodity price risk. Hedge accounting will be appropriate if the futures contract is designated as a hedge of that risk and it is expected to be effective. Hedge effectiveness would normally require that the futures contract cover the same number of gallons of heating oil as the amount being hedged and that the price underlying the futures contract is for the same grade of heating oil and at the same location.[30] Under hedge accounting, the carrying value of the heating oil inventory would be adjusted for changes in its fair value. The commodity futures contract would be reported at fair value. Accompanying and offsetting gains and losses on changes in the fair value of the heating oil inventory and on the futures contract would be reported in earnings. There would be a net earnings effect only to the extent the hedge was ineffective.

Fair Value Hedge of Commitment to Buy Heating Oil Inventory

The heating oil company could also use a short position in a heating oil futures contract to hedge a firm commitment to buy heating oil at a fixed price. The firm purchase commitment creates commodity price risk. The company would incur a loss on the fixed-price purchase commitment if heating oil prices were to fall and would enjoy a gain if heating oil prices were to rise.

In the absence of hedge accounting, losses on the purchase commitment would be recorded, though gains would not. If the heating oil futures contract is designated as a fair value hedge of the firm purchase commitment and the criteria for hedge accounting are met, changes in fair value, including gains and losses on both the firm purchase commitment and the futures contract, would be reported in earnings. There would be no net earnings effect except to the extent the hedge was ineffective.

Fair Value Hedge of Fixed-Rate Debt

In an earlier example, a company used a receive-fixed, pay-variable interest rate swap to convert its fixed-rate debt into a variable-rate obligation. The company could designate the interest rate swap as a fair value hedge of its fixed-rate debt. The risk being hedged is interest rate risk. When interest rates rise, the fair value of fixed-rate debt decreases. Decreases in interest rates cause the fair value of fixed-rate debt to increase. However, the decrease in interest rates will result in an increase in the value of the interest rate swap. Assuming the interest rate swap has the same notional amount as the principal amount of the debt and the swap and debt have the same maturity dates, the swap could be designated as an effective fair value hedge of the fixed-rate debt. Hedge accounting would be appropriate.

Under hedge accounting, both the fixed-rate debt and the receive-fixed, pay-variable interest rate swap would be carried at market value. Gains and losses on both financial instruments, offsetting in amount, would be reported in income. A net gain or loss would appear in income only to the extent the hedge was ineffective.

What is particularly striking about this example is that while in the absence of a fair value hedge the fair value of fixed-rate debt would be disclosed, changes in that fair value would not be recognized. By hedging the debt, those gains and losses are now recognized, but are offset by losses and gains recognized on the hedging instrument. The net effect of hedge accounting is that gains and losses on the financial derivative are recognized only to the extent that they are ineffective as a fair value hedge.

Cash Flow Hedges

In a cash flow hedge, a company designates a financial derivative as hedging its exposure to variability in expected future cash flows that are attributable to a particular risk. That exposure may be associated with an existing recognized asset or liability, such as interest payments on variable-rate debt, or a forecasted transaction, such as an expected sale of a common stock investment. To qualify an existing recognized asset or liability or a forecasted transaction for hedge accounting, several criteria must be met. The following six points summarize these criteria:

1. There must be a formal documentation of the hedging relationship and the entity's risk management objective and strategy for undertaking the hedge, including identification of the hedging instrument, the hedged transaction, the nature of the risk being hedged, and how the hedging instrument's effectiveness in hedging the exposure to the hedged transaction's variability in cash flows attributable to the hedged risk will be assessed.

2. Both at inception of the hedge and on an ongoing basis, the hedging relationship is expected to be highly effective in achieving offsetting cash flows. An assessment of effectiveness is required whenever financial statements or earnings are reported, and at least every three months.

3. The hedged transaction must be specifically identified, and if a forecasted transaction, it must be a probable event.

4. The hedged transaction may be a group of individual transactions that share the same risk exposure for which they are designated as being hedged.

5. The hedged transaction presents an exposure to variations in cash flow attributable to the hedged risk that could affect reported earnings.

6. A nonderivative instrument, such as a Treasury note, may not be designated as a hedging instrument in a cash flow hedge.

When the criteria for hedge accounting are met, gains and losses on the effective portion of a qualifying cash flow hedge are accounted for in the other comprehensive income component of shareholders' equity. Amounts accumulated in other comprehensive income are reclassified into earnings in the same period during which the hedged forecasted transaction affects earnings. If a cash flow hedge is discontinued because it is probable that the original forecasted transaction will not occur, then any gain or loss on the hedging instrument that has been accumulated in other comprehensive income should be recognized in earnings. Gains and losses on the ineffective portion of a cash flow hedge are reported in earnings immediately and are not funneled through other comprehensive income. A series of examples are provided to demonstrate the application of hedge accounting to cash flow hedges.

Cash Flow Hedge of a Forecasted Sale of an Equity Security

If the holder of the stock in Dell Computer identified a future date on which sale of the stock was probable, then a put option strategy used to hedge the cash flow to be received from the sale of the company's investment would be considered to be a cash flow hedge. Assuming the put option strategy is designated as a hedge of variability in the cash flows to be received from the sale of the investment due to changes in its market value, that it is an effective strategy, and that its effectiveness is monitored, then hedge accounting is appropriate.

Under hedge accounting, a company with the stock investment would continue accounting for its investment as it always had. That is, assuming the investment is considered to be available for sale, it would be carried at market value with changes in market value—gains and losses—accumulated in other comprehensive income. The purchased put options would also be carried at market value with gains and losses offsetting those on the common stock investment accumulated in other comprehensive income. Any portion of the option strategy that was ineffective in hedging the common stock investment would be recognized currently in earnings. Ultimate sale of the common stock investment would result in the transfer to earnings from other comprehensive income of the accumulated and netted gains and losses on the stock and the purchased put options.

Cash Flow Hedge of Forecasted Purchase of Heating Oil Inventory

In an earlier example, a company with heating oil inventory entered into a firm commitment to purchase additional inventory. A short sale of a heating oil futures contract to hedge the inherent commodity price risk was considered to be a fair value hedge of the heating oil purchase commitment. If instead of entering into a firm commitment to buy the inventory the company identified a probable date of purchase, then the short position in the heating oil futures contract would be considered to be a cash flow hedge, a hedge of the cash flows to be paid on the purchase of the heating oil inventory. The underlying risk being hedged is commodity price risk.

Assuming the short position in the heating oil futures contract is considered to be a hedge of the cash flows to be paid on the expected purchase of the heating oil inventory, that it is an effective hedge, and that its effectiveness is monitored, then hedge accounting is appropriate. As it is an expected transaction, the company would not record its planned inventory purchase. The short position in the heating oil futures contract would, however, be reported at fair value. Resulting gains and losses on that contract would be reported in other comprehensive income. Gains and losses on any portion of the futures contract deemed to be ineffective as a hedging mechanism would be reported in earnings. When the purchased inventory is ultimately sold and the inventory's cost is transferred to cost of goods sold, then any net gains or losses on the heating oil futures contract that had been accumulated in other comprehensive income would be reported in earnings.

Cash Flow Hedge of Variable-Rate Debt

In an earlier example, a company used a receive-fixed, pay-variable interest rate swap as a fair value hedge of its fixed-rate debt. If instead of fixed-rate debt, the company had a variable-rate obligation, it could use a receive-variable, pay-fixed interest rate swap as a cash flow hedge of its variable interest payments. The underlying risk being hedged is interest rate risk.

If the company were to designate its interest rate swap as a cash flow hedge of the interest payments to be made on its variable-rate debt, and assuming that the hedge were effective and that its effectiveness were monitored, then hedge accounting would be appropriate. Under hedge accounting the company would not change how it accounts for its variable-rate debt. Interest expense and cash interest payments would rise and fall with changes in interest rates. Interest rate changes would also alter the receipt stream generated by the interest rate swap agreement. These changes would be reflected in income and cash flow and offset changes in interest expense and payments on the variable-rate debt.

The interest rate swap agreement itself would be carried at fair value. Gains and losses on adjusting the agreement to fair value would be reported in the other comprehensive income component of shareholders' equity. These gains and losses would net to zero when the swap agreement matured. If the debt were settled early, any gains and losses on the swap agreement that had been accumulated in other comprehensive income would be recognized in earnings. If the swap were terminated early, before settlement of the debt, any gains and losses accumulated in comprehensive income would continue to be carried there. These accumulated gains and losses would be recognized in earnings in the same periods during which the hedged debt affected earnings, resulting in an adjustment to interest expense.

Foreign Currency Hedges

The topic of foreign currency reporting is sufficiently broad and important to financial analysis as to warrant a separate chapter. Accordingly, we only introduce the topic of foreign currency hedges in the paragraphs below. A richer discussion of the topic, complete with more detailed examples, is provided in Chapter Seven.

Depending on the item or transaction being hedged, a foreign currency hedge can be a fair value hedge, a cash flow hedge, or a hedge of a net investment in a foreign operation. Highlights of the accounting for all three types of foreign currency hedges are provided below.

Foreign Currency Fair Value Hedges

A foreign currency fair value hedge can be a hedge of an unrecognized foreign currency firm commitment or of the foreign currency exposure of an available-for-sale security. A firm commitment to buy inventory at an agreed-upon price denominated in a foreign currency creates a foreign currency–denominated purchase commitment. Such a commitment creates foreign currency risk.[31] Like any foreign currency–denominated liability, in terms of an entity's own currency the value of the obligation changes with changes in the foreign currency's exchange rate. Losses accrue with increases in the exchange rate and gains result from decreases in the rate.

This foreign currency purchase commitment can be hedged with many financial derivatives, including a long position in a foreign currency forward contract, futures contract, or foreign currency call option.[32] To qualify for hedge accounting, the same criteria must be met as with non–foreign currency–denominated fair value hedges. Generally, the hedging instrument must be designated as a hedge of the foreign currency risk, the hedge must be effective and its effectiveness must be monitored. With hedge accounting, changes in the fair value of the purchase commitment would be recorded in earnings. The financial derivative used to hedge the commitment would be carried at fair value with resulting gains and losses, offsetting those generated by the purchase commitment, also recorded in earnings.

Foreign currency risk also arises when an available-for-sale investment position is taken in a foreign currency–denominated debt or equity security.[33] This asset-related foreign currency risk can be hedged with short positions in foreign currency forward contracts, futures contracts, and with purchased foreign currency put options.

The foreign currency available-for-sale security would be carried at market value. A hedging item would be similarly valued. To the extent the available-for-sale security is unhedged, changes in its market value would be recorded in other comprehensive income. However, if the criteria for hedge accounting are met, changes in the market value of the security attributable to changes in foreign currency exchange rates would be recorded in earnings and netted against the earnings effect of the hedging instrument.

Earlier in this chapter we provided an example of a U.S. company that incurred an obligation of 100,000 British pounds payable on September 1, 1999. The company hedged its foreign currency risk with a foreign currency forward exchange contract to purchase 100,000 British pound for delivery on September 1, 1999. Under current accounting guidelines, the British pound obligation is adjusted for changes in foreign currency exchange rates, resulting in gains and losses. Those gains and losses are recorded in earnings. The forward exchange contract is similarly adjusted, resulting in the recording of offsetting gains and losses in earnings. No special hedge accounting provisions are needed.

Foreign Currency Cash Flow Hedges

Foreign currency cash flow hedges are hedges of the foreign currency exposure to variability in the cash flows associated with forecasted foreign currency–denominated transactions. Example transactions include a probable export sale or a forecast purchase of inventory, in which the sale price and purchase price, respectively, are denominated in a foreign currency.

Both transactions can be hedged with foreign currency–denominated financial derivatives, including forward contracts, futures contracts, and options. For hedge accounting treatment, the foreign currency hedges must fulfill the criteria for cash flow hedges. Generally, the hedging instrument must be designated as a hedge of the foreign currency risk, the hedge must be effective, and effectiveness must be monitored.

No special accounting treatment is afforded the forecast transactions. The transactions are recorded when they occur. The hedging items are accounted for at fair value. If the criteria for hedge accounting treatment are met, resulting gains and losses are accumulated in other comprehensive income. These gains and losses are recorded in earnings when the forecast transactions are prematurely terminated or, if not prematurely terminated, when they ultimately affect earnings. If the hedges are terminated early, any gains and losses accumulated in other comprehensive income are carried there until the earnings effect is recorded on the underlying hedged item.

Hedges of Net Investments in Foreign Operations

As will be discussed in Chapter Seven, a company with a foreign subsidiary, or with an equity-accounted investment located in a foreign country, will have foreign currency risk. Such investments are typically translated at the current exchange rate and the effects of changes in the exchange rate are accumulated in other comprehensive income. Hedges of the foreign currency risk inherent in these investments might be undertaken with a foreign currency forward contract, futures contract, or an option. Another likely hedging instrument would be a nonderivative. For example, a foreign currency–denominated obligation would hedge a net investment in a foreign operation.

If the financial derivative or nonderivative is designated and effective as a hedge of the investment in a foreign operation and if that effectiveness is monitored, the hedging instrument will qualify for hedge accounting. Hedge accounting does not change the accounting applied to the foreign investment itself. Changes in the carrying value of the investment due to changes in exchange rates are accumulated in other comprehensive income. The hedging instrument will be carried at fair value. Resulting gains and losses will also be accumulated in other comprehensive income and will not be recorded in earnings until some or all of the investment is sold or the investment affects earnings in some other way.

Transition to SFAS No. 133

Because SFAS No. 133 brings onto the financial statements many financial derivative positions that had previously been excluded, a carefully planned transition to the new standard was needed. The standard uses a transition adjustment to capture the total financial statement effects of the difference between the old and new way of accounting for financial derivatives. Included in this transition adjustment are the following items calculated on the date of initial application of SFAS No. 133:

- The difference between a derivative's previous carrying amount and its fair value. Netted from this component of the transition adjustment will be offsetting gains and losses arising from adjusting the carrying amounts of hedged items to fair value.

- Any gains or losses on derivatives that had previously been deferred under superseded accounting standards
- Any gains or losses on derivatives designated as fair value hedges that were previously reported in other comprehensive income.

The transition adjustment resulting from adopting the new standard will be reported as a cumulative effect of a change in accounting principle. That cumulative effect amount will appear in net income or other comprehensive income, depending on whether the financial derivatives giving rise to the transition adjustment were used as hedging instruments, and if so, the nature of the hedge. A transition adjustment arising from financial derivatives that are not employed as hedging instruments and those used in fair value hedges will be reported as a cumulative effect–type adjustment of net income. A transition adjustment arising from financial derivatives that are used in cash flow hedges will be reported as a cumulative effect adjustment of other comprehensive income.[34]

DISCLOSURE REQUIREMENTS FOR FINANCIAL DERIVATIVES

The disclosure requirements for financial derivatives found in SFAS No. 133 supplement those found in SFAS No. 107, "Disclosures about Fair Value of Financial Instruments." That standard provides disclosure requirements for all financial instruments, including financial derivatives.

SFAS No. 107 defines financial instruments broadly. In its definition, the standard includes cash, evidence of an ownership interest in an entity, or a contract that imposes on an entity a contractual obligation to deliver cash or another financial instrument or exchange financial instruments on potentially unfavorable terms, or conveys to an entity a contractual right to receive cash or another financial instrument or exchange financial instruments on potentially favorable terms. This definition includes just about every conceivable financial item, whether recognized in the financial statements or not. Examples include cash, accounts receivable, loans receivable, investments, accounts payable, deposit liabilities, and short- and long-term debt, as well as financial derivatives.

According to the disclosure requirements of SFAS No. 107, companies must disclose, either in the body of the financial statements or in the notes, the fair value of financial instruments for which it is practicable to estimate that value.[35] Also to be disclosed is the method and significant assumptions used to estimate fair value. If it is not practicable to estimate fair value, then a company must disclose all pertinent information for estimating fair value, such as the carrying amount, effective interest rate, and maturity, and it must provide the reasons why it is not practicable to estimate fair value.

SFAS No. 107 was then amended by SFAS No. 133 to include one additional disclosure requirement and one encouraged disclosure. The added disclosure requirement is the requirement that companies disclose information on concentrations about the credit risk of its financial instruments. Such concentrations could arise from an individual counterparty or groups of counterparties that are engaged in similar activities or that have similar economic characteristics. The encouraged disclosure is quantitative information about the market risk of a company's financial instruments.

SFAS No. 133 added to these requirements disclosures that are specifically relevant for financial derivatives. At the top of the FASB's list is the requirement that companies disclose their objectives for holding or issuing derivative instruments, the context needed to understand those objectives, and its strategies for achieving those objectives. A company's derivatives-related disclosures must include an identification of those derivatives designated as fair value hedges, as cash flow hedges, as hedges of the foreign currency exposure of a net investment in a foreign operation, and other derivatives that are not held for hedging purposes. A company must also indicate its risk management policy for each type of hedge, including a description of the items or transactions for which risk is being hedged. For derivatives not designated as hedges, a company must indicate the purpose of this derivative activity.

The accounting standard also includes earnings-related disclosure requirements for each type of hedge. For fair value and cash flow hedges, companies are required to disclose the net gain or loss recognized in earnings during the reporting period and a description of where the net gain or loss is reported in the financial statements. For cash flow hedges, that net gain or loss represents the amount of the hedges' ineffectiveness or the amount of the hedges' gain or loss that was purposefully excluded from the hedging activity. Companies are also required to disclose the amount of any net gain or loss recognized in earnings when a hedged item no longer qualifies for hedge accounting.

For cash flow hedges, companies have additional disclosure requirements. Reporting firms with cash flow hedges must provide a description of the transaction or event that will result in the reclassification into earnings of gains and losses that are reported in accumulated other comprehensive income, and the amount expected to be reclassified within the next 12 months. Companies with cash flow hedges must also disclose the maximum length of time over which the firm is hedging its exposure to the variability in future cash flows for forecasted transactions.

For hedges of the foreign currency exposure of a net investment in a foreign operation, companies must disclose the net amount of gains or losses included in the cumulative translation adjustment during the reporting period. This translation adjustment is included with the accumulated other comprehensive income component of shareholders' equity.

Disclosure Examples

As noted, SFAS No. 133 is not effective until fiscal years beginning after June 15, 2000. For calendar-year companies, this effective date means that companies will not apply the new standard until the year ending December 31, 2001. Their annual reports, including application of the new accounting and reporting requirements, will not appear until early 2002. Although the FASB does encourage early application of SFAS No. 133, at the time of this writing, we do not have financial statement examples of the new disclosures to provide. What we do have are the accounting policy and fair value disclosures of financial instruments, including financial derivatives, made pursuant to SFAS No. 105, "Disclosure of Information about Financial Instruments with Off-Balance-Sheet Risk and Financial Instruments with Concentrations of Credit Risk"; SFAS No. 107, "Disclosures about Fair Value of Financial Instruments"; and SFAS No. 119, "Disclosure about Derivative Financial Instruments and Fair Value of Financial Instruments."[36] With the examples provided, we will identify how the accounting will differ and what additional disclosures companies will make as the new accounting rules are adopted.

Accounting Policy Note: Philip Morris Companies, Inc.

Philip Morris Companies, Inc. makes reference to the new accounting standard for financial derivatives with the following statement:

> During 1998, the Financial Accounting Standards Board issued Statement of Financial Accounting Standards ("SFAS") No. 133, "Accounting for Derivative Instruments and Hedging Activities," which must be adopted by the Company by January 1, 2000. SFAS No. 133 requires that all derivative financial instruments be recorded on the consolidated balance sheets at their fair value. Changes in the fair value of derivatives will be recorded each period in earnings or other comprehensive earnings, depending on whether a derivative is designated as part of a hedge transaction and, if it is, the type of hedge transaction. Gains and losses on derivative instruments reported in other comprehensive earnings will be reclassified to earnings in the periods in which earnings are affected by the hedged item. The Company has not yet determined the impact that adoption or subsequent application of SFAS No. 133 will have on its financial position or results of operations.[37]

The statement notes how the Company will account for financial derivatives once it begins to apply the provisions of SFAS No. 133. More specifically, it notes that derivative financial instruments will be recorded on the balance sheet at fair value with changes in fair value being recorded in earnings or other comprehensive income, depending on whether the derivative in question is a hedge, and if so, the type of hedge it is. Further, it notes that gains and losses reported in other comprehensive income will be reclassified to earnings in those periods in which earnings are affected by the hedged items. As a way to see how these new provisions will alter extant accounting and reporting practices for financial derivatives, in the following paragraphs we contrast the company's current accounting policies for its financial derivatives with those policies expected to be in place once the new accounting standard is adopted.

Philip Morris begins its accounting policy note for financial derivatives with the following statement on hedging:

> **Hedging instruments:** The Company utilizes certain financial instruments to manage its foreign currency, commodity and interest rate exposures. The Company does not engage in trading or other speculative use of these financial instruments. To qualify as a hedge, the Company must be exposed to price, currency or interest rate risk and the financial instrument must reduce the exposure and be designated as a hedge. Additionally, for hedges of anticipated transactions, the significant characteristics and expected terms of the anticipated transaction must be identified and it must be probable that the anticipated transaction will occur. Financial instruments qualifying for hedge accounting must maintain a high correlation between the hedging instrument and the item being hedged, both at inception and throughout the hedged period.[38]

In this statement, the Company fulfills many of the disclosure requirements of SFAS No. 133. It discloses its objectives for holding financial derivatives, ". . . to manage its foreign currency, commodity and interest rate exposures . . . the Company does not engage in trading or other speculative use of these financial instruments," and notes the kinds of risk being hedged, "price, currency or interest rate risk." The Company also provides a statement about how it assesses and monitors hedge effectiveness, ". . . financial instruments qualifying for hedge accounting must maintain a high correlation between the hedging instrument and the item being hedged, both at inception and throughout the hedged period."

The Company then provides a description of its accounting practices for financial derivatives. The Company describes its hedge accounting policy for foreign currency exposure as follows:

> The Company uses forward contracts, options and swap agreements to mitigate its foreign currency exposure. The corresponding gains and losses on those contracts are deferred and included in the basis of the underlying hedged transactions when settled.[39]

Given that foreign currency gains and losses are currently being deferred, this policy appears to refer to the company's accounting for financial derivatives used to mitigate foreign currency risk associated with firm commitments denominated in foreign currencies. Current accounting standards permit deferral of foreign currency gains and losses in such situations. Under SFAS No. 133, this arrangement would be considered a foreign currency fair value hedge of an unrecognized firm commitment. In such a hedge arrangement, the financial derivative would be carried at fair value with changes in fair value, offset by the effects of exchange rate changes on the firm commitment, recorded in earnings.

To the extent the Company has foreign currency exposure associated with existing foreign currency denominated account balances, such as receivables, payables, and debt obligations, then financial derivatives used to mitigate such foreign currency exposure would not be considered hedges under SFAS No. 133. In such situations, no assessment of hedge effectiveness would be needed. Nonetheless, the financial derivatives used to mitigate the foreign currency exposure would be carried at fair value and resulting gains and losses would be recorded in earnings. Similarly, the foreign currency denominated account balances would be translated and reported at the current exchange rate. Any changes in the translated balance amounts would also be recorded in earnings, and would be offset by gains and losses on the derivatives.

The Company describes its accounting policies for hedges of net investments in foreign operations as follows:

> Foreign currency and related interest rate swap agreements are used to hedge certain foreign currency net investments. Realized and unrealized gains and losses on foreign currency swap agreements that are effective as hedges of net assets in foreign subsidiaries are offset against currency translation adjustments as a component of stockholders' equity. The interest differential to be paid or received under the currency and related interest rate swap agreements is recognized over the life of the related debt and is included in interest and other debt expense, net. Gains and losses on terminated foreign currency swap agreements, if any, are recorded as currency translation adjustments, which is a component of stockholders' equity.[40]

The Company records gains and losses on foreign currency swap agreements used to hedge its net assets in foreign subsidiaries in the translation adjustment within shareholders' equity. The same practice would be followed under SFAS No. 133. That is, the foreign currency swap agreements would be reported at fair value with resulting gains and losses recorded in the foreign currency translation adjustment component of accumulated other comprehensive income. The Company also records gains and losses on terminated foreign currency swap agreements in the translation adjustment component of shareholders' equity. Under SFAS No. 133, the treatment is the same. Any gain or loss accumulated in other comprehensive income on a terminated hedge position would be carried in the accumulated other comprehensive income component of shareholders' equity until the foreign investment was sold or impacted earnings in some other way. The Company's current treatment of interest differentials paid or received under the interest rate swap agreements related to its foreign operations would continue to be recognized in interest expense under SFAS No. 133.

The Company provides the following accounting policy statement regarding its interest rate swaps:

> Interest rate swap agreements are accounted for on an accrual basis with the net receivable or payable recognized as an adjustment to interest expense. Gains and losses on terminated interest rate swaps, if any, are recognized over the remaining life of the arrangement, or immediately, if the hedged items do not remain outstanding. The fair value of the interest rate swap agreements and changes in these fair values as a result of changes in market interest rates are not recognized in the consolidated financial statements.[41]

These interest rate swaps are cash flow hedges of variable interest payments on the Company's outstanding debt. In the note, the Company discloses that any gains and losses on terminated interest rate swaps are recognized over the remaining life of the debt arrangement, or immediately if the debt arrangement does not remain outstanding. Under SFAS No. 133, gains and losses on terminated swaps would be carried in accumulated other comprehensive income and would be recognized as an adjustment to interest expense over the remaining life of the debt arrangement. Consistent with the company's current policy, they would be recognized immediately in earnings if the underlying debt arrangement were no longer outstanding.

In the note, the Company also discloses that currently, the fair value of the interest rate swap agreements and changes in that value are not recognized. Under SFAS No. 133, the swaps would be carried at fair value and changes in that value, assuming the swaps serve as cash flow hedges, would be reported in other comprehensive income.

The company discloses use of commodity futures and forward contracts to hedge its commodity price risk:

> Commodity futures and forward contracts are used by the Company to procure raw materials, primarily coffee, cocoa, sugar, wheat and corn. Commodity futures and options are also used to hedge the price of certain commodities, primarily coffee and cocoa. Realized gains and losses on commodity futures, forward contracts and options are deferred as a component of inventories and are recognized when related raw material costs are charged to cost of sales. If the anticipated transaction were not to occur, the gains and losses would be recognized in earnings currently.

The Company is using these financial derivatives as cash flow hedges of expected commodity-based inventory transactions.[42] Realized gains and losses on the derivatives are deferred as a component of the inventories and recognized when the inventories are sold. Under SFAS No. 133, the earnings effect of this policy would not be changed. Under the new standard, the derivatives would be carried at fair value with accompanying gains and losses recognized in other comprehensive income, that is, excluded from earnings. The accumulated gains and losses would be recognized in earnings when the inventory was sold. Under the new standard, the company will continue to recognize in earnings gains and losses on financial derivatives intended as hedges of anticipated transactions that do not occur.

Finally, the Company discloses the use of options to hedge anticipated transactions:

> Options are used to hedge anticipated transactions. Option premiums are recorded generally as other current assets on the consolidated balance sheets and amortized to interest and other debt expense, net over the lives of the related options. The values of options, excluding their time values, are recognized as adjustments to the related hedged items. If anticipated transactions were not to occur, any gains or losses would be recognized in earnings currently.

These policies will change under SFAS No. 133. Rather than amortizing option premiums, the company will carry option contracts at fair value. Changes in the fair value of any portion of the option that is designated as a hedge of an anticipated transaction would be recorded in other comprehensive income. Amounts accumulated there would be recorded in earnings when the anticipated hedged item is recognized in earnings. Changes in the fair value of any portion of the

option that is not designated as a hedge, and this would include changes in the
option's time value, would be recorded in earnings currently.

In other footnotes to its annual report, Philip Morris provided disclosures of
the fair value and carrying value of its financial instruments, including financial
derivatives. The following added disclosures are expected to accompany the company's adoption of SFAS No. 133:

- The amount of gains and losses recognized on the company's fair value hedges
  and discontinued hedges and an identification of where these items are reported
  in the financial statements
- A description of the transaction or event that will result in the reclassification
  into earnings of gains and losses that are reported in accumulated other comprehensive income and the amount expected to be reclassified within the next
  12 months
- The maximum length of time over which the company is hedging its exposure
  to the variability in future cash flow for forecasted transactions
- The amount of gains or losses included in accumulated other comprehensive
  income for hedges of foreign currency exposure of net investments in foreign
  operations

Fair Value and Carrying Value Disclosures of Financial Derivatives: AT&T Corporation

In the notes to its annual report, AT&T Corporation provided a summary of the
notional amounts, valuation methods used, and the fair value and carrying value
for its financial derivatives. Excerpts from the Company's disclosures are provided
in Exhibit 6.1.

Many of AT&T's disclosures will remain after the company adopts SFAS No.
133. The company is identifying its financial derivatives, showing how they are
valued, and presenting fair value amounts. In particular, what will change under
the new guidelines are the carrying values for the financial derivatives. Because
they will be carried at fair value, there will be no need to disclose different carrying
values.

Loss on a Hedge Agreement: Georgia Gulf Corp.

On its 1998 consolidated statement of income, Georgia Gulf Corp. reports a "Loss
on interest rate hedge agreement" of $9 million. An accompanying footnote de-
scribes the loss as follows:

> In June 1998, the Company filed a shelf registration with the Securities and Exchange
> Commission for the issuance of $200,000,000 of long-term bonds. Shortly after the
> filing, the Company entered into an agreement to lock in interest rates on a portion

Exhibit 6.1.   Disclosures of Financial Derivatives: AT&T Corp., Excerpts from Footnotes to Financial Statements, for the Year Ended December 31, 1998 (Millions of Dollars)

Fair Values of Financial Instruments Including Derivative Financial Instruments

The following table summarizes the notional amounts of material financial instruments. The notional amounts represent agreed-upon amounts on which calculations of dollars to be exchanged are based. They do not represent amounts exchanged by the parties and, therefore, are not a measure of our exposure. Our exposure is limited to the fair value of the contracts with a positive fair value plus interest receivable, if any, at the reporting date.

Derivatives and Off-Balance-Sheet Instruments

	1997 *Contract/Notional Amount*	1998 *Contract/Notional Amount*
Interest rate swap agreements	$671	$702
Foreign exchange:		
Forward contracts	426	244
Option contracts	2	—
Letters of credit	63	184
Guarantees of debt	242	237

The following tables show the valuation methods, carrying amounts and estimated fair values of material financial instruments.

Financial Instrument	*Valuation Method*
Debt excluding capital leases	Market quotes or based on rates available to us for debt with similar terms and maturities
Letters of credit	Fees paid to obtain the obligations
Guarantees of debt	There are no quoted market prices for similar agreements available
Interest rate swap agreements	Market quotes obtained from dealers
Foreign exchange contracts	Market quotes

For debt excluding capital leases, the carrying amounts and fair values were $11,875 and $12,312, respectively, for 1997; and $6,691 and $7,136, respectively, for 1998.

	1997			
	Carrying Amount		*Fair Value*	
	Asset	*Liability*	*Asset*	*Liability*
Interest rate swap agreements	$3	$10	$5	$31
Foreign exchange forward contracts	$—	$21	$3	$33

(continued)

Exhibit 6.1.   (Continued) Disclosures of Financial Derivatives: AT&T Corp., Excerpts from Footnotes to Financial Statements, for the Year Ended December 31, 1998 (Millions of Dollars)

	1998			
	Carrying Amount		*Fair Value*	
	Asset	*Liability*	*Asset*	*Liability*
Interest rate swap agreements	$5	$13	$—	$19
Foreign exchange forward contracts	$7	$7	$13	$4

Source: AT&T Corp., annual report, December 1998, pp. 62–63.

of the long-term bonds. During the third quarter of 1998, treasury yields dropped to their lowest levels in 30 years, while at the same time, investors' preference for treasury bonds and weakened demand for corporate bonds limited the Company's ability to issue longer term bonds. As a result, the Company's plans to issue long-term bonds were postponed indefinitely and the interest rate lock agreements were terminated, resulting in a pretax loss of $9,500,000 in the third quarter of 1998.

The company had entered into a cash flow hedge of an expected transaction. Had the borrowing been effected, under SFAS No. 133, the loss on the interest rate hedge would have been accumulated in other comprehensive income. However, given its termination, the loss would be reported as an earnings charge, just as the company handled the loss in this example.

ANALYSIS

Financial derivatives have straightforward implications for analysis when considered from the standpoint of financial quality. Because of their nonrecurring character, gains and losses recognized in earnings on derivatives' positions that are not used as hedges will affect earnings quality on the persistence dimension. A nonrecurring gain will impair earnings quality on the persistence dimension, but a nonrecurring loss will enhance it. Moreover, since the vast majority of derivatives-related instruments settle either daily or in the near term, these gains and losses tend to be cash backed. By definition, financial derivatives require only nominal initial net investments. Accordingly, the amount of cash received from a gain position or paid due to a loss position will be very close in amount to the gain or loss recorded. As a result, these gains and losses will have immaterial implications for earnings quality on the cash dimension. The gains will be approximately equal to the cash received. The losses will be approximately equal to the cash paid.

Consider the $9.5 million loss recognized by Georgia Gulf on a terminated interest rate lock agreement. The loss is a nonrecurring loss and appeared to entail a cash payment of the same amount. As such, the loss enhances earnings quality on the persistence dimension, but has no implications for earnings quality on the cash dimension.

Prior to adoption of SFAS No. 133, financial derivatives offer situations where carrying values differ from fair values, impacting position quality. For example, in Exhibit 6.1, AT&T disclosed at December 31, 1998, the existence of interest rate swaps with a net liability carrying value of $8 million (an asset carrying value of $5 million less a liability carrying value of $13 million). On the same date, the fair value of this net liability was $19 million. Position quality was impaired, though given the company's size, by an immaterial amount. Also on December 31, 1998, the company disclosed that the net carrying value of its foreign exchange forward contracts was zero (an asset carrying value of $7 million less a liability carrying value of $7 million). On the same date, the fair value of the foreign exchange forward contracts was a net asset position of $9 million ($13 million for the asset less $4 million for the liability). Here, position quality was enhanced, though again by an immaterial amount. Combining the position-quality effects of the interest rate swap agreements and the foreign exchange forward contracts results in a slight impairment of position quality.

Once SFAS No. 133 is adopted, any position-quality effects of financial derivatives will be eliminated. With the new standard, all financial derivatives, whether held as hedges or for investment purposes, will be reported at fair value. There will no longer be differences between carrying value and fair value.

The analysis of financial derivatives goes well beyond the issues of earnings and position quality. Financial derivatives used as hedges provide a well-tested approach for reducing corporate risk. As they reduce risk, they also reduce earnings volatility. However, when financial derivatives are used for speculative gain, there is also the risk of substantial loss. Examples such as the derivatives-related losses taken by Dell Computer and Procter & Gamble attest to the inherent risk created by speculative derivatives trades. A careful analysis of financial derivatives requires an assessment of the objectives for positions taken in financial derivatives, their contribution to financial results, and a company's exposure to future loss.

The American Institute of Certified Public Accountants (AICPA) has developed a series of questions designed to help managements and boards of directors gain a better understanding of their entity's derivatives activities. These questions are also helpful for equity and credit analysts in better understanding the objectives for a firm's use of financial derivatives and the company's exposure to future loss. The AICPA's questions are reproduced below.

1. Has the board established a clear and internally consistent risk management policy, including risk limits (as appropriate)?

   Are our objectives and goals for derivatives activities clearly stated and communicated? To what extent are our operational objectives for derivatives being achieved? Are derivatives used to mitigate risk or do they create additional risk? If risk is being assumed, are trading limits established? Is the entity's strategy for derivatives use designed to further its economic, regulatory, industry, and/or operating objectives?

2. Are management's strategies and implementation policies consistent with the board's authorization?

Management's philosophy and operating style create an environment that influences the actions of treasury and other personnel involved in derivatives activities. The assignment of authority and responsibility for derivatives transactions sends an important message. Is that message clear? Is compliance with these or related policies and procedures evaluated regularly? Does the treasury function review itself, or is it evaluated, as a profit center?

3. Do key controls exist to ensure that only authorized transactions take place and that unauthorized transactions are quickly detected and appropriate action is taken?

Internal controls over derivatives activities should be monitored on an ongoing basis, and should also be subject to separate evaluations. Who is evaluating controls over derivatives being identified and reported upstream? Are duties involving execution of derivatives transactions segregated from other duties (for example, the accounting and internal audit functions)?

4. Are the magnitude, complexity, and risks of the entity's derivatives commensurate with the entity's objectives?

What are the entity's risk exposures, including derivatives? Internal analyses should include quantitative and qualitative information about the entity's derivatives activities. Analyses should address the risks associated with derivatives, which include:

- Credit risk (the possible financial loss resulting from a counterparty's failure to meet its financial obligations)
- Market risk (the possible financial loss resulting from adverse movements in the price of a financial asset or commodity)
- Legal risk (the possible financial loss resulting from a legal or regulatory action that could invalidate a financial contract)
- Control risk (the possible financial loss resulting from inadequate internal control structure)

Are our derivatives transactions standard for their class (that is, plain vanilla) or are they more complex? Is the complexity of derivatives transactions inconsistent with the risks being managed? The entity's risk assessment should result in a determination about how to manage identified risks of derivatives activities. Has management anticipated how it will manage potential derivatives risks before assuming them?

5. Are personnel with authority to engage in and monitor derivative transactions well qualified and appropriately trained?

Who are the key derivatives players within the entity? Is the knowledge vested only in one individual or a small group? The complexity of derivatives activities should be accompanied by development of personnel. For example, do employees involved in derivatives activities have the appropriate technical and professional expertise? Are other employees being appropriately educated before they become involved with derivatives transactions? Does the entity have personnel that have been cross-trained in case of the absence or departure of key personnel involved with derivatives activities? How do we ensure the integrity, ethical values, and competence of personnel involved with derivatives activities?

6. Do the right people have the right information to make decisions?

What information about derivatives activities are we identifying and capturing, and how is it being communicated? The information should address both external and internal events, activities, and conditions. For example, are we capturing and communicating information about market changes affecting derivatives transactions and about changes in our strategy for the mix of assets and liabilities that are the focus of risk management activities involving derivatives? Is this information being communicated to all affected parties?

Are the analysis and internal reporting of risks the company is managing and the effectiveness of its strategies comprehensive, reliable, and well designed to facilitate oversight? The board should consider derivatives activities in the context of how related risks affect the achievement of the entity's objectives—economic, regulatory, industry, or operating. For example, do derivatives activities increase the entity's exposure to risks that might frustrate, rather than further, achievement of these objectives?

Do we mark our derivatives transactions to market regularly (and, if not, why not)? Do we have good systems for marking transactions to market? Have the systems been tested by persons independent of the derivatives function? Do we know how the value of our derivatives will change under extreme market conditions? Is our published financial information about derivatives being prepared reliably and in conformity with generally accepted accounting principles?[43]

While the AICPA's questions are helpful to analysts in better understanding a company's objectives for its use of financial derivatives and the company's exposure to loss, the questions do not address the contribution of financial derivatives to reported results. In analyzing the effects of derivatives on a company's results, it is important to note (a) the amount of net gains or losses resulting from derivatives activities appearing in the income statement, and (b) the amount of nets gains or losses accumulated in other comprehensive income plus the projected timing of their inclusion in earnings. Disclosures provided by SFAS No. 133 will provide needed information for both items.

Gains and losses appearing in the income statement currently are inherently nonrecurring and should be removed when calculating sustainable earnings. Financial institutions that maintain a trading desk are a possible exception, though in periods of outsized gains or losses, similar steps should be taken. Gains and losses accumulated in other comprehensive income are the result of cash flow hedges and hedges of net investments in foreign operations. Although these amounts will appear in earnings, it must be remembered that they will also be offset by the earnings effects of related hedged items.

SUMMARY

The purpose of this chapter is to provide the analyst with a broader understanding of financial derivatives—their mechanics, their accounting and reporting requirements, and how to analyze their risk exposure and earnings effects. The following points are made in the chapter:

- Financial derivatives are financial instruments that derive their value from the price or rate of an underlying financial contract or index. The underlying financial contract or index can be a security price, foreign exchange rate, commodity price, interest rate, or an index of prices or rates. Settlement is effected through the receipt or payment of cash outside the contract, or through delivery of another asset. The terms of settlement are calculated using a notional amount—a number of shares, currency units, principal amount, or other measure of size or volume. The acquisition of a financial derivative requires either no net investment or a net investment that is smaller than the notional amount or one that is determined by applying the notional amount to the underlying financial contract or index. Examples include common stock call and put options, foreign currency forward exchange contracts, commodity futures contracts, and interest rate swaps.
- Financial derivatives are often used to manage or hedge risk—replacing one risk with another, reducing risk to a lower level, or in some instances, eliminating risk altogether.
- Risk is uncertainty or potential variability of financial outcomes. Companies face many and varied kinds of risk. Four types of risk for which financial derivatives are useful in hedging are (a) commodity price risk, (b) foreign currency risk, (c) interest rate risk, and (d) market value risk.
- In addition to using financial derivatives to hedge risk, companies can also use natural hedges. With a natural hedge, existing or newly created financial instruments are used to manage risk.
- In addition to being used to manage risk, financial derivatives can also be used as vehicles for speculative gain. The large amount of leverage inherent in derivatives contracts makes it possible to earn outsized gains on them. However, that same leverage can result in significant losses. There is always the opportunity to incur substantial losses when a company carries speculative derivatives positions.

- Accounting and disclosure requirements for financial derivatives have recently changed. Accounting requirements for financial derivatives are provided in SFAS No. 133, "Accounting for Derivative Instruments and Hedging Activities," which is effective for fiscal years beginning after June 15, 2000.[44] Under the new standard, financial derivatives are to be carried at fair value. Resulting gains and losses are reported in income or the other comprehensive income component of shareholders' equity depending on whether the derivatives serve as hedges and the nature of those hedges. Gains and losses on financial derivatives that do not serve as hedges are recognized in earnings. Gains and losses on financial derivatives that serve as fair value hedges of on-balance-sheet assets and liabilities and of firm commitments are also recognized in earnings and serve to offset gains and losses recognized on the hedged items. Gains and losses on financial derivatives that serve as cash flow hedges of on-balance-sheet items and expected transactions are accumulated in other comprehensive income. These gains and losses are recognized in earnings when the hedged items affect earnings.

- Financial derivatives can also be used in foreign currency fair value and cash flow hedges and to hedge a net investment in a foreign operation. Foreign currency fair value and cash flow hedges are accounted for in the same manner as non–foreign currency fair value and cash flow hedges. A foreign currency hedge of a net investment in a foreign operation is carried at fair value. Gains and losses on that hedge are accumulated in other comprehensive income and offset translation gains and losses on the foreign investment. A more in-depth consideration of the translation of foreign currency transactions and foreign currency financial statements, including the use of hedges to minimize foreign currency risk, is provided in Chapter Seven.

- Disclosure requirements for financial derivatives are provided in SFAS No. 107, "Disclosures about Fair Value of Financial Instruments," and in SFAS No. 133.[45] Companies must disclose the fair value of financial instruments, including derivatives, the method used to estimate fair value, and information about the credit risk of its financial instruments. For financial derivatives, companies must disclose their objectives for holding derivatives and strategies for achieving those objectives, an identification of the derivatives designated as fair value hedges, as cash flow hedges, and as hedges of foreign currency exposure of net investments in foreign operations, and their risk management policy for each type of hedge, including a description of the items or transactions for which risk is being hedged. For derivatives not designated as hedges, companies must indicate the purpose of their derivative activity.

- SFAS No. 133 also includes earnings-related disclosure requirements for each type of hedge. For fair value and cash flow hedges, companies must disclose the net gain or loss recognized in earnings during a reporting period and a description of where that net gain or loss is reported.

- For cash flow hedges, companies must also provide a description of the transaction or event that will result in the reclassification into earnings of gains and losses that are reported in accumulated other comprehensive income, and the amount expected to be reclassified within the next 12 months. Companies with cash flow hedges must also disclose the maximum length of time over which the firm is hedging its exposure to the variability in future cash flows for forecasted transactions.

- For hedges of the foreign currency exposure of a net investment in a foreign operation, companies must disclose the net amount of gains or losses included in accumulated other comprehensive income.

- Financial derivatives have limited implications for financial quality. Derivatives-related gains impair earnings quality on the persistence dimension, losses enhance it. Because derivatives transactions are typically settled in cash for amounts roughly equal to the gains and losses reported, their implications for earnings quality on the cash dimension are, in most cases, immaterial. Under SFAS No.133, financial derivatives are carried at fair value. As such, they do not impact position quality.

- Beyond the issues of financial quality, derivatives have far-reaching implications for analysis. Derivatives used for speculative gain carry the risk of substantial loss. Analysts must carefully assess the derivatives-related risk exposure of the companies they analyze and because of their inherent nonrecurring quality, understand the contribution of derivatives to earnings.

GLOSSARY

Call option A contract that gives its holder the right but not the obligation to buy an asset, typically a financial instrument, at a specified price through a specified date.

Cash flow hedge A hedge used to reduce exposure to variability in expected future cash flows of a recognized asset or liability, an expected transaction, or a foreign currency expected transaction, that are due to a particular risk.

Clearinghouse An organization interposed between buyers and sellers of options and futures. All trades are actually sales to or purchases from the clearinghouse.

Commodity price risk The risk that market forces will change the prices of commodities, such as oil and natural gas, coal, industrial metals, precious metals, and agricultural commodities.

Comprehensive income The change in equity of a business enterprise during a period from transactions and other events and circumstances from nonowner sources. It includes all changes in equity during a period except those resulting from investments by owners and distributions to owners.

Counterparty The opposite party in a financial transaction.

Fair value The amount at which an asset could be purchased or sold or a liability incurred or settled in a current transaction between willing and informed parties. When a quoted market price is available, fair value is the product of the number of units in question times that market price. That product is also referred to as the item's market value. For traded securities, the terms fair value and market value are synonymous. When no quoted market price is available for the item in question, fair value must be estimated.

Fair value hedge A hedge used to reduce exposure to change in the fair value of all or a part of a recognized asset or liability, an unrecognized firm commitment, or a foreign currency firm commitment or available-for-sale security that is due to a particular risk.

Financial derivative A financial instrument that derives its value from the price or rate of an underlying financial contract or index.

Financial instrument Cash, evidence of an ownership interest in an entity, or a contract that imposes on an entity a contractual obligation to deliver cash or another financial instrument or exchange financial instruments on potentially unfavorable terms, or conveys to an entity a contractual right to receive cash or another financial instrument or exchange financial instruments on potentially favorable terms.

Firm commitment An agreement with an unrelated party, binding on both parties and usually legally enforceable, that includes all relevant terms and a disincentive for nonperformance that is sufficiently large to make performance probable.

Forecasted transaction A transaction that is expected to occur, but for which there is no firm commitment. Because no transaction or event has yet occurred and the transaction or event when it occurs will be at the prevailing market price, a forecasted transaction does not give an entity any present rights to future benefits or a present obligation for future sacrifices.

Foreign currency forward exchange contract A forward contract to buy or sell foreign currency at a specified future date and at a specified exchange rate.

Foreign currency hedge A hedge used to reduce exposure to variability in the fair value of a foreign currency firm commitment, or an available-for-sale security, or used to hedge variability in expected future cash flows of a forecast foreign currency transaction, or used to hedge variability in the foreign currency–translated amount of a net investment in a foreign operation.

Foreign currency risk The risk of changes in foreign currency exchange rates on the fair values and cash flows associated with foreign currency–denominated assets and liabilities.

Forward contract A privately negotiated agreement to buy or sell a commodity or financial instrument at a specified future date and at a specified exchange price.

Forward rate An agreed-to rate for future exchange of commodities or financial instruments in a forward contract.

Futures contract   An agreement with standardized provisions, leaving variable only price and delivery month, to purchase or sell a commodity for future delivery.

Hedge   A financial position taken to reduce or eliminate risk or to replace one type of risk with another.

Hedge effectiveness   The extent to which a hedge shields an asset or liability from fair value and cash flow changes associated with an identified risk.

Hedge ineffectiveness   The extent to which a hedge does not shield an asset or liability from fair value and cash flow changes associated with an identified risk.

Interest rate risk   The risk of changes in interest rates on the fair values and cash flows associated with company assets and liabilities.

Interest rate swap   An agreement between two parties to exchange interest payments based on an agreed-upon principal or notional amount. Interest rate swaps are used to change fixed-rate obligations to variable rates or variable-rate obligations to fixed rates.

Intrinsic value   The amount by which the exercise price of a call option on a stock is exceeded by the market price of the underlying stock, or the amount by which the exercise price on a put option on a stock exceeds the market price of the underlying stock.

London Interbank Offered Rate (LIBOR)   The rate at which banks in London exchange Eurocurrencies and/or Eurodollars with each other. It is a prime bankers' rate often used in international banking as a basic interest rate.

Market value   A quoted market price per unit times the number of units being valued. Synonymous with fair value for financial instruments for which a quoted market price is available.

Market value risk   The risk of changes in market values on the fair values and cash flows associated with company assets and liabilities.

Natural hedge   The use of an existing or newly created financial instrument, as opposed to a financial derivative, to reduce or eliminate risk or to replace one type of risk with another.

Notional amount   A physical or financial measure upon which the terms of performance and settlement of a financial derivative are based. A notional amount can be a number of currency units, shares, bushels, pounds, or other units specified in a derivative instrument.

Other comprehensive income   Revenues, expenses, gains, and losses that are included in comprehensive income but are excluded from net income. Examples include unrealized gains and losses on available-for-sale investment securities, translation adjustments on net investments in foreign operations, minimum liability adjustments for underfunded pensions, and gains and losses on financial derivatives considered to be cash flow hedges and hedges of net investments in foreign operations. Other comprehensive income is accumulated and reported as a component of shareholders' equity.

Put option   A contract that gives its holder the right but not the obligation to sell an asset, typically a financial instrument, at a specified price through a specified date.

Risk   Uncertainty or potential variability of financial outcomes.

Spot rate   The existing market rate for exchange of commodities or financial instruments.

Time value   The portion of the fair value of an option that exceeds its intrinsic value.

Underlying   The price or rate of a contract or index from which a financial derivative derives its value. Examples include a security price, foreign exchange rate, commodity price, interest rate, or an index of prices or rates.

NOTES

1. M. Mayer, "The Dangers of Derivatives," The *Wall Street Journal,* Editorial Commentary (May 20, 1999).

2. SFAS No. 52, "Foreign Currency Translation" (Stamford, CT: Financial Accounting Standards Board, December 1981); SFAS No. 80, "Accounting for Futures Contracts" (Stamford, CT: FASB, August 1984); SFAS No. 105, "Disclosure of Information about Financial Concentrations of Credit Risk" (Norwalk, CT: FASB, March 1990); SFAS No. 107, "Disclosures about Fair Value of Financial Instruments" (Norwalk, CT: FASB, December 1991); and SFAS No. 119, "Disclosure about Derivative Financial Instruments and Fair Value of Financial Instruments" (Norwalk, CT: FASB, October 1994).

3. SFAS No. 133, "Accounting for Derivative Instruments and Hedging Activities" (Norwalk, CT: FASB, June 1998).

4. This rate was obtained using rates on futures contracts of similar terms. Because a forward exchange contract is an agreement negotiated privately, the forward exchange rates can vary and will differ slightly from rates on futures contracts.

5. In actuality, a payment will be received by the company only for the net difference in the two amounts, $2,500 ($17,500 less $15,000) in this example.

6. E. Comiskey, C. Mulford, and D. Turner, "Bank Accounting and Reporting Practices for Interest Rate Swaps," *Bank Accounting & Finance* (Winter 1987–1988), pp. 3–14.

7. Advanced Energy Industries, Inc., annual report, December 1997. Information obtained from Disclosure, Inc., *Compact D/SEC: Corporate Information on Public Companies Filing with the SEC* (Bethesda, MD: Disclosure, Inc., March 1999).

8. Belco Oil and Gas Corp., annual report, December 1997. Information obtained from Disclosure, Inc., *Compact D/SEC: Corporate Information on Public Companies Filing with the SEC* (Bethesda, MD: Disclosure, Inc., March 1999).

9. Walsh International, Inc., annual report, June 1997. Information obtained from Disclosure, Inc., *Compact D/SEC: Corporate Information on Public Companies Filing with the SEC* (Bethesda, MD: Disclosure, Inc., March 1999).

10. PNC Bank Corp., annual report, December 1997. Information obtained from Disclosure, Inc., *Compact D/SEC: Corporate Information on Public Companies Filing with the SEC* (Bethesda, MD: Disclosure, Inc., March 1999).

11. Fair value is the amount at which an asset could be purchased or sold or a liability incurred or settled in a current transaction between willing and informed parties. When no quoted market price is available for the item in question, fair value must be estimated. When a quoted market price is available, fair value is the product of the number of units in question times that market price. That product is also referred to as the item's market value. For traded securities, the terms fair value and market value are synonymous.

12. Baker Hughes, Inc., annual report, December 1997. Information obtained from Disclosure, Inc., *Compact D/SEC: Corporate Information on Public Companies Filing with the SEC* (Bethesda, MD: Disclosure, Inc., March 1999).

13. Anderson's, Inc., annual report, December 1997. Information obtained from Disclosure, Inc., *Compact D/SEC: Corporate Information on Public Companies Filing with the SEC* (Bethesda, MD: Disclosure, Inc., March 1999).

14. Century Aluminum Co., annual report, December 1997. Information obtained from Disclosure, Inc., *Compact D/SEC: Corporate Information on Public Companies Filing with the SEC* (Bethesda, MD: Disclosure, Inc., March 1999).

15. Barrick Gold Corp., annual report, December 1997. Information obtained from Disclosure, Inc., *Compact D/SEC: Corporate Information on Public Companies Filing with the SEC* (Bethesda, MD: Disclosure, Inc., March 1999).

16. UAL Corp., annual report, December 1997. Information obtained from Disclosure, Inc., *Compact D/SEC: Corporate Information on Public Companies Filing with the SEC* (Bethesda, MD: Disclosure, Inc., March 1999).

17. Data General Corp., annual report, September 1998. Information obtained from Disclosure, Inc., *Compact D/SEC: Corporate Information on Public Companies Filing with the SEC* (Bethesda, MD: Disclosure, Inc., March 1999).

18. Cendant Corp., annual report, December 1997. Information obtained from Disclosure, Inc., *Compact D/SEC: Corporate Information on Public Companies Filing with the SEC* (Bethesda, MD: Disclosure, Inc., March 1999).

19. Chevron Corp., annual report, December 1997. Information obtained from Disclosure, Inc., *Compact D/SEC: Corporate Information on Public Companies Filing with the SEC* (Bethesda, MD: Disclosure, Inc., March 1999).

20. Mellon Bank Corp., annual report, December 1997. Information obtained from Disclosure, Inc., *Compact D/SEC: Corporate Information on Public Companies Filing with the SEC* (Bethesda, MD: Disclosure, Inc., March 1999).

21. Belden, Inc., annual report, December 1997. Information obtained from Disclosure, Inc., *Compact D/SEC: Corporate Information on Public Companies Filing with the SEC* (Bethesda, MD: Disclosure, Inc., March 1999).

22. First Virginia Banks, Inc., annual report, December 1997. Information obtained from Disclosure, Inc., *Compact D/SEC: Corporate Information on Public Companies Filing with the SEC* (Bethesda, MD: Disclosure, Inc., March 1999).

23. M. Mayer, "The Dangers of Derivatives," *The Wall Street Journal,* Editorial Commentary (May 20, 1999).

24. Nextel Communications, Inc., annual report, December 1997. Information obtained from Disclosure, Inc., *Compact D/SEC: Corporate Information on Public Companies Filing with the SEC* (Bethesda, MD: Disclosure, Inc., March 1999).

25. *The Wall Street Journal* (April 22, 1994), p. B10.

26. Procter & Gamble Co., annual report, September 1994, p. 23.

27. *Ibid.,* p. 5.

28. *The Wall Street Journal* (October 15, 1998), p. A3.

29. SFAS No. 133, "Accounting for Derivative Instruments and Hedging Activities" (Norwalk, CT: FASB, June 1998).

30. Note that if the company were hedging its heating oil inventory until a planned date of sale, it would be a cash flow hedge of a forecasted transaction. Cash flow hedges are discussed in a subsequent section of this chapter.

31. Note that this foreign currency risk is separate and apart from commodity price risk.

32. Firm commitments can also be hedged with nonderivative financial instruments.

33. To qualify for hedge accounting, a foreign currency equity security must not trade on an exchange where trades are denominated in the investor's currency. This assumption is needed to ensure that the primary risk being hedged is foreign currency risk and not simply the risk of changes in market value.

34. SFAS No. 33 does not mention specifically the handling of the transition for hedges of foreign currency exposure of net investments in foreign operations. Gains and losses on these items and offsetting hedge effects were already included in other comprehensive income and require no transition to a new method of accounting.

35. Trade accounts, such as accounts receivable and accounts payable were exempted from the disclosure requirements for fair value when their carrying amounts approximate fair value.

36. SFAS No. 105, "Disclosure of Information about Financial Concentrations of Credit Risk" (Norwalk, CT: FASB, March 1990); SFAS No. 107, "Disclosures about Fair Value of Financial Instruments" (Norwalk, CT: FASB, December 1991); and SFAS No. 119, "Disclosure about Derivative Financial Instruments and Fair Value of Financial Instruments" (Norwalk, CT: FASB, October 1994).

37. Philip Morris Companies, Inc., annual report, December 1998, p. 44. Note that after the company made the statement that SFAS No. 133 must be adopted by the company by January 1, 2000, the FASB delayed the effective date for one additional year.

38. *Ibid.,* p. 43.

39. *Ibid.*

40. *Ibid.,* p. 44.

41. *Ibid.*

42. There is also a possibility that these purchase transactions would rise to the level of commitments. If this were the case, then their treatment as fair value hedges would be in order.

43. As included in *New Developments Summary* (New York: Grant Thornton & Co., July 25, 1994).

44. SFAS No. 133, "Accounting for Derivative Instruments and Hedging Activities" (Norwalk, CT: FASB, June 1998).

45. SFAS No. 107, "Disclosures about Fair Value of Financial Instruments" (Norwalk, CT: FASB, December 1991).

Chapter 7

Foreign Exchange Reporting and Analysis

The market rightfully gave Coke's stock price only a slight haircut for the yen's move (down), though. Foreign currency translation doesn't affect the actual cash flow of Coke's Japanese subsidiary. It does affect the value of Japan-generated earnings that Coke brings back to the United States, but it's not likely that all Japanese earnings are shuttled to America.[1]

If you have a strong marketing position, you can play the hardball game of saying, I want to be paid in my own currency.[2]

While once simply hyperbole, the global economy is a clear reality of the twenty-first century. Our economy is dramatically affected, for both good and ill, by developments in countries and regions that are thousands of miles from our shores. Moreover, economic and political turmoil in key regions of the world can produce dramatic changes in the value of our currency as well as those of our key trading partners. For example, in the late 1990s a virtual meltdown of currency values took place in a number of Southeast Asian countries, for example, Indonesia, Malaysia, South Korea, and Thailand. In 1998, the Indonesian rupiah depreciated from around 2,300 rupiah per dollar to about 16,000 per dollar, a drop of about 85 percent. Countries in several other regions also experienced similar declines in the value of their currencies.

Changes in currency values, even by far less dramatic proportions than those experienced in Southeast Asia, can have a significant impact on the competitive position and financial performance of U.S. firms. For example, the market position of the U.S. domestic textile and apparel industry was battered by the decline in Southeast Asian currencies. These declines in currency values reduced demand from Southeast Asian countries for imports from the United States, and at the same time increased the competitiveness of their exports into our domestic markets. Moreover, the value of investments in domestic plant and equipment was reduced as production was shifted to these lower-cost foreign countries.[3]

These somewhat global effects of changing exchange rates manifest themselves in many specific ways in the underlying financial statements of companies. Those most directly affected are firms that either: (1) engage in transactions with firms in other countries or that (2) have operations abroad. The effects of the foregoing are normally characterized as transaction or translation foreign currency effects, respectively. The treatment of foreign currency issues in this chapter uses this standard dichotomy.

Transaction reporting includes accounting for transactions, such as purchases and sales by U.S. companies, which are denominated in foreign currencies. The employment of foreign currency derivatives is also included within the scope of transaction reporting. Translation reporting involves the restatement of the financial statements of foreign subsidiaries or branches from the local foreign currency into the reporting currency of the parent company. Because the financial statements of foreign subsidiaries are normally prepared in their local foreign currency, the statements must be translated into the reporting currency of the parent before consolidation can take place.

This chapter opens with some discussion of exchange rates and the nature of currency risk. In addition, some sources of transaction gains and losses will be briefly discussed and illustrated. The hedging of foreign currency exposures is discussed both within the setting of transaction as well as translation exposure.[4] Following the discussion of foreign currency transactions and the hedging of transactional exposures, the topic of statement translation will be treated. Because of the extensive background on derivatives in Chapter Six, including coverage of the requirements of the new derivatives standard, Statement of Financial Standards (SFAS) No. 133, "Accounting for Derivative Instruments and Hedging Activities," this material is not repeated in this chapter.[5] For those with little or no knowledge on derivatives, it will be useful to read Chapter Six as background for the discussion and illustration of the hedging of foreign currency exposure.

As preparation for the discussion of both transaction and translation reporting and analysis, some basic foreign currency background and terminology is provided in the next section.

KEY FOREIGN CURRENCY BACKGROUND AND TERMINOLOGY

Much terminology that is relevant to this chapter was covered in Chapter Six and is discussed here only when it seems essential. Alternative forms of the foreign exchange rates are discussed here as well as the sources and nature of currency exposure. Common foreign currency derivatives are also identified and briefly discussed.

Foreign Exchange Rates

Foreign exchange rates express the value of one unit of currency in terms of another. This expression can be in terms of (1) the U.S. dollars, or portion thereof, that are equivalent to one unit of the foreign currency or (2) the foreign currency, or portion thereof, that is equivalent to one U.S. dollar. The first expression is referred to as the *direct rate* and the second as the *indirect rate*. Examples of both forms of expression are found in the financial press. Exhibit 7.1 presents some exchange rates for selected currencies from *The Wall Street Journal*.

Where more than one exchange rate is provided in Exhibit 7.1, the first rate is the spot rate. The additional rates, where listed, are those for the currencies in

Exhibit 7.1. Foreign Exchange Rates: Direct and Indirect Expressions

	Direct Rate		Indirect Rate	
	9/7/99	9/8/99	9/7/99	9/8/99
Britain (pound)	$1.6042	$1.6185	.6234	.6179
1-month forward rate	1.6048	1.6188	.6231	.6177
3-month forward rate	1.6058	1.6193	.6227	.6176
6-month forward rate	1.6076	1.6196	.6220	.6174
Ecuador (sucre)	$.00009007	$.00008999	11102.50	11112.50
Germany (mark)	$.5413	$.5419	1.8474	1.8455
1-month forward rate	.5427	.5432	1.8427	1.8409
3-month forward rate	.5466	.5471	1.8296	1.8279
6-month forward rate	.5544	.5548	1.8037	1.8024
Indonesia (rupiah)	$.0001198	$.0001156	8350.00	8650.00
Japan (yen)	$.009023	$.009005	110.83	111.06
1-month forward rate	.009067	.009047	110.29	110.53
3-month forward rate	.009192	.009171	108.79	109.03
6-month forward rate	.009466	.009443	105.64	105.90
Thailand (baht)	$.02548	$.02524	39.625	39.245
Euro	$1.0587	$1.0599	.9446	.9435

Source: The Wall Street Journal (September 9, 1999), p. C17.

forward contracts with terms of one, three, and six months, respectively. At September 7, 1999, the British pound was worth $1.6042 dollars—the direct rate. Alternatively, the dollar is worth .6234 of a pound—the indirect rate. The direct rate can be derived from the indirect rate by simply dividing one by the indirect rate: direct rate equals 1/.6234 or $1.6042. That is, the direct rate is the reciprocal of the indirect rate.

On September 8, 1999, the pound appreciated against the dollar, as the direct rate went from $1.6042 to $1.6185. The British pound increased in value by about 1.4 cents ($1.6185 − $1.6042 = $0.014). However, the corollary is that the dollar depreciated against the pound. Notice that when using the indirect rate the dollar was worth .6234 parts of a pound on September 7, but only .6179 at the end of September 8, 1999.

The Ecuadorian sucre depreciated against the dollar between September 7 and September 8. The direct rate for the sucre went from $.00009007 to $.00008999. The sucre was worth a smaller fraction of a dollar at the end of September 8, 1999. From the indirect rate information, a dollar could be acquired for 11,102.5 sucres on September 7, 1999, but it would take 11,112.5 sucres on September 8, 1999. The dollar appreciated against the sucre, and the sucre depreciated against the dollar.

Exhibit 7.2. Changes in Exchange Rates and the Value of the Dollar

	Change in the Value of the Dollar	
Change in the Exchange Rate	Direct Rate	Indirect Rate
Increases	Dollar depreciates	Dollar appreciates
Decreases	Dollar appreciates	Dollar depreciates

Unless one has some ongoing experience with exchange rates, it often takes some deliberation to determine whether an exchange rate movement indicates that the dollar has appreciated or depreciated. Depreciation of the dollar is indicated by either the direct rate's getting larger or the indirect rate's getting smaller. When the direct rate for the German mark increased from $.5413 to $.5419, the dollar depreciated because a larger fraction of a dollar was needed to acquire each mark. Alternatively, the dollar appreciates when the direct rate for the foreign currency declines. However, with the indirect rate, the change in the rate has the opposite meaning. Notice that the indirect rate for the Indonesian rupiah increased from 8,350 to 8,650. It took 300 additional rupiah to acquire a dollar at the end of September 8, 1999. The dollar is appreciating when the indirect rate is increasing and vice versa.

The preceding examples reveal that changes in the direct rates have a direct relationship with changes in the value of the foreign currency, but an indirect relationship with changes in the value of the dollar. That is, increases in direct rates indicate appreciation in the foreign currency and decreases indicate depreciation. But, changes in the indirect rates have a direct relationship with changes in the value of the dollar. Increases in indirect rates indicate appreciation in the dollar and decreases indicate depreciation.

The alternative expressions of exchange rates, and the implications of changes in these rates for appreciation and depreciation in the dollar, are summarized in Exhibit 7.2.

Forward rates represent the prices at which foreign currencies can be exchanged at future dates. Forward contracts are one of the most popular foreign currency derivatives used by firms to hedge currency risk.[6] Notice that the 6-month forward rate for the pound sterling, at September 8, 1999, is $1.6196, while the spot rate is only $1.6185. The forward rate is at a premium to the spot rate.

A U.S. firm might sell pounds through a forward contract in order to protect the dollar value of a pound account receivable. Because the forward rate is at a premium to the spot rate, the amount received from the forward sale will exceed the amount received if the currency were currently available to be sold in the spot market. Alternatively, a U.S. firm might buy pounds to fix the dollar burden of an account payable in the pound sterling. In this case, the premium represents a payment beyond that required if currency were purchased currently in the spot market.

If the forward rates are below the spot rates, then the currency is at a discount in the forward market. The implications of discounts for the examples above are exactly the opposite. Cash received from forward sales is less than what would be received in the spot market. Similarly, the cash required for forward purchases is less than would be required if currency were purchased in the spot market.

The existence and size of forward contract premiums and discounts are traditionally viewed as due mainly to interest rate differences between countries. These differences are usually explained in terms of the following interest-rate parity theorem:

> The interest rate differential between two countries will be equal to the difference between the forward-exchange rate and the spot-exchange rate.[7]

The logic behind this theorem is that it would otherwise be possible to earn returns that are greater than those available in local currencies by making investments in countries with higher interest rates. Realization of this higher return, putting aside the possibility of credit risk, could be assured by hedging the investment through the forward market. This would protect the local currency value of the investment from adverse movements in the foreign currency. However, under the interest rate parity theorem, the forward contract discount or premium adjusts so that no excess return is earned.

Consider the investment of $1 million in a British investment offering a 7 percent rate against the availability of only 5 percent on comparable U.S. investments. Assume that the spot value of the pound sterling is $1.60. Under interest rate parity, the annual forward rate is approximated as the spot rate times the ratio of one plus the domestic interest rate over one plus the foreign rate: $1.60 $\times$ (1.05/1.07) = $1.57.[8] The forward rate would be at a discount to the spot rate in this case because the foreign interest rate is above the domestic rate. This discount will be just sufficient to eliminate the excess of the return at the foreign interest rate over the return available domestically.

Assume that the $1 million is placed in a pound sterling investment offering a 7 percent annual return. Further, assume that an effort is made to protect this return by selling the sterling amount of the investment at the forward rate of $1.57. The outcome of this investment is summarized in Exhibit 7.3.

The data in Exhibit 7.3 show that the 7 percent sterling investment of $1 million produces a dollar return of about $50,000, for an annual percentage return of 5 percent. Notice that this is the domestic return and not the 7 percent offered on the pound sterling investment. The example in Exhibit 7.3 assumes the operation of interest rate parity. That is, market forces produce forward rates that remove the possibility of producing higher risk-free returns by investing in countries with higher interest rates and then hedging the currency risk with a forward contract. If an investment is hedged through a forward contract, then the domestic return, barring a credit risk problem, will be earned without regard to whether the foreign investment rate is above or below the domestic rate.

Exhibit 7.3. Forward Contract Rates, Interest-Rate Parity and Investment Returns

Dollars invested	$1,000,000
Times the indirect-rate for the pound at the date of the investment: (1/$1.60)	0.625
Sterling investment	625,000
Plus interest for one year at 7%: 625,000 pounds × .07 =	43,750
Maturity value of investment in pounds	668,750
Times the one-year forward contract rate of	$1.57
Maturity value in dollars	$1,049,937
Investment return: ($1,049,937 − $1,000,000)/$1,000,000 =	5%

It is of course possible to invest in 7 percent pound sterling instruments and earn either more or less than 7 percent. If the investment is left unhedged, a return beyond 7 percent could be achieved if the pound appreciated against the dollar. For example, assume that no hedge is initiated and that the pound has appreciated to $1.62 when the investment matures. Then, total proceeds will equal the pounds received of 668,750 times the spot rate for the pound of $1.62, or $1,083,375. On a $1,000,000 investment, this represents a return of about 8.3 percent— [($1,083,375 − $1,000,0000) / $1,000,000]. However, a lower return, or even an overall loss, could result if, instead, the pound depreciated against the dollar.

Currency Risk and Exposure

Chapter Six defines foreign currency risk as "The risk of changes in foreign currency exchange rates on the fair values and cash flows associated with foreign currency denominated assets and liabilities." Assets and liabilities that are denominated in foreign currencies will expand and contract as exchange rates change. Whether a given exchange rate change results in a gain or loss depends on the net position in that currency. That is, is the firm's net position an asset or a liability? The term *foreign currency exposure* is often used interchangeably with *foreign currency risk*.

The effects of exchange rate changes, conditional upon whether a firm has asset or liability exposure, are summarized in Exhibit 7.4. While framed in terms of assets and liabilities, these terms should be seen to include future cash inflows and outflows that are not yet reflected on the balance sheet. Firms view the potential expansion or contraction of these cash flow streams as also creating currency risk.

Appreciation of a foreign currency in which a firm has a net asset position is good news because the foreign currency assets are then worth more in dollars. However, the same currency movement is bad news if the firm has a net liability

Exhibit 7.4. Foreign Currency Exposure, Exchange Rate Changes, and Foreign Currency Gains and Losses

	Exposure in the Foreign Currency	
Movement of the Foreign Currency	Net Asset	Net Liability
Appreciates	Gain	Loss
Depreciates	Loss	Gain

Exhibit 7.5. Rankings of Alternative Hedging Objectives

Hedging Objective	Percent Ranking the Objective as Most Important
1. To manage volatility in cash flows	49%
2. To manage volatility in accounting earnings	42%
3. To manage market value of the firm	8%
4. To manage balance sheet accounts or ratios	1%
	100%

Source: G. Bodnar, G. Hayt, and R. Marston "The Wharton Survey of Derivatives Usage by U.S. Non-Financial Firms," *Financial Management* (Winter 1996), pp. 114–115.

position in the foreign currency. The corollary of appreciation of the foreign currency is depreciation of the dollar. A loss results because more dollars are then required to discharge the foreign currency liability.

Hedges and Hedging Instruments

Hedges are discussed extensively in Chapter Six and are also commented on here, but the focus is exclusively on foreign currency derivatives and hedges of foreign currency exposure. Hedges are designed to create gains and losses to offset those that result from foreign currency exposure. That is, an effective hedge will produce a gain when a loss is experienced on the foreign currency exposure. Alternatively, an effective hedge will produce a loss when a gain results from the foreign currency exposure.[9] The primary derivative instruments used to hedge currency risk or exposure, by their relative frequency of use, are forward contracts, over-the-counter options, currency swaps, and futures contracts.[10]

Information on the hedging of different currency exposures is quite consistent. The Wharton survey of derivatives usage provides survey data on the percentage of derivative users who identified selected hedging objectives as the most important. The ranking and percentage of respondents selecting each hedging objective as the most important are presented in Exhibit 7.5.

With the contemporary emphasis on cash flows, some might find the closeness of the support for managing cash flows and earnings somewhat surprising. The authors of the Wharton survey felt the need to comment on this matter. They observed that:

> While in many cases the impact of hedging on reported earnings and cash flows may be similar, the popularity of this objective (hedging earnings volatility) may suggest that some firms focus hedging strategy more on stabilizing the reported numbers presented to investors than on stabilizing the actual economic internal cash flows.[11]

Additional attention is given to the hedging of currency risk, and the use of alternative derivative instruments in hedging currency exposure, in subsequent sections of this chapter.

TRANSACTION REPORTING AND ANALYSIS

Some of the more typical foreign currency transactions are purchases, sales, investments, and borrowings in which one side of the transaction is denominated in a foreign currency. For example, a U.S. electronics retailer makes a purchase from a Japanese manufacturer of electronics, and the U.S. firm is invoiced in the Japanese yen. The U.S. firm has a foreign currency transaction, but the Japanese supplier does not. The U.S. firm has an account payable that is denominated in the Japanese yen. As the value of the dollar rises and falls against the yen, the dollar burden of the yen accounts payable will decrease and increase for the U.S. firm. A U.S. bank loans money to a Philippine firm, and the transaction is denominated in the U.S. dollar. The Philippine firm has a foreign currency transaction, but the U.S. bank does not.[12] This dollar obligation of the Philippine firm will expand or contract as the Philippine peso depreciates or appreciates, respectively, against the U.S. dollar.

The appreciation and depreciation in currency values affects the earnings and cash flows of firms with foreign currency transactional exposure. These unpredictable increases or decreases in future earnings and cash flows create what is referred to as *foreign currency risk* in Chapter Six. To reduce this risk, firms often employ foreign currency derivatives for hedging purposes.

The treatment of foreign currency transaction and translation reporting and analysis in the balance of this chapter is organized as follows:

- Examples of sources of foreign currency transactional exposure from company reports are provided.
- The accounting and reporting for unhedged transactional exposure is illustrated.
- The accounting and reporting for hedged transactional exposure is illustrated.
- Examples of company policies on the hedging of transactional exposure are provided.
- Implications for financial analysis are integrated throughout these discussions.

Examples of Transactional Exposures from Company Reports

The existence of foreign currency exposure adds an element of risk and uncertainty to a firm's future earnings and cash flow. As a result, it is important to be aware of the source and significance of currency exposure. Fortunately, companies provide reasonably good disclosure of their currency exposures. Most information on currency exposure is found in (1) a section dealing with market or currency risk in the management's discussion and analysis section of the annual report, (2) in a note to the financial statements on foreign currency, and (3) in a note to the financial statements on derivatives. Exhibit 7.6 presents a sampling of the sources of transaction exposure disclosed in recent company annual reports. Because the disclosed items create currency risk, they should all be considered denominated in foreign currencies.

The most common source of transaction exposure is that associated with sale and purchase transactions. These create foreign currency asset (accounts receivable) and liability (accounts payable) exposure, respectively. Commitments of various types are also frequently identified as giving rise to currency risk. For example, purchase commitments are a common source of currency risk, even though a liability is typically not recorded on the balance sheet of the purchaser until the actual purchase occurs.[13] During the commitment period, exposure is represented by the possibility that the foreign currency will rise against the dollar, thereby increasing the dollar cost of the goods. After the transaction is recorded and a foreign currency account payable is recorded, currency risk or exposure represents the possibility that the foreign currency might increase further in value, thus requiring an even larger number of dollars to discharge the obligation. Currency risk during the commitment period as well as while the foreign currency payable is on the books is commonly hedged.

Intercompany loans, future foreign currency cash inflows or outflows from a variety of sources, and borrowings in foreign currencies, make up the balance of the disclosed transaction exposures.

The manner in which some of the above transactions affect earnings and cash flows is best illustrated by reviewing the accounting for an unhedged purchase or sale transaction. The next section illustrates such a transaction and its associated accounting treatment.

Accounting and Reporting for Unhedged Foreign Currency Transactions

Generally accepted accounting principles (GAAP) require that transactions giving rise to foreign currency assets or liabilities be revalued to the current exchange rate when financial statements are prepared.[14] Such accruals give rise to noncash gains and losses that will, if sufficiently material, be disclosed as adjustments to

Exhibit 7.6. Company Disclosures of the Sources of Transaction Exposure

---

Alberto-Culver Company (1998)
Inventory payments
Royalty payments

Armstrong World Industries (1997)
Anticipated events, e.g., sales, royalties, service fees, and dividends
Intercompany loans

BARRA, Inc. (1999)
Accounts receivable

ConAgra, Inc. (1999)
Purchase and sales commitments

Goodyear Tire and Rubber Company (1998)
Accounts payable and receivable
Intercompany loans
Firm commitments
Swiss franc debt

Newport Corporation (1998)
Accounts receivable

Tenneco, Inc. (1998)
Intercompany loans

Vishay Intertechnology, Inc. (1998)
An agreement to purchase a German company, with the purchase price denominated in the
  Deutsche mark

Western Digital Company (1998)
Operating expense commitments in foreign currencies

Sources: Companies' annual reports. The year following each company name designates the annual report from which each example was drawn.

net income in the operating activities section of the statement of cash flows. In addition, the accrual of these foreign currency gains and losses usually creates temporary differences and associated deferred tax liabilities and assets.

Exhibit 7.7 summarizes data on an unhedged foreign currency purchase transaction and illustrates application of GAAP to the transaction.

Importer, Inc. has currency risk in the Exhibit 7.7 example because it has been invoiced in the Indonesian rupiah, and not the U.S. dollar. This results in liability exposure in the rupiah. Good news would be if the dollar increased in value against the rupiah, and it did. As a result, the dollars needed to acquire 100 million rupiah declined significantly between the purchase and settlement dates. The rupiah fell by about 67 percent against the dollar.

The reduction in the rupiah account payable at the end of 2000 puts an unrealized gain of $14,085 into the income statement of Importer, Inc., and results

Exhibit 7.7. An Unhedged Purchase Transaction in a Foreign Currency

Importer, Inc., a U.S. company, purchases shoes from an Indonesian supplier and is invoiced 100,000,000 rupiah. The purchase is recorded on 11/30/2000 and payment is made on 2/1/2001. Both direct (dollars per rupiah) and indirect (rupiah per dollar) exchange rates are given below:

Spot rates	Direct	Indirect
Sale-date exchange rate—11/30/2000	$.00026247	3,810
Year-end exchange rate—12/31/2000	$.00012162	8,222
Settlement-date rate—2/1/2001	$.00008658	11,550

Accounting Treatment

Date of sale, 11/30/2000

Purchase recorded	$26,247*
Account payable recorded	$26,247

*100,000,000 rupiah times the 11/30/2000 direct exchange rate of $.00026247 equals $26,247.

End of year, 12/31/2000

Reduction in previously recorded account payable	$14,085*
Foreign exchange transaction gain	$14,085

*100,000,000 times ($.00026247 - $00012162) equals $14,085.

Settlement date, 2/1/2001

Reduction in accounts payable balance from 12/31/2000	$12,162
Foreign exchange transaction gain	$3,504*
Reduction in cash	$8,658**

*100,000,000 rupiah times ($.00012162 - $.00008658) equals $3,504.
**100,000,000 rupiah times the spot rate of .00008658 equals $8,658

---

in a new lower accounts payable balance of $12,162 ($26,247 − $14,085). This gain is noncash and would be deducted from Importer's year 2000 net income in computing cash flows from operating activities. Moreover, the gain represents a taxable temporary difference and would require the recording of a deferred tax provision of about $5,634 (assumes a 40 percent tax rate) and an offsetting deferred tax liability in the same amount. The deferred tax provision would be added back to Importer's net income as a noncash expense. On balance, the cash quality of Importer's earnings is impaired somewhat by a net noncash gain of $8,451 ($14,085 − $5,634). If we assume that Importer, Inc. regularly makes purchases that are denominated in foreign currencies, then this gain might be treated as a recurring item in assessing earnings quality in terms of persistence.

By settlement date on 2/1/2001, the rupiah has fallen further and an additional gain of $3,504 is recorded. Importer, Inc. had unhedged liability exposure in a currency that depreciated against the dollar. A liability that was initially recorded

Exhibit 7.8. Identifying Profit Trends in the Face of Foreign Exchange Losses: Goodyear Tire and Rubber, Years Ending December 31, 1993–1995 (Thousands of Dollars)

	1993	*1994*	*1995*
Pretax earnings before foreign exchange losses	$898,000	$943,300	$943,200
Foreign exchanges losses	$113,100	$77,600	$17,400
Pretax results after foreign exchange losses	$784,900	$865,700	$925,800

Source: Goodyear Tire and Rubber Company, Form 10-K annual report to the Securities and Exchange Commission (December 1995), p. 33.

at $26,247 was discharged with a cash payment of only $8,658. A total foreign currency transaction gain of $17,589 was realized.

A decision not to hedge in the face of significant transaction exposure increases the uncertainty associated with future earnings and cash flows. While presumably such decisions are based on expectations for future exchange rate movements and an evaluation of the costs and benefits of hedging, a substantial unhedged position could have severe negative consequences for firms. For example, BARRA, Inc. disclosed that it did not hedge its foreign currency exposure and cautioned readers of its financial statements about the potential consequences of this failure to hedge currency exposure:

> Our management has considered its exposures to foreign currency fluctuations. To this point we have decided not to engage in hedging or managing exposures to foreign currency fluctuations . . . Because we do not engage in hedging, a strengthening of the U.S. dollar versus other non-U.S. currencies could have a material adverse affect on our business, results of operations and financial condition.[15]

In the absence of hedging, the transaction gains and losses that could be incurred by Importer, Inc. could be viewed as recurring operating items. They represent a continuing feature of operating in an international environment. Therefore, it might be inappropriate to characterize the persistence dimension of earnings quality as being either enhanced or impaired by transaction losses or gains, respectively. However, it is common for the earnings of firms with unhedged foreign currency exposure to become very volatile in the face of significant changes in currency values. At some point, highly volatile transaction gains and losses can obscure underlying trends in a firm's performance. As a case in point, consider the effect of foreign currency losses on the results of Goodyear Tire and Rubber over the period 1993 through 1995, as set out in Exhibit 7.8.

Goodyear Tire and Rubber is a large international company and it has incurred net foreign exchange gains or losses in each year from 1993 through 1998 (1996 through 1998 included a loss of $7.4 million in 1996, and gains of $34.1 million and $2.6 million in 1997 and 1998, respectively).[16] As a result, it becomes difficult to label these gains and losses as nonrecurring. However, notice the strong growth in earnings in both 1994 and 1995 when foreign exchange losses are included in results. But, with the foreign exchange losses excluded, the 1993 through 1995 results are flat. Moreover, the reported earnings growth of $60.1 million in 1995 could be seen as being produced by the $60.2 million decline in the foreign currency loss in 1995: $77.6 million in 1994 minus $17.4 million in 1995 equals $60.2 million. These data indicate that underlying profit trends may become more evident when irregular, but recurring, amounts of foreign exchange gains and losses are removed from reported results.[17]

The unhedged transaction summarized in Exhibit 7.7 resulted in a substantial foreign exchange gain because the importer had liability exposure in a currency that fell in value. If the importer had, instead, been an exporter to Indonesia and invoiced customers in the rupiah, then a substantial loss would have resulted. To avoid foreign currency risk in such cases, it is common for firms to hedge part or all of their exposure. For example, in an apparent reference to mainly transactional exposure, Becton, Dickenson & Company stated that:

> During 1997 and 1998, the Company hedged substantially all of its foreign exchange exposures primarily through the use of forwards and currency options.[18]

The accounting for hedged foreign currency transaction exposure is illustrated in the next section.

Accounting and Reporting of Hedged Foreign Currency Transactions

A hedge is an arrangement by which offsetting foreign currency exposures are created. In a perfect hedge, the offsetting gains and losses are equal. Most hedging involves the use of the derivative instruments that were the subject of Chapter Six. However, as discussed earlier in Chapter Six, it is also possible to achieve a hedge without using derivative instruments. Such an arrangement is usually referred to as a natural hedge and is discussed with respect to foreign currency hedging later in this chapter. In the hedging examples illustrated in this section, only forward contracts are employed. This is designed to focus on the key features of hedging applications without adding the complexity associated with the consideration of a variety of foreign currency derivatives. Moreover, forward contracts appear to be the leading financial derivative currently being used to hedge currency risk. Finally, these forward contract illustrations can largely be generalized to the other principal foreign currency derivatives.

Transaction Hedges under SFAS No. 133

The foreign currency hedging applications covered by SFAS No. 133, "Accounting for Derivative Instruments and Hedging Activities," that involve transaction exposure include the following:

- Hedges of foreign currency–denominated firm commitments
- Hedges of available-for-sale securities
- Hedges of forecasted foreign currency–denominated transactions[19]

Under SFAS No. 133, items one and two are termed *fair value* hedges and item three a *cash flow* hedge.

Hedges of Firm Commitments

The gains or losses on a foreign currency derivative used to hedge a firm commitment, as well as the gains or losses on the firm commitment, are recognized in earnings in the same period. This creates the simultaneous offsetting of gains and losses that characterize a hedge. The gain or loss on the derivative results from its restatement to fair value. The gain or loss on the firm commitment also results from the accrual of changes in the value of the commitment. However, with the firm commitment, only the gains and losses and not the value of the firm commitment are recorded. The gains and losses on both the derivative and the firm commitment are based on the same changes in forward rates.

Prior to the requirements of SFAS No. 133, hedges of firm commitments were treated differently. Whereas gains and losses on the changing value of the forward contract were recognized, changes in the value of the firm commitment were not. This meant that there was an absence of offsetting gains and losses on a period-by-period basis. As an off-balance-sheet item, the firm commitments were not revalued. As a result, no gains or losses were recognized to offset those being recognized on the forward contract.

The lack of recognized offsetting gains and losses was handled by deferring the gains and losses that were recognized on the forward contracts.[20] Later, when the firm commitment became a recognized transaction (e.g. a purchase or a sale), the gain or loss deferred on the forward contract was treated as an adjustment to the amount of the purchase or sale. An example of this accounting, which is not permitted under SFAS No. 133, is provided in Exhibit 7.9.

Western Digital Corporation uses forward contracts to hedge commitments for operating expenses denominated in foreign currencies. Because Western Digital wanted to fix the dollar burden of these future foreign currency cash outflows, the Company purchased the foreign currencies through forward contracts. At the end of fiscal 1998, Western Digital disclosed $17.1 million of unrealized losses that were deferred and reported as assets on its balance sheet. Losses on forward contracts to purchase foreign currencies result when the foreign currency falls in value. A contract to purchase a foreign currency at a fixed price is worth less when the foreign currency falls in value.

In the disclosures in Exhibit 7.9, Western Digital indicates that the forward contracts do function as hedges. These disclosures note that when the hedged transactions actually take place, the deferred losses are offset by the reduced U.S. dollar value of the local currency operating expenses (i.e., the offsetting gain).

Exhibit 7.9. Gain and Loss Deferral with a Firm Commitment Hedge:
Western Digital Corporation, Year Ending June 27, 1998 (Amounts in Millions,
Except Average Contract Rate)

As of June 27, 1998, the Company had outstanding the following purchased foreign currency forward contacts:

	Contract Amount	Weighted Average Contract Rate	Unrealized Loss*
Foreign currency forward contracts:			
Singapore dollar	$178.9	1.60	$8.8
Malaysian ringgit	61.4	3.66	8.3
British pound sterling	1.6	1.63	—
	$241.9		$17.1

*The unrealized losses on these contracts are deferred and recognized in the results of operations in the period in which the hedged transactions are consummated, at which time the loss is offset by the reduced U.S. dollar value of the local currency operating expense.

Source: Western Digital Corporation, annual report, June 1998, p. 27.

Unlike previous GAAP, SFAS No. 133 calls for "special accounting" that recognizes gains and losses on both the forward contract and the firm commitment. The offsetting gains and losses are included in earnings at the same time. The deferral of gains and losses on the forward contracts is no longer either necessary or permitted under SFAS No. 133.

Hedges of Foreign Currency Available-for-Sale Securities

As outlined in Chapter Eight, available-for-sale securities are carried on the balance sheet at fair value and the unrealized gains and losses from marking them to fair value are initially included in other comprehensive income. However, if currency risk of an available-for-sale security is hedged, then the offsetting gains and losses on both the forward contract and the hedged currency risk of the securities are included in earnings. This "special accounting" called for under SFAS No. 133 differs from previous GAAP, which called for the offsetting gains and losses to be included in other comprehensive income and not net earnings.[21]

Hedges of Forecasted Foreign Currency–Denominated Transactions

Hedges of forecasted transactions, cash flow hedges, are distinguished from hedges of firm commitments (a fair value hedge), under the reporting requirements of SFAS No. 133.[22] A forecasted transaction might involve, for example, probable future sales or purchases of a firm's products. The dollar value of these forecasted cash flows can be protected by either selling (a forecasted sale transaction) or buying (a forecasted purchase transaction), respectively, the forecasted foreign currency amounts through forward contracts.

Special accounting is required in these cases because the forecasted transactions do not give rise to recognized gains and losses as exchange rates change. However, marking the associated forward contracts to fair value does produce foreign currency gains or losses. As gains and losses on the forward contracts are recognized, SFAS No. 133 calls for their initial inclusion in other comprehensive income and not earnings. Subsequently, when the forecasted transaction affects earnings, the net gains or losses on the foreign currency derivative, which had previously been included in other comprehensive income, are reclassified into the determination of earnings.

As an example, assume a forecasted purchase of goods in a foreign currency. A hedge of this future cash requirement would be achieved by buying the foreign currency thorough the forward contract. When the forecasted purchase actually takes place, it will be recorded at the existing spot value of the foreign currency. Finally, when the purchased goods are sold, the net gain or loss accumulated in other comprehensive income will be either added to (an accumulated net loss) or deducted from (an accumulated net gain) cost of sales.

The following section illustrates the hedge of (1) an exposed net asset position and (2) a forecasted purchase transaction.

Hedge of an Exposed Net Asset Position: A Fair Value Hedge

Exhibit 7.10 illustrates a case of asset exposure that resulted from an export sale by a U.S. firm, Exporter, Inc., to a German customer. The dollar value of the mark accounts receivable is protected by a forward contract that fixes the future value of the German marks in terms of U.S. dollars. This is accomplished by entering into a forward on 12/2/2000 to sell the marks for U.S. dollars, with delivery to take place on 1/30/2001.

Notice that the forward rates in Exhibit 7.10 for the mark are at a premium to the spot rate. This is consistent with German interest rates typically being lower than U.S. rates, an issue discussed earlier in this chapter. An example explaining the spot/forward differences was provided in Exhibit 7.3.

On the date of the sale, 12/2/2000, Exporter, Inc. records the German mark accounts receivable at the spot value of the mark (i.e., $.5413). A sale in the same amount is also recorded. A cost-of-sales amount would also be recorded, but is not included in this illustration.

On this same date, the forward contract is also recorded at the 90-day forward rate of $.5427. Notice that Exporter, Inc. will actually receive more through the forward contract sale than would have been received if the marks were available to sell in the spot market, where the rate is only $.5413. That is, the forward rate is at a premium to the spot. However, if the forward rate had been at a discount to the spot, then less would be received from the sale through the forward contract.

The forward contract is a derivative instrument under SFAS No. 133 and any changes in its fair value must be recorded by Exporter, Inc.[23] As is typically true of derivatives, the forward contract has no initial net fair value.[24] The illustration

Exhibit 7.10.   A Sale Transaction Hedged with a Forward Contract: Exporter, Inc.

Exporter, Inc., a U.S. company, sells a machine tool to a German customer and invoices the customer for 6,000,000 German marks (DM). The sale is recorded on 12/2/2000 and payment is received on 1/30/2001. A forward contract is entered into to deliver 6,000,000 DM on 1/30/2001. Relevant direct-exchange-rate information, both spot and forward rates, is given below. At the maturity date of the forward contract, both the spot rate and forward rate will be the same. Foreign currency balances, which must be periodically revalued at changing spot or forward rates, are designated by "fx" after the account title.

DM direct exchange rates

Date	Spot rates	Forward Rates
Sale-date exchange rate—12/2/2000	$.5413	90-day rate $.5427
Year-end exchange rate—12/31/2000	$.5425	60-day rate $.5441
Settlement-date rate—1/30/2001	$.5460	0-day rate $.5460

Accounting Treatment

Date-of-sale balances recorded—12/2/2000

Sales revenue	$3,247,800*
DM account receivable (fx)	$3,247,800

*6,000,000 DM times the 12/2/2000 spot rate of $.5413

Forward contract receivable	$3,256,200*
Forward contract payable (fx)	$3,256,200

*6,000,000 DM times the 12/2/2000 90-day forward rate of $.5427

End of year balances recorded and adjusted—12/31/2000

Foreign exchange loss on the forward contract	$8,400*
Increase in forward contract payable (fx)	$8,400
Foreign exchange gain on DM account receivable	$7,200**
Increase in the DM account receivable (fx)	$7,200

*6,000,000 DM times ($.5441 − .5427)
**6,000,000 DM times ($.5425 − $5413)

Settlement date—1/30/2001

Foreign exchange loss on forward contract	$11,400*
Increase in the forward contract payable (fx)	$11,400
Foreign exchange gain on DM receivable	$21,000**
Increase in DM account receivable (fx)	$21,000

*6,000,000 DM times ($.5460 − $.5441)
**6,000,000 DM times ($5460 − $.5425)

(*continued*)

Exhibit 7.10. (Continued) A Sale Transaction Hedged with a Forward Contract: Exporter, Inc.

Increase in foreign currency from collection of the DM account receivable (fx)	$3,276,000*	(fx)
Decrease in DM account receivable (fx)	$3,276,000	
Reduction in foreign currency delivered to satisfy the forward contact payable (fx)	$3,276,000	
Decrease in forward contract payable (fx)	$3,276,000	
*6,000,000 DM times the spot rate of $.5460		
Collection of dollars in exchange for 6,000,000 DM delivered to settle the forward contract receivable	$3,256,200*	
Decrease in forward contract receivable (fx)	$3,256,200	
*6,000,000 times the original forward rate of $.5427		

in Exhibit 7.10 records the forward contract at the 90-day forward rate, $.5427, times the notional amount of the contract, 6 million marks in this example.[25] This results in the initial recording of an offsetting asset and liability, which is consistent with this foreign currency derivative having no initial net value.

In practice, offsetting asset and liability balances are not typically recorded upon inception of the forward contract. Rather, only the subsequent changes in the fair value of the contract are recorded. The initial recording of offsetting assets and liabilities is done here to aid understanding of the nature of the hedging process.

The dollar value of the deutsche mark (DM) account receivable is measured using the spot rate. Because the forward contract and the DM account receivable are revalued at different rates, the resulting gains and losses will not offset each other on a period-by-period basis. However, upon the maturity of the forward contract and collection of the DM account receivable, the net income statement effect is simply the original difference between the spot and forward rate: $.5427 minus $.5413 times 6,000,000 DM or $8,400.

At year-end, both the forward contract payable and the DM receivable must be revalued. The forward contract is revalued to the 12/31/2000 forward rate for a contract with a remaining term of 60 days—12/31/2000 to 1/30/2001. The DM receivable is revalued to the new spot rate at 12/31/2000. As illustrated in Exhibit 7.10, revaluing the forward contract calls for increasing the contract payable balance and recording a foreign exchange loss. However, revaluation of the DM account receivable to the new spot rate calls for recording a foreign exchange gain on the DM account receivable and increasing its carrying value.

A loss is recorded on the forward contract because the contract payable balance is revalued to the new forward contract rate of $.5441, up from $.5427. For Exporter, Inc. to settle the forward contract would cost about $8,400. The contract to sell a currency at $.5427 creates a loss when the new forward rate for a contract with the same maturity rises to $.5441. There is no change in the recorded value of the forward contract receivable because its value is fixed at the initial 90-day forward rate of $.5427. The net value of the forward contract receivable at the end of the year is: forward contract receivable of $3,256,200 minus forward contract payable of $3,264,600 equals a net liability balance of $8,400. The gain of $7,200 on the DM receivable results from the increase in the spot value of the mark of from $.5413 to $.5425. The spot value of the mark has increased and with it the U.S. dollar value of the DM account receivable.

Again, in a departure from practice designed to aid understanding, the example in Exhibit 7.10 shows the delivery of the foreign currency to the exchange broker and the collection in turn of the promised forward contract amount. In practice, derivatives normally involve a net settlement. Exporter, Inc. would record collection of the 6 million DM and record them at their spot value of $3,276,000. However, the agreed forward contract rate was only $.5427 or $3,256,200, and a loss of $19,800 ($8,400 + $11,400) has accrued on the forward contract. The net settlement method would simply involve a net payment of $19,800 by Exporter, Inc., with Exporter, Inc. retaining the total $28,200 of appreciation on the DM receivable. Exporter's net income statement benefit of $8,400 ($28,200 − $19,800) is equal to the original forward contract premium.

By selling the DM through a forward contract, Exporter, Inc. ensured that it would realize $3,256,200 upon collection of its DM accounts receivable—the initial forward contract receivable amount recorded in Exhibit 7.10 at 12/2/2000. GAAP require that both the DM account receivable and the forward contract payable be periodically revalued. The DM account receivable is revalued to the new spot rate, and the forward contract payable is revalued to the new forward rate for a contract with a term equal to the remaining term of the original 90-day contract. These revaluations produce the following foreign currency transaction gains and losses:

DM account receivable:		
Gain at 12/31/2000 revaluation to new spot rate	$7,200	
Gain at 1/30/2001 revaluation to the new spot rate	21,000	
Total gain		$28,200
DM forward contract:		
Loss at the 12/31/2000 revaluation to the new forward rate	8,400	
Loss at the 1/30/2001 revaluation to the new forward rate	11,400	
		19,800
Net income statement effect—a gain		$8,400

Again, this final net income statement effect equals the difference between the spot and forward rate at inception of the 90-day forward contract. There has been an offsetting of gains and losses that is characteristic of a hedge. However, the original forward contract premium of $8,400 remains as the net income statement effect.[26]

One feature of SFAS No. 133 is omitted from the illustration in Exhibit 7.10. The Statement calls for recording the present value of forward contract gains and losses instead of their undiscounted amounts. This reflects the fact that these amounts are future cash payments or receipts. However, in most cases, the effects of such discounting will probably be relatively small. As a result, and in an effort to focus on the central aspects of hedging, this feature is not part of the above discussion.

Hedge of a Forecasted Purchase Transaction: A Cash Flow Hedge

A forecasted transaction differs in an important way from a transaction that is firmly committed. With a committed transaction, the commitment is revalued, resulting in transaction gains and losses to offset those resulting from the forward contract position. With each side of the transaction being revalued on an ongoing basis, the gains and losses offset each other. The hedge of a commitment is classified under SFAS No. 133 as a fair value hedge.[27] However, SFAS No. 133 classifies the hedge of a forecasted transaction as a cash flow hedge.

A forecasted or anticipated transaction does not have the degree of likelihood required to permit the recognition, on an ongoing basis, of transaction gains and losses on the forecasted amounts. However, if a forward contract is used to hedge such exposure, then this foreign currency derivative must be marked to market value on an ongoing basis. "Special accounting" is required in this case because there are no recognized gains or losses on the forecasted transaction to offset the gains or losses that are recognized on the forward contract. SFAS No. 133 provides "special accounting" to deal with this lack of symmetry in the timing of the recognition of gains and losses.

The special accounting applied to this cash flow hedge calls for initial inclusion of the gains or losses on the forward contracts in other comprehensive income as they accrue. Subsequently, when the forecasted transaction is included in the determination of earnings, the forward contract gains or losses are reclassified from accumulated other comprehensive income into the determination of earnings. This procedure continues to recognize the changing fair values of foreign currency derivatives as they accrue, and also ensures that transaction gains or losses on both the forward contract and the forecasted transaction are included in earnings in the same period.

For convenience, the foreign exchange rates in Exhibit 7.10 are also used in this illustration. The details on the forecasted transaction are provided in Exhibit 7.11.

Again, for purposes of effective illustration, the forward contract is recorded at inception with offsetting receivable and payable balances measured at the 90-day forward rate of $.5427. As before, the forward contract receivable and payable balances are equal; the derivative has no initial net value. At the end of the year, the forward contract receivable is increased to reflect the increase of from $.5427 to $.5441 in the forward rate for the remaining 60-day term of the original 90-

Exhibit 7.11.   Anticipated/Forecasted Purchase Transaction Hedged
with a Forward Contract: A Cash Flow Hedge

Importer, Inc., a U.S. company, expects to be invoiced for a 10,000,000 German mark
(DM) purchase at the end of January, 2001. To hedge this cash flow exposure, Importer
enters into a 90-day forward contract on November 2, 2000, to purchase 10,000,000 DM.
The purchase of goods takes place 90 days later, and is recorded on 1/30/2001, with
payment for the purchase to be made on 3/31/2001. Relevant direct-exchange-rate information, both spot and forward rates, is given below. At the maturity date of the forward
contract, both the spot rate and forward rate will be the same. Foreign currency balances,
which must be periodically revalued at changing spot or forward rates, are designated by
"fx" after the account title.

DM direct exchange rates

Date	Spot rates	Forward rates
Forward contract purchase—11/2/2000	$.5413	90-day rate $.5427
Year-end exchange rate—12/31/2000	$.5425	60-day rate $.5441
Forward contract settlement and purchase—1/30/2001	$.5460	0-day rate $.5460
Payment date for purchase—3/31/2001	$.5430	NA

Accounting Treatment

Forward contract purchase—11/2/2000

Forward contract receivable (fx)	$5,427,000*
Forward contract payable	$5,427,000

*10,000,000 DM times the 90-day forward rate of $.5427

End of year forward contract adjustment—12/31/2000

Foreign exchange gain on the forward contract—other comprehensive income	$14,000*
Increase in forward contract receivable (fx)	$14,000

*10,000,000 DM times ($.5441 − .5427)

Adjustments at forward contract maturity—1/30/2001

Foreign exchange gain on the forward contract—other comprehensive income	$19,000*
Increase in the forward contract receivable (fx)	

*10,000,000 DM times ($.5460 − $.5441) | $19,000

Settlement with the foreign currency broker—1/30/2001

Cash payment to foreign currency broker	$5,427,000*
Reduction in forward contract payable	$5,427,000

*Original 90-day forward rate of $.5427 times 10,000,000 DM

(*continued*)

Exhibit 7.11. (Continued) Anticipated/Forecasted Purchase Transaction Hedged with a Forward Contract: A Cash Flow Hedge

Receipt of foreign currency from currency broker—1/30/2001		
Foreign currency—DM (fx)	$5,460,000*	
Reduction in forward contract receivable (fx)	$5,460,000	
*10,000,000 DM times spot rate for the DM of $.5460		
Recording the purchase of goods—1/30/2001		
Inventory	$5,460,000*	
Accounts payable increase	$5,460,000	
*10,000,000 DM times $.5460		

day forward contract. While the forward had no value at inception, it now has a net fair value of $14,000 and a gain is recorded. The right to acquire a currency at a fixed rate grows in value when the currency appreciates—as it did between 11/2/2000 and 12/31/2000.

Following the guidance of SFAS No. 133, the $14,000 gain is included in other comprehensive income and not in earnings for the year.[28] The purchase has not been recorded, and it is only an anticipated and not a committed transaction. There is no recognized loss to offset the gain on the forward contract if the forward contract gain were included in earnings. Therefore, the gains or losses on the forward contract are included in accumulated other comprehensive income until the anticipated transaction has both (1) taken place and (2) been included in the determination of earnings. For the purchase of goods that will subsequently be sold, inclusion of the accumulated gain on the forward contract will take place when the purchased goods are sold and a cost of sales amount is recorded.

A further forward contract gain of $19,000 is recorded upon the maturity of the forward contract. This results because the forward rate, which upon maturity is equal to the spot rate, increased still further between 12/31/2000 and 1/30/2001.

Upon settlement of the forward contract, Importer, Inc. makes a payment to the currency broker of $5,427,000, which is the 10,000,000 DM purchased through the forward contract at the original 90-day rate of $.5427. In return, Importer, Inc. receives foreign currency worth $5,460,000 at the spot rate of $.5460. The differences between these two rates, the spot value of $.5460 for the DM upon contact maturity and the original 90-day forward of $.5427, results in the total forward contract gain of $33,000 ($14,000 + $19,000): ($.5460 − $.5427) times 10,000,000 DM equals $33,000.

However, notice that the spot rate cost of the purchased goods increased over the 90-day period by $47,000: spot rate at purchase date for the goods of $.5460 minus the original spot rate at 11/2/2000 of $.5413 times 10,000,000 DM equals $47,000. This growth in cost was not fully offset by the matching forward contract because of the forward contract premium of $14,000. That is, it cost $.5427 to purchase the 10,000,000 DM through the 90-day forward contract. This exceeded the spot rate of $.5413 at 11/2/2000 by $.0014, or a total of $14,000.

Transaction beyond the Purchase Date

To achieve closure on this illustration, assume that the purchase recorded on 1/30/2001 is, contrary to original plans, paid for on the very same day and that the goods are simultaneously sold. The recording of (1) the cost of sale and (2) the reclassification of the total gain on the forward contract of $33,000 out of accumulated other comprehensive income are described below:

- The goods booked into inventory on 1/30/2001 at $5,460,000 are transferred into cost of sales.
- The foreign currency gain of $33,000 is reclassified out of other accumulated other comprehensive income and deducted from cost of sales.

The net cost of sales becomes the original amount booked of $5,460,000 minus the reclassified gain on the forward contract of $33,000, or $5,427,000.

If payment were not to take place until 3/31/2001, then Importer, Inc. would have some other decisions to make. If Importer both took delivery and held the 10 million DM, then it will have still have a hedge in place. The gains and losses on the 10 million DM account payable will be offset by gains and losses on the 10 million cash DM balance. Alternatively, if there had simply been a net settlement with the foreign exchange broker, then Importer, Inc. would not be holding 10 million DM. To hedge its 10 million DM liability exposure, Importer could enter into a new forward contract to buy 10 million DM. No special accounting would be necessary in this case. The gains and losses on the periodic revaluation of the DM account payable and the DM forward contract would simply offset each other in earnings. In any event, whenever the acquired goods are sold, the $33,000 gain on the cash flow hedge must be reclassified out of accumulated other comprehensive income and included in the determination of net income.

Recap of the Hedge of an Anticipated Purchase Transaction

Importer, Inc. fixed the cost of an anticipated or forecasted purchase transaction by entering a forward contract to buy the needed foreign currency. The forward rate was at a premium to the spot and this caused the gains and losses on the revaluation of the forward contract to fail to be fully offsetting. Under current GAAP, the hedge of an anticipated or forecasted transaction is classified as a cash flow hedge. As they accrue, gains or losses on the forward contract are included in other comprehensive income. They are only included in the determination of earnings when and as the original hedged item is included in the determination of earnings.

Beyond the commitment period, Importer, Inc. could either hold German marks to hedge its now recorded German mark account payable or enter into a new forward contract to buy German marks. In either case, these hedges would be considered to be fair value hedges and their respective gains and losses would be included in the determination of net income as they accrue.

With these detailed illustrations of a fair value and a cash flow hedge, the next section provides examples of disclosures by companies of their policies for hedging foreign currency transactional exposure.

Company Hedging of Transactional Exposure

Large public companies usually provide disclosures of the key sources of transactional exposure and their associated hedging policies. Some also provide disclosures of exposure and associated hedging by currency.[29] Exhibit 7.12 provides examples, beyond those provided earlier in Exhibit 7.6, of transactional exposure that is hedged as well as the foreign currency derivatives used in hedging these exposures.

Relative Use of Alternative Foreign Currency Derivatives

The information in Exhibit 7.12 is designed to provide examples of transaction exposures that are hedged and the foreign currency derivatives that are used. The dominance of forward contracts and options in Exhibit 7.12 is representative of their relative use, based on large-sample surveys of hedging practices.[30] Results from the annual Wharton survey of derivatives usage provide additional insight into the use of foreign currency derivatives:

- More than 75 percent of firms rank the forward contract as one of their three top choices.
- About 50 percent of firms choose over-the-counter (OTC) options as one of their top three choices.[31]

The popularity of forward contracts is usually attributed to their tailoring characteristics. That is, both the size of the contract and its maturity can be tailored to specific hedging requirements. OTC options, which are privately negotiated as opposed to exchange traded, can likewise be tailored.

Hedging Objectives

Survey data on hedging objectives were presented earlier in Exhibit 7.5. These data highlighted the dominance of managing the volatility of cash flows and earnings, with 49 percent and 42 percent, respectively, ranking cash flows and earnings as the most important. Firms often make statements in their annual reports on the objectives of their hedging activities. Exhibit 7.13 provides a sampling of these disclosures.

The data in Exhibit 7.13 are consistent with the Wharton survey results summarized earlier in Exhibit 7.5. Reducing the volatility of cash flows and earnings

Exhibit 7.12. Examples of Hedged Transaction Exposures and Associated Derivatives

---

Alberto-Culver Co. (1998)

Transaction exposures	Inventory purchases and royalty payments
Foreign currency derivatives	Forwards

Archer Daniels Midland Co. (1998)

Transaction exposures	Substantially all foreign currency transactions, except for amounts considered permanently invested
Foreign currency derivatives	Exchange-traded futures and forwards

Becton, Dickenson & Co. (1998)

Transaction exposures	Receivables, payables, and short-term borrowings
Foreign currency derivatives	Forwards and options

Brown-Forman Corporation (1999)

Transaction exposures	Sale and purchase cash flows
Foreign currency derivatives	Options and forwards

C.R. Bard, Inc. (1998)

Transaction exposures	Intercompany transactions
Foreign currency derivatives	Forwards and options

ConAgra, Inc. (1999)

Transaction exposures	Fixed purchase and sales commitments
Foreign currency derivatives	Forwards

Tenneco, Inc. (1998)

Transaction exposures	Intercompany and third-party trade payable and receivables
Foreign currency derivatives	Forwards

TOYS "R" US, INC. (1998)

Transaction exposures	Trade payables, and a Swiss franc note payable
Foreign currency derivatives	Forward contracts and currency swaps

UAL, Inc. (1998)

Transaction exposures	Yen and French franc liabilities and Hong Kong revenues
Foreign currency derivatives	Forwards and put options

Sources: Companies' annual reports. The year following each company name designates the annual report from which each example was drawn.

Exhibit 7.13. Company Disclosures of Foreign Currency Hedging Objectives

---

Armstrong World Industries, Inc. (1998)

The Company uses foreign currency forward contracts to reduce the risk that future *cash flows* from transactions in foreign currencies will be affected unfavorably by changes in exchange rates.

Brown-Forman Corp. (1999)

The Company uses foreign currency options and forward contracts as protection against the risk that the eventual U.S. dollar *cash flows* resulting from the sale and purchase of goods in foreign currencies will be adversely affected by changes in exchange rates.

Goodyear Tire and Rubber Co. (1998)

In order to reduce the impact of changes in foreign exchange rates on consolidated *results of operations* and future foreign currency denominated *cash flows,* the Company was a party to various forward exchange contracts.

H. J. Heinz Co. (1999)

The company's *cash flow and earnings* are subject to fluctuation due to exchange rate variation. When appropriate, the company may attempt to limit its exposure to foreign exchange rates through both operational and financial market actions.

Johnson and Johnson (1998)

The Company uses financial instruments to manage the impact of interest rate and foreign exchange rate changes on *earnings and cash flows.*

The Quaker Oats Company (1998)

The Company uses foreign currency options and forward contracts to manage the impact of foreign currency fluctuations recognized in the Company's *operating results.*

VF Corporation (1998)

The Company enters into short-term foreign currency forward exchange contracts to manage exposures related to specific foreign currency transactions or anticipated *cash flows.*

Sources: Company annual reports, emphasis is added. The year following each company name designates the annual report from which each example is drawn.

appears to be the dominant objective, and typically the joint goals of currency hedging programs.

Natural Hedges

As a final hedge-related item in this transactions-oriented section, it should be noted that some firms hedge their currency exposure by creating what are termed *natural hedges.* This term is used in a fairly broad manner and it includes arrangements that create offsetting gains and losses, but that do not employ foreign currency derivatives. To supplement earlier discussion in Chapter Six, some recent examples of natural hedges are listed in Exhibit 7.14. Some of these examples

Exhibit 7.14.   Examples of Natural Hedges

Amcol International Corp. (1998)

The Company's various exposures often offset each other, providing a *natural hedge* against currency risk.

Baltek Co. (1998)

In 1998, the Company continued to borrow money for working capital purposes in local currency (sucre) denominated loans as a natural hedge of the net investment in Ecuador.

Burr Brown Corporation (1998)

Netting foreign currency receivables and payables due from subsidiaries creates a *natural hedge*.

Belden, Inc. (1998)

A *natural hedge* is created by borrowing in the same currency as the currency of anticipated cash flows from foreign operations.

Marquette Medical Systems, Inc. (1998)

Natural hedges are created by entering into foreign loans to offset similar amounts of foreign accounts receivable and incurring operating expenses in yen, which mitigate the exposure to yen denominated sales in Japan.

Philippine Long Distance Telephone Co. (1997)

The Company's operating revenues are substantially linked to the U.S. dollar. Accordingly, this constitutes a *natural hedge* for its short-term foreign currency denominated liabilities which are mainly in U.S. dollars.

CSR, Ltd. (1998)

U.S. dollar liabilities provide a *natural hedge* against the CSR Group's United States based assets.

Source: Companies' annual reports, emphasis added. The year following each company name designates the annual report from which each example is drawn.

report the application of natural hedges to both translation as well as transaction exposure.

The Amcol International entry in Exhibit 7.14 appears to be a true *natural hedge.* Offsetting of currency exposures is simply a byproduct of their operations and does not involve recording balances for the purpose of creating a "natural" hedge. The Baltek Company appears to be a case of entering into a particular borrowing arrangement with the purpose, at least in part, of creating a hedge. However, this is still properly classified a "natural hedge" because it does not involve using a foreign currency derivative. However, it would seem to be less "natural" than the Amcol International hedge.

Some of the natural hedges in Exhibit 7.14 appear to be designed to hedge translation and not transaction exposure. This appears to be the case with both Baltek Company and CSR, Ltd. It seems to be a clear advantage if a company's own operations create offsetting currency exposures. This reduces the need to use foreign currency derivatives and incur additional costs in the process.

The above completes the treatment in this chapter of the financial reporting and analysis of foreign currency transactions. Attention is now turned to foreign currency translation.

TRANSLATION REPORTING AND ANALYSIS

Generally accepted accounting principles require that virtually all majority-owned subsidiaries be consolidated.[32] Exceptions include situations in which control is likely to be temporary or does not rest with the majority owner. An example of the latter would be the case of a majority-owned subsidiary that is under the control of the courts because it is in a legal reorganization or in bankruptcy. There are no exemptions from the consolidation requirement because a subsidiary is located in another country.[33]

In the typical case, a foreign subsidiary's own financial statements will be in the local foreign currency. Before consolidation can take place, these statements must be translated into the reporting currency of the parent, the U.S. dollar in the case of subsidiaries of U.S. parents. The remainder of this chapter is devoted to illustrating the process of statement translation and considering the implications of the translated financial information for financial analysis. Some attention is also devoted to company hedging of currency exposure associated with foreign subsidiaries.

Translation of Foreign Subsidiary Financial Statements

In the strict technical sense, there is only a single translation method applied to foreign subsidiaries under SFAS No. 52, "Foreign Currency Translation."[34] This is the "all current" translation method. This method is applied in cases in which the functional currency of the subsidiary is its own domestic currency. This will normally be the case "For an entity with operations that are relatively self-contained and integrated within a particular country."[35] The all-current translation method is described in SFAS No. 52 as follows:

> For assets and liabilities, the exchange rate at the balance sheet date shall be used. For revenues, expenses, gains, and losses, the exchange rate at the dates on which those elements are recognized shall be used. Because translation at the exchange rates at the dates the numerous revenues, expenses, gains, and losses are recognized is generally impractical, an appropriately weighted-average exchange rate for the period may be used to translate those elements.[36]

Application of the above translation method begins with the financial statements in the local (functional) foreign currency. After translation of each financial statement balance with the appropriate current or average exchange rate, a translation adjustment will result.[37] Under the requirements of SFAS No. 130, "Reporting Comprehensive Income," these translation adjustments are included in other comprehensive income.[38] Prior to the issuance of SFAS No. 130, translation adjustments resulting from translation under the all-current method were reported directly in shareholders' equity.[39]

The trial balances in Exhibit 7.15 are simply listings of all of Foreign Sub's accounts. The accounts listed in the foreign current units (FC) trial balance are translated (i.e., multiplied by an exchange rate), following the all-current method described above. This translation results in the U.S. dollar trial balance in Exhibit 7.15.

All of the assets and liabilities are translated at the current exchange rate at 12/31/2001 of $.66—hence the label "all-current" method. This is the direct exchange rate for the currency of the subsidiary. However, because they are assumed to be distributed evenly over the year, the revenue and expense accounts are translated using the average exchange rate for 2001 of $.62. The common stock balance, neither an asset nor a liability, is translated at the (historical) exchange rate at the date that the shares were issued, or $.58 at 1/1/2001.

Illustration of the All-Current Translation Method

The basic information used to illustrate the all-current translation is found in Exhibit 7.15.

If the sum of the translated asset and expense accounts is computed and the sum of the liability, revenue, and shareholders' equity accounts is also totaled, with the exception of the translation adjustment account, the result is a U.S. dollar trial balance that does not balance. That is, the sum of the asset and expense account balances does not equal the sum of the liability, revenue, and shareholders' equity account balances. This difference is computed below:

Translated sum of Foreign Sub asset and expense balances	$2,092
Minus translated sum of Foreign Sub liability, revenue, and shareholders' equity balances	2,005
Difference	$87

The above difference is the initial translation adjustment. Under SFAS No. 130, "Reporting Comprehensive Income," this translation adjustment is an unrealized gain, and it is included in other comprehensive income.

The emergence of other comprehensive income from the translation of Foreign Sub can be explained. Consider Foreign Sub as simply a net investment in a foreign currency, with the investment equal to the excess of Foreign Sub's assets over its liabilities. At the beginning of the year, but after the initial stock issue, the net investment in Foreign Sub amounted to 1,000 FC. This net investment represents asset exposure in a foreign currency that appreciated in value across the year from $.58 to $.66. The effect of this increase on just the initial net

Exhibit 7.15. An All-Current Translation Illustration: Basic Information

1. Foreign Sub was formed on January 1, 2001, with an initial funding from a share issue that netted 1,000 FC (FC = foreign current units).
2. Selected exchange rates were:

At January 1, 2001	$.58
Average for 2001	$.62
At December 31, 2001	$.66

3. The trial balances of Foreign Sub, both in FC and translated into U.S. dollars following the all-current method, are provided below. Asset and expense balances are grouped first followed by liability, shareholders' equity and revenue balances.[40]
4. Trial Balance in FC and Translated into US$ at December 31, 2001:

Accounts	FC	Exchange Rates	US$
Cash	200	.66	132
Accounts receivable	100	.66	66
Inventory	300	.66	198
Property and equipment	1,800	.66	1,188
Cost of sales	600	.62	372
Selling and administrative expense	100	.62	62
Income tax provision	120	.62	74
Totals	3,220		$2,092
Accounts payable	200	.66	132
Notes payable	1,020	.66	673
Common stock	1,000	.58	580
Retained earnings	0		0
Translation adjustment	0		87
Sales	1,000	.62	620
Totals	3,220		$2,092

investment of 1,000 FC would account for $80 of the total translation adjustment (i.e., other comprehensive income: $.66 − $.58 × 1,000 FC = $80). The $7 remaining balance is explained by the growth in net assets across the year as a result of Foreign Sub's net income of 180 FC. Foreign Sub's net income is only translated to the average exchange in producing the U.S. dollar income statement. However, the translated balance sheet includes all assets and liabilities at year-end exchange rates. Therefore, to measure the full growth in net assets due to net income for the year, the net income of 180 FC must be adjusted to the end-of-year exchange rate from the average rate for the year: 180 FC times (year-end rate of $.66 − average rate of $.62) equals $7. To summarize the translation adjustment of $87:

Growth across the year in the initial net investment of Foreign Sub
  of 1,000 FC: ($.66 − $.58) × 1,000 FC = $80

Additional growth in net investment resulting from the effect of
  foreign currency appreciation of from a $.62 rate used to translate
  Foreign Sub's net income to $.66 used to translate the growth in net
  assets due to this net income:

($.66–$.62) × 180 FC =   7

Translation adjustment $87

The U.S. dollar income statement and balance sheet for Foreign Sub are developed
from the translated trial balance data in Exhibit 7.15 and are presented in Exhibit
7.16. Total comprehensive income of $199 includes the translation adjustment for
the year of $87. That is, it is composed of realized net income of $112 plus the
translation adjustment of $87 for a total of $199.

It should be noted that the translation of the statement data of Foreign Sub
and the preparation of U.S. dollar statements is necessary in order to produce
consolidated financial statements. Beyond this the Financial Accounting Standards
Board (FASB), in SFAS No. 52, "Foreign Currency Translation," states that translation should accomplish the following objectives:

1. Provide information that is generally compatible with the expected economic
   effects of a rate change on an enterprise's cash flows and equity.
2. Reflect in consolidated statements the financial results and relationships of the
   individual consolidated entities as measured in their functional currencies in
   conformity with U.S. GAAP.[41]

Whether translation under the all-current method achieves objective one would
be difficult to establish. However, the achievement of objective two, as it relates
to results and relationships is not difficult to confirm. Financial relationships include key balance sheet ratios such as the current ratio (the ratio of current assets
to current liabilities) and an important income statement measure, the gross margin
(sales minus cost of sales divided by sales). Translation under the all-current
method does preserve these relationships from the foreign currency financial statements into the U.S. dollar statements:

	FC	US$
Current ratio	600/200 = 3/1	396/132 = 3/1
Gross margin	400/1,000 = 40%	248/620 = 40%

Each of the preceding financial statistics is exactly the same in the foreign currency
as they are in the translated U.S. dollar amounts.

The exclusion of the translation adjustment from net income is explained in
SFAS No. 52, as follows:

Exhibit 7.16.   Statement Translation under the All-Current Method

Income Statement	FC	Exchange Rates	US$
Sales	1,000	.62	620
Less cost of sales	600	.62	372
Gross margin	400	.62	248
Less selling and administrative expense	100	.62	62
Pretax profit	300		186
Less tax provision	120	.62	74
Net income	180		112
Other comprehensive income			87
Comprehensive income			$199

Balance Sheet	FC	Exchange Rates	US$
Cash	200	.66	132
Accounts receivable	100	.66	66
Inventory	300	.66	198
Property and equipment—net	1,800	.66	1,188
Total assets	2,400		$1,584
Accounts payable	200	.66	132
Notes payable	1,020	.66	673
Common stock	1,000	.58	580
Retained earnings	180		112
Accumulated other comprehensive income			87
Total liabilities and shareholders' equity			
	2,400		$1,584

The economic effects of an exchange rate change on an operation that is relatively self-contained and integrated within a foreign country relate to the net investment in that operation. Translation adjustments that arise from consolidating that foreign operation do not impact cash flows and are not included in net income.[42]

The above characterization of the subsidiary's operations being, "relatively self-contained and integrated within a foreign country," implies application of the all-current translation method. However, where this is not the case, then the all-current translation procedure is not applied. Rather, a process referred to as re-measurement under the temporal method is used to restate the foreign currency statements into the reporting currency of the U.S. parent. In contrast to translation under the all-current method, SFAS No. 52 states:

The economic effects of an exchange rate change on a foreign operation that is an extension of the parent's domestic operations relate to individual assets and liabilities and impact the parent's cash flows directly. Accordingly, the exchange gains and losses in such an operation are included in net income.[43]

The process of statement remeasurement under the temporal method is considered next.

Statement Remeasurement under the Temporal Method

In applying the all-current method, it was assumed that the functional currency of Foreign Sub was the local currency of the foreign country. However, if the U.S. dollar were the functional currency, then the foreign subsidiary's income statement and balance sheet amounts are remeasured into the reporting currency (i.e., the U.S. dollar), using the temporal method. Remeasurement is designed to produce U.S. dollar statements that parallel those that would have resulted if all transactions of the foreign subsidiaries had been recorded as they occurred on the books of the U.S. parent.

The functional currency is defined in SFAS No. 52 as "the currency of the primary economic environment in which the entity operates; normally, that is the currency of the environment in which an entity generates and spends cash."[44]

Functional Currency Determinants

Indicators that the local foreign currency is the subsidiary's functional currency include the following:

- Cash flows related to the foreign entity's individual assets and liabilities are primarily in the foreign currency and do not directly impact the parent company's cash flows.
- Sales prices are determined more by local competition or local government regulation.
- There is an active local sales market for the foreign entity's products.
- Financing is primarily denominated in the foreign currency.
- Labor, materials, and other costs for the foreign entity's products or services are primarily local costs.
- There is a low volume of intercompany transactions and there is not an extensive interrelationship between the operations of the foreign entity and the parent.[45]

Leslie Fay Company, Inc. is an example of a company whose operations in the Far East did not satisfy the above indicators. Leslie Fay explained why the U.S. dollar, as opposed to the local foreign currencies, was its functional currency:

> The Company's Far East subsidiaries were financed by U.S. dollar advances and all of their finished goods sales were to the parent. Accordingly, the functional currency of the Far East subsidiaries was the U.S. dollar, and remeasurement gains and losses were included in determining net income for the period.[46]

The FASB, in SFAS No. 52, views the cash flow implications of translation under the all-current method and remeasurement under the temporal method as quite different. Translation adjustments under the all-current method are not seen to have any cash flow effects. However, the view of cash flows and remeasurement is, to repeat, quite different.

> The economic effects of an exchange rate change on a foreign operation that is an extension of the parent's domestic operations relate to individual assets and liabilities and impact the parent's cash flows directly. Accordingly, the exchange gains and losses in such an operation are included in net income.[47]

Functional Currency in Highly Inflationary Economies

In addition to cases such as Leslie Fay Company, Inc., the functional currency is not considered to be that of the foreign country in which the subsidiary is located if that country is considered highly inflationary. "For purposes of this requirement, a highly inflationary economy is one that has cumulative inflation of approximately 100 percent or more over a 3-year period."[48] The logic of not treating the local currency as the functional currency in this case is spelled out in SFAS No. 52 as follows:

> A currency in a highly inflationary environment is not considered stable enough to serve as a functional currency and the more stable currency of the reporting parent is to be used instead.[49]

Remeasurement and the Temporal Method

Remeasurement of the statements of foreign entities differs in important ways from translation under the all-current method. Remeasurement under the temporal method is accomplished as follows:

- All monetary assets and liabilities are remeasured at current exchange rates.
- All nonmonetary assets, liabilities, and equity balances are remeasured at historical exchange rates.
- Revenues and expenses are typically remeasured at average exchange rates for the period. However, cost of sales and depreciation expense are remeasured at the historical rates used to remeasure the related inventory and fixed asset balances.

In addition to the above differences from translation under the all-current method, the gains or losses that emerge from remeasurement are included in the determination of net income. They are not included in other comprehensive income as is the case for translation adjustments under the all-current method. The inclusion of remeasurement gains and losses in net income is consistent with the view that the exchange rate changes that result in the translation adjustments under the temporal method "impact the parent's cash flows directly."[50]

Exhibit 7.17.   Statement Remeasurement under the Temporal Method: Basic Information

1. Foreign Sub is formed on January 1, 2001, with an initial funding from a share issue that netted 1,000 FC (FC = foreign current units).
2. Selected exchange rates were:

At January 1, 2001	$.58
Average for 2001	$.62
At December 31, 2001	$.66

3. Property and equipment was acquired when the exchange rate was $.58 and inventory at the exchange rate of $.62. Depreciation of 60 FC is removed from Selling and administrative expense and set out separately because it is remeasured at a different exchange rate.
4. The trial balances of Foreign Sub, both in FC and remeasured into U.S. dollars under the temporal method, are provided below. Asset and expense balances are grouped first, followed by liability, shareholders' equity and revenue balances.
5. Trial Balance in FC and Translated US$ at December 31, 2001:

Accounts	FC	Exchange Rates	US$
Cash	200	.66	132
Accounts receivable	100	.66	66
Inventory	300	.62	186
Property and equipment—net	1,800	.58	1,044
Cost of sales	600	.62	372
Selling and administrative expense	40	.62	25
Depreciation	60	.58	35
Tax provision	120	.62	74
Remeasurement loss			71
Totals	3,220		$2,005
Accounts payable	200	.66	132
Notes payable	1,020	.66	673
Common stock	1,000	.58	580
Retained earnings	0		0
Sales	1,000	.62	620
Totals	3,220		$2,005

Illustration of Statement Remeasurement under the Temporal Method

The basic information used in this illustration is found in Exhibit 7.16 and is the same information found in Exhibit 7.15 and used to illustrate all-current translation. However, because the temporal method requires some balances to be remeasured at historic exchange rates, some additional information is provided. Remeasurement under the temporal method is illustrated in Exhibit 7.17.

Key differences between the translation and remeasurement of Foreign Subs statements are the remeasurement of property and equipment and inventory at their historical rates of $.58 and $.62, respectively. Moreover, the associated depreciation expense balance is also remeasured at the same historical rate of $.58. In this case, the remeasurement rate applied to cost of sales is the same average rate applied under the all-current translation in this case.

Because only Foreign Sub's monetary assets and liabilities are remeasured at the changing current exchange rate, foreign currency exposure is also different. Currency exposure under the all-current method is the net investment in Foreign Sub. Net investment is the excess of all of Foreign Sub's assets over its liabilities. The net investment is the measure of exposure because all assets and liabilities are translated at the changing current exchange. None of the assets or liabilities is frozen in value at historic exchange rates. The net asset exposure under the all-current method, combined with appreciation in the foreign currency, explains the translation adjustment gain of $87 that was included in other comprehensive income in Exhibit 7.16.

However, with remeasurement under the temporal method, Foreign Sub's exposure changes from asset (the net investment) exposure under the all-current method to net liability exposure under temporal remeasurement. Because only monetary assets and liabilities are remeasured at the current rate, exposure is determined by the relationship between monetary assets and monetary liabilities. With a significant excess of monetary liabilities over monetary assets, Foreign Sub has net liability exposure. Liability exposure combined with depreciation in the U.S. dollar resulted in a remeasurement loss of $71. This loss appears in both the remeasured trial balance in Exhibit 7.17 and in the remeasured income statement in Exhibit 7.18.

Foreign Sub's net liability exposure is evident by reviewing its balance sheet in Exhibit 7.18. At the end of 2001, the monetary assets (i.e., cash and accounts receivable), totaled only 300 FC. However, monetary liabilities (i.e., accounts payable and notes payable), totaled 1,220 FC.

The difference in comprehensive income under all-current translation and under temporal remeasurement is reconciled below:

Comprehensive income under the all-current translation		$199
Reduction in selling and administrative expense resulting from remeasurement of depreciation at the historical rate of $.58 versus the average rate of $.62:		
($.58 − $.62) times 60 FC equals		2
Difference in translation and remeasurement adjustments		
Translation adjustment (gain) under all-current translation	$(87)	
Minus the remeasurement loss under the temporal method	71	(158)
Temporal method net income		$43

The all-current and temporal methods are applied in different circumstances, and they can produce quite different financial results. In particular, as shown above, the translation adjustments are different because currency exposure is altered under these two methods. Moreover, translation adjustments under the all-current method are consigned to other comprehensive income and are not part of conventional net income that is the focus of most statement users. Whether there are real economic differences that justify financial statement effects that can be so different is an issue on which there is little evidence. Some of the implications of these different outcomes are discussed in the balance of this chapter, where selected company disclosures of translation and remeasurement policies are examined.

Selected Company Translation and Remeasurement Disclosures

The above discussion and illustration of statement translation and remeasurement is designed to provide an overview of translation and remeasurement methods and their impact on translated and remeasured statements. The discussion is supplemented in this section by some selected disclosures of translation and remeasurement policies as well as their effects on company financial statements.

Disclosures of translation policies by large firms usually include references to the use of both the all-current translation method as well as remeasurement under the temporal method. However, for most firms the functional currency of its foreign subsidiaries is the local foreign currency and the all-current translation method is applied. The translation disclosures below of H. J. Heinz Company are typical:

> **Translation of Foreign Currencies:** For all significant foreign operations, the functional currency is the local currency. Assets and liabilities of these operations are translated at the exchange rate in effect at each year-end. Income statements accounts are translated at the average exchange rate prevailing during the year. Translation adjustments arising from the use of differing exchange rates from period to period are included as a component of shareholders' equity.[51]

The H. J. Heinz Company apparently has some foreign operations for which remeasurement under the temporal method is applied. Their characterization of the all-current method is consistent with the illustration of the all-current method in Exhibits 7.15 and 7.16. The H. J. Heinz disclosures refer to the translation adjustments being "included as a component of shareholders' equity." That component is, of course, accumulated other comprehensive income.

As is permitted under SFAS No. 130, "Reporting Comprehensive Income," the H. J. Heinz Company discloses accumulated comprehensive income and its change each year in its consolidated statement of shareholders' equity. The cumulative balances and changes each year from 1997 through 1999 are presented in Exhibit 7.18.

Notice that H. J. Heinz Company has translation losses in each year from 1997 through 1999. Across just these three years, these losses have reduced shareholders' equity by a total of about $309 million. If we assume that most of the

Exhibit 7.18. Statement Remeasurement under the Temporal Method

Income Statement	FC	Exchange Rates	US$
Sales	1,000	.62	620
Less cost of sales	600	.62	372
Gross margin	400		248
Less: Selling and administative expense	40	.62	25
Depreciation	60	.58	35
Remeasurement loss		(Exhibit 7.17)	71
Pretax profit	300		117
Less tax provision	120	.62	74
Net income	180		$43
Balance Sheet	FC	Exchange Rates	US$
Cash	200	.66	132
Accounts receivable	100	.66	66
Inventory	300	.62	186
Property and equipment—net	1,800	.58	1,044
Total assets	2,400		1,428
Accounts payable	200	.66	132
Notes payable	1,020	.66	673
Common stock	1,000	.58	580
Retained earnings	180	(above)	43
Total liabilities and shareholders' equity	2,400		$1,428

accumulated other comprehensive loss at May 1, 1996, resulted from translation losses, then the reduction in shareholders' equity rises to about $497 million or approximately 28 percent of shareholders' equity at April 28, 1999.

The presence of these losses, in the face of the net asset exposure that is typical of translation under the all-current method, implies that the currencies have, on balance, depreciated in the countries in which H. J. Heinz Company operates. Recall that the exclusion of these losses from the determination of net income turns on their noncash character. However, a review of the H. J. Heinz Company statements of cash flows will show no additions for these noncash losses. This is because the statement of cash flows begins with net income and not comprehensive income. The H. J. Heinz other comprehensive losses are not deducted in arriving at net income unless and until they are realized.

Notice that the other comprehensive income information for 1997 reveals the reclassification of a $13,758,000 realized translation adjustment. This indicates that one of the foreign subsidiaries, which gave rise to a portion of the accumulated translation adjustment, was sold or otherwise disposed of, in whole or in part.

H. J. Heinz Company did in fact disclose that it sold its New Zealand ice cream business during 1997 for about $150 million. When this occurs, the associated accumulated translation adjustment is considered realized and is included in the determination of the gain or loss on the disposition of the foreign subsidiary.

The size of the H. J. Heinz Company translation losses may raise the issue of why this exposure was not hedged. A review of the Company's disclosures of the use of foreign currency derivatives refers to the hedging of intercompany cash flows, purchases and sales, and foreign currency denominated obligations.[52] In a section of its management's discussion and analysis, the Company states that, "The company manufacturers and sells its products in a number of locations around the world, and hence foreign currency risk is well diversified."[53] This diversification has obviously not protected it from substantial translation adjustments.

The apparent absence of hedging by H. J. Heinz Company of its translation exposure is not surprising in light of the survey data on hedging practices discussed earlier in this chapter. The dominant hedging objectives center on the protection of cash flow and earnings. No surveys are available since SFAS No. 130, "Reporting Comprehensive Income," brought translation adjustments into an expanded measure of income (i.e., comprehensive income). However, important statement users (e.g., lenders and security analysts), appear to be continuing their focus on traditional net income, which does not include these translation adjustments. Therefore, the willingness of H. J. Heinz Company to leave its substantial net investment or translation exposure unhedged is not surprising.

Albany International Corporation: All-Current Translation and Temporal Remeasurement

The H. J. Heinz Company disclosed its all-current translation adjustments within the statement of shareholders' equity and not in a comprehensive income statement format. This treatment is by far the most common method of implementing the requirements of SFAS No. 130. However, Albany International Corporation follows the minority practice of including its translation adjustments in an income statement format. Albany also discloses the use of both the all-current translation method and remeasurement under the temporal method. These disclosures are provided in Exhibit 7.19.

Putting translation losses into the comprehensive income statement format highlights these items, unlike the more common practice of disclosing them in the statement of changes in shareholders' equity. Albany International's translation adjustments, combined with the adjustments for its underfunded pensions, result in a comprehensive income series that is much weaker than the net income series. However, anecdotal evidence again suggests that key statement users are continuing to rely principally on the traditional net income series.

Albany International disclosed that it had operations in both Mexico and Brazil. Either or both of these countries were considered highly inflationary during some part of the three-year period covered by the information in Exhibit 7.19.

Exhibit 7.19.   Translation Adjustment in Accumulated Other Comprehensive
Income: The H. J. Heinz Company, Years Ending April 30, 1997, April 29,
1998, and April 28, 1999 (Thousands of Dollars)

	1997	1998	1999
Accumulated other comprehensive loss at May 1, 1996	$(188,303)		
Other comprehensive income (loss) net of tax:			
Minimum pension liability, net of $3,282 tax	5,588		
Unrealized translation adjustments	(41,353)		
Realized translation reclassification adjustment	(13,758)		
Other comprehensive income (loss)	(49,523)		
Accumulated other comprehensive loss at April 30, 1997	$(237,826)		
Accumulated other comprehensive loss at May 1, 1998		$(237,826)	
Other comprehensive income (loss), net of tax:			
Minimum pension liability, net of $1,428 tax		2,433	
Unrealized translation adjustments		(180,284)	
Other comprehensive income (loss)		(177,851)	
Accumulated other comprehensive loss at April 29, 1998		$(415,677)	
Accumulated other comprehensive loss at April 30, 1998			$(415,677)
Other comprehensive income (loss), net of tax:			
Minimum pension liability, net of $6,975 tax benefit			(11,880)
Unrealized translation adjustments			(88,040)
Other comprehensive income (loss)			(99,920)
Accumulated other comprehensive loss at April 28, 1999			$(515,597)

Source: H. J. Heinz Company, annual report, April 1999, pp. 42–43.

Adjustments from the remeasurement of the foreign currency statements of such
operations are included in net income, as the accounting policy note in Exhibit
7.19 reveals.

   Like H. J. Heinz Company above, Albany International has incurred significant translation losses in recent years. Albany International discloses a total of
$83,736,000 of accumulated translation adjustments (losses) in the shareholders'

equity section of its 1998 balance sheet. This accumulated translation loss amounted to about 27 percent of Albany International's 1998 shareholders' equity.

Unlike the H. J. Heinz Company, Albany International's accounting policy note on derivatives reveals that it does hedge the net asset exposure of foreign operations translated under the all-current method:

> Gains and losses on forward exchange contracts that are designated a hedge of a foreign operation's net assets and/or long-term intercompany loans are recorded in "Translation adjustments," a separate component of shareholders' equity.[54]

Albany International's hedging of its noncash net investment exposure could be influenced by the highlighting of its translation adjustments in its consolidated statements of comprehensive income. Some additional disclosures bearing on the hedging of translation and remeasurement exposures are presented and discussed in the next section.

On the Hedging of Translation and Remeasurement Exposures

The hedging survey data discussed earlier in this chapter reveal that the major focus of hedging is on protecting cash flows and earnings. As no survey data are yet available since SFAS No. 130 became effective, it is unclear whether firms will switch their hedging focus from net income to comprehensive income.[55] However, given the noncash character of the these translation adjustments, and the relatively low profile being given to the disclosure of comprehensive income data, hedging will probably continue to focus on protecting cash flows and traditional net income.

It is not uncommon for firms to disclose that they do not hedge either translation or remeasurement exposure. Some examples of such disclosures are presented in Exhibit 7.20. The motivations are implicit in some cases and explicit in others. Becton, Dickinson & Company makes it clear that its absence of hedging is due to the absence of an effect upon earnings and cash flow. The focus of Smurfit-Stone Container Corp. is on an absence of an impact of translation on earnings.

A review of hedging disclosures suggests that firms have a somewhat greater inclination to hedge remeasurement exposure. A logical inference is that this is because remeasurement adjustments do affect net earnings whereas translation adjustments under the all-current method do not.

SUMMARY

The focus of this chapter has been to overview the financial reporting and analysis of foreign currency transactions and statement translation. Transactional exposure has been the major focus of the technical treatment of foreign currency hedging.

Exhibit 7.20. Translation Adjustments in a Comprehensive Income Statement Format: Albany International Corp., Years Ending December 31, 1996–1998 (Thousands of Dollars)

Consolidated Statements of Comprehensive Income For the Years Ended December 31	1996	1997	1998
Net income	$48,306	$49,059	$31,772
Other comprehensive income (loss) before tax:			
Foreign currency translation adjustments	(12,063)	(42,011)	615
Pension liability adjustments	(101)	12,483	(16,868)
Income taxes related to items of other			
Comprehensive income (loss)	303	—	—
Comprehensive income	$36,445	$19,531	$15,519

Translation of Financial Statements: Assets and liabilities of non-U.S. operations are translated at year-end rates of exchange, and the income statements are translated at the average rates of exchange for the year. Gains or losses resulting from translating non-U.S. currency financial statements are accumulated in a separate component of shareholders' equity.

For operations in countries that are considered highly inflationary economies, gains and losses from translation and transactions are determined using a combination of current and historical rates and are included in net income.

Source: Albany International, annual report, December 1998, pp. 12, 15.

However, the issue of hedging and translation exposure has also been addressed. The following are key points for the reader to consider:

- Transactional exposure typically results from sales, purchases, or borrowings that are denominated in a foreign currency. The use of foreign currency derivatives, for either speculative or hedging purposes, is also considered to represent a foreign currency transaction.
- Hedging of transactional exposure is very common and the focus is usually on cash flow exposures associated with sales and purchases that are denominated in foreign currencies. The hedging of exposure associated with firm commitments and forecasted transactions or cash flows is also common.
- Survey data reveal that the objectives of transactional hedging are mainly to protect future cash flows or earnings. Firms have a very limited inclination to hedge exposure that does not have the potential to impact either cash flows or net income
- The most popular foreign currency derivatives used in hedging transactional exposure are forward contracts and OTC options. The tailoring features of both

Exhibit 7.21.   Disclosures of Policies not to Hedge Translation
or Remeasurement Exposures

Becton, Dickinson & Company (1997)

The Company does not generally hedge these translation exposures since such amounts
are recorded as cumulative currency translation adjustments, a separate component of shareholders' equity, and do not affect earnings or current cash flow.

Henry Schein, Inc. (1998)

The Company considers its investments in foreign operations to be both long-term and
strategic. As a result, the Company does not hedge the long-term translation exposure in
its balance sheet.

Smurfit-Stone Container Corp. (1998)

The Company's investments in foreign subsidiaries with a functional currency other than
the U.S. dollar are not hedged. The net assets in foreign subsidiaries translated into U.S.
dollars using the year-end exchange rates were approximately $1,070 million at December
31, 1998. The potential loss in fair value resulting from a hypothetical 10% adverse change
in foreign currency exchange rates would be approximately $107 million at December 31,
1998. Any loss would be reflected as a cumulative translation adjustment in Accumulated
Other Comprehensive Income and would not impact net income of the Company.

VF Corporation (1998)

VF does not hedge the translation of foreign currencies into the U.S. dollar.

Source: Companies' annual reports. The year following each company name designates the annual
report from which each example is drawn.

of these instruments, in terms of both notional amounts and maturities, play a
major role in their popularity.

- Transactional gains and losses are frequently the result of revaluing balance
sheet positions to reflect changes in either spot or forward rates. Therefore, the
resulting foreign currency gains and losses are noncash items. Hence, the cash
quality of earnings may be affected. In addition, these recognized but unrealized
gains and losses often create temporary differences and therefore call for the
recording of deferred tax liabilities and assets, respectively. Finally, some transactional gains and losses may be considered to be nonrecurring in nature. In
these cases, the gains or losses should be considered in assessing the persistence
dimension of earnings quality.

- Not all hedging of transactional exposure calls for the use of foreign currency
derivatives. The "natural" hedge often reduces transactional exposure by offsetting (i.e., netting) expected foreign currency inflows and outflows in the same
foreign currencies. Some somewhat less "natural" hedges, which do not involve
the use of financial derivatives, may involve engaging in a transaction that is

designed to reduce exposure. An example would be denominating borrowings in a currency in which an asset exposure already exists in the same foreign currency.

- Statement translation is necessary before a foreign operation can be consolidated with its domestic parent. As the consolidation of controlled foreign subsidiaries is required, translation is in turn essential. Translation is also necessary when a foreign entity is accounted for by the equity method.

- The standard translation procedure is the all-current method and it is applied if (a) the functional currency of a foreign subsidiary is its local currency and (b) the subsidiary is not located in a highly inflationary economy. Under the all-current method, all assets and liabilities are translated at current or end-of-period exchange rates. Revenues and expenses are typically translated at average exchange rates for the period. Paid-in capital is translated at historical rates. The translation adjustments that result from statement translation are included in other comprehensive income. Exposure under the all-current method is measured by the net investment in the foreign entity. The exclusion of translation adjustments from regular net income is based on their unrealized and noncash character. Accumulated translation adjustments are reclassified into net income when realized as the result of a sale or other disposition.

- If a foreign subsidiary's functional currency is not its own local currency, or if it is located in a highly inflationary economy, then its statements are remeasured into the reporting currency of its parent using the temporal method. Under the temporal method, monetary assets and liabilities are remeasured at current exchange rates and nonmonetary assets and liabilities, including paid-in capital, are remeasured using historical exchange rates.

  Revenues and expenses are normally remeasured at average exchange rates for the period. However, costs or expenses associated with nonmonetary assets, such as inventory and plant and equipment, are remeasured at the same rates as these assets. Exposure under temporal method remeasurement is equal to the net of monetary assets and monetary liabilities. Gains and losses from remeasurement are included in the determination of net income. Unlike translation adjustments under the all-current translation method, remeasurement gains and losses are viewed as having a direct impact on the parent's cash flows.

- Hedging translation exposure under the all-current method or remeasurement exposure under the temporal method is far less common than the hedging of transaction exposure. This is due to the threat to cash flow posed by transaction exposure that is not present with all-current translation, and perhaps not even in the case of temporal remeasurement. In addition, unhedged transaction exposure creates gains and losses that may increase the volatility of net income. Only gains and losses under remeasurement with the temporal method are included in net income.

GLOSSARY

Note: As the discussion below relates to foreign currency matters, "foreign currency" will be used as a prefix only when it is an important part of the listed terms.

All-current translation method　The translation method that restates all assets and liabilities of a subsidiary at the current exchange rate of its parent. Paid-in capital amounts are translated at historical rates and income statement amounts at representative average rates for the period. The translation adjustment of each period is included in other comprehensive income. Accumulated translation adjustments are included in accumulated other comprehensive income and are classified as part of shareholders' equity.

Cash flow hedge　A hedge of exposure resulting from the variability of expected future cash flows. This exposure may be the result of existing assets or liabilities or of a forecasted transaction.

Conversion　The exchange of one currency for another.

Currency exposure　The potential for the expansion or contraction of assets, liabilities, and future cash flows as a result of changes in exchange rates.

Currency risk　The potential for expansion or contraction in foreign currency assets or liabilities or future cash flows as a result of changes in exchange rates.

Current exchange rate　The spot rate for a currency. Also referred to as the closing rate or end-of-period rate.

Direct exchange rate　The value (price) of a foreign currency expressed in units of a domestic currency. For example, in recent years the direct exchange rate of the pound sterling has been about $1.50.

Discount or premium　The difference between the spot and forward rate. A discount exists when the forward rate is less than the spot rate upon entering into a forward contract to purchase a foreign currency. A premium exists when the forward rate exceeds the spot rate.

Exposure　Balance sheet amounts, income statement amounts, commitments, forecasted foreign currency amounts, and so on, that will expand or contact in terms of the domestic currency with changes in the exchange rates of foreign currencies. A broader concept of exposure would include both positive and negative effects on a firm's competitive position that result from either increases or decreases in domestic currency values. That is, increases in the value of the dollar may harm the competitive position of an American exporter because the firm's products will be more expensive in the foreign currency. However, a decrease in the value would have the opposite effect.

Fair value hedge　A hedge of the changing values of a firm commitment or of an available-for-sale security.

Foreign currency transaction　A transaction in which assets, liabilities, revenues, or expenses are recorded in a domestic currency but which are actually denominated in a foreign currency. *Example:* A U.S. firm makes a sale to a

Germany customer and the transaction is denominated in the German mark. The U.S. firm has a foreign currency transaction but the German firm does not.

Forward contract A derivative contract to either buy or sell a foreign currency, at an agreed exchange rate, for future delivery or receipt.

Forward exchange rate The agreed rate at which foreign currency will either be acquired or delivered in the future.

Functional currency The currency of the economic environment in which a firm conducts its business.

Futures contract A derivative contract to either receive or deliver a foreign currency at an agreed future date. Gains and losses on this exchange-traded derivative are normally settled in cash on a daily basis.

Hedge A foreign currency position that typically produces gains or losses when a related position produces offsetting losses and gains. Purchase of a foreign currency through a forward contract produces gains to offset transaction losses on a related accounts payable in a case where the foreign currency appreciates in value.

Hedge inefficiency A transaction gain or loss that results when the terms of a derivative used to achieve a hedge differ from the underlying exposure.

Historical exchange rate The exchange rate existing at the time that a transaction took place.

Indirect exchange rate The value of a foreign currency expressed in units of the foreign currency per unit of the domestic currency.

Interest rate parity A theorem that holds that interest rate differential between two countries will be equal to the difference between the forward exchange rate and the spot exchange rate.

Monetary/nonmonetary method A translation method that translates monetary assets and liabilities (e.g., accounts receivable and long-term debt) at the current exchange rate and nonmonetary assets and liabilities (e.g., inventory and property and equipment) at historical exchange rates.

Monetary assets and liabilities Items that are expressed in a fixed amount of currency. Examples would include cash, accounts receivable, accounts payable, and notes payable.

Natural hedge Narrowly, a natural hedge represents offsetting exposure (e.g., a German mark account receivable and a German mark account payable) that is simply a result of a firm's operations. However, in practice the expression "natural hedge" is also applied to transactions that are executed, at least in part, for the purpose of creating a hedge. For example, a U.S. bank with a Swiss franc liability makes a loan that is denominated in the Swiss franc.

Nonmonetary assets and liabilites Items whose value is not fixed in terms of a given amount of currency. Examples would include inventory, plant and equipment, and deferred income.

Notional amount of a derivative   The number of currency units, shares, bushels, pounds, or other units specified in the contract.

Option contract   A derivative contract to either purchase (a call option) or sell (a put option) a foreign currency at an agreed price (i.e., the strike price).

Partial hedge   A hedge that only offsets a portion of foreign currency exposure.

Remeasurement   Restatement of the financial statement amounts of a foreign subsidiary from its local foreign currency into its functional currency. In most cases, once restatement into the functional currency has been achieved, the statements are in the reporting currency of the parent. That is, where the local foreign currency of the subsidiary is not its functional currency, the functional currency is that of the parent.

Reporting currency   Generally the currency of a parent company that has foreign subsidiaries. The foreign subsidiaries keep their books in their local currencies, but they are consolidated by their parent and the results and position are ultimately reported in the currency of their parent.

Special accounting   The inclusion of gains and losses on foreign currency derivatives in other comprehensive income until such time as the offsetting transaction is included in income determination. Also, the revaluation of a foreign currency commitment so that its gain or loss will offset the loss or gain on a foreign currency derivative being used to hedge such exposure. The recognition of a transaction gain or loss on an available for sale investment in net income to offset the loss or gain on a foreign currency derivative being used to hedge such exposure is also an example of special accounting.

Speculation   The use of a foreign currency derivative in an effort to benefit from expected movements in exchange rates. Speculative use of a currency derivative is distinguished from use of the same contract to hedge or to reduce risk.

Spot rate   The exchange rate for current transactions in a currency. This is distinguished from the forward rate which is the rate that applies to agreements to exchange currencies at future dates.

Swap   An exchange of currencies, which includes an agreement to re-exchange the currencies at a later date at an agreed rate.

Temporal method   A method of statement remeasurement, or translation, that remeasures all monetary assets and liabilities at current exchange rates, nonmonetary assets and liabilities at historical rates, revenues and expenses at representative average rates, with the exception of cost of sales and depreciation, which are remeasured at the same rates as associated inventory and fixed assets. Resulting remeasurement gains and losses are included in net income—not other comprehensive income.

Trading position   Same as a speculation.

Translation   The restatement of the financial statement amounts of a foreign subsidiary into the currency of its parent. Restatement into the currency of the parent is necessary before consolidation of the foreign subsidiary with its domestic parent can take place. Restatement of a foreign currency into its domestic equivalent is by either multiplication of the foreign currency amount by the direct exchange rate or division of the foreign currency amount by the indirect rate.

Translation gain or loss   A gain or loss resulting from the translation of the statements of a foreign subsidiary. Used narrowly, this term refers to the translation adjustments that result from translation with the all-current method. However, in practice, it would usually be seen to include remeasurement gains and losses from the application of the temporal method.

NOTES

1. "A Weakened Yen for Coke," *The Mobile Register* (June 21, 1998), p. 6F.

2. L. Scism, "U.S. Firms Abroad Ride Shifting Waves of Currency," *The Wall Street Journal* (August 6, 1993), p. B2.

3. This shifting of production to other countries is most pronounced in those domestic textile and apparel companies that are labor, as opposed to capital, intensive. Lower foreign labor costs provide a competitive advantage for foreign producers as well as a cost-savings incentive for the movement of production out of the U.S. by domestic companies.

4. Much more hedging is done of transaction than of translation exposure. Hence, the hedging focus is mainly on transactional exposure.

5. SFAS No. 133, "Accounting for Derivative Instruments and Hedging Activities" (Norwalk, CT: The Financial Accounting Standards Board, June 1998). The effective date of this statement has been deferred to fiscal years beginning after June 15, 2000. See SFAS No. 137, "Accounting for Derivative Instruments and Hedging Activities—Deferral of Effective Date of FASB Statement No. 133" (Norwalk, CT: The Financial Accounting Standards Board, June 1999).

6. G. Bodnar, G. Hayt, and R. Marston, "The Wharton Survey of Derivatives Usage by U.S. Non-Financial Firms," *Financial Management* (Winter 1996), pp. 113–133.

7. S. Ross, R. Westerfield, and J. Jaffe, *Corporate Finance* (New York: Irwin/McGraw-Hill, 1999), p. 860.

8. Proportional adjustments would need to be made to these annual results for periods other than a year.

9. An exception to this gain and loss symmetry is found in the case of foreign currency options. If an option contract is used to hedge exposure, then a gain will result if there is an adverse movement in the value of the foreign currency. However, no loss is incurred on the option contract if the currency movement is favorable to the hedged exposure. In this case the option simply expires without value. However, a cost equal to the option premium or investment is incurred. Because of the absence of symmetrical gains and losses when options are used for hedging, options are usually referred to as one-sided arrangements.

10. Data on the relative use of different foreign-currency derivatives are from G. Bodnar, G. Hayt, and R. Marston, "The Wharton Survey of Derivatives Usage by U.S. Non-Financial Firms," *Financial Management* (Winter 1996), pp. 114–115.

11. *Ibid.,* p. 117.

12. This is not to suggest that the U.S. bank would be indifferent to or unaffected by changes in the value of the Philippine peso. A devaluation of the peso makes it more costly for the Philippine firm to purchase the dollars to pay off its U.S. dollar debt. This increases the possibility of a bad debt for the bank.

13. An exception is the accrual of a liability in cases where the current cost of the items covered by a purchase commitment fall in value. A liability equal only to the amount of the loss, and not the full amount of the purchase commitment, is recorded. However, under SFAS No. 133, assets and liabilities will be recorded as gains and losses are recorded on purchase commitments that are denominated in foreign currencies. But, this will only be the case where a fair value hedge of this exposure is in place.

14. The relevant GAAP include: SFAS No. 52, "Foreign Currency Translation" (Stamford, CT: Financial Accounting Standards Board, December 1981); and SFAS No. 133, "Accounting for Derivative Contracts and Hedging" (Norwalk, CT: Financial Accounting Standards Board, June 1998).

15. BARRA, Inc., annual report, March 1999, p. 25.

16. Goodyear Tire and Rubber Company, annual report, December 1998, p. 32.

17. The sustainable earnings worksheet introduced in Chapter Three includes line items to remove both foreign exchange gains and losses in the development of a sustainable earnings series.

18. Becton, Dickenson & Company, annual report, September 1998, p. 37.

19. SFAS No. 133, "Accounting for Derivative Contracts and Hedging" (Norwalk, CT: Financial Accounting Standards Board, June 1998), para. 18.

20. SFAS No. 52, "Foreign Currency Translation" (Stamford, CT: Financial Accounting Standards Board, December 1981), para. 21.

21. SFAS No. 133, "Accounting for Derivative Contracts and Hedging" (Norwalk, CT: Financial Accounting Standards Board, June 1998), paras. 37–39.

22. *Ibid.,* paras. 30–35.

23. SFAS No. 133, "Accounting for Derivative Contracts and Hedging Activities" (Norwalk, CT: Financial Accounting Standards Board, June 1998), pp. 1–3.

24. The exception to the rule would be the case of foreign currency options. Upon inception, an option premium is paid that represents the initial fair value of the option.

25. The notional amount is the number of currency units, shares, bushels, pounds, or other units specified in the contract. SFAS No. 133, "Accounting for Derivative Contracts and Hedging" (Norwalk, CT: Financial Accounting Standards Board, June 1998), p. 3.

26. Under the previous requirements of SFAS No. 52, "Foreign Currency Translation" (Stamford, CT: Financial Accounting Standards Board, December 1981), para. 18, the forward contract premium was accounted for separately and amortized over the term of the contract. As a result, the changing spot rates would have been used to revalue both the DM account receivable and the forward contract payable. In this case, the periodic gains and losses on the two positions would exactly offset. The final income statement effect is the same under both approaches, but the period by period result would differ.

27. SFAS No. 133, "Accounting for Derivative Contracts and Hedging" (Norwalk, CT: Financial Accounting Standards Board, June 1998), paras. 28–32.

28. *Ibid.,* para. 30.

29. Both Armstrong World Industries, Inc. and Dupont (E.I. du Pont de Nemours and Company) provide schedules of the currency exposures by amount and currency. In addi-

tion, these schedules also reveal hedging of these currencies by currency and their net unhedged exposure. See Armstrong World Industries, Inc., annual report, December 1998, p. 42; and E. I. du Pont de Nemours, annual report, December 1998, p. 33.

30. G. Bodnar, G. Hayt, and R. Marston, "The Wharton Survey of Derivatives Usage by U.S. Non-Financial Firms," *Financial Management* (Winter 1996), pp. 114–115.

31. *Ibid.,* pp. 114–115.

32. SFAS No. 94, "Consolidation of All Majority-Owned Subsidiaries" (Stamford, CT: Financial Accounting Standards Board, October 1997).

33. See Chapter Nine of this book, the section on "Changes in the Definition of Control," for an update on FASB activity in proposing changes in the concept of control used to determine whether or not consolidation is required.

34. SFAS No. 52, "Foreign Currency Translation" (Stamford, CT: Financial Accounting Standards Board, December 1981).

35. *Ibid.,* para. 5.

36. SFAS No. 52, "Foreign Currency Translation" (Stamford, CT: Financial Accounting Standards Board, December 1981), para. 12.

37. In a strictly mechanical sense, the translation adjustment is the amount by which a trial balance of the firm's accounts is out of balance after translation of all account balances, other than the translation adjustment itself.

38. SFAS No. 130, "Reporting Comprehensive Income" (Norwalk, CT: Financial Accounting Standards Board, June 1997), para. 29.

39. As a historical note, prior to SFAS No. 52, SFAS No. 8, "Accounting for the Translation of Foreign Transactions and Foreign Currency Statements" (Stamford, CT: Financial Accounting Standards Board, October 1975) provided statement translation requirements. Under SFAS No. 8, a different translation method was required (i.e., the temporal method), and all translation adjustments were included in the income statement. This approach created significant earnings volatility for large U.S. multinationals. Opposition to SFAS No. 8 was fierce, and it was replaced about seven years later by SFAS No. 52. Under SFAS No. 52, translation adjustments resulting from application of the all-current method bypassed the income statement and were disclosed directly in shareholders' equity. Now, under SFAS No. 130, "Reporting Comprehensive Income" these translation adjustments are included in other comprehensive income.

40. These account groupings are standard, and they reflect the fact that the asset and expense accounts have the same type of balance (i.e., a debit balance), and the liability, shareholders' equity, and revenue accounts all have credit balances.

41. SFAS No. 52, "Foreign Currency Translation" (Stamford, CT: Financial Accounting Standards Board, December 1981), from the Summary.

42. SFAS No. 52, "Foreign Currency Translation" (Stamford, CT: Financial Accounting Standards Board, December 1981), from the Summary.

43. *Ibid.*

44. SFAS No. 52, "Foreign Currency Translation" (Stamford, CT: Financial Accounting Standards Board, December 1981), para. 162.

45. *Ibid.,* para. 42.

46. Leslie Fay Co., Inc., annual report, December 1996. Information obtained from Disclosure, Inc. *Compact D/SEC: Corporate Information on Public Companies Filing with the SEC* (Bethesda, MD: Disclosure, Inc., June 1999). Leslie Fay Co. subsequently disposed of these operations.

47. SFAS No. 52, "Foreign Currency Translation" (Stamford, CT: Financial Accounting Standards Board, December 1981), from the Summary.

48. *Ibid.,* para. 11.

49. SFAS No. 52, "Foreign Currency Translation" (Stamford, CT: Financial Accounting Standards Board, December 1981), from the Summary.

50. *Ibid.*

51. H. J. Heinz Company, annual report, April 1999, p. 45.

52. *Ibid.,* p. 46.

53. *Ibid.,* p. 35.

54. Albany International Corp., annual report, December 1998, p. 16.

55. SFAS No. 130, "Reporting Comprehensive Income" (Norwalk, CT: Financial Accounting Standards Board, June 1997).

Chapter 8

Investment Reporting and Analysis I: Debt and Equity Securities

Presidential Life Corp. will restate several years of financial results
to reflect a mark-down of some junk securities in its portfolio as part
of a settlement with the Securities and Exchange Commission.[1]

Accounting standards for investments in debt and equity securities have changed markedly in recent years. Contributing to the changes, at least in part, were abuses of former accounting rules. Those rules, especially in the case of debt securities, were linked strongly to cost. As with the investments in debt securities of Presidential Life Corporation above, regulators and accounting standard setters were concerned that fair market values were being ignored, often to the peril of financial statement usefulness, even when those market values departed significantly from cost. In those cases in which market values were employed to account for investments, the strong presence of conservatism dictated that those investments were not to be written up above cost.[2]

Beginning with fiscal years starting in 1994, changes in accounting standards for investments became effective. No single company's financial statements reflect more clearly the potentially significant impact of those changes in accounting than the financial statements of SunTrust Banks, Inc. For decades, SunTrust carried its investment in the common stock of the Coca-Cola Company unchanged at $110,000, the market value of those shares when they were received as part compensation for underwriting work performed in 1919. In 1993, SunTrust elected early adoption of the new rules, writing its investment in Coca-Cola up to $1,076,946,000. Together with gains on other investment securities, the new rules raised SunTrust's shareholders' equity by approximately 27 percent. As of December 31, 1997, SunTrust's Coca-Cola shares were worth $3,218,772,000, and total investment gains had augmented the company's shareholders' equity by 65 percent—a noteworthy amount.

Although investments accounting today is often referred to loosely as being market-value driven, such a view is not totally correct and can be misleading. Market-value or fair-value accounting is an important component of contemporary accounting standards for investments; however, many investments are not carried at market.[3] Depending on the nature of the instrument involved, management's intent with respect to the timing of its disposal, and the investment's size relative to the underlying issuer, cost, amortized cost, or the equity method, assuming the position is insufficient to provide control, might be used. Moreover, under these alternatives to market-value accounting, there are circumstances in which declines in market value are nonetheless taken into account. And even with market-value accounting, resulting gains and losses are sometimes taken to the income statement and included in the computation of net income, and are sometimes taken directly to other comprehensive income, being reported outside of net income.

Besides the confusion that the new rules can engender, the many and varied methods of accounting for investments create opportunities for differences between carrying value and market value to arise, with accompanying implications for position quality. Also, depending on whether or not recognized gains and losses are taken to income, investments accounting can affect earnings quality on both the cash and persistence dimensions.

The purpose of this chapter and Chapter Nine is to clarify contemporary accounting and reporting standards for investments and identify their implications for analysis. In this chapter, the focus is on investments in debt securities and equity securities in which the investor's ownership position is insufficient to provide control. In Chapter Nine attention is directed to accounting for business combinations in which the investor–investee relationship becomes one of parent–subsidiary.

INVESTMENTS IN DEBT AND EQUITY SECURITIES

The focus here is on investments in securities. More specifically, a security represents a share or interest in a property or an enterprise. A security interest might be an instrument, such as a stock certificate or a bond, though if not, to be a security, it must be registered in books maintained to record transfers by or on behalf of the issuer. Securities are of a type that are commonly dealt in on securities markets and are divisible into classes of shares, participations, or obligations.[4] For example, while common stock issues and bonds are securities, equity interests in private partnerships and auto loan receivables are not. Securitization is the process whereby securities are created backed by pools of nonsecuritized assets. For example, an issuer might pool such assets as auto loans or credit card receivables and sell shares in the pool backed by these assets. Investors would receive interest and principal payments from cash flows generated by the pool of assets and would account for the investment as an investment in a security.

Determining how an investment in a security is to be accounted for is dependent on the nature of that investment and the timing of management's intent with respect to its disposal. The nature of an investment in a security refers to whether it is a debt or equity security and for equity securities, whether or not it has a readily determinable fair market value and whether or not the ownership position taken is sufficient to provide the investor with significant influence over operating and financial policies of the investee.[5]

Debt securities represent a creditor relationship with an enterprise. They include U.S. government securities, municipal securities, corporate bonds, convertible debt, commercial paper, and all securitized debt instruments such as the pools of auto loan receivables discussed above, or, for example, collateralized mortgage obligations (CMOs), real estate mortgage investment conduits (REMICs), and interest-only and principal-only strips. A preferred stock issue that must be redeemed by the issuing enterprise or is redeemable at the option of the investor— redeemable preferred stock—is also considered to be a debt security for accounting purposes. Equity securities represent an ownership interest in an enterprise, including such issues as common stock and preferred stock, though excluding redeemable preferred. An ownership interest in a mutual fund would be accounted for as an equity security. Equity securities also include rights to acquire an ownership interest at fixed or determinable prices such as warrants, rights, and call options, and rights to dispose of equity interests, such as put options. Because they do not offer rights to acquire ownership interests in an enterprise, futures and options on futures are not considered to be equity securities. The accounting for these derivatives, or securities that derive their value from other underlying securities, is discussed in Chapter Six.

An equity security has a readily determinable market value if sales prices or bid-and-asked quotations are currently available on a securities exchange registered with the Securities and Exchange Commission (SEC) or in the over-the-counter (OTC) market. Quotes from the OTC market must be publicly reported by the National Association of Securities Dealers Automated Quotations (NASDAQ) systems or by the National Quotation Bureau. Typically, when market value is used to value securities for balance sheet purposes, the closing market price is used. As stated by Kaye Group, Inc., "the fair value of equity securities is based on the closing sale price on December 31."[6]

Restricted stock, or stock whose sale is restricted by government or contractual requirement for a period exceeding one year is not considered to have a readily determinable market value. Equity securities traded in foreign markets are considered to have readily determinable market values provided those foreign markets are of a breadth and scope comparable to markets in the United States. Whether a readily determinable market value is available for debt securities is not of concern in accounting for debt securities because, when needed, fair value can be estimated using a risk-adjusted present-value framework—the present value of the cash flows represented by the debt security is calculated using a risk-adjusted discount rate. Such an approach may not be applied in determining an estimate of the fair value of equity securities.

Whether an investment in an equity security provides the investor with significant influence over the operating and financial policies of the investee is a function of the size of ownership position taken. The presumption is that a 20 percent ownership stake, in the absence of evidence to the contrary, is sufficient to confer significant influence. More is said about significant influence and accounting for investments in equity securities where significant influence exists in a later section of this chapter, "Accounting for Investments under the Equity Method."

Accounting and financial reporting practices for investments in debt securities and equity securities, excluding those conferring significant influence, vary depending on management's intent with respect to the investments' disposal. Investments might be considered to be held to maturity, held for trading purposes, or held as available for sale. Each of the accounting methods are explained below and are accompanied with recent financial statement examples.

Held-to-Maturity Securities

Only debt securities and redeemable preferred stock can be classified as held to maturity because, by definition, equity securities have no maturity value. A debt security should be classified as held to maturity if the reporting entity has both the positive intent and the ability to hold those securities to maturity. If a firm's intent is to hold a debt security for an indefinite period of time, it should not be classified as held to maturity. Similarly, an investment should not be classified as held to maturity if the firm anticipates that a sale might be necessary due to changes in interest rates, foreign currency risk, liquidity, or other asset-liability management needs.

Held-to-maturity securities are accounted for at amortized cost. That is, at cost, including any unamortized purchase premium or discount. A premium or discount from par arising at purchase is amortized to interest income over the holding period to maturity, with any premium reducing interest income and discount increasing it. By the maturity date, the security should be reported at par. Interest income on held-to-maturity debt securities is included in income as it accrues. Dividend income on redeemable preferred stock is included in income when a dividend is declared by the issuer.

BankAmerica Corporation (BAC) describes its accounting for held-to-maturity securities as follows:

> BAC's securities portfolios include U.S. Treasury and other government agency securities, mortgage-backed securities, state, county, municipal, and foreign government securities, equity securities and corporate debt securities.
>
> Debt securities for which BAC has the positive intent and ability to hold to maturity are classified as held-to-maturity and reported at amortized cost. Debt securities that BAC may not hold to maturity and marketable equity securities are classified as available-for-sale securities unless they are considered to be part of trading-related activities.
>
> Dividend and interest income, including amortization of premium and accretion of discount, for both securities portfolios are included in interest income.[7]

The Company's balance sheet as of December 31, 1997, reported held-to-maturity securities carried at $3,667,000,000. Disclosed parenthetically on the balance sheet on the same date, the market value of these securities was reported to be $3,744,000,000. The Company accompanied the balance sheet amounts with a

Exhibit 8.1.   Amortized Cost and Fair Value of Held-to-Maturity Securities:
BankAmerica Corp., Excerpts from Footnotes to Financial Statements, for the
Year Ended December 31, 1997 (Millions of Dollars)

	Held-to-Maturity Securities			
	Amortized Cost	Gross Unrealized Gains	Gross Unrealized Losses	Fair Value
December 31, 1997				
U.S. Treasury and other government agency securities	$16	$—	$—	$16
Mortgage-backed securities	1,877	41	2	1,916
State, county, and municipal securities	306	13	1	318
Foreign governments	1,105	51	35	1,121
Corporate and other debt securities	363	18	8	373
	$ 3,667	$123	$46	$3,744

Source: BankAmerica Corp., annual report, December 1997, p. 66.

footnote detailing cost and fair-value information. An excerpt from that note is
provided in Exhibit 8.1. Note that because the securities were carried at amortized
cost, the gross unrealized gains and gross unrealized losses disclosed in the note
were not included in balance sheet amounts reported as assets.

In addition to the required disclosures of amortized cost, fair value, and gross
unrealized gains and losses on its held-to-maturity portfolio, BankAmerica also
disclosed, as required, the contractual maturities of its held-to-maturity debt securities.[8] While only a general disclosure requirement for nonfinancial institutions,
for financial institutions, the reporting requirement of contractual maturities is
more stringent, requiring four maturity groupings: (1) within one year, (2) after
one year, (3) after five years through ten years, and (4) after ten years. Bank-
America fulfilled this reporting requirement in its 1997 annual report with the
display provided in Exhibit 8.2.

The disclosure of contractual maturities is useful information in assessing a
company's exposure to interest rate risk. The longer the contractual maturity dates,
the more susceptible are the fair values of its debt securities to changes in interest
rates. Most of BankAmerica's debt securities that are held-to-maturity have contractual maturities exceeding 10 years. Any meaningful rise in interest rates would
have a dramatic negative effect on the fair values of these securities. Though
because the securities are accounted for at amortized cost, those temporary declines would not be taken into account.

The use of amortized cost and not fair value in accounting for held-to-maturity
securities is made clear in the BankAmerica example. The reason for not using
fair value is that if management intends to hold the securities until maturity, then

Exhibit 8.2. Contractual Maturities of Held-To-Maturity Securities:
BankAmerica Corp., Excerpts from Footnotes to Financial Statements,
for the Year Ended December 31, 1997 (Millions of Dollars)

The following is a summary of the contractual maturities of held-to-maturity securities at
December 31, 1997:

	Amortized Cost	*Fair Value*
Due in one year or less	$295	$296
Due after one year through five years	285	290
Due after five years through ten years	830	855
Due after ten years	2,257	2,303
	$3,667	$3,744

Source: BankAmerica Corp., annual report, December 1997, p. 67.

fair value is not relevant for measuring and evaluating the cash flows associated
with them. There is, however, an important exception to this rule. When the fair
value of a held-to-maturity security declines below amortized cost and that decline
is considered to be other than temporary, the security is to be written down to fair
value with the accompanying loss included in earnings for the period. The new,
reduced valuation is to become the new cost basis and is not changed for subsequent market-value recoveries.

Deciding whether a decline in fair value is an other-than-temporary decline
requires judgment on the part of management. An important factor in this decision
is whether the investor will be unable to collect all amounts due according to the
contractual terms of the security.

In 1996, the fair value of BankAmerica's held-to-maturity securities was below cost. That year, the company reported its held-to-maturity securities at an
amortized cost amount of $4,138,000,000. Disclosed parenthetically on the bal-
ance sheet was the market value of these securities, $3,920,000,000. In an accom-
panying footnote the detail of the company's investments in these securities and
its unrealized gains and losses was provided. That note is reported in Exhibit 8.3.
Because the company considered the decline in fair value to be a temporary condition, some or all of the unrealized losses were not taken into account.

Berkshire Hathaway's investment in USAir Group, Inc. provides an insightful
example into one management's determination of when a decline in fair value of
a security is other than temporary. In a footnote to its 1994 annual report, the
Company provided the following description of its investment in preferred stock
of USAir:

> Investments in securities with fixed maturities include 358,000 shares of USAir Group,
> Inc. Series A Cumulative Convertible Preferred Stock ("USAir Preferred Shares").
> The USAir Preferred Shares were acquired in 1989 for $358 million. If not called or
> converted prior to August 7, 1999, the USAir Preferred Shares are mandatorily re-

Exhibit 8.3. Amortized Cost and Fair Value of Held-to-Maturity Securities. Amortized Cost Exceeds Fair Value: BankAmerica Corp., Excerpts from Footnotes to Financial Statements, for the Year Ended December 31, 1996 (Millions of Dollars)

	Held-to-Maturity Securities			
	Amortized Cost	Gross Unrealized Gains	Gross Unrealized Losses	Fair Value
December 31, 1996				
U.S. Treasury and other government agency securities	$19	$—	$—	$19
Mortgage-backed securities	2,163	31	15	2,179
State, county, and municipal securities	423	14	6	431
Foreign governments	1,160	9	261	908
Corporate and other debt securities	373	21	11	383
	$4,138	$75	$293	$3,920

Source: BankAmerica Corp., annual report, December 1997, p. 66.

deemable by USAir Group, Inc. ("USAir") at $1,000 per share ($358 million in the aggregate), plus accrued dividends.

For the past five years USAir has incurred very significant loses. On September 29, 1994, USAir announced that it was deferring the quarterly dividend payment due September 30, 1994, on the USAir Preferred Shares. As of March 7, 1995 neither the quarterly dividend due September 30, 1994, or December 31, 1994, had been received. USAir has publicly stated that its ability to survive in the low fare competitive environment is contingent upon USAir's ability permanently to reduce its operating costs through reductions in personnel costs and other cost saving initiatives. USAir management is currently engaged in discussion with the leadership of its unionized employees to achieve its goal of reducing personnel costs. While USAir's management has stated they are committed to reaching an agreement with the labor groups, both the timing and the outcome of the negotiations are uncertain.

As a result of the extended period of losses and the uncertainty surrounding the outcome of the labor negotiations, Berkshire management has concluded that an other than temporary decline in the value of the USAir Preferred Shares has arisen. Accordingly, the 1994 Consolidated Statement of Earnings includes a charge of $268.5 million to reflect the decline.[9]

Berkshire Hathaway considered several factors in its decision to view the decline in the fair value of its investment in USAir to be an other-than-temporary event. As provided in the footnote, USAir had reported "very significant losses," the company had suspended its quarterly dividend payments, and had publicly stated that its very ability to survive in the low-fare competitive environment was contingent on its ability to reduce its operating costs through personnel reductions and other cost-saving initiatives—actions whose outcome was uncertain. As a result, company management decided to record a write-down of the investment and record an income statement charge.

One final observation should be made on the Berkshire Hathaway investment in USAir. From its acquisition in 1989 until just before the decision to record a charge to the income statement for an other-than-temporary decline in the investment's market value, Berkshire Hathaway's investment in the redeemable preferred stock of USAir had been accounted for as a held-to-maturity security. That designation was used because of the issue's mandatory redemption feature. As noted, redeemable preferred stock is considered to be a debt security for accounting purposes. During 1994, Berkshire Hathaway transferred the investment to its available-for-sale portfolio. Accounting for such transfers is discussed in a subsequent section of this chapter.

Referring to this chapter's opening quotation, the SEC forced Presidential Life to write down the company's investments in "junk securities," or below-investment-grade debt securities. As many of the issuers of these securities were in or near bankruptcy, the case for an other-than-temporary decline in market value was an easy one to make.

For companies providing a classified balance sheet, classification of held-to-maturity investments in debt securities is dependent on the maturity date.[10] Investments in securities maturing within one year of the balance sheet date would be classified as current assets. Investments in securities maturing beyond one year would be classified as noncurrent.

Cash equivalents are closely related to investments in held-to-maturity securities. Cash equivalents are short-term, highly liquid investments that are both (1) readily convertible into known amounts of cash and (2) so near their maturity that they present insignificant risk arising from potential changes in interest rates.[11] Generally such investments, including Treasury bills, commercial paper, and money market funds, have original maturities of three months or less. Such investments are used for short-term cash management and are accounted for at cost.

Trading Securities

Investments in debt and equity securities that are made with the intention of selling them in a short period of time are considered trading securities. Trading means frequent buying and selling in an effort to generate profits from short-term changes in price. Holding periods for investments in trading securities are typically less than three months and might be measured in terms of days or even hours. For example, the purchase of zero-coupon Treasury bonds in the morning in anticipation of a decline in interest rates accompanying an easing of monetary policy by the Federal Reserve Board later that day would constitute an investment in a trading security.

Investments in trading securities are reported at fair value. Unrealized holding gains and losses arising from the net change in the fair value of a trading security from one period to the next are included in income as they arise. Deferred income tax expense on these unrealized gains and losses are also recorded and included in income. Although interest income is accrued on a debt security held in a trading portfolio, any discount or premium from par on that investment is not amortized to income. Dividends on equity securities held in a trading portfolio are included in income when declared by the issuer.

When debt and equity securities are actively traded, any gains or losses that result, both realized and unrealized, are considered part of the company's operating results. As such, the reasoning is, they should be included in the calculation of net income.

Investments in debt and equity securities considered trading securities are common among financial institutions such as commercial and investment banks, insurance companies, and brokerage firms. In fact, for many such firms, trading gains and losses are an important component of operating profit.

Returning, for example, to BankAmerica Corporation, the company's footnotes to its 1997 annual report included a note titled "Trading Account Assets," which provided the following statement:

> Trading account assets, which are generally held for the short term in anticipation of market gains and resale, are carried at their fair values. Realized and unrealized gains and losses on trading account assets are included in trading income.[12]

That policy is consistent with the accounting guidelines for trading securities. The company's balance sheet reported trading account assets of $12,205,000,000 and $15,551,000,000 as of December 31, 1996 and 1997, respectively. The amounts reported were, of course, at fair value. They comprised approximately five percent and six percent, respectively, of total assets at December 31, 1996 and 1997.

While the company's trading account asset balances included trading investments in debt and equity securities, they also likely included other trading positions such as interest rate futures and options on futures, interest rate swaps, and foreign currency positions. A detailed description of these positions was not apparent. This lack of disclosure was not surprising given the short-term nature of these investments.

BankAmerica's income statement reported trading income of $630 million in 1996 and $692 million in 1997. These trading income amounts included much more than simply gains and losses on the company's trading portfolio of debt and equity securities. In an effort to help the reader to understand better the contribution of debt and equity investments to trading income, footnotes did provide the following disclosure:

> During the year ended December 31, 1997, trading income included a net unrealized holding loss of $15 million. For the years ended December 31, 1996 and 1995, trading income included net unrealized holding gains on trading securities of $1 million and $37 million, respectively.[13]

While not common, some industrial firms will disclose the existence of a trading portfolio. Intel Corporation provides a case in point as it disclosed in the footnotes to its 1997 annual report:

> **Trading assets.** During 1996, the Company began purchasing securities classified as trading assets. Net gains on the trading asset portfolio were $37 million and $12 million in 1997 and 1996, respectively. The Company maintains its trading asset portfolio to generate returns that offset changes in certain liabilities related to deferred compensation arrangements. The trading assets consist of marketable equity securities and are stated at fair value. Both realized and unrealized gains and losses are included in other income or expense and generally offset the change in the deferred compensation liability, which is also included in other income or expense.

Intel's trading portfolio is small and was apparently established for a specific reason—to offset the income effects of changes in the company's deferred compensation liability. More specific information about how this was achieved was not noted.

One small nonfinancial company, which was subsequently taken private, and which reported a significant trading portfolio for its size, was Bay Tact Corporation. Bay Tact, a financial information and publishing firm, described its accounting policy for its trading investments in marketable securities as follows:

> Marketable securities consist of investments in equity stocks less the amount due on margin. At December 31, 1993, the Company appropriately adopted FASB 115 "Accounting for Certain Investments in Debt and Equity Securities" and the securities are shown at market value less the amount due on margin. The Company freely trades these securities and correspondingly records the net unrealized gains and losses in its statement of income.[14]

In its annual report the company provided a disclosure of the cost and market value of its investment portfolio and of resulting unrealized gains and losses. That disclosure is reproduced in Exhibit 8.4.

At December 31, 1993, the market value of Bay Tact's total portfolio before margin debt was a significant 35 percent of total assets and 43 percent of shareholders' equity. Much of the firm was clearly at risk to the vagaries of the stock market. Certainly, market exposure to this extent is out of the ordinary. After apparently gaining a greater appreciation for the risk associated with such significant trading exposure, the firm reduced it markedly by December 31, 1994.

Available-for-Sale Securities

The available-for-sale classification is the default classification for all investments in debt and equity securities not classified as held-to-maturity or trading. As such, the classification is quite large and will likely include, especially for nonfinancial firms, the largest portion of a company's investment securities. In fact, the majority of nonfinancial firms will classify virtually all of their investments in debt and equity securities as available-for-sale securities.

Exhibit 8.4. Cost and Market Value of Trading Securities: Bay Tact Corp., Excerpts from Footnotes to Financial Statements, for the Years Ended December 31, 1993 and 1994

| | *1993* | | *1994* | |
	Cost	*Market Value*	*Cost*	*Market Value*
Total	$286,647	$283,662	$8,200	$9,500
Less—amount due on margin	91,302	91,302	—	—
Net marketable securities	$195,345	$192,360	$8,200	$9,500

Unrealized gains and losses at December 31, are as follows:

	1993	*1994*
Unrealized gains	$24,632	$1,300
Unrealized losses	(27,617)	—
Net Unrealized Gains (Losses)	$(2,985)	$1,300

Source: Bay Tact Corp., annual report, December 1994, p. 15.

To be included with available-for-sale securities, a firm need not have plans for sale of an investment. It must simply be an investment that is not held to maturity, which is not possible for equity securities, and which is not part of the company's trading positions. SunTrust Banks' investment in the common stock of Coca-Cola, described earlier in the chapter, is a case in point. The Company has held the investment in Coca-Cola since 1919. It has no apparent plans to sell it, and yet, it is classified as available for sale.

Investments in both debt securities and equity securities that are classified as available-for-sale are reported at fair value, whether that fair value measure is above or below cost. However, unlike trading securities where unrealized gains and losses are included in net income, unrealized gains and losses on available-for-sale securities bypass the income statement and are taken directly to other comprehensive income. Because accumulated other comprehensive income is reported as a component of shareholders' equity, it is accurate to think of unrealized gains and losses on available-for-sale securities also as components of shareholders' equity. And as these unrealized gains and losses are recorded on the books—albeit the balance sheet—and not the tax return, deferred income taxes are also recorded against them. That is, an unrealized gain or loss is reported in other comprehensive income net of any related income tax effect even though those taxes will not be due or saved until the underlying securities are sold and the gain or loss is realized. More is said about deferred income taxes in Chapter Five.

While the recording of unrealized gains and losses on available-for-sale securities in shareholders' equity is the norm, that procedure is appropriate for losses only when they are considered to be temporary in nature. Like debt securities that are held to maturity, when declines in the market value of available-for-sale securities are considered to be other than temporary, those unrealized declines are recorded in income. Kaye Group, Inc. provided a clear statement of this policy and insight into the company's views as to when a decline in the value of an investment is other than temporary:

> If a decline in fair value of an investment is considered to be other than temporary, the investment is reduced to its net realizable value and the reduction is accounted for as a realized investment loss. In evaluating whether a decline is other than temporary, management considers the duration and extent to which the market value has been less than cost, the financial condition and near-term prospects of the issuer, including events that may impact the issuer's operations and impair the earnings potential of the investment, and management's ability and intent to hold an investment for a sufficient period to allow for an anticipated recovery in fair value.[15]

Interest income on debt securities carried as available-for-sale is included in income as it accrues. Any purchase premium or discount is not amortized. Dividend income on equity securities carried as available for sale is included in income when declared by the issuer.

Delta Air Lines, Inc. provided the following footnote disclosure of its investments in available-for-sale securities in its 1997 annual report:

> The Company's investments in Singapore Airlines Limited (Singapore Airlines) and Swissair, Swiss Air Transport Company Ltd. (Swissair), which are accounted for under the cost method, are classified as available-for-sale under SFAS 115, and are recorded at aggregate market value. At June 30, 1997 and 1996, the gross unrealized gain on the Company's investment in Singapore Airlines was $134 million and $190 million, respectively, and the gross unrealized gain on the Company's investment in Swissair was $32 million and $16 million, respectively. The $101 million and $126 million unrealized gains, net of the related deferred tax provision, on these combined investments at June 30, 1997 and 1996, respectively, are reflected in shareholders' equity. Delta's right to vote, to transfer or to acquire additional shares of the stock of Singapore Airlines and Swissair is subject to certain restrictions. Delta's other investments in available-for-sale securities are recorded as short-term investments in the Company's Consolidated Balance Sheets. At June 30, 1997, these investments consisted of government agency debt (23%) and corporate debt securities (77%) with average stated maturities of 4 months and 6 months, respectively.[16]

As disclosed in the footnote, the company's investments in both debt and equity securities were considered to be available-for-sale. The largest part of these investments was in the equity securities of Singapore Airlines and Swissair. The company noted that these investments were accounted for "under the cost method." That is not to say that they were accounted for at cost. In fact, the company did indicate that the investments were recorded at market value. The reference to the cost method was their way of saying that the firm's ownership position was insufficient to provide them with significant influence in the operating and financial affairs of those firms. As a result, the equity method was not being used. The cost method was referred to by them, and is done so by others, though use of the term is confusing, as indicating nonuse of the equity method. The underlying investments were still, however, recorded at fair value.

Delta classified its investments in Singapore Airlines and Swissair as non-current assets. The company did disclose the existence of other available-for-sale securities, in particular government agency debt and corporate debt securities, that were classified as short-term investments. These investments were included with current assets on the balance sheet. Thus, available-for-sale securities can be classified as either short-term or long-term, depending on the intended timing of the investment and its maturity date.

Delta noted that at June 30, 1997, its gross unrealized gains on its Singapore Airlines and Swissair investments were $134 million and $32 million, respectively. It was then disclosed that combined, these gains were $101 million, net of the related deferred tax provision. Before tax, the combined gain was $166 million. Thus, there was a deferred tax provision of $65 million ($166 million − $101 million) recorded on the gross combined gain. That tax, which was calculated at a 39 percent combined federal and state rate ($65 million ÷ by $166 million) was included with deferred tax liabilities on the company's balance sheet. The use of ordinary income tax rates and not capital gains rates on these unrealized capital gains reflects the fact that capital gains treatment is not available to corporate taxpayers. The $101 million gain, net of tax, was included with shareholders' equity.

As noted in the introductory section of this chapter, SunTrust Banks has sizable investments in available-for-sale securities. The company referred to these securities as "investment securities" and provided the following accounting policy description for them:

> Investment securities are classified as available-for-sale and are carried at market value with unrealized gains and losses, net of any tax effect, added to or deducted from realized shareholders' equity to determine total shareholders' equity.[17]

SunTrust separated realized shareholders' equity—common stock, additional paid-in capital, retained earnings, and treasury stock—from the component of shareholders' equity arising from its available-for-sale securities. This treatment emphasized the fact that the gains on the available-for-sale securities were, in fact, unrealized.

SunTrust used the display presented in Exhibit 8.5 to report the amortized cost, fair value, and unrealized gains and losses on its available-for-sale portfolio as of December 31, 1996 and 1997.

For SunTrust, the pretax net unrealized gains, or unrealized gains less unrealized losses, totaled $2,588,907,000 at December 31, 1996, and $3,311,979 at December 31, 1997. From Exhibit 8.5, these net unrealized gains, which are cumulative through the date indicated, can also be calculated as fair value less amortized cost. In its tax note, the company disclosed deferred tax liabilities related

Exhibit 8.5.   Amortized Cost and Fair Value of Available-for-Sale Securities: SunTrust Banks, Inc., Excerpts from Footnotes to Financial Statements, for the Years Ended December 31, 1996 and 1997 (Thousands of Dollars)

Investment securities at December 31:	1996			
	Amortized Cost	Fair Value	Unrealized Gains	Unrealized Losses
U.S. Treasury and other U.S. government agencies and corporations	$3,277,833	$3,290,850	$24,306	$11,289
States and political subdivisions	749,077	773,197	25,183	1,063
Mortgage-backed securities	3,750,505	3,748,583	27,043	28,965
Common stock of the Coca-Cola Company	110	2,540,024	2,539,914	—
Other securities	184,734	198,512	15,108	1,330
Total investment securities	$7,962,259	$10,551,166	$2,631,554	$42,647

Investment securities at December 31:	1997			
	Amortized Cost	Fair Value	Unrealized Gains	Unrealized Losses
U.S. Treasury and other U.S. government agencies and corporations	$2,875,007	$2,896,354	$24,717	$3,370
States and political subdivisions	622,386	642,092	19,955	249
Mortgage-backed securities	4,031,451	4,049,922	34,291	15,820
Trust preferred securities	662,993	674,346	17,397	6,044
Common stock of the Coca-Cola Company	110	3,218,772	3,218,662	—
Other securities	225,372	247,812	22,702	262
Total investment securities	$8,417,319	$11,729,298	$3,337,724	$25,745

Source: SunTrust Banks, Inc., annual report, December 1997, p. 44.

to "Unrealized gains on investment securities" in the amount of $987,129,000 and $1,263,098,000 at December 31, 1996 and 1997, respectively. These deferred taxes were calculated using a combined federal and state income tax rate of 38 percent. The net unrealized gains, net of income taxes, were thus $1,601,778,000 and $2,048,881,000 at December 31, 1996 and 1997, respectively. The company reported these amounts in the shareholders' equity section of its balance sheet as presented in Exhibit 8.6.

Because Statement of Financial Accounting Statement (SFAS) No. 130, "Reporting Comprehensive Income," was not effective for fiscal years ending in 1997, SunTrust did not report its unrealized gains on investment securities as "accumulated other comprehensive income" within shareholders' equity.[18] As seen in Exhibit 8.6, the gains were reported instead as "Unrealized gains on investment securities, net of taxes." Nonetheless, the impact of the gains on shareholders'

Exhibit 8.6. Shareholders' Equity Section of Consolidated Balance Sheets: SunTrust Banks, Inc., for the Year Ended December 31, 1996 and 1997 (Thousands of Dollars, Except Shares)

	1996	1997
Preferred stock, no par value; 50,000,000 shares authorized; none issued	$—	$—
Common stock, $1 par value; 350,000,000 shares authorized	225,608	211,608
Additional paid in capital	310,612	296,751
Retained earnings	2,972,900	2,751,645
Treasury stock and other	(230,918)	(109,503)
Realized shareholders' equity	3,278,202	3,150,501
Unrealized gains on investment securities, net of taxes*	1,601,778	2,048,881
Total shareholders' equity	$4,879,980	$5,199,382

Source: SunTrust Banks, Inc., annual report, December 1997, p. 39.

*The original report made reference to the investment securities footnote, provided here as Exhibit 8.5.

equity was the same. In a cumulative fashion, they increase shareholders' equity. The net increase in the gains between 1996 and 1997, $447,103,000 in this example ($2,048,881,000 − $1,601,778,000) appeared in the company's statement of shareholders' equity. For the bank's fiscal year ending December 1998, any net change in the unrealized gain, whether up or down, will appear within shareholders' equity as a component of "other comprehensive income" for the year.

Included with the disclosures for its available-for-sale portfolio, SunTrust also reported contractual maturities for its available-for-sale debt securities. This is a reporting requirement as was the case for held-to-maturity securities.[19] Because available-for-sale securities are reported at fair value, the effects of changes in interest rates on the fair value of available-for-sale securities will be reported on the balance sheet. Thus, the balance sheet is more exposed to the risk associated with extended maturities for available-for-sale securities than it was for securities that are held to maturity where positions are reported at amortized cost. SunTrust's disclosure of the contractual maturities of its available-for-sale securities is provided in Exhibit 8.7.

When available-for-sale securities are sold, the realized gain or loss, net of income tax, is included in net income. Any unrealized gain or loss that had previously been included in the accumulated other comprehensive income component of shareholders' equity is removed. Thus, if an available-for-sale security is sold for the same amount at which that security had been carried on the balance sheet, the sale will have no net effect on shareholders' equity even though an accompanying gain or loss will be included in net income. Rather, within shareholders'

Exhibit 8.7. Contractual Maturities of Available-For-Sale Securities: SunTrust Banks, Inc., Excerpts from Footnotes to the Financial Statements, for the Year Ended December 31, 1997 (Thousands of Dollars)

The amortized cost and fair value of investments in debt securities at December 31, 1997, by contractual maturities, are shown below. Expected maturities will differ from contractual maturities because borrowers may have the right to call or prepay obligations with or without call or prepayment penalties.

	Amortized Cost	Fair Value
Due in one year or less	$1,269,502	$1,271,523
Due after one year through five years	2,097,194	2,127,316
Due after five years through ten years	152,102	160,265
Due after ten years	641,588	653,688
Mortgage-backed securities	4,031,451	4,049,922
	$8,191,837	$8,262,714

Source: SunTrust Banks, Inc., annual report, December 1997, p. 44.

equity, the gain or loss, net of taxes, will simply be transferred from accumulated other comprehensive income to retained earnings.

Among the disclosure requirements for sales of available-for-sale securities are the proceeds from sale and the gross realized gains and losses. These disclosure requirements were satisfied by SunTrust in the following note:

> Proceeds from the sale of investments in debt securities were $634.9, $736.5 and $1,206.9 million in 1997, 1996 and 1995.Gross realized gains were $.2, $.2 and $1.4 million, and gross realized losses on such sales were $2.2, $3.2 and $8.0 million in 1997, 1996 and 1995.[20]

Delta Air Lines disclosed its realized gains and losses and proceeds from sales of available-for-sale securities as follows:

> During fiscal 1997, 1996 and 1995, the proceeds from sales of available-for-sale securities were $610 million, $626 million and $926 million, respectively, which resulted in a realized gain of less than $1 million for fiscal 1997, and realized losses of $1 million and $4 million for fiscal 1996 and 1995, respectively. The unrealized losses on these investments were less than $1 million and were reflected in shareholders' equity at June 30, 1997 and 1996, respectively.[21]

As noted, the company had already included in shareholders' equity unrealized losses on the investments sold.

Sales of available-for-sale securities provide an opportunity for companies to recognize gains in income that had been accumulated in shareholders' equity while excluding losses. The prospects for such "cherry picking"—choosing winners for

Exhibit 8.8.   Summary of Accounting Guidelines for Investments

Characteristics of Classification	*Accounting Treatment*
Held to Maturity	
Firm has the positive intent and ability to hold the security to maturity	Accounted for at amortized cost. Marked down to a lower fair value if a decline in value below cost is judged to be *other than temporary*. The write-down establishes a new cost basis and is included in the income statement.
Trading	
Bought and held principally for the purpose of selling in the near term. Active and frequent buying and selling	Carried at fair value with increases and decreases in value included in the income statement.
Available for Sale	
The default category for securities that do not meet the classification characteristics for either of the other two categories.	Carried at fair value with increases and decreases in value included in other comprehensive income.

sale to boost income while not selling losers—is, in the views of some, a drawback to current accounting principles for investments.[22]

Summary of Accounting Guidelines for Investments

Exhibit 8.8 summarizes accounting guidelines for investments in debt and equity securities across all three classifications, held-to-maturity, trading, and available-for-sale.

Transfers between Investment Categories

Events arise, conditions change, and companies must reconsider original investment classifications. For example, a company with debt securities reported as available-for-sale may decide that a trading classification is more appropriate.

Companies are generally allowed to transfer securities between investment classifications. However, specific guidelines are offered when transfers involve moving securities from the held-to-maturity category. The concern is that possibly the securities were improperly classified as held to maturity in the first place. As noted earlier, if a firm's intent at the time of purchase is to hold a debt security for an indefinite period of time, or if it anticipates that a sale might be necessary due to changes in interest rates, foreign currency risk, liquidity, or other asset or liability management needs, then the held-to-maturity classification was inappropriate in the first place. A transfer from the held-to-maturity classification for any of these reasons might be considered an error in the original prior-year classification. But transfers from the held-to-maturity classification because of a significant deterioration in the issuer's creditworthiness, a change in the tax law, a major business combination or disposition, or a change in regulatory requirements, are appropriate and are not inconsistent with the original held-to-maturity classification.

American Country Holdings, Inc. justified its transfer of debt securities from the held-to-maturity classification to available-for-sale as follows:

> FASB Statement No. 115 allows companies to transfer securities between categories for events that are isolated, nonrecurring, and unusual that could not have been reasonably anticipated. Accordingly, in connection with the Acquisition, the Company chose to reclassify all held to maturity securities to available for sale. As a result, the Company transferred $23,000,000 of held to maturity fixed maturities to available for sale resulting in a $300,000 increase to unrealized investment gains. The Company no longer holds any fixed maturities as held to maturity.[23]

The Company's decision to transfer the securities due to an acquisition is well within the guidelines for when such a transfer is appropriate.

Because the accounting for unrealized gains and losses in the various investment categories—held to maturity, trading, and available for sale—is different, a question arises as to how to account for transfers of securities between investment classifications. Generally, transfers are accounted for at fair value. However, a key issue that arises is whether or not to include resulting unrealized gains and losses in income. The answer depends on the transfer being made.

Transfers into and from the Trading Classification

Investments in debt and equity securities that are transferred into the trading classification should be recorded at fair value at the time of the transfer. Any unrealized gain or loss should be recognized in income at that time. When securities are transferred from the trading classification, any unrealized gain or loss will already have been recognized in income.

There are no restrictions on which specific securities can be transferred into a trading portfolio. Thus, as with sales of securities, transfers into the trading classification allow firms to recognize in income previously unrecognized, unrealized gains while excluding from income unrealized losses. This can be done by selecting for transfer into the trading classification only those securities that have unrealized gains while not transferring those securities with unrealized losses. Of course, once the transfer into the trading classification is made, a near term sale of the security should be expected.

Transfers into Available-for-Sale Classification from Held-to-Maturity

Debt securities transferred into the available-for-sale classification from the held-to-maturity classification should be adjusted to fair value at the time of transfer. Recall that securities carried as held to maturity are reported at amortized cost. Any resulting unrealized gain or loss calculated at the time of the transfer, net of related income tax effects, should be recorded as a component of accumulated other comprehensive income within shareholders' equity.

The Berkshire Hathaway investment in the redeemable preferred stock of USAir provides an example of such a transfer. Berkshire Hathaway had carried this investment as a held-to-maturity security at its cost, $3.58 billion. There was no premium or discount; however, if there were, it would not be amortized because premium or discount is not amortized on equity issues, whether they are redeemable or not. At the time of the transfer to an available-for-sale classification, the fair value of the investment was $1.79 billion. The resulting unrealized loss, viewed as temporary in nature, was charged against shareholders' equity. Additional losses were recorded as the fair value of the investment continued to decline. Ultimately, the investment was reduced in value to $89.5 million. These losses and the significant deterioration of USAir's financial position were sufficient reasons to warrant a transfer of the investment from the held-to-maturity classification. As disclosed by the company in its 1994 annual report:

> Effective March 31, 1994, investments in securities with fixed maturities were classified as available-for-sale and carried at fair value with the net after-tax unrealized gain or loss reported as a component of shareholders' equity. Accordingly, at March 31, 1994, the carrying value of the USAir preferred Shares was adjusted to reflect its then estimated fair value of $179.0 million. At September 30, 1994, the estimate was adjusted downward to $89.5 million which also represents the estimated fair value as of December 31, 1994.[24]

As noted earlier, Berkshire Hathaway ultimately decided that its losses on USAir were other than temporary and the company charged the unrealized loss on its investment to the income statement. As reported by the company:

> While the aforementioned charge to earnings was recorded in the fourth quarter of 1994; the charge to shareholders' equity, however, had been recorded in earlier reporting periods.[25]

Another example of a transfer of debt securities from the held-to-maturity classification to the available-for-sale category is provided below. In its 1997 annual report, Bancorp Connecticut made the following statement:

> During 1997, the entire securities held-to-maturity portfolio, which totaled $53,454,786, was transferred to the securities available-for-sale portfolio. The transfer was performed by the Corporation to provide the flexibility to actively manage the investment portfolio for optimal return. The transfer resulted in a gross unrealized gain of $162,930.[26]

The transfer was made to allow the company to have more flexibility to actively manage its investments. Presumably, there was no such intent when the original decision to classify the securities as held-to-maturity was made. The resulting unrealized gain would now be reported in shareholders' equity.

Transfers into Held-to-Maturity Classification from Available-for-Sale

A decision to transfer securities to the held-to-maturity classification from available for sale must be made carefully. Once again, the firm must have the intent and ability to hold the securities transferred until maturity. The consideration of such factors is not to be taken lightly.

The debt securities transferred to the held-to-maturity classification are adjusted to fair value at the date of transfer. Any unrealized gain or loss is recorded in accumulated other comprehensive income within shareholders' equity and will remain there after the transfer. However, that unrealized gain or loss will be amortized to interest income, much like a purchase premium or discount, over the remaining term to maturity.

The 1997 annual report of Conseco, Inc. provided a good summary of its accounting policies for transfers of debt securities, referred to by them as fixed maturity investments, between classifications, including transfers to the held-to-maturity classification from available for sale. In the footnote to the company's annual report, which is reproduced below, available-for-sale securities are referred to as "actively managed" investments:

> When there are changes in conditions that cause us to transfer a fixed maturity investment to a different category (i.e., actively managed, trading or held to maturity), we transfer it at its fair value on that date. We account for the security's unrealized gain or loss (such amounts were immaterial in 1997) as follows: For a transfer to the trading category—we recognize the unrealized gain or loss immediately in earnings. For a transfer from the trading category—we do not reverse the unrealized gain or loss already recognized in earnings. For a transfer to actively managed from held to maturity—we recognize the unrealized gain or loss immediately in shareholders' equity. For a transfer to held to maturity from actively managed—we continue to report the unrealized gain or loss at the date of transfer in shareholders' equity, but we amortize the gain or loss over the remaining life of the security as an adjustment of yield.[27]

Investments in Nonmarketable Equity Securities

The accounting guidelines provided for equity securities are only relevant for equity securities that have a readily determinable market value. More specifically, there are posted prices or bid-and-asked quotations available on a securities exchange or the over-the-counter market. Such prices or quotes are necessary in order to value equity securities carried in a trading or available-for-sale classification at fair value. Such prices are not needed for debt securities given the relative ease with which fair value can be estimated using present value calculations when prices or quotes are not available.

Nonmarketable equity securities should be accounted for at cost. There are no adjustments to estimates of fair value, whether up or down. However, if evidence is obtained that indicates that fair value of a nonmarketable equity security has fallen below cost and that decline is other than temporary, then the security should be written down. An accompanying loss should be recorded in income. The new valuation should be treated as the investment's cost basis. Moreover, the security should not be written up even if evidence indicates that fair value has recovered. Thus, the accounting for nonmarketable equity securities is similar to that of debt securities carried in the held-to-maturity classification.

In its 1997 annual report, Green Street Financial Corporation characterized its accounting for nonmarketable investments as follows:

> The Association accounts for its investments in accordance with Statement of Financial Accounting Standards ("SFAS") No. 115 Accounting for Certain Investments in Debt and Equity Securities. Accordingly, equity securities, which are nonmarketable, do not require classification under SFAS No. 115 and continue to be carried at cost.[28]

In its 1997 report, MBLA Financial Corporation provided an example of a nonmarketable equity security—an investment in the Federal Home Loan Bank:

> Equity securities that are nonmarketable are carried at cost. Nonmarketable equity securities held by the Association consist of their patronage equity in the Financial Information Trust (a computer service bureau) and stock in the Federal Home Loan Bank. The Association, as a member of the Federal Home Loan Bank system, is required to maintain an investment in capital stock of the Federal Home Loan Bank in an amount based on its outstanding loans and advances.[29]

Financial Quality and Investments in Debt and Equity Securities

The manner in which companies account for investments in debt securities and marketable and nonmarketable equity securities have very direct implications for financial quality—earnings quality and position quality.

Held-to-Maturity Securities and Financial Quality

The income derived from held-to-maturity securities is interest income and is, for the most part, all cash. Thus, earnings quality is neither enhanced nor impaired on a persistence or cash basis. However, to the extent that interest income earned on such investments entails the amortization of a significant discount, as with a zero-coupon bond, then earnings quality is impaired on the cash dimension. Here cash will not be received for the investment income until the bond matures.

When a held-to-maturity security is sold or transferred to a trading portfolio, any resulting gain or loss would impact earnings quality. Securities sold would enhance earnings quality on the cash dimension, but their gains would impair earnings quality on the persistence dimension, and their losses would enhance it. Transfers to a different classification do not provide cash flow. As a result, reported gains would impair earnings quality on both the cash and persistence dimensions. Losses would enhance earnings quality.

Until it is deemed to be an other-than-temporary decline, the fair value of a held-to-maturity security is not taken into account. As a result, these securities may be carried at amounts greater or less than fair value. If fair value exceeds amortized cost, position quality is enhanced. If amortized cost exceeds fair value, position quality is impaired.

Trading Securities and Financial Quality

To the extent that trading gains reported on the income statement are unrealized, earnings quality is impaired on a cash dimension. Unrealized losses would enhance earnings quality on a cash dimension. However, the very nature of a trading portfolio would suggest that unrealized gains and losses will be realized in the very near term. Thus, such trading gains and losses have only minor implications for cash quality.

On the surface, it would appear that because trading portfolios are typically carried by financial institutions, where trading desks are an important component of company operations, net trading gains would take on a more recurring quality. As such, the results of trading debt and equity securities would have no significant implications for earnings quality on a persistence dimension. However, trading in debt and equity securities does not provide a smooth stream of earnings. For example, in the case of SunTrust, the company disclosed trading account profits and commissions in 1995 of $10.6 million, in 1996 of $13.3 million, and in 1997 of $18 million. Results such as these would appear to warrant traditional considerations of earnings quality on a persistence dimension, with earnings quality being impaired when out-sized gains are reported and enhanced with the reporting of out-sized losses.

Position quality is a nonissue for trading securities. Because they are carried at fair value, position quality is neither enhanced nor impaired.

Available-for-Sale Securities and Financial Quality

While they are held, the only income derived from available-for-sale debt and equity securities is interest income and dividend income. This income is primarily cash or near-term cash and has a recurring quality. Thus, it has no significant impact on earnings quality on the cash or persistence dimensions. Gains and losses on the sale of available-for-sale securities enhance earnings quality on the cash dimension. Gains from sales impair earnings quality on the persistence dimension while losses enhance quality. Transfers to a trading portfolio result in noncash gains and losses being reported on the income statement. Such gains impair earnings quality on the cash and persistence dimension while losses due to transfers enhance earnings quality on both dimensions.

Investments in debt and equity securities classified as available-for-sale are reported at fair value. As a result, position quality is not affected.

Future Directions for Investments Accounting

Accounting for investments in debt and equity securities, like accounting for all financial assets and liabilities, is moving inexorably toward fair value. Since the release of SFAS No. 115, we have seen significant strides in this regard with investments classified as trading assets or available for sale.

New rules requiring disclosure of fair value for all financial assets and liabilities became effective as early as years ending in 1993. SFAS No. 107, "Disclosures about Fair Value of Financial Instruments," added significant disclosure requirements and was effective for fiscal years ending after December 15, 1992.[30] That standard required firms to disclose the fair value of all financial instruments, both assets and liabilities, including those on and off the balance sheet, for which it was practicable to estimate fair value. Investments in debt and equity securities were clearly included within these disclosure requirements.

However, *disclosure* of fair value for investments is not the same thing as *accounting* for investments at fair value. Disclosure does not necessarily mean that fair value has been taken into account in the company's financial statements. Thus, we saw firms such as BankAmerica Corporation disclosing the fair value of held-to-maturity securities in Exhibit 8.1 and Exhibit 8.3. Even though these securities were accounted for at amortized cost, the company fulfilled the reporting requirements of SFAS No. 107 with disclosure of the fair value of these securities.

Research evidence on the usefulness of fair value accounting, at least for investments in debt and equity securities, is encouraging, though not totally consistent. Barth examined whether fair value disclosures of investments and fair value securities gains and losses—unrealized and unrecognized gains and losses—have incremental power over traditional historical cost measures in explaining the market value of equity and annual stock returns, respectively.[31] Earlier studies had found somewhat mixed results on the usefulness of fair value accounting. Barth attributed that lack of significant findings to problems of measurement error in estimating fair values and noise introduced in studying firms across several industries. To alleviate these potential confounding factors, the author used actual disclosed fair value measures for firms in a single industry, commercial banks. She found that the fair value of investment securities provides incremental explanatory power in explaining variations in the market value of equity across firms. The results for unrealized securities gains and losses were less convincing. The gains did not provide more explanatory power than realized gains and losses and earnings before securities gains and losses. The author viewed this lack of significance as a potential problem in measuring unrealized gains and losses.

Nelson extended Barth's work with commercial banks.[32] She looked at the usefulness of all fair value disclosures for financial instruments, including investments. Among other disclosures of fair value available for bank assets and liabilities was information on loans, deposits, long-term debt, and net off-balance-sheet financial instruments. Her objective was to determine whether accounting measures using fair values of financial instruments better explained variations in market value of equity than traditional historical cost–based measures. She found no incremental explanatory power for financial instruments beyond investments. Then, once she controlled for two indicators of future profitability captured by traditional historical cost measures, return on equity and growth in book value of equity, even the incremental power of the fair value of investments, dissipated.

Thus, research results on the usefulness of fair value accounting for financial instruments, including investments, are not unequivocal. Theoretically, the use of fair value to account for investments appears to have merit. A very limited number of studies with mixed results looking at a single industry are probably not sufficient to guide accounting policy. More research appears to be needed.

Meanwhile, the Financial Accounting Standards Board (FASB) is moving ahead with plans to require companies to *account for* all financial assets and liabilities, including investments in debt and equity securities, at fair value. This would require the inclusion in earnings of changes in the fair value of these items. The proposal is consistent with the concerted move the FASB is making toward fair value accounting. For example, the recently issued accounting pronouncement on derivatives and hedge accounting, SFAS No. 133, "Accounting for Derivative Instruments and Hedging Activities," requires fair value accounting and the inclusion in income of the resulting gains and losses. However, only firms with financial derivatives or that are engaged in hedging activities have been affected. The new proposal to account for all financial assets and liabilities has quite sweeping implications for all companies. The proposal will likely be met with much opposition from firms loath to introduce the increased volatility into earnings that would likely accompany expansion in fair value accounting. Only time will tell where this proposal leads.

ACCOUNTING FOR INVESTMENTS UNDER THE EQUITY METHOD

The equity method is applied when an equity ownership position in voting stock is sufficient to provide the investor with significant influence over the operating and financial policies of the investee. To apply the equity method, the underlying equity securities need not have a readily determinable market value—the method is appropriate for both publicly traded and privately held stock.

Measuring Significant Influence

Significant influence on the part of an investor can be indicated in many ways. These might include, for example, representation on the board of directors, participation in policy-making processes, material intercompany transactions, interchange of managerial personnel, and technological dependency. Also important is the extent of ownership on the part of the investor relative to the concentration of other shareholders. Certainly judgment is needed in deciding whether an investor has significant influence. In order to achieve a reasonable level of uniformity in the application of this rule, the relevant standard, Accounting Principles Board Opinion No. 18, "The Equity Method of Accounting for Investments in Common Stock," indicated that, "An investment (direct or indirect) of 20 percent or more of the voting stock of an investee should lead to a presumption that in the absence of evidence to the contrary an investor has the ability to exercise significant influence over an investee."[33] And because ownership interests of over 50 percent are sufficient to warrant consolidation, the equity method is appropriate for ownership interests of between 20 percent and 50 percent, inclusive.

There remains room for judgment in deciding whether to apply the equity method. While many consider the 20 percent to 50 percent rule as being somewhat inflexible, it is not so. Companies with ownership interests of below 20 percent that consider their positions sufficient to exert significant influence will use the equity method. Consider, for example, the case of Burlington Northern, Inc. In its 1995 annual report, the Company provided the following description of its method of accounting for its investment in Santa Fe Pacific Corporation:

> Burlington Northern, Inc. has a 17 percent ownership interest in Santa Fe Pacific Corp. The Company accounts for its investment in Santa Fe Pacific Corp. under the equity method.[34]

Another example is that of Promus Hotel Corporation. As the company indicated in its 1997 annual report:

> Investments in partnerships and ventures are accounted for using the equity method of accounting when the Company has a general partnership interest or its limited partnership interest exceeds 5% and the Company does not exercise control over the venture.

Other companies with ownership positions of greater than 20 percent will not use the equity method if they consider their position to be insufficient to exert significant influence. In its 1996 annual report, Advanta Corporation provided the following description of its accounting policy for certain investment positions of greater than 20 percent:

> For investments that are not publicly traded, estimates of fair value have been made by management that consider several factors including the investees' financial results, conditions and prospects, and the values of comparable public companies. Because of the nature of these investments, the equity method of accounting is not used in situations where the Company has a greater than 20 percent ownership interest.[35]

It was not clear from the Company's report what the nature of these investments was that rendered the company's position as lacking in significant influence. The lack of public trading is not such a reason.

Examples provided by the FASB of cases in which an investment of 20 percent or more might not enable an investor to exert significant influence include:

- The investee opposes the investor's acquisition of its stock (e.g., the investee files a legal suit against the investor).
- The investor and investee sign an agreement under which the investor surrenders significant shareholder rights (e.g., when the investee is resisting a takeover attempt by the investor).
- The investor's ownership share does not result in "significant influence" because majority ownership of the investee is concentrated among a small group of shareholders who operate the investee without regard to the views of the investor.
- The investor needs or wants more financial information than is publicly issued by the investee, tries to obtain it from the investee, and fails.
- The investor tries and fails to obtain representation on the investee's board of directors.[36]

Notwithstanding the identified exceptions to application of the 20 percent rule in applying the equity method, the use of an ownership position between 20 percent and 50 percent remains the primary criterion in deciding whether an investor has significant influence. For the majority of companies, when an ownership position reaches 20 percent, the equity method is applied. When an ownership position falls below 20 percent, the equity method is not applied. Alternatives are accounting for the investment as available for sale if it has a readily determinable market value, or at cost if it does not.

Evidence of the widespread use of the 20 percent ownership percentage criterion was provided in our own earlier research.[37] We screened the stock data records for over 8,000 firms to determine stock ownership. Positions were recorded when ownership fell between 5 percent and 50 percent, inclusive. The yield was a distribution of 1,255 ownership percentage data points. The objective was to determine whether investment positions occur with unusual frequency in the vicinity of 20 percent. A "best-fit" regression equation was superimposed on the ownership percentage distribution, where the number of firms observed was regressed upon the ownership percentage. The pattern of ownership and the fitted line are graphed in Exhibit 8.9.

Exhibit 8.9 indicates that the number of firms with ownership percentage positions in other companies declines as the size of the ownership percentage increases. This is to be expected given the increasing level of resources needed to command greater ownership levels. Note, however, that a there is a much higher than expected concentration of firms from just below 20 percent to just above it. The concentration of firms in the 19 to 24 percent range was significantly greater than chance. This finding was attributed to the existence of the 20 percent rule. That rule pushed companies to move their ownership positions to just below 20

Exhibit 8.9. Ownership Percentage Distribution: 1982 Data

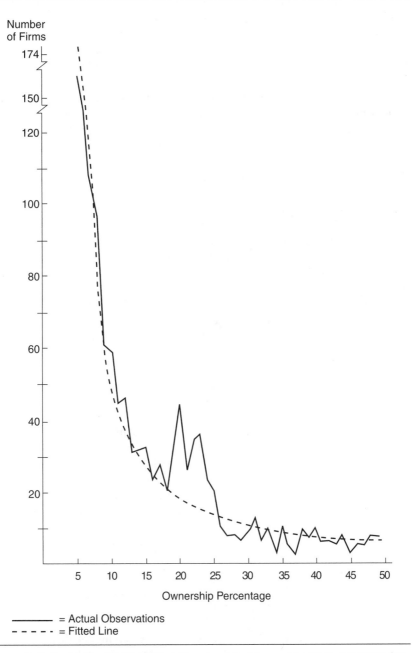

Source: E. E. Comiskey and C. W. Mulford, "Investment Decisions and the Equity Accounting Standard," *The Accounting Review* (July 1986), p. 521. Reprinted with permission.

percent when they wanted the greatest ownership percentage possible without having to apply the equity method. The rule also moved ownership positions to just above 20 percent when they wanted to minimize an ownership level while still applying the equity method.

Adding to our argument, we also looked at a similar distribution using data from 1969, a year prior to the existence of the 20 percent rule. For this data, no significant concentration of ownership positions was noted around 20 percent.

The 20 percent ownership rule for application of the equity method has also been incorporated into international accounting standards.[38] Among the countries adopting a 20 percent rule are Singapore and Malaysia. We surveyed 200 annual reports of Singaporean and Malaysian firms and found a concentration of ownership interests around 20 percent for these companies. This is the same result as in the case of the study of U.S. companies.[39]

Applying the Equity Method

Under the equity method, the investment is recorded initially at cost. Each accounting period, the investment is increased by the investor's proportionate share of the earnings of the investee or decreased by the investor's proportionate share of losses. The investor's share of earnings or losses are reported as equity method income or loss on the investor's income statement. Dividends declared by the investee are not reported as income to the investor but as a reduction in the investment account. In this way, dividends are accounted for as a return of investment.

Basic Example: SUPERVALU, INC.

As an example, SUPERVALU, Inc. uses the equity method to account for its 46 percent interest in ShopKo Stores, Inc. The investment appeared on the company's balance sheet as of its fiscal year end in February 1996 and 1997 at $193,975,000 and $209,788,000, respectively. SUPERVALU described its investment in ShopKo as follows: "The company's ownership in ShopKo, a mass merchandise discount retailer, is 46 percent and is accounted for under the equity method."[40] SUPERVALU provided summarized information on the financial results for ShopKo. Those results are reproduced in Exhibit 8.10.

The SUPERVALU income statement and cash flow statement are provided in Exhibits 8.11 and 8.12, respectively.

Referring to Exhibit 8.10, it is noted that ShopKo generated net earnings of $44,946,000 during 1997. With a 46 percent ownership interest, SUPERVALU's share of those earnings is approximately $20,675,000. On its income statement, presented in Exhibit 8.11, SUPERVALU reported in 1997 "Equity in earnings of ShopKo" in the amount of $20,675,000. The equity in earnings of Shopko reported for 1995 and 1996 can be calculated in a similar manner, by multiplying SUPERVALU's 46 percent share times ShopKo's net earnings. However, there may be

Exhibit 8.10. Summarized Financial Results of Equity-Accounted Investment ShopKo Stores, Inc.: SUPERVALU, Inc., Years Ending February 25, 1995, February 24, 1996, and February 22, 1997 (Thousands of Dollars)

	1995	1996	1997
Sales	$1,852,929	$1,968,016	$2,333,407
Gross profit	488,016	501,283	549,666
Net earnings	37,790	38,439	44,946
		1996	1997
Current assets		$476,191	$565,172
Noncurrent assets		641,769	668,720
Current liabilities		260,795	333,315
Noncurrent liabilities		435,534	439,713

Source: SUPERVALU, Inc. Form 10-K annual report to the Securities and Exchange Commission (February 1997), p. 30.

slight differences due to rounding in the ownership percentage. Thus, the equity income reported is SUPERVALU's share of ShopKo's net income.

Referring to Exhibit 8.12, it is noted that ShopKo subtracted "Equity in earnings of ShopKo" from net earnings in calculating cash flow from operating activities for each year, 1995 through 1997. Then in each year, the company added "Dividends received from ShopKo" to net earnings in computing cash flow from operating activities. Recall that the investor's share of an investee's earnings is included in net income of the investor. Those earnings are cash-backed only to the extent that they are collected in the form of dividends. By subtracting equity in earnings but adding dividends received, SUPERVALU is including in operating cash flow only the component of equity method income that is backed by cash flow. Often, rather than presenting the equity in earnings as a subtraction and dividends received as an addition on a cash flow statement, companies will report "Undistributed equity in earnings" or "Equity in earnings in excess of dividends" as a net subtraction on the cash flow statement. That net subtraction represents the excess of equity method income over dividends received. If dividends received exceeded equity method income, then a net addition on the cash flow statement would have a title such as "Dividends received in excess of equity in earnings."

At year-end 1996, SUPERVALU carried its investment in ShopKo at $193,975,000. Adding the company's share of ShopKo's 1997 net income resulted in an increase in the investment of $20,675,000 during 1997. Subtracting from the investment balance dividends received by SUPERVALU from ShopKo during 1997 would reduce the investment by $4,862,000. The end result is an investment balance of $209,788,000, the amount at which SUPERVALU carried the investment at year-end 1997.

Exhibit 8.11. Equity Method in the Income Statement: SUPERVALU, Inc., Consolidated Statements of Earnings, Years Ending February 25, 1995, February 24, 1996, and February 22, 1997 (Thousands of Dollars)

	1995	1996	1997
Net sales	$16,563,772	$16,486,321	$16,551,902
Costs and expenses:			
Cost of sales	15,040,117	14,906,602	14,885,249
Selling and administrative expenses	1,169,843	1,212,967	1,286,121
Restructuring and other charges	244,000	—	—
Interest			
Interest expense	135,383	140,150	136,831
Interest income	24,112	23,472	16,136
Interest expense—net	111,271	116,678	120,695
Total costs and expenses	16,565,231	16,236,247	16,292,065
Earnings (loss) before equity in earnings of ShopKo and income taxes	(1,459)	250,074	259,837
Equity in earnings of ShopKo	17,384	17,618	20,675
Earnings before income taxes	15,925	267,692	280,512
Provision (benefit) for income taxes:			
Current	113,505	36,692	77,591
Deferred	(140,914)	64,567	27,877
Income tax expense (benefit)	(27,409)	101,259	105,468
Net earnings	$43,334	$166,433	$175,044

Source: SUPERVALU, Inc., Form 10-K annual report to the Securities and Exchange Commission (February 1997), p. 24.

The SUPERVALU example is useful in describing how the equity method works. The example also demonstrates some of the important disclosure requirements for equity-method accounting. In particular, required disclosures include the name of each investee and the percentage of common stock owned, the accounting policy applied to the investment, and if material, summarized information about assets, liabilities, and results of operations of the investee. Also required, though not provided here is the market value, if available, of the investor's share of the underlying stock of the investee.

Investee Losses Exceed Carrying Amount: Athanor, Inc.

Whereas net income of the equity-accounted investee increases the investment balance, losses reduce it. Occasionally, investee losses can cause the investor's investment balance to be reduced to zero, and potentially, below zero. If this

Exhibit 8.12.   Equity Method in the Cash Flow Statement: SUPERVALU, Inc., Consolidated Statements of Cash Flows, Operating Activities Section, Years Ending February 25, 1995, February 24, 1996, and February 22, 1997 (Thousands of Dollars)

	1995	1996	1997
Cash Flows from Operating Activities			
Net earnings	$43,334	$166,433	$175,044
Adjustments to reconcile net earnings to net cash provided by operating activities:			
Equity in earnings of ShopKo	(17,384)	(17,618)	(20,675)
Dividends received from ShopKo	6,482	6,482	4,862
Depreciation and amortization	198,718	219,084	232,071
Provision for losses on receivables	1,627	2,269	8,851
Restructuring and other charges	244,000	—	—
Gain on sale of property, plant, and equipment	(3,689)	(12,215)	(3,530)
Deferred income taxes	(140,914)	64,567	27,877
Treasury shares contributed to employee incentive plan	525	107	430
Changes in assets and liabilities, excluding effect from acquisitions:			
Receivables	(14,862)	17,865	(30,509)
Inventories	52,296	79,880	(58,658)
Other current assets	4,638	(2,671)	12,408
Direct financing leases	9,517	8,302	9,111
Accounts payable	18,444	(59,218)	(53,872)
Other liabilities	(49,804)	(51,569)	25,379
Net Cash Provided by Operating Activities	$352,928	$421,698	$328,789

Source: SUPERVALU, Inc., Form 10-K annual report to the Securities and Exchange Commission (February 1997), p. 28.

happens, the investor should suspend application of the equity method when the investment balance reaches zero. This treatment assumes the investor has limited liability with respect to its investment—that its losses are limited to amounts invested. Once the investee has returned to profitable operations and has earned sufficient amounts to cover the investor's losses, the equity method should be applied once again.

In some cases, the investor's share of the investee's losses is not limited. This may be due to guarantees or contractual obligations to cover investee losses. In such cases, the investor should continue recording its share of the investee's losses even though it would result in carrying the investment at a negative amount. That negative investment amount would be reported as a liability on the investor's balance sheet.

Consider the case of Athanor Group, Inc. In the Company's 1997 annual report, the following description of its equity-accounted investment in Core Software Technology was provided:

> The Company accounts for its investment in Core Software Technology (Core) on the equity method that requires the Company to record its share of Core's earnings or losses. The investment in Core has been reduced to zero due to Core's accumulated losses. During 1996 and 1995, the Company advanced $149,739 and $123,500, respectively, to Core which were subsequently written off.[41]

As a result of a series of losses, Athanor reduced its investment in Core to zero. Even new investments in Core made in 1995 and 1996 were written off as Core had sufficient losses to cover even those amounts.

The Equity Method and Premiums and Discounts from Book Value

In the SUPERVALU example, the Company's investment was equal to its share of ShopKo's shareholders' equity. This is the same as carrying its investment at book value. For example, it can be seen in Exhibit 8.10, that as of February 22, 1997, ShopKo reported current assets of $565,172,000, noncurrent assets of $668,720,000, current liabilities of $333,315,000, and noncurrent liabilities of $439,713,000. ShopKo's shareholders' equity can be calculated by adding together current and noncurrent assets and subtracting from the subtotal current and noncurrent liabilities. The resulting shareholders' equity amount is $460,864,000. Multiplying that shareholders' equity figure by SUPERVALU's 46 percent share, the underlying book value of SUPERVALU's investment can be computed. The resulting amount is $211,997,000, which, after a small difference, likely located in the ownership percentage, is approximately equal to SUPERVALU's reported investment balance of $209,788,000 at that date.

It is more typical for an investment to be made at an amount that is not equal to the investor's share of the investee's shareholders' equity. Usually, the investor pays an amount that is greater than book value, occasionally less.

When an investor pays an amount that is greater than book value, the excess is attributed to two components: a revaluation of identifiable net assets of the investee and goodwill. That excess, or premium, is carried in the investment balance—it is not reported separately on the balance sheet. Moreover, the excess is amortized against equity-method income over the estimated useful lives of the revalued identifiable net assets and goodwill. A portion of the excess is expensed each period, reducing equity-method income. Often, it is not practical to obtain information to revalue identifiable net assets of the investee. In such cases, the entire excess paid is attributed to goodwill. Identifying the excess as goodwill also permits an extended amortization period because the maximum amortization period allowed for goodwill is 40 years.

An example of accounting for an equity-method purchase premium is provided by Coca-Cola's investment in Coca-Cola Amatil Limited. The Company described its investment in Amatil as follows:

> We own approximately 33 percent of Coca-Cola Amatil, an Australian-based bottler of our products that operates in 18 countries. Accordingly, we account for our investment in Coca-Cola Amatil by the equity method. The excess of our investment over our equity in the underlying net assets of Coca-Cola Amatil is being amortized on a straight-line basis over 40 years. The balance of this excess, net of amortization, was approximately $64 million at December 31, 1997.[42]

According to this note, Coca-Cola owns 33 percent of Coca-Cola Amatil and uses the equity method to account for its investment. As of December 31, 1997, there was an unamortized excess of cost over the Company's share of net assets of Amatil in the amount of $64 million. That excess was being amortized using the straight-line method over a 40-year period. The Company also provided a summary of financial information for Coca-Cola Amatil. That summary is reproduced in Exhibit 8.13.

In referring to the balance sheet information provided in Exhibit 8.13, at December 31, 1997, Coca-Cola Amatil had shareholders' equity measured at book value in the amount of $3,455,000,000. Coca-Cola's 33 percent share of that book value was $1,140,150,000. Adding the $64 million unamortized excess to Coca-Cola's share of book value, brings it up to $1,204,150,000—Coca-Cola's disclosed investment balance, rounded to the nearest $1 million. Thus, any unamortized excess of the price paid for an investment over the underlying book value of that investment is carried in the investment balance on the balance sheet.

In referring to the income statement information provided in Exhibit 8.13, for the year ended December 31, 1997, Coca-Cola Amatil reported net income of $89 million. Coca-Cola's 33 percent share of that income was $29,370,000. In the exhibit, Coca-Cola disclosed equity-method income from Coca-Cola Amatil of $27 million. The difference, $2,370,000, can be attributed to amortization of the excess of the purchase price over Coca-Cola Amatil's book value. It is the $27 million amount that appears on Coca-Cola's income statement as equity-method income.

In some instances, the investor pays an amount that is less than its share of the investee's underlying book value. That discount is carried in the investment balance and is amortized to equity-method income. In contrast to a purchase excess or premium, which reduces equity-method income, amortization of a discount increases it. The 1996 annual report of Worthington Industries provides an example:

> At May 31, 1996, the Company's share of the underlying net assets of Rouge exceeded the carrying amount included in investment in unconsolidated affiliates of $101,134,000 by $9,106,000. The excess is being amortized into income by increasing equity in net income of unconsolidated affiliates using the straight-line method over the remaining 12 years.[43]

Exhibit 8.13. Summarized Financial Information for Equity-Method Investment in Coca-Cola Amatil Limited: The Coca-Cola Co., Excerpts from Footnotes to the Financial Statements, for the Year Ended December 31, 1995, 1996, and 1997 (Millions of Dollars)

Balance Sheet Data		1996	1997
Current assets		$1,847	$1,470
Noncurrent assets		2,913	4,590
Total assets		$4,760	$6,060
Current liabilities		$1,247	$1,053
Noncurrent liabilities		1,445	1,552
Total liabilities		$2,692	$2,605
Share-owners' equity		$2,068	$3,455
Company equity investment		$881	$1,204
Income Statement Data	1995	1996	1997
Net operating revenues	$2,193	$2,905	$3,290
Cost of goods sold	1,311	1,737	1,856
Gross profit	$882	$1,168	$1,434
Operating income	$214	$215	$276
Cash operating profit*	$329	$384	$505
Net income	$75	$80	$89
Company equity income	$28	$27	$27

*Cash operating profit is defined as operating income plus depreciation expense, amortization expense, and other noncash operating expenses.

Source: The Coca-Cola Co., annual report, December 1997, p. 50.

The Equity Method and the Market Value of Underlying Shares

Coca-Cola disclosed market value information for its investment in Coca-Cola Amatil:

> If valued at the December 31, 1997, quoted closing price of publicly traded Coca-Cola Amatil shares, the calculated value of our investment in Coca-Cola Amatil would have exceeded its carrying value by approximately $918 million.[44]

Thus, even though there remained an unamortized excess of purchase price over book value, as was the case in Coca-Cola's investment in Coca-Cola Amatil, the market value of those shares exceeded the investment carrying value under the equity method by $918 million. Routine application of the equity method does

not take the market value of the underlying shares into account, whether that market value increases above the carrying value of the investment or falls below it.

However, if the market value of the underlying shares of a security accounted for using the equity method fell below carrying value and the decline in value were considered to be an other-than-temporary decline, then the investment should be written down to market value. The write-down should be taken as a loss on the income statement. Cone Mills Corporation provides an example. The company provided the following footnote in its 1997 annual report:

> In 1993, Cone Mills purchased 20% of Compania Industrial de Parras S.A. (CIPSA), the largest denim manufacturer in Mexico. The initial investment was $24 million and an additional $12.4 million was invested to maintain the 20% ownership when CIPSA issued additional shares. A large portion of the investment in CIPSA was treated as goodwill. CIPSA incurred substantial losses in 1995 and its share value declined sharply. This reversal of fortunes was largely due to the effect of the devaluation of the peso (the peso fell quickly from 3.45 to 6.38 and continued to decline) coupled with the substantial dollar-denominated debt owed by CIPSA. As a result of this deterioration in CIPSA's prospects, Cone Mills accelerated its write-off of acquisition goodwill and also took a additional charge of $7.3 million in 1995 to reduce the carrying value of the investment to expected net realizable value. At the end of 1995, Cone Mills reduced its stake in CIPSA to 18% and reported that it would account for the investment by the cost method in future periods.[45]

Cone Mills wrote its equity-accounted investment down to take into account the investment's decline in market value. Moreover, with the write-down, the company discontinued application of the equity method.

Share Issues by Equity-Accounted Investees

Under the equity method, the investor's share of investee's shareholders' equity is reflected in the investment balance. The investment balance is adjusted upward for increases in that equity due to investee earnings and adjusted downward for decreases due to investee losses or dividends. When an investee increases shareholders' equity because of an offering of stock, the investor must also adjust the investment balance to reflect its share of the increase in the investee's underlying equity. The increase in the investment balance accompanying the issue of shares by the investee is accompanied by a gain reported on the investor's income statement.

For example, assume an investor owns 300 of an investee's 1,000 outstanding shares. The underlying book value of the 1,000 shares is $1,000 and the investor carries its equity-accounted 30 percent ownership investment at $300. The investee issues 200 additional shares to the public at $3 per share. The investor did not buy additional shares. The investee's shareholders' equity is increased by $600 to $1,600. The number of shares outstanding is increased by 200 shares to 1,200 shares. The investor now has 300 out of 1,200 shares, or 25 percent. A 25 percent ownership of $1,600 in shareholders' equity indicates an ownership of underlying equity in the amount of $400 (25 percent $\times$ $1,600). The investor would record a gain on the issue of stock by the investee in the amount of $100, the increase in the underlying equity of its investment.

In recent years, the Coca-Cola Co. has reported gains from such transactions. One example involves the equity-accounted investment examined earlier, Coca-Cola Amatil. Coca-Cola entered 1996 with a 39 percent ownership interest in Coca-Cola Amatil and used the equity method to account for it. That year, the company's ownership interest in Coca-Cola Amatil was reduced when Coca-Cola Amatil issued shares. Coca-Cola provided the following description of the transaction:

> Also in the third quarter of 1996, Coca-Cola Amatil issued approximately 46 million shares in exchange for approximately $522 million. The issuance reduced our Company's ownership percentage in Coca-Cola Amatil from approximately 39 percent to approximately 36 percent. This transaction resulted in a noncash pretax gain of $130 million for our Company. We have provided deferred taxes of approximately $47 million on this gain.[46]

As a result of the issue of stock by Coca-Cola Amatil, Coke's percentage ownership of its investment was reduced. While Coke did not sell any of its shares, a reduction in its ownership interest is tantamount to such an act. Because the market value of Coca-Cola Amatil's shares had increased since Coca-Cola purchased its investment, Coke had gained. An increase in the market value of the shares and a reduction in its ownership interest provide support for Coke's recognition of a gain on the share issue by its equity-accounted investment. Note that if the share price of Coca-Cola Amatil had not increased since Coca-Cola purchased its shares, no gain would have been recorded. Moreover, if the share price had fallen in the interim, it would have resulted in a loss.

Coca-Cola described the gain as a noncash gain. Certainly, Coca-Cola Amatil received cash for the shares issued. But, as an investor in Coca-Cola Amatil, Coke did not receive this cash.

Changing from and to the Equity Method

If an investor's level of interest or ownership falls below that necessary for continued use of the equity method, a change must be made to account for the investment as available for sale. If the shares have a readily determinable market value, they will be carried at market value; if not, then they are carried at cost. The carrying value of the investment at the time of the change becomes the investment's cost basis. The investor's share of earnings and losses recognized in previous periods are not adjusted. Henceforth, dividends received from the investment are accounted for as dividend income. However, any dividends received in excess of the investor's share of the investee's earnings should be accounted for as a reduction in the investment's carrying value.

An example of a change away from the equity method is provided in the 1997 report of Worthington Industries:

> In the first quarter of 1997, the Company irrevocably converted Class B shares (2.5 votes per share) of Rouge Steel Company common stock for Class A shares (1 vote per share) of Rouge Steel Company common stock which reduced its voting interest in Rouge to below 20%. In addition, the Company's seats on the Board of Directors of Rouge, and its future right to those seats, were relinquished. As a result of these two steps, the Company has no ability to exercise significant influence over Rouge. Therefore, the Company's investment in Rouge no longer qualifies for the equity method of accounting and was changed to the cost method. As a result, after May 31, 1996, the Company's equity share of Rouge earnings is no longer included in reported earnings or earnings per share. In addition, the investment in Rouge common stock was transferred from investment in unconsolidated affiliates and is shown separately in 1997. This investment is adjusted to market value as an "available-for-sale" security with a net of tax adjustment to shareholder's equity.[47]

A change to the equity method provides more of an accounting challenge. Here a retroactive adjustment is necessary to adjust the carrying value of the investment to include the investor's share of cumulative net earnings of the investment less dividends since the date of acquisition. The adjustment amount is also recorded in retained earnings. Any unrealized holding gain or loss recorded in accumulated other comprehensive income within shareholders' equity is also removed. Prior-year financial statements are restated to the new presentation format.

Financial Quality and the Equity Method

Earnings quality on the cash dimension depends on the extent to which an investor's share of investee earnings are supported by the receipt of dividends. In most cases, assuming a less than 100 percent payout of earnings by the investee, dividends are less than equity income. In such instances, earnings quality is diminished on the cash dimension. When dividends received by the investor exceed equity method income, earnings quality is enhanced on the cash dimension.

The impact of equity method income on earnings quality on the persistence dimension is dependent on the source of the investee's earnings. To the extent those earnings are generated from recurring sources, earnings quality on the persistence dimension is not affected. When those underlying earnings are derived from nonrecurring sources, earnings quality is diminished on the persistence dimension.

Gains on sales of equity-accounted investments, and gains from issues of stock by equity-accounted investees impair earnings quality on the persistence dimension. And because the investor does not receive cash when an underlying investee issues shares, any gain recognized from such a transaction would diminish earnings quality on the cash dimension. Losses on the sale of equity-accounted investments, and losses from issues of stock by equity-accounted investees enhance earnings quality on both the cash and persistence dimensions.

The impact of the equity method on position quality depends on the market value of the underlying shares. When the market value exceeds the carrying value of the equity-accounted investment, position quality is enhanced. Position quality is impaired when the carrying value of the investment exceeds the market value of the underlying shares.

SUMMARY

The reader should consider the following key points:

- Accounting for investments in securities depends on whether the investments are in debt or equity securities, management's intent with respect to disposal, and for equity securities, whether they have readily determinable market values, and whether the ownership positions taken are sufficient to provide significant influence.
- Nonmarketable equity securities are accounted for at cost.
- Accounting for debt securities and equity securities that have readily determinable market values and for which significant influence does not exist depends on whether the investment is classified as held to maturity, trading, or available for sale.
- Held-to-maturity debt securities are accounted for at amortized cost. Interest, adjusted for amortization of any premium or discount, is accrued to income.
- Trading securities, debt and equity, are accounted for at fair value. Unrealized gains and losses are recorded in income as market values change. Interest income is accrued. Dividend income is recognized when declared.
- Debt securities and equity securities that are held as available for sale are accounted for at fair value. Unrealized gains and losses are recorded in accumulated other comprehensive income within shareholders' equity. Interest income on debt securities is accrued, dividend income is recognized when declared.
- Investments in equity securities providing the investor with significant influence over the operating and financial policies of the investee are accounted for using the equity method. The investment is recorded initially at cost and subsequently adjusted for the investor's share of the income or loss of the investee and for dividends received from the investee. There can be, and often is, goodwill buried in an investment balance accounted for under the equity method. This goodwill is amortized to equity-method income over an assumed useful life, not to exceed 40 years.
- All investments are subject to write down when market value has fallen below carrying value and the decline is considered to be an other-than-temporary decline. The accompanying loss is taken to the income statement. The new, lower valuation becomes the investment's cost basis.

Exhibit 8.14. Summary of Accounting Methods for Debt Securities and Equity Securities

Accounting Methods

Nature of the Investment	Cost	Amortized Cost	Market: Gains and Losses to Income	Market: Gains and Losses to Other Comp. Income*	Equity Method
Equity: nonmarketable, no significant influence	X				
Debt: held to maturity		X			
Debt and Equity: marketable, held for trading no significant influence			X		
Debt and equity: marketable, neither held to maturity nor trading, no significant influence				X	
Equity: significant influence, either marketable or nonmarketable					X

*Other comprehensive income, within shareholders' equity.

The accounting methods appropriate for investments in debt and equity securities are summarized in Exhibit 8.14.

GLOSSARY

Amortized cost Cost of a security adjusted for the amortization of any purchase premium or discount.

Available-for-sale security A debt or equity security not classified as a held-to-maturity security or a trading security. Can be classified as a current or noncurrent investment depending on the intended holding period.

Collateralized Mortgage Obligation (CMO) A mortgage-backed security that gives the holder a security interest in, but not ownership of, underlying mortgage instruments.

Debt security A security representing a debt relationship with an enterprise, including a government security, municipal security, corporate bond, convertible debt issue, and commercial paper. For accounting purposes, redeemable preferred stock is also considered to be a debt security.

Equity method   The accounting method for an equity security where the level of ownership provides an investor with a voting interest that is sufficient to permit the investor to have significant influence over the operating and financial policies of an investee. The investor recognizes its share of the earnings and losses of the investee. Dividends are treated as a recovery of investment and reduce the investment balance on the balance sheet; they are not included in the investor's earnings.

Equity security   An ownership interest in an enterprise, including preferred and common stock.

Fair market value   Market value.

Fair value   The amount at which an asset could be purchased or sold or a liability incurred or settled in a current transaction between willing and informed parties. When a quoted market price is available, fair value is the product of the number of units in question times that market price. That product is also referred to as the item's market value. For traded securities, the terms fair value and market value are synonymous. When no quoted market price is available for the item in question, fair value must be estimated, but only in the case of debt instruments.

Held-to-maturity security   A debt security for which the investing entity has both the positive intent and the ability to hold until maturity.

Junk security   Debt security that is considered to be below investment grade.

Market value   A quoted market price per unit times the number of units being valued. Synonymous with fair value for financial instruments for which a quoted market price is available.

National Association of Securities Dealers Automated Quotations (NASDAQ) system   A computerized network for the over-the-counter market that processes quotes and trades for member institutions and individuals.

Nonmarketable security   A debt or equity security for which there is no posted price or bid-and-asked quotation available on a securities exchange or over-the-counter market.

Redeemable preferred stock   A preferred stock issue that must be redeemed by the issuing enterprise or is redeemable at the option of the investor. Considered a debt security for accounting purposes.

Real Estate Mortgage Investment Conduit (REMIC)   A mortgage-backed security with a special tax-preferred structure created in the Tax Reform Act of 1986 that allows remittance to investors of the cash flow from the underlying pool of mortgages to be controlled such that tax consequences can be minimized.

Restricted stock   Stock whose sale is restricted by government or contractual requirement.

Securitization   The process whereby securities are created backed by pools of assets, such as accounts receivable, credit card receivables, and mortgages.

Security   A share or an interest in a property or an enterprise such as a stock certificate or a bond.

Significant influence   The extent of influence of an investor over the operating and financial policies of an investee. Typically inferred when an investor has a voting interest of between 20 percent and 50 percent of an investee's voting shares. However, can also be inferred as a result of such factors as board representation, participation in management, material intercompany transactions, or technological dependency.

Trading security   A debt or equity security bought and held for sale in the near term to generate income on short-term price changes.

NOTES

1. *The Wall Street Journal,* March 2, 1993, p. B3.

2. Conservatism is a constraint on the application of accounting principles that requires that special care be taken to avoid overstating assets and revenues or understating liabilities and expenses. While the conservatism constraint has not been repealed in present-day accounting, the relevance of market value to accounting for investments has been more greatly acknowledged.

3. The Financial Accounting Standards Board is debating this issue and is considering requiring that all investments, in fact, all financial assets as well as financial liabilities be carried at market value.

4. Adapted from SFAS No. 115, "Accounting for Certain Investments in Debt and Equity Securities" (Norwalk, CT: Financial Accounting Standards Board, 1993), para. 137.

5. Accounting guidance is provided by SFAS No. 115, "Accounting for Certain Investments in Debt and Equity Securities" (Norwalk, CT: Financial Accounting Standards Board, 1993). Fair value is the amount at which an asset could be purchased or sold or a liability incurred or settled in a current transaction between willing and informed parties. When a quoted market price is available, fair value is the product of the number of units in question times that market price. That product is also referred to as the item's market value. For traded securities, the terms fair value and market value are synonymous. When no quoted market price is available for a debt instrument, then fair value must be estimated. The term fair market value here is used to mean market value.

6. Kaye Group, Inc., annual report, December 1997. Information obtained from Disclosure, Inc. *Compact D/SEC: Corporate Information on Public Companies Filing with the SEC* (Bethesda, MD: Disclosure, Inc., June 1998).

7. BankAmerica Corp., annual report, December 1997, p. 60.

8. SFAS No. 115, "Accounting for Certain Investment in Debt and Equity Securities" (Norwalk, CT: Financial Accounting Standards Board, 1993), para. 20.

9. Berkshire Hathaway, Inc., annual report, December 1994, p. 30.

10. Actually the definition for classifying current assets uses one year, or the operating cycle, whichever is longer. The operating cycle is the time period needed for a company to move from cash, through to inventory, accounts receivable, and back to cash. Contractors often have operating cycles exceeding one year.

11. SFAS No. 95, "Statement of Cash Flows" (Norwalk, CT: Financial Accounting Standards Board, 1987).

12. BankAmerica Corp., annual report, December 1997, p. 60.

13. *Ibid.,* p. 67.

14. Bay Tact Corp., annual report, December 1994, p. 15.

15. Kaye Group, Inc., annual report, December 1997. Information obtained from Disclosure, Inc. *Compact D/SEC: Corporate Information on Public Companies Filing with the SEC* (Bethesda, MD: Disclosure, Inc., June 1998).

16. Delta Air Lines, Inc., annual report, December 1997. Information obtained from Disclosure, Inc. *Compact D/SEC: Corporate Information on Public Companies Filing with the SEC* (Bethesda, MD: Disclosure, Inc., June 1998).

17. SunTrust Banks, Inc., annual report, December 1997, p. 42.

18. SFAS No. 130, "Reporting Comprehensive Income" (Norwalk, CT: Financial Accounting Standards Board, 1997). A detailed discussion of this accounting standard and its reporting requirements is provided in Chapter Two.

19. SFAS No. 115, "Accounting for Certain Investment in Debt and Equity Securities" (Norwalk, CT: Financial Accounting Standards Board, 1993), para. 20.

20. SunTrust Banks, Inc., annual report, December 1997, p. 45.

21. Delta Air Lines, Inc., annual report, December 1997. Information obtained from Disclosure, Inc. *Compact D/SEC: Corporate Information on Public Companies Filing with the SEC* (Bethesda, MD: Disclosure, Inc., June 1998).

22. The ability to recognize gains in income while deferring losses led two members of the seven-member Financial Accounting Standards Board to vote against SFAS No. 115. The standard was approved anyway.

23. American Country Holdings, Inc., annual report, December 1997. Information obtained from Disclosure, Inc. *Compact D/SEC: Corporate Information on Public Companies Filing with the SEC* (Bethesda, MD: Disclosure, Inc., June 1998).

24. Berkshire Hathaway, Inc., annual report, December 1994, p. 30.

25. *Ibid.*

26. Bancorp Connecticut, Inc., annual report, December 1997. Information obtained from Disclosure, Inc. *Compact D/SEC: Corporate Information on Public Companies Filing with the SEC* (Bethesda, MD: Disclosure, Inc., June 1998).

27. Conseco, Inc., annual report, December 1997. Information obtained from Disclosure, Inc. *Compact D/SEC: Corporate Information on Public Companies Filing with the SEC* (Bethesda, MD: Disclosure, Inc., June 1998).

28. Green Tree Financial Corp., annual report, September 1997. Information obtained from Disclosure, Inc. *Compact D/SEC: Corporate Information on Public Companies Filing with the SEC* (Bethesda, MD: Disclosure, Inc., June 1998).

29. MBLA Financial Corp., annual report, June 1997. Information obtained from Disclosure, Inc. *Compact D/SEC: Corporate Information on Public Companies Filing with the SEC* (Bethesda, MD: Disclosure, Inc., June 1998).

30. SFAS No. 107, "Disclosures about Fair Value of Financial Instruments" (Norwalk, CT: Financial Accounting Standards Board, 1991).

31. M. E. Barth, "Fair Value Accounting: Evidence from Investment Securities and the Market Valuation of Banks," *The Accounting Review* (January 1994), pp. 1–25.

32. K. K. Nelson, "Fair Value Accounting for Commercial Banks: An Empirical Analysis of SFAS No. 107," *The Accounting Review* (April 1996), pp. 161–182.

33. Accounting Principles Board Opinion No. 18, "The Equity Method of Accounting for Investments in Common Stock" (New York: Accounting Principles Board, 1971).

34. Burlington Northern, Inc., annual report, December 1995. Information obtained from Disclosure, Inc. *Compact D/SEC: Corporate Information on Public Companies Filing*

with the SEC (Bethesda, MD: Disclosure, Inc., June 1998). Burlington Northern, Inc. and Santa Fe Pacific Corp. have merged since this example was taken.

35. Promus Hotel Corp., annual report, December 1996, Information obtained from Disclosure, Inc. *Compact D/SEC: Corporate Information on Public Companies Filing with the SEC* (Bethesda, MD: Disclosure, Inc., June 1998).

36. FASB Interpretation No. 35, "Criteria for Applying the Equity Method of Accounting for Investments in Common Stock" (Norwalk, CT: Financial Accounting Standards Board, 1981).

37. E. E. Comiskey and C.W. Mulford, "Investment Decisions and the Equity Accounting Standard," *The Accounting Review* (July 1986), pp. 519–525.

38. International Accounting Standard No. 28, "Accounting for Investments in Associates" (London: International Accounting Standards Committee, 1988).

39. E. E. Comiskey and C. W. Mulford, "Investment Decisions and Equity Accounting Standards: The Cases of Singapore and Malaysia," *Advances in International Accounting* (1990), pp. 61–70.

40. SUPERVALU, Inc., Form 10-K annual report to the Securities and Exchange Commission (February 1997), p. 30.

41. Athanor Group, Inc., annual report, October 1997, p. 24.

42. The Coca-Cola Co., annual report, December 1997, p. 50.

43. Worthington Industries, Inc., annual report, May 1996. Information obtained from Disclosure, Inc. *Compact D/SEC: Corporate Information on Public Companies Filing with the SEC* (Bethesda, MD: Disclosure, Inc., March 1997).

44. The Coca-Cola Co., annual report, December 1997, p. 50.

45. Cone Mills Corp., annual report, December 1997, Information obtained from Disclosure, Inc. *Compact D/SEC: Corporate Information on Public Companies Filing with the SEC* (Bethesda, MD: Disclosure, Inc., June 1998).

46. The Coca-Cola Co., annual report, December 1997, pp. 51–52.

47. Worthington Industries, Inc., annual report, May 1996. Information obtained from Disclosure, Inc. *Compact D/SEC: Corporate Information on Public Companies Filing with the SEC* (Bethesda, MD: Disclosure, Inc., June 1998).

Chapter 9

Investment Reporting and Analysis II: Business Combinations

> Control—the ability of an entity to direct the policies and management that guide the ongoing activities of another entity so as to increase its benefits and limit its losses from that other entity's activities.[1]

> Some regulators have taken a dim view of what they consider the excesses of such stock deals—especially those that get the kind of favorable accounting treatment known as pooling of interests.[2]

> The rulemaking body, the Financial Accounting Standards Board, is weighing a proposal that would give companies that pay cash for acquisitions more discretion in how they account for goodwill.[3]

After years of being left alone by regulators and accounting standard setters, accounting for business combinations—mergers and acquisitions—is on the threshold of significant change. Much of the accounting guidance for this area dates to the early 1970s and even as far back as the late 1950s.[4] It is from these early pronouncements that we have a working definition of control, that we have provisions for use of the purchase and pooling methods, and that we have guidance on permitted amortization periods for goodwill. As suggested by the quotations opening this chapter, all three of these pillars of contemporary accounting for business combinations are being reconsidered and will likely be revised in the not-too-distant future.

The purpose of this chapter is to continue the discussion of accounting for investments begun in Chapter Eight. In fact, this chapter is the next logical step in accounting for equity securities. In Chapter Eight, it was shown that when investments in marketable equity securities are insufficient to provide significant influence, classification as available for sale is appropriate unless the investment is made for trading purposes. Such available for sale investments are reported at fair value with unrealized gains and losses reported in the accumulated other comprehensive income component of shareholders' equity. When an equity investment captures a sufficient amount of voting interest to provide the investor with significant influence over the operating and financial policies of the investee, equity-method accounting is appropriate. Such positions are, for the most part, between 20 percent and 50 percent, inclusive, of the investee's voting equity.

This chapter examines equity investments that constitute more than 50 percent of the voting equity of an investee. Such a position is sufficient, using the extant definition, to provide the investor with control over the affairs of the investee. As such, in most instances a full consolidation of the investee's financial statements with those of the investor is warranted.

This chapter is designed around current accounting guidelines for business combinations. The chapter does, however, detail the changes in those guidelines that are in process, how those changes might alter accounting practice, and what their potential implications are for corporate policy concerning business combinations.

THE STRUCTURE OF BUSINESS COMBINATIONS

A business combination occurs when two or more businesses are brought together into one accounting entity.[5] The single entity carries on the activities of the previously separate, independent enterprises. The assets of the combined entity are derived from the assets of the previously separate entities and the claims (i.e., liabilities and shareholders' equity) on those assets are derived from the holders of claims in the previously separate entities.

The Meaning of *Control*

In a business combination, one entity gains control over the affairs of the other combining entities. Although the definition of *control* is evolving, the current definition is very clear:

> The usual condition for a controlling financial interest is ownership of a majority voting interest, and therefore, as a general rule ownership by one company, directly or indirectly, of over fifty percent of the outstanding voting shares of another company is a condition pointing toward consolidation.[6]

Using this definition, an ownership interest of 50 percent plus would be sufficient to provide control. There are exceptions to this rule, however. For example, a controlled entity should not be combined with a controlling entity for reporting purposes if control is likely to be temporary. This was the case recently with Cendant Corporation with its over 50 percent ownership of Avis Rent A Car, Inc. According to Cendant:

> Upon entering into a definitive merger agreement to acquire Avis in 1996, the Company announced its strategy to dilute its interest in ARAC [a subsidiary of Avis that controlled the company's rental car operations] while retaining assets associated with the franchise business, including trademarks, reservation system assets and franchise agreements with ARAC and other licensees. Since the Company's control was planned to be temporary, the Company accounted for its 100% investment in ARAC under the

equity method. The Company's equity interest was diluted to 27.5% pursuant to an initial public offering by ARAC in September 1997 and was further diluted to 20.4% as a result of a secondary offering in March 1998.[7]

Even though Cendant owned 100 percent of Avis, presumably rendering the issue of control moot, Cendant did not treat its position in Avis as one of control. The company had plans for reducing its ownership in Avis to a level that was less than 50 percent. However, because Cendant planned to retain sufficient ownership to exert significant influence, the company used the equtiy method to account for its investment.

In some instances, ownership of over 50 percent does not provide a share-holder with control, even when the position is not viewed as temporary in nature. This may occur, for example, when a majority-owned entity is in legal reorgani-zation or in bankruptcy. Several years ago, before its demise, Eastern Airlines, Inc. owned a controlling financial interest in Continental Airlines, Inc. However, because Continental was, for a time, in bankruptcy proceedings, Eastern did not report with Continental as a combined entity but used the equity method to account for the company instead. Control of Continental rested with the bankruptcy trustee and not with Eastern.

There may be instances in which an entity owns more than 50 percent of another and does not even have significant influence over the investee. Such a situation may occur when an owned entity is located in a foreign country and the foreign government is hostile to or has repudiated the investor's rights of control. An investment in such a difficult situation would be accounted for as available for sale if the shares were readily marketable, or at cost, likely reduced for value impairment, if they were not.

The Financial Accounting Standards Board (FASB) has proposed a new def-inition of control, summarized in the opening quotations to this chapter. The def-inition, as provided in the opening quotes to this chapter, states:

> Control—the ability of an entity to direct the policies and management that guide the ongoing activities of another entity so as to increase the benefits or limit the losses from that other entity's activities.[8]

Clarifying its position, the FASB indicated that for accounting purposes, con-trol involves the presence of two essential characteristics:

1. A parent's nonshared decision-making ability that enables it to guide the on-going activities of its subsidiary

2. A parent's ability to use that power to increase the benefits that it derives and limit the losses that it suffers from the activities of that subsidiary.[9]

Note that in defining control, an ownership percentage of over 50 percent is not used. In the view of the FASB, a controlling interest need not be represented by an ownership position of more than 50 percent. For example, according to the FASB:

> A parent's decision-making powers may stem from a subsidiary's governing instrument (articles of incorporation, partnership agreement, or trust indenture), contractual arrangements with holders of voting rights, a voting trust, or other legal device, while its ability to derive benefits stems from a holding of nonvoting equity shares or other beneficial interest.[10]

Moreover, the FASB observes that there may be limits on control, but such limits do not necessarily eliminate it:

> The definition of control does not require unlimited decision-making powers. Control rarely, if ever, exists without restrictions on a parent's decision-making power and its ability to derive benefits from its subsidiary. Even control of a wholly owned subsidiary with no debt may be restricted to some degree by law, regulations, and the nature of the subsidiary's assets.[11]

Continuing to expand on its proposed definition of control, the FASB has proposed three presumptions of control. Absent evidence to the contrary, the existence of any one of the following situations would provide evidence of the existence of control. According to the proposed definition, the existence of control of a corporation shall be presumed if an entity:

- Has a majority voting interest in the election of a corporation's governing body or a right to appoint a majority of the members of its governing body
- Has a large minority voting interest in the election of a corporation's governing body and no other party or organized group of parties has a significant voting interest
- Has a unilateral ability to (1) obtain a majority voting interest in the election of a corporation's governing body or (2) obtain a right to appoint a majority of the corporation's governing body through the present ownership of convertible securities or other rights that are currently exercisable at the option of the holder and the expected benefits from converting those securities or exercising that right exceeds its expected cost.[12]

While this proposed definition of control is just that—a proposal—it is clear that the FASB is moving away from the simple use of ownership of voting stock as its definition of control. Such a change in definition, which is not scheduled to become effective until fiscal years ending on or after December 2000, could have wide-reaching financial statement effects. Companies with significant ownership positions that are below 50 percent may find themselves obliged to report in a combined fashion with previously noncombined entities.

One company that could be affected by this proposal is the Coca-Cola Co. At February 20, 1998, that company owned approximately 43.7 percent of the outstanding shares of Coca-Cola Enterprises, Inc. Only one other shareholder owned more than five percent of the shares on that date, with an ownership position of 8.6 percent. Coca-Cola Enterprise's board of directors, which consists of 13 members, has three members who are either management personnel of Coca-Cola Co or consultants to that company.

Does Coca-Cola *control* Coca-Cola Enterprises? Using a legal definition of owning over 50 percent of the outstanding shares, it does not. Effective control, however, would appear to be a possibility. One of the presumptions of control, as noted, is that an entity has a "large minority voting interest in the election of a corporation's governing body and no other party or organized group of parties has a significant voting interest."[13] Coke's 43.7 percent interest could be viewed as fulfilling this requirement. Moreover, Coca-Cola Enterprises is an important component of the distribution network for Coca-Cola's products. Coke has a vested interest in maintaining a significant say over Coca-Cola Enterprise's operations. Considering these factors, it would appear to us that a case of effective control by Coca-Cola over Coca-Cola Enterprises could be made.

The impact on Coke's financial statements of redefining its relationship with Coca-Cola Enterprises as being one of control would be significant. For reporting purposes, Coca-Cola would combine the financial statements of Coca-Cola Enterprises with its own and report as a single company. Coke currently accounts for Coca-Cola Enterprises using the equity method. Thus, Coca-Cola Enterprises appears as an investment on Coke's balance sheet. Coke's share of Coca-Cola Enterprises' net income appears on Coke's income statement as equity-method income. Reporting Coca-Cola and Coca-Cola Enterprises as a single company would bring 100 percent of Coca-Cola Enterprises' assets and liabilities, excluding intercompany account balances, onto Coke's balance sheet. Using figures available as of December 31, 1997, the net result would be a doubling of Coke's assets and a 163 percent increase in Coke's liabilities.[14] The share of Coca-Cola Enterprises' net assets or shareholders' equity not owned by Coke would be reported on Coke's balance sheet as a noncontrolling interest in subsidiaries. The combined entity's shareholders' equity would not change. The new, combined Coca-Cola entity would appear to be a much more highly levered firm.

Reporting as a single company would also bring 100 percent of Coca-Cola Enterprises' revenues and expenses, excluding intercompany accounts, onto Coke's income statement. For 1997, Coke's revenues would increase by approximately 60 percent. Expenses would also increase and the portion of Coca-Cola Enterprises' earnings not controlled by Coke would be reported as a noncontrolling (minority) interest. Combined net income would remain unchanged. As a result, net profit margin would decline from approximately 22 percent for Coca-Cola in 1997 to approximately 14 percent for the combined entity.[15] The company would appear to be a much less profitable operation. More is said about the financial statement effects of consolidation versus use of the equity method in a subsequent section of this chapter.

If Coca-Cola were considered to have a controlling financial interest in Coca-Cola Enterprises, the company could avoid the undesirable effects of consolidation by reducing its ownership in Coca-Cola Enterprises. The key would be to reduce it below a level that is considered to be a "large minority voting interest."

As is to be expected, the proposed new rule defining control is not without controversy, most of which focuses on the subjectivity of the new definition. According to Pat McConnell of Bear, Stearns & Co., "There's a risk here that the FASB has fixed things for the worse."[16]

One company that has applied the new, broader definition of control to an investment is Arkansas Best Corporation. The company consolidates its interest even though its investment position is less than 50 percent. In its annual report, Arkansas Best provides the following description of its investment in Treadco, Inc.:

> At December 31, 1997, the Company's percentage ownership of Treadco was 46%. The Company's consolidated financial statements reflect full consolidation of the accounts of Treadco, with the ownership interests of the other stockholders reflected as minority interest, because the Company controls Treadco through stock ownership, board representation and management services provided under a transition services agreement.[17]

Different Business Combination Structures

In a business combination, the combining entities may or may not retain their precombination legal status. In a combination known as a *statutory combination*—combinations fulfilling the legal or state statute definition of a combination structure—one or more precombination entities are liquidated and cease to exist. In a combination known as a nonstatutory combination, precombination entities are not liquidated as part of the combination transaction.

Statutory and nonstatutory combinations can be structured as either mergers or consolidations. The use of these terms to describe business combinations depends on whether a new entity is created to effect the transactions.

Statutory and Nonstatutory Mergers

In a merger transaction, two or more companies are combined, with one of the combining firms surviving the combination. For example, A + B = A. In a statutory merger, or a combination that fulfills the legal definition of a merger, the acquired firm—B in this example—is liquidated and ceases to exist. As an example, consider the acquisition of Gloucester County Bankshares, Inc. by Fulton Financial Corporation. Fulton Financial provided the following description of the transaction:

> On February 29, 1996, the Corporation completed its acquisition of Gloucester County Bankshares, Inc. (Gloucester) of Woodbury, New Jersey. As provided under the terms

of the merger agreement, Gloucester was merged with and into the Corporation and each of the outstanding shares of the common stock of Gloucester was converted into 1.91 shares of the Corporation's common stock. The Corporation issued 2.0 million shares of its common stock in connection with the merger.[18]

In a nonstatutory merger, the acquired firm is not liquidated. It continues to exist and operate, but as a subsidiary of A. Thus, in a nonstatutory merger, a parent–subsidiary relationship is created. Moreover, for purposes of financial reporting, accounting steps must be taken to combine companies A and B into a single reporting entity, company C. These accounting steps are known as an accounting consolidation or worksheet consolidation of A and B. Through this reporting process, the combination will appear to be a merger of A and B to create A, even though the legal definition of a merger is not fulfilled. More is said about the worksheet consolidation process in subsequent sections of this chapter. An example of a nonstatutory merger was also provided by Fulton Financial:

> On August 31, 1997, the Corporation completed its acquisition of The Peoples Bank of Elkton (Elkton) of Elkton, Maryland. As provided under the terms of the merger agreement, Elkton became a wholly-owned subsidiary of the Corporation and each of the outstanding shares of the common stock of Elkton was converted into 4.158 shares of the Corporation's common stock.[19]

In a merger, the acquiring company can acquire the assets or stock of the acquired firm. In an asset acquisition, A distributes assets or stock to B (not to B's shareholders) in return for B's assets. Such a transaction is, by its nature, equivalent to a statutory merger. By acquiring the assets of the acquired firm, there will be no need to proceed with a worksheet consolidation of the two companies. The assets of the acquired firm are held directly by the acquiring firm. Though again, to fulfill the legal definition of a merger, B would need to be liquidated by distributing the assets or stock received from A to its own shareholders. An example of an asset acquisition is provided by the Rare Hospitality International Inc. acquisition of Lone Star Steaks, Inc. Rare Hospitality provided the following description of the transaction:

> During 1995, the Company purchased certain assets and trademark rights of Lone Star Steaks, Inc. for a purchase price, including acquisition expenses, of $3,402,000. The purchase price included cash consideration of $2,152,000 and 96,153 newly issued shares of the Company's common stock. These shares had a market value at the time of the transaction of $1,250,000.[20]

In this transaction, Rare Hospitality acquired the assets, including trademark rights, of Lone Star and not the Company's stock. Note that Lone Star would now have assets consisting of the cash paid the company by Rare Hospitality and the newly issued Rare Hospitality shares. Because only "certain assets" were purchased by Rare Hospitality, Lone Star was also likely to be left with other assets as well. The company kept its previous shareholder structure and continued as a separate entity.

In an acquisition of stock, A distributes assets or issues shares to the shareholders of B and receives their shares in return. Such a transaction is a statutory merger if B is liquidated and a nonstatutory merger if B is not liquidated.

The combination of WorldCom, Inc. and MCI Communications Corporation fits the definition of a merger. WorldCom issued 1.2439 shares of its stock to the shareholders of MCI for each MCI share held. In effect, WorldCom plus MCI equals WorldCom (though the company's name was changed to MCI WorldCom, Inc). And because of plans to cancel the shares of MCI held by WorldCom, the combination appeared to fit the definition of a statutory merger. As stated by WorldCom in a recent filing with the Securities and Exchange Commission (SEC):

> As a result of the Merger and without any action on the part of the holders thereof, at the Effective Time, all shares of MCI Common Stock shall cease to be outstanding and shall be canceled and retired and shall cease to exist . . .[21]

In a merger structured as A + B = A, A is typically the acquiring firm and B the acquired, though this is not always the case. If A were to issue a controlling number of shares to the shareholders of B to effect the combination, it is in actuality an acquisition of A by B. Deciding which firm is the acquiring firm and which is being acquired is important in business combinations accounted for as purchases because the acquired firm is revalued to market value. The acquiring firm is not revalued. More is said about this topic later in the chapter.

Consider a proposed agreement by MicroFrame, Inc. to acquire Solcom Systems, Ltd. In a footnote to its annual report, MicroFrame provided the following information about the proposed transaction:

> On June 23, 1998, the Company entered into an agreement to acquire Solcom Systems, Ltd. ("Solcom"), a developer of remote monitoring technology, for approximately 5.6 million shares and options to purchase shares of the Company's common stock. The acquisition is expected to be completed in the second quarter of 1999.[22]

On the surface, this proposed transaction appears to be an acquisition of Solcom by MicroFrame. However, prior to the transaction, MicroFrame had 4,849,531 shares outstanding. Thus, by issuing 5 million new shares, MicroFrame is, in effect, proposing to be acquired by Solcom. There is, however, one other wrinkle. MicroFrame had options outstanding to purchase 1,794,796 of its shares. With the exercise of these options—a likely event given their in-the-money status— MicroFrame will have 6,644,327 shares outstanding. As a result, the shareholders of MicroFrame will own over half of the outstanding shares of the newly combined company.

Statutory and Nonstatutory Consolidations

In a consolidation transaction, two or more companies are combined, but neither of the combining firms survives the combination. Rather, a new entity is created to acquire the combining entities. For example, A + B = C. In a statutory consolidation, the acquired firms, A and B in this example, are liquidated and cease to exist. In a nonstatutory consolidation, A and B are not liquidated. The companies continue to exist and operate as subsidiaries of C. Here again, a parent–subsidiary relationship is created. And for purposes of financial reporting, a worksheet consolidation must be used to combine companies A and B into a single firm, company C.

In a consolidation, like a merger, the newly formed company can acquire the assets or stock of the combining firms. Because a consolidation involves the creation of a new entity, C, a company without assets, to effect the combination, a consolidation typically involves the issue of shares. These newly created shares might be issued directly to the combining companies, A and B, to acquire their assets. However, it is more likely that these shares will be issued to the shareholders of the combining companies to acquire their stock.

While in a merger it is reasonably clear who the acquiring and acquired firms are, this is not the case in a consolidation. While a consolidation is structured as A + B = C, one of the combining companies, A or B is actually acquiring the other. The company whose shareholder group ends up with control of more shares of the combined entity after the combination is complete is the acquiring company. For example, assume that in a consolidation, a new company, C, issues 400 shares to the shareholders of A to acquire their shares and 600 shares to the shareholders of B to acquire their shares. In this transaction, because the shareholders of B have 60 percent of the total, B has actually acquired A. This is the case even though the newly combined entity will be called C.

Consider, for example, the combination of NationsBank Corporation and BankAmerica Corporation. The transaction involved the combination of the two companies to create a *new* Bank of America Corporation. Stock in the new corporation was issued to the shareholders of each of the combining companies—a consolidation. Shareholders in NationsBank received one share of the new company's stock for each share of NationsBank they held. Shareholders in Bank of America received 1.1316 shares of the new company's stock for each of their BankAmerica shares. However, even though the new company is called Bank of America, the shareholders in NationsBank own 54 percent of the new company. As a result, the transaction was in actuality an acquisition of the original BankAmerica by NationsBank.

ACCOUNTING FOR BUSINESS COMBINATIONS

Although many terms can be used to describe a business combination, such as *acquisition, merger, consolidation,* or *combination,* to name a few, there are but two ways to account for all combinations. A business combination can be accounted for as either a purchase transaction or a pooling of interests. However, the choice of accounting method is not something that the combining firms can

Exhibit 9.1. Relative Use of Pooling of Interests and Purchase Accounting for Combinations

Pooling-of-Interests method	1993	1994	1995	1996	1997
Prior-year statements restated	11	7	19	17	7
Prior-year statements not restated*	10	12	13	15	12
Total	21	19	32	32	19
Purchase method	200	215	244	256	215

*The failure to restate prior-year statements, required under generally accepted accounting principles for poolings of interests, is usually due to the lack of materiality of such restatements.

Source: Accounting Trends and Techniques: Annual Survey of Accounting Practices Followed in 600 Stockholders' Reports, 52nd ed. (New York: American Institute of Certified Public Accountants, 1998), p. 67.

simply choose as they wish. The accounting method applied to a business combination is determined by the terms of the combination agreement. If the transaction's terms meet the requirements for a pooling of interests, it is to be accounted for as such. If the transaction does not meet the requirement for a pooling, then it is to be accounted for as a purchase.

We have seen an increase in the number of business combinations accounted for as poolings in recent years, though this trend reversed somewhat in 1997. As will be seen in subsequent sections, poolings require that the combination is accomplished with stock and as share prices have traded up in recent years, the net cost to acquiring firms has declined. Also, poolings have a less negative impact on the acquiring firm's results of operations.

However, as can be seen by examining Exhibit 9.1, the increase in poolings notwithstanding, purchase accounting remains the most common form of business combination accounting. Explaining the dominance of this method is the fact that purchases do not place onerous terms on the combining parties and, as a result, are the easiest transactions to effect.

Purchase Accounting

When a business combination is considered to be a purchase, the acquiring firm is viewed as being the purchaser of the acquired company. Accordingly, net assets (i.e., assets less liabilities of the acquired firm) are recorded at their acquisition cost. Acquisition cost is the fair value of the consideration given in the transaction plus any costs incurred to effect the combination. Such costs include attorneys' and accountants' fees as well as underwriting fees for issuing debt and equity securities. However, while the acquired firm is combined at fair value, the acquiring firm, which was not purchased, is combined at its precombination book value. Such treatment is consistent with the accounting treatment afforded the purchase of any asset. The purchased asset is recorded at its current cost.

Goodwill and Other Intangibles

In purchase accounting, the fair value of the consideration given in the acquisition is assigned to two items—identifiable net assets of the acquired firm and goodwill. In a first step, the acquired firm's identifiable net assets are revalued to fair value. For some previously unrecognized assets, this may result in recognition for the first time. For current assets and current liabilities, such a revaluation is not difficult. Cash, cash equivalents, and investments carried at market value are left at carrying values. Accounts receivable are valued at amounts expected to be collected. Inventory is valued at current cost, which can be approximated roughly with first-in, first-out (FIFO) cost. Amounts that are expected to be realized are used for other current assets. Most current liabilities—accounts payable, accrued expenses payable, and notes payable that are currently due—can in most instances be left at book value. Noncurrent assets—buildings, land, property, plant, and equipment—require appraisals. Estimates of fair value are also required for identifiable intangible assets—patents, copyrights, and franchises—and nonmarketable investments. Other noncurrent assets should be valued at amounts that are expected to be realized. Book value might be an appropriate measure. Long-term liabilities should be valued using a present value calculation and existing market rates of interest. As a last step, a value is assigned to goodwill for the difference between the fair value of the consideration given in the acquisition and the computed fair value of all identifiable net assets.

As an example, consider the following two acquisitions made by Mother's Work, Inc.:

> On April 5, 1995, the Company acquired A Pea in the Pod, Inc. (Pea) for $25,487,000, in cash, including transaction costs, and the assumption of $2,459,000 in funded debt. The purchase price and the repayment of the funded debt was financed with borrowings from a bank and an insurance company. The purchase price was allocated to the fair value of the net assets acquired, with $21,524,000 allocated to goodwill under the purchase method of accounting.
>
> On August 1, 1995, the Company acquired Motherhood Maternity Shops, Inc. (Motherhood) for $33,985,000, including transaction costs, and the assumption of $20,000,000 in funded debt and accrued interest. Approximately $22,485,000 was paid in cash and $11,500,000 was paid with newly issued preferred stock. The purchase price was allocated to the fair value of the net assets acquired with $18,471,000 allocated to goodwill under the purchase method of accounting.[23]

In the April 1995 transaction, Mother's Work acquired A Pea in the Pod for $25,487,000 in cash. For that amount, Mother's Work acquired A Pea in the Pod's net assets, or assets less liabilities. In addition to the amount paid to acquire the company's net assets, Mother's Work also assumed A Pea in the Pod's liabilities. Thus, the total price paid to get control of A Pea in the Pod's assets was the price paid of $25,487,000 to acquire the company's net assets plus $2,459,000 in liabilities assumed. Note too that the cash paid to acquire A Pea in the Pod was described as including transactions costs. Transactions costs, which include such costs as investment bankers' commissions, accountants' and attorneys' fees, underwriting and other financing fees, are added to the purchase price in a transaction accounted for as a purchase. Of the price paid to acquire the target's net assets, $25,487,000, $3,963,000 was assigned to the fair value of identifiable net assets. The bulk of the purchase price, $21,524,000 in this example, was allocated to goodwill.

In Mother Work's August 1995 acquisition, $33,985,000 was paid, including transaction costs, to acquire the net assets of Motherhood Maternity. In addition to this purchase price, the company assumed $20 million in liabilities. Most of the purchase price, $22,485,000, was paid in cash, with the remainder paid with newly issued preferred stock. A purchase transaction can be completed using any form of currency acceptable to the acquired company, such as cash, common or preferred stock, or debt. In this example, the fair value of net assets acquired was $15,514,000, with $18,471,000 being allocated to goodwill.

In a recent acquisition, CBS Corporation disclosed, in careful detail, the fair value of identifiable assets and liabilities and of goodwill. That information is provided in Exhibit 9.2.

Exhibit 9.2 points out clearly that goodwill is the difference between the purchase price, or the fair value of the consideration paid in an acquisition, which was $1,550,000,000 in this example, and the fair value of net assets, or assets less liabilities, received. The exhibit also indicates that the fair value of assets and liabilities, and the amount recorded as goodwill, were both based on preliminary estimates. This is how the valuation process works. As new information is received regarding valuations on the date of acquisition, the amounts recorded should be revised, resulting in changes in the valuations assigned to the various assets acquired and to goodwill.

A trend in recent years in purchase accounting has been to assign a valuation to a greater number of intangibles, not just goodwill. In so doing, the acquiring company provides a more accurate representation of the assets acquired. An example provided by AAF McQuay, Inc. is reproduced in Exhibit 9.3.

One "intangible" that is very prevalent in business combinations accounted for as purchases, especially among technology firms, is purchased in-process research and development (R&D). Although purchased in-process R&D has value to the acquiring firm, accounting principles dictate that it is to be expensed immediately at the time of acquisition. The reasoning is that the realizability of in-process R&D, like R&D generally, cannot be adequately assessed to warrant the recording of an asset.[24] Many acquiring firms welcome such treatment. Because of the special charge, financial performance looks very poor in the acquisition year; however, the stage is set for better measured performance in future years.

Representative of the accounting afforded purchased in-process R&D are a series of business combinations entered into by Cisco Systems, Inc. during 1997. In these transactions, the bulk of the purchase prices paid were assigned to pur-

Exhibit 9.2. Detail of Acquisition Purchase Price Provided in a Footnote to the Financial Statements: CBS Corp.: Year Ended December 31, 1997 (Millions of Dollars)

On September 30, 1997, the Corporation acquired Gaylord's two major cable networks: TNN and CMT. The acquisition included the domestic and international operations of TNN, the U.S. and Canadian operations of CMT, and approximately $50 million in working capital. The total purchase price of $1.55 billion was paid through the issuance of 59 million shares of the Corporation's common stock. The acquisition was accounted for under the purchase method. Based on preliminary estimates, which may be revised at a later date, the excess of the consideration paid over the estimated fair value of net assets acquired of approximately $1.2 billion was recorded as goodwill and is being amortized on a straight-line basis over 40 years.

	TNN and CMT at September 30, 1997
Cash	$8
Receivables	63
Program rights	22
Investments	—
Assets held for sale	—
Property and equipment	49
Identifiable intangible assets:	
FCC licenses	—
Cable license agreements	506
Other	—
Goodwill	1,177
Other assets	4
Liabilities for talent, program rights, and similar contracts	(8)
Debt	—
Deferred income taxes	(200)
Other liabilities	(71)
Total purchase price	$1,550

Source: CBS Corp., annual report, December 1997. Information obtained from Disclosure, Inc. *Compact D/SEC: Corporate Information on Public Companies Filing with the SEC* (Bethesda, MD: Disclosure, Inc., September 1998).

chased in-process R&D. Cisco Systems provided the following description of the transactions:

> In July 1997, the Company completed the acquisition of Skystone Systems Corporation ("Skystone"), an innovator of high-speed Synchronous Optical Network/Synchronous Digital Hierarchy (SONET/SDH). Under the terms of the agreement, shares of the Company's common stock worth approximately $69.4 million, and $22.7 mil-

Exhibit 9.3. Detail of Intangibles Acquired in Business Combinations: AAF McQuay, Inc., Year Ended June 30, 1996 and 1997 (Thousands of Dollars)

Intangible assets consist of the following:	1996	1997
Cost in excess of net assets acquired	$154,964	$159,977
Other intangibles:		
Technology	12,676	14,304
Trademarks	61,161	61,161
Drawings	54,000	54,000
Workforce	18,417	18,417
Total other intangibles	146,254	147,882
Less accumulated amortization	29,378	41,075
	$271,840	$266,784

Source: AAF McQuay, Inc., annual report, *Compact D/SEC: Corporate Information on Public Companies Filing with the SEC* (Bethesda, MD: Disclosure, Inc., June 1998).

lion in cash has been exchanged for all outstanding shares, warrants, and options of Skystone. As part of this transaction, the Company recorded approximately $89.4 million in purchased research and development expense.

In July 1997, the Company acquired Ardent Communications ("Ardent"), a designer of combined communications support for compressed voice, LAN, data, and video traffic across public and private Frame Relay and ATM networks. Under the terms of the agreement, shares of the Company's stock worth approximately $165.3 million have been exchanged for the outstanding shares and options of Ardent. As part of this transaction, the Company recorded approximately $163.6 million in purchased research and development expense.

Also in July 1997, the Company acquired Global Internet Software Group ("Global Internet"), a wholly owned subsidiary of Global Internet.Com and a pioneer in the Windows NT network security marketplace. Approximately $40.2 million in cash was exchanged for all of the outstanding shares of Global Internet. As part of this transaction, the Company recorded approximately $37.6 million in purchased research and development expense.[25]

Regulators, such as the SEC, have become concerned over the extensive use of purchased in-process R&D write-offs in acquisition transactions. Recent developments at the FASB indicated that the standard-setting body would prefer to eliminate the ability of acquiring firms to take these write-offs. In a proposed standard that was planned for publication during 1999, the FASB was to require that such purchased in-process R&D be recorded as an intangible asset and amortized over its expected useful life. Amortization, as opposed to immediate expensing, would result in a considerable drag on future earnings of many firms. However, later in 1999, the FASB announced that it would take no near-term action on this matter.

Negative Goodwill

Occasionally, the fair value of identifiable net assets acquired in a business combination accounted for as a purchase exceeds the purchase price. This might happen in the purchase of a distressed company, such as one in bankruptcy, or a firm with significant off-balance-sheet contingent obligations. When such a "bargain purchase" occurs, the discount amount should first be applied toward reducing proportionately the values assigned to noncurrent assets, except for long-term investments in marketable securities, received in the transaction. The reasoning for this action is that because values assigned to noncurrent assets entail subjective valuations such as appraisals, they might not provide accurate representations of fair value in such a bargain purchase. Because investments in marketable securities have quoted market prices, fair value can be objectively established. Moreover, fair value can be established in a reasonably objective way for current assets. If the discount amount is sufficiently large such that noncurrent assets are reduced to zero, any additional discount should be reported as negative goodwill, a deferred credit.

An example of negative goodwill that arose in a purchase transaction is provided in the disclosures of Brake Headquarters USA, Inc:

> In November 1997, in a series of transactions, the Company acquired by way of merger substantially all of the assets and certain liabilities of WAWD, a wholly-owned subsidiary of Echlin, Inc., for a total purchase price (including acquisition costs) of $8,431,400 million in cash and 130,000 shares of the Company's common stock valued at $961,250. Fifty thousand of the shares issued are being held in escrow for up to 15 months as security for certain indemnification obligations. The shares held in escrow retain all voting and dividend rights and are included in common shares outstanding at December 31, 1997. The Company has accounted for the acquisition of WAWD under the purchase method of accounting and the results of operations of WAWD have been included in the 1997 statement of operations since its date of acquisition. The excess of the estimated fair market value of the net assets acquired over the purchase price was first utilized to reduce long-term assets acquired with the remaining excess of $3,732,100 recorded as a deferred credit (negative goodwill), which is being amortized over a 10 year period.[26]

There continues to be an open debate concerning the accounting for negative goodwill. An alternative treatment to that described above has been proposed by Moville and Petrie.[27] The authors disagree with reducing the values assigned to noncurrent assets, except for long-term investments, in bargain purchase transactions. Rather, they would consolidate all assets at fair value and recognize within shareholders' equity the total negative goodwill amount as a component of other comprehensive income. In their view, this treatment would better enable investors to assess the cash flow implications of the bargain purchase. As it is based on fair value and not on an arbitrary reduction in the values assigned to certain noncurrent assets, their proposed accounting treatment is appealing.

Another alternative treatment proposed by the FASB is to recognize negative goodwill as an extraordinary item. This proposal is only tentative and we do not expect it to be adopted.

Amortization of Intangibles

Intangible assets, including goodwill and other intangibles acquired in a business combination, are subject to amortization, or a periodic expensing over their estimated useful lives. The relevant accounting standard indicates:

> . . . the value of intangible assets at any one date eventually disappears and the recorded costs of intangible assets should be amortized by systematic charges to income over the periods estimated to be benefited.[28]

Factors used in determining the appropriate amortization period include legal provisions that may limit maximum useful life, provisions for renewal or extension, effects of obsolescence, demand, and competition and expected actions of competitors. However, amortization is not to exceed a 40-year period.[29]

Clearly, these factors entail the use of judgment on the part of management. This use of judgment results in varied amortization periods as is clear in the following amortization periods chosen for goodwill by several companies in the medical supplies industry:

- **Allergan, Inc.:** Goodwill represents the excess of acquisition costs over the fair value of net assets of purchased businesses and is being amortized on a straight-line basis over periods from 7 to 30 years.[30]
- **Biomet, Inc.:** Excess acquisition costs over fair value of acquired net assets (goodwill) are amortized using the straight-line method over periods ranging from 8 to 15 years.[31]
- **Healthdyne Technologies, Inc.:** The excess of cost over net assets of businesses acquired (goodwill) is being amortized using the straight-line method over periods ranging from 15 to 40 years.[32]
- **St. Jude Medical, Inc.:** Goodwill is amortized on a straight-line basis over 20 years.[33]

Amortization of intangibles reduces earnings. The longer the chosen useful life, the lower the annual charge against income. The examples of many and varied amortization periods for goodwill noted above notwithstanding, many companies use the maximum permitted 40-year period. The CBS case provided earlier is one such example. It should be noted, however, that if at some future date the amount of unamortized goodwill is considered to be value-impaired—that the amount invested in goodwill will not be recovered from related cash flows—that goodwill is subject to writedown.[34] The result is a potentially significant one-time charge to earnings. Companies choosing longer useful lives are more likely to record such special charges.

In its 1997 annual report, Eli Lilly & Co. provided an example of a special charge to write-down goodwill that had become value impaired. The net result was a special charge of $2 billion:

> Subsequently, pursuant to SFAS No. 121, "Accounting for the Impairment of Long-Lived Assets and for Long-Lived Assets to Be Disposed Of," the company evaluated the recoverability of the long-lived assets, including intangibles, of its PCS healthcare-management businesses. While revenues and profits are growing and new capabilities are being developed at PCS, the rapidly changing, competitive and highly regulated environment in which PCS operates has prevented the company from significantly increasing PCS' operating profits from levels that existed prior to the acquisition. In addition, since the acquisition, the health-care-industry trend toward highly managed care has been slower than originally expected and the possibility of selling a portion of PCS' equity to a strategic partner has not been realized. In the second quarter of 1997, concurrent with PCS' annual planning process, the company determined that PCS' estimated future undiscounted cash flows were below the carrying value of PCS' long-lived assets. Accordingly, during the second quarter of 1997, the company adjusted the carrying value of PCS' long-lived assets, primarily goodwill, to their estimated fair value of approximately $1.5 billion, resulting in a noncash impairment loss of approximately $2.4 billion ($2.21 per share). The estimated fair value was based on anticipated future cash flows discounted at a rate commensurate with the risk involved.[35]

Whereas amortization of intangible assets entails charges against earnings, amortization of negative goodwill results in periodic credits to earnings. Thus, in the Brake Headquarters example, amortization of negative goodwill will increase earnings. The fact that amortization of the negative goodwill amount will increase earnings may have been the reason the company chose an amortization period of only 10 years. The shorter the amortization period for negative goodwill, the greater the credit to earnings.

Tax Implications of Goodwill Amortization

When properly structured, goodwill amortization is a tax-deductible expense. When a purchase transaction is structured as an asset acquisition, goodwill, like other acquired intangibles, can be amortized for tax purposes over a 15-year period. Other intangibles that might be acquired in a business combination that are deductible over this same 15-year period include covenants not to compete, patents, copyrights, franchises, supply contracts, and other permits and rights.

When a purchase transaction is structured as an acquisition of stock, goodwill may still be tax deductible. The key is that an Internal Revenue Code Section 338 election must be made to effect a deemed liquidation of the target company. Here, the acquiring and target corporations agree to a two-step acquisition of the target corporation's assets. First, the target corporation's shareholders sell their stock to the acquiring corporation. For financial statement purposes, a stock acquisition is accounted for as a purchase by the acquiring company. However, for tax purposes, the acquiring corporation makes a deemed liquidation election with respect to the acquisition of the target corporation's stock. This election results in a hypothetical sale of the old target corporation's assets, including intangibles, to a new target corporation for their fair value. The new target has acquired the assets of the old target. Such a transaction requires the old target corporation to recognize and pay tax on gains and losses from the sale of assets. However, as a result of the sale transaction, the tax bases of the old target corporation's assets are stepped up to fair value on the books of the new target corporation. Intangible assets are also recognized on the books of the new target corporation. The new target and, indirectly, the acquiring firm, then receives tax deductions for these stepped-up assets as they are amortized over appropriate useful lives.[36]

Other Accounting and Reporting Issues Related to Purchase Accounting

In a purchase transaction, the fair value of the acquired firm's net assets and goodwill, if any, are combined with the book value of the net assets of the acquiring firm on the date of acquisition. Combined retained earnings on the date of acquisition equal those of the acquiring firm only. Retained earnings of the acquired firm are not carried forward into the combined entity. Earnings in the year of acquisition include the results of the acquiring firm plus the acquired firm from the date of acquisition. Any goodwill amortized and increased expenses relating to amortization of revaluations of the net assets of the acquired firm are charged against combined earnings. Prior-year financial statements are not restated. However, *pro forma* results are presented of the combined entity as though the combination had been in effect since the beginning of the previous year.

Compass Plastics and Technologies, Inc. provided *pro forma* disclosures accompanying a purchase transaction entered into during the company's 1996 fiscal year. Those disclosures are reproduced in Exhibit 9.4.

Leveraged Buyouts

Closely related to the business combination accounted for as a purchase is the leveraged buyout (LBO) transaction. An LBO often results in the change in control of a firm, but it does not entail an acquisition of one entity by another in the traditional way. Rather, an LBO is more like a financial restructuring that replaces much of a firm's shareholders' equity with debt.

As the name *leveraged buyout* suggests, debt is used to finance some or all of an LBO transaction. Sometimes, the assets of the target firm itself are used as loan collateral. In an LBO, a new shareholder group, which may be management of the target firm, acquires the shares of the old shareholder group. The shares might be paid for with cash, borrowed funds, or even shares in the reconstituted firm. If more than 80 percent of the purchase price is paid for with funds derived

Exhibit 9.4.   *Pro Forma* Disclosures Accompanying Business Combination
Accounted for as a Purchase: Compass Plastics and Technologies, Inc.,
52-Week Periods Ended October 29, 1995, and October 27, 1996

The following are the *pro forma* operating results for the 52-week period ended October
27, 1996, and October 29, 1995, as if the acquisition by the Company described above had
occurred on October 30, 1995, and October 31, 1994, respectively. The *pro forma* results
give effect to changes in amortization and deferred income taxes from valuing the acquired
net assets at estimated fair value and recording the excess of purchase price over the net
assets acquired.

	1995	*1996*
Revenue	$42,678,959	$39,345,443
Operating income	$2,034,526	$2,420,065
Other expenses	$1,065,390	$1,223,059
Net income	$535,450	$670,644
Net income per share	$0.15	$0.19
Weighted average common stock and common		
stock equivalents outstanding	3,600,000	3,600,000

The *pro forma* results of operations are not necessarily indicative of the actual operating
results that would have occurred had the acquisition been consummated at the beginning
of the period.

Source: Compass Plastics and Technologies, Inc., annual report, October 1996. Information obtained
from Disclosure, Inc. *Compact D/SEC: Corporate Information on Public Companies Filing with the
SEC* (Bethesda, MD: Disclosure, Inc., September 1998).

from sources other than borrowings against the assets of the target itself, then a
change in control is deemed to have occurred.[37] When such a change in control
occurs, there are grounds for a new accounting basis. That is, assets are revalued
to fair value and goodwill is recorded as in any combination accounted for as a
purchase. Without a change in control, the transaction is more of a recapitalization,
and the target firm's book values are carried forward.

Amtrol, Inc. accounted for its LBO as a change in control:

> The Merger was accounted for as a purchase transaction effective as of November 13,
> 1996, in accordance with Accounting Principles Board Opinion No. 16, Business
> Combinations, and EITF Issue No. 88–16, Basis in Leveraged Buyout Transactions
> and, accordingly, the consolidated financial statements for the periods subsequent to
> November 12, 1996 reflect the purchase price, including transaction costs, allocated
> to tangible and intangible assets acquired and liabilities assumed, based on their es-
> timated fair values as of November 12, 1996. The excess of the purchase price over
> the fair value of net assets acquired has been allocated to goodwill.[38]

In contrast, the LBO of Apex PC Solutions, Inc. did not entail a change in control.
As described by the company, there was no basis for revising asset and liability
valuations to fair value:

The new investors did not acquire substantially all of the shares representing voting interests of the Company. The voting interests of new investors represented 50% of the voting interests of the Company after the leveraged recapitalization. Accordingly, the transaction has been recorded as a recapitalization with amounts distributed to the selling shareholder recorded as charges to shareholders' equity (deficit). The transaction did not result in a new basis of accounting for the assets and liabilities of the Company because it would not have been appropriate under EITF Issue No. 88–16, "Basis in Leveraged Buyout Transactions" or pushdown accounting guidelines of the Securities and Exchange Commission ("SEC").[39]

Financial Quality Implications of Purchase Accounting

Because it entails the revaluation of assets, recognition of goodwill, and the amortization of these revalued amounts, purchase accounting has very real implications for both earnings and position quality.

Amortization of goodwill and other intangibles recognized in a purchase transaction are noncash expenses. As they reduce earnings without reducing cash flow, such charges enhance earnings quality on the cash dimension. Operating cash flows exceed reported earnings. Also enhancing earnings quality on the cash dimension are other purchase-related noncash charges such as acquistion-related asset write-downs and purchased in-process R&D. Because of their nonrecurring nature, these latter charges also enhance earnings quality on the persistence dimension.

Because purchase accounting results in a revaluation of the acquired firm's assets and liabilities to fair value, it tends to eliminate any precombination enhancement of position quality. Undervalued assets and overvalued liabilities are now reported at fair value. Moreover, any goodwill recognized in a purchase transaction will impair position quality because of its limited recoverable value in the event of financial difficulties. Negative goodwill, if any, which is reported as a deferred credit along with other of the acquiring firm's liabilities, will enhance position quality because it implies that valuable assets have been written off.

Pooling-of-Interests Accounting

By the time this book appears in print, pooling-of-interests accounting may no longer be part of U.S. generally accepted accounting principles (GAAP). However, it will continue to occupy a prominent place in the history of financial reporting in this country. For years, the SEC has decried the fact that upwards of 40 percent of the time of the chief accountant's staff was consumed dealing with companies seeking to have transactions cleared for pooling-of-interests treatment. In addition, even when it is removed from GAAP, thousands of transactions that have been accounted for on a pooling basis will continue to affect the statements of U.S. companies. Undervaluations of assets in business combinations structured as poolings, as opposed to purchases, will continue to affect assessments of position quality. Also, the absence of asset revaluations and the recognition of goodwill

will continue for decades to cause earnings of combinations that received pooling treatment to be far higher than they would have been if they had been accounted for as purchases.

A business combination that is accounted for as a pooling of interests does not entail, for accounting purposes, the purchase of one company by another. Instead, the transaction is viewed as a comingling of the ownership interests of the combining corporations. Because there has been no purchase of one company by another, there is no basis for establishing new acquisition costs on that date. Rather, the net assets of the acquired company are recorded by the firm making the acquisition at the book values of the firm being acquired. Moreover, the net assets of the acquiring firm are left at book value. In maintaining and accounting for the transaction at book value, any costs incurred to effect the combination are expensed as incurred.

Requirements for Pooling-of-Interests Accounting

There are 12 criteria that must be met by the terms of a business combination for the transaction to be accounted for as a pooling of interests. In fact, if a business combination, regardless of its legal form, meets all 12 criteria, it must be accounted for as a pooling of interests. If not, it must be treated as a purchase transaction. The 12 pooling criteria, grouped into three broad categories, are identified below.

A. *Attributes of the combining entities.* In a pooling of interests, independent ownerships are combined to continue previously separate operations.

1. Each of the combining companies is autonomous and has not been a subsidiary or division of another corporation within two years before the plan of combination is initiated. A new company meets this criterion as long as it is not a successor to a nonindependent company.

2. Each of the combining companies is independent of the other combining companies. No more than 10 percent of any combining company is held by any other combining company(ies).

B. *Nature of combining transaction.* The combination is effected through an exchange of stock.

3. The combination is effected in a single transaction or is completed in accordance with a specific plan within one year after the plan is initiated.

4. A corporation offers and issues only common stock with rights identical to those of the majority of its outstanding voting common stock in exchange for substantially all of the voting common stock interests of another company at the date the plan of combination is consummated. Substantially all is interpreted to mean at least 90 percent of the outstanding shares. Cash may be used for partial shares.

5. None of the combining companies changes the equity interest of the voting common stock in contemplation of effecting the combination either within

two years before the plan of combination is initiated or between the dates the combination is initiated and consummated. Changes in contemplation of effecting the combination may include distributions to stockholders and additional issues, exchanges, and retirements of securities.

6. Each of the combining companies reacquires shares of voting common stock only for purposes other than business combinations, and no company reacquires more than a normal number of shares, as determined by past acquisitions, between the dates the plan of combination is initiated and consummated.

7. The ratio of the interest of an individual common stockholder to those of other common stockholders in a combining company remains the same as a result of the exchange of stock to effect the combination.

8. The voting rights to which the common stock ownership interests in the resulting combined corporation are entitled are exercisable by the stockholders. The stockholders are neither deprived of nor restricted in exercising those rights for a period.

9. The combination is resolved at the date the plan is consummated and no provisions of the plan relating to the issue of securities or other consideration are pending.

C. *Absence of planned transactions.*

10. The combined corporation does not agree directly or indirectly to retire or reacquire all or part of the common stock issued to effect the combination.

11. The combined corporation does not enter into other financial arrangements for the benefit of the former stockholders of a combining company, such as a guaranty of loans secured by stock issued in the combination, which in effect negates the exchange of equity securities.

12. The combined corporation does not intend or plan to dispose of a significant part of the assets of the combining companies within two years after the combination other than disposals in the ordinary course of business of the formerly separate companies and to eliminate duplicate facilities or excess capacity.[40]

Examples of Pooling-of-Interests Combinations

The announced combination of Crestar Financial Corporation with SunTrust Banks, Inc. is one example of a planned pooling-of-interests transaction. In a press release, the following information was provided:

ATLANTA (Dow Jones)—SunTrust Banks Inc. (STI) signed a definitive agreement to merge with Crestar Financial Corp. (CF) in stock swap valued at $9.5 billion. In a press release Monday, the companies said each Crestar share will be exchanged for

0.96 SunTrust shares. Based on Friday's closing price on SunTrust shares of $87.44 and Crestar's 113.5 million diluted shares outstanding, each Crestar share is valued at $83.94. The merger, which will be accounted for as a pooling-of-interests, is expected to add to SunTrust's earnings beginning in 1999. Following the merger, Crestar will be a unit of SunTrust but will retain its current name and management.[41]

As described, this transaction appears to be a nonstatutory merger. SunTrust is acquiring the stock and control of Crestar by issuing SunTrust shares. Crestar will not be legally liquidated, but will be operated as a subsidiary of SunTrust. The companies claim that the transaction will be afforded pooling treatment. Apparently, in addition to the use of stock to effect the deal, the other criteria for pooling-of-interests treatment will be fulfilled.

The acquisition of Chrysler Corporation by Daimler-Benz AG is another example of a pooling of interests. Some of the terms of the transaction were detailed in the following newspaper article:

NEW YORK—(Dow Jones)—Shareholders of Chrysler Corp. and Germany's Daimler-Benz AG Friday approved the auto makers' planned $38 billion merger but the meetings raised some thorny issues, such as executive pay, Daimler's World War II record, fears that Daimler's Mercedes brand will disappear in the combined company and Chrysler holders' rights in the new company. Both votes were overwhelmingly in favor of the deal. Chrysler shareholders who voted in favor of the deal represented 97.5% of the shares voted. According to Daimler, some 350 million shares were cast in favor of the deal while only 367,000 voted against. The companies hope to complete the deal by early December. Daimler Chairman Juergen Schrempp said the real work starts now—in selling the deal to shareholders. At the Daimler meeting in Stuttgart, Germany, executives endured an almost 12-hour question and answer marathon. Still, some shareholders will likely lodge a complaint against Daimler under German law because they think Daimler didn't give them enough time to address their questions.

During the stock swap period from Sept. 24 to Oct. 23, Daimler hopes that 90% of all shares will be swapped for shares in the new DaimlerChrysler AG. Daimler will need the 90% mark in order to take advantage of the "pooling of interests" practice under U.S. accounting. Pooling would allow the new company to keep a 54 billion mark ($31.82 billion) goodwill charge off its balance sheet. The charge would lower earnings. If less than 75% agree to the swap, Daimler and Chrysler say they will cancel the whole deal.[42]

The combination, as described, is a consolidation. Stock in a new company, DaimlerChrysler AG, is to be swapped for the shares of Chrysler and Daimler-Benz AG. Whether the combining companies will be liquidated or operated as separate entity/subsidiaries is unclear.

The article makes clear the need for 90 percent of the combining shareholders to agree to the deal as a condition for pooling treatment. In fact, according to the information provided, the transaction would likely be scuttled if sufficient shareholders did not agree to accept the offered shares.

One interesting aside to the Daimler-Benz and Chrysler combination was the need for Chrysler to reissue 28 million shares that had been repurchased in a two-year period prior to the announcement of the deal with Daimler-Benz. Those share repurchases were sufficient to violate one of the 12 pooling-of-interests criteria. By reissuing the shares, the Company was able to fulfill the pooling criteria.

Other Accounting and Reporting Issues Related to Pooling of Interests

Because a pooling of interests is accounted for at book value, there is no revaluation of the net assets of the acquired firm. Moreover, there is neither goodwill nor negative goodwill recorded. The financial statements of the two companies are effectively combined, with earnings for the year of the combination reflecting the results of the combining firms for the entire year. Retained earnings of the acquired firm are carried forward so that combined retained earnings will equal the sum of the retained earnings of the combining companies. Prior-year financial statements are restated to give the appearance that the combination had been in effect since the earliest year presented.

The acquisition of Bugaboo Steak House, Inc. by Rare Hospitality International, Inc. was accounted for as a pooling of interests. The manner in which the transaction was effected and accounted for were consistent with the points raised here:

> On September 13, 1996, the Company exchanged approximately 3,179,000 newly issued shares of its common stock for all of the outstanding shares of Bugaboo Creek Steak House, Inc. and certain affiliated entities (2,939,000 shares for Bugaboo Creek Steak House, Inc. and 240,000 shares for other nonpublic affiliated enterprises). Bugaboo Creek Steak House, Inc. operated 14 Bugaboo Creek Steak Houses and five The Capital Grille restaurants, and managed three specialty concept restaurants at the time of the merger.
>
> The exchange of shares was accounted for as a pooling of interests, and accordingly, the accompanying consolidated financial statements have been restated to include the accounts and operations of Bugaboo Creek for all periods presented.[43]

Corporate Spinoffs

Corporate spinoffs can be thought of as a reverse pooling of interests. In a spinoff, a company separates a portion of its business into a newly created subsidiary and distributes shares in that entity to its shareholders as a dividend. The assets and liabilities of the subsidiary that is spun off are removed from the balance sheet of the parent company at book value. They are reported at this same amount on the balance sheet of the entity spun off. Shareholders' equity of the parent company is reduced by the net assets distributed.

In effect, in a spinoff, the parent company pays a dividend to its shareholders. But because that dividend is in the form of stock in an entity owned by the parent, it is nontaxable to the receiving shareholders.

General Motors Corporation accounted for the spin-off of Electronic Data Systems Corporation in this way. The company described the transaction as follows:

On June 7, 1996, General Motors split-off Electronic Data Systems Corporation (EDS) to General Motors Class E stockholders on a tax-free basis for U.S. federal income tax purposes. Under the terms of the split-off, each share of General Motors former Class E common stock was exchanged for one share of EDS common stock.[44]

Financial Quality Implications of Pooling-of-Interests Accounting

When business combinations are accounted for as poolings of interests, assets and liabilities are left at book value. Moreover, goodwill is not recognized. Thus, the accounting method has less of an impact on earnings and position quality than does accounting for business combinations using the purchase method.

Without amortization of goodwill and other intangibles, earnings quality on the cash dimension is not impacted as it was with purchase accounting. There are no acquisition-related special charges such as in-process R&D. However, any costs incurred to effect a pooling-of-interests transaction—attorneys' and accountants' fees, and the fees of underwriters—are expensed as incurred. These costs are nonrecurring and would enhance earnings quality on the persistence dimension.

Because assets and liabilities remain at book value in a pooling of interests, precombination position quality is not affected by the combination. Position quality will be enhanced to the extent that assets are undervalued or liabilities are overvalued.

Summary of Purchase and Pooling-of-Interests Methods

Exhibit 9.5 summarizes key features of accounting for business combinations using the purchase and pooling-of-interests methods.

Given the need to record and amortize goodwill and other intangibles in a purchase transaction, many companies undertaking business combinations seek pooling-of-interests treatment. However, because of the difficulty in fulfilling the twelve pooling-of-interests criteria, such accounting treatment is often difficult to obtain.

As discussed earlier, the FASB plans to eliminate the pooling-of-interest accounting method. There is a growing interest in coordinating the accounting for business combinations with the rest of the world where pooling-of-interest accounting is not permitted. Moreover, by eliminating or strongly restricting poolings, financial results will be more comparable across companies and potential overpayments in acquisitions will not be as readily hidden.

Research Results: Purchase versus Pooling of Interests

Several studies have examined the stock market's reaction to the use of the purchase and pooling-of-interests methods of accounting for business combinations. To control for the tax implications of these business combinations, studies in this area typically look at all-stock transactions that are considered to be tax-free reorganizations under the Internal Revenue Code. As a result, the purchase versus

Exhibit 9.5.   Key Features of Purchase and Pooling-of-Interests Methods

Purchase Accounting
1. Most common acquisition accounting treatment.
2. Purchase price can be paid with any currency—cash, stock, debt, or any combination thereof.
3. Actual cost of the acquisition is recorded.
4. Assets and liabilities of acquired company are combined at fair value.
5. Goodwill is typically recorded and occasionally negative goodwill is recorded.
6. Amortization of revalued assets and goodwill reduce earnings.
7. Retained earnings of the acquired company at the date of acquisition are not included in combined retained earnings.
8. Earnings of the acquired firm are included from the date of acquisition.
9. Previous-year financial statements are not restated.
10. Prior-year *pro forma* results of the combined entity are provided.

Pooling-of-Interests Accounting
1. Stringent criteria limit use.
2. Purchase price must be paid in common stock and at least 90% of outstanding shares must be acquired.
3. Actual cost of the acquisition is suppressed and is not recorded.
4. Assets and liabilities of acquired company are combined at book value.
5. Neither goodwill nor negative goodwill are recorded.
6. No amortization of revalued assets or goodwill to reduce future earnings.
7. Retained earnings of the acquired company at the date of acquisition are included in combined retained earnings.
8. Earnings of the acquired firm are included from the beginning of the acquisition year.
9. Previous-year financial statements are restated.
10. No prior-year *pro forma* results.

pooling-of-interests business combinations differ on the amounts of bid premiums paid and postcombination measures of net income while controlling for postcombination after-tax cash flows to acquiring-firm shareholders.

Hong, Kaplan, and Mandelker examined monthly price movements around the effective date for a sample of 122 pooling-of-interests and 37 purchase-method mergers.[45] All of their sample transactions consisted of mergers in which the market value of the securities issued exceeded the book value of the net assets acquired. As a result, firms using the purchase method reported higher depreciation and amortization charges and, accordingly, lower net income than firms using the pooling-of-interests method. Interestingly, the purchase-method firms experienced significant positive abnormal returns in the 12 months surrounding the effective date of their mergers. The pooling firms experienced no such positive return. However, as was noted in a later study by Davis, the use of the effective date and not the announcement date to center the statistical test and a small and potentially time period–sensitive sample of purchase-method firms may have affected Hong and colleagues' results.

In his study, Davis addressed these shortcomings and confirmed the findings of Hong, Kaplan, and Mandelker.[46] Davis also found positive abnormal returns for the purchase-method firms. This was in a time period leading up to merger announcement dates. Although the pooling firms also experienced positive abnormal returns, those returns were not statistically significant. On closer examination, he found evidence to indicate that the poolings entailed higher bid premiums, implying lower returns to the acquiring firms. This finding confirms results of a study by Robinson and Shane, which found that business combinations employing the pooling-of-interests method entailed higher bid premiums than similar combinations accounted for as purchases.[47] Vincent also looked at valuation differences between purchase and pooling-of-interests business combinations.[48] In her study, however, the focus was on the period following the acquisition rather than on the acquisition announcement or effective dates. The author's results indicate that pooling firms enjoy an equity valuation advantage over purchase firms. However, she was unable to attribute this relative advantage to differences in financial reporting and concluded that inherent differences in the types of firms involved in poolings and purchase transactions may be a more likely explanatory factor.

CONSOLIDATED FINANCIAL STATEMENTS

When a business combination results in a parent–subsidiary relationship, such as in a nonstatutory merger or consolidation, accounting steps must be taken to combine the companies under common control into a single reporting entity. As noted earlier, these accounting steps are known as an accounting consolidation or worksheet consolidation. When completed, the combined companies will appear to be a single entity.

Consolidating Worksheet

An accounting or worksheet consolidation is conducted on a consolidating worksheet. The worksheet has columns for each of the combining companies, including the parent. Financial statement accounts are summed horizontally across the worksheet and adjusted for intercompany stock ownership and intercompany transactions. The process of combining the entities must take into account the method used to effect the original business combination, that is, whether it was a purchase or a pooling of interests.

A simple example is used to demonstrate how a consolidating worksheet is completed under both the purchase and pooling methods. In both cases, the same business combination terms are used. It is assumed that Pluto Corporation (the

Exhibit 9.6. Preacquisition Financial Statement Data, Pluto Corp. and Saturn, Inc., as of December 31, 2000 (Thousands of Dollars, Except Per-Share Amounts)

	Pluto Corp.		Saturn, Inc.	
	Book Value	Fair Value	Book Value	Fair Value
Tangible assets	$20,000	$25,000	$10,000	$12,000
Liabilities	$12,000	$12,000	$4,000	$3,000
Common stock ($1 par)	$1,000		$1,000	
Retained earnings	$7,000		$5,000	
Net assets	$8,000	$13,000	$6,000	$9,000
Earnings (year-to-date)	$1,000		$1,000	
Market price per share	$25		$10	
Earnings per share	$1.00		$1.00	
Price-to-earnings (P/E) ratio	25/1		10/1	

parent company) acquires 90 percent of the outstanding shares of Saturn, Inc. (the subsidiary) on December 31, 2000, by issuing one share of Pluto for every two shares of Saturn acquired. Because Saturn had 1,000 shares outstanding prior to the acquisition, Pluto issued 450 shares to acquire its 900 Saturn shares. Preacquisition financial statement data for the two companies are provided in Exhibit 9.6.

The Purchase Method and the Date-of-Acquisition Consolidating Worksheet

If the purchase method had been used to account for the acquisition, Pluto would have recorded its investment in Saturn at the fair value of the shares issued. Using Pluto's $25 share price, that would entail recording the investment at $11,250,000 ($25 × 450 shares). In recording the shares issued in making the investment, Pluto's common stock would be increased for $450,000 ($1 par per share × the 450 shares issued), and additional paid-in-capital would have been increased for the balance of $10,800,000 ($11,250,000 − $450,000). The purchase method consolidating worksheet is provided in Exhibit 9.7.

In completing the purchase-method date-of-acquisition consolidating worksheet, the two companies—Pluto, the parent company; Saturn, the subsidiary—are reported as if they are a single entity. Their assets and liabilities are combined and Pluto's share of the assets and liabilities of Saturn are revalued to fair value. Goodwill is recorded. Consolidated shareholders' equity reflects the equity of Pluto immediately after the acquisition of Saturn. Reported as minority interest is the portion of the shareholders' equity of Saturn owned by third-party shareholders and not by Pluto. As the business combination was effected at the end of the year, earnings for the combined entity for the year ended December 31, 2000, would be $1,000—Pluto's separate-company earnings.

Exhibit 9.7 Purchase-Method Date-of-Acquisition Consolidating Worksheet
(Thousands of Dollars)

	Pluto	Saturn	Adjustments Eliminations	Consolidated
Tangible assets	$20,000	$10,000	(b) 1,800	$31,800
Investment in Saturn	11,250		(a) (5,400)	
			(b) (5,850)	
Goodwill			(b) 3,150	3,150
Total	$31,250	$10,000		$34,950
Liabilities	12,000	4,000	(b) (900)	15,100
Common stock	1,450	1,000	(a) (900)	
			(c) (100)	1,450
Retained earnings	7,000	5,000	(a) (4,500)	7,000
			(c) (500)	
Additional paid-in capital	10,800			10,800
Minority (noncontrolling) interest in equity			(c) 600	600
Total	$31,250	$10,000	0	$34,950

Description of adjustments and eliminations:

(a) Eliminates the 90% of book value of Saturn's shareholders' equity owned by Pluto and the book value component of the Investment in Saturn account:

Book value of Saturn's common stock	$900	(90% × $1,000)
Book value of Saturn's retained earnings	+4,500	(90% × $5,000)
Book value component of Investment in Saturn	$5,400	

(b) Reclassifies the excess of the purchase price paid for the shares in Saturn over their book value from the Investment in Saturn account to a revaluation of Saturn's identifiable assets and liabilities and goodwill:

Investment in Saturn at fair value of consideration given	$11,250	(450 shares × $25)
Book value component of Investment in Saturn	−5,400	(90% × $6,000)
Excess of purchase price paid over book value	$5,850	

(continued)

Exhibit 9.7   (continued) Purchase-Method Date-of-Acquisition Consolidating Worksheet (Thousands of Dollars)

This $5,850 excess can be attributed to a revaluation of Saturn's assets in the amount of $1,800, a revaluation of Saturn's liabilities in the amount of $900, and to goodwill in the amount of $3,150, calculated as follows:

Fair value of Saturn's identifiable assets	$12,000	(Exhibit 9.6)
Book value of Saturn's identifiable assets	− 10,000	(Exhibit 9.6)
Excess of fair value over book value of identifiable assets	$2,000	
Pluto's share of excess of fair value over book value of identifiable assets	$1,800	(90% × $2,000)
Fair value of Saturn's identifiable liabilities	$3,000	(Exhibit 9.6)
Book value of Saturn's identifiable liabilities	− 4,000	(Exhibit 9.6)
Excess of book value over fair value of identifiable liabilities	$1,000	
Pluto's share of excess of book value over fair value of identifiable liabilities	$900	(90% × $1,000)
Investment in Saturn at fair value of consideration given	$11,250	(450 shares × $25)
Fair value of Saturn's identifiable net assets	− 8,100	(90% × $9,000)
Goodwill	$3,150	

(c) Reclassifies as minority (noncontrolling) interest the 10% of book value of shareholders' equity of Saturn not owned by Pluto.

Book value of Saturn's common stock not owned by Pluto	$100	(10% × $1,000)
Book value of Saturn's retained earnings not owned by Pluto	+ 500	(10% × $5,000)
Minority interest	$600	

The Pooling-of-Interests Method and the Date-of-Acquisition Consolidating Worksheet

If the pooling-of-interests method had been used to account for the acquisition, Pluto would have recorded its investment in Saturn at the book value of the shareholders' equity received. The book value of Saturn's shareholders' equity on the date of acquisition was $6 million, consisting of $1 million common stock and $5 million retained earnings. Pluto's 90 percent share of this book value is $5.4 million. In recording the shares issued in making the investment, Pluto's common stock would be increased for $450,000 ($1 par per share times the 450 shares issued), retained earnings would be increased for $4.5 million (Saturn's

Exhibit 9.8. Pooling-of-Interests Method Date-of-Acquisition Consolidating
Worksheet (Thousands of Dollars)

	Pluto	Saturn	Adjustments Eliminations	Consolidated
Tangible assets	$20,000	$10,000		$30,000
Investment in Saturn	5,400		(a) (5,400)	
Total	$25,400	$10,000		$30,000
Liabilities	12,000	4,000		16,000
Common stock	1,450	1,000	(a) (900)	
			(b) (100)	1,450
Retained earnings	11,500	5,000	(a) (4,500)	
			(c) (500)	11,500
Additional paid-in capital	450			450
Minority (noncontrolling) interest in equity			(c) 600	600
Total	$25,400	$10,000	0	$30,000

Description of adjustments and eliminations:

(a) Eliminates the 90% of book value of Saturn's shareholders' equity owned by Pluto
and the book value component of the Investment in Saturn account:

Book value of Saturn's common stock	$900	(90% × $1,000)
Book value of Saturn's retained earnings	+4,500	(90% × $5,000)
Book value component of Investment in Saturn	$5,400	

Because the Investment in Saturn account was recorded at Saturn's book value, this
adjustment eliminates the entire investment balance. There is no revaluation of
identifiable assets, identifiable liabilities, or goodwill to be reclassified.

(b) Reclassifies as minority interest the 10 percent of book value of shareholders' equity
of Saturn not owned by Pluto.

Book value of Saturn's common stock not owned by Pluto	$100	(10% × $1,000)
Book value of Saturn's retained earnings not owned by Pluto	+500	(10% × $5,000)
Minority (noncontrolling) interest	$ 600	

retained earnings of $5 million × Pluto's 90 percent share), and additional paid-
in capital would have been increased for the balance of $450,000 ($5.4 million
− $450,000 − $4,500,000). The pooling-of-interests method consolidating worksheet is provided in Exhibit 9.8.

In completing the pooling-of-interests method date-of-acquisition consolidating worksheet, the two companies—Pluto, the parent company; Saturn, the

subsidiary—are again reported as if they are a single entity. However, in the pooling-of-interests consolidation, the two companies' assets are combined at book value. No goodwill is recorded. Consolidated shareholders' equity reflects the equity of Pluto as it existed immediately after the acquisition of Saturn. Reported as minority or noncontrolling interest is the portion of the shareholders' equity of Saturn owned by third-party shareholders and not by Pluto. Earnings for the combined entity for the year ended December 31, 2000, would be $1,900, the combined results for the two companies as though they had been combined for the entire year presented, less the minority (noncontrolling) interests' 10 percent share of Saturn's net income. More is said about minority or noncontrolling interests later in this chapter.

Eliminating Intercompany Transaction Balances

The date-of-acquisition consolidating worksheets focused on consolidating the balance sheets of the combining companies. As time passes and combining companies transact with one another, intercompany transactions must also be eliminated. These eliminations can involve both the balance sheet and the income statement. Moreover, the eliminations are largely the same whether the business combination was accounted for as a purchase or as a pooling of interests.

For example, Saturn, the subsidiary company, might sell inventory at a markup to Pluto, the parent. On its separate-company financial statements, Saturn would record sales revenue and cost of goods sold, while reducing inventory for the cost of inventory sold. Pluto would, on its separate-company financial statements, record the purchase of inventory at an inflated purchase price—a price consisting of Saturn's cost plus the markup. The consolidating worksheet would need to reduce consolidated sales revenue and cost of goods sold for the amounts reported by Saturn on the intercompany transaction. Any gross profit recorded by Saturn on the sale, which had not been confirmed by Pluto's sale of the inventory to a third party, would also need to be eliminated from the consolidated inventory balance.

As another example, Pluto might make an intercompany loan to Saturn. On its separate-company financial statements, Pluto would report a loan receivable and interest income, and Saturn would report a loan payable and interest expense. All of the effects of the intercompany loan would need to be eliminated on a consolidating worksheet. The loan receivable would be eliminated against the loan payable while the interest income would be eliminated against the interest expense. The end result is to report the combined entity's financial results as though no such transaction took place.

There are numerous examples of other intercompany transactions that might be entered into. Generally, entities under common control cannot report increased revenues, expenses, assets, or liabilities as a result of transacting with one another. The purpose of the consolidating worksheet is to remove the effects of such transactions.

Consolidated Financial Statements versus the Equity Method

The equity method of accounting for investments, used when the investing company has significant influence but not control over the operating and financial policies of the investee, can be considered a one-line consolidation—one line to consolidate the balance sheet and one line to consolidate the income statement. On the balance sheet, the investor nets its share of all of the assets and liabilities of the investee into a single amount. That amount, assuming no purchase premium on the acquistion, equals the investor's share of the investee's net assets (i.e., investee's shareholders' equity). This balance is reported on the investor's balance sheet as the investment in the subsidiary. The investor also nets all of the investee's revenues and expenses. The investor's share of this net amount, which is the investor's share of the investee's net income, is reported on the investor's income statement as equity income.

Because the investor records its share of investee net income, the investor's net income and shareholders' equity under the equity method are no different from a full consolidation of the investee once the portion of the investee's net income attributable to minority (noncontrolling) interests is excluded. What is different under the equity method versus full consolidation is the amount of detail added to the financial statements. On the balance sheet, full consolidation replaces a single investment account with the detail of all of the assets and liabilities of the investee. On the income statement, full consolidation replaces equity-method income with the detail of the investee's revenues and expenses.

As an example, as supplemental information to its 1996 financial statements, DIMON, Inc. provides separate financial statements for the parent company and its subsidiaries in a combining, consolidation worksheet format. On the parent company's balance sheet, the subsidiaries are reported as Investment in consolidated subsidiaries in the amount of $288,533,000. That balance sheet reports total assets of $541,652,000, total liabilities of $225,804,000, and shareholders' equity of $315,848,000. The consolidated balance sheet reports no investment in consolidated subsidiaries, total assets of $1,020,014,000, and total liabilities of $704,166,000. Shareholders' equity is unchanged from the parent-company-only amount of $315,848,000. On the supplemental consolidating income statement, the parent company reports sales and other operating revenues of $10,541,000, and a separate line for equity in loss of subsidiary companies in the amount of $13,344,000. A net loss of $30,165,000 is reported. On the consolidated income statement, Sales and other operating revenues are reported at $1,941,188,000 and no equity in loss of subsidiary companies. The consolidated net loss remains unchanged at $30,165,000.[49]

While net income and shareholders' equity are the same under full consolidation and the equity method, the detail added by consolidation alters some measures of profitability and leverage of the reporting consolidated entity. For example, consolidation results in an increase in revenues and total assets with no accompanying change in net income. As a result, net profit margin and return on assets are reduced. However, because consolidation does not change shareholders' equity, return on equity is unaffected by consolidation. Measures of financial leverage are increased because consolidation increases reported liabilities with no change in shareholders' equity.

A Closer Look at Minority (Noncontrolling) Interests

In the consolidation worksheet examples provided earlier, Pluto Corporation acquired 90 percent of the outstanding shares of Saturn, Inc. In the consolidation process, Pluto consolidated all of Saturn's assets and liabilities with its own. The portion of net assets of Saturn not owned by Pluto was separated from consolidated shareholders' equity and reported as minority (noncontrolling) interest in equity. That minority (noncontrolling) interest was reported at $600, or 10 percent of the book value of Saturn's net assets.[50]

We are using the terms *minority interest* and *noncontrolling interest* interchangeably. Technically, the term *minority interest* is an appropriate designation for the interests of noncontrolling or third-party shareholders when the controlling shareholder has a majority voting interest. The term *noncontrolling interest* is a broader term, encompassing the interests of noncontrolling or third-party shareholders whether or not the controlling shareholder has a majority voting interest. The FASB prefers the broader designation of noncontrolling interest.

Minority (noncontrolling) interest in equity reflects the portion of shareholders' equity owned by third-party investors, or investors outside the consolidated entity. It represents a valid claim of outsiders on the shareholders' equity of a consolidated subsidiary.

Minority (noncontrolling) interest in equity is typically reported on the balance sheet between liabilities and shareholders' equity. Such reporting reflects a general disagreement on what the claim represents. We have surveyed numerous lenders and financial analysts on whether they consider minority (noncontrolling) interest in equity to be a liability or shareholders' equity. The responses we have received tend to be split rather evenly between the two. If there is a consensus view, it is that for a going concern, minority (noncontrolling) interest in equity is more of an equity claim. It represents a shareholders' claim, even though it is a subsidiary's shareholders' claim. It does not have a scheduled maturity nor does it require the accrual of interest as would a liability.[51] However, for a financially troubled subsidiary, one that may face liquidation, the minority (noncontrolling) interest claim takes on more of the characteristics of a liability. It is a valid claim on the net assets of the subsidiary and must be settled upon liquidation of that entity. If viewed as a liability, however, it is certainly a subordinated claim—subordinated to the claims of all other liabilities.

Minority (noncontrolling) interest in income is an attribution to third-party shareholders of their share of a consolidated subsidiary's net income. It is reported on a consolidated income statement as a reduction in income, much like an expense. The parent company has consolidated all of the revenues and expenses of

Exhibit 9.9. Minority (Noncontrolling) Interest in Income Presented
in Summarized Consolidated Statement of Income and Statement of Cash
Flows: Repro-Med Systems, Inc.: Year Ended February 28, 1998

Summarized Consolidated Statement of Income	
Sales	$2,225,342
Costs and expenses	2,594,473
(Loss) from operations	(369,131)
Nonoperating (expense)	(66,699)
(Loss) before minority interest	(435,830)
Minority interest in (income) of subsidiary	(161,669)
(Loss) before income taxes	(597,499)
(Benefit for income taxes)	(307,315)
Net (loss) after income taxes	$(290,184)

Summarized Consolidated Statement of Cash Flows—Operating Section	
Net (loss)	$(290,184)
Adjustment to reconcile net (loss) to net cash provided by operating activities:	
Income of minority interests	161,669
Depreciation and amortization	134,747
Other changes in working capital accounts	(331,944)
Net cash (consumed) by operating activities	$(325,712)

Source: Repro-Med Systems, Inc., Form 10-K annual report to Securities and Exchange Commission
(February 1998), pp. 41–42.

the subsidiary, even though the subsidiary is not wholly owned. The portion of
net income of the subsidiary not owned by the parent company is subtracted from
consolidated net income.[52] In a similar fashion, because it involves an attribution
of their share of a subsidiary's loss, minority (noncontrolling) interest in loss
would be added to consolidated net income.

Continuing our earlier consolidation example, though ignoring the income-
reducing effects due to amortization of goodwill and asset revaluations in the
purchase example, assume that in the year ended December 31, 2001, Saturn, Inc.
reported revenues of $3,000, expenses of $1,800, and net income of $1,200.
Pluto's 90 percent share of Saturn's earnings would be $1,080. Pluto would con-
solidate all of the revenues and expenses of Pluto, which adds $1,200 to consoli-
dated earnings. Then, on its consolidated income statement, Pluto would subtract
10 percent of Saturn's net income, or $120, reducing its share of Saturn's net
income to $1,080.

Minority (noncontrolling) interest in income or loss does not involve cash
payments or receipts. The only cash flow involved is the payment of a dividend
by a consolidated subsidiary to the minority shareholders. As such, on an indirect-

method cash flow statement, minority (noncontrolling) interest in income is added back to net income, while minority (noncontrolling) interest in loss is subtracted from net income in calculating operating cash flow. Dividends paid to minority or noncontrolling shareholders, if any, are reported in the financing section of the cash flow statement. More is said about the cash flow statement in Chapter Thirteen.

Repro-Med Systems, Inc., owns 58.3 percent of its consolidated subsidiary, Gamogen, Inc. A summarized consolidated income statement and cash flow statement for the company for the year ended February 28, 1998, are provided in Exhibit 9.9.

In reviewing Exhibit 9.9, it can be seen that Repro-Med's minority (noncontrolling) interest in income of $161,669 is subtracted from consolidated net income. The purpose is to assign to the minority (noncontrolling) shareholders their share of the subsidiary's net income. Then, because minority (noncontrolling) interest in income is a noncash reduction in earnings, it is added back to net income in deriving operating cash flow.

SPECIAL TOPICS IN ACCOUNTING FOR BUSINESS COMBINATIONS

Two topics that are closely related to business combinations are financial reporting for business segments and the specialized topic of push-down accounting. Accounting guidelines for business-segment reporting have changed recently. With respect to push-down accounting, little in the way of formal accounting guidelines has been established.

Segment Reporting

Business combinations result in the loss of financial statement detail. The components of financial position and performance are lost as companies are combined and reported as one. The purpose of segment reporting is to release hidden data from consolidated financial information, providing more insight into differing levels of profitability, growth, and risk possessed by different business components of a consolidated whole. For example, in the absence of segment data, the higher growth prospects of E. I. DuPont de Nemours and Company's Life Sciences division or the extent of insurance business written by General Electric Company's Specialty Insurance division would potentially be lost from view.

Guidance on segment reporting is provided by SFAS No. 131, "Disclosures about Segments of an Enterprise and Related Information."[53] That standard defines an operating segment as a component of an enterprise:

• That engages in business activities from which it may earn revenues and incur expenses (including revenues and expenses relating to transactions with other components of the same enterprise)

- Whose operating results are regularly reviewed by the enterprise's chief operating decision maker to make decisions about resources to be allocated to the segment and assess its performance
- For which discrete financial information is available[54]

This definition leaves it up to management's judgment to determine operating segment classifications. Though the standard does provide guidelines to assist companies in determining which operating segments are reportable.

Generally, a segment is considered to be reportable if it is significant to the enterprise as a whole. A segment is significant to the enterprise as a whole if one of three quantitative tests is met:

1. Its unaffiliated and intersegment revenue is at least 10 percent of combined revenue of all reported operating segments.
2. The absolute value of its operating profit or loss, consisting of unaffiliated and intersegment revenue less expenses, is at least 10 percent of the greater, in absolute value terms, of the combined operating profits of all segments reporting a profit or the combined operating losses of all segments reporting a loss.
3. Segment assets, which exclude assets held for general corporate use, are at least 10 percent of combined assets of all operating segments.

In addition to these 10 percent tests, the combined unaffiliated revenue of all reportable segments must be at least 75 percent of combined unaffiliated revenue of all operating segments. If this last requirement is not met, additional segments must be designated as reportable until this test is satisfied.

Required segment disclosures consist of the following:

- An explanation of how management identified the enterprise's reportable segments and a description of the types of products and services from which each reportable segment derives its revenue
- Descriptive information on the revenue and expense items included in segment profit and loss, on the determination of segment assets, and on the basis of measurement for each
- A reconciliation of segment amounts to consolidated totals
- An inclusion of segment disclosures in interim financial statements

In addition to these segment disclosures, certain enterprise-wide disclosures are also required. These disclosures include information on revenue generated from external customers for each general category of product or service. However, revenue disclosures by segment will typically fulfill this requirement. Also required is information on revenue from external customers and long-lived assets attributable to domestic and foreign operations. Finally, if the amount of revenue generated by sales to any external customers exceeds 10 percent of consolidated revenue, this must be disclosed together with the segment generating those sales. The segment disclosures provided in the footnotes to the 1998 annual report of Cooper Industries, Inc. and summarized in Exhibit 9.10 provide a good example of new segment-reporting requirements.

The value of segment disclosures for determining corporate earning power can be seen in the detail provided by Cooper Industries displayed in Exhibit 9.10. For example, in reviewing the exhibit, it can be seen that the bulk of the company's revenue and operating earnings growth is derived from its electrical products segment. Revenue and operating earnings for that segment were up 17.3 percent across the two years ended in 1998, versus a decline of 15.0 percent and .9 percent, respectively, for revenue and operating earnings of the tools and hardware segment over that same time frame. However, helping to explain the poor performance of the tools and hardware segment was the disclosed disposition of the Kirsch division in May 1997. The detail provided regarding nonrecurring charges is also helpful in determining earning power. While the company's consolidated income statement discloses nonrecurring charges of $53 million in 1998, it is disclosed in the segment note that the bulk of that charge, $42 million in 1998, was attributable to the electrical products segment.

Push-Down Accounting

Push-down, or new basis accounting, is used to reflect a revaluation of the assets and liabilities of an acquired company based on the price paid by the acquirer. The accounting method comes into effect only when the acquired company reports separately from the parent. The method has no effect on consolidated financial statements. For example, in applying push-down accounting to the separate financial statements of an acquired entity, assets and liabilities would be revalued to fair value as of the acquisition date and goodwill calculated on that date would also be reported.

There is no official accounting guidance for the application of push-down accounting. The FASB carried it on its agenda for many years and has now shelved the topic. The SEC has permitted, and in some instances required, push-down accounting for separately filed financial statements of acquired subsidiaries where the change in control resulted from a 100 percent change in common stock ownership. The method has not been required in instances where the change in ownership was less than 100 percent. Thus, when and how to apply the method remains well within the realm of professional judgment.

An example of push-down accounting is provided in the footnotes to the financial statements of ITC DeltaCom, Inc., formerly DeltaCom, Inc., and a subsidiary of ITC Holding, Inc., a company set up to effect the acquisition of DeltaCom.

Exhibit 9.10. Segment Disclosures: Cooper Industries, Inc., for the Years Ended December 31, 1996, 1997, and 1998 (Millions of Dollars)

Note 7: Industry Segments and Geographic Information

The Company's continuing operations are organized into two segments as follows:

The **Electrical Products** segment manufactures and markets electrical and electronic distribution and circuit protection products and lighting fixtures for use in residential, commercial, and industrial construction, maintenance, and repair; and products for use by utilities and industries for primary power distribution and control.

	1996	1997	1998
Revenues by Destination:			
Domestic	$1,828.9	$1,955.6	$2,145.5
International	578.6	612.7	678.9
	$2,407.5	$2,568.3	$2,824.4
Operating Earnings			
Before Nonrecurring Items[a]	$408.3	$461.6	$479.0
Total Assets	$1,976.0	$2,441.7	$2,473.3
Other Data:			
Sales backlog	$241.9	$249.4	$306.4
Capital expenditures	$79.1	$79.2	$95.9
Number of employees	17,200	19,000	20,400

The **Tools & Hardware** segment produces and markets tools and hardware items for use in residential, commercial, and industrial construction, maintenance, and repair; and for general industrial and consumer use. This segment also manufactured and marketed window treatments through May 30, 1997.

	1996	1997	1998
Revenues by Destination[b]:			
Domestic	$615.8	$527.7	$540.2
International	357.2	319.6	286.6
	$973.0	$847.3	$826.8
Operating Earnings			
Before Nonrecurring Items[a,b]	$113.4	$104.4	$112.4
Total Assets	$787.3	$561.7	$903.8
Other Data:			
Sales backlog	$103.7	$74.2	$78.7
Capital expenditures	$32.7	$37.0	$45.3
Number of employees	9,500	7,000	7,400

[a]The respective 1996, 1997, and 1998 operating earnings amounts exclude nonrecurring charges of $3.0 million, $15.9 million, and $42.6 million for the Electrical Products segment and $2.0 million, $22.5 million, and $8.7 million for the Tools & Hardware segment.

[b]The Tools & Hardware segment includes revenues and operating earnings for the Company's Kirsch division through May 30, 1997. Revenues were $252.9 million and $97.4 million in 1996 and 1997, respectively. Operating earnings before nonrecurring items were $22.0 million and $4.8 million in 1996 and 1997, respectively.

Source: Adapted from Cooper Industries, Inc. annual report, December 1998, p. 33.

On January 29, 1996 (the "Acquisition Date"), DeltaCom was purchased by ITC Holding for total consideration of $71,362,213, including cash acquired of $1,828,121 (the "Acquisition"). The consideration included $65,362,213 in cash and $6,000,000 in common stock of ITC Holding. Simultaneously, ITC Holding refinanced $8,643,384 of DeltaCom's outstanding debt by borrowing against its own line of credit and contributing the proceeds to DeltaCom, which then repaid all of its outstanding debt. The Acquisition was accounted for under the purchase method of accounting, and the purchase accounting entries have been "pushed down" to the Company's financial statements. The purchase price was allocated to the underlying assets purchased and liabilities assumed based on their estimated fair values at the Acquisition Date. The acquisition costs exceeded the fair market value of net tangible assets acquired by $54,645,063, of which $5,464,506 has been allocated to identifiable intangible assets and the remainder has been recorded as goodwill in the accompanying consolidated balance sheets. Amounts recorded in connection with the "pushdown" include the $49,180,557 in goodwill, $5,464,506 in customer base, $74,005,598 in debt related to the Acquisition and debt refinancing, and $6,000,000 in paid-in capital.[55]

SUMMARY

The following are key points for the reader to consider:

- The definition of control is changing from one that employs a strict majority ownership–based measure to one that employs effective control through such measures as a large minority ownership, a majority representation on the board of directors, or contractual arrangements.
- Business combinations can be structured as mergers, where A + B = A, or consolidations, where A + B = C. Statutory business combinations entail legal liquidation of one or more combining entities. Combining entities are not liquidated in nonstatutory combinations, and a consolidating worksheet is needed to combine their financial statements.
- Business combinations are accounted for as either purchases or poolings of interest. A purchase transaction is accounted for at fair value, with goodwill, and in some instances, negative goodwill being recorded. Poolings of interest are accounted for at book value, with no revaluation and no goodwill being recorded.
- Goodwill recorded in a purchase transaction is amortized over its estimated useful life. Currently, that estimated useful life is not to exceed 40 years, though in the future, the maximum amortization period will likely be reduced to 20 years.
- Acquiring companies in purchase transactions often charge to earnings a significant portion of the purchase price as purchased in-process research and development. As a result, the amount of goodwill recorded is reduced. Though in the future, the ability to record an immediate writedown of purchased in-process research and development may be severely restricted should the FASB decide to issue a new standard on this subject.

- The amortization of goodwill and the writedown of purchased in-process research and development typically enhances earnings quality on the cash dimension. A nonrecurring charge from writing down purchased in-process (R&D) enhances earnings quality on the persistence dimension. The revaluation of the acquired company's assets and liabilities to fair value eliminates the existence of either enhanced or diminished position quality for that firm. However, a case can be made that position quality is enhanced by an off-balance-sheet asset (i.e., the purchased in-process R&D).

- Twelve criteria must be met before a business combination can be accounted for as a pooling of interests. One of the more important criteria is that the transaction must be an all-stock deal with only limited amounts of cash. If a business combination does not meet these 12 criteria, it must be accounted for as a purchase transaction.

- Except for nonrecurring charges related to the costs of effecting a business combination, poolings have little effect on earnings quality. Because the balance sheet is not revalued, the existence of either enhanced or diminished position quality of the acquired firm, if any, is maintained under the pooling treatment.

- Because it offers the ability to avoid future charges related to the amortization of goodwill and asset revaluations, the popularity of poolings has increased. Though recent developments indicate that the use of pooling treatment will be severely restricted or eliminated in the near future.

- Minority interest in income reflects the claims of third parties on the earnings of a consolidated subsidiary. It is reported as a reduction from consolidated net income. Minority interest in equity reflects the claims of those same third parties on the equity of a consolidated subsidiary. Reflecting general disagreement on the nature of that claim, it is reported on the balance sheet between liabilities and shareholders' equity.

- Detail is lost when parent and subsidiary companies are consolidated as one. Segment reporting helps restore the information lost in that consolidation and is useful in financial statement analysis.

- Push-down accounting is sometimes used to reflect fair value when the financial statements of a subsidiary are published separately.

GLOSSARY

Business combination   The combining of two or more entities under common control into a single accounting entity.

Consolidating worksheet   An accounting worksheet used to combine two or more entities under common control into a single entity.

Consolidation   A combination of two or more companies where a new entity is created to acquire the combining firms and neither of the combining firms survives the combination. A + B = C.

Control   The ability of an entity to direct the policies and management that guide the ongoing activities of another entity so as to increase the benefits or limit the losses from that other entity's activities.

Goodwill   An intangible asset representing the amount paid, in the acquisition of either significant influence or control of an entity, over and above the fair value of the acquired entity's identifiable net assets.

Leveraged buyout (LBO)   A transaction in which a new shareholder group, often a company's management, acquires the shares of an old shareholder group. Debt is typically used to finance the purchase and the company's own assets often serve as loan collateral.

Merger   A combination of two or more companies with one of the combining firms surviving the combination. $A + B = A$.

Minority (noncontrolling) interest in equity   The interest in the equity of an entity that reflects the portion of shareholders' equity owned by noncontrolling or third-party investors, or investors outside the consolidated entity.

Minority (noncontrolling) interest in income   The interest in the income of an entity that reflects the portion of net income attributed to noncontrolling or third-party investors, or investors outside the consolidated entity.

Negative goodwill   A bargain purchase where the fair value of identifiable net assets acquired in a business combination accounted for as a purchase exceed the purchase price. The discount is first applied toward reducing proportionately the values assigned to noncurrent assets, except for long-term investments. Any remaining negative goodwill is recorded as a deferred credit.

Net assets   Shareholders' equity. Total assets less total liabilities.

Noncontrolling interest   Generally minority interest. However, the term is used to reflect minority shareholder interest when the definition of control is extended beyond a simple majority share ownership interest.

Nonstatutory consolidation   Consolidation in which acquired firms are not liquidated but operate as subsidiaries of the acquiring firm.

Nonstatutory merger   Merger in which acquired firms are not liquidated but operate as subsidiaries of the acquiring firm.

Pooling of interests   A business combination accounted for as a comingling of the ownership interest of combining corporations. The transaction is accounted for at book value. No goodwill is recognized.

Purchase   A business combination where the acquiring firm is viewed as being the purchaser of the acquired firm. Identifiable net assets of the acquired firm are revalued to fair value and goodwill, if any, is recognized.

Push-down accounting   New basis accounting used to reflect a revaluation of the assets and liabilities of an acquired company based on the price paid by an acquirer. Used when an acquired firm issues its own separate financial statements.

Segment   The component of an enterprise that engages in business activities from which it may earn revenue and incur expenses, whose operating results are regularly reviewed by management, and for which discrete financial information is available.

Spin-off   A separate portion of a company's business is formed into a subsidiary, and the shares of that subsidiary are distributed to shareholders in the form of a dividend.

Statutory consolidation   Consolidation that fulfills the legal definition of a consolidation, in which acquired firms are liquidated and cease to exist.

Statutory merger   Merger that fulfills the legal definition of a merger, in which acquired firms are liquidated and cease to exist.

NOTES

1. Proposed Statement of Financial Accounting Standards, "Consolidated Financial Statements: Purpose and Policy" (Norwalk CT: Financial Accounting Standards Board, February 23, 1999), p. 3.

2. *The Wall Street Journal* (July 14, 1998), p. C1.

3. *Ibid.,* April 27, 1998, p. A3.

4. Three key accounting pronouncements that guide accounting for business combinations are as follows: Accounting Research Bulletin No. 51, "Consolidated Financial Statements" (New York: Committee on Accounting Procedure, August 1959); Accounting Principles Board Opinion No. 16, "Business Combinations" (New York: Accounting Principles Board, August 1970); and Accounting Principles Board Opinion No. 17, "Intangible Assets" (New York: Accounting Principles Board, August 1970).

5. Accounting Principles Board Opinion No. 16, "Business Combinations" (New York: Accounting Principles Board, 1970). While this definition would work for any form of business organization, the focus here is on corporations.

6. Accounting Research Bulletin No. 51, "Consolidated Financial Statements" (New York: Committee on Accounting Procedure, 1959), para. 2. The reference here to consolidation is a generic term for business combination.

7. Cendant Corp., annual report, December 1997. Information obtained from Disclosure, Inc., *Compact D/SEC: Corporate Information on Public Companies Filing with the SEC* (Bethesda, MD: Disclosure, Inc., June 1998).

8. Proposed Statement of Financial Accounting Standards "Consolidated Financial Statements: Purpose and Policy" (Norwalk, CT: Financial Accounting Standards Board, February 23, 1999), p. 3.

9. *Ibid.,* p. 4.

10. *Ibid.*

11. *Ibid.,* p. 19.

12. *Ibid.,* p. 7. The FASB notes that a minority voting interest is large when it exceeds 50 percent of the votes typically cast in a corporation's election of directors. As an example, if typically only 60 percent of the eligible votes are cast in elections of directors, a minority holding of 35 percent would be deemed large; however, that holding would not be deemed large if typically 80 percent of the eligible votes are cast.

13. *Ibid.*

14. At December 31, 1997, combination would add Coca-Cola Enterprises' assets of $17,283,000,000, which is net of Coca-Cola's investment account balance to Coke's assets

of $16,490,000,000 and add Coca-Cola Enterprises' liabilities of $15,705,000,000 to Coke's liabilities of $9,629,000,000.

15. For 1997, combination would add Coca-Cola Enterprise' revenues of $11,278,000,000 to Coke's revenues of $18,868,000,000. Prior to combination, Coke's net income was $4,129,000 for a net profit margin of 22 percent. On a combined basis, revenues would be $30,146,000,000. Combination of two companies to replace equity method accounting does not alter net income. With net income unchanged, the net profit margin would be approximately 14 percent.

16. *The Wall Street Journal* (March 3, 1999), p. C12.

17. Arkansas Best Corp., annual report, December 1997, p. 23.

18. Fulton Financial Corp., Form 10-K annual report to the Securities and Exchange Commission (December 1997), p. 22.

19. *Ibid.*

20. Rare Hospitality International, Inc., Form 10-K annual report to the Securities and Exchange Commission (December 1996), p. 39.

21. WorldCom, Inc. Form 8-K report to the Securities and Exchange Commission (November 9, 1997), p. 4.

22. MicroFrame, Inc., annual report on Form 10-K to the Securities and Exchange Commission (March 1998), p. F-20.

23. Mother's Work, Inc., annual report, September 1997. Information obtained from Disclosure, Inc. *Compact D/SEC: Corporate Information on Public Companies Filing with the SEC* (Bethesda, MD: Disclosure, Inc., September 1998).

24. SFAS No. 2, "Accounting for Research and Development Costs" (Stamford, CT: Financial Accounting Standards Board, October 1974).

25. Cisco Systems, Inc., annual report, July 1997. Information obtained from Disclosure, Inc. *Compact D/SEC: Corporate Information on Public Companies Filing with the SEC* (Bethesda, MD: Disclosure, Inc., September 1998).

26. Brake Headquarters USA, Inc., annual report, December 1997. Information obtained from Disclosure, Inc. *Compact D/SEC: Corporate Information on Public Companies Filing with the SEC* (Bethesda, MD: Disclosure, Inc., September 1998).

27. W. Movile and A. Petrie, "Accounting for a Bargain Purchase in a Business Combination," *Accounting Horizons* (September 1989), pp. 38–43.

28. Accounting Principles Board Opinion No. 17, "Intangible Assets" (New York: Accounting Principles Board, August 1970), para. 27.

29. The FASB has proposed reducing the amortization period to 20 years. Refer to Proposed Statement of Financial Accounting Standards, "Business Combinations and Intangible Assets" (Norwalk, CT: FASB, September 7, 1999).

30. Allergan, Inc., annual report, December 1997, p. 37.

31. Biomet, Inc., annual report, May 1996, p. 24.

32. Healthdyne Technologies, Inc., annual report, December 1996. Information obtained from Disclosure, Inc. *Compact D/SEC: Corporate Information on Public Companies Filing with the SEC* (Bethesda, MD: Disclosure, Inc., September 1998).

33. St. Jude Medical, Inc., annual report, December 1996, p. 32.

34. SFAS No. 121, "Accounting for the Impairment of Long-Lived Assets" (Norwalk, CT: Financial Accounting Standards Board, March 1995).

35. Eli Lilly & Co., annual report, December 1997. Information obtained from Disclosure, Inc. *Compact D/SEC: Corporate Information on Public Companies Filing with the SEC* (Bethesda, MD: Disclosure, Inc., September 1998).

36. J. L. Kramer, T. R. Pope, and L. C. Phillips, Federal Taxation 1997 (Upper Saddle River, New Jersey: Prentice Hall, 1996), pp. 7-5–7-7 (Corporations).

37. Emerging Issues Task Force, "Basis in Leveraged Buyout Transactions" (Norwalk, CT: Financial Accounting Standards Board, 1988).

38. Amtrol, Inc., annual report, December 1997. Information obtained from Disclosure, Inc. *Compact D/SEC: Corporate Information on Public Companies Filing with the SEC* (Bethesda, MD: Disclosure, Inc., September 1998).

39. Apex PC Solutions, Inc., annual report, December 1997. Information obtained from Disclosure, Inc. *Compact D/SEC: Corporate Information on Public Companies Filing with the SEC* (Bethesda, MD: Disclosure, Inc., September 1998).

40. Adapted from Accounting Principles Board Opinion No. 16, "Business Combinations" (New York: Accounting Principles Board, August 1970).

41. Dow Jones News Service (New York: Dow Jones & Co., Inc., July 20, 1998).

42. Dow Jones News Service (New York: Dow Jones & Co., Inc., September 19, 1998).

43. Rare Hospitality International, Inc., Form 10-K annual report to the Securities and Exchange Commission (December 1997), pp. 39–40.

44. General Motors Corp., annual report, December 1996, p. 64.

45. H. Hong, R. Kaplan, and G. Mandelker, "Pooling vs. Purchase: The Effects of Accounting for Mergers on Stock Prices," *The Accounting Review* (January 1978), pp. 31–47.

46. M. Davis, "Differential Market Reaction to Pooling and Purchase Methods," *The Accounting Review* (July 1990), pp. 696–709.

47. J. Robinson and P. Shane, "Acquisition Accounting Method and Bid Premia for Target Firms," *The Accounting Review* (January 1990), pp. 25–48.

48. L. Vincent, "Equity Valuation Implications of Purchase Versus Pooling Accounting," *The Journal of Financial Statement Analysis* (Summer 1997), pp. 5–19.

49. DIMON, Inc., annual report, December 1996, pp. 44–45.

50. Under the purchase method, some preparers of financial statements revalue even the minority interest's share of the net assets of the acquired firm. As the minority shareholders have not sold their interests, revaluation does not appear warranted. However, both approaches are permitted under extant accounting principles.

51. A recent proposal from the FASB calls for minority (noncontrolling) interest to be reported as a component of shareholders' equity. Refer to Proposed Statement of Financial Accounting Standards, "Consolidated Financial Statements: Policy and Procedures" (Norwalk, CT: Financial Accounting Standards Board, October 16, 1995), para. 22.

52. A recent proposal from the FASB calls for minority (noncontrolling) interest in income to be treated as a distribution of net income as opposed to an expense in computing net income. Refer to Proposed Statement of Financial Accounting Standards, "Consolidated Financial Statements: Policy and Procedures" (Norwalk, CT: Financial Accounting Standards Board, October 16, 1995), para. 23.

53. SFAS No. 131, "Disclosures About Segments of an Enterprise and Related Information" (Norwalk, CT: Financial Accounting Standards Board, June 1997).

54. *Ibid.*, pp. 3–4.

55. ITC DeltaCom, Inc., annual report, December 1996. Information obtained from Disclosure, Inc. *Compact D/SEC: Corporate Information on Public Companies Filing with the SEC* (Bethesda, MD: Disclosure, Inc., March 1999).

Chapter 10

Lease Reporting and Analysis

> In October, the start-up carrier had to scale back to one plane and a
> limited schedule after plane lessor Viscount Air Services took back
> one of its aircraft in the middle of the night at the Pittsburgh airport."[1]

Leasing, or the possession and use of assets without having ownership, is probably far more pervasive than most would imagine. An annual survey conducted by the American Institute of Certified Public Accountants (AICPA) reveals that about 90 percent of surveyed companies disclosed some leasing activity.[2] Leasing plays a major role in making possible the acquisition and use of a vast range of assets by firms in virtually all industries. The scope and scale of leasing cause its financial reporting treatment and implications for financial analysis to be of significant importance to financial statement producers as well as users.

LEASING BACKGROUND

The principal focus of this chapter, as well as all other chapters in this book, is on reporting treatments and the implications for analysis of each topic covered. Leasing is a subject about which many people have varying degrees of knowledge and understanding. In many cases, this may be due to the dramatic growth in auto leasing in recent years. However, for key producers and users of financial information, extensive background is necessary in order to evaluate the implications of leasing for both the financial performance and financial position of firms engaged in leasing.

In an interesting case in point, a number of years ago a bankruptcy hearing was held in Atlanta for a regional carrier, Air Atlanta. A number of interested parties were engaged in conversation prior to the beginning of the proceedings. In the course of these conversations, someone remarked that there was hope for recovering some of what they were owed by Air Atlanta because it had $40 million of aircraft on its balance sheet. This view was immediately challenged by someone pointing out that these aircraft were all leased, and that they had been repossessed by the aircraft owners (i.e., lessors). The original commentator was clearly nonplussed by this information and demanded to know how the aircraft could be on Air Atlanta's balance sheet if Air Atlanta did not own them. Answering this and similar questions is central to the objectives of this chapter.

Leasing Motivation

There is a range of motivations for leasing, as opposed to outright purchase and financing through the use of other forms of debt or of equity. Some of the more common reasons cited for leasing include the following:

- To permit the shifting of the tax benefits of ownership to the lessor, in return for attractive leasing terms[3]
- To avoid the risk of obsolescence
- To achieve a less costly form of financing than conventional borrowing
- To achieve full tax deductibility of lease payments
- To obtain off-balance-sheet financing[4]
- To reduce the likelihood of violating of debt agreement covenants
- To avoid the alternative minimum tax (AMT)[5]

Income taxes are listed first above because of the central role that they play in decisions to lease and, in the view of some, to the very existence of much of today's leasing activity. This point is made by Westerfield and Jaffe and is found in the statement below:

> Leasing allows the transfer of tax benefits from those who need equipment, but cannot take full advantage of the tax benefits associated with ownership, to a party who can. If the corporate income tax were repealed, long-term leasing would virtually disappear.[6]

An opportunity to test this view is unlikely since the corporate income tax is no doubt here to stay. However, although many of the above leasing incentives are directly or indirectly tax-based, some are not. Therefore, leasing would probably continue, albeit at a reduced level, even in the absence of the corporate income tax.

Some additional factors motivating the choice to lease are the flexibility of payment structures, the absence of substantial up-front cash requirements (i.e., down payments), and the simplicity of lease application and documentation. Especially in the case of smaller firms, leasing may make possible the acquisition of assets not readily available through other forms of financing.

Consistent with the above listings, bankers prospecting for leasing business have told us that they look for several things in a leasing prospect:

1. Are they already doing some leasing?
2. Is the prospect's effective tax rate lower than that of the bank?
3. Is the prospect in an (alternative minimum tax) AMT position?

While related to point two above, a determination of whether the prospect is currently in a taxpaying position is also a useful screening question.

Examples of Leased Assets and Their Characteristics

Virtually any asset can be leased. However, some items are leased with greater frequency than others. Examples would include airplanes, computers, railroad rolling stock, shipping containers, cars and trucks, medical diagnostic equipment, and automotive diagnostic and repair equipment.

Certain features make some items more attractive for leasing than others. A high potential residual value, which can be realized through the re-leasing or sale of assets, is often a key source of overall profitability for the lessor. Assets that are essential to the operation of the lessee's business provide strong pressure to give lease payments a high payment priority. Equipment that is both new and state-of-the-art is especially appealing, as are nonspecialized assets, which have broader potential for re-leasing when they come off lease. Serial numbers, or some other means of unambiguous identification, are important in the event that it becomes necessary to recover a leased asset.

Assets that are subject to rapid wear and tear or abuse are less attractive leasing candidates. Examples would include signs (bored motorists sometimes shoot at them), vending machines (unsatisfied customers frequently subject them to abuse), and carpeting. Assets with low maintenance costs are also more likely to remain in good condition.

FINANCIAL REPORTING BY LESSEES[7]

This presentation of the financial reporting requirements of lease transactions is organized as follows: (1) basic lessee transactions; (2) basic lessor transactions; (3) sale-type leases; and (4) sale and leaseback transactions. Both the financial reporting for leases and their implications for financial analysis are considered.

The principal current generally accepted accounting principles (GAAP) requirements for leases are found in two statements of financial accounting standards: SFAS No. 13, "Accounting for Leases," and SFAS No. 28, "Accounting for Sales with Leasebacks."[8] The original expectation was that SFAS No. 13 would result in substantial assets and liabilities being recorded on the balance sheet, where disclosure was previously confined to the footnotes. However, the lease classification criteria of the Statement provided considerable room for maneuver.[9] If a lessee does not wish to record an additional asset and liability on its balance sheet, then creative structuring of the lease contract can usually keep the arrangement off-balance-sheet.[10] In a sense, SFAS No. 13 appears to have been simply looked upon as a challenge that had to be met and overcome.

As a result of the maneuvering by both lessors and lessees, the Financial Accounting Standards Board (FASB) found it necessary to deal repeatedly with issues associated with the implementation of the original leasing standard, SFAS No. 13. The FASB recently released a 450-page document, "Accounting for Leases—A Codification as of October 1, 1998."[11] In addition to reproducing both

SFAS Nos. 13 and 28, the document also includes five other lease-related statements of financial accounting standards, six FASB interpretations, 11 FASB technical bulletins, and 31 abstracts produced by the Emerging Issues Task Force.[12] Given the number and variety of items affecting GAAP for leasing, the FASB felt that it was essential to provide a single source that included all items dealing with lease reporting.

The discussion below deals with the central aspects of lease reporting. For many of the more detailed technical aspects of lease reporting, the reader is referred to "Accounting for Leases—A Codification as of October 1, 1998."

Reporting of Basic Lessee Transactions

Most of the attention devoted to leasing has focused on the treatment by the lessee (i.e., the party using the asset) as opposed to the lessor (i.e., the party who owns the asset). Central to the formation of GAAP for leasing has been the goal of having the accounting and reporting reflect the economic substance of leasing arrangements, and not simply their legal form. Viewed from a legal perspective, a lease could simply be viewed as an executory arrangement, which gives rise to neither an asset nor a liability. This would lead to accounting that simply records an expense as and when the payment obligation accrues.

Where leases are in substance an installment purchase of an asset, then failure to account for them as such results in both off-balance-sheet liabilities as well as assets. However, from a financial analysis perspective, relevant literature has emphasized the reduction in position quality resulting from failure to record the liability.

The key conceptual issue of SFAS No. 13, which guides the classification and accounting for leases, is outlined as follows:

> The provisions of this Statement derive from the view that a lease that transfers substantially all of the benefits and risks incident to the ownership of property should be accounted for as the acquisition of an asset and the incurring of an obligation by the lessee and as a sale or financing by the lessor. . . . In a lease that transfers substantially all of the benefits and risks of ownership, the economic effect on the parties is similar, in many respects, to that of an installment purchase.[13]

To make the above concept operational, SFAS No. 13 includes four lease classification criteria. If a lease arrangement satisfies any one of the four criteria, then the lease is classified as and accounted for as a capital lease. If not, then the lease is classified as and accounted for as an operating lease. In brief, classification as a capital lease requires the lessee to record an asset and associated liability upon inception of the lease. Subsequently, lease expense is made up of both interest on the lease liability and amortization of the leased asset. Operating lease classification calls for the recording of neither an asset nor a liability; rent expense is simply recorded as incurred.

Lease Classification Criteria

The lease classification criteria are as follows[14]:

1. The lease transfers ownership of the property to the lessee by the end of the lease term.
2. The lease contains a bargain purchase option.[15]
3. The lease term is equal to 75 percent or more of the estimated economic life of the leased property.
4. The present value at the beginning of the lease term of the minimum lease payments equals or exceeds 90 percent of the fair value of the leased property.

Application of criteria one and two above is generally unambiguous. Transfer of title, criterion number one, means that the lease is effectively an installment purchase of the asset. Under criterion number two, SFAS No. 13 characterizes a bargain purchase option as one that is "sufficiently lower than the expected fair value of the property at the date the option becomes exercisable that exercise of the option appears, at the inception of the lease, to be reasonably assured."[16] As an example of a bargain purchase option, Armstrong World Industries, Inc. disclosed the following on a lease of plant and related equipment: "The lease agreement contains a purchase option of $1 until 2018. As a result, the present value of the remaining future minimum lease payments is recorded as a capitalized lease asset and related capitalized lease obligation."[17]

The logic underlying criterion three is that the right to use an asset for three-fourths or more of its useful life effectively makes the lessee the "economic" owner of the asset. Therefore, the lease should be accounted for much like an installment purchase of the asset, even though the lessee may never plan to become the legal owner of the asset.

Criterion four involves similar logic. Conveying an amount to the lessor for the use of an asset, which amounts to 90 percent or more of the value of the leased asset, appears very much like an installment purchase. If either criterion three or four is satisfied, it seems reasonable to consider that the risks and rewards of ownership have been transferred to the lessee.

Characteristics of the Lessee Accounting Alternatives: Operating and Capital

A lease is classified and accounted for as an operating lease if it fails to satisfy any one of the four lease classification criteria listed above. The key features of operating lease accounting are:

- Neither an asset nor a liability is recorded upon the inception of the lease.
- Annual lease expense is simply recorded as lease payments are made or accrued.

A lease that does satisfy at least one of the four lease classification criteria is classified as a capital lease and accounted for as follows:

- Both an asset and a liability are recorded upon inception of the capital lease. The asset and liability are recorded at the present value of the minimum lease payments for the lease term.
- The lease expense for each year is equal to a combination of amortization of the leased asset and interest on the lease obligation.

In most cases the amortization of the leased asset is on a straight-line basis over the lease term. The interest expense on the lease obligation will decline over time as the lease obligation itself is reduced. It is common for capital leases to produce temporary differences between lease expense in the books and in the income tax return. The combination of straight-line amortization of the leased asset, plus a pattern of accelerated interest expense recognition, results in an initial excess of book lease expense over that deducted in the tax return. The differences between book and tax return lease expense are temporary and deferred tax assets must be recorded.

The tax disclosures of Southwest Airlines indicate the presence of temporary differences and deferred tax assets associated with both capital and operating leases.[18] Southwest's schedule of deferred tax assets and liabilities included deferred tax assets labeled "Capital and operating leases" of $62 million and $61 million for 1997 and 1998, respectively. The presence of deferred tax assets means that Southwest's expense recognition for its leases is accelerated on its books compared to that in its tax return.

Lessee Accounting Illustrated

The basic features of lease accounting are illustrated here with an example. The following data are assumed:

- The lease term is five years.
- The lease finance rate is 10 percent.
- The useful life of the leased asset is five years.
- The annual end-of-year lease payments are $100,000.
- The lessor's cost and fair value of the asset is $379,079.
- The residual value of the asset is zero.
- The lease does not transfer title at its termination.
- The lease does not contain a bargain purchase option.

Based on the above data, this lease would be classified as a capital lease, and an asset and liability would be recorded at its inception. The lease satisfies two of the four lease classification criteria. First, the lease term is 100 percent of the useful life of the asset, well above the 75 percent of useful life threshold. Second, using the above lease finance rate of 10 percent, the present value of the lease payments is $379,079 or 100 percent of the fair value of the leased asset, well above the 90 percent threshold.

In determining present value, SFAS No. 13 requires that the discount rate be the lower of the interest rate implicit in the lease or the lessee's incremental borrowing rate. For simplicity, we assume that these rates are equal. Using the lower of the two rates increases the likelihood that a lease is classified a capital lease because the use of a lower discount rate increases present value. This in turn increases the likelihood of the lease present value exceeding the 90 percent of fair value threshold, lease classification criterion four above.

While the above lease would be classified as a capital lease, for purposes of illustration and comparison, both capital and operating lease treatments are illustrated below.

Operating Lease

There is no recording of assets or liabilities required upon inception of the lease, unless a security or other deposit is required. If such a deposit is made, the deposit is recorded as a separate asset. At the end of each of the five years, a lease payment of $100,000 is made and lease expense in the same amount is recorded.[19] Again, as noted earlier, the operating lease treatment is typically the method used in the tax return, without regard to how the lease is classified under GAAP for shareholder reporting purposes.

Capital Lease

Upon lease inception, an asset and liability, equal in amount to the present value of the stream of lease payments, are recorded.[20] The effect, as shown below, on the balance sheet is that assets and liabilities are each increased by the present value of the lease:

Assets	=	Liabilities	+	Shareholders' Equity
Leased property $379,079	=	Lease obligation $379,079		

Because liabilities increase with no change in shareholders' equity, financial leverage (e.g., the ratio of liabilities to equity) is increased. Increased financial leverage is often seen to be a disadvantage and, as a result, efforts are sometimes taken to structure leases so that they do not satisfy any of the four lease classification criteria.[21] This structuring avoids capital lease classification and the associated increase in reported financial leverage. Although a common view, the position that keeping a lease off-balance-sheet (i.e., reporting as operating leases) does not affect financial leverage is challenged by evidence on the debt equivalence of leases.[22]

Exhibit 10.1. Accounting for a Capital Lease

	Payment	Interest Expense[a]	Liability Reduction[b]	Liability
Inception				$379,079
Year 1	$100,000	$37,908	$62,092	316,987
Year 2	100,000	31,699	68,301	248,686
Year 3	100,000	24,869	75,131	173,555
Year 4	100,000	17,355	82,645	90,910
Year 5	100,000	9,090	90,910	0
	$500,000	$120,921	$379,079	

[a]Interest is simply 10% multiplied times the beginning liability balance of each year. Year 1 interest is .10 × $379,079 or $37,908.
[b]The liability reduction is that portion of the payment not treated as interest. The year 1 reduction is $100,000 − $37,908 or $62,092.

Over the five-year lease term, accounting for the lease involves: (1) recording the cash payment, (2) computing the portion of the payment that is treated as interest expense, (3) reducing the lease liability by the excess of the payment over the portion treated as interest, and (4) amortizing the leased property. In addition, to the extent that book treatment of the lease differs from that in the tax return, deferred taxes are recorded. Accounting for the lease payments and interest expense for the five-year lease term is summarized in Exhibit 10.1.

The amortization of the leased asset normally follows the straight-line approach. This means that the annual amortization expense will be $75,816, or $379,079 divided by five years. In the first year, the leased asset will decline by $75,816, whereas the lease liability (see Exhibit 10.1) will be reduced by only $62,092. During these early years, less of the lease payment goes to reduce the lease liability. Because in the early years the lease liability is higher, more of the lease payment is treated as interest.

For firms that are growing and replacing expiring leases with new leases, it is common for the capital lease assets, net of accumulated amortization, to be continually less than the total present value of the lease liability. For example, in its 1998 annual report, PHYCOR, Inc. discloses net capital lease assets of $9,484,000 and capital lease liabilities of $11,705,000.[23] Recall, in the example in Exhibit 10.1, that the leased asset and lease liability are identical at inception of the capital lease. Subsequently, the leased asset declines by $75,816 each year, but the lease liability only declines by $62,092 at the end of year one. Thus, the net leased asset is smaller than the liability at the end of year one by $75,816 minus $62,092 or $13,724.

In anticipation of the tax issue that will be raised shortly, for book purposes there is a net liability balance of $13,724—lease liability of $316,987 minus lease

Exhibit 10.2. Comparison of Capital and Operating Lease Expenses

	Capital Lease			Operating Lease Payment	Expense Difference
Year	Amortization	Interest	Total		
1	$75,816	$37,908	$113,724	$100,000	$13,724
2	75,816	31,699	107,515	100,000	7,515
3	75,816	24,869	100,685	100,000	685
4	75,816	17,355	93,171	100,000	(6,829)
5	75,815	9,090	84,905	100,000	(15,095)
	$379,079	$120,921	$500,000	$500,0000	0

asset of $303,263—at the end of year one. However, for income tax purposes neither the leased asset nor the lease liability are recognized. Therefore, on this $13,724 "basis difference," a deferred tax asset of $5,490 is required, assuming a flat 40 percent income tax rate.

Comparison of Capital and Operating Lease Expense Patterns

At the end of the five-year lease term, the total lease expense is the same under both the capital and operating lease classifications. However, the pattern of expense recognition is accelerated under the capital lease treatment. Exhibit 10.2 summarizes the two expense patterns.

While expense recognition differs each year under the two methods, total lease expense is the same for each method at the end of the lease term.

In the tax return, lessees generally follow the operating lease method and deduct the lease payment as expense each year. When the capital lease treatment is employed for book purposes, this results in a temporary difference between lease expense in the books and tax return. In years one through three, when capital lease expense (the book lease expense) exceeds the operating lease expense (the tax return expense), a deferred tax asset is recorded each year. This deferred tax asset would grow each year for the first three years by the originating temporary difference times the tax rate. In years four and five the temporary difference reverses, and the deferred tax asset is amortized.

Lessee Financial Statement Disclosures

Lessee disclosures of leasing activities are extensive.[24] In the discussion below a standard and complete set of disclosures is first presented and then a sampling from lease disclosures of other companies is provided.

A Standard Set of Lessee Disclosures: Delta Air Lines

The lease disclosures of Delta Air Lines, Inc. are presented in Exhibit 10.3. The schedules of lease payments for both capital and operating leases are valuable information in assessing the future cash requirements of the firm. Note that op-

Exhibit 10.3.   A Standard Set of Lease Disclosures: Delta Air Lines Lease
Disclosures, Years Ended June 30, 1997–1998 (Millions of Dollars)

Note 7. Lease Obligations

The Company leases certain aircraft, airport terminal and maintenance facilities, ticket offices and other property and equipment. Rent expense is generally recorded on a straight-line basis over the lease term. Amounts charged to rental expense for operating leases were $0.9 billion in fiscal 1998, 1997 and 1996.

At June 30, 1998, the Company's minimum rental commitments under capital leases (primarily aircraft) and noncancelable operating leases with initial remaining terms of more than one year were as follows:

Years Ending June 30 (in Millions)	Capital Leases	Operating Leases
1999	$100	$950
2000	67	950
2001	57	940
2002	57	960
2003	48	960
After 2003	71	10,360
Total minimum lease payments	$400	$15,120
Less: Amounts representing interest	88	
Present value of future minimum capital lease payments	312	
Less: Current obligations under capital leases	63	
Long-term capital lease obligations	$249	

As of June 30, 1998, Delta leased 219 aircraft. These leases have remaining terms ranging from 18 months to 19 years and expiration dates ranging from 1999 to 2017.

Certain municipalities and airport authorities have issued special facility revenue bonds to build or improve airport terminal and maintenance facilities that Delta leases under operating leases. Under these lease arrangements, the Company is required to make rental payments sufficient to pay principal and interest on the bonds as they become due.

Source: Delta Air Lines, Inc., annual report, June 1998, p. 45.

erating lease expense is recognized on a straight-line basis.[25] For fiscal 1999, Delta is scheduled to make minimum lease payments of $950 million. For its capital leases, Delta's scheduled minimum payment for fiscal 1999 is $100 million.

From the illustration in Exhibit 10.3, we know that a portion of the capital lease payment in 1999 will be treated as interest and the balance will reduce the capital lease obligation. Delta's total capital lease obligation at the end of fiscal 1998 was $312 million. This amount is broken down and disclosed in Delta's 1998 balance sheet as a $63 million current portion of the liability and a $249 million long-term amount.

Exhibit 10.4.   Net Capital Lease Assets: Delta Air Lines, Inc., Years Ended June 30, 1997–1998 (Millions of Dollars)

	1997	*1998*
Flight equipment under capital leases	$523	$515
Less: Accumulated amortization	176	216
	347	299

Source: Delta Air Lines, Inc., annual report, June 1998, p. 34.

Exhibit 10.5.   Approximation of 1999 Total Capital Lease Expense: Delta Air Lines, Inc., Years Ended June 30, 1997–1998 (Millions of Dollars)

	1999
1999 capital lease interest expense ($100 − $63)	$37
1999 capital lease amortization	40
Estimated 1999 total capital lease expense	$77

Source: Data from Exhibits 10.3 and 10.4.

Capital lease expense is composed of two elements: interest expense and the amortization of the capital lease asset. The 1999 interest component of capital lease expense of $37 million is computed by deducting the current portion of the lease liability, $63 million, from the total 1999 lease payment of $100 million. The amortization component of capital lease expense cannot be as readily calculated from standard lease disclosures. However, we can approximate the amount of amortization expense in 1998 from information disclosed in Delta's 1997 and 1998 balance sheets on accumulated amortization of the capital lease assets, which is presented in Exhibit 10.4.

In the absence of any additions or expirations of capital leases in 1997, the 1998 amortization recorded on Delta's capital lease would have been equal to the growth in the accumulated amortization balance: $216 million − $176 million = $40 million.

If we assume that the amortization expense for 1999 will also be about $40 million, the amount computed above for 1998, then we can approximate Delta's 1999 total capital lease expense as outlined in Exhibit 10.5.

Combining the estimated capital lease expense above with the scheduled operating lease payment for 1999 suggests a total lease expense of about $1,027,000,000 ($77,000,000 + $950,000,000) for 1999.

Other Lessee Disclosures
The standard set of lessee disclosures found in the case of Delta Air Lines is often supplemented by other information. Examples of (1) purchases options and (2) renewal options are provided below.

Bargain Purchase Option Disclosure: La-Z-Boy, Inc.
La-Z-Boy, Inc. leases trucks for use in transporting its furniture. These leases are classified as capital leases. This classification is not surprising because the La-Z-Boy disclosures reveal bargain purchase options, the second of the four lease classification criteria. From the La-Z-Boy annual report: "The majority of the leases include bargain purchase options."[26] The expectation is that the bargain purchase option will be exercised and that the trucks will then be owned by La-Z-Boy. A lease with a bargain purchase option is properly viewed as the equivalent of an installment purchase.[27]

Fair Market Value Renewal and Purchase Options: AMR Corporation
The noncancelable term of a lease is important in deciding on classification as operating versus capital. Recall that lease classification criterion three calls for capital lease classification if the noncancelable lease term is equal to or greater than 75 percent of the useful life of the leased asset. If renewals are available at fair market value rates, then the renewal terms are not considered to be part of the noncancelable lease term. However, if the renewal terms can be considered a bargain, then these renewal periods are included in determining the original noncancelable term of a lease. AMR's lease disclosures contain the following:

> The aircraft leases can generally be renewed at rates based on *fair market value* at the end of the lease term for one to five years. Most aircraft leases have purchase options at or near the end of the lease term at *fair market value* (emphasis added).[28]

AMR's lease commitments at the end of 1997 were about $21 billion, and of this about 90 percent was for operating leases. If AMR prefers leases that are accounted for as operating and not capital leases, then the fair market value options help to achieve this objective. Bargain renewal options would extend the noncancelable lease term and increase the likelihood that the 75 percent threshold of lease classification criterion three would be triggered. Of course, the presence of a bargain purchase option, criterion two alone, would call for a capital lease classification. In fact, in addition to the fair market value purchase options identified above, AMR disclosed the presence of bargain purchase options on what had originally been operating leases for 12 Boeing 767-300 aircraft:

> Upon expiration of the amended leases, American can purchase the aircraft for a nominal amount. As a result, the aircraft are recorded as flight equipment under capital leases.[29]

A Penalty for Nonrenewal and the Determination of Lease Term:
AirLease, Ltd.
Presence of a bargain renewal option results in inclusion of the renewal period in the computation of the original lease term. The original lease term will also include the renewal period if a significant penalty is applied should the lease not be re-

newed. As with a bargain renewal option, this increases the likelihood of renewal and usually will call for including the renewal period in the original lease term. AirLease, Ltd., a lessor, disclosed the impact of such a feature and its effect on its lease term, and presumably on that of its lessees:

> The lessee is required to pay a substantial additional amount if it does not renew the lease for three years at the end of the initial 12-year term (1998); accordingly, the lease is accounted for as a 15-year lease.[30]

While no surprise, in a subsequent 10-K report (1997), AirLease reported that the lessee, US Airways, Inc., had exercised its option to renew the lease for an additional three years at the end of the initial 12-year term (1998).[31]

FINANCIAL ANALYSIS OF LESSEES

The lessee disclosures presented above provide information that users should evaluate as they assess the strength of a lessee's financial position and its prospects for the generation and use of future earnings and cash flow. This section focuses on a range of financial analysis issues: (1) leases and future cash flows, (2) leases and fixed-charge coverage ratios, (3) leases and leverage ratios, (4) leases and other covenants, (5) leases as off-balance-sheet asset sources, and (6) leases and profitability analysis.

Future Cash Flows

Standard lessee disclosures provide very useful information as users develop projections of a firm's future cash flows (refer to the Delta Air Lines disclosures in Exhibit 10.3).[32] GAAP require that schedules of minimum lease payment commitments be provided. While the standard disclosure combines lease payment data for the years beyond year five, this information remains very valuable to the process of projecting future cash flows.

Users should be aware that the schedules of lease commitments are only for leases in effect at the date of the balance sheet. Actual future cash outlays may differ from these amounts as a result of entering into new leases. In addition, contingent lease payments may also raise actual lease payments above the amount of the minimum commitments.

The presence of contingent payment features in lease agreements should be considered in using lease disclosures to make cash flow projections. Contingent payment provisions may result in increases in lease payments above the disclosed minimum payments. Contingent payments are generally tied to either some measure of usage of the leased asset or the level of revenues produced by its use.

For example, Avado Brands, Inc., a firm in the restaurant business, explains that some of its leases contain provisions for "contingent rentals payable based on a percentage of sales in excess of stipulated amounts for restaurant facilities."[33]

Exhibit 10.6.   Contingent Rental Disclosures: Vulcan Materials Company, for Years Ended December 31, 1996–1998 (Thousands of Dollars)

Total rental expense of nonmineral leases, exclusive of rental payments made under leases of one month or less, is summarized as follows (thousands of dollars):

	1996	*1997*	*1998*
Minimum rentals	$17,188	$17,894	$18,725
Contingent rentals (based principally on usage)	10,677	11,840	15,410
Total	$27,865	$29,734	$34,135

Source: Vulcan Materials Company, annual report, December 1998, p. 49.

Further, Avado discloses the contingent portion of its operating lease payments: "Rental expense included contingent rentals of $900,000 in 1996, $1,000,000 in 1997 and $2,300,000 in 1998."[34] These contingent payments represented an average of about 6 percent of Avado's total lease payments. However, in other cases contingent payments could be much more substantial.

Vulcan Materials Company made the contingent lease payment disclosures provided in Exhibit 10.6. Vulcan's contingent payments are clearly a significant addition to the minimum rent payments. Projections of cash outflows for lease payments should augment the minimum rentals by the likely level of the contingent payment.

Fixed-Charge Coverage Ratios

Estimating a firm's coverage of its fixed charges is a common feature of financial analysis. Moreover, financial covenants calling for firms to maintain minimum coverage ratios are a key feature of most credit agreements and bond indentures. The interest associated with capital leases is included in interest expense in the income statement. However, under standard GAAP disclosures, no portion of operating lease payments is treated as interest; rather, it is disclosed as rent expense. Analysis that is focused on the substance of transactions could reasonably view a portion of operating lease payments as equivalent to interest. In fact, it is common to include some or all of operating lease payments in computations of fixed-charge coverage ratios.

Leases and Fixed-Charge Coverage Disclosures under Securities and Exchange Commission Requirements

A fixed-charge coverage ratio includes a measure of earnings or cash flow in the numerator and of fixed charges in the denominator. The ratio of earnings before interest and taxes (EBIT) to interest expense is a common coverage ratio. To illustrate, as part of its quarterly Securities and Exchange Commission (SEC) filing

Exhibit 10.7.   Statement of Computation of Ratio of Earnings to Fixed
Charges: Delta Air Lines, Six months ended December 31, 1997–1998
(Millions of Dollars)

	Six Months Ended December 31	
	1997	*1998*
Earnings before income taxes	$730	$858
Add (deduct) fixed charges from below		
Fixed charges from below	397	410
Interest capitalized	(18)[a]	(22)
Earnings as adjusted	1,109	1,246
Fixed charges:		
Interest expense	99	92
Portion of rental expense representative of interest factor	298	318
Total fixed charges	397	410
Unadjusted ratio of earnings to fixed charges	8.19[b]	10.09
Adjusted ratio of earnings to fixed charges	2.79[c]	3.04

[a]Capitalized interest is deducted from pretax earnings, as originally reported, to ensure that earnings bear the full burden of all interest incurred. For this analytical process, an evaluation of fixed-charge (interest only in this case) calls for undoing the effects of the interest capitalization procedure.
[b]The unadjusted coverage ratio for 1997 is computed as: ($730 + $99 – 18) ÷ $99 = 8.19.
[c]The adjusted ratio for 1997 is computed as: ($1,109 ÷ $397) = 2.79.
Source: Delta Air Lines, Form 10-Q quarterly report to the Securities and Exchange Commission (December 1998), p. 11.

requirements on Form 10-Q, Delta Air Lines presents a schedule that displays the computation of its EBIT coverage ratio. For the six months ending on December 31, 1997 and 1998, respectively (Delta has a June 30 year end), an adapted version of Delta's EBIT disclosure is provided in Exhibit 10.7.

The disclosures in Exhibit 10.7 are required by the SEC.[35] In the definition of fixed charges, the SEC declares that:

The term "fixed charges" shall mean the total of (a) interest, whether expensed or capitalized; (b) amortization of debt expense and discount or premium relating to indebtedness, whether expensed or capitalized; (c) such portion of rental expense as can be demonstrated to be representative of the interest factor in the particular case; and (d) a preferred stock dividend requirement of majority-owned subsidiaries and fifty-percent-owned persons, excluding in all cases items which would be or are eliminated in consolidation.[36]

If no portion of its rentals is treated as interest, then Delta's unadjusted coverage ratios are 8.19 and 10.09 in 1997 and 1998, respectively. The comparable adjusted numbers are 2.79 and 3.04, respectively. While no part of rentals is treated as interest under GAAP, a quite different perspective can be taken for purposes of financial analysis.

Approximating the Interest Component of Lease Payments

Many leases classified as operating differ only slightly from capital leases. Therefore, a focus on substance as opposed to form supports treating a portion of operating lease expenses (rentals) as interest. It has long been common for firms to simply multiply operating lease expense by one-third in arriving at "such portion of rental expense as can be demonstrated to be representative of the interest factor . . ."[37] As with all rules of thumb, this one is designed to be both simple and to provide a reasonable approximation of the interest element of operating lease payments.

Capital lease disclosures can be used as a benchmark for the interest portion of operating lease expense. A sampling from a set of airlines and a variety of other companies is reported in Exhibit 10.8. Two approaches are used: (1) total remaining interest on capital leases is simply divided by total remaining capital lease payments; and (2) the projected interest expense associated with next year's lease payment (payment minus the portion that is listed as current in the year-end balance sheet) is divided by next year's payment.

These two estimates are labeled single payment and total payments, respectively. The first measure provides an aggregate measure of the level of interest in relationship to total future lease payments. The second method provides a near-term measure of the relationship between the lease payment and interest.

The information in Exhibit 10.8 is based on only a small number of companies and is not necessarily representative of the larger universe of lessees. The information is simply developed as a basis for discussion of the one-third of lease payments as a rule of thumb for estimating interest.

While neither the airlines nor diversified group averages deviate widely from one-third, the individual company percentages vary over a wide range. Deviations could reflect differences in such factors as interest rates, remaining maturities, and the pattern of remaining lease payments (i.e., increasing, decreasing, or flat). An inspection of the payment schedules of some of the firms listed is revealing.

Among the airlines, Southwest Airlines Company actually has interest that represents one-third of the upcoming lease payment. Its payment pattern is declining over the first five-year interval and the total life of the leases appears to be about 13 years. The average interest rate on its capital leases is about eight percent.[38] Interest represents 50 percent of the next capital lease payment of Northwest Airlines Corporation. It appears that the leases continue for only one or two years beyond the first five-year interval. Their pattern is relatively flat. The average interest rate on Northwest's capital leases is also about eight percent.

Among the other firms, Mead Corporation shows 94 percent of the next year's payment as interest. Its average interest rate on its capital leases is only about four

Exhibit 10.8. The Interest Component of Capital Lease Payments

Airlines	Interest as a % of	
	Total Payments	Single Payment
Company		
Southwest Airlines Company	37	33
AMR Corporation	32	53
Northwest Airlines Corporation	29	50
Delta Air Lines, Inc.	22	37
Hawaiian Airlines, Inc.	18	21
Average	28	39
Diversified		
Western Power and Equipment Corporation	62	8
Mead Corporation	55	4
Smithfield Foods, Inc.	25	50
PHYCOR, Inc.	10	14
Go-Video, Inc.	9	11
Average	32	17

Sources: Based on the 1998 annual report of each listed company.

percent. Mead's disclosures reveal that its capital leases do not mature until the year 2028. The payments within the first five years, and then from 2003 to 2028, are a total of $41 million and $343 million, respectively.

While only a limited sampling, the above would suggest that use of one-third to represent the average interest component in operating lease payments may miss the mark by a wide margin in some cases. This appears to be especially true if leases have a very long remaining term. This may also be the case if the remaining lease terms are very short and the payment pattern is declining very sharply. Variation is less with the airline sample. This may reflect the fact that leases are a central part of the airline financing and that the pattern of ongoing growth may keep the average lease maturity somewhere in the middle of the total life of the typical lease.

Notice that in the example in Exhibit 10.1, in which the interest rate is 10 percent and the lease term five years, interest approximates one-third of the lease payment in year two: interest of $31.7 million divided by the lease payment of $100 million equals 32 percent. In a series of spreadsheet computations, some insight is developed into the interest expense to lease payment relationship. A small set of these results is presented Exhibit 10.9. These data show that the year in which the one-third relationship exists is positively related to the interest rate. With the higher interest rates, the interest percentage exceeds one-third of the total lease payment prior to reaching the one-third relationship.

Exhibit 10.9. Interest Rates, Lease Maturities, and the Interest Expense
to Payments Relationship

Lease Interest Rate	Year in Which Interest Percentage Approximates 1/3
4%	1
6%	4
8%	5
10%	6
12%	7 ·

Source: Spreadsheet computations performed by the authors.

Like any rule of thumb, approximating the interest component of an operating
lease payment will frequently miss the mark by a considerable margin. Moreover,
differences in interest rates and lease maturities make it very difficult to improve
on the estimation of the interest component of lease payments with available
disclosures. However, for firms like airlines, with substantial and sustained leasing
activities, it may be possible to develop more accurate interest percentages by
employing approximations of lease interest rates and average lease maturities in
spreadsheet calculations. Although judgments will necessarily be required, the
results may be sufficiently more accurate than those derived from use of the one-
third benchmark to be worthwhile.

One alternative to use of the one-third rule is to simply treat the entire lease
payment as a fixed charge and not attempt to approximate the interest component.
Standard and Poor's has used this approach in developing a coverage ratio that is
characterized as "pretax fixed charge coverage including rents."[39]

Another approach to approximating the interest component of operating lease
payments would be to estimate the present value of the operating leases and then
compute the interest expense directly. The computation is identical to that illustrated in Exhibit 10.5. There, the current liability portion of the capital lease
liability is deducted from the lease payment to arrive at the interest expense.

The integration of the interest component of operating lease payments, or of
the payments themselves, in fixed-charge coverage ratios is one approach used by
analysts to recognize the debt-like characteristics of operating leases. A complementary analysis attempts to approximate the present value of off-balance-sheet
operating lease commitments in order to include them in such measures as debt-
to-equity ratios. These techniques are outlined in the next section.

Leases and Balance Sheet–Based Leverage Ratios

It is generally accepted in financial analysis, and documented in available research,
that operating leases are more or less economically equivalent to capital leases in
terms of their contribution to financial leverage.[40] Any request of key statement

users for examples of off-balance-sheet liabilities will find operating leases at the top of their lists. Off-balance-sheet operating lease payments need to be brought into balance-sheet leverage analysis, just as they are included in the more income statement–oriented coverage analysis in the previous section. To do this requires that estimations be made of the obligation represented by operating lease commitments.

Estimating Operating Lease Obligations

Efforts to estimate the present value or debt equivalence of operating lease commitments use the standard set of lease disclosures as input. In illustrating estimation alternatives, the lease disclosures from the 1998 annual report of Southwest Airlines Company are used. Relevant data from Southwest's lease disclosures and its balance sheet are included in Exhibit 10.10.

Direct Estimation of Present Value

One direct approach to the estimation of the present value of operating leases, used by securities rating firms such as Standard and Poor's and by other analysts and researchers, involves the even distribution of the payments scheduled beyond the first five years. That is, the sum of the lease payments beyond the first five years are simply distributed in level amounts over the estimated remaining lease term. Refer to the Southwest disclosures in Exhibit 10.10 for an example of this disclosure.[41]

Estimation of the present value of the operating leases requires (1) a discount (i.e., interest rate) and (2) a year-by-year schedule of lease payments. For computational convenience, we will assume that lease payments are made at the end of each year. An interest rate of 8 percent is selected because it is the approximate average interest rate of Southwest's capital leases. Calculation of this discount rate is outlined in Exhibit 10.11.

The year-by-year operating lease payments are already available in Exhibit 10.10. The remaining term of the operating leases beyond 2003 is approximated by dividing the last separately scheduled lease payment, $190,925,000, into the remaining lease payments beyond 2003 (i.e., $1,901,005,000). This yields a rounded 10 years as the estimate of the lease term beyond 2003: $1,901,005,000/ $190,925,000 $\approx$ 10. This estimated term is then divided into the operating lease payments beyond 2003 to develop a level lease payment for the years 2004 to 2013: $1,901,005,000/10 = $190,100,000.

Determining the total present value of above involves finding the present value at the end of 1998 of (1) each of the separately scheduled payments from 1999 to 2003, and (2) an annuity of 10 equal payments of $190,100,000. Again, a discount rate of 8 percent is used. This direct approach yields a total present value of $1,759,265,000. The stream of off-balance-sheet operating lease payments is the equivalent of $1,759,265,000 of debt. The computation is presented in Exhibit 10.12.

Exhibit 10.10.   Data for Estimating the Present Value of Operating Leases: Southwest Airlines, Year Ended December 31, 1998 (Thousands of Dollars)

Partial Lease Note

Future minimum lease payments under capital leases and noncancelable operating leases with initial or remaining terms in excess of one year at December 31, 1998 were:

Year	Capital Leases	Operating Leases
1999	$20,245	$247,208
2000	16,871	235,955
2001	17,391	222,688
2002	17,561	208,311
2003	17,750	190,925
After 2003	120,049	1,901,005
Total minimum lease payments	209,867	$3,006,092
Less amount representing interest	76,677	
Present value of minimum lease payments	133,190	
Less current portion	9,400	
Long-term portion	$123,790	

From the Southwest Airlines 1998 Balance Sheet

Total liabilities (includes deferred taxes, deferred sale and leaseback gains and other deferred liabilities)	$2,318,078
Total stockholders' equity	$2,397,918
Unadjusted ratio of total liabilities to stockholders' equity	0.97/1

Source: Southwest Airlines, Inc., Form 10-K annual report to the Securities and Exchange Commission (December 1998), pp. 31–32.

Exhibit 10.11.   Estimation of the Capital Lease Interest Rate of Southwest Airlines, Year Ended December 31, 1998 (Thousands of Dollars)

Scheduled 1999 capital lease payment	$20,245
Minus current portion	9,400
Interest portion of the 1999 payment	10,845
Divide by end of December 31,1998, capital lease liability	133,190
Equals average interest rate on capital lease liability	8.1%

Source: Data in Exhibit 10.10.

Exhibit 10.12. The Debt-Equivalence of Southwest Airlines' Operating Leases, December 31, 1998 (Dollars in Thousands)

	Payment	×	Present-Value Factor	=	Present Value
1999	$247,208		.92593		$228,897
2000	235,955		.85734		202,294
2001	222,688		.79383		176,776
2002	208,311		.73503		153,171
2003	190,925		.68058		129,984
2004–2013	190,100		4.56677*		868,143
Total					$1,759,265

Source: Data in Exhibits 10.10 and 10.11 as well as text above.

*This present value factor is for 15 periods at 8% minus the factor for 5 periods at 8%. This provides the same present value as computing the present value of the 2004–2013 payment stream and then bringing this present value back to the end of 1998. This is the point in time at which the debt-equivalence of the operating lease payments is being computed.

If added to the total liabilities already on Southwest's December 31, 1998, balance sheet, then Southwest's adjusted ratio of total liabilities to total stockholders' equity is as follows:

Original, as reported, liabilities	$2,318,978,000
Plus present value of operating lease commitments	1,759,265,000
Equals new adjusted total liabilities	4,078,243,000
Divide by the unchanged stockholders' equity	2,397,918,000
Equals adjusted ratio of liabilities to stockholders' equity of	1.70/1

The leverage ratio of 1.70/1 above compares to only .97/1 on an unadjusted basis; Southwest Airlines is much more highly levered than its unadjusted balance sheet would indicate.

Operating lease commitments represent one of the more common, and typically more significant, off-balance-sheet liabilities. They can be a major source of reduction in the quality of financial position. Even within a single industry, firms will differ in the extent of their use of capital versus operating leases. As a result, adjustments such as the above are essential in order to properly compare the relative degrees of financial leverage among firms.

Other Approaches to Estimation of Operating Lease Present Values

A simple rule of thumb has been used for many years in estimating the present value of operating lease commitments.[42] The most recent operating lease expense, or an average of scheduled operating lease payments, is multiplied by a factor of 7 or 8 to approximate the present value of the operating lease payments. Appli-

Exhibit 10.13. Interest Rates and Associated Lease Payment Multipliers

Interest Rate	Multiplier
14%	7.1
12	8.3
10	10.0
8	12.5
6	16.7

cation of such a multiplier is equivalent to finding the present value of a perpetuity.[43] A perpetuity is a payment stream that continues forever. The formula for the value of a perpetuity is: present value = annual lease expense/interest rate. This formulation can also be rearranged as: present value = 1/interest rate times annual lease expense

Consider an operating lease payment of $100. Using the formula for a perpetuity, and a discount rate of 10 percent yields: $100/.10 = $1,000. Moreover, a factor based on the second formulation above can also be applied: $100 times 1/.10 = $1,000. The factor is the reciprocal of the interest rate. The multiplication of $100 times 1/.10 is same as simply multiplying $100 times 10; 1/.10 equals 10. The multiplication of payment by the factor of 10 is the equivalent of finding its present value as a perpetuity. Other interest rates can be equated to their multipliers. A selection of rates and multipliers is provided in Exhibit 10.13. Whereas rounded values are used in practice, these multipliers have been carried out to one decimal place.

Notice that the multipliers increase as the interest rates decrease. That is, present value rises as the discount interest rate falls. Alternatively, the present value falls as the interest rate rises.

Application of the multiplier consistent with an 8 percent interest rate to Southwest's operating lease commitments (i.e., 12.5 per Exhibit 10.13) results in the following estimate of present value:

Average of scheduled payments for 1999 to 2003	$221,017,000
Times multiplier from the above schedule for 8 percent	× 12.5
Equals the estimate of the operating lease obligation	$2,762,712,500

This estimate compares to the direct estimate of $1,759,265,000 in Exhibit 10.12. The estimate using a multiplier of 12.5 results in an obligation that is about $893 million greater than the direct estimate in Exhibit 10.8.

One obvious reason for this excess is the fact that the computation in Exhibit 10.12 is based on a finite set of future lease payments. However, a payment stream that lasts forever is implicit in the multiplier approach used. That is, the payment stream is not finite; it is assumed to continue forever at about $221 million per year in the Southwest Airlines example. This would, in principle, lead to overestimation of operating lease obligations. This overestimation would be greater the shorter the remaining lease term, that is, the further it is removed from being a perpetuity.

However, an alternative view can be taken of the apparent overestimation of the Southwest Airlines operating lease liability. If maturing leases are continually replaced by new leases, then the concept of the payments as a perpetuity becomes more plausible.

In practice, the multiplier used to approximate the debt equivalence of operating leases is typically 7 or 8.[44] A multiplier of 12.5 was used above because it was consistent with the average interest rate of 8 percent in Southwest's capital leases. Use of a multiplier of 8, a number frequently used in practice, results in a liability estimate of only $1,768,136,000. This amount is only slightly greater than the $1,759,265,000 estimate developed using direct present-value calculation of Exhibit 10.12.

Estimating the Lease Obligation Using Capital Lease Relationships

As a final approach to estimating the debt equivalence of the operating leases, the ratio of the present value of the capital leases to the total capital lease payments can be used. If also applied to the Southwest Airlines operating lease data, the following results:

Present value of capital leases	÷	Total capital lease payments	×	Total operating lease payments	=	Estimated lease liability
$133,190,000		$209,867,000		$3,006,092,000		$1,907,786,000

The precision of the preceding estimation method will be determined mainly by the conformity of the capital and operating lease payment patterns and remaining maturities. If they are very similar, and if it is reasonable to assume the same interest rate for both types of leases, then the reliability of the liability estimate should be quite good. Note that the $1,907,786,000 liability estimate is very close to the $1,759,265,000 direct calculation in Exhibit 10.12.

Some Relevant Research on Lease Liability Estimation

There is a good deal of variability in the above estimates. A summary of the liability estimates is provided below:

Direct present value estimation	$1.7 billion
Payment multiplier of 8 (consistent with 12.5 percent interest rate)	$1.8 billion
Payment multiplier of 12.5 (consistent with 8 percent interest rate)	$2.8 billion
Use of present value of capital leases to payments relationship	$1.9 billion

For the example using the data of Southwest Airlines, the direct estimation of present value, Exhibit 10.12, results in the lowest liability estimate. This outcome is consistent with the broader research results of a study by Imhoff, Lipe, and Wright.[45] The authors compared estimations of operating lease liabilities for samples of 51 grocery firms and 29 airlines. They developed liability estimates using the direct present-value approach and the multiple of rents technique, employing a multiplier of 8. They determined that the median liability estimate using a factor of 8 times rents resulted in a much larger estimated liability than with the direct-present-value estimation procedure. For the grocery firms, the liability estimate using the multiple of rents was 65 percent greater than with the direct-present-value method and 103 percent higher for the airlines.

Lease Liability Overstatement with Multiple-of-Rents Method

The apparent tendency toward overstatement of operating lease liabilities is influenced by a number of factors. The 8-times-rents method assumes that current rents will continue forever. Actual lease payment schedules are, however, for finite periods. This will result in a tendency toward liability overstatement. However, the common use of payment multiples such as 7 and 8 should, in today's interest rate environment, lead to liability understatements. That is, multiples of 7 and 8 imply interest rates of 14 and 12 percent, respectively. These high rates, when used to find present value, will tend toward liability understatement.

Market Behavior and Alternative Lease Liability Estimates

Interestingly, the work of Imhoff, Lipe, and Wright indicates that market behavior is consistent with analysts using the simple multiple of rents technique as opposed to the direct present-value procedure of Exhibit 10.12. These authors studied the association of unadjusted and adjusted ratios of debt to assets (i.e., a measure of financial leverage) with measures of security risk. Financial leverage is expected to be positively associated with the uncertainty or risk of security returns. Using their samples of airline and grocery firms, Imhoff, Lipe, and Wright developed the results summarized in Exhibit 10.14.

In reviewing Exhibit 10.14, it can be noted that all the correlations based on adjusted leverage ratios (i.e., ratios adjusted to include estimates of operating lease liabilities) are more highly correlated with return volatility than are the unadjusted ratios. This implies that the market treats operating leases as debt in the assessment of financial leverage.

Also, the measures of market volatility are more highly associated with the leverage ratios developed using the multiple-of-rents method than with the direct-present-value approach. Imhoff, Lipe, and Wright see this as suggesting that "the market may be using an inefficient heuristic, i.e., rule of thumb, to assess firm risk."[46] That is, it appears that market estimates of financial leverage use a technique that typically overstates the debt represented by operating leases.

An alternative view to that of the Imhoff, Lipe, and Wright would have two key arguments. First, one could hold that superior estimates, from a going-concern perspective, of operating lease liabilities are produced with the multiple-of-rents

Exhibit 10.14. Alternative Lease Liability Estimations and the Association of Financial Leverage with Return Variability

	Airlines	Groceries
Rank correlations of unadjusted leverage ratios with stock price volatility:		
Rank correlation with ratios unadjusted for operating leases:	0.402	0.462
Rank correlation with ratios adjusted for operating leases:		
1. Direct present value method	0.615	0.472
2. Multiple of rents—8 times—method	0.650	0.552

Source: E. Imhoff, R. Lipe, and D. Wright, "Is Footnote Disclosure an Adequate Alternative to Financial Statement Recognition," *The Journal of Financial Statement Analysis* (Fall 1995), p. 78.

method. Second, the higher correlations found between measures of market risk and leverage measures incorporating the multiple-of-rents method simply confirm the superiority of the multiple-of-rents method.

It is widely held that the current accounting treatment of operating leases fails to capture their economic substance. To deal with this shortcoming in GAAP, analysts attempt to incorporate operating leases into revised measures of fixed-charge coverage as well as adjusted balance sheet measures of financial leverage. Rules of thumb are widely used, but by their very nature they have shortcomings. The multiple-of-rents method appears to provide rather inaccurate liability estimates if the accuracy benchmarks are liability measures developed by the direct calculation of present value. However, the results of Imhoff, Lipe, and Wright suggest that market measures of security risk are most closely associated with adjusted leverage measures that employ the multiple-of-rents method.

The case for the incorporation of estimated operating lease liabilities in producing various adjusted financial statistics appears compelling. Alternative approaches to estimating the debt represented by operating leases can produce quite different results, and there is a good deal of diversity in practice when it comes to estimating operating lease liabilities. Further, there does not appear to be a body of research that points to one estimation method as being superior to all others. However, in the face of this uncertainty, the greatest error would be to omit off-balance-sheet operating leases from assessments of financial leverage. It is better to have an admittedly crude estimation of the debt represented by operating leases than to simply omit them from the analysis.

In addition to assessing the implications of leasing for a firm's financial position and financial performance, creditors often attempt to deal with the off-balance-sheet nature of operating leases through financial covenants in their credit agreements. Some of these approaches to controlling operating leases are discussed below.

Control of Leasing with Debt Covenants

Financial covenants in credit agreements sometimes include capital lease obligations that place limitations on the incurring of additional debt. An example of the wording of such a covenant follows:

> The borrower may not incur or assume indebtedness for borrowed money, other than to Bank ABC, or act as a guarantor for indebtedness of others in an aggregate amount greater than $XXX. For the purpose hereof, sale of accounts receivable and/or *entering into capital leases* (emphasis added) of personal property shall be deemed the incurring of indebtedness for borrowed money.[47]

The preceding wording considers capital leases to be borrowings, but not operating leases. It offers one explanation for why lessees sometimes insist that a lease be structured to avoid capital lease classification. This covenant is an invitation to avoid the borrowing limitation by entering into operating leases.

There are examples of efforts to directly control operating lease commitments. Earlier discussion illustrated the inclusion of a portion of operating lease payments in the computation of fixed-charge coverage ratios. Financial covenants calling for some or all of operating lease payments to be included in the measurement of fixed-charge coverage ratios represents a somewhat indirect approach to controlling operating lease activity. A more direct approach would involve the use of a debt-to-equity covenant that includes estimates of the present value of operating lease commitments within the scope of the definition of debt. An example of this type of covenant, which appears to directly limit operating lease activity, is provided below:

> The Company's debt agreements require, among other things, that the Company: (a) meet certain working capital requirements; (b) limit the type and amount of indebtedness incurred; (c) *limit operating lease rentals* (emphasis added) . . . [48]

Limitations on operating lease commitments by lenders are evidence that operating lease commitments are viewed as debt equivalents. Financial analysis does place major reliance on GAAP-based statements. However, financial analysis is not bound by the definitions and classifications in these statements. The movement of financial analysis beyond GAAP definitions and classifications, in order to engage issues of form versus substance, is exemplified by the treatment of leases.

Leases as Sources of Off-Balance-Sheet Assets

Discussions of the balance sheet effects of leasing have typically focused on the reduction in financial position quality due to the off-balance-sheet liabilities associated with operating leases. However, disclosures of company acquisitions often reveal portions of the purchase price being assigned to favorable leases.

Favorable lease positions could result from either capital or operating leases. The label simply indicates that the lease terms are better than could be obtained in a newly negotiated lease of the same asset. Acquisitions accounting, under the purchase method, requires that such assets be measured and recorded.

Favorable lease positions represent off-balance-sheet assets in the case of operating leases and simply undervalued assets in the case of capital leases. In each case their presence enhances the quality of financial position.

Strengthened position quality carries with it an improvement in financial flexibility. This became manifest during the inflation-driven boom in real estate values in the late 1970s. Many firms were able to generate substantial amounts of cash by either subleasing their properties or by permitting themselves to be bought out by their lessors. In New York City, the typical pattern was to cash out of the favorable lease and move to New Jersey.

Analysts should be alert to the possibility of additional financial strength that could be represented by favorable lease positions. These could be especially important for firms that are downsizing or restructuring and are no longer in need of leases on very attractive real estate.

Profitability Issues and Lease Financial Analysis

Most of the above discussion has centered on the off-balance-sheet liability dimension of operating leases, and their implications for the measurement of financial leverage and fixed-charge coverage. This parallels the traditional emphasis by both accountants and financial analysts on these issues. However, as the example summarized in Exhibit 10.2 reveals, profits are also affected by the classification of a lease as capital versus operating. Further, both an asset and liability are omitted under the operating lease treatment asset. The combination of differences in net income and total assets has the potential to affect profitability measures such as return on asset (ROA) and return on equity (ROE).

To the extent that operating leases are viewed as the economic equivalent of capital leases, ROA statistics for firms with a significant reliance on operating leases may provide less reliable measures of profitability. Further, the use of ROA statistics to compare profitability among firms would also be affected.

A comparison of profits under the capital versus operating lease treatments shows net income under the capital lease method to be below that of the operating lease method, at least during the early years of the lease term. The combination of interest expense and asset amortization generally results in accelerated expense recognition and therefore lower income levels. At the firm level, and not at the level of the individual lease, this lower income tends to be sustained over time. This is a product of a combination of growth and lease replacement. The lower income level with capital leases is indicated by the presence of deferred tax asset positions for firms that account for some or all of their leases as capital leases.[49]

Leasing Alternatives and Return-on-Asset Measures

ROA measures generally employ EBIT. This is designed to gauge performance independent of the manner in which the firm is financed. EBIT will be higher, at least during the early years of the lease term, when leases are accounted for as capital as opposed to operating leases. To illustrate, the example in Exhibit 10.2 shows interest expense of $37,908 in year one and asset amortization of $75,816, for a total capital lease expense of $113,724. Assume that earnings before taxes are $75,000 under the operating lease treatment. This would mean that earnings under the capital lease treatment would be $61,276. This earnings difference is equal to the $13,724 excess of capital lease expense over operating lease expense. EBIT under the two lease accounting methods would be:

	Reporting Treatment	
	Capital Lease	Operating Lease
Earnings before income tax	$61,276	$75,000
Add interest expense	37,908	—
EBIT	$99,184	$75,000

If there were no differences in assets between the capital and operating lease treatments, then the ROA would be higher under the capital lease method. This results because EBIT is higher under the capital lease treatment than under the operating lease method: $99,184 versus $75,000. The key is the addition of interest expense of $37,908 to earnings before taxes under the capital lease treatment. Because there is no interest, as such, recorded on operating leases, there is no such addition to earnings in arriving at EBIT under the operating lease treatment.

However, while EBIT is higher under the capital lease alternative, total assets are also higher. Depending on the difference in total assets under the two methods, the ROA increase under the capital lease method, which results from the addition of interest expense to income, could be wholly or partly offset. As a result, the ultimate effect of alternative lease treatments on ROA statistics is uncertain.

Leasing Alternatives and Return-on-Equity Measures

With ROE measures, interest is not added back. This means that the earnings used to measure ROE will typically be lower under the capital lease method. However, stockholders' equity will also be lower because of this reduced level of net income. So, once again, the ultimate impact of the two lease accounting methods is uncertain.

Fortunately, there is some research that helps to anticipate what the effects on ROA and ROE statistics would be if operating leases were instead treated as capital leases. Imhoff, Lipe, and Wright report the effects of capitalization of operating leases on ROA and ROE measures for some individual case studies.[50] Their qualified conclusions regarding the effect of operating lease capitalization on ROA and ROE can be summarized as follows:

Return on Assets

1. Constructive capitalization of operating leases (i.e., the treatment of operating leases as capital leases), always increases operating income because depreciation expense on the leased asset replaces the lease payment.[51] The lease payment is greater than the amount of depreciation because the payment includes the equivalent of interest and principal. Holding assets constant, the increase in operating income increases ROA.

2. However, in addition to the increase in operating income, there is an increase in total assets from constructive capitalization. Holding operating income constant, the increase in total assets reduces the ROA.

3. Where operating leases are growing significantly, the reduction in ROA from the increase in assets will dominate the increase in operating income, thus lowering ROA.

Return on Equity

1. Constructive capitalization will result in a lower shareholders' equity.

2. If operating leases are in the first two-thirds of their terms, then constructive capitalization will decrease net income.

3. Again, where operating lease commitments are significant and growing, capitalization of operating leases will usually reduce ROE.

Most of the attention given to operating leases has been on the effects of operating leases, and their constructive capitalization, on measures of financial leverage and not on earnings measures. The work summarized above reveals that the effects of constructive capitalization on return measures such as ROA and ROE can be somewhat uncertain. Whether ROA and ROE are higher or lower as a result of constructive capitalization of operating leases may depend on where the collective leases are in their lease terms. Moreover, the level of growth in the operating leases also plays a role.

The degree of uncertainty surrounding the effects of lease classification on ROA and ROE measures appears to be greater than in the case of estimating the effects of constructive capitalization (i.e., treating operating leases as if that were capital leases) of operating leases on measures of financial leverage. Analysts have traditionally shown less concern with the effects of alternative lease accounting methods on measures of profitability than with their potential effects on measures of financial leverage. Hence, the uncertainty surrounding the influence of lease reporting alternatives on measures of return may be a somewhat less serious matter.[52]

FINANCIAL REPORTING BY LESSORS

The basic principles that guide lessee reporting also apply to lessor transactions. A modification in terminology is found on the lessor side: The term *operating lease* is used, but the term *finance lease* is normally substituted for capital lease. Lessor reporting is largely a mirror image of the lessee accounting. However, it is important to note that SFAS No. 13, "Accounting for Leases," does not require that lessees and lessors classify and account for a lease in the same way.

Characteristics of the Lessor Accounting Alternatives: Operating and Finance Leases

The lease classification criteria that apply in distinguishing operating from capital leases for lessees also apply to operating and finance (or capital) leases for lessors.[53] However, two additional criteria have to be satisfied for the lessor to classify the lease as a finance lease:

1. Collectibility of the minimum lease payments is reasonably predictable.
2. No important uncertainties surround the amount of unreimbursable costs yet to be incurred by the lessor.[54]

The key accounting and reporting features of operating and finance leases for the lessor are:

Operating Lease

1. The lessor retains the leased asset on its books.
2. Lease revenue is recognized on a straight-line basis and depreciation is recorded following the lessor's normal depreciation policy.[55]

Finance Lease

1. The lessor removes the carrying value of the leased asset and replaces it with the sum of the lease payments receivable plus any unguaranteed residual value accruing to the benefit of the lessor.
2. The difference between the gross investment in the lease (1 above) and the sum of the present value of the two components of the gross investment in the lease is recorded as unearned income.
3. The net investment in the lease is the gross investment (1 above) minus the unearned income balance.
4. The unearned income is amortized into earnings so as to produce a constant periodic rate of return on the net investment in the lease.[56]

Some general characterizations of commonly leased assets were provided at the beginning of this chapter. Specific examples of assets leased by selected lessors are provided in Exhibit 10.15. It is important to recognize that lessors differ in that some (1) manufacture their leased assets and also perform the leasing function, whereas others (2) simply purchase the leased asset from a manufacturer or dealer and perform the leasing function. However, even for some lessors who are neither manufacturers nor dealers, the presence of a difference between the cost and fair value of assets may permit a lease to be treated as a sale. The topic of sale-type leases is considered later in the chapter.

Of the companies included in Exhibit 10.15, GPA Group, PLC, and International Lease Finance Corporation are lessors who lease aircraft but are clearly not aircraft manufacturers. Caterpillar, Inc. and Navistar International Corporation both manufacture and lease equipment, though in both cases their leasing activities are conducted through consolidated financial subsidiaries.

Basic Lessor Accounting Illustrated

The basic features of lease accounting are illustrated with the same data used in the earlier illustration of lessee accounting (Exhibit 10.1). The only additional information provided is the cost to the lessor of the leased asset.

- The lease term is five years.
- The lease finance rate is 10 percent.
- The useful life of the leased asset is five years.
- The annual end-of-year lease payments are $100,000.
- The lessor's cost and fair value of the asset is $379,079.
- The residual value of the asset is zero.
- There is neither a bargain purchase option nor a title transfer at the end of the lease.

The above lease meets two of the four lease classification criteria: (1) the lease term is over 75 percent of the useful life of the leased asset: five-year lease term and five-year useful life; and (2) the present value of the lease receipts exceeds 90 percent of the fair value of the leased asset: present value of the lease receipts equals $379,079 and the fair value of the leased asset is also $379,079.

To be classified as a finance lease, the agreement must also satisfy the two additional criteria identified earlier that are related to (1) the likelihood of collectibility of lease receipts and (2) unreimbursable costs yet to be incurred. In illustrating finance lease accounting below, we assume that these additional criteria are satisfied.

Operating Lease Accounting

Operating lease accounting by the lessor is relatively simple, just as it is with the lessee. In the current example, the lessor would simply recognize revenue equal to the annual lease receipt of $100,000 and also deduct depreciation of the leased asset. If we assume straight-line deprecation, then the annual depreciation is the asset's cost to the lessor of $379,079, divided by the useful life of five years, results in annual depreciation of $75,816. Earnings for each of the five years, ignoring any other associated costs, will be:

Annual lease revenue	$100,000
Depreciation expense	75,816
Annual earnings	$24,184

In most cases, operating lease accounting approximates the treatment accorded the lease by the lessor in its income tax return. However, deferred taxes will normally still result because of depreciation-related taxable temporary differences. The leased assets, still on the books of the lessor, are typically depreciated on a straight-line basis, whereas tax return depreciation will be on a more accelerated basis. As a result, deferred tax liabilities will be recorded.

Finance Lease Accounting

Accounting for the above lease as a finance lease is summarized in Exhibit 10.16. A level rate of return is produced on the lease by multiplying the net lease investment at the beginning of each year by the interest rate in the transaction. The net investment in the lease will decline each year by the difference between the lease receipt and the portion of the receipt treated as interest income. The expected decline in the net investment is typically listed as a current asset if the lessor presents a classified balance sheet.[57] The reduction in the net lease investment is analogous, on the books of the lessee, to the portion of a capital lease obligation that is extinguished when a lease payment is made. As with the lessor, this portion is classified as current in the lessee's balance sheet.

The amount of interest income declines over time in line with the reduction in the net lease investment. This accelerated pattern of income recognition normally leads to taxable temporary differences and the recording of deferred tax liabilities. A temporary difference results because lease income is usually recognized more slowly in the tax return, where the accounting treatment approximates that of the operating lease method.

Income recognized under the finance lease and operating lease treatments is compared in Exhibit 10.17. As illustrated at the beginning of this section, the operating lease income is the same each year and is simply equal to the lease receipt of $100,000 minus straight-line depreciation of $75,816 each year or $24,184.

Exhibit 10.15. Selected Lessors and the Assets They Lease

Company	Assets Leased
American United Global, Inc.	Construction equipment
Berthel Fisher & Co. Leasing, Inc.	Telecommunication, agricultural, and general equipment
Capital Associates, Inc.	Equipment: transportation, materials handling, manufacturing, office automation, medical, and mining
Cardinal Health, Inc.	Point-of-use pharmacy systems
Caterpillar, Inc.	Heavy construction equipment
Cort Business Services Corp.	Office furniture and accessories
Cronos, Inc.	Intermodal marine containers
Dia Met Minerals, Ltd.	Helicopters
GATX Corp.	Railcars and tankage
GPA Group, PLC	Commercial aircraft
International Lease Finance Corp.	Commercial jet aircraft
Latin American Casinos, Inc.	Slot machines
Leasing Solutions, Inc.	Personal computers
McGrath Rentcorp	Electronic test and measurement instruments
Mitcham, Inc.	Seismic data acquisition
Modern Medical Modalities Corp.	Magnetic resonance imaging and computerized axial tomography
National Equipment Services, Inc.	Construction equipment
Navistar International Corp.	Trucks
OEC Compression Corp.	Gas compression equipment
Westar Financial Services, Inc.	Automobiles
Williams Scotman, Inc.	Mobile office units and modular structures

Sources: 1997 and 1998 annual reports of the listed companies.

The accelerated income recognition is seen by some lessors as an incentive to structure leases so that they qualify for finance lease accounting. This is especially true of bank lessors. Banks are subject to regulatory capital requirements, with shareholders' equity being the principal component of capital. Finance lease treatment recognizes income sooner and, therefore, bolsters measured regulatory capital.

If we assume that the finance lease treatment is applied to the books and the operating lease treatment in the tax return, then the excess of finance lease income in each of years one through three represents originating taxable temporary differences (see Exhibit 10.17). Moreover, the excess of operating lease income over finance lease income in years four and five represents the reversal of these taxable

Exhibit 10.16. Accounting by the Lessor for a Finance Lease

	Lease Receipt	Interest Income	Investment Reduction	Net Investment
Inception				$379,079[c]
Year 1	$100,000	$37,908[a]	$62,092[b]	316,987
Year 2	100,000	31,699	68,301	248,686
Year 3	100,000	24,869	75,131	173,555
Year 4	100,000	17,355	82,645	90,910
Year 5	100,000	9,090	90,910	0
	$500,000	$120,921	$379,079	

[a]Interest is 10% times the beginning of the year net investment. Year 1 interest is .10 times $379,079 or $37,908.

[b]The net investment reduction is that portion of the receipt not treated as interest. The year 1 reduction is $100,000 minus $37,908 or $62,092.

[c]The initial net investment in the lease is equal to the lease payments receivable of $500,000 minus the initial unearned income of $120,921 or $379,079. The unearned income is equal to the lease payments receivable of $500,000 minus the cost to the lessor of the leased asset of $379,079 or $120,921.

Exhibit 10.17. Comparison of Finance and Operating Lease Income Patterns

Year	Finance Lease	Operating Lease	Difference
1	$37,908	$24,184	$13,724
2	31,699	24,184	7,515
3	24,869	24,184	685
4	17,355	24,184	(6,829)
5	9,090	24,185	(15,095)
	$120,921	$120,921	0

temporary differences. The tax effects of these temporary differences are summarized in Exhibit 10.18.

The cash quality of results in years one through three is enhanced because of the noncash deferred tax provisions in these years. However, cash quality is reduced in years four and five because the taxable temporary differences reverse and the deferred tax liability is paid down.

Exhibits 10.16 through 10.18 illustrate the accounting for a single lease transaction. As a lease moves through its term, temporary differences originate and then reverse. However, for most lessors the reversing temporary differences are more than offset by a growing number of new leases on which temporary differ-

Exhibit 10.18. Lessor Accounting and Deferred Income Taxes

Year	Temporary Difference	Deferred Tax Provision	Deferred Tax Liability
1	$13,724[a]	$5,489[b]	$5,489
2	7,515	3,006	3,006
3	685	274	274
4	(6,829)	(2,731)	(2,731)
5	(15,095)	(6,038)	(6,038)
	$ —	$ —	$ —

[a]The differences between finance lease income and operating lease income per Exhibit 10.17.
[b]An assumed tax rate of 40% times the temporary difference of $13,724.

ences are originating. This means that the cash quality of results for the firm can remain enhanced over very long periods of time. It typically takes a significant and sustained decline in the level of business for temporary differences at the firm level to reverse. Normally, lease-related tax deferrals provide lessors with a significant strengthening in the cash quality of their earnings.

Lessor Financial Statement Disclosures

Lessors disclose information on expected lease receipts, and in the case of finance leases, on the net investment in finance leases. The net investment in the lease is comparable to the present value of a lessee's capital lease obligation. In the discussion below a standard set of disclosures is first presented and then a sampling from lease disclosures of other companies is provided.

Standard Lessor Disclosures

Exhibit 10.19 contains the major features of the leasing disclosures of IBM Credit Corporation.[58] Disclosures with respect to leveraged leases have been omitted. IBM Credit Corporation is a wholly owned subsidiary of International Business Machines.

Notice that IBM Credit's direct financing leases have typical terms of three to four years and the operating leases from two to four. These relatively limited terms no doubt reflect the short useful lives of the information processing products that are the subject of these leases. Given the similarity of the lease terms, close calls must be required in classifying leases as either direct financing or operating leases.[59] Recall that one of the lease classification criteria calls for finance lease treatment if the lease term is equal to or greater than 75 percent of the useful life of the leased asset. If the same types of products are the subjects of both the finance and operating leases, then it is not surprising that the operating leases have

Exhibit 10.19. Lease Disclosures: IBM Credit Corporation, Years Ended December 31, 1997–1998 (Thousands of Dollars)

NET INVESTMENT IN CAPITAL LEASES:

The Company's capital lease portfolio includes direct financing and leveraged leases. The Company originates financing for customers in a variety of industries and throughout the United States. The Company has a diversified portfolio of capital equipment financings for end users.

Direct financing leases consist principally of IBM advanced information processing products with terms generally from three to four years. The components of the net investment in direct financing leases at December 31, 1997 and 1998, are as follows:

(Thousands of Dollars)	1997	1998
Gross lease payments receivable	$4,922,989	$5,278,060
Estimated unguaranteed residual values	327,239	397,529
Deferred initial direct costs	36,325	30,634
Unearned income	(502,564)	(571,168)
Allowance for receivable losses	(52,373)	(65,644)
	$4,731,616	$5,069,411

The scheduled maturities of minimum lease payments outstanding at December 31, 1998, expressed as a percentage of the total, are due approximately as follows:

Within 12 months	48%
13 to 24 months	33
25 to 36 months	15
37 to 48 months	3
After 48 months	1
	100%

EQUIPMENT ON OPERATING LEASES:

Operating leases consist principally of IBM advanced information processing products with terms generally from two to four years. The components of equipment on operating lease at December 31, 1997 and 1998, are as follows:

(Thousands of Dollars)	1997	1998
Cost	$6,640,874	$7,046,757
Accumulated depreciation	(3,057,233)	(3,427,172)
	$3,583,641	$3,619,585

Minimum future rentals were approximately $3,346.6 million at December 31, 1998. The scheduled maturities of the minimum future rentals at December 31, 1998, expressed as a percentage of the total, are due approximately as follows:

Within 12 months	55%
13 to 24 months	31
25 to 36 months	11
37 to 48 months	2
After 48 months	1
	100%

Source: IBM Credit Corporation, Form 10-K annual report to the Securities and Exchange Commission (December, 1998), pp. 27–28.

Exhibit 10.20. Schedule of Deferred Tax Assets and Liabilities: IBM Credit Corporation, Years Ended December 31, 1997–1998 (Thousands of Dollars)

	1997	*1998*
Deferred tax assets (liabilities):		
Provision for receivable losses	$75,477	$87,623
Lease income and depreciation	(1,014,615)	(1,017,373)
Other, net	51,958	(43,936)
Deferred income taxes	$(887,180)	$(973,686)

Source: IBM Credit Corporation, Form 10-K annual report to the Securities and Exchange Commission (December, 1998), p. 35.

slightly shorter terms. This presumably results in their terms falling below the 75 percent threshold.

In line with accounting requirements for finance leases, note that IBM Credit does not include the leased assets on its books. Rather, upon inception of the lease, the leased assets are replaced by five different components that make up IBM Credit's net investment in the direct financing leases. However, in the case of the operating leases, the leased assets remain on the books of IBM Credit and depreciation is recorded. However, regardless of whether the lease is accounted for as a finance lease or an operating lease, IBM Credit would still own the leased assets for income tax purposes and would record depreciation on the leased assets in its tax return.

IBM Credit Corporation's Lease Accounting and Deferred Taxes

IBM Credit Corporation reports that its assets under operating leases are depreciated on its books using the straight-line method, but it also reports that depreciation is on an accelerated basis in IBM's consolidated tax return. In addition, it is likely that IBM recognizes income on its finance leases on a more accelerated basis on its books than in its tax return.

In the case of the operating lease assets, the use of straight-line depreciation on its books and accelerated depreciation in its tax return creates taxable temporary differences. Similarly, the accelerated recognition of finance lease income on the books, combined with an essentially straight-line recognition procedure in the tax return, creates taxable temporary differences. As taxable temporary differences, both of these items give rise to deferred tax liabilities.

The importance of the tax deferrals associated with IBM Credit's lease accounting is evident from a review of its schedule of deferred tax assets and liabilities, provided in Exhibit 10.20.

Exhibit 10.20 reveals that IBM Credit Corporation has a $974 million net deferred tax liability at December 31, 1998. The schedule shows that virtually all of this net liability results from the two lease-related temporary differences previously discussed. To put the size of the net liability into perspective, IBM Credit's shareholders' equity was $1.9 billion at December 31, 1998.[60]

A strong case can be made that the position quality of IBM Credit is enhanced by its cumulative net tax deferral of $974 million. If the lease portfolio of IBM Credit continues to grow, then the net deferred tax liability should likewise continue to grow. This liability bears no interest and is, in fact, overstated due to current GAAP requirements that do not call for carrying the net deferred tax liability at its present value.

The cash quality of IBM Credit's earnings is enhanced by its significant tax-deferral capacity. This enhancement of cash quality is evident from the detailing of its tax provision into current and deferred components in Exhibit 10.21. In 1998, about $87 million of IBM Credit's total tax provision of $201 million was deferred. This deferral enhances the cash quality of earnings by reducing the portion of the total tax provision that requires a current cash payment. The percentage of IBM Credit's tax provision that was deferred was 53 percent, 63 percent, and 43 percent in 1996, 1997, and 1998, respectively.

Components of Net Investment in Finance Leases

IBM Credit's net investment in its finance leases includes more items that were included in the earlier outlining of lessor accounting (Exhibit 10.16). At the end of the lease terms, IBM Credit can take possession of the leased assets. As these assets are expected to still have value, the present value of the estimated residual value is included as part of the net investment in the finance leases. If the residual value were guaranteed by the lessee, then the amount of the guarantee would have been included in the lease payments receivable.[61] The direct costs associated with originating a lease must be capitalized and treated as part of the net investment.[62] The allowance for losses on the leases simply reflects the credit risk exposure associated with any receivable.

Lessors and Balance Sheet Classification

As a financial firm, IBM Credit does not classify its balance sheet and, as a result, the current portion of its net investment in leases is not disclosed. Disclosure of the current portion of the net investment in leases makes it possible to approximate the average rate of return being earned on the finance leases. An example of this disclosure from the financial statements of Mail Boxes, Etc. is provided in Exhibit 10.22.

While Mail Boxes' disclosures are for its sales-type leases, these disclosures are identical to those found with finance leases. Once the sale portion of the sales-type lease is recorded, the accounting for a sales-type lease and a direct finance lease are the same.

The lease disclosures of Mail Boxes make it possible to identify (1) the portion of next year's lease receipts that will be treated as interest income, and to compute (2) the average interest return being earned on the net investment in the lease.

Exhibit 10.21. The Cash Quality of Earnings and Deferred Taxes: IBM Credit Corporation, Years Ended December 31, 1996–1998 (Thousands of Dollars)

	1996	*1997*	*1998*
Federal:			
Current	$60,741	$32,401	$93,164
Deferred	83,637	100,332	74,081
	144,378	132,733	167,245
State and local:			
Current	19,216	8,575	20,900
Deferred	12,528	21,907	12,603
	31,744	30,482	33,503
Total provision	$176,122	$163,215	$200,748

Source: IBM Credit Corporation, Form 10-K annual report to the Securities and Exchange Commission (December 1998), p. 35.

Exhibit 10.22. Disclosures of the Current Portion of Net Lease Investments: Mail Boxes, Etc., Years Ended April 30, 1996–1997 (Thousands of Dollars)

3. Net Investment in Sales-Type Leases

The Company leases various types of office and computer equipment to franchisees under three to eight-year lease agreements. The following summarizes the components of the net investment in sales-type leases at April 30:

	1996	*1997*
Total minimum lease payments to be received	$13,241	$10,980
Less unearned income	(3,309)	(2,591)
Net investment in sales-type leases	9,932	8,389
Less portion due within one year	(2,414)	(2,322)
Net investment in leases	$7,518	$6,067

Annual minimum lease payments subsequent to April 30, 1997, are as follows (in thousands): 1998—$3,307; 1999—$2,736; 2000—$2,031; 2001—$1,330; 2002—$778; and thereafter—$798.

Source: Mail Boxes, Etc., Form 10-K annual report to the Securities and Exchange Commission (April 1997), p. F-15.

The expected 1998 interest income, for just those leases on the books at the end of fiscal 1997, is simply the 1998 lease receipt, disclosed in Exhibit 10.22, minus the current portion of the net investment in the leases at the end of fiscal 1997: $3,307,000 − $2,322,000 = $985,000. This interest income amount can be converted into the annual return on the lease investment by dividing the expected fiscal 1998 interest income of $985,000 by the net investment in the leases at the end of fiscal 1997 (i.e., beginning of fiscal 1998): $985,000/$8,389,000 = 11.7 percent.

The lease return of about 11.7 percent may appear to be rather high. However, the leases are of relatively small items of office equipment used in the operations of the businesses. Credit risk associated with leases to the business operators may be above average, and residual values, should leased assets need to be repossessed, could be below their unrecovered cost.

A variation on the direct finance lease is the sales-type lease. Once the lease has initially been recorded, the accounting for the sales-type lease is the same as the finance lease. The sales-type lease is discussed next.

Financial Reporting of Sales-Type Leases

If a lease satisfies one of the four lease classification criteria and, in addition, there is a material difference between the lessor's cost and the fair value of the leased asset, then the lease will be accounted for as a sale, that is, a sales-type lease.[63] Although it may usually be the case, accounting for a lease as a sale (i.e., as a sales-type lease) does not require that the lessor be either a manufacturer or dealer. As explained in SFAS No. 13:

> Normally, sales-type leases will arise when manufacturers or dealers use leasing as a means of marketing their products. Leases involving lessors that are primarily engaged in financing operations will normally not be sales-type leases if they qualify under paragraphs 7 and 8, but will most often be direct financing leases . . . However, a lessor need not be a dealer to realize dealer's profit (or loss) . . . if a lessor, not a dealer, leases an asset that at the inception of the lease has a fair value that is greater or less than its cost or carrying amount, if different, such a transaction is a sales-type lease, assuming the criteria referred to are met.[64]

The key difference between a sales-type lease and a direct financing lease is that, upon inception of the lease, a sale and associated cost of sale are recorded. That is, the lease is accounted for as if it were a sale. In addition, the recognition of profit is accelerated compared to the operating lease treatment.

Some examples of lessors and the assets they lease under sales-type leases are provided in Exhibit 10.23. A review of the companies and assets leased reveals that most are firms that produce what they lease. However, sales-type treatment extends to dealers and lessors who are not manufacturers. For example, B.T. Office Products leases but does not manufacture copiers. Again, if a lease qualifies under the finance lease criteria, and the asset's value is different from its carrying value, then sales-type lease treatment is in order.

Exhibit 10.23. Examples of Assets in Sales-Type Leases

Lessor	Assets under Sales-Type Leases
Acuson Corp.	Electro-medical equipment
Affinity Technology Group, Inc.	Software for electronic technologies
Alcatel USA, Inc.	Telephone and telegraph equipment
Beckman Coulter, Inc.	Laboratory apparatus, analytical instruments, etc.
B.T. Office Products, International, Inc.	Copiers
Cambex Corp.	Computer storage devices
Gull Laboratories, Inc.	Analytical instruments
Hudson's Grill of America, Inc.	Restaurant equipment
Illinois Tool Works, Inc.	Transportation, mining, and paper processing equipment
International Business Machines, Inc.	Computer hardware
Kronos, Inc.	Labor management systems
McClain Industries, Inc.	Truck trailers and special industrial equipment
Med Waste, Inc.	Refuse systems
PMT Services, Inc.	Point-of-sale equipment
Printware, Inc.	Plate-setter systems
Sentry Technology Corp.	Security systems
Sonic Corp.	Restaurant related buildings and equipment
Techforce Corp.	Channel extension and data network hardware
Tennant Company	Floor maintenance equipment
USCS International, Inc.	Software
Vari Lite International, Inc.	Automated lighting systems

Sources: 1997 annual reports of the listed companies.

In illustrating the sales-type lease reporting, we use the same data as in the finance lease example of Exhibit 10.16. The only addition is that the cost of the leased asset is assumed to be $300,000.

Upon inception, sales revenue equal to the present value of the stream of lease receipts of $379,079 is recorded. In addition, the $300,000 cost of the leased asset is charged to cost of sales.[65] The result is the following recognized gross profit:

Sale	$379,079
Less cost of sale	300,000
Gross profit	$79,079

After the initial recording of the lease, the subsequent accounting is identical to the case of the finance lease in Exhibit 10.16. Income reported under both operating and sales-type lease accounting during the five-year term is summarized in Exhibit 10.24. For operating lease purposes, depreciation is computed on a straight-line basis.

Income recognition is accelerated under the sales-type versus both the direct finance and operating lease treatments. This income acceleration usually creates a substantial temporary difference, along with an associated noncash deferred tax provision and deferred tax liability. Again, the temporary difference results because operating lease treatment, or its equivalent, is normally used in the tax return, while the sales-type method is used in the books.

FINANCIAL ANALYSIS OF LESSORS

Lessor financial statements, and their associated financial analysis, have traditionally raised less controversy than the financial statements of lessees. However, lessor financial statements and the associated lease reporting options do raise some important issues of financial analysis. These range across the key dimensions of financial quality outlined in Chapter One. Some financial analysis issues have already been engaged in the course of outlining the financial reporting treatments applied to leases by lessors. Some additional attention is given to other financial analysis issues in this section.

Persistence of Lessor Earnings

The classification of a lease as direct financing or sales-type, versus an operating lease, typically results in a significant acceleration of lease income.[66] If a lessor's prospects are for smooth, but rather moderate growth, then the lease reporting alternatives have limited implications for the persistence or sustainability of earnings. However, in general, accelerated recognition of income results in an earnings stream with increased volatility. This volatility will be most pronounced when a lessor experiences significant growth combined with sharp fluctuations in revenues.

Research by Comiskey and colleagues demonstrated that increased earnings volatility resulted when fluctuations in business volume were combined with accelerated income recognition policies.[67] Although the setting involved finance companies and not lessors, the matter of interest was the same: assessing the impact on earnings of accounting policies that accelerated recognition of income.

The earnings of lessors who have a large portion of leases accounted for as finance leases will have greater volatility and a lower degree of earnings persistence than lessors with an emphasis on operating leases. The usual caveat of "other things being equal" must be added. Vari Lite International, Inc., a lessor of automated lighting systems, offers a cautionary note on the relationship between sales-type leases and the volatility of its earnings:

> Because most sales-type lease revenues are recorded in their entirety at the inception of the lease, wide variations in revenues and earnings in any given quarter can occur.[68]

Exhibit 10.24. Income Recognition under Sales-Type
and Operating Lease Methods

	Income Recognized					
	Year 1	Year 2	Year 3	Year 4	Year 5	Total
Sales-Type Lease						
Gross profit	$79,079[a]					
Interest income	37,909[b]	$31,698	$24,869	$17,355	$9,090	
Total income	116,988	31,698	24,869	17,355	9,090	$200,000
Operating Lease						
Lease receipt	$100,000	$100,000	$100,000	$100,000	$100,000	
Less depreciation	60,000[c]	60,000	60,000	60,000	60,000	
Total income	40,000	40,000	40,000	40,000	40,000	$200,000

[a]The present value of the lease payments receivable minus the cost of the leased asset.
[b]See computations in the Exhibit 10.16 illustration of a direct financing lease.
[c]The cost of the leased asset of $300,000 divided by its useful life of five years. No salvage value.

Cash Quality of Lessor Earnings

The pattern of cash inflows is not directly affected by the classification of leases as finance versus operating. However, as discussed and illustrated earlier, the pattern of income recognition is quite different. The relationship between cash inflows and earnings under the finance and operating lease accounting methods is depicted in Exhibit 10.25.

During the early years of the lease term, the excess of lease receipts over finance lease income is smaller than in the later years. As a result, cash quality is not as strong if the lessor with an emphasis on finance leases is located in region (a) of the graph. If, instead, that same lessor is located in region (b), cash quality—the relationship between lease income and lease receipts—is relatively stronger. For the operating lease, the relationship between lease receipts and lease income is constant over the lease term.

If a lessor is growing and expanding its portfolio of leases, then the average lease will probably be in the first half of its initial term. Here, region (a) in the graph, cash quality, is lower than it is in region (b) for the lessor with a finance lease emphasis. Therefore, in the typical case, the cash quality of a firm with a high concentration of finance leases will be somewhat lower than for the firm with a greater emphasis on operating leases. That is, the excess of lease cash inflows over lease income is greater for the operating leases in region (a).

The excess of lease receipts over lease income, be it under the finance or operating lease method, is due to associated leasing costs. The primary cost in

Exhibit 10.25. Earnings and Their Cash Quality: Finance versus Operating Leases

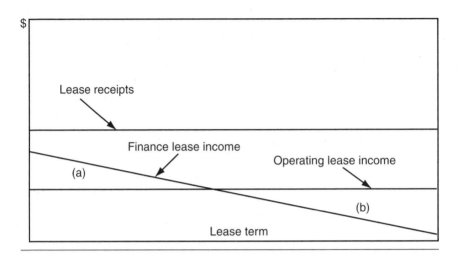

each case is normally the cost to the lessor of the leased asset. With an operating lease, lease income is the excess of total lease revenues over the cost of the leased asset. In the lessor's income statement, these elements appear as operating lease revenue and depreciation expense. With the finance lease, total income is also the excess of lease receipts over the cost of the leased asset. However, in the lessor's income statement, income is presented on a net basis. The finance lease income reflects the net of total lease receipts minus the cost of the leased asset, recognized on a constant yield basis over the term of the lease.

Lessors and the Quality of Financial Position

The implications for financial position quality is affected by whether leases are classified as operating or finance leases. In principle, position quality should be lower for lessors who emphasize finance as opposed to operating leases. Because income is recognized on an accelerated basis with finance leases, it follows that the net investment in finance leases is greater than the net carrying amount of the operating lease assets, that is, principally cost minus accumulated depreciation. If we assume that a lease portfolio's value is not affected by its book accounting treatment, then any excess of portfolio value over the carrying value of the lease portfolio should be less where finance leases dominate the portfolio. That is, position quality is weaker in the finance versus operating lease case.

Operating Leases

Operating leases are represented on the balance sheet by the undepreciated cost of the leased assets.[69] In the income statement, the operating leases appear in the form of lease revenue and associated depreciation expense. If straight-line depreciation is used in the books, and a more accelerated method is used in the tax return, then the income statement will also include a noncash deferred tax provision and the balance sheet will include a deferred tax liability.

To the extent that the lessor continues to grow and replace depreciating assets, then it is common for the deferred tax liability to be a somewhat permanent item on the lessor's balance sheet. As this liability does not bear interest, and it is not carried at present value under current GAAP, position quality is enhanced. As indicated earlier, cash quality also benefits from the deferred tax liability growth and the associated noncash deferred tax provision.

As with finance leases discussed below, position quality can be affected by estimates made about the residual value of leases. This is important with operating leases because there is often no expectation that the full investment in the leased asset will be recovered in a single leasing. Instead, full investment recovery usually requires remarketing activity in order to place the asset on a new or renewed lease or to sell the asset. Overestimates of residual values can result in significant asset write-downs or losses on sales.

Finance Leases

Even with finance leases, in which full payout status is more likely, estimates of residual value are crucial to the reliability of lessor profit measures. As with operating leases, remarketing activities when assets come off lease play a major role in ultimate full lease investment recovery. Selected lessor commentary on the role of residual value is provided in Exhibit 10.26.

In evaluating residual values, analysts should review the lessor's history of gains and losses from the remarketing of leased assets. Moreover, the nature of the assets leased should be considered. Lessors who emphasize high-technology equipment may be much more vulnerable to shrinkage in residual values than those who lease assets that are not as likely to suddenly become obsolete. Limited-use or highly specialized assets may also have a narrow market when they come off lease.

Financial analysts should give special attention to cases in which unguaranteed residual values are material in amount. In these cases, substantial shrinkage in residual values could seriously threaten the viability of the firm. As an example of substantial residual value, GATX Capital Corporation disclosed total residual values for direct finance and leveraged leases of about $484 million and $179 million at the end of 1997 and 1998, respectively.[70] These residual values represented 132 percent and 45 percent, respectively, of 1997 and 1998 shareholders'

Exhibit 10.26.   Residual Values of Leased Assets: Lessor Commentary

Company	Commentary
Airlease, Ltd. (1998)	Residual valuation, which is reviewed annually, represents the estimated amount to be received from the disposition of aircraft after lease termination. If necessary, residual adjustments are made which result in an immediate charge to earnings and/or a reduction in earnings over the remaining term of the lease.
Berthel Fisher & Co. Leasing (1997)	Realization of residual values depends on many factors, several of which are not within the Company's control, including general market conditions at the time of the original lease contract's expiration, whether there has been unusual wear and tear on, or use of, the equipment, the cost of comparable new equipment, the extent, if any, to which the equipment has become technologically or economically obsolete.
Leasing Solutions, Inc. (1996)	The Company's focus is on operating leases because such leases provide the opportunity for the Company to realize substantial return through residuals received upon remarketing the equipment to the original customer at the end of the initial lease term.
Linc Capital, Inc. (1997)	Residual values are estimated at the inception of the lease and reviewed periodically over the term of the lease. Estimated residual values of leased equipment may be adjusted downward, but not increased . . . To date, the Company has not had a net loss from the realization of residual values for any quarterly period.
Phoenix Leasing, Inc. (1997)	Operating leases, which generally have terms of shorter duration than full payout leases, are leases that will return to the lessor an amount less than the purchase price of the equipment. Upon expiration of the initial lease term, it is necessary to extend the lease term with the existing lessee, enter into a new lease with another lessee or sell the equipment

Sources: Companies' annual reports to shareholders. The year following each company name designates the annual report from which the example was drawn.

equity of GATX Capital. Unanticipated shrinkage in these residual values could result in substantial losses and associated reductions in shareholders' equity.

For many lessors, the remarketing of assets coming off lease has been a significant source of profitablity. Consistent gains on the sale of such leased assets indicate a source of potentially enhanced position quality. That is, asset sales at gains document that the assets were undervalued on the lessor's balance sheet. Moreover, such gains imply some level of understatement of previously reported earnings. Nonetheless, analysts should also see these residual value estimates as susceptible to substantial shrinkage if, for example, new technologies emerge that are either unexpected or ahead of schedule.

SALE AND LEASEBACK TRANSACTIONS

A somewhat unique class of lease transaction is the sale and leaseback. This transaction involves the sale of an asset, combined with its immediate leaseback. This is a very common transaction, and it is typically viewed to be a financing vehicle. The financing view is supported by the practice of displaying the sale proceeds in the financing activities section of the statement of cash flows.

Motivation for Sale and Leasebacks

In a review of a selection of sale and leaseback transactions, the recurrent themes are their use as either a source of financing or a means of paying down existing debt. Several examples are included in Exhibit 10.27, which indicate the use of the sale-leaseback proceeds.

Beyond their use as a financing vehicle, the possibility of recognizing gains on sale and leaseback transactions could be a motivating factor. For example, during the difficult 1980s and early 1990s in the banking industry, some sale and leasebacks appeared to be prompted by the need to increase bank regulatory capital. In its darkest hours, the Bank of America sold and leased back its world headquarters building in San Francisco. By selling and leasing the building back, the Bank of America was able to recognize an immediate gain of about $300 million, while deferring another $250 million for recognition over the term of the leaseback. The recognized gain of $300 million was added to its shareholders' equity, which is the principal component of a bank's regulatory capital.[71]

Some recent examples of sale and leaseback transactions are provided in Exhibit 10.28. There is a good deal of variety in assets that are sold and leased back.

A recent collection of anecdotes on the reasons underlying sale and leaseback transactions adds to the preceding.[72] A key reason noted for recent transactions involving real estate was the sense that the market may have peaked and that it was time to capture accumulated gains. Other factors that appeared to be influencing decisions to do sale and leasebacks were:

Exhibit 10.27.   Sale and Leaseback Motivations

Company	Use of Sale and Leaseback Proceeds
American Mobile Satellite Corp. (1997)	Refinanced computer hardware components
American Restaurant Group, Inc. (1997)	Sold and leased back land and building; used proceeds mainly to pay down debt and the balance for capital expenditures
Big 5 Corporation (1997)	Sold land and warehouse and repaid debt
Foodarama Supermarkets, Inc. (1997)	Sold supermarket assets and repaid debt
Great Lakes Aviation, Ltd (1997).	Repaid debt
IVC Industries, Inc. (1998)	Used proceeds to repay debt on a warehouse and distribution facility that was the subject of the sale and leaseback
Praxair, Inc. (1998)	Sold and leased back storage equipment and used the proceeds to repay debt

Sources: Companies' annual reports to shareholders. The year following each company name designates the annual report from which the example was drawn.

- A desire to free up capital to reinvest in core businesses
- A desire to dispose of excess properties as a result of mergers and downsizings
- A desire for an alternative, and cost-efficient means of raising cash without using the debt and equity markets
- A belief that real estate should be owned by firms that are in the real estate business
- A belief that little credit is given for real estate assets in assessing financial strength because of their illiquid character
- A desire to lower debt as a means of increasing return on invested capital
- A desire to shed assets as a means of increasing ROA
- A belief that a lower ratio of debt to equity, made possible by the sale and leaseback, will lower the cost of debt

Accounting for Sale and Leaseback Transactions

Accounting for sale and leaseback transactions is guided by SFAS No. 28, "Accounting for Sales with Leasebacks."[73] In some cases SFAS No. 28 permits immediate recognition of part or all of the gain on a sale and leaseback transactions. However, full deferral of a sale and leaseback gain is typically required, combined with the subsequent amortization of the gain through the income statement. Im-

Exhibit 10.28.   Assets Sold in Sale and Leaseback Transactions

Company	Assets Sold and Leased Back
Action Industries, Inc.	Headquarters facility
American Mobile Satellite Corp.	Computer hardware
Arizona Public Service Co.	Palo Verde generating unit
Artisoft, Inc.	Computer equipment and software
Asarco, Inc.	Mining equipment
Beazer Homes USA, Inc.	Model homes
Cinergi Pictures Entertainment, Inc.	Rights to films: *Judge Dredd* and *Evita*
Denamerica Corp.	Restaurants
Foodarama Supermarkets, Inc.	Buildings
GATX Capital Corp.	Rail equipment and steel production facility
Greyhound Lines, Inc.	Buses
Intime Systems International, Inc.	Computer equipment
Laser Storm, Inc.	Laser systems, arenas, and restaurant equipment
Panamsat Corp.	Satellite transponders
Questech, Inc.	Equipment
Rheometric Scientific, Inc.	Corporate headquarters and main manufacturing facility
Santa Fe Gaming Corp.	Gaming equipment
SDW Holdings Corp.	Paper machine
Sentry Technology Corp.	Company headquarters
Southwest Air Lines, Co.	Aircraft

Sources: Companies' annual reports for the year 1997.

mediate recognition of the full gain is permitted only where a minor leaseback is involved.[74] Some, but not all, of the gain may be recognized immediately in cases where the leaseback is for more than a minor but less than substantially all of the use of the asset.[75]

SFAS No. 28 provides guidelines for determining whether a leaseback is considered minor or substantially all. A minor leaseback is one in which the present value of the leaseback is less than 10 percent of the fair value of the asset sold. The substantially all threshold is guided by the 90 percent lease classification criterion of SFAS No. 13, "Accounting for Leases." A leaseback for substantially all of the remaining use of the asset would result if the present value of the leaseback amounted to 90 percent or more of the fair value of the leased asset. In turn, a minor leaseback would exist if the present value of the leaseback were for 10 percent or less of the fair value of the leased asset.[76]

The Bank of America transaction, discussed earlier, fell between the minor and substantially all categories. It was a leaseback that was more than minor but less than substantially all of the remaining use of the asset. Therefore, the Bank of America was able to recognize part of the gain immediately, and the remainder was deferred and amortized into earnings over the term of the leaseback.

Illustration of Sale and Leaseback Accounting

The accounting for sale and leaseback transactions is illustrated with the use of the following example:[77]

- The carrying value of an airplane that was sold and leased back is $100,000.
- The selling price is $600,000.
- The airplane's remaining life is 10 years and the leaseback period is three years.
- The lease does not transfer title and does not contain a bargain purchase option.
- The interest rate implicit in the lease as computed by the lessor is 12 percent.
- The annual monthly lease payments are $6,330.
- The present value of the leaseback, $6,330 at month for 36 months at 12 percent, is $190,581.

Failure of the lease to either transfer title or include a bargain purchase option, criteria one and two of the four lease classification criteria, keeps the leaseback from being considered a capital lease. Moreover, the leaseback term of only three years falls well short of the lease classification criterion which calls for capital lease treatment if the lease term is 75 percent or more of remaining useful life of the assets. Finally, the fourth lease classification criterion calls for capital lease treatment only if the lease present value is 90 percent or more of the fair value of the airplane. As the plane was sold for $600,000, it would be reasonable to assume that this is representative of its fair value. The leaseback present value of $190,581 is well short of 90 percent of fair value of $600,000.

The present value above is computed using the 12 percent rate implicit in the lease transaction. SFAS No. 13 requires the use of the lower of this implicit rate or the lessee's incremental borrowing rate.[78] The assumption in this case is that the implicit rate of 12 percent is in fact lower than the lessee's incremental borrowing rate. Using the lower of the two rates results in a larger present value and increases the likelihood that an agreement will be classified as a capital lease.

This lease does not satisfy any of the four lease classification criteria and is, therefore, classified as an operating lease. Further, the leaseback is classified as "more than minor" because the present value of the leaseback, $190,581, exceeds 10 percent of the fair value of the asset sold (.10 × $600,000 = $60,000). In addition, the lease is also less than "substantially all" because the lease present value of $190,581 is not equal to or greater than 90 percent of the $600,000 fair value of the leased asset. Therefore, this leaseback is considered to be "more than minor" but "less than substantially all." The pretax accounting for this case is summarized in Exhibit 10.29.

Exhibit 10.29. Accounting for a Sale and Leaseback Transaction

	Year 1	Year 2	Year 3
Initial gain recognized	$(309,419)[a]	$	$
Lease payments expensed	75,960[b]	75,960	75,960
Amortization of deferred gain	(63,527)[c]	(63,527	(63,527)
Net lease (gain) expense	$(296,986)	$12,433	$12,433

[a]The initial recognized gain is equal to the total gain realized minus the initial present value of the leaseback: [$600,000 − $100,000] − $190,581 = $309,419.
[b]The monthly lease payment of $6,330 times 12 months equals $75,960.
[c]Total gain of $500,000 minus the initial gain recognized of $309,419 equals the total deferred gain of $190,581. Total deferred gain of $190,581 divided by 3 equals the $63,527 of the deferred gain amortized each year.

Following the requirements of SFAS No. 28, the initial gain recognized of $309,419 is the excess of the realized gain over the present value of the leaseback.

Total gain realized on the sale ($600,000 − $100,000)	$500,000
Less the present value of the leaseback	190,581*
Gain recognized in year one income statement	309,419

*Thirty-six payments of $6,330 discounted at an annual rate of 12 percent.

The portion of the gain recognized immediately in earnings is only the $309,419 excess of the realized gain over the present value of the leaseback. The logic is that this portion of the gain could not be viewed as having been financed through the leaseback. Alternatively, the portion of the gain equal to the present value of the leaseback, $190,581, is viewed as being financed through the lease-back. Hence, immediate recognition in earnings of $190,581 of the gain is not permitted.

The portion of the total gain that is deferred, $190,581, is carried in the liability section of the balance sheet. It is amortized on a straight-line basis over the three-year lease term, and treated as a reduction in lease expense, as illustrated in Exhibit 10.29.[79] Note that the net lease expense is only $12,433, after offsetting the amortization of deferred gain each year against the annual lease payments: $75,960 minus the annual amortization of the deferred gain of $63,527 equals $12,433.

If the preceding leaseback had instead been classified as a minor leaseback, then the entire gain would have been recognized in the year of the sale. Alternatively, if the leaseback had been held to be for substantially all of the property, then the entire gain would have been deferred and amortized over the term of the leaseback.

The summary in Exhibit 10.29 does not include income taxes. The income tax and book treatments from Exhibit 10.29 are summarized in Exhibit 10.30.

Exhibit 10.30. Summary of Book and Tax Return Treatment of the Sale and Leaseback

	Book Treatment	Tax Return Treatment	Temporary Difference
Year 1			
Initial gain recognized	$(309,419)	$(500,000)	$(190,581)
Net lease expense	12,433	75,960	63,527
Net gain	(296,986)	(424,040)	(127,054)
Year 2			
Net lease expense	12,433	75,960	63,527
Year 3			
Net lease expense	12,433	75,960	63,527
Totals	$(272,120)	$(272,120)	$0

Exhibit 10.31. Current and Deferred Tax Elements of the Tax Provision

	Year 1	Year 2	Year 3
Book net (gain) or expense from Exhibit 10.30	$(296,986)	$12,433	$12,433
Tax provision (benefit) at 40%	118,794	(4,973)	(4,973)
Current provision	169,616[a]	(30,384)	(30,384)
Deferred provision (benefit)	(50,822)[b]	25,411	25,411
Total	118,794	(4,973)	(4,973)

[a]The current provision is the 40% tax rate multiplied by the taxable income (tax return treatment column in Exhibit 10.30) of each year. Year one: $424,040 times 40% or $169,616.

[b]The deferred provision (benefit) is the 40% tax rate multiplied times the temporary differences of each year (right hand column, Exhibit 10.30). Year one: $127,054 times 40% equals $50,822.

    Title to the airplane that was sold and leased back is transferred to the lessor. Moreover, the lessee received full cash payment for the airplane. Income tax authorities will treat the gain as a fully realized gain and consider it taxable in the year of the sale. However, GAAP require that a portion of the gain be deferred and amortized into the book income statement over the term of the leaseback.

    The difference between the book and tax return treatments result in an originating temporary difference in year one of $127,054. The temporary difference then reverses in equal amounts, $63,527, in years two and three. Assuming a combined 40 percent income tax rate, a deferred tax asset of $50,822 ($127,054 × .40) is recorded in year one and amortized in equal amounts, $25,411, in years two and three.

Exhibit 10.32. Sale and Leaseback Transaction: FiberMark, Inc., December 31, 1998

In April 1994, FiberMark entered into a sale-leaseback agreement with CIT Group, Inc. (CIT). FiberMark sold CIT $7,813,000 in fixed assets for a purchase price of $25,000,000. As a result FiberMark recorded a deferred gain of $17,187,000, which is amortized on a straight-line basis over the life of the 10-year lease. In 1998, 1997, and 1996 the company amortized $1,719,000, $1,718,000, and $1,719,000, respectively, of the deferred gain into income. At December 31, 1998 and 1997, the deferred gain amounted to $9,166,000 and $10,855,000 net of accumulated amortization of $8,021,000 and $6,302,000, respectively.

In connection with the sale-leaseback transaction, CIT leased back the fixed assets to FiberMark utilizing a 10-year operating lease. The lease requires quarterly payments of $843,000 for the first five years and quarterly payments of $690,000 for the remaining five years of the lease.

Source: FiberMark, annual report, December 1998, p. 37.

The tax effects from Exhibit 10.30. are summarized in Exhibit 10.31, in which the total tax provision in each of the three years is divided into current and deferred components.

With this background on the GAAP requirements for sale and leaseback transactions, we turn to an actual sale and leaseback example and explore its implications for financial quality.

A Sale and Leaseback Transaction: FiberMark, Inc.

FiberMark, Inc. executed a sale and leaseback transaction in 1994. Its 1998 annual report contained the disclosures provided in Exhibit 10.32 on the transaction.

Notice that FiberMark deferred the entire gain of $17,187,000 ($25,000,000) sale price minus the $7,813,000 book value of the assets sold) on this sale and leaseback. The leaseback is far too substantial to be considered minor. A minor leaseback (i.e., a present value of 10 percent or less of the fair value of the leased asset) would permit immediate recognition of the full gain. Further, the present value of the 10-year leaseback must have exceeded the total gain. Otherwise, some portion of the gain, as outlined in Exhibit 10.29, could have been recognized immediately and the balance deferred.

The gain on the sale and leaseback documents that fact that the quality of FiberMark's financial position was enhanced prior to the sale and leaseback. The sale price of $25 million, on an asset carried on the books at $7,813,000 (the gain of $17,187,000 on a sale price of $25 million implies a $7,813,000 book value for the assets sold), reveals previously unrecognized value. Prior to the sale and leaseback transaction, FiberMark's position quality was enhanced. Its balance sheet was stronger than it appeared to be because of the presence of significantly undervalued assets. However, after the transaction, the balance sheet has been marked to market value for these assets. This marking-to-market is outlined below:

Cash added to the balance sheet	$25,000,000
Book value of assets sold removed from balance sheet	7,813,000
Net increase, to market value, of the balance sheet	$17,187,000

As discussed in the earlier example, FiberMark's gain will be taxed on a current basis. FiberMark's lease and tax disclosures indicate that the gain was taxed at a combined federal and state rate of about 38 percent. FiberMark's schedule of deferred tax assets and liabilities reveals a deferred tax asset for deferred gains of $3,492,000 at the end of 1998. The deferred gain at that same date was $9,166,000. Dividing the remaining deferred tax asset of $3,492,000 by the remaining deferred gain of $9,166,000 results in a combined tax rate of 38.1 percent (i.e., the tax rate used in computing the tax on the gain).

Position Quality and FiberMark's Sale and Leaseback

As outlined above, FiberMark's balance sheet is marked-to-market when the sale and leaseback takes place. Position quality is no longer enhanced by the presence of these particular undervalued assets. However, the gain realized on these assets should raise questions about the possibility of other significantly appreciated assets. These would make it possible to both obtain financing and to increase the amount of shareholders' equity at the same time. These undervalued assets would add to FiberMark's financial flexiblity.

Flexibility in the sale and leaseback of appreciated assets may be restricted if the assets have already been pledged to secure earlier borrowings. Moreover, it is common for credit agreements to include covenants that restrict sale and leaseback transactions.

Beyond the possibility of other undervalued assets that the sale and leaseback signals, the initial classification of all of the realized gain among the liabilities on the balance sheet merits consideration. The assets were sold, cash was received, and title to the assets was passed to the lessor. From a financial analysis perspective, this has all of the characteristics of shareholders' equity (i.e., retained earnings). It is not uncommon for analysts to treat deferred sale and leaseback gains as an equity component for purposes of evaluating financial leverage.[80]

Earnings Quality and FiberMark's Sale and Leaseback

All of the cash associated with FiberMark's sale of assets was received in the year of the sale and leaseback. As a result, in years subsequent to the sale, the increase in earnings due to the amortization of the deferred gain results in a noncash increase in earnings. This noncash component of earnings is highlighted in the operating activities section of the FiberMark cash flow statement where it is deducted from net income in arriving at cash from operating activities. The relevant portion of the operating activities section of the statement of cash flows is provided in Exhibit 10.33.

In each year, the deferred gain is subtracted from net income in arriving at cash flows from operating activities. The cash quality of earnings is clearly re-

Exhibit 10.33. Cash Quality of Earnings and Amortization of Deferred Sale-Leaseback Gains: FiberMark, Inc., Partial Statements of Cash Flows, Years Ended December 31, 1996–1998 (Thousands of Dollars)

	1996	1997	1998
Cash flows from operating activities:			
Net income	$7,217	$6,169	$11,509
Adjustments to reconcile net income to net cash provided by operating activities:			
Depreciation and amortization	3,651	7,393	8,953
Amortization of deferred gain	(1,719)	(1,718)	(1,719)

Source: FiberMark, Inc., annual report, December 1998, p. 28.

duced as FiberMark amortizes deferred gains. Moreover, while the deferred gains contribute to earnings over a 10-year period, this earnings increase has a definite termination point. Therefore, within the framework of the analysis of earnings quality, earnings quality might also be considered to be somewhat diminished in terms of persistence. This reduction in earnings quality in terms of persistence would be greater if the remaining amortization period were shorter.

SUMMARY

Leasing is a topic that raises many issues related to both financial reporting and financial analysis. It is rich in implications that relate to the theme of assessing financial quality. A summary of some of the key points raised in this chapter follow.

- Lessee accounting and reporting turns on whether a lease transfers the risks and rewards of ownership to the lessee. Four lease classification criteria are employed to make this determination: transfer of title, bargain purchase option, length of lease term, and lease present value in relationship to fair value of the leased asset.
- Satisfaction of any one of the four classification criteria calls for recording an asset and associated liability by the lessee upon lease inception. That is, the lease is classified and accounted for as a capital lease. Otherwise, the lease is classified and accounted for as an operating lease.
- Under an operating lease, neither an asset nor a liability is recorded upon lease inception. Lease expense is normally recognized on a straight-line basis over the term of the lease.

- Expense recognition under the capital lease treatment is accelerated compared to the straight-line recognition pattern of the operating lease. Capital lease expense includes both interest and amortization of the leased asset.

- In most cases, the tax return treatment of a lease approximates that of an operating lease. Where a lease is classified as capital on the books, this will mean that temporary differences will emerge and deferred tax assets will be recorded.

- Treatment of a lease as operating results in an off-balance-sheet obligation. In practice, analysts estimate the debt equivalence of the operating lease commitments and include this amount in the assessment of a firm's financial leverage.

- Some credit agreements attempt to control the incurrence of additional operating lease commitments by treating then as comparable to debt. In addition, a portion of operating lease payments may be included within the definition of fixed charges in an effort to control operating lease commitments through a required fixed-charge coverage requirement.

- Attention is typically focused on the off-balance-sheet debt represented by operating leases. However, operating leases also affect various profitability measures, such as return on asset and return on equity.

- In some cases a lease may be the source of enhanced position quality because a lessee has lease terms that are more favorable than terms that could be negotiated currently. Where such leased assets are no longer required, lessees may be able to receive payments from the lessor to buy out the lessee or it may be possible for the lessee to sublease the asset at rates that are higher than those currently paid by the lessee.

- Lessor reporting treatments include operating lease, direct-finance lease, and leveraged lease. A sales-type lease is simply a variation on a direct-finance lease that involves the initial recording of a manufacturing or dealer margin, in addition to subsequent interest income. A leveraged lease has a lessee, lessor, and one or more suppliers of nonrecourse financing.

- A lease is classified as a finance lease if it satisfies at least one of the four lease classification criteria and also satisfies two other criteria: (1) No important uncertainties surround unreimbursable costs yet to be incurred, and (2) collectibility of lease payments is reasonably predictable. Finance lease income is recognized at a constant rate of return on the net investment in the lease. Where a sales-type finance lease is involved, a manufacturing or dealer profit margin is also recognized at inception of the lease.

- Income recognition by the lessor on an operating lease is generally on a straight-line basis.

- Finance lease recognition on the books is generally accelerated in relationship to that in the tax return. As a result, a temporary difference emerges and a deferred tax liability is recorded.

- Acceleration of income recognition under finance lease treatment can result in a higher degree of volatility in the lessor's earnings stream than would be the case under the operating lease method. This may diminish the lessor's earnings quality in terms of persistence.

- Where unguaranteed residual value is a major element of net lease investment, active monitoring of recoverability is essential in assessing the quality of a lessor's financial position.
- Sale and leaseback transactions result in the balance sheet being marked-to-market and also in the deferral of gain on the sale. Subsequently, the deferred gain is amortized through the income statement. The increase in earnings from gain amortization is not associated with any current cash inflow, and the cash quality of earnings is therefore impaired.

GLOSSARY

Bargain purchase option   Provides the lessee with the right to acquire the leased asset at the end of the lease term for an amount that is clearly below fair market value. Presence of a bargain purchase option requires a lease agreement to be classified and accounted for as a capital lease.

Bargain renewal option   Permits the lessee to renew the lease at expiration for amounts that are below fair market value. Presence of a bargain renewal option requires the renewal periods to be added to the noncancelable term of a lease for purposes of testing whether or not the lease term is for 75 percent or more of the useful life of the leased asset.

Closed-end lease   A lease in which the lessee bears no risk for residual value of the leased asset; residual-value risk is borne by the lessor.

Conditional sale lease   Treats the lease as essentially an installment purchase. The lessee is treated as the owner for income tax purposes and the tax benefits of ownership go to the lessee and not the lessor.

Contingent rentals   Increases or decreases in lease expense that are usually tied to some level of activity in or utilization of the leased asset.

Constructive capitalization   Capitalization of a lease that has properly been classified and accounted for as an operating lease. The objective is to assess the effects that capitalization of operating leases would have on, for example, measures of profit performance or financial leverage.

Direct finance lease   Transfers the risks and rewards of ownership to the lessee based on satisfaction of one or more of the four lease classification criteria and, in addition, satisfies the requirements that (1) collectibility of minimum lease payments is reasonably predictable and (2) no uncertainties surround amounts of unreimbursable costs to be incurred by the lessor.

Executory costs   The costs of maintenance, insurance and taxes, whether or not paid by the lessee or lessor.

Fair market value purchase option   Permits the lessee to acquire the leased asset for an amount considered to approximate fair market value.

Finance lease   Transfers the risks and rewards of ownership to the lessee. Finance leases can take two forms: a direct finance lease and a leveraged finance lease.

Full payout leases   Results in the noncancellable rental payments during the initial term of the lease being sufficient to allow the lessor to recover its full investment in the leased asset.

Full-service leases   Calls for the lessor to be responsible for maintenance, insurance, and taxes associated with the leased asset.

Gross lease   See Full-Service Leases above.

Guaranteed residual value   Requires, in some cases, the lessee to make up any shortfall between the guaranteed value and actual fair market value of the leased asset upon expiration of the lease. In other cases, it is the lessor who secures the guarantee of residual value from a third party.

Hell or high water provisions   Require the lessee to make the lease payments under any and all circumstances.

Implicit lease interest rate   The discount rate that causes the present value of the lease payments at the beginning of the lease to equal the lessor's fair value of the leased asset. This rate is comparable to the internal rate of return on an investment.

Incremental borrowing rate   The current rate(s) that would be paid by the lessee on additional borrowings.

Initial direct costs   Direct (i.e., incremental) costs associated with the origination of a lease. Included are costs of credit analysis of a prospective lessee, evaluating and recording guarantees, collateral, etc. Guiding GAAP are found in SFAS No. 91, "Accounting for Nonrefundable Fees and Costs Associated with Originating or Acquiring Loans and Initial Direct Costs of Leases."

Leveraged lease   A finance lease that involves three parties: the lessor, the lessee, and a provider or providers of nonrecourse long-term debt financing.

Net leases   The lessee pays taxes, maintenance, and insurance. The lease payments to the lessor are net of these costs. Also referred to as a triple net lease.

Open-end lease   A lease in which the lessee guarantees that the lessor will realize some minimum value on resale of the leased asset at the end of the lease. The lessee bears the residual value risk.

Operating lease   A lease that does not transfer the risks and rewards of ownership to the lessee. The operating lease does not satisfy any of the four lease classification criteria.

Renewal option   A right held by the lessee to renew the lease at the end of its noncancelable term.

Residual value insurance   Provides the lessee or lessor with protection in the event that the residual value of the lease falls short of expectations. Sometimes secured by lessors in order to raise the level of guaranteed lease receipts so that the 90 percent of fair value threshold (lease classification criterion four) is triggered and finance lease treatment is then possible.

Sale and Leaseback Involves a sale followed by a leaseback of the asset sold by it previous owner. Generally accepted accounting principles restrict the immediate recognition by the seller of gain, but not loss, on these transactions.

Sale-type lease A lease satisfying the finance lease criteria, but also involving a significant difference between the leased asset's cost and fair value. A manufacturing or dealer profit margin is recognized upon inception of the lease. Sale and cost of sale amounts are recorded.

TRAC lease A lease with a terminal rental adjustment clause. This clause shifts the residual value risk to the lessee.

Triple net leases A lease agreement that requires the lessee to make all payments for taxes, maintenance, and insurance.

True lease Qualifies as a lease under the Internal Revenue Code, thus permitting the lessee to deduct the lease payments in its tax return and the lessor to deduct depreciation of the leased asset in its tax return.

NOTES

1. R. Ho, "Nations Air to Begin Adding Planes Again: Dispute with Lessor Settled Out of Court," *The Atlanta Journal Constitution,* January 3, 1996, p. E3.

2. *Accounting Trends and Techniques,* 52nd ed. (New York: American Institute of Certified Public Accountants, 1998), p. 255. This annual survey of 600 firms draws on 33 different industries. Banks, leasing and real estate companies, plus insurance firms are not represented in the sample.

3. Some of the listed items were identified in a survey by T. Mukherjee, "A Survey of Corporate Leasing Analysis," *Financial Management* (Autumn 1991), p. 105.

4. There is evidence that leasing is a debt substitute. That is, leasing, whether it is on or off the balance sheet, uses up some of a firm's debt capacity. See F. Marston and R. Harris, "Substitutability of Leases and Debt in Corporate Capital Structures," *Journal of Accounting, Auditing & Finance* (Spring 1988), pp. 147–164. The desire for off-balance-sheet financing is sometimes based on the assumption that debt capacity is not displaced, or at least at less than dollar for dollar. This argument in favor of off-balance-sheet lease financing is somewhat suspect.

5. The alternative minimum tax (AMT) is designed to negate some of the benefits that are part of the regular tax law. The goal is to increase the likelihood that firms do not avoid tax payments altogether by using extensive tax-reducing features of the law. For example, as part of a complex calculation, the excess of accelerated over straight-line depreciation is added back to taxable income as computed under the regular tax law. A rate of 20 percent is then applied to this new higher income number. If the result is a tax that is greater than the tax under the regular tax system, then the higher amount must be paid. Leasing, by replacing depreciation with rent expense, helps a firm to avoid the AMT.

6. R. Westerfield and J. Jaffe, *Corporate Finance,* 5th ed. (New York: Irwin Mc-Graw-Hill, 1999), p. 620.

7. Lessees are the parties who possess and use but do not own the leased asset. Lessors are the owners of the asset.

8. SFAS No. 13, "Accounting for Leases" (Stamford, CT: Financial Accounting Standards Board, November 1976); and SFAS No. 28, "Accounting for Sales with Leasebacks" (Stamford, CT: Financial Accounting Standards Board, May 1979).

9. C. Reither, "What Are the Best and Worst Accounting Standards," *Accounting Horizons,* September 1998, pp. 283–292. This survey was conducted by Cheri Reither of the FASB. Subjects were participants at the 1996 AAA/FASB Financial Reporting Issues Conference. SFAS No. 13 was judged to be the "worst" standard. The ability to "game" the standard was the key criticism.

10. However, off-balance-sheet status may come at a cost. For example, one technique used to avoid on-balance-sheet treatment of a lease is to shorten the lease term in relationship to the asset's useful life. Shortening the lease term generally increases the cost of the lease.

11. "Accounting for Leases—A Codification as of October 1, 1998" (Norwalk, CT: Financial Accounting Standards Board, October 1998).

12. The purpose of the Emerging Issues Task Force (EITF) of the FASB is to attempt to reach a consensus on how to account for new financial transactions that have proved difficult to deal with or which have been accounted for in a variety of different ways. Unlike the extended deliberative process of the FASB, the EITF deals rather quickly with somewhat more narrow reporting issues.

13. SFAS No. 13, "Accounting for Leases," para. 60.

14. SFAS No. 13, para. 7.

15. Under SFAS No. 13, para. 5(d), a bargain purchase option is "a price sufficiently lower than expected fair value of the property at the date the option becomes exercisable that exercise of the option appears, at the inception of the lease, to be reasonably assured."

16. SFAS No. 13, para. 5(d).

17. Armstrong World Industries, Inc., annual report, December 1998, p. 65.

18. Southwest Airlines Company, annual report, December 1998. Information obtained from Disclosure, Inc., *Compact D/SEC: Corporate Information on Public Filing with the SEC* (Bethesda, MD: Disclosure, Inc., June 1999).

19. In the case of interim results, the annual lease expense would of course need to be apportioned across the four quarters.

20. If the present value of the lease exceeds the fair value of the leased asset, then both the leased asset and the lease liability should be recorded at fair value. See SFAS No. 13, para. 10.

21. As an example, the issue of the useful life of the leased asset is certainly subject to judgement. Lease classification criteria three might be avoided by extensions in expected useful life, which could thus avoid the lease term being held to be 75 percent or more of useful life of the asset. Similarly, classification criterion four might be avoided by increases in the discount rate which, in turn, reduce the present value of lease payments.

22. M. Bayless and J. Diltz, "An Empirical Study of the Debt Displacement Effects of Leasing," *Financial Management* (Winter 1986), pp. 53–60; and F. Marston and R. Harris, "Substitutability of Leases and Debt in Corporate Capital Structures," *Journal of Accounting, Auditing and Finance* (Spring 1988), pp. 147–164.

23. PHYCOR, Inc., annual report, December 1998, p. 35.

24. Illustrations of lease disclosure requirements can be found in SFAS No. 13, "Accounting for Leases," para. 122.

25. SFAS No. 13 generally calls for straight-line recognition of operating lease expense, even in cases where rental payments are not made on a straight-line basis: SFAS No. 13, para. 15.

26. La-Z-Boy Inc., annual report, April 1998, p. 23.

27. For income tax purposes, a bargain purchase option will probably call for the transaction to be accounted for as a conditional sale. The asset will be recorded and depreciated by the lessee-purchaser. Such a transaction would not transfer tax benefits from a lessee to the lessor. As such, it is not considered to be a tax-oriented lease.

28. AMR Corporation, annual report, December 1997, p. 55.

29. *Ibid.*

30. AirLease, Ltd., Form 10-K annual report to the Securities and Exchange Commission (December 1996), p. 43.

31. AirLease, Ltd., Form 10-K annual report to the Securities and Exchange Commission (December 1997), p. 40.

32. SFAS No. 13, para. 122.

33. Avado Brands, Inc., annual report, January 1999, p. 30.

34. *Ibid.,* p. 30.

35. Securities and Exchange Commission, Regulation S-K, Reg. §229.503, item 503.

36. *Ibid.,* §229.503, item 503, (4)(i).

37. *Ibid.*

38. Determined by dividing the 1999 lease payment minus the current portion by the present value of the capital lease payments at the end of 1998: ($20,245,000 − $9,400,000) / $133,190,000 = 8.1 %.

39. Standard and Poor's, *Standard and Poor's Corporate Finance Criteria* (New York: Standard and Poor's Corporation, 1991), p. 69.

40. Some references: R. Bowman, "The Debt Equivalence of Leases: An Empirical Investigation," *The Accounting Review* (April 1980), pp. 237–253; F. Marston and R. Harris, "Substitutability of Leases and Debt in Corporate Capital Structures," *Journal of Accounting, Auditing & Finance* (Spring 1988), pp. 147–164; and M. Bayless and J. Diltz, "An Empirical Study of the Debt Displacement Effects of Leasing," *Financial Management* (Winter 1986), pp. 53–60.

41. Two papers by Imhoff and others provide substantial detail on estimation procedures and other issues: E. Imhoff, R. Lipe, and D. Wright, "Operating Leases: Impact of Constructive Capitalization," *Accounting Horizons* (March 1991), pp. 51–63; and E. Imhoff, R. Lipe, and D. Wright, "Operating Leases: Income Effects of Constructive Capitalization," *Accounting Horizons* (June 1997), pp. 12–32. The technique outlined by Imhoff et al. is also found in a report in Standard and Poor's *Creditweek,* June 8, 1992, pp. 5–16.

42. For a discussion on rules of thumb applied to operating leases, see S. Cottle, F. Murry, and F. Block, *Graham and Dodd's Security Analysis,* 5th ed. (New York: McGraw-Hill, 1988), pp. 305–310.

43. Our experience working with analysts reveals that they often use these multipliers to estimate present value without understanding what the multipliers imply about either interest rate levels or the length of the payment stream.

44. The multipliers of 7 and 8, consistent with discount rates of about 14.2% and 12.5%, respectively, may simply have originated in a period of higher interest rates than those in the late 1990s.

45. E. Imhoff, R. Lipe, and D. Wright, D. "Is Footnote Disclosure an Adequate Alternative to Financial Statement Recognition," *The Journal of Financial Statement Analysis* (Fall 1995), p. 77.

46. *Ibid.,* p. 79.

47. From an anonymous source.

48. Haverty Furniture Companies, Inc., Form 10-K annual report to the Securities and Exchange Commission (December 1998), p. 17.

49. When a lease is accounted for as a capital lease on the books, it is generally treated as an operating lease in the tax return. Tax disclosures of lessees will often reveal deferred tax assets resulting from temporary differences created by capital leases. Deferred tax assets result when cumulative book profit is lower than cumulative tax return profits. This results if, on a cumulative basis, capital lease expense per the books has exceeded operating lease expense in the tax return.

50. E. Imhoff, R. Lipe, and D. Wright, "Operating Leases: Income Effects of Constructive Capitalization," *Accounting Horizons* (June 1997), pp. 13–32.

51. Imhoff et al. approach the choice of the income measure used in measuring ROA in a somewhat different manner. The more conventional measure is income before both interest and taxes (i.e., EBIT). However, Imhoff et al. use a measure of operating income that is before interest but after taxes.

52. This should be seen as a qualified statement. It may be that the difficulty of assessing the effects of lease classification on return measures has some negative consequences. However, we are not aware of any research that demonstrates this to be the case. It should be noted that lease classification and profitability issues have traditionally received more attention in the case of lessors as opposed to lessees.

53. It is common to see the term *direct* finance lease used, as opposed to simply finance lease. There are in fact two classes of finance lease. The direct finance lease simply involves two parties—a lessor who owns the asset and the lessee. Alternatively, in the case of a leveraged lease, which is a finance lease, there are three parties—a lessor who owns the asset, another party or parties who provided nonrecourse financing to the lessor, and the lessor. Because the focus here is on direct finance leases, we simply employ the term finance lease.

54. SFAS No. 13, "Accounting for Leases" para. 8.

55. *Ibid.,* para. 19.

56. *Ibid.,* paras. 18–19.

57. In the case of lessors who are financial firms, classified balance sheets are typically not provided.

58. IBM Credit uses the caption "capital leases" to cover both its direct finance and leveraged leases. It is not uncommon to see this usage. However, the "capital lease" caption is usually employed on the lessee side of the transaction for leases that have been brought on to the balance sheet (i.e., capital leases).

59. Upon initiation, many of the finance leases are presumably also classified as sales-type leases by IBM Corporation, IBM Credit Corporation's parent. The profit margin, represented by the difference between the sales value and the cost of the leased products, would be recognized by IBM Corporation. IBM Credit, in providing financing, only recognizes finance income. There will be more of this matter later in the chapter.

60. IBM Credit Corporation discloses a further deferred tax liability of $175 million, at December 31, 1998, in a schedule detailing its net investment in leveraged leases.

61. A residual value guarantee adds to the lease payments receivable and increases the likelihood that a lease will be classified as a finance lease. Lessors sometimes obtain insurance on residual values, from parties other than the lessee, as a means of obtaining a finance lease classification.

62. SFAS No. 91, "Accounting for Nonrefundable Fees and Costs Associated with Originating or Acquiring Loans and Initial Direct Costs of Leases" (Stamford, CT: Financial Accounting Standards Board, December 1986).

63. SFAS No. 13, para. 17.

64. *Ibid.,* para. 6.

65. If there is an unguaranteed residual value, its present value is deducted from the asset's cost in arriving at the cost of sales amount. SFAS No. 13, para. 17(c). Guaranteed residual values are also included in minimum lease payments receivable.

66. Income acceleration is only for purposes of determining pretax financial (i.e., book income). In the tax return, a lessor will normally elect to recognize income as slowly as possible, subject to requirements of the tax law.

67. E. Comiskey and F. Mlynarczyk, "Recognition of Income by Finance Companies," *The Accounting Review* (April 1968), pp. 248–256; and E. Comiskey and C. Colantoni, "Accounting Alternatives and Finance Company Earnings," *Financial Analysts Journal* (March–April 1969), pp. 55–59.

68. Vari Lite International, Inc., annual report, December 1998. Information obtained from Disclosure, Inc., *Compact D/SEC: Corporate Information on Public Filing with the SEC* (Bethesda, MD: Disclosure, Inc., June 1999).

69. Occasionally, the costs of originating operating leases will also be included on the balance sheet.

70. GATX Capital Corporation, annual report, December 1998. Information obtained from Disclosure, Inc., *Compact D/SEC: Corporate Information on Public Filing with the SEC* (Bethesda, MD: Disclosure, Inc., June 1999).

71. A sale and leaseback transaction might be used to produce profit in a firm's tax return in order to avoid the expiration of a loss carryforward. This would be considered a tax-planning strategy under the provisions of SFAS No. 109, "Accounting for Income Taxes" (Norwalk, CT: Financial Accounting Standards Board, February 1992), para. 21.

72. B. Martinez, "Why Own? Sell It and Then Lease Back the Space," *The Wall Street Journal* (April 20, 1999), p. A2.

73. SFAS No. 28, "Accounting for Sales with Leasebacks" (Stamford, CT: Financial Accounting Standards Board, May 1979).

74. SFAS No. 28, para. 23.

75. SFAS No. 28, para. 25.

76. See SFAS No. 28, paras. 3 and 24.

77. Adapted from an example in SFAS No. 28, para. 26.

78. The incremental borrowing rate of the lessee is used in computing present value unless the implicit interest rate computed by the lessor is lower. SFAS No.13, "Accounting for Leases" (Stamford, CT: Financial Accounting Standards Board, November 1976), para. 7(d). Also see paras. 5(k) and 5(l) for discussion of the implicit rate in the lease and the lessee's incremental borrowing rate.

79. Under SFAS No. 28, para. 3, amortization of the deferred gain is in proportion to the asset amortization in the case of a capital lease leaseback and in proportion to gross rental expense in the case of an operating lease leaseback.

80. An example is found in Standard and Poor's *Creditweek,* June 8, 1992, pp. 5–16. The debt-to-capital analysis of UAL, Inc. includes deferred gains along with conventional shareholders' equity.

Chapter 11

Reporting and Analysis of Pensions and Other Postretirement Benefits

"We deal with many companies who have surplus assets, but it's hush-hush—none of them wants to discuss it publicly"[1]

Through the mid-1980s, pensions and other postretirement benefits were a ghostly presence in financial statements. Disclosures were rather limited, and benefit plans that appeared to create obligations did not receive financial statement recognition.[2] All this changed with the issuance of Statement of Financial Accounting Standards (SFAS) No. 87 (1985), "Accounting for Pensions," and SFAS No. 88 (1985), "Employers' Accounting for Settlements and Curtailments of Defined Benefit Plans and for Termination Benefits." These two statements deal mainly with the accounting for defined-benefit pension plans.

About five years later, an additional pair of standards was issued that cover the accounting for postretirement and postemployment benefits: SFAS No. 106 (1990), "Employers Accounting for Postretirement Benefits Other Than Pensions," and SFAS No. 112 (1992), "Employers' Accounting for Postemployment Benefits."[3] SFAS Nos. 106 and 112 focus on other postretirement and postemployment benefits (OPEB).[4] Postretirement refers to nonpension benefits received after retirement. Examples include health care and life insurance benefits. Postemployment refers to nonpension benefits that begin after employment has ended, but before retirement benefits are received. These benefits cover employees who, although they have ceased working, are not yet eligible for conventional retirement benefits.

More recently, an additional disclosure-related standard has been issued: SFAS No. 132, "Employers' Disclosures about Pensions and Other Postretirement Benefits."[5] This statement is confined to required pension and OPEB disclosures, but changes none of the measurement requirements of previous standards.

The key issues addressed by both the pension and OPEB standards are those of matching, liability recognition, and disclosure. Prior to this newer set of benefit standards, cash-basis accounting was often applied, especially in the case of postretirement benefits. Expenses were recognized only as cash was disbursed to pay for benefits. In addition, in the case of pension plans, no obligations were recognized in the presence of earned but unfunded or underfunded benefits. With postretirement benefits, it is common for such plans to be totally unfunded.[6] Further, prior to SFAS No. 106, "Employers' Accounting for Postretirement Benefits Other Than Pensions," plan sponsors did not record an obligation for benefits as they were earned. This resulted in the omission of very large obligations from the balance sheets of many firms.

Both pension and OPEB plans can have important implications for financial analysis. However, before effective financial analysis of pension and OPEB plan disclosures can be conducted, a solid grounding in pension measurement and disclosure requirements is necessary. This chapter first outlines the reporting and disclosure requirements for conventional defined-benefit pension plans. The implications of pension plans and associated disclosures for financial analysis are integrated with this treatment of pension financial reporting. A short overview of the role of selected government entities in pension regulation will also be provided. Following this focus on pensions, attention will be turned to OPEB benefits. Many of the concepts underlying pension reporting also apply to OPEB reporting. Therefore, the treatment of OPEB benefits requires somewhat less attention to the reporting requirements. As with pensions, implications for financial analysis will be integrated with the coverage of reporting and disclosure requirements.

PENSION REPORTING AND ANALYSIS

There is a considerable body of terminology that is unique to pension plans. The glossary at the end of this chapter includes the more commonly encountered pension-related terms. These terms are also explained and illustrated as issues of reporting and analysis are engaged. Some basic pension-related terms are discussed below, followed by an overview of key accounting and reporting issues.

Basic Pension Concepts and Terminology

The major pension plans fall into one of two categories: defined contribution or defined benefit. The plan features create significant differences in financial reporting as well as their implications for financial analysis.

Defined-Contribution Plans

In a defined-contribution plan, the plan sponsor simply agrees to contribute a defined amount of money or other assets on behalf of the employee.[7] The eventual pension benefit is determined by the amount of money or other assets contributed on each employee's behalf and the return earned on these assets. The employees are the beneficiaries of the pension trust. The sponsor's principal responsibility for the defined-contribution plan is discharged when the agreed contributions are made on behalf of the eligible employees.

The definition of required contributions is typically tied to the employee's level of compensation. A sampling of some contribution policies is provided in Exhibit 11.1.

Exhibit 11.1.   Contribution Policies of Defined-Contribution Pension Plans

Company	Contribution Policy
Acme Metals, Inc.	Company contributions to the defined-contribution plan and the employee stock ownership plan (ESOP) are based on 7.5% and 3.5%, respectively, of eligible compensation.
Alliant Techsystems, Inc.	The two principal defined-contribution plans are Company-sponsored 401(k) plans to which employees may contribute up to 18% of their pay. The Company contributes in Company stock or cash amounts equal to 50% of employee contributions up to 4% or 6% of the employee's pay.
FiberMark, Inc.	The defined-contribution plan is a 401(k) ERISA and IRS-qualified plan covering substantially all employees, which permits employee salary deferrals up to 16% of salary with the company matching 50% of the first 6%.
WHX Corporation	The defined-contribution plans provide for contributions based on a rate per hour worked for hourly employees.

Sources: 1998 company annual reports of each of the above firms.

Some of the above defined-contribution plans involve only a contribution by the employer. This appears to be true for WHX Corporation in Exhibit 11.1. Others—typically the 401(k) plans—are also contributory plans. That is, contributions may be made by both the employer and the covered employee. The plans of Alliant TechSystems, Inc. and FiberMark, Inc. are examples of such plans.

Little attention is given to defined-contribution plans in the balance of this chapter because they raise few issues of reporting and analysis. Again, the plan sponsor's primary responsibility is discharged when the defined contribution is made on behalf of covered employees. Pension expense is recognized when the contribution is made, and its amount is confined to the contribution. As we will see, the case of defined-benefit pension plans is far more complex.

Defined-Benefit Plans

In a defined-benefit plan, the plan defines the benefit that the employee will receive upon retirement. The plan sponsor commits to providing the funds necessary to meet this obligation. Most defined-benefit plans are pay related. That is, the eventual benefit is based on the amount of compensation earned by employees.

While most defined-benefit pension plans are pay related, Brown-Forman Corporation discloses both pay-related and non–pay-related defined-benefit plans as follows:

Exhibit 11.2.   Selected Benefit Policies of Defined-Benefit Pension Plans

Company	Defined-Benefit Policy
Ecolab, Inc.	The company has a noncontributory defined-benefit plan covering substantially all of its U.S. employees. Plan benefits are based on years of service and highest average compensation for five consecutive years of employment.
General Electric Company	Generally, benefits are based on the greater of a formula recognizing career earnings or a formula recognizing length of service and final average earnings.
Regions Financial Corp.	Regions has a defined-benefit pension plan covering substantially all employees. The benefits are based on years of service and the employee's highest five years of compensation during last 10 years of employment.

Sources: 1998 company annual reports of each of the above firms.

> The benefits for these plans are based primarily on years of service and employees' pay near retirement for salaried employees and stated amounts for each year of service for union and hourly employees.[8]

The defined benefits for the union and hourly employees of Brown-Forman are simply based on years of service and are not pay related.

A selection of company policies dealing with the definition of pension benefits under defined-benefit plans is provided in Exhibit 11.2.

The defined-benefit plan creates a degree of uncertainty regarding the ultimate cost of the promised benefits that is not true of the defined-contribution plans. Once the employee has earned benefits under the plan, the employer has an obligation to provide sufficient resources to meet this commitment. The ultimate cost of providing the agreed benefits is based on a large number of assumptions concerning such items as future compensation, returns on pension assets, and the like. Alternatively, under the defined-contribution plan, the plan defines (and by so doing, limits) the cost of providing the earned benefits. However, from the employee's perspective, uncertainty surrounding ultimate pension benefits is greater with the defined-contribution plans. With the defined-contribution plan, the ultimate benefits received depend entirely on the contributions made, how they are invested, and how well the investments perform.

Contributory versus Noncontributory Plans

In most pension plans, the plan sponsor makes contributions to pension funds. However, in some cases, the employee also makes a contribution. Such plans are termed contributory plans. Notice that some of the defined-contribution plans referenced in Exhibit 11.1, especially the Section 401(k) plans, may involve contributions by both the employer and employee. Ecolab, Inc., in Exhibit 11.2, characterizes its defined-benefit plans as noncontributory. That is, only Ecolab, and not its employees, makes contributions to the pension trust. It is quite common for government-sponsored defined-benefit plans to require contributions by covered employees.

Qualified Plans

Qualified pension plans must meet certain requirements of the Internal Revenue Code.[9] Qualified status has the following results:

- Contributions by plan sponsors to pension funds, within limits, are deductible when made.
- Contributions by plan sponsors to pension funds create no immediate taxable income for plan participants.
- The earnings of the pension fund assets are taxed to neither the plan sponsor nor participants as earned. Rather, such earnings are generally taxable income of participants only when they receive pension benefits.

Defined-contribution plans present few issues with respect to either financial reporting or analysis. The obligations of plan sponsors are limited primarily to making the agreed contributions and fulfilling any other fiduciary responsibilities. However, sponsors of defined-benefit plans have responsibilities that extend well beyond the making of periodic contributions to the pension plan. There are important issues such as expense measurement, measurement and disclosure of pensions obligations, ongoing funding decisions, and so on. Moreover, plan sponsors are required to ensure that sufficient resources are available in the pension trusts to provide the defined benefits. As a result, the remaining pension plan discussion will focus only on defined-benefit plans.

Defined-Benefit Pension Plans

Beyond the above introductory discussion, there is a significant body of terminology that is unique to pension plans. The glossary at the end of this chapter explains much of this terminology, and it is also defined, discussed, and illustrated throughout the balance of this chapter. Also, most of the terminology and underlying concepts and procedures discussed here also apply to OPEB plans.

Relationships among Plan Sponsors, Pension Plan, and Participants

It is important to have a clear sense of the relationships and roles of the several parties involved with defined-benefit plans. These plans involve three parties: the

Exhibit 11.3. Pension Plan Relationships: Sponsor, Pension Plan, and Retirees

Plan sponsor makes contributions to the pension fund	→	Pension fund management invests fund assets and pays benefits to retirees	→	Retirees receive benefits from the pension fund

sponsor (usually the employer) of the plan, the pension fund or pension trust, and the plan participants (current and retired employees and beneficiaries). Their relationships are outlined in Exhibit 11.3.

The plan sponsor bears the responsibility for making the necessary contributions to the defined-benefit trust (i.e., pension fund). The plan sponsor has the responsibility for investment of the funds in order to ensure that sufficient resources are available to satisfy the promises made under the defined-benefit agreements. The plan participants are the beneficiaries of the pension trust assets in the case of defined-contribution plans. For example, if the pension funds are not sufficient to meet benefit requirements, then the employer must provide for any shortfall. However, if pension plans become overfunded, plan sponsors may benefit from this overfunding by either making reduced contributions to the pension trusts or by plan terminations and the recovery of excess assets.[10]

A Complete Set of Defined-Benefit Plan Disclosures: Adolph Coors

A complete set of required pension disclosures is provided in Exhibit 11.4 (as well as Exhibits 11.7 through 11.14). Initial issues related to generally accepted accounting principles (GAAP) requirements are discussed, using these disclosures for purposes of illustration. Matters that extend beyond this single set of disclosures will be illustrated with additional examples and exhibits.

Basic Plan Description
A description of the Coors' pension plans is provided in Exhibit 11.4. This disclosure reveals defined-benefit plans that are pay related. The disclosed pension funding policy is tied to the requirements of pension law (ERISA—Employee Retirement Income Security Act of 1974) as well as the income tax law.

The presence of a savings and investment (thrift) plan, to which Coors makes matching contributions, is also disclosed. This represents a form of defined-contribution plan that supplements the main defined-benefit plans.

Pension Plan Contributions
The Company contributes at least as much as ERISA requires, but no more than the amount that is deductible for tax purposes. A pension contribution of $48 million is disclosed that was not actually made until January 1999. This contribution is specifically tied to an increase in the pension obligations due to an amendment to the pension plans. Subsequent disclosures will reveal that Coors

Exhibit 11.4. Basic Pension Plan Description: Adolph Coors Company,
December 31, 1998

Note 7: Employee Retirement Plans

The Company maintains several defined-benefit pension plans for the majority of its
employees. Benefits are based on years of service and average base compensation levels
over a period of years. Plan assets consist primarily of equity, interest-bearing investments,
and real estate. The Company's funding policy is to contribute annually not less than the
ERISA minimum funding standards, nor more than the maximum amount that can be
deducted for federal income tax purposes. Total expense for all these plans was $24.8
million in 1996, $14.1 million in 1997, and $11.9 million in 1998. These amounts include
the Company's matching contributions for the savings and investment (thrift) plan of $5.7
million in 1996, $5.8 million in 1997, and $6.1 million in 1998. The steady decrease in
pension expense from 1996 through 1998 is primarily due to the improvement in the funded
position of the Coors Retirement Plan over that period. In November 1998, the ACC board
of directors approved changes to one of the plans. The changes, which will result in an
amendment to the plan, will be effective July 1, 1999, and will increase the projected
benefit obligation at the effective date by approximately $48 million. To offset the increase
in the projected benefit obligation of the defined-benefit plan, the Company made a $48
million contribution to the plan in January 1999.

Notice that the settlement rates in the table that follows were selected for use at the end
of each of the years shown. The Company's actuary calculates pension expense annually
based on data available at the beginning of each year, which includes the settlement rate
selected and disclosed at the end of the previous year.

Source: Adolph Coors Company, annual report, December 1998, pp. 35–36.

made a 1998 contribution of $2.7 million. This relatively small contribution is
due to the well-funded position of their defined-benefit pension plans.

This Coors funding policy is fairly typical. A selection of funding policies of
other firms is provided in Exhibit 11.5. Notice that the funded status (i.e., the
relationship between plan assets and obligations) of the General Electric Company
(GE) plans has resulted in GE's making no pension contributions since 1988. At
the end of 1998, GE's pension plans were overfunded by about $16 billion.[11]

Composition of Pension Fund Assets

The Coors disclosures provide a very general characterization of the type of assets
in the pension funds. Typically, little information on the relative proportions of
debt and equity investments is provided. However, disclosure of investments in
the sponsor's own securities is provided. There are limitations on the proportion
of plan assets that can be represented by the sponsor's own securities. Some
sample disclosures of the nature of plan assets are provided in Exhibit 11.6.

Unlike Bethlehem Steel in Exhibit 11.6, very few plans provide numerical
details on the distribution of plan assets.[12] Bethlehem's disclosure is helpful in

Exhibit 11.5. Selected Pension Funding Policies

Company	Funding Policy
General Electric Company	Funding policy for the GE Pension Plan is to contribute amounts sufficient to meet minimum funding requirements as set forth in employee benefit and tax laws plus such additional amounts as GE may determine to be appropriate. GE has not made contributions since 1987 because the fully funded status of the GE Pension Plan precludes current tax deduction and because any GE contribution would require payment of annual excise taxes.
Graco, Inc.	The Company funds these plans annually in amounts consistent with minimum funding requirements and maximum tax deduction limits.
Navistar International Corp.	The Company's policy is to fund its pension plans in accordance with applicable U.S. and Canadian government regulations and to make additional payments as funds are available to achieve full funding of the accumulated benefit obligation.

Sources: 1998 annual reports for each of the listed companies.

evaluating the level of the assumed rate of return on plan assets. For example, its asset distribution tilt in the direction of equity securities would make a somewhat higher return assumption more reasonable.[13]

Role of Actuaries
The plan descriptions include a reference to the Company's "actuary," who calculates the pension expense. In making such a computation, actuaries rely on a number of actuarial assumptions. Examples include: (1) retirement age, (2) mortality, (3) employee turnover, (4) future salary levels, (5) vesting provisions, (6) investment returns, (7) benefits, and (8) interest-rate levels. Their work, in addition to determining the pension expense for accounting purposes, also provides information on the level of pension obligations as well as guidance on funding needs.

Components of Net Periodic Pension Cost
Exhibit 11.7 details the elements of the net pension cost or expense.[14] This schedule includes a range of influences that bear on pension cost determination that is far more extensive than in the case of most other expenses.

The pension cost components are defined and discussed in Exhibit 11.8. However, some summary comments may also be useful. Item one, the service cost component, is developed on the basis of a number of actuarial assumptions. These tend to be long-term in nature and actual experience will always vary to some

Exhibit 11.6. Composition of Pension Fund Assets

Company	Fund Composition		
Bethlehem Steel Corporation (1997)	Plan assets at fair value (millions):		1997
	Fixed-income securities		$1,552
	Equity securities		3,102
	Cash and marketable securities		276
	Total plan assets		$4,930
FiberMark, Inc. (1998)	Plan assets are invested principally in equity securities, government and corporate debt securities, and other fixed-income obligations.		
Milicron, Inc. (1998)	The plans' assets consist principally of stocks, debt securities, and mutual funds. The U.S. plan also includes common shares of the company with a market value of $28.0 million in 1998 and $25.4 million in 1997 (*Note:* company shares amount to about 5% of total plan assets).		
Oregon Steel Mills, Inc. (1998)	Plan assets are invested in common stock and bond funds (96%), marketable fixed-income securities (1%), and insurance company contracts (3%) at December 31, 1998.		

Sources: Companies' annual reports. The year following each company name designates the annual report from which the example was drawn.

degree from these assumptions. Item two simply represents the growth in the pension obligations due to the combination of interest and the passage of time. However, items three through six all result from a key feature of current pension GAAP: smoothing.

Smoothing represents an effort to insulate the net pension cost from volatility that would result if changes in pension assets and obligations were included as they occurred in the determination of net pension cost.[15] The indicators of smoothing are terms such as deferral, amortization, and recognition. The term *deferral* refers to the delayed recognition of a change in pension assets or obligations in the determination of net pension cost. These deferred asset and obligation changes are usually labeled deferred gains and losses. Deferred gains result from increases in assets or decreases in obligations. Deferred losses result from decreases in assets or increases in obligations.

Amortization results from the decision to defer the change in pension assets or obligations over a number of future periods. *Recognition* represents the subsequent inclusion, termed amortization, in pension cost of previously deferred, gains and losses. Again, these gains and losses are the previously deferred changes in pension assets and obligations.

Exhibit 11.7. Components of Net Periodic Pension Cost: Adolph Coors Company, 1996–1998 (Thousands of Dollars)

	For Years Ended		
	December 29, 1996	*December 28, 1997*	*December 27, 1998*
Components of net periodic pension cost:			
Service cost—benefits earned during the year	$12,729	$11,234	$14,449
Interest cost on projected benefit obligation	31,162	32,730	33,205
Expected return on plan assets	(29,676)	(36,176)	(42,498)
Amortization of prior service cost	2,274	2,274	2,274
Amortization of net transition amount	(1,690)	(1,690)	(1,691)
Recognized net actuarial loss (gain)	4,279	(111)	28
Net periodic pension cost	$19,078	$8,261	$5,767

Source: Adolph Coors Company, annual report, December 1998, pp. 35–36.

The changes in pension assets and obligations that are deferred include (1) actual experience that differs from actuarial assumptions, (2) the effects of changes in actuarial assumptions, (3) retroactive changes in plan benefits, and (4) under or overfunded amounts that existed upon initial adoption of SFAS No. 87, "Employers' Accounting for Pension Costs."[16]

Deferral takes place only with respect to the statements of the employer or pension plan sponsor. All changes in pension assets and obligations are reflected as they occur in the financial statements of the pension plan.

The logic of the deferral of pension-related gains and losses is that defined benefit plans are long-term arrangements and that over time these pension gains and losses should be largely offsetting. Further, from a pragmatic perspective, firms objected to new reporting standards that would increase the volatility of their reported earnings and make it more difficult for the investment community to forecast their results accurately.

Changes in the Projected Benefit Obligation

Exhibit 11.9 displays the beginning and ending balances of the projected benefit obligation (PBO) and details the changes during each year. The requirement to present this schedule was introduced with SFAS No. 132, "Employers' Disclosures about Pensions and Other Postretirement Benefits."[17] Again, the PBO is the actuarial present value of the future benefit payments. Measurement of this obligation incorporates the estimated growth in pension benefits that result from changes in compensation levels. Exhibit 11.14 displays the assumed rates of increase in compensation used in the development of the PBO. These rates were 5.00 percent, 4.5 percent, and 4.5 percent in 1996, 1997, and 1998, respectively.

Exhibit 11.8.   Net Periodic Pension Cost Components: Adolph Coors
Company, 1996–1998

1. **Service cost**: Service cost represents the growth in the projected benefit obligation that
   results from pension benefits earned during the year. The pension obligation is the
   present value of the future cash payments that will go to the beneficiaries of plan. Hence,
   service cost is the present value of the increase in payments that result from employee
   service during the year.
2. **Interest on projected benefit obligation (PBO)**: Because the PBO is measured at
   present value, the passage of each year results in a growth in the obligation by interest.
   The earlier description of the Coors' plans states that the "Company's actuary calculates
   pension expense annually based on data available at the beginning of each year, which
   includes the settlement (discount) rate selected and disclosed at the end of the previous
   year." Use of the end of 1997 (also the beginning of 1998) discount rate of 7.25%
   (disclosed in Exhibit 11.14) times the beginning of 1998 PBO, $465,229,000 (disclosed
   in Exhibit 11.9), yields interest of $33,729,102. This is very close to the $33,205,000
   listed in the schedule of pension cost components (Exhibit 11.7). It is not possible to
   compute the interest amount exactly with the information provided. For example, the
   PBO grows during the year as a result of service cost and this would add to the amount
   of interest. Also, the PBO is reduced during the year as benefit payments are made.
      The PBO is distinguished from the accumulated benefit obligation (ABO)—not dis-
   closed by Coors—in that it incorporates an assumed rate of increase in compensation.
   The ABO is simply based on historic rates of compensation. The PBO is used to gauge
   funded status (the excess or shortfall of plan assets in relationship to plan obligations)
   for GAAP purposes and, for pay-related plans, it is always larger than the ABO.
3. **Expected return on plan assets:** The expected return is the product of pension assets
   (found in Exhibit 11.10) and the expected rate of return on plan assets (found in Exhibit
   11.17). The return assumptions at the end of 1997 and 1998 were 10.25% and 10.50%,
   respectively. If the rate at the beginning of 1998 of 10.25% is used, then the estimate
   of expected return is 10.25% times the beginning of 1998 assets of $465,494,000 or
   $47,713,135.[a] There is more divergence here than in the case of the interest calculation
   above. However, the use of the beginning of the year assets does not reflect the timing
   of asset increases from returns during the year or asset decreases due to benefits paid
   to retirees during the year. Nevertheless, the calculation illustrates the manner in with
   the expected return is computed.[b]
      Credit is taken for expected return in computing periodic pension cost, and not actual
   return. The difference between actual and expected return is deferred. The deferred
   return for 1997 was the actual return of $78,163,000 (disclosed in Exhibit 11.10) minus
   the expected return of $36,176,000 (disclosed in Exhibit 11.7) or $41,987,000. In 1998,
   the expected return of $42,498,000 exceeded the actual return of $33,006,000. This
   return shortfall of $9,492,000 was likewise deferred. Credit for the expected return of
   $42,498,000 was taken in arriving at net pension cost. The expected pension returns
   recognized by Coors from 1996 to 1998 grew mainly because of the increase in pension

(Continued)

Exhibit 11.8. (Continued) Net Periodic Pension Cost Components: Adolph Coors Company, 1996–1998

---

assets. The deferral of returns that deviate from expected is designed to smooth pension cost. This in turn insulates earnings from the volatility that would result if actual pension returns or losses were included in the computation of each year's pension cost.

4. **Amortization of prior service cost**: Changes are often made in plan benefits, with benefit increases being more common than decreases, and such changes are usually retroactive. With a benefits increase, there is an immediate associated increase in the pension plan obligation. However, rather than include the benefit increase immediately in pension cost, GAAP permit this additional cost to be amortized into pension cost over the remaining service periods of the affected plan participants.[c]

   Amortization of the cost of retroactive benefit increases over future years is an additional example of the smoothing feature of pension GAAP. Including the total cost of benefit improvements in pension cost for the year would induce significant earnings volatility. This could serve as a disincentive for employers to provide such benefit improvements. It is evident from the Exhibit 11.7 disclosures that Coors is amortizing its prior service cost on a straight-line basis. Note that the disclosed amount is $2,274,000 in each year from 1996 to 1998.

5. **Amortization of net transition amount**: The transition amount refers to the funded status of a pension plan when SFAS No. 87, "Employers' Accounting for Pensions," was initially adopted.[d] Funded status is determined by comparing plan assets to the projected benefit obligation. A transition asset or obligation is associated with an overfunded, assets exceed the PBO, or underfunded, assets are less than the PBO, position, respectively. SFAS No. 87 does not require that this asset or liability balance be immediately included in the calculation of periodic pension cost. Rather, this amount is to be amortized (included in pension cost) over the remaining service period of employees expected to receive benefits under the plan.[e] This feature also serves to smooth earnings by creating a less volatile pension cost stream. Exhibit 11.7 reveals an annual amortization of a net transition amount of about $1,690,000. Unlike amortization of prior service cost in 4 above, this recognition of an overfunded status upon adoption of SFAS No. 87 decreases net pension cost.

6. **Recognition of net actuarial loss (gain)**: Actuarial gains and losses result from either changes in actuarial assumptions or pension outcomes that deviate from the actuarial assumptions. For example, the 1998 schedule of the change in projected benefit obligation shows an actuarial loss of $40,932,000 (Exhibit 11.9). This indicates a change in the obligation due to either a change in an assumption or experience different from that assumed. Note that the schedule of rate assumptions (Exhibit 11.14) reveals a 0.25 decrease in the discount rate, between 1997 and 1998, used to compute the present value of the PBO. This reduction in the discount rate produces an immediate increase in the PBO.[f] However, consistent with the smoothing theme of SFAS No. 87, there is no requirement that this loss be recognized immediately in the computation of pension cost. Also, note that the actual return on plan assets in 1998 (see Exhibit 11.10) was

(Continued)

Exhibit 11.8. (Continued) Net Periodic Pension Cost Components: Adolph
Coors Company, 1996–1998

$33,006,000 but the expected return (Exhibit 11.7) was about $42,489,000. This
$9,492,000 shortfall of actual in relation to expected return also is an actuarial loss. The
schedule of funded status (Exhibit 11.11) shows an accumulated unrecognized net actuarial loss of $28,836,000 at the end of 1998, compared to a $21,560,000 gain at the
end of 1997. This change of about $50,396,000 is approximately equal to the
$50,424,000 sum of the actuarial loss of $40,932,000 disclosed in the schedule detailing
the 1998 change in the PBO plus the $9,492,000 shortfall in actual pension returns
identified above.

The concept underlying the deferral of actuarial gains and losses is that deviations
from actuarial assumptions are temporary and will zero out over time. However, if
unrecognized actuarial gains or losses become too large, then SFAS No. 87, *Employers'
Accounting for Pensions,* calls for their recognition in the calculation of pension cost.[g]
The threshold used to define large is 10% of the larger of plan assets or the PBO. To
the extent that the unrecognized actuarial gain or loss exceeds this amount, then the
excess must be included in pension cost, either reducing pension cost if a gain or
increasing pension cost if a loss. The minimum amortization is the excess divided by
the remaining service life of affected employees.[h] Some of the individual Coors' plans
must have exceeded the 10% threshold because portions of previously unrecognized
actuarial gains and losses were recognized in the computation of net pension cost (Exhibit 11.7) in each year from 1996 through 1998.[i]

[a]Pension assets at the end of 1997 are also the pension assets on the first day of 1998.

[b]An outline of the computation of actual pension return is: ending plan assets + benefit payments –
plan contributions – beginning plan assets.

[c]SFAS No. 87, "Employers' Accounting for Pensions" (Stamford, CT: Financial Accounting Standards
Board, December 1985), paras. 24–28.

[d]Most firms initially adopted SFAS No. 87 within the 1985 to 1987 time period.

[e]SFAS No. 87, para. 77. If the remaining service period is less than 15 years, then a 15-year amortization period may be used.

[f]In finding the present value of the future pension payments, an increase in the discount rate decreases
the PBO and a decrease increases the PBO.

[g]SFAS No. 87, paras. 32–33.

[h]SFAS No. 87, paras. 32–34.

[i]If Coors had a single defined benefit pension plan, then it is unlikely that any of the previously
unrecognized actuarial gains or losses would have been recognized in either 1997 or 1998. The
actuarial gains and losses fall well below the recognition threshold of 10 percent of the higher of either
plan assets or the projected benefit obligation.

The linkage between pension cost elements and changes in the PBO are evident in Exhibit 11.9. The 1998 service cost of $14,449,000 and interest cost of
$33,205,000 create identical increases in the PBO during 1998. In addition, the
.25 reduction in the discount rate, which is disclosed in Exhibit 11.14, results in
an increase of $40,932,000 in the PBO. The remaining change during the year is

Exhibit 11.9. Changes in Projected Benefit Obligation: Adolph Coors Company (Thousands of Dollars)

	December 28, 1997	December 27, 1998
Change in projected benefit obligation:		
Projected benefit obligation at beginning of year	$422,516	$465,229
Service cost	11,234	14,449
Interest cost	32,729	33,205
Actuarial loss	22,660	40,932
Benefits paid	(23,910)	(21,259)
Projected benefit obligation at end of year	$465,229	$532,556

Source: Adolph Coors Company, annual report, December 1998, pp. 35–36

the reduction of $21,259,000 resulting from benefits paid. The payment of benefits discharges a portion of the pension obligation.

In terms of financial analysis, the PBO is most relevant in evaluating the financial position of the firm from a going-concern perspective. The PBO includes the effects of any expected future increases in rates of compensation. While Coors does not disclose the accumulated benefit obligations (ABOs) of its plans, these obligations are more relevant in the event of a plan termination or in the case of financial difficulties of the plan sponsor. If a pension plan is terminated, then there will be no further accrual of benefits. Hence, the PBO is not relevant. Rather, the current burden of the pension plan is approximated by the ABO.

Changes in Plan Assets

The requirement to present the schedule of changes in pension plan assets, found in Exhibit 11.10, was also introduced with SFAS No. 132, "Employers' Disclosures about Pensions and Other Postretirement Benefits."[18] Unlike the schedule of changes in the PBO, none of the changes in pension assets links directly to net pension cost. The actual return on plan assets is displayed, but only the expected return is included in the determination of net pension cost. The other two items, employer contributions and benefit payments simply increase and decrease, respectively, pension plan assets. Note that the 1998 benefits paid of $21,259,000 also appear in Exhibit 11.9 as reducing the PBO by this same amount.

Pension Plan Funded Status

The difference between the PBO and plan assets is used to characterize the funded status of pension plans. Funded status of the Coors plans is presented in Exhibit 11.11. The Coors plans were overfunded by $265,000 at the end of 1997, but were underfunded by $52,556,000 at the end of 1998. The reasons for this change to underfunded status can be found in the earlier disclosures and are summarized in Exhibit 11.12—a schedule prepared by the authors and not presented by Adolph Coors.

Exhibit 11.10. Changes in Plan Assets: Adolph Coors Company (Thousands of Dollars)

	December 28, 1997	December 27, 1998
Change in plan assets:		
Fair value of assets at beginning of year	$394,206	$465,494
Actual return on plan assets	78,163	33,006
Employer contributions	17,035	2,759
Benefits paid	(23,910)	(21,259)
Fair value of plan assets at end of year	$465,494	$480,000

Source: Adolph Coors Company, annual report, December 1998, pp. 35–36.

Exhibit 11.11. Pension Plan Funded Status: Adolph Coors Company (Thousands of Dollars)

	December 28, 1997	December 27, 1998
Funded status—(shortfall) excess	$265	$(52,556)
Unrecognized net actuarial loss (gain)	(21,560)	28,836
Unrecognized prior service cost	16,577	14,303
Unrecognized net transition amount	(4,110)	(2,419)
Accrued benefit cost	$(8,828)	$(11,836)

Source: Adolph Coors Company, annual report, December 1998, pp. 35–36.

In 1998, the actual return on pension assets was only about $33 million (Exhibit 11.10), but the expected return was about $42.5 million, a $9.5 million shortfall from expectations (Exhibit 11.7). In addition, the reduction of .25 percentage points in the discount rate (Exhibit 11.14) increased the PBO by about $40.9 million (Exhibit 11.9). The combination of these two items alone reduced funded status by their sum of $50.4 million.

The decline in funded status in 1998 is detailed in Exhibit 11.12 in the "actual" column. In the "*pro forma*" column, the effect of the actuarial loss of $40.9 million is removed from growth in the PBO, and the return shortfall of $9.5 million is added to the change in assets ($40.9 million + $9.5 million = $50.4 million).

In spite of the actual change in 1998 to an underfunded position of $52.5 million, there appears to be little reason for concern about the funded status of the plans. As shown in Exhibit 11.12, in the absence of the change in the discount rate and the return shortfall, the changes in plan assets and obligations would have been a shortfall of $2.4 million. The funded strength of the Coors plans called for only $2.7 million of pension contributions in 1998. Moreover, the $48 million increase in the PBO that resulted from plan amendments (Exhibit 11.4), which became effective in July 1999, has already been fully funded by a $48 million

Exhibit 11.12.   Analysis of the Changes in Funded Status of the Coors
Pension Plans, December 27, 1998 (dollars in millions)

	Actual 1998	*Pro Forma 1998*
Changes in plan assets:		
Return on plan assets	$33.0	$42.5
Employer contributions	2.7	2.7
Benefits paid	(21.2)	(21.2)
Total	14.5	$24.0
Changes in the PBO:		
Service cost	$(14.4)	$(14.4)
Interest on projected benefit obligation	(33.2)	(33.2)
Actuarial loss	(40.9)	—
Benefits paid	21.2	21.2
Total	(67.3)	(26.4)
Decline in funded status	$(52.8)	$(2.4)

Sources: Exhibits 11.7, 11.9, 11.10, and 11.11.

Exhibit 11.13.   Reconciliation of Pension Funded Status to Sponsor's
Financial Statements: Adolph Coors Company, December 27, 1998 (Thousands
of Dollars)

Funded status per the statements of the pension plans—	
underfunded	$(52,556)
Add:	
Actuarial loss recognized by the pension plan but not on	
the books of Coors	28,836
Unrecognized prior service cost recognized by the	
pension plan but not on the books of Coors	14,303
Deduct:	
Unrecognized transition amount recognized by the	
pension plan but not on the books of Coors	(2,419)
Accrued benefit cost (a liability) on the balance	
sheet of Coors	$(11,836)

Source: Information in Exhibit 11.11.

pension contribution in January 1999. Finally, while additional reductions in interest rate levels are always possible, further increases in the PBO from such rate reductions would seem less likely than reductions in the PBO from rate increases.

The combined Coors plans were underfunded by $52,556,000 at the end of 1998: the PBO of $532,556,000 minus pension assets of $480,000,000. The presentation of funded status, Exhibit 11.11, also includes a reconciliation of (1) the net underfunded position per the pension plan and (2) the pension liability on the books of Coors. The underfunded status of $52,556,000 is reconcilied to the accrued benefit liability of only $11,836,000 on the balance sheet of the Adolph Coors Company. This schedule serves the same purpose as does a bank reconciliation. The funded status of the pension plan, the bank, is reconciled to the pension plan balance carried on the books, checkbook, of Coors in Exhibit 11.13. Exhibit 11.13 is an annotated version of Exhibit 11.11, prepared by the authors.

On a cumulative basis, $28,836,000 and $14,303,000 of pension obligations are recognized on the financial statements of the Coors *pension plans* that have not been recognized by *Coors* in the determination of its net pension cost. This has reduced the benefit liability on the books of Coors in relationship to the pension plans by a total of $43,139,000. That is, the Coors balance sheet appears somewhat stronger than the financial statement of the pension plans. This results from the practice of the plan sponsor's (i.e., Coors), deferring some of the changes in pension obligations for later recognition in net pension cost.

The $2,419,000 of unrecognized transition amount has been deferred, that is, not yet recognized by Coors in the computation of net pension cost. This is the unamortized amount by which the Coors plans were overfunded at initial adoption of SFAS No. 87, "Employers' Accounting for Pensions."[19] Notice that this overfunded amount is being recognized as a reduction in net pension cost at the rate of $1,690,000 per Exhibit 11.7. The delayed recognition of this overfunding results in the balance sheet of Coors being marginally weaker than the financial statements of the pension plans.

Issues related to pensions and the recognition of pension liabilities by plan sponsors will be discussed and illustrated later in this chapter. However, it should be recognized that in relationship to PBO, the Coors pension plans are underfunded by $52,556,000 per Exhibit 11.11. The quality of financial position of Coors could be considered to be somewhat diminished because its balance sheet includes accrued benefit cost, a pension liability of only $11,836,000 at the end of 1998.

Pension Plan Actuarial Rate Assumptions
Actuarial rate assumptions are the final pension plan disclosures provided by Coors. Exhibit 11.14 includes the discount rate, rate of compensation increase, and the expected rate of return on plan assets.

Discount rate assumptions
The decline in the discount rate across the period of 1996 through 1998 resulted in actuarial losses and associated increases in the PBO, as discussed above. SFAS

Exhibit 11.14. Pension Plan Rate Assumptions: Adolph Coors Company, for the Years 1996–1998

	1996	*1997*	*1998*
Weighted-average assumptions as of year-end:			
Discount (settlement) rate	7.75%	7.25%	7.00%
Rate of compensation increase	5.00%	4.50%	4.50%
Expected return on plan assets	10.25%	10.25%	10.50%

Source: Adolph Coors Company, annual report, December 1998, pp. 35–36.

No. 87 states that discount rates should "reflect the rates at which the pension benefits could be effectively settled."[20]

Expected rate of return assumptions

The increase in the expected rate of return on plan assets reduces net periodic pension cost. Recall that the expected return is the product of the expected rate of return multiplied by plan assets. As shown in Exhibit 11.8, the expected return reduces net pension cost. Alternatively, a decrease in the rate would increase pension cost. The expected rate of return is characterized in SFAS No. 87 as "the average rate of earnings expected on funds invested or to be invested to provide for benefits . . ."[21] The Coors 1998 rate assumption of 10.5 percent is high in relationship to typical rates. Some sample data, presented later in this chapter, indicate an average rate of 9.0 percent in 1998.

Rates of increase in compensation

The rate of compensation increase was constant between 1997 and 1998, but it did fall between 1996 and 1997. This change in actuarial assumption would reduce the PBO. However, because the ABO is based on historical and not projected compensation levels, the 1997 rate reduction would not affect the ABO. In general, the higher the assumed rate of compensation increase, the greater the excess of the PBO over the ABO. Coors did not disclose the amount of its ABO because it is not required to do so under the disclosure requirements of SFAS No. 132, "Employers' Disclosures about Pensions and Other Postretirement Benefits."[22]

With this overview of pension plan reporting and related disclosures, we now move on to a more exclusive focus on the implications of pension plans for financial analysis. However, some consideration will be given to reporting issues that were not raised by the pension disclosures of Adolph Coors.

PENSION PLANS AND FINANCIAL ANALYSIS

A number of the relationships between pension plans and pension plan sponsors have implications for financial analysis. Examples include:

- The funded status of pension plans
- Pension income versus net pension cost
- The level of actuarial assumptions
- Pension poison pills
- The regulatory role of selected government entities

Financial Analysis and the Funded Status of Pension Plans

Under current pension GAAP, the funded status of pension plans is measured by comparing plan assets to the PBO. Where plans are either over- or underfunded, the analyst should determine the extent to which the over- or underfunded amounts are already reflected on balance sheet of the plan sponsor as a prepaid pension asset or accrued pension liability, respectively. In the routine application of accrual accounting, prepaid pension assets will emerge when pension contributions exceed net periodic pension cost. Alternatively, an accrued pension liability results when the pension cost accrual exceeds pension contributions.

The pension asset or liability balances on the books of a pension plan sponsor are seldom equal to the amount of over or underfunding based on the statements of the pension plans. These differences result from the process of deferral that was discussed and illustrated earlier.

A disclosure of funded status, which is a GAAP requirement, by comparing plan assets to the PBO is implicitly adopting a going-concern perspective. A firm with pension plans that are fully funded on this basis has strong position quality. The pension funds contain sufficient assets to fulfill the firm's promises under its defined-benefit plans, even after allowing for higher future compensation levels. Moreover, cash flow is often strengthened by either reduced or eliminated pension contributions.

A determination of funded status by making a comparison of plan assets to the ABO is implicitly adopting a liquidation perspective. If a pension plan were terminated, then the ABO would approximate the obligation to be satisfied. A firm can be underfunded on a going concern basis but overfunded from a liquidation standpoint. There is a requirement, in some cases, for firms with underfunded plans to make additional minimum liability adjustments. In these cases, funded status is determined by comparing plan assets to the ABO and not the PBO.

Under SFAS No. 87, disclosure of both the ABO and PBO was required.[23] However, under the more recent SFAS No. 132, only the PBO is routinely disclosed. The ABO is generally disclosed only in cases in which one or more plans have assets that are less than the ABO.[24]

Examples of overfunded and underfunded pension plans are presented below to both explore their implications for financial analysis as well as to continue outlining GAAP governing pension reporting.

Overfunded Pension with Most Overfunding Recognized: Sherwin-Williams Company

The pension plans of the Sherwin-Williams Company were overfunded by $323,285,000 at the end of 1998. An abridged display of funded status is presented in Exhibit 11.15. At the end of 1998, $302,475,000 of the overfunded amount had already been recognized in the financial statements of Sherwin-Williams simply through the application of pension GAAP. For example, the unrecognized net asset at adoption of SFAS No. 87 has almost all been recognized over the intervening years. Moreover, as the level of pension assets continued to grow, the expected return on plan assets likewise increased. The high level of expected return is principally responsible for the net pension benefit in each of the years from 1996 through 1998, as disclosed in Exhibit 11.16.

The net pension benefit is a key source of the $302,475,000 of recognized overfunding at the end of 1998. As the Sherwin-Williams pension plans have become increasingly overfunded, the expected return has become large enough to more than offset the positive elements of net pension cost (i.e., mainly service and interest cost). No funds are distributed to Sherwin-Williams in the face of its net pension benefit. Instead, this benefit is recognized through increasing the net pension asset recognized on the Sherwin-Williams balance sheet. The $30,851,000 pension benefit in 1998 explains almost all of the $31,709,000 increase, ($302,475,000 − $270,766,000), in the net pension asset between the beginning and end of 1998, as is outlined in Exhibit 11.17.[25] The $858,000 difference in Exhibit 11.17 is probably explained by some small pension accruals.

The overfunded position of the Sherwin-Williams pension plans is a strong positive for their financial position. However, there is little improvement in the quality of financial position, as defined in Chapter One, because most of the overfunded amount has already been recognized in the Sherwin-Williams balance sheets. That is, of the overfunded amount of about $323,285,000, $302,475,000 has already been recognized by Sherwin-Williams through its inclusion in the computation of net pension cost and it, the $302,475,000, is on the Sherwin-Williams balance sheet at the end of 1998.

Notice that no pension contributions are reported by Sherwin-Williams in Exhibit 11.15 for either 1997 or 1998. This was made possible by the overfunded status of the pension plans. In the absence of this overfunding, Sherwin-Williams would be reporting a much reduced pension benefit and would probably be making cash outlays for pension contributions. The pension overfunding strengthens the cash flow of Sherwin-Williams.

The net pension benefit currently being recognized contributes to Sherwin-Williams' earning performance. This pension benefit is largely the result of the substantial overfunding of the pension plans. While the overfunding may continue, and with it the pension benefit, it would seem more likely, especially in the face of Sherwin-Williams' not making any current plan contributions, that the overfunding will decline over time. This means that the current level of benefit being

Exhibit 11.15. Overfunded Pension with Overfunding Largely Recognized: Sherwin-Williams, Years Ended December 31, 1997–1998 (Thousands of Dollars)

	1997	1998
Benefit Obligations		
Balance at the end of year	$175,204	$169,099
Plan assets		
Balance at the beginning of year	391,865	446,271
Actual return on plan assets	60,143	71,188
Acquisitions	10,574	—
Other—net	2,037	(759)
Benefits paid	(18,348)	(24,316)
Balance at the end of year	446,271	492,384
Excess plan assets (funded status)	271,067	323,285
Unrecognized net asset	(4,304)	(2,792)
Unrecognized actuarial (gain) loss	3,195	(20,348)
Unrecognized prior service cost	808	2,330
Net asset recognized in the consolidated balance sheets	$270,766	$302,475

Source: Adapted from Sherwin-Williams, annual report, December 1998, p. 27.

Exhibit 11.16. Net Periodic Benefit: Sherwin-Williams Company, Years Ended December 31, 1996–1998 (Thousands of Dollars)

	1996	1997	1998
Net periodic benefit:			
Service and interest cost	$14,449	$14,429	$14,506
Net amortization and deferral	(145)	(1,008)	(2,524)
Expected return on assets	(29,602)	(33,594)	(37,531)
Settlement gain	—	—	(5,302)
Net periodic benefit	$(15,298)	$(20,173)	$(30,851)

Source: Sherwin-Williams, annual report, December 1998, p. 27.

recognized should be viewed as impairing somewhat the quality of the Sherwin-Williams earnings in terms of persistence. The persistence dimension of earnings quality in 1998 is also diminished somewhat by the nonrecurring "Settlement" gain of $5,302,000.

    The pension benefit also does not result in any cash inflow to Sherwin-Williams from its overfunded pension plans. In this sense, the pension benefit represents noncash income and could be seen as reducing earnings quality in terms

Exhibit 11.17. Recording Pension Benefits on the Employers' Books: Sherwin-Williams Co., Years Ended December 31, 1997–1998 (Thousands of Dollars)

Net pension benefit for 1998		$30,851
Net pension asset on the 1998 balance sheet	$302,475	
Net pension asset on the 1997 balance sheet	270,766	
Net pension asset increase		31,709
Difference		$858

Source: Information found in Exhibits 11.15 and 11.16.

of cash content. However, there is a cash benefit being realized, and it takes the form of Sherwin-Willams currently not being required to make contributions to its pension plans. Under these circumstances, the cash quality of earnings should probably not be considered to be impaired.

Pension Asset Exceeds Overfunded Amount: VF Corporation

VF Corporation's pension plans are overfunded by $3,114,000, but the Company carries a pension asset on its balance sheet of $35,164,000 at the end of 1998. Information on the funded status of these plans is provided in Exhibit 11.18. The difference of $32,050,000 ($35,164,000 − $3,114,000) between the amount recognized on VF's balance sheet and the overfunding of its pension plans is mainly due to the deferred recognition by VF Corporation of $29,943,000 of prior service cost.

The retroactive improvement in pension benefits results in an immediate increase in the PBO in the financial statements of the pension plans. However, VF Corporation deferred, consistent with pension GAAP, recognition of this increase in its PBO. It is recognizing (i.e., amortizing) the cost of this benefit improvement and including it in the determination of net pension cost over future years.[26]

The increase in the PBO obligation from this plan amendment is real and must eventually be funded by VF Corporation. For purposes of financial analysis, it would be more realistic to consider the asset associated with overfunding to be the $3,114,000 based on the pension plan disclosures instead of the $35,164,000 that results from deferring recognition of the PBO increase. VF Corporation's position quality should be considered somewhat diminished due to this asset overvaluation.

In addition to the issue of recognition of funded status by the plan sponsor, the pension disclosures of VF Corporation illustrate how quickly the funded status of a firm's pension plans can change. The VF pension plans were overfunded by $52,147,000 at the end of 1997. However, this overfunding was reduced to only $3,144,000 at the end of 1998, a decline of $49,033,000. This change reflected

Exhibit 11.18. Pension Asset Exceeds Overfunded Amount: VF Corporation, Years Ending December 31, 1997–1998 (Thousands of Dollars)

	1997	1998
Plan Assets		
Fair value of plan assets, beginning of year	$405,000	$526,087
Actual return on plan assets	115,805	28,013
Company contributions	27,000	20,400
Benefits paid	(21,718)	(20,909)
Fair value of plan assets, end of year	$526,087	$553,591
Benefit Obligations		
Benefit obligations, beginning of year	$411,295	$473,940
Service cost	16,726	19,738
Interest cost	33,577	36,370
Plan amendments	2,896	19,005
Actuarial loss	31,164	22,333
Benefits paid	(21,718)	(20,909)
Benefits obligations, end of year	473,940	550,477
Funded status, end of year	52,147	3,114
Unrecognized net actuarial (gain) loss	(37,483)	2,107
Unrecognized prior service cost	16,117	29,943
Unrecognized net transition asset	(3,068)	—
Pension asset recorded in Other Assets	$27,713	$35,164

Source: Adapted from VF Corporation annual report, January 1999, p. 28.

an increase in the PBO of $76,537,000, against an increase in pension assets of only $27,504,000.

Asset growth was sharply reduced in 1998 because the actual return on plan assets was only $28,013,000, compared to a return of $115,805,000 in 1997. In addition, plan amendments and an actuarial loss increased the pension obligation by $41,338,000 in 1998.

Substantial Unrecognized Overfunded Amount: General Electric Company

Prior to the stock market boom of the 1980s and 1990s, the chief pension plan concern was underfunding. Now, the typical plan is overfunded.[27] While a fairly extreme example in terms of absolute dollar amounts, General Electric's (GE) funded status is not unusual. Information on pension assets and obligations is provided in Exhibit 11.19. The funded status of the General Electric plans is presented in Exhibit 11.20. Unlike VF Corporation above, GE has only recognized about half of its overfunded amount.[28]

Exhibit 11.19. Substantial Unrecognized Overfunding: General Electric Company, Years Ended December 31, 1997–1998 (Millions of Dollars)

	1997	1998
Projected Benefit Obligation		
Balance at January 1	$23,251	$25,874
Service cost, net of participant contributions	596	625
Interest cost on benefit obligation	1,686	1,749
Participant contributions	120	112
Plan amendments	136	—
Actuarial loss	1,388	1,050
Benefits paid	(1,715)	(1,838)
Special early retirement cost	412	—
Balance at December 31	$25,874	$27,572
Fair Value of Assets		
Balance at January 1	$33,686	$38,742
Actual return on plan assets	6,587	6,363
Employer contributions	64	68
Participant contributions	120	112
Benefits paid	(1,715)	(1,838)
Balance at December 31	$38,742	$43,447

Source: General Electric Company annual report, December 1998, p 51.

Exhibit 11.20 reveals that GE is overfunded by $15,875,000,000 at the end of 1998. This overfunding represents an increase of $3,007,000,000 in a single year: $15,875,000,000 overfunding at the end of 1998 and an overfunding of only $12,868,000,000 at the end of 1997. In an adaptation of GE's actual disclosure, the recognized versus unrecognized portions of the overfunding have been aggregated and disclosed separately in Exhibit 11.20.

Recognized amounts have been included in the determination of net pension cost on the books of GE; unrecognized amounts have been recognized only in the separate financial statements of the GE pension plans. In general, the unrecognized amounts will be recognized in the determination of net pension cost in future years.[29]

At the end of 1998, GE's pension plans are overfunded by about $15,875,000,000. However, as Exhibit 11.20 reveals, only $7,752,000,000 was recognized as an asset on the GE balance sheet. The quality of GE's financial position is enhanced by this unrecognized value.

The source of GE's unrecognized overfunding is detailed in what it terms "unrecognized" balances in its own schedule of funded status. This schedule is provided in Exhibit 11.21.

Exhibit 11.20. Funded Status of Pension Plans: General Electric Company, Years Ended December 31, 1997–1998 (Millions of Dollars)

	1997	1998
Fair value of plan assets	$38,742	$43,447
Less projected benefit obligation	25,874	27,572
Funded status	$12,868	$15,875
Recognized as a prepaid pension asset on the balance sheet of General Electric	6,574	7,752
Unrecognized by General Electric	6,294	8,123
Funded status	$12,868	$15,875

Source: Adapted from General Electric Company, annual report, December 1998, p. 52.

Exhibit 11.21. Funded Status of the General Electric Pension Plans: December 31, 1998 (Millions of Dollars)

	1997	1998
Fair value of plan assets	$38,742	$43,447
Add (deduct) unrecognized balances		
SFAS No. 87 transition gain	(462)	(308)
Net actuarial gain	(7,538)	(9,462)
Prior service cost	1,003	850
Projected benefit obligation	(25,874)	(27,572)
Pension liability	703	797
Prepaid pension asset	$6,574	$7,752

Source: Adapted from General Electric, annual report, December 1998, p. 52.

A substantial portion of the overfunded amount resulted from investment returns on pension assets that have been far in excess of the assumed rate of return (i.e., 9.5 percent for 1996 through 1998). For example, Exhibit 11.19 discloses the actual pension returns for 1997 and 1998, of $6,587,000,000 and $6,363,000,000, respectively. These amounts compare to expected returns of only $2,721,000,000 and $3,024,000,000 for 1997 and 1998, respectively.[30] If we convert the actual return amounts to rates of return, by dividing the dollar returns by beginning of the year assets, the results are 19.6 percent for 1997 and 16.4 percent for 1998. The total excess of actual over expected returns for just 1997 and 1998 was $7,205,000,000.

In its computation of net periodic pension benefit, plan sponsors only take credit for expected and not actual returns. However, if such deferred gains become sufficiently large, then a portion of the deferred gains is recognized in the determination of net pension cost or, in the case of GE, net pension income.

Although not disclosed in the above exhibits, GE reported pension income of $709 million, $331 million, and $1,016,000,000 in 1996, 1997, and 1998, respectively. Included in this income amount were recognized actuarial gains of $210 million, $331 million, and $365 million in 1996, 1997, and 1998, respectively. The threshold for recognition of deferred gains is 10 percent of the higher of plan assets or the PBO. That is, if the deferred gains exceed the higher of 10 percent of plan assets or the PBO, then a portion must be recognized in the determination of pension cost or pension income. This rule also applies in the case of deferred actuarial losses.[31]

A review of the level of GE's pension assets reveals why it has been recognizing a portion of previously deferred actuarial gains in recent years. At the end of 1998, 10 percent of plan assets is about $4.3 billion and 10 percent of the PBO is about $2.8 billion. Unrecognized actuarial gains at the end of 1998 total about $9.5 billion. The excess of actuarial gains over 10 percent of plan assets, $5.2 billion (actuarial gains of $9.5 billion − 10 percent of the plan assets of $4.3 billion) must be included in the subsequent year's determination of net pension income. The recognition of portions of its actuarial gains both contribute to GE's annual net pension benefit and also increase its net prepaid pension asset. In this way, portions of the overfunding in the pension plan are recognized on the balance sheet of GE.

GE's position quality is significantly enhanced by the unrecognized pension overfunding of $8,123,000,000 at the end of 1998. To put this into perspective, GE's total shareholders' equity at the end of 1998 was about $38.9 billion. GE has made only nominal pension contributions in recent years because of the extent of its overfunding. This strengthens its cash flow.

As discussed earlier in the case of the Sherwin-Williams Company, the contribution to earnings made by GE's overfunded plans would generally not be considered operating income. However, if the overfunded position is maintained, then this earnings component could be expected to continue. Hence, the reduction in earnings quality in terms of persistence is not significant.[32]

Realizing the Value of an Overfunded Pension

Because of its overfunded status, GE reports that it has made only limited pension contributions since 1987.[33] As noted immediately above, this has had a clear positive effect on the level of GE's cash flow. Absent this overfunded condition, pension cost and not pension income would have been recorded and regular contributions would have been made to the pension plans. Beyond the benefit associated with not being required to make pension contributions, there are other avenues by which plan sponsors can benefit from an overfunded plan.

Acquisition by a Firm with Underfunded Plans

DeSoto Corporation had a significantly overfunded plan, and for some time there were discussions about this making DeSoto an attractive takeover target. In 1997, DeSoto merged with Keystone Consolidated Industries, Inc. In its 1997 10-K report, Keystone reported that:

> The DeSoto acquisition included the concurrent merger of Keystone's three under-funded defined benefit pension plans with and into DeSoto's overfunded defined ben-efit pension plan, which resulted in an overfunded plan for financial reporting pur-poses.[34]

In its 1997 10-K report, Keystone disclosed pension plans that were now overfunded by about $62 million. To provide some perspective, Keystone's total shareholders' equity at the end of 1997 was only $44 million. One would expect that DeSoto's overfunded pension plans were priced into the value the DeSoto shareholders received for their shares.

Transfers from Overfunded Pension Plans to OPEB Plans

Beyond realizing the benefits of an overfunded plan through a merger, some firms have transferred assets to OPEB plans and used them to pay OPEB benefits. The practice is permitted by Section 420 of the Internal Revenue Code. Allegheny Teledyne, Inc., an entity that was created by the merger of Allegheny Ludlum and Teledyne, reports making such transfers:

> Cash from excess pension assets of $30,500,000 in 1996, $31,900,000 in 1997, and $37,400,000 in 1998 was transferred pre-tax under Section 420 of the Internal Revenue Code from the Company's defined benefit pension plans to the Company. The Internal Revenue Code permits transfers annually of an amount not to exceed the Company's actual expenditures on retiree health care benefits. While not affecting reported op-erating profit, cash flow increased by the after-tax effect of the transferred amount.[35]

Use to Fund Retirement Incentives and Related Items

Another avenue for benefiting from an overfunded plan is to fund retirement incentives associated with early retirement options. Enriching pension benefits employs excess assets already in the pension funds. The plan sponsor realizes a benefit from the use of the plan assets without incurring any tax obligation. The presence of excess pension assets creates financial flexibility that can be used to achieve employee reductions designed to create more economically viable entities. Further, it is far more tax efficient than obtaining excess assets through a plan termination.

Asset Reversions from Plan Terminations

Although far less common than in earlier years, a plan termination is a direct way to access excess pension plan assets. The plan sponsor must provide for accrued pension benefits before any pension assets are withdrawn. In the past, this has typically been handled by using pension assets to purchase annuity contracts from insurance companies. The remaining assets then revert to the plan sponsor, but they are subject to onerous taxation.

Both federal and state income taxes generally apply to asset reversions and their combination could amount to 40 percent or more of the value of the withdrawn assets. In addition, a federal excise tax of 20 percent also applies in cases where, subject to Internal Revenue Code requirements, a replacement plan is instituted or pension benefits are increased. In the absence of the replacement plan or benefit increases, the federal excise tax rises to 50 percent.[36] This means a total tax of up to 90 percent in the case of a termination that does not satisfy the replacement plan or increased benefits provisions of the Code. The objective of these excise taxes appears to have been to discourage plan terminations; it appears to be working.

Recent anecdotal evidence suggests that the limited number of firms terminating overfunded plans are avoiding the 50 percent excise tax by satisfying the replacement plan or increased benefits provisions. Both Montgomery Ward and Edison Brothers Stores have terminated overfunded plans and avoided the 50 percent excise tax on asset reversions by establishing replacement plans.[37]

Compliance with the "qualified replacement plan" requires, among other things, that a direct transfer from the terminated plan be made to the replacement plan before any employer reversion. Further, the transfer must be in an amount equal to at least 25 percent of the maximum amount that the employer could receive as an employer reversion.[38] Compliance with the "benefit increases" provision requires, among other things, *pro rata* increases in the accrued benefits of all qualified participants that have an aggregate present value of not less than 20 percent of the maximum amount that the employer could receive as an employer reversion.[39]

The above discussion has emphasized reporting and analysis in the case of overfunded pension plans. This emphasis is consistent with the current predominance of overfunded plans. However, pension reforms that were instituted in the early 1970s, plus the new GAAP requirements of the mid-1980s, were driven by concerns related to under and not overfunding. Also, market reversals or a severe general economic decline, could quickly throw large numbers of firms into underfunded status. The following discussion considers the GAAP requirements associated with underfunded plans, the implications of underfunded plans for financial analysis, and selected government regulatory activity in the area of pensions.

GAAP Requirements and Underfunded Pension Plans

Prior to the issuance of SFAS No. 87, "Employers' Accounting for Pensions," in December 1985, there was no requirement that a liability be recognized for an underfunded pension plan. The requirement to record a liability on the books of the plan's sponsor was one of the standard's key contributions.[40]

Exhibit 11.22. Underfunded Plans and the Additional Minimum
Pension Liability

1. Accumulated benefit obligation	A
2. Minus plan assets at their fair value	− B
3. Equals pension underfunding	= C
4. Minus existing pension liability	− D
or	
Plus existing prepaid pension asset	+ E
5. Equals additional minimum pension liability adjustment	= F

Instituting a requirement to record an additional liability in the case of underfunded pensions faced very strong opposition from the business community.
However, research by Dhaliwal supported the position that even before the issuance of SFAS No. 87, the market incorporated these off-balance-sheet pension
obligations into its assessment of financial leverage.[41] Dhaliwal's results indicated
that "the effect of unfunded vested pension liabilities on market-perceived risk of
the firm is not significantly (statistically) different from that of debt and other
liabilities."[42]

The Minimum Pension Liability Adjustment

Funded status is currently assessed by comparing plan assets to the PBO. However,
the requirement to record an additional pension liability is determined by comparing plan assets with the ABO. Where required, the liability increase is referred
to as the "additional minimum pension liability" adjustment.[43] The formula for
the additional minimum liability adjustment is outlined in Exhibit 11.22.

GAAP require that the sponsor's balance sheet include a net liability position
for underfunded plans. This net liability must be at least equal to the underfunded
amount, line 3 in Exhibit 11.22. In the absence of (a) an unrecognized transition
obligation or (b) unrecognized prior service cost, the entire required adjustment
must be recorded as (1) a decrease in other comprehensive income and (2) an
offsetting increase in pension liability. Deferred tax effects of the adjustment must
also be recorded. However, the charge to other comprehensive income is reduced,
up to the amount of the combination of unrecognized transition obligation and
unrecognized prior service cost.[44]

Operation of the minimum pension liability adjustment is best understood
with a numerical example. The minimum liability adjustment is illustrated in Exhibit 11.23.

The net effect of the adjustments in Exhibit 11.23 is to increase the pension
liability balance by $150,000, bringing it up to the $200,000 of pension underfunding. This requires a minimum liability adjustment of only $150,000 because
a pension liability accrual of $50,000 already existed on the plan sponsor's balance
sheet.

Exhibit 11.23.   Illustration of the Minimum Pension Liability Adjustment

Data	
Accumulated benefit obligation	$1,000,000
Plan assets at fair value	800,000
Minimum required liability	200,000
Accrued pension liability prior to the adjustment	50,000
Unrecognized prior service cost	80,000
Combined income tax rate	40%

Statement Effects

Minimum pension liability adjustment:

Minimum liability		$200,000
Existing liability		50,000
Required minimum pension liability adjustment		150,000
Charge to other comprehensive income:		
Minimum pension liability adjustment		$150,000
Unrecognized prior service cost		80,000
Pretax charge to other comprehensive income		70,000
Minus tax benefit of the charge (.40 × $70,000)		28,000
Net charge to other comprehensive income		42,000
Other balance sheet account changes:		
Increase in deferred tax assets (offset to tax benefit above)		$28,000
Increase in intangible pension asset:		
Minimum pension liability adjustment	150,000	
Pretax charge to other comprehensive income	70,000	80,000

In addition to the liability increase, shareholders' equity is reduced as a result of the after-tax charge of $42,000 made against other comprehensive income. This charge is $70,000 on a pretax basis, but is reduced by the $28,000 ($70,000 × 40 percent) potential tax savings associated with the charge. A deferred tax asset of $28,000 is recorded in view of the unrealized nature of this potential tax savings. Finally, an intangible pension asset of $80,000 is also recorded on the balance sheet of the plan sponsor. Note that the intangible asset is limited in this case to the amount of the unrecognized prior service cost.

The above adjustments must be updated in future periods as the pension becomes either more or less underfunded. The intangible pension asset will increase or decrease in the future with increases and decreases, respectively, in the minimum pension liability adjustment. However, the intangible pension asset is not amortized and included in the determination of net pension cost.

Intangible Pension Assets

The recognition of an intangible asset in the face of an underfunded pension is rather difficult to rationalize. However, it is consistent with pressure on the FASB to limit reductions in earnings or shareholders' equity upon the recognition of previously off-balance-sheet obligations. Beyond this, while somewhat strained, the case is made that an intangible asset is a by-product of the decisions that create unrecognized prior service cost. This cost results from retroactive improvements in pension benefits. Benefit improvements lead in turn to expectations of improvements in employee morale and productivity. This provides the logic for the emergence of an intangible pension asset.[45]

An alternative view is that recognition of an additional minimum pension liability should result in a reduction in shareholders' equity, either by a charge against earnings or a direct reduction in shareholders' equity. The additional liability is often the result of retroactive benefit improvements, and the argument that future benefits will result from this action is very tenuous. For purposes of financial analysis, a reduction in shareholders' equity should provide financial statement data that are more consistent with the fundamental economics of the pension commitments.

An Underfunded Pension Plan: Albany International Corporation

Disclosures related to the minimum pension liability adjustment of Albany International are provided in Exhibit 11.24. Albany International reported that in 1998 "the Company was required to accrue an additional minimum liability for those plans for which accumulated plan benefits exceed plan assets."[46]

Once again, the intangible pension asset is not amortized through the income statement. Rather, this asset is simply increased or decreased as the pension plan(s) become either more or less underfunded. The expectation is probably that over time initially underfunded plans would become fully funded, especially in view of the oversight roles now played by several government agencies.[47]

The FASB took an important stand in requiring that a liability be recorded in the case of underfunded pensions.[48] An even stronger stance would have called for taking a going-concern perspective and gauging underfunding against the projected as opposed to the lower accumulated benefit obligation. However, this concession reflects the compromises that are part of any process that has political dimensions.

From a financial analysis perspective, the intangible pension asset, recorded in cases in which the additional minimum pension liability exceeds unrecognized prior service cost, would seem to rank near the bottom of all intangibles. Unlike some other intangibles (e.g., patents), this asset has no separable value. A strong case could be made that these intangible pension assets should be deducted from shareholders' equity in computing any leverage-oriented financial ratio. Further, for creditors looking to the balance sheet for support in the case that earnings and cash flow dry up, an intangible pension asset will provide little solace.

Exhibit 11.24. Minimum Pension Liability Adjustment: Albany International Corporation, December 31, 1998 (Thousands of Dollars)

The Company was required to accrue an additional minimum liability for those plans for which accumulated plan benefits exceeded plan assets. The liability at December 31, 1998 of $21,680 was offset by an asset amounting to $4,812 (included in intangibles) and a direct charge to equity of $16,868. There was no additional liability required at December 31, 1997.

The projected benefit obligation, accumulated benefit obligation, and fair value of plan assets for the pension plans with accumulated benefit obligation in excess of plan assets were $19,357, $13,396, and none, respectively, for 1997, and $155,168, $128,355, and $102,258, respectively for 1998.

Amounts recognized in the balance sheet are as follows*:

	1997	1998
Accrued pension (liability) asset	$6,718	$(27,876)
Intangible asset	—	4,812
Accumulated other comprehensive income	—	16,868
Net amount recognized at year end	$6,718	$(6,196)

*This balance of $16,868,000 appears both in the other comprehensive income section of the 1998 Albany income statement as well as in the shareholders' equity section of the 1998 balance sheet as a reduction of accumulated other comprehensive income.

Source: Albany International Corporation, annual report to shareholders, December 1998, p. 23.

Exhibit 11.25 provides two examples of the potential effects on total liability-to-equity ratios of charging off intangible pension assets. In each of these cases, charging off the intangible pension asset results in a significant increase in the ratio of debt to equity.

Pension Income versus Pension Cost

The implications of pension income for earnings quality were discussed to some extent in the earlier case examples. However, the growing frequency and significance of pension income versus pension cost merits additional discussion and illustration.

Pension income is almost always a product of overfunded pension plans. Overfunding has resulted mainly from the combination of a sustained bull market and a significant portion of pension assets being in equity securities. The influence of declining interest rates also played a role by increasing the market value of debt instruments.[49] Substantial service cost and interest components of net pension cost can easily be offset by the expected return on significantly overfunded pension plans.

Exhibit 11.25. Intangible Pension Assets and Debt-to-Equity Ratios (Millions of Dollars)

Company	Under SFAS No. 87	Charge-off with No Tax Benefit	Charge-off with Tax Benefit
Navistar International Corp. (1998)	7.03	9.49	8.37*
Northwestern Steel & Wire Co. (1997)	3.42	4.14	3.83

*The leverage ratios of Navistar reflect the high level of debt employed by its financial service activities. A combined federal and state income tax rate of 40% was used to compute the potential tax benefit from the write-off of the pension intangible assets.

Sources: The 1998 annual report of Navistar International and the 1997 annual report of Northwestern Steel and Wire Company.

Exhibit 11.26. A Case of Substantial Pension Income: Allegheny Teledyne, Inc., Years Ended December 31, 1996–1998 (Millions of Dollars)

	1996	1997	1998
Pension income:			
Service cost—benefits earned during the year	$34.4	$37.0	$37.3
Interest cost on benefits earned in prior years	125.1	131.9	132.2
Expected return on plan assets	(203.7)	(207.8)	(230.8)
Amortization of prior service cost	9.5	10.4	12.5
Amortization of unrecognized transition asset	(30.5)	(30.5)	(30.5)
Amortization of net actuarial gain	(1.2)	0.4	(2.0)
Total pension income	$(66.4)	$(58.6)	$(81.3)

Source: Allegheny Teledyne, Inc., annual report, December 1998, pp. 42–43.

Overfunded Pension Plans and Pension Income: Allegheny Teledyne, Inc.

The pension plans of Allegheny Teledyne, Inc. are overfunded and the firm discloses net pension income.[50] Selected information from its pension disclosures is provided in Exhibits 11.26 and 11.27.

For perspective, the 1998 pension income of $81.3 million represents about 21 percent of Allegheny Teledyne's 1998 pretax income of $391 million. At the end of 1998, the pension plans are overfunded by $812 million. Of this amount, a net prepaid pension asset of $398.9 million has been recognized on the 1998 balance sheet of Allegheny Teledyne. The unrecognized overfunding of $413.3 million ($812.2 million − $398.9 million) enhances the quality of Allegheny Teledyne's financial position.[51]

The Allegheny Teledyne pension income results primarily from (1) an overfunded position upon initial adoption of SFAS No. 87 (i.e., the transition asset),

Exhibit 11.27. Significantly Overfunded Pension Plans: Allegheny Teledyne, Inc., Years Ended December 31, 1997–1998 (Millions of Dollars)

	1997	1998
Pension funded status:		
Funded status of the plan	$691.5	$812.2
Unrecognized net actuarial gain	(278.0)	(403.5)
Unrecognized transition asset	(131.2)	(100.7)
Unrecognized prior service cost	86.2	90.9
Net prepaid pension asset	$368.5	$398.9

Source: Allegheny Teledyne, Inc., annual report, December 1998, pp. 42–43.

plus (2) subsequent increases in overfunding from investment returns in excess of those expected. From the disclosures in Exhibit 11.26, the transition asset is being recognized at the rate of $30.5 million each year. Also, Exhibit 11.27 reveals a transition asset of $100.7 million remaining unrecognized at the end of 1998. Hence, at the rate of $30.5 million a year, this source of net pension income will run out in early 2002 ($30.5 million in each year from 1999 to 2001 equals $91.5 million, with the balance of $9.2 million remaining to be recognized in 2002). This nonrecurring component of net pension income reduces the quality of Allegheny Teledyne's earnings in terms of persistence. Moreover, there is no direct cash inflow associated with the component of pretax earnings.[52]

The other principal contribution to the overfunded position results from returns on pension assets well in excess of those expected. Most of the $403.5 million of unrecognized net actuarial gain at the end of 1998 is probably due to excess returns on pension assets. However, there are, no doubt, some other actuarial gains and losses in this balance.

The net pension cost that would have resulted in the absence of the overfunding is approximated as outlined in Exhibit 11.28.

While Allegheny Teledyne's overfunding is more material than the typical overfunded plan, overfunding is widespread and substantial. Earnings analysis in these cases should consider two issues:

1. Will the pension income be sustained?
2. Is the income supported by a cash benefit?

The above discussion has already noted that the pension income will decline by $30.5 million after 2002 when the remaining transition asset is fully recognized. Moreover, recognition of this component of pension income involves no direct cash inflow. Earning quality should be seen as impaired on both the cash and persistence dimensions.

However, the reduction in pension income when the transition asset is fully recognized may be offset to some extent by at least two other factors. Pension

Exhibit 11.28. Net Pension Cost in the Absence of Overfunding: Allegheny Teledyne, Inc., Year Ended December 31, 1998 (Millions of Dollars)

1998 pension income			$(81.3)
Add:			
Amortization of transition asset		$30.5	
Expected return on plan overfunding:			
Total overfunding	$812		
Times 1998 expected rate of return	.09	73.1	
Amortization of net actuarial gain		2.0	105.6
1998 net pension cost in the absence of plan overfunding			$24.3

Source: Based on disclosures in the Allegheny Teledyne, Inc., annual report, December 1998, pp. 42–43.

income may continue to rise if the overfunding of the Allegheny Teledyne plans continues to grow. That is, the product of an assumed rate of return and rising plan assets will result in larger expected returns. As shown in Exhibit 11.28, the 1998 expected return on plan overfunding amounts to about $73.1 million. This $73.1 million currently offsets about 43 percent of the $169.5 million total of service cost and interest cost on the PBO for 1998—disclosed in Exhibit 11.26.

However, a recent use of pension assets by Allegheny Teledyne may offset some of the asset growth from excess investment returns. In both 1997 and 1998, the Company transferred assets from the Allegheny Teledyne pension funds to pay other postretirement benefits. In 1997 and 1998, a total of $69 million of pension assets was transferred out of the pension plans to pay such benefits. Such asset transfers are currently permitted under Section 420 of the Internal Revenue Code.[53]

In addition to benefits from future excess returns on pension assets, increasing portions of the 1998 unrecognized net actuarial gains of $403.5 million will be recognized in the determination of net pension cost or income. These deferred gains are well above the recognition threshold of 10 percent of the higher of plan assets or the PBO. At the end of 1998, plan assets were about $2.8 billion and the PBO was about $2 billion. The recognition threshold in this case would be 10 percent of the plan assets or $280 million. This means that about $123.5 million of the actuarial gains could be subject to recognition during 1999 and subsequent years: unrecognized actuarial gains of $403.5 million minus the recognition threshold of $280 million equals $123.5 million.[54]

There is, of course, no direct cash inflow associated with the pension income. In the Allegheny Teledyne case, the pension income is simply recorded by increasing a prepaid pension asset account. The growth in this asset is, in turn, subtracted from net income in arriving at cash flow from operating activities. However, the extent of overfunding has relieved Allegheny Teledyne of the need to make pension contributions. Further, the cash flow requirements of the OPEB benefits have been satisfied by asset transfers from the overfunded pension plans. Because the transfers are not taxable to Allegheny Teledyne, they represent a very tax-efficient way to realize the benefits of an overfunded pension. Cash not used for pension plan contributions or OPEB payments is available for other purposes. Overfunded pension plans clearly strengthen cash flow and as well as adding to financial flexibility.

Levels of Actuarial Assumptions

The analysis of funded status and net pension cost or income should involve a review of disclosed actuarial rate assumptions: expected returns, discount (settlement) rates, and rates of increase in compensation. The levels of these rates, as well as changes therein, can have a significant effect on the level of pension cost or income and benefit obligations.

Differences in investment return assumptions may simply reflect differences in policies governing the investment of pension assets. Some firms may decide to assume somewhat more risk in an effort to increase returns and lower pension costs. Others, in an effort to preserve a significantly overfunded position, may adopt more conservative investment policies.

Differences in expected rates of increase in compensation could reflect such factors as industry, age and skill levels of the workforce, geographic location, and a host of other influences. However, discount or settlement rates should show little interfirm variability because they reflect general economic conditions rather than firm-specific circumstances.

The means, medians, and ranges of rate assumptions for a diversified group of 100 companies are presented in Exhibit 11.29. The data cover the years 1996 to 1998, plus data from a study of the 1992 rate assumptions of 100 firms are also included. The distributions of the rate assumptions are very narrow. Only two or three firms are at the extremes of any of the rate ranges.

The implications of rate assumptions that are at the extreme of these distributions should be considered in evaluating both pension plan and the sponsoring firm's financial performance and position. Some extreme rates can be readily explained by a careful review of the pension disclosures. For example, in Exhibit 11.29, the 2 percent lower limit of the range of compensation-rate assumptions for 1996 to 1998 represents a U.S. firm with only two defined-benefit plans, each of which is located in Germany. Moreover, extremely low assumed rates of return are usually explained by high concentrations of pension investments in fixed-return securities.

Discount rates can have a direct effect on the funded status of pension plans. The higher the discount rate, the lower the benefit obligation. The lower the benefit obligation, the stronger the disclosed funded status of the plans. However, there is a trade-off in that a higher discount rate results, other things equal, in an increase in interest on the PBO, thus increasing net pension cost. Other things are, of course, not equal because the higher discount rate is applied to a lower PBO. The

Exhibit 11.29.   Actuarial Rate Assumptions from Two 100-Firm Samples

	1992	1996	1997	1998
Assumed rate of return:				
Mean	9.25	8.60	9.00	8.80
Median	9.00	9.00	9.00	9.00
Range	6.00–12.10	7.50–11.00	7.00–11.00	7.00–11.00
Discount (settlement) rate:				
Mean	8.25	7.60	7.00	6.80
Median	8.50	7.50	7.25	6.80
Range	5.80–9.10	7.00–8.50	6.00–7.25	5.50–7.50
Rate of compensation increase:				
Mean	5.50	4.40	4.40	4.30
Median	5.50	4.50	4.50	4.50
Range	4.00–6.90	2.00–7.00	2.00–6.00	2.00–6.00

Source: 1998 annual reports to shareholders for the 1996 to 1998 data. The 1992 data are from E. Comiskey and C. Mulford, "Understanding Pension Cost: A Guide for Lenders," *Commercial Lending Review* (Spring 1994), pp. 46–48.

effects of reduced discount rate levels are exactly the opposite of those for discount rate increases.[55] Estimation of the potential future effect of discount rate changes on pension cost and funded status entail computational expertise that falls within the purview of actuaries.

Firms with relatively high assumed rates of return will, other things equal, report lower net pension cost, or higher pension income. In general, an unusually high return assumption should be associated with a higher concentration of plan assets in equity securities.[56] Notice that the median return assumption in Exhibit 11.29 has been flat at 9 percent. This rate was well below the actual returns earned by many pension funds for most of the 1990s. However, unlike the discount rate, the return assumption is chosen to reflect long-term average rates of return on pension assets. As most pension funds are a blend of debt and equity investments, 9 percent is probably a realistic rate from a long-term perspective.

Exhibit 11.29 shows that mean (median) discount rates fell from 7.60 (7.50) to 6.80 (6.80) between 1996 and 1998. These rates compare to mean (median) rates of 8.25 (8.50) in 1992. The somewhat steady decline in discount rates has increased pension obligations. This has in turn offset some of the dramatic improvement in the funded status of U.S. defined-benefit pension plans that has resulted from investment returns consistently exceeding assumed rates of return. If significant inflation were to return and interest rates were to rise, then funded status would improve because of the resulting reduction in benefit obligations. However, there would no doubt be an offsetting influence from an associated decline in the value of both debt and equity investments.

The sample data on increases in compensation have been stable in recent years at about 4.5 percent. Compensation rate increases that are significantly different from 4.50 percent might bear some follow up. The higher the rate, the greater the difference between the ABO and the PBO, and vice versa.

The implications of rate assumptions for financial analysis are somewhat limited. However, it is useful to at least compare a firm's rate assumptions with those used by other firms. Data such as that in Exhibit 11.29 can be used in such a review. Explanations can be sought for rate assumptions that deviate significantly from broader averages. In addition, a firm's discount rate assumption could temper the interpretation of its overfunded pension plan. The overfunded pension of a firm with an unusually high discount rate should probably be viewed as adding less strength to its financial position than the case of a firm with an overfunded position and a discount rate at the average level or below. That is, a high discount rate lowers the PBO and in turn increases the funded position of the pension plan. Moreover, a pension cost level that is reduced by the use of an unusually high assumed rate-of-return could reduce the quality of a firm's earnings in terms of persistence. If the return level is not achieved over the longer term, then future earnings will be reduced.

Pension Poison Pills

The tendering by DeSoto, Inc. shareholders of their shares to Keystone Consolidated Industries, Inc., in a merger transaction, was described earlier in this chapter. Part of DeSoto's appeal to Keystone Consolidated was its overfunded pension plan. Some firms do not wish an overfunded plan to increase their attractiveness as takeover targets.[57] As a result, they initiate pension poison pills that are designed to deny the overfunded amount to acquiring firms. Exhibit 11.30 provides several examples of these arrangements.

As with any poison pill, questions may arise as to whose interests are served. There was no poison pill in the DeSoto merger example, and it seems reasonable to assume that DeSoto's overfunded pension plan was priced into the value received by DeSoto shareholders when they tendered their shares to Keystone Consolidated. That is, the overfunded pension was reflected in the cash price or common stock exchange ratio negotiated in the transaction.

If, as in the case of some of the examples in Exhibit 11.30, a pension poison pill calls for excess pension assets to be used to increase pension benefits, then shareholders of the acquired firm would seem unlikely to benefit from the overfunded amounts. The presence of pension poison pills would appear to reduce the potential value of a firm in an acquisition transaction.

Pensions and the Regulatory Role of Government Entities

As the final topic in this treatment of pensions, the roles currently played by some federal governmental entities are outlined. In the opening of this chapter, there is

Exhibit 11.30.   Examples of Pension Poison Pills

RR Donnelley and Sons, Inc. (1997)
In the event of Plan termination, the Plan provides that no funds can revert to the company and any excess assets over Plan liabilities must be used to fund retirement benefits.

Mead Corporation (1998)
The Company's pension plans require the allocation of excess plan assets to plan members if the plans are terminated, merged, or consolidated following a change in control (as defined) of the Company opposed by the Board of Directors of the Company. Amendment of these provisions after such a change in control would require approval of plan participants.

Olin Corporation (1998)
The pension plan of Olin Corporation provides that if, within three years following a change of control of the Company, any corporate action is taken or filing made in contemplation of, among other things, a plan termination or merger or other transfer of assets or liabilities of the plan, and such termination, merger, or transfer thereafter takes place, plan benefits would automatically be increased for affected participants (and retired participants) to absorb any plan surplus.

Whirlpool Company (1997)
The U.S. pension plans provide that in the event of a plan termination within five years following a change in control of the company, any assets held by the plans in excess of the amounts needed to fund accrued benefits would be used to provide additional benefits to plan participants. A change in control generally means one not approved by the incumbent board of directors, including an acquisition of 25% or more of the voting power of the company's outstanding stock or a change in a majority of the incumbent board.

Source: Companies' annual reports to shareholders. The year following the company name designates the annual report from which the example was drawn.

discussion of new accounting standards introduced in the mid-1980s that were designed to improve the quality of pension financial reporting. The need to change and improve pension reporting was prompted in part by pension legislation that was enacted about a decade earlier.

Employee Retirement Income Security Act of 1974 (ERISA)

In the early 1960s, there were prominent cases of firms being unable to satisfy their pension commitments. In some instances, this involved firms that went into bankruptcy and were liquidated. These cases sparked a decade of public debate and congressional activity that led in 1974 to passage of the Employee Retirement Income Security Act (ERISA). As its title suggests, ERISA was designed to protect pension benefits.

Some of the key features of ERISA are (1) minimum pension funding requirements, (2) restrictions on the period of time that employees must work before their pension benefits become vested, and (3) the creation of the Pension Benefit Guaranty Corporation (PBGC).

Minimum funding requirements increase the likelihood that, upon retirement, funds will be available to fulfill defined-benefit pension promises. Vesting gives an employee the legal right to accrued pension benefits upon retirement, even if they leave their current employment. Prior to ERISA there were stories of long-serving employees being dismissed just prior to their becoming vested. These actions were alleged to have been motivated by the desire to avoid being required to pay the employee the pension benefits earned by years of service. Now, employees must be fully vested in their earned benefits after five years of service.

The Pension Benefit Guaranty Corporation

To provide an even greater level of pension security, the PBGC was also created.[58] The PBGC guarantees a pension benefit in cases where pension plans have insufficient funds to provide the promised benefits. In 1999, the PBGC coverage extended to over 44,000 private-sector defined-benefit plans covering about 42 million workers and retirees.[59]

The PBGC is funded by a per-capita premium on employees that is paid by plan sponsors. All single-employer pension plans pay an annual basic flat-rate premium of $19 per participant. Underfunded pension plans pay an additional variable-rate charge of $9 per $1,000 of unfunded vested benefits.[60] These funds are used to protect plan participants in the event that a pension plan is terminated without sufficient funds to satisfy the pension obligations.

Prior to a plan termination, the PBGC can take over a pension plan if it is deemed to be necessary to protect the plan participants. In addition, in the event of the termination of an underfunded plan, PBGC can bring a claim against the sponsoring firm to satisfy the funding shortfall. This claim can be for up to 30 percent of the net assets of the plan sponsor, or the amount of the funding shortfall, whichever is smaller. This is a powerful claim since it has the standing of a tax lien.

Short of a plan takeover, the PBGC can take other actions such as securing a potential claim with assets of the plan sponsor or requiring the sponsor to make additional contributions to the pension plans.[61] The following illustrate the recent exercise of some these options:

> **Galey & Lord, Inc.** Pursuant to an agreement with the Pension Benefit Guaranty Corporation ("PBGC"), the Company has given the PBGC a first priority lien of $10 million on certain land and building assets of the Company to secure payment of any liability to the PBGC that might arise if one or more pension plans are terminated.[62]

> **Tultex Corporation.** The Company has agreed in principle with the Pension Benefit Guaranty Corporation to provide $5.5 million in supplemental contributions to the pension plan, in excess of the minimum required annual contributions, over the next three years for the protection of plan participants.[63]

Both of the above examples highlight why the funded status of pension plans must be carefully considered. This assessment must extend beyond the positive implications for a firm's financial position when pension plans are overfunded. In both of the above cases, weak pension funding positions gave the PBGC an opportunity to step in and take actions to protect its position in the event that Galey & Lord, Inc. and Tultex Corporation should be unable to meet their pension promises.

In the case of Galey & Lord, Inc., the PBGC now has a first priority lien on $10 million of previously unencumbered assets. In addition, Tultex Corporation now has a commitment to make $5.5 million of supplemental pension contributions over the next five years. Each of these actions weaken the financial flexibility of these firms and they also diminish somewhat the support available for claims against Galey & Lord and Tultex held by other creditors.

REPORTING AND ANALYSIS OF OTHER POSTRETIREMENT BENEFITS (OPEB)

The reporting and analysis of OPEB is similar to that of pension plans.[64] Actuarial assumptions, the deferral of actuarial gains and losses, the amortization of deferred changes in plan assets and obligations, and the reconciliation of funded status to sponsor asset or liability balances are all treated in a similar manner. However, there are key differences related to the funding of benefits and the extent to which benefits can be unilaterally changed by plan sponsors. Moreover, OPEB benefits are not covered by ERISA or protected by the PBGC.

Accounting Prior to the Current OPEB Standards

The present accounting and disclosure requirements for OPEB plans are SFAS No. 106, "Employers' Accounting for Postretirement Benefits Other than Pensions," and SFAS No. 112, "Employers' Accounting for Postemployment Benefits."[65] These statements were introduced five and seven years, respectively, after the principal pension accounting standards: SFAS No. 87, "Employers' Accounting for Pensions," and SFAS No. 88, "Employers' Accounting for Settlements and Curtailments of Defined Benefit Pension Plans and for Plan Terminations."

Prior to issuance of the OPEB standards, these plans were primarily accounted for on a cash basis. Expense was recognized, and deductible for income tax purposes, only when benefit payments were made. No obligations were recognized on the books of plan sponsors as benefits were being earned. Also, because the contributions to fund OPEB plans are typically not deductible as made for tax purposes, these plans are usually not funded. Prior to adoption of the OPEB standards, the omission of liabilities from the balance sheets of plan sponsors clearly reduced the quality of financial position.

Accounting under the OPEB Standards

There was fierce opposition by the business community to the FASB proposal to apply accrual accounting to OPEB plans. In the end, the OPEB statements called for the same accrual-basis accounting already required for pension plans. However, just as with pension plans, the OPEB standards permit delays in the recognition of previously unrecognized obligations. Moreover, changes in plan assets and obligations due to experience different from actuarial assumptions, changes in actuarial assumptions, and increases or decreases in benefits are deferred and recognized in OPEB cost in subsequent periods.

Postretirement versus Postemployment Benefits

The distinction between postretirement and postemployment benefits is made clear in the statements below from the 1998 annual report of Avon Products, Inc. The postretirement benefits are like pension benefits in that they are received only after retirement. However, the postemployment benefits are received mainly during an interval between the end of employment and the beginning of retirement.

> *Postretirement benefits*
>
> Avon provides health care, in excess of Medicare coverage, and life insurance benefits for the majority of employees who retire under Avon's retirement plans in the United States and certain foreign countries. The cost of such health care benefits is shared by Avon and its retirees.[66]
>
> *Postemployment benefits*
>
> Avon provides postemployment benefits that include salary continuation, severance benefits, disability benefits, continuation of health care benefits and life insurance coverage to former employees after employment but before retirement.[67]

Legal Protections of OPEB versus Pension Benefits

Compared to pension benefits under defined-benefit plans, OPEB benefits do not share the protections introduced with ERISA in 1974. Somewhat telling is the frequent reference by plan sponsors to their apparent unilateral ability to alter or reduce OPEB benefits. Moreover, some firms take the position that, although they may be required to record them under GAAP, OPEB liabilities are not legal obligations. A sampling of these statements is provided in Exhibit 11.31. The statement by General Motors Corporation, made upon its initial adoption in 1992 of SFAS No. 106, is the strongest on the legal status of OPEB obligations.[68]

Since SFAS No. 132, "Employers' Disclosures about Pensions and Other Postretirement Benefits," it has been common for firms with both pension and OPEB plans to provide a single display with the disclosures for both sets of plans. However, in order to focus on the OPEB plans, only the OPEB portion of these disclosures are presented in this discussion.

Exhibit 11.31. On the Liability Status of Accrued OPEB Benefits

Alexander & Baldwin, Inc. (1998)	The Company does not prefund these benefits and has the right to modify or terminate certain of these plans in the future.
Crown Cork and Seal, Inc. (1998)	The Company reserves the right, subject to existing agreements, to change, modify, or discontinue the plans.
Delta Air Lines, Inc. (1998)	The Company has reserved the right to modify or terminate the medical plans for both current and future retirees.
General Motors (1998)	The Corporation has disclosed in the consolidated financial statements certain amounts associated with estimated future postretirement benefits other than pensions and characterized such amounts as accumulated postretirement benefit obligations, liabilities, or obligations. Notwithstanding the recording of such amounts and the use of these terms, GM does not admit or otherwise acknowledge that such amounts or existing postretirement-benefit plans of GM (other than pensions) represent legally enforceable liabilities of GM.
Tenneco, Inc. (1998)	All of these benefits (OPEB) may be subject to deductibles, copayment provisions, and other limitations, and Tenneco has reserved the right to change these benefits. Tenneco's postretirement-benefit plans are not funded.

Source: Companies' 1998 annual reports to shareholders.

Underrecognized OPEB Obligation: Illinois Tool Works, Inc.

The OPEB disclosures of Illinois Tool Works, Inc. (ITW) are presented in Exhibit 11.32. As is typical of these plans, they are not funded. Moreover, contributions to fund OPEB benefits are generally only deductible to the extent that they are made to pay for current benefits. Absent any funding, the funded position of the ITW plans at the end of 1998 is simply the benefit obligation of $141,289,000. This absence of funding is a key difference between defined-benefit pension plans and OPEB plans.

While the funded status of the plans is a liability of $141,289,000, Exhibit 11.32, the funded status schedule, reveals an accrued benefit cost of only $50,018,000 on ITW's 1998 balance sheet. The principal explanation for this difference is the unrecognized net transition amount of $100,831,000. Upon adoption of SFAS No. 106, firms were given the option of either (1) recording the entire unrecognized obligation and associated income statement charge, or (2) amortizing the obligation to expense over future periods.[69]

By a significant margin, firms elected to recognize the entire obligation and charge it against earnings immediately upon adoption of SFAS No. 106. For example, upon adoption of SFAS No. 106, General Motors recorded a previously unrecognized OPEB obligation of approximately $33 billion and an after-tax reduction in earnings of $21 billion.[70] While electing immediate charge-off of the previously unrecognized obligations can sharply reduce current earnings, it does relieve future earnings of this burden. Where amortization of the transition amount is elected, it is to take place over the remaining service life of active plan participants. However, if this period is less than 20 years, then 20 years may be used.

Unlike General Motors, ITW elected to amortize the transition obligation, which is taking place at the rate of $7,306,000 each year, as revealed by the detailing of the net periodic benefit cost in Exhibit 11.32. The amortization option is an example of the deferral and smoothing features that are also a part of the pension accounting standards. ITW also disclosed an unrecognized actuarial gain of $9,560,000. The reduction in the unrecognized gain from $21,631,000 at the end of 1997 to $9,560,000 at the end of 1998 is mainly the result of the reduction in the discount rate of from 7.50 percent to 6.75 percent between 1997 and 1998. This discount rate reduction produced the $11,305,000 increase in the benefit obligation identified as "due to an actuarial loss." While this liability increase is registered immediately in the statement of the OPEB plan, its recognition is deferred in the computation of ITW's net benefit cost. A small portion of the decline in unrecognized gain resulted from amortization of $766,000 of the gain in 1998.[71]

The quality of ITW's financial position is diminished by the delayed recognition of $91,271,000 of the total benefit obligation of $141,289,000 at the end of 1998: $141,289,000 − $50,018,000 = $91,271,000.[72] However, the cash quality of ITW's earnings is marginally strengthened in both 1997 and 1998 because the net benefit cost exceeds the company's cash contributions to pay for current benefits.

ITW's disclosures of its health care cost trend rates, and the effects of a one-percentage-point change in these rates on benefit costs and benefit obligations, are also presented in Exhibit 11.32. These disclosures provide information that could be very helpful in forecasting future earnings or financial position under varying health care cost rate assumptions. Disclosing the sensitivity of a cost or obligation is a fairly unique disclosure in financial reporting. However, some current disclosure requirements for derivatives call for similar information.

The health care cost trend rates are analogous to the expected compensation increase in the case of defined-benefit pension plans.[73] Increases in these rates increase benefit costs and obligations and decreases have the opposite effect. A review of company disclosures reveals some divergence in these rates. Unlike discount rates, these rates are affected by a variety of company or industry-specific factors that could influence the expected rate of cost increase, for example, composition and location of the workforce, nature of the work performed, or geo-

Exhibit 11.32. A Standard Set of OPEB Disclosures: Illinois Tool Works, Inc., Years Ended December 31, 1996–1998 (Thousands of Dollars)

	1996	1997	1998
Components of net periodic benefit cost:			
Service cost	$2,253	$2,381	$2,647
Interest cost	9,182	9,246	9,264
Amortization of actuarial gain	(1,239)	(1,172)	(766)
Amortization of transition amount	7,306	7,306	7,306
Net periodic benefit cost	$17,502	$17,761	$18,451
Change in benefit obligation:			
Benefit obligation at beginning of year		$124,805	$129,328
Service cost		2,381	2,647
Interest cost		9,246	9,264
Participant contributions		3,220	3,472
Actuarial loss		3,755	11,305
Benefits paid		(14,079)	(14,727)
Benefit obligation at end of year		$129,328	$141,289
Change in plan assets:			
Fair value of plan assets at beginning of year		$—	$—
Company contributions		10,859	11,255
Plan participant contributions		3,220	3,472
Benefits paid		(14,079)	(14,727)
Fair value of plan assets at end of year		$—	$—
Funded status		$(129,328)	$(141,289)
Unrecognized net actuarial gain		(21,631)	(9,560)
Unrecognized net transition amount		108,137	100,831
Accrued benefit cost		$(42,822)	$(50,018)
Rate assumptions:			
Discount rate	7.75%	7.50%	6.75%
Current and ultimate health care cost trend rate	5.00%	5.00%	5.00%

Assumed health care cost trend rates can have a significant affect on the amounts reported for the health care plans. A one-percentage-point change in assumed health care cost trend rates would have the following effects:

	1-Percentage point increase	1-Percentage point decrease
Effect on total of service and interest cost components	$1,700	$(1,360)
Effect on postretirement benefit obligation	17,944	(14,411)

Source: Illinois Tool Works, Inc. annual report, December 1998, pp. 31–32.

Exhibit 11.33. Sample Health Care Cost Rate Assumptions (All percentages Except for Dates)

| | Rate Assumptions | |
Company	Current rate	Future rate & date
Alexander & Baldwin, Inc.	10.0	5.0, 2002
Dimon, Inc.	7.5	5.5, 2002
Emerson Electric Company	8.0	5.0, 2004
Giant Cement Holdings, Inc.	8.0	5.0, 2001
Hasbro, Inc.	7.5	4.5, 2012
H. B. Fuller Company	6.6	4.3, 2002
Maytag Corporation	6.5	5.0, 2001
Cincinnati Milicron, Inc.	8.8	5.0, 2005
Regions Financial Corporation	9.1	5.1, 2007
SAFECO Corporation	10.0	6.0, 2003
Stewart & Stevenson Services, Inc.	10.0	6.0, 2001

Source: 1998 annual reports in each of the above cases.

graphic location. Some examples of health care cost rate assumptions are provided in Exhibit 11.33.

The assumptions about current health care cost rates in Exhibit 11.33 range from 10.0 percent down to 6.5 percent. The data reveal that further declines are expected and, while the point at which such decline is expected to bottom out varies, the expected rate at the low point appears to be about five percent. Little can be said about the variation in current rates in the absence of the specific information that would be available to a health care actuary. However, substantial differences in rates of firms in the same industry would merit some investigation.

Overrecognized OPEB Obligation: Maytag Corporation

An abridged presentation of Maytag's OPEB plan funded status is presented in Exhibit 11.34. Maytag's total benefit obligation at the end of 1998 is $424,244,000. However, the benefit obligation recorded on Maytag's balance sheet is $460,599,000.

Maytag disclosed two items in reconciling the funded status of the Maytag plans and the OPEB liability recorded on its December 31, 1998, balance sheet: unrecognized actuarial gain and unrecognized prior service cost. Each of these items represents reductions in the benefit obligations that were registered immediately in the statements of the plans, but have not yet been recognized in Maytag's computation of its periodic postretirement-benefit cost.

Maytag has been recognizing portions of the unrecognized benefits in the determination of its annual periodic postretirement cost. This recognition reduces Maytag's postretirement cost over the period 1996 through 1998, as can been seen

Exhibit 11.34. Overrecognition of Benefit Obligation: Maytag Corporation, Years Ended December 31, 1997–1998 (Thousands of Dollars)

	1997	1998
Benefit obligation at end of year	$381,690	$424,244
Change in plan assets:		
Fair value of plan assets at beginning of year	—	—
Employer contribution	21,408	22,544
Benefits paid	(21,408)	(22,544)
Fair value of plan assets at end of year	—	—
Funded status of plan	(381,690)	(424,244)
Unrecognized actuarial gain	(53,861)	(26,491)
Unrecognized prior service cost	(18,839)	(9,864)
Postretirement-benefit liability	$(454,390)	$(460,599)

Source: Maytag Corporation, annual report, December 1998, p. 50.

Exhibit 11.35. Recognition of Actuarial Gains and Prior Service Benefits: Maytag Corporation, Years Ended December 31, 1996–1998 (Thousands of Dollars)

	1996	1997	1998
Components of net periodic postretirement cost:			
Service cost	$15,453	$12,491	$12,895
Interest cost	28,498	26,588	26,613
Amortization of prior service cost (benefit)	(8,130)	(10,168)	(8,975)
Recognized actuarial gain	—	(1,550)	(1,780)
Net periodic postretirement cost	$35,821	$27,361	$28,753

Source: Maytag Corporation annual report, December 1998, p. 51.

from the cost reductions in Exhibit 11.35. While the title is perhaps misleading, the prior service cost represents a benefit. That is, the retroactive change in the plans reduced employee benefits. Prior service benefit would be a more descriptive label.

The actuarial gains and prior service cost benefits have not been fully recognized (i.e., amortized) in the computation of postretirement cost. Therefore, they create the difference of $36,355,000 between the 1998 benefit obligation of $424,244,000 per the OPEB plan and the $460,599,000 plan liability recorded on the Maytag balance sheet.

From an economic perspective, the OPEB plan obligation at the end of 1998 is $424,244,000. Because of the deferral features in SFAS 106, Maytag has a liability on its balance sheet of $460,599,000. Maytag's financial position quality should be considered to be enhanced by this liability overrecognition, just as it would be considered impaired if the liability were underrecognized. There is also some limited improvement in the cash quality of Maytag's results because benefit payments in 1997 and 1998 fall short of postretirement cost by about $5,953,000 and $6,209,000 million, respectively. However, earnings quality in terms of persistence is diminished somewhat because (1) the remaining unrecognized gains dropped by about $36,345,000 during 1998 ($72,700,000 − $36,355,000) and (2) the remaining unrecognized gains will only reduce postretirement cost, and increase pretax earnings, for a limited future period. The unrecognized prior service cost, at the recent annual amortization rate of about $9 million, will be almost fully amortized in the next year. Continued recognition of the actuarial gain is problematic because its amount at the end of 1998 is less than the 10 percent amortization threshold of SFAS 106: Unrecognized actuarial gains of $26,491,000 are less than 10 percent times the benefit obligation of $424,244,000.

SUMMARY

Pensions and other postretirement and employment benefits are topics rich in unique terminolgy and important issues of financial reporting and analysis. A summary of some of the key points raised in this chapter follow.

• Defined-benefit, as opposed to defined-contribution, pension plans raise many challenging issues for financial reporting and analysis. Key income-related issues center on the measurement of periodic net pension cost or income and the recognition of changes in plan assets and obligations that result from either changes in actuarial assumptions or performance that deviates from actuarial assumptions. The principal balance sheet–related issues center on the recognition of assets or liabilities in the case of overfunded or underfunded plans, respectively.

• A key feature in the measurement of both net pension and OPEB cost or income is the deferral of changes in assets and liabilities that result from experience different from actuarial assumptions and from plan amendments. Both pension and OPEB GAAP allow for the allocation of the income statement effects of these items so as to reduce the volatility of net benefit cost or income and, as a result, net income.

• In general, funded status of pension and OPEB plans is determined by the relationship of the plan assets, if any, and the benefit obligation. The over- or underfunded amount on this basis will seldom equal the asset or liability balance recorded on the balance sheet of the plan sponsor. This is principally due to the deferrals of gains and losses referred to above.

• A liability adjustment may be required in the case of underfunded pension plans. However, the underfunding in this case is judged by the relationship of plan assets to the accumulated benefit obligations (ABO) and not the projected benefit obligations (PBO). If required, the liability increase is referred to as the minimum liability adjustment.

- Where an additional minimum liability adjustment is required, and the amount of the adjustment is less than the sum of (1) unrecognized prior service cost and (2) unrecognized transition obligation, then an intangible pension asset offsets the establishment of the additional pension liability. Where the required adjustments exceeds the sum of unrecognized prior service cost and transition obligation, this excess is included as a charge, after-tax, against other comprehensive income.

- With the expansion of overfunded pension plans, sustained and significant amounts of net pension income are common. With substantial overfunded amounts, net pension income may be sustained. However, its sustainability should be considered to be less secure than that income produced from operations.

- The presence of pension income, instead of pension cost, is typically the result of an overfunded position. A fully or overfunded position often means that no pension plan contributions are required. This is a cash savings that strengthens the sponsor firm's cash flow and adds to its financial flexibility.

- In the measurement of net pension cost or income, credit is taken for the expected and not the actual return on plan assets. Differences between actual and expected returns are deferred.

- The concept of deferral, a prominent feature of pension reporting, does not extend to the financial statement of the pension or other postretirement benefits (OPEB) plan. Changes in plan assets and obligations are always registered immediately in the statements of the pension plan. Deferral applies only to the financial statements of the plan sponsor. Such deferrals, and their subsequent amortization, explain the differences between funded status based on statements of the pension plan and the net asset or liability recorded on the balance sheet of the plan sponsor.

- In addition to making it possible to avoid making pension plan contributions, the realization of benefits represented by an overfunded pension plan may result from (a) the transfer of funds assets to pay other postretirement benefits; (b) a plan termination and reversion of excess assets, after tax; (c) the use of plan assets to pay for employee buyout programs; and (d) an acquisition of the firm with overfunded plans by a firm with underfunded plans.[74]

- OPEB plans employ most of the same features found in the accounting for pension plans. The deferred recognition in the determination of net periodic postretirement-benefit cost of actuarial gains and losses, as well as prior service costs and benefits, is a feature of both pension and OPEB accounting.

- Transition obligation positions of OPEB plans could either be recognized immediately upon adoption of SFAS 106 or amortized into the computation of postretirement cost in the future. Most firms elected to recognize the entire transition obligation of adoption of SFAS 106. Position quality will be diminished for firms that elected to defer recognition of the transition obligation.

- Unlike pension plans, OPEB plans are typically not funded. The inability to deduct, for tax purposes, contributions beyond those required to pay for current benefits is the major explanation for the absence of funding.
- Substantial differences are common between the funded status of OPEB plans and the liabilities recognized on the balance sheets of plan sponsors. Where the plan sponsor recognizes a liability that is less than the funded status (i.e., the plan's benefit obligation minus any plan assets), then the sponsor firm's position quality is diminished. Where the opposite is true, position quality is enhanced.
- It is common for the cash quality of the earnings of an OPEB sponsor to be enhanced. This is due to the typical excess of the postretirement cost over the current employer contribution. The contribution covers only the cost of retirees, but benefits are also being earned by a typically larger number of current employees.

GLOSSARY

Accumulated benefit obligation   The actuarial present value of the pension benefits earned to date. Measurement is based on historical compensation rates for pay-related plans.

Actual return on plan assets   The growth in the value of plan assets, reduced by contributions and increased by payments to plan beneficiaries.

Actuarial assumptions   Estimates necessary to measure pension cost and to develop an appropriate funding plan for benefits. Examples include: mortality rates, employee turnover, interest rates, discount rates, expected rates of return on plan assets, future compensation levels, etc.

Actuarial gains and losses   Changes in plan assets or liabilities resulting from either changes in actuarial assumptions or actual experience that deviates from these assumptions.

Actuarial present value   The present value of future benefit payments adjusted for the probability of payment.

Additional minimum pension liability adjustment   The addition to the plan sponsor's recorded pension liability required to create a net pension liability equal to plan underfunding. Underfunding is measured by the excess of the accumulated benefit obligation over plan assets. The liability is increased or decreased in the future as underfunding increases or decreases.

Amortization   Under pension and related GAAP, this refers to the inclusion of deferred gains or losses in the determination of net pension cost or income. It differs from the conventional use of the term because there is no asset or liability on the books of the plan sponsor that is being amortized.

Amortization of actuarial gains and losses   Inclusion of a portion of actuarial gains or losses in the determination of net pension cost or income. Inclusion of these gains and losses is only required if the net accumulated gain or loss exceeds 10 percent of the greater of the projected benefit obligation or the fair value of plan assets. Amortization of the excess of the actuarial gains and losses above the 10 percent threshold is usually over the remaining service life of employees expected to receive benefits under the plan

Amortization of unrecognized prior-service cost or benefit   Inclusion of a portion of prior-service cost or benefit in the determination of net pension cost or income.

Amortization of unrecognized net transition asset or obligation   Inclusion of a portion of the transition (date of adoption of SFAS No. 87, "Employers' Accounting for Pensions") asset or obligation in the determination of net pension cost or income. Amortization is usually over the remaining service life, at adoption of SFAS No. 87, of employees expected to receive benefits under the plan.

Asset reversions   Assets recovered from overfunded pension plans after accrued pension benefits have been funded.

Corridor rule   The requirements that actuarial gains and losses be amortized as part of net benefit cost when, at the beginning of the period, they exceed the higher of 10 percent of plan assets or the projected benefit obligation (ABO in the case of SFAS 106). The plus or minus 10 percent region is the corridor. Also see "amortization of actuarial gains and losses" above.

Deferred gains and losses   Changes in the value of plan assets and obligations that deviate from expectations based on actuarial assumptions. The deferred gains and losses are included in the asset and obligation values in the statement of funded status of the pension plan, but not in the computation of net periodic pension cost or income. Deferred gains and losses are amortized if they exceed the higher of 10 percent of the PBO or the value of plan assets. Also see "corridor rule" above.

Defined-benefit pension plans   Pension plans providing specified retirement benefits, typically based on age, years of service, and level of compensation. The plan sponsor bears the responsibility of ensuring that sufficient assets are available in the pension funds to provide the defined benefits. These plans may or may not be contributory.

Defined contribution plans   Pension plans that contribute defined sums on behalf of employees. Ultimate pension benefits are determined by the contributed assets and investment performance of the fund. The plan defines the contribution to the plan and does not commit to a specified benefit upon retirement.

Discount or settlement rate   The interest rate used to compute accumulated and projected benefit obligations. The rate used approximates that available on annuity contracts that could be used to settle pension obligations (settlement rate) or rates of return on high quality fixed-income investments.

Employee Retirement Income Security Act of 1974 (ERISA) Pension legislation of great historical significance. ERISA instituted significant reforms in such areas as mandatory funding, vesting requirements, etc.

Expected or assumed long-term rate of return on plan assets The average return expected to be earned on pension assets over a period of years. Expected return is the product of the long-term rate of return and pension assets. The expected return is deducted from service and interest costs in the computation of net periodic pension cost or income.

Fair and market-related value of plan assets Fair value is the amount realizable on sale of an investment between a willing buyer and seller. Market-related value recognizes changes in the value of investments over a period of years—not to exceed five.

Financial flexibility The capacity ". . . to survive bad times, to recover from unexpected setbacks, and to take advantage of profitable and unexpected investment opportunities. Generally, the greater the financial flexibility, the lower the risk of enterprise failure."[75]

Funded status The excess or shortfall of pension assets in relation to pension obligations. A plan termination or liquidation perspective would focus on funded status in terms of the accumulated benefit obligation. A going concern view would be based on the projected benefit obligation.

Health care cost trend rate An assumed annual rate of change in the cost of health care benefits.

Intangible pension asset Recorded to offset the additional minimum pension obligation to the extent that the additional minimum pension obligation does not exceed the sum of any unamortized prior service cost and unamortized transition obligation; any excess is charged against other comprehensive income.

Interest on projected benefit The growth in the projected benefit obligation due to the passage of time only. In concept, computed as the discount (or settlement) rate times the projected benefit obligation at the beginning of the period.

Market-related asset value Generally refers to an approach to the valuation of pension plan assets that does not simply use end-of-period market or fair values for a single period. Rather, a market-related value may recognize (i.e., smooth) changes in market value over a period not to exceed five years.

Minimum pension liability The excess of the accumulated benefit obligation, both vested and nonvested, over plan assets. If the sponsor's books do not already carry a net pension liability equal to or greater than the minimum pension liability, then an adjustment is recorded to establish such minimum net liability balance.

Net amortization and deferral A single line item included in the computation of net periodic pension cost or income. Main elements: the difference between actual and expected return on pension assets, amortization of prior service cost, amortization of transition asset or obligation, and amortization of deferred gains or losses.

Net periodic pension cost or income   The summation of (service cost) + (interest) − (expected return on pension assets) + or − (amortization of prior service cost) + or − (amortization of actuarial losses or gains) and + or − (amortization of transition obligation or asset).

Pension Benefit Guaranty Corporation (PBGC)   A government agency, funded by a per-capita insurance premium on participants in covered plans, which insures guaranteed pension benefits.

Pension plan contributions   Contributions of assets to the pension plan by plan sponsors, and in the case of contributory plans, by plan participants. Contributions are typically of cash, but on occasion involve other assets, including securities of the sponsor firm.

Pension poison pill   A provision typically designed to prevent those mounting hostile takeovers to benefit from overfunded pension plans of target firms. The procedure normally involves a requirement that excess assets be used to enrich pension benefits of plan beneficiaries in the event of such a takeover.

Plan amendment   A change in the terms of a pension plan. For example, benefits might be increased by providing a larger pension credit for each year of service.

Plan assets   Assets invested and held to provide for the payment of benefits to current and future retirees. Plan assets are measured at fair or market-related value and accounted for in separate financial statements of the plan and not of the plan sponsor (i.e., the employer).

Plan curtailment   The reduction or elimination of the accrual of benefits for future service.

Plan sponsor   The company, or other entity, providing the pensions benefits and making the necessary contributions to the pension trust.

Plan termination   Benefit accruals cease and all accrued benefits are typically funded through annuity arrangements with insurance companies. Excess assets are often recovered by the plan sponsor. Replacement plans may or may not be put in place.

Prior-service cost   Increases or decreases in plan obligations due to amendments that provide increases or decreases in benefits on a retroactive basis. While unusual, prior-service cost can represent a benefit in a case where benefits are retroactively reduced. Benefit decreases and prior-service benefits as opposed to costs have been far more common in the case of OPEB plans.

Projected benefit obligation   The actuarial present value of all benefits earned to date, in which future compensation levels are incorporated into the estimation of the plan obligation.

Qualified defined-benefit plan   A plan meeting specified requirements of the tax law. Qualification normally ensures that contributions are deductible when made by sponsors, returns on pension assets are not taxed to beneficiaries as accrued, and beneficiaries are taxed only when pension benefits are received.

Rate of increase in compensation   The expected rate of increase in compensation over the period of employment. The greater the rate of increase, the larger the difference between the projected and accumulated benefit obligations in the case of pay-related defined-benefit plans.

Reconciliation of funded status   A section of the statement of funded status that reconciles funded status of the pension plan to the pension asset or liability carried on the balance sheet of the plan sponsor. Reconciling items include: unrecognized gains or losses, unrecognized prior service cost or benefit, and unrecognized transition asset or obligation positions.

Service cost   The growth in the PBO due to additional benefits earned by employees for a specified period.

Section 401(k) plan   A defined-contribution plan that typically involves contributions by employees that are matched to some extend by their employers. The facilitating tax law is found in section 401(k) of the *Internal Revenue Code*.

Statement of funded status   A financial report listing, among other things, the assets and obligations of the pension or OPEB plan. The summary of funded status is typically designated as the excess or shortfall of plan assets over the projected benefit obligation (ABO in the case of OPEB plans). This excess or shortfall is also reconciled to the pension or OPEB asset or liability carried on the balance sheet of the plan sponsor.

Transition asset or obligation   The excess (asset) or shortfall (obligation) of plan assets in relation to the projected benefit obligation at the date of initial adoption of SFAS No. 87, "Employers' Accounting for Pensions."

Unrecognized initial (transition) asset or obligation   The portion of the original transition asset or obligation not yet amortized as part of the calculation of net periodic pension cost or income.

Unrecognized net gains or losses   The portion of actuarial gains and losses not yet amortized as part of the calculation of net periodic pension cost or income by the plan sponsor.

Unrecognized prior service cost   The portion of the original prior service cost not yet amortized as part of the calculation of net periodic pension cost or income.

Vested accumulated benefit   That portion of the accumulated benefit obligation to which employees have a legal right, even if employment is terminated prior to retirement.

NOTES

1. S. Woolley, "Corporate America's Clean Little Secret," *Business Week* (March 18, 1996), pp. 104–105. The quote from this article is attributed to Alan A. Nadel, a partner in Arthur Andersen, LLP.

2. Older GAAP requirements included: Accounting Principles Board Opinion (APB) No. 8, "Accounting for the Cost of Pension Plans," (New York: American Institute of

Certified Public Accountants, November 1966); SFAS No. 35, "Accounting and Reporting by Defined Benefit Pension Plans" (Stamford, CT: Financial Accounting Standards Board, May 1980); SFAS No. 36, "Disclosure of Pension Information" (Stamford, CT: Financial Accounting Standards Board, May 1980); and SFAS No. 81, "Disclosure of Postretirement Health Care and Life Insurance Benefits" (Stamford, CT: Financial Accounting Standards Board, November 1984).

3. Key GAAP includes: SFAS No. 87, "Employers' Accounting for Pensions" (Stamford, CT: Financial Accounting Standards Board, December 1985); SFAS No. 88, "Employers' Accounting for Settlements and Curtailments of Defined Benefit Pension Plans and for Termination Benefits" (Stamford, CT: Financial Accounting Standards Board, December 1985); SFAS No. 106, "Employers Accounting for Postretirement Benefits Other Than Pensions" (Norwalk, CT: Financial Accounting Standards Board, December 1990); and SFAS No. 112, "Employers' Accounting for Postemployment Benefits" (Norwalk, CT: Financial Accounting Standards Board, November 1992).

4. The tradition has been to use the label OPEB for both postretirement and postemployment benefits.

5. SFAS No. 132, "Employers' Disclosures about Pensions and Other Postretirement Benefits" (Norwalk, CT: Financial Accounting Standards Board, February 1998).

6. The absence of funding in the case of OPEB plans is due to the lack of current tax-deductibility of funding contributions.

7. In addition to cash, firms sometimes contribute their own common shares to plans.

8. Brown-Forman Corporation, annual report, April 1998, p. 34.

9. Qualified plans are covered in Sections 401–416 of the Internal Revenue Code. Achieving qualified status is important because of the tax benefits, for both employers and employees, that result. An example of one of the features required for qualified status is that employee benefits must vest within specified periods of time. Vesting means that the employee has a legal right to earned benefits even if they leave their current employer. The general requirement is that earned benefits must be fully vested after five years of service. An alternative provides for phased vesting of 20 percent after three years and increases of 20 percent in each subsequent year, with full vesting achieved after seven years. Section 411(a) of the Internal Revenue Code.

10. D. Kieso and J. Weygandt, in *Intermediate Accounting,* 9th ed. (New York: Wiley, 1998), pp. 1094–1095, point out that the employer or plan sponsor is the beneficiary of a defined-benefit-plan trust, whereas the employees are the beneficiaries of a defined-contribution-plan trust. This point on the differences in pension trust beneficiaries does not appear to be well known. Where the exact nature of the legal relationship between pension plans and plan sponsors it at issue, legal counsel should be consulted.

11. General Electric Company, annual report, December 1998, p. 51.

12. Bethlehem Steel did not provide this asset detailing in its 1998 annual report.

13. Research reported by E. Amir and S. Benartzi in "The Expected Rate of Return on Pension Funds and Asset Allocation as Predictors of Portfolio Performance," *The Accounting Review* (July 1998), pp. 335–352, documents a stronger predictive relationship between pension fund performance and the portion of the fund invested in equities than with the expected rate of return. Hence, information on the portion of the fund invested in equities may be of value in predicting pension returns.

14. M. Barth, W. Beaver, and W. Landsman, "The Market Valuation Implication of Net Periodic Pension Components," *The Journal of Accounting and Economics* (July 1991), pp. 27–62.

15. Changes in pension assets and liabilities that result from contributions to the pension funds and the payment of pension benefits are not included within the scope of changes referred to in this discussion. Rather, included are the changes that result from actual results that deviate from actuarial assumptions, changes in actuarial assumptions, or retroactive changes in benefits.

16. SFAS No. 87, "Employers' Accounting for Pensions" (Stamford, CT: Financial Accounting Standards Board, December 1985).

17. SFAS No. 132, "Employers' Disclosures about Pensions and Other Postretirement Benefits" (Norwalk, CT: Financial Accounting Standards Board, February 1998), para. 5(a).

18. *Ibid.,* para. 5(b).

19. SFAS No. 87, Para. 77.

20. *Ibid.,* para. 44. This paragraph also indicates that rates implicit in the current prices of annuity contracts may be used to estimate the discount rate. Rates of return on high-quality fixed-income investments are also identified as a source of information to guide the selection of the discount rate.

21. *Ibid.,* para. 45.

22. SFAS No. 132. In illustrations of the application of this standard, para. 63, SFAS No. 132 does disclose the accumulated benefit obligation in the case of a pension plan that is required to record an additional minimum pension liability. This case is discussed later in the chapter.

23. SFAS No. 87, para. 54.

24. SFAS No. 132, para. 6.

25. Even though Sherwin-Williams ends up with a pension benefit (income) each year, no assets are distributed to Sherwin-Williams from the pension trust. Hence, to record the pension income, a pension asset is booked. For those inclined to debits and credits: debit pension asset and credit pension income.

26. Recognition of prior service cost is to be over the future service periods of employees expected to receive benefits under the plan—SFAS No. 87, para. 25. The Statement supports recognition over future periods because ". . . plan amendments are granted with the expectation that the employer will realize economic benefits in future periods. . . ," para. 24.

27. A recent *The Wall Street Journal* article reported that the top ten U.S. corporate pension plans were overfunded by over $100 billion dollars: E. Schultz, "Companies Reap a Gain Off Fat Pension Plans: Fattened Earnings" (June 15, 1999), pp. A1, A6.

28. The recognition by General Electric of only half of its overfunded amount is not motivated by an active desire to be conservative. Neither should the recognition of a pension asset far in excess of the overfunded amount be taken as evidence of aggressive asset recognition by VF Corporation. These results simply flow from application of the GAAP that govern pension accounting and reporting.

29. Some of the unrecognized amounts may be offset by subsequent changes in actuarial assumptions or in experience that differs from the actuarial assumptions.

30. The expected returns were disclosed in GE's schedule of the effect of its pension plans on its operating income, General Electric Company, annual report, December 1998, p. 51.

31. SFAS No. 87, para. 32.

32. While not provided in the exhibits that were provided from the GE annual report, the Company did disclose that a $412 million nonrecurring early retirement cost was de-

ducted in arriving at 1997 pension plan income. This strengthens 1997 net income in terms of persistence.

33. General Electric Company, annual report, December 1998, p. 51. However, General Electric's pension disclosures show pension contributions of $64 million and $68 million in 1997 and 1998, respectively.

34. Keystone Consolidated Industries, Inc., Form 10-K annual report to the Securities and Exchange Commission (December 1997, p. F-11).

35. Allegheny Teledyne, Inc., annual report, December 1998, p. 44.

36. See §4980 of the Internal Revenue Code for details on the tax on the reversion of qualified plan assets to employers.

37. E. Schultz, "Pension Terminations: '80's Replay," *The Wall Street Journal* (June 15, 1999), pp. C1, C19.

38. Internal Revenue Code, §4980, (d)(B)(i). A complete and careful study of Section 4980 is essential to develop a full understanding of these provisions.

39. Internal Revenue Code, §4980, (d)(A)(i).

40. SFAS No. 87, paras. 32–38.

41. D. Dhaliwal, "Measurement of Financial Leverage in the Presence of Unfunded Pension Obligations," *The Accounting Review* (October 1986), pp. 651–662.

42. *Ibid.,* p. 651.

43. SFAS No. 87, paras. 36–38.

44. SFAS No. 87, paras. 36–38; and SFAS No. 130, "Reporting Comprehensive Income" (Norwalk, CT: Financial Accounting Standards Board, June 1997), para. 17, and SFAS No. 132, para. 63.

45. SFAS No. 87, para. 159.

46. Albany International Corporation, annual report, December 1998, p. 23.

47. These agencies include the Pension Benefit Guaranty Corporation (PBGC), the Internal Revenue Service (IRS), and the Department of Labor (DOL).

48. In a survey of opinions about the best and worst accounting standards, conducted by the FASB, SFAS No. 87 ranked as fourth best out of 47 standards issued by the FASB and the previous standard-setting body, the Accounting Principles Board (APB). The recognition of previously off-balance-sheet pension liabilities was the key basis for the Standard's ranking. C. Reither, "What are the Best and Worst Accounting Standards," *Accounting Horizons* (September 1998), pp. 283–292.

49. The growth in bond values from declining interest rates is offset to some extent by increases in pension obligations that result from the use of lower discount rates in determining their present value.

50. Most of this overfunding comes from the Teledyne side of Allegheny Teledyne. Allegheny Teledyne was formed by the merger of Teledyne, Inc. and Allegheny Ludlum Corporation.

51. If the unrecognized pension overfunded were added, pretax, to shareholders' equity, the Allegheny Teledyne ratio of liabilities to equity would decline to 1.05/1 from 1.37/1, or to 1.15/1 on an aftertax basis.

52. The absence of a cash flow associated with the recognition of $30.5 million of transition assets reduces the cash quality of earnings as outlined in Chapter One. However, the increase in overfunding due to the transition asset also makes it possible for Allegheny Teledyne to avoid the need to make pension plan contributions. Therefore, there is a real, but indirect, cash flow benefit from the annual $30.5 of recognized transition assets.

53. This feature of the Code is scheduled to expire for transfers made after December 31, 2000. Of course, it may be extended.

54. The minimum amortization of the actuarial gains is the excess of the gains over the recognition threshold divided by the average remaining service period of active employees expected to receive benefits under the plan—SFAS No. 87, paras. 31–34.

55. The effects of changes in discount rates are more complex than this discussion might suggest. Discount rate changes may well be linked to changes in rates of inflation in the economy. Thus, discount rate changes could also affect rates of increase in compensation as well as returns on pension assets.

56. Some available research highlights the importance of the percentage of equity securities in pensions portfolios in predicting future pension returns: E. Amir and S. Benartzi, "The Expected Rate of Return on Pension Funds and Asset Allocation as Predictors of Portfolio Performance," *The Accounting Review* (July 1998), pp. 335–352. Their findings indicate that the percentage of equity securities in pension portfolios is more predictive of future returns than the expected rates of return of the plans.

57. Allegheny Ludlum and Teledyne were combined in 1996. This transaction also involved the merger of their pension plans, with Teledyne's being significantly overfunded and Allegheny Ludlum's being uderfunded. The combined plans are now overfunded. In addition, excess assets are now being transferred, with no negative tax consequences, from the overfunded pension plans to OPEB plans in order to pay retiree health benefits.

58. Extensive information about the PBGC can be obtained from its website: PBGC.gov.

59. Pension Benefit Guaranty Corporation, *About PBGC: Mission and Background* (March 1999), p. 1.

60. Pension Benefit Guaranty Corporation, *FACTS: Pension Insurance Premiums* (March 1999), p. 1.

61. In an apparently active period, the PBGC reported that "In the last three years (1992 to 1995), PBGC has negotiated 36 major settlements that have provided more than $14 billion in new pension contributions and protections for 1.3 million workers." This was reported in PBGC News, no. 96-40, April 1, 1996, p. 1.

62. Galey & Lord, Inc., annual report, October 1998, p. 38.

63. Tultex Corporation, annual report, January 1999, p. 13.

64. A comprehensive comparison of pension and OPEB accounting is provided in SFAS No. 106, "Employers Accounting for Postretirement Benefits Other Than Pensions" (Norwalk, CT: Financial Accounting Standards Board, December 1990), Appendix B.

65. By a significant margin, SFAS No. 106 was ranked as the best standard issued by either the Accounting Principles Board or the Financial Accounting Standards Board. See C. Reither, "What Are the Best and Worst Accounting Standards," *Accounting Horizons* (September 1998), pp. 283–292. A typical survey response illustrates why SFAS No. 106 made the top of the "Best" list: "Recognized a liability that had been previously unrecognized and moved from cash to accrual basis of accounting."

66. Avon Products, Inc., annual report, December 1998, p. 55.

67. Avon Products, Inc., p. 56.

68. This statement also appeared as late as early 1999 in the General Motors Corporation annual report for 1998.

69. SFAS No. 106, paras. 110–112.

70. General Motors Corporation, annual report, December 1993, p. 38.

71. There is the same requirement for the amortization of actuarial gains and losses for OPEB plans as there is for defined-benefit pension plans: SFAS No. 106, paras. 58–59.

72. Available research is not wholly consistent on the valuation implications of unrecognized or off-balance-sheet OPEB obligations. Work by E. Amir, "The Effect of Accounting Aggregation on the Value-Relevance of Financial Statement Disclosures: The Case of SFAS No. 106," *The Accounting Review* (October 1996), pp. 573–590, finds that ". . . there is no evidence of an association between market-to-book ratios and either unrecognized gains and losses . . . or amortizations of unrecognized amounts, indicating that off-balance-sheet OPEB liabilities may not be relevant to investors. . ." (p. 588).

73. The health care cost trend rates differ from expected increases in compensation by their reduced reliability. The substantial uncertainty surrounding health care cost increases produces substantial uncertainty in the estimation of OPEB obligations. This may have contributed to the somewhat unexpected results of Amir's work cited in the immediately preceding footnote.

74. Item (c) assumes that the amount by which the pension is overfunded is priced and included in the value of cash or securities distributed to the shareholders of the acquired firm.

75. D. E. Kieso and J. J. Weygandt, *Intermediate Accounting,* 9th ed. (New York: Wiley, 1998), p. 205.

Chapter 12

Adjusted Balance Sheet Analysis

Often have you heard it that told, all that glitters is not gold.[1]

We don't get hung up over the inadequacies of conventional accounting since those who understand our business appreciate that customer lists are among Unistar's most important assets.[2]

Chapter Three, "Analyzing Business Earnings II," illustrates adjustments that exclude the effects of nonrecurring items of revenue or gain and expense or loss from reported net earnings or loss. The resulting adjusted (sustainable) earnings series provides a more reliable indicator of trends in the underlying operating performance of the firm. This series serves as a better foundation for, among other things, making earnings projections. Adjustments to as-reported financial position may likewise be necessary in order to develop a more realistic representation of financial position. In particular, the presence of valuation differences and off-balance-sheet assets and liabilities must be considered.

Some individual cases of valuation differences and off-balance-sheet assets and liabilities were reviewed by topical area (e.g., inventories, income taxes, investments, leases, and pensions) in the earlier chapters of this book. The separate influence of these items on various balance sheet ratios, especially liquidity and leverage ratios, was examined. This chapter will focus on adjusted financial ratios that incorporate, on a more comprehensive basis, the effects of disclosed valuation differences and off-balance-sheet items on financial position. The objective is to incorporate the effects of these valuation differences and off-balance-sheet assets and liabilities into revised balance sheet ratios, particularly liability to equity ratios.

The balance of this chapter is organized around the following points:

- Developments in financial reporting standards that have affected the range and significance of off-balance-sheet assets and liabilities and valuation differences are reviewed.

- Examples of key off-balance-sheet assets and liabilities and valuation differences are presented and discussed.

- Off-balance-sheet assets and liabilities and valuation differences that are recognized in purchase accounted business acquisitions are examined.

Exhibit 12.1. Off-Balance-Sheet Assets and Liabilities and Valuation
Differences: The Effects of FASB Standards

SFAS No. 2, "Accounting for Research and Development Costs" (October 1974):
Called for the immediate expensing of amounts spent on research and development.
SFAS No. 5, "Accounting for Contingencies" (May 1975):
Established guidelines for the recognition of contingent obligations.
SFAS No. 13, "Accounting for Leases," (November 1976):
Required some leases to be recorded on the balance sheet as liabilities.
SFAS No. 87, "Employers' Accounting for Pensions" (December 1985):
Required liabilities to be accrued for underfunded pension plans.
SFAS No. 94, "Consolidation of All Majority-Owned Subsidiaries" (October 1987):
Brought previously off-balance-sheet liabilities of unconsolidated subsidiaries into
    consolidated totals by requiring full consolidation of all majority-owned subsidiaries.
SFAS No. 106, "Employers' Accounting for Postretirement Benefits Other than
    Pensions" (December 1990):
Required liabilities to be accrued for previously unrecognized benefit obligations and the
    ongoing accrual of liabilities for benefits as earned.
SFAS No. 109, "Accounting for Income Taxes" (February 1992):
Called for the recording of deferred tax assets on all deductible temporary differences as
    well as loss and tax-credit carryovers.
SFAS No. 115, "Accounting for Certain Investments in Debt and Equity Securities"
    (May 1993):
Called for certain investments previously carried at cost to be recorded at fair value.
SFAS No. 121, "Accounting for the Impairment of Long-Lived Assets" (March 1995):
Established guidance for the identification and write-down of impaired assets.
SFAS No. 133, "Accounting for Derivative Instruments and Hedging Activities" (June
    1998):
Among other things, the Statement called for the recording of all derivative instruments
    at fair value as opposed to cost.

• Revised balance sheet ratios are developed from comprehensive adjustments for
  off-balance-sheet assets and liabilities and valuation differences of selected companies.

ACCOUNTING STANDARDS, OFF-BALANCE-SHEET ASSETS, LIABILITIES, AND VALUATION DIFFERENCES

Some perspective is useful in considering off-balance-items and valuation differences. Since the inception of the Financial Accounting Standards Board (FASB),
a number of its accounting standards have affected both the range and significance
of off-balance-sheet items and valuation differences. While in no sense all-inclu-
sive, some of the more important standards are listed in Exhibit 12.1.

Some of these standards increased and some decreased the range and significance of off-balance-sheet items and valuation differences. For example, the immediate expensing of research and development (R&D) costs under Statement of Financial Accounting Standards (SFAS) No. 2, "Accounting for Research and Development Costs," created additional off-balance-sheet assets.[3] That is, prior to this Statement, some firms had R&D assets on their balance sheets because they were capitalizing and amortizing these expenditures. Under SFAS No. 2, R&D assets were no longer recorded.

Available research on R&D and security valuation suggests that the market values these off-balance-sheet R&D assets. The leading work in this area by Lev and Sougiannis concluded that:

> The major outcomes of these adjustments—the corrections to reported earnings and book values for R&D capitalization—were found to be strongly associated with stock prices and returns, indicating that the R&D capitalization process yields value-relevant information to investors.[4]

Other work by Sougiannis reports that:

> The study finds that, on average, a one-dollar increase in R&D leads to a two-dollar increase in profit over a seven-year period and a five-dollar increase in market value.[5]

A plan by the FASB to require that acquired R&D, as opposed to internal R&D expenditures, be recorded on the balance sheet and amortized against future earnings has been abandoned for the time being. Off-balance-sheet R&D assets will therefore continue to require adjustments.

In a survey study to identify the best and worst accounting standards, SFAS No. 2 was included among the five worst. Failing to permit the recognition of assets associated with R&D spending was its key weakness.[6]

Some of the Statements in Exhibit 12.1 called for bringing previously off-balance-sheet liabilities onto the balance sheet. SFAS No. 5, "Accounting for Contingencies," increased the recognition of uncertain obligations.[7] SFAS No. 13, "Accounting for Leases," added some previously off-balance-sheet lease commitments to the balance sheet.[8] Both SFAS No. 87, "Employers' Accounting for Pensions," and SFAS No. 106, "Employers' Accounting for Postretirement Benefits Other than Pensions," called for the recognition of additional pension-related obligations.[9] SFAS No. 94, "Consolidation of All Majority-Owned Subsidiaries," brought substantial amounts of new liabilities into consolidated totals by expanding consolidation requirements to include such highly leveraged firms as finance and leasing subsidiaries.[10]

Of the above standards, SFAS Nos. 5, 87, and 106 were included among the five best standards in a survey conducted on the subject.[11] Bringing liabilities on to the balance sheet and standardizing accounting in each of these areas were the key strengths of these standards. However, SFAS No. 13, "Accounting for Leases," was included among the five worst. Its key weakness was failing to

Exhibit 12.2.   Examples of Valuation Differences and Off-Balance-Sheet Items (Millions of Dollars)

Topical Area and Company	Off-Balance-Sheet Item or Valuation Difference	Amount and Percentage of Shareholders' Equity[a]
Chiquita Brands International, Inc. (1998)	Foreign currency derivatives	$14/not significant
Investments/Coca-Cola Co. (1998)	Undervalued equity-accounted investments	$6,423/76%
Inventory/Deere & Co. (1998)	Undervalued LIFO inventory	$1,050/26%
Leases/Delta Air Lines, Inc.[b] (1998)	Unrecognized operating lease commitments	$7,847/195%
Purchased in-process R&D/ E.I. DuPont de Nemours Co. (1998)	Expensed in-process R&D	$2,921/21%
Pensions/General Electric Co. (1998)	Unrecognized pension overfunding	$8,123/21%
Other postretirement benefits/Illinois Tool Works, Inc. (1998)	Unrecognized other postretirement benefits obligation	$91/3%

[a]The percentages of shareholders' equity are pretax.

[b]The unrecognized lease obligation of Delta Air Lines, Inc. is based on the direct present-value calculation procedure, outlined in Chapter 10.

Sources: Companies' annual reports. The year following each company name designates the annual report from which each example is drawn.

achieve the objective of bringing more lease commitments onto the balance sheet as liabilities. The use of "bright-line" rules determining whether to record a lease as an obligation were also seen to open the way to abuse of the Statement.

As in the case of off-balance-sheet R&D assets, there is a body of research that suggests that financial markets were incorporating these off-balance-sheet obligations into the financial analysis of firms prior to the issuance of these standards by the FASB.[12]

Of the last four standards in Exhibit 12.1, each falls mainly within the valuation differences category. However, the tax accounting standard, SFAS No. 109, "Accounting for Income Taxes," does call for the recognition of off-balance-sheet assets in the case of deferred tax assets associated with tax loss and tax credit carryforwards.[13] SFAS No. 115, "Accounting for Certain Investments in Debt and Equity Securities," requires the measurement of some investments at fair value that had previously been carried on the balance sheet at cost.[14] SFAS No. 121, "Accounting for the Impairment of Long-Lived Assets," made the ongoing evaluation of the recoverability of the carrying value of assets a generally accepted accounting principles (GAAP) requirement.[15] Properly implemented, this State-ment should reduce the presence of valuation differences associated with over-valued assets.

There is relevant research related to the market assessment of valuation dif-ferences prior to the issuance of SFAS No. 115. Work by Barth studied how the disclosed fair values of banks' investment securities were reflected in share prices compared with historical costs. Barth concluded that:

> The findings indicate that investment securities' fair values have explanatory power beyond historical costs. Strikingly, historical costs have *no* explanatory power incre-mental to fair values.[16]

The results of this study indicate that the market incorporated the fair value of securities in the share prices of the banks in the study, as opposed to simply their historical cost. This implies that the valuation differences in these cases (i.e., fair value − historical cost) were incorporated into the share prices of the banks in the study, even before the issuance of SFAS No. 115.

SFAS No. 133, "Accounting for Derivative Instruments and Hedging Activ-ities," extends the reach of fair-value accounting initiated by SFAS No. 115.[17] This Statement requires that all financial derivatives now be recorded at fair value in the balance sheet.

The Statements in Exhibit 12.1 either have or will reduce the range and sig-nificance of off-balance-sheet items and valuation differences. However, off-bal-ance-sheet items and valuation differences remain. The next section illustrates important examples of these items.

Disclosed Valuation Differences and Off-Balance-Sheet Items from Company Reports

As noted above, both the range and significance of off-balance-sheet items and valuation differences have been reduced over the years by the standard-setting activities of the FASB. However, important areas still exist that affect the assess-ment of the quality of financial position. This section provides a number of ex-amples from recent company reports.

A listing of some off-balance-sheet items and valuation differences is pro-vided in Exhibit 12.2. Some similar cases have been provided in earlier chapters; however, it should be useful to summarize and review examples from a number of topical areas before more comprehensive balance sheet restatements are con-sidered.

Chiquita Brands International: Financial Derivative Valuation Difference

Chiquita Brands International, Inc. is included in Exhibit 12.2 to illustrate the fact that financial derivatives have been sources of valuation differences, or in some cases off-balance-sheet assets and liabilities. Once SFAS No. 133, "Accounting for Derivative Instruments and Hedging Activities," is adopted, financial derivatives will no longer be sources of valuation differences and off-balance-sheet assets and liabilities. They will be carried on the balance sheet at their fair value. The presence of a valuation difference is evident in the following Chiquita Brands disclosure[18]:

December 31, 1998

	Carrying value	Estimated fair value
Foreign currency option contracts	$5,890,000	$(800,000)

The carrying value of the currency options is an asset in the amount of $5,890,000, but the estimated fair value is a liability of $800,000, a valuation difference of $6,690,000. Again, under SFAS No. 133 there will no longer be valuation differences in these cases because all financial derivatives will all be carried at fair value.

The Coca-Cola Company: Investments Valuation Difference

The Coca-Cola Company provides a dramatic example of understatement of shareholders' equity related to its accounting for selected investments under current GAAP. This valuation difference of $6.4 billion at the end of 1998 is equal to 76 percent of the shareholders' equity of Coca-Cola. While stated here in pretax terms, if this valuation difference were actually realized, then the net contribution to earnings and shareholders' equity would be reduced by a charge for taxes. However, even if placed on an after-tax basis, the unrecognized value is very material.

The Coca-Cola investments are in bottling companies whose shares are traded, and the holdings are sufficient to provide Coca-Cola with significant influence. Therefore, the equity method of accounting is applied and the investments are carried at cost, adjusted for Coca-Cola's share of profits minus its share of dividends. These investments are not carried at their fair value.[19] In gauging the financial leverage of Coca-Cola, the case would seem compelling to include this unrecognized value, in whole or in part and on a pretax or after-tax basis, in a revised amount of shareholders' equity.

Consider how Coca-Cola's balance sheet would differ if its holdings were below the 20 percent threshold of the equity method. In addition, assume that the less than 20 percent holding resulted in the *absence of significant influence* over these investee companies. Ignoring the difference in the absolute scale of these investments, the unrecognized value would then be recognized and included in other comprehensive income, thus also becoming part of total shareholders' equity.

Deere & Company, Inc.: LIFO Inventory Valuation Difference

The undervaluation of inventory due to the use of the last-in, first-out (LIFO) inventory method by Deere & Company is one of the most common disclosed valuation differences. This disclosure is required for public companies by the Securities and Exchange Commission (SEC).[20]

Delta Air Lines, Inc.: Off-Balance-Sheet Lease Commitments

For analysts, unrecognized lease commitments top the list of off-balance-sheet liabilities. These commitments are very large in the case of Delta Air Lines, but heavy reliance on operating leases is a common feature of the airline industry. In noting the size of the estimated present value of Delta's operating leases, it is important to remember that this is but a single item that would be part of a comprehensive restatement of their shareholders' equity.

At the end of fiscal 1998, Delta Air Lines had unrecognized appreciation on equity investments of $877 million. Moreover, by the end of fiscal 1999, Delta Air Lines disclosed that it held warrants to purchase 18.6 million shares of Priceline.com's common stock for $.93 per share. Delta has little or no investment in these warrants. At August 13, 1999, the value of the Priceline.com shares underlying these warrants was about $1.2 billion.[21] Finally, Delta Air Lines also had deferred sale and leaseback gains of about $643 million at the end of fiscal 1999.[22] Combined, and put on an after-tax basis with a combined tax rate of 40 percent, just these two fiscal 1999 items would add about $1,106,000,000 to Delta's shareholders equity: ($1.2 billion + $643 million) × (1 − .40) = $1,106,000,000.[23] The additional shareholders' equity amounts to about 25 percent of Delta Air Lines' reported shareholders' equity at the end of fiscal 1999.

E. I. DuPont de Nemours Company (DuPont): Off-Balance-Sheet Research and Development

Over just the period 1996 through 1998, DuPont charged off about $2.9 billion of purchased in-process research and development (R&D). On a pretax basis, this amounts to about 21 percent of DuPont's 1998 shareholders' equity. As earlier discussion has outlined, there is evidence that the market incorporates these and other off-balance-sheet items and valuation differences in the determination of share prices.

General Electric Company: Unrecognized Pension Overfunding

The General Electric pension plans were overfunded by about $8.1 billion at the end of 1998. General Electric benefits on an ongoing basis from all of its overfunding amount by not being required to make pension contributions. Moreover, in some cases these overfunded amounts may be used for certain postretirement benefits.

Illinois Tool Works, Inc.: Valuation Difference on Other Postretirement Benefit Obligations

Like the General Electric Company, Illinois Tool Works also has a valuation difference. However, in its case it is a liability and not an asset that is underrecognized. Although not very large in this case, this condition does serve to weaken the reported strength of the Illinois Tool Works balance sheet.

The above examples provide a review of some of the major topical areas that can still give rise to either off-balance-sheet amounts or valuation differences. It is not uncommon for other examples of off-balance-sheet items and valuation differences to emerge in the process of accounting for company acquisitions accounted for using the "purchase" method. The next section provides a sampling of such items and discusses their possible implication for adjusted balance sheet analysis.

Acquisitions Accounting and Off-Balance-Sheet Items and Valuation Differences

Under the purchase method of accounting for acquisitions, the purchase price is assigned to identifiable net assets acquired on the basis of their fair values. Any residual that remains at the end of this process is assigned to goodwill.[24] Acquisition disclosures usually do not enumerate these individual revaluations. Acquired assets that often require revaluation include land, plant and equipment, patents, and inventory accounted for with the LIFO method.

In addition to the recognition of valuation differences, it is also common to record new assets that did not appear on the books of the acquired company. Exhibit 12.3 presents a sampling of these mainly intangible assets that were recorded as part of purchase acquisitions. Most of these items are disclosed as part of descriptions of acquisitions accounting or listings of intangible assets.

Access Worldwide Communications, Inc.: Assembled Workforce

Costs associated with the recruitment and training of a workforce would have been expensed as incurred. Therefore, the assembled workforce represents an off-balance-sheet asset. It is common for companies to declare that, "People (employees) are our most important asset." Employees are not purchased as such in an acquisition. However, if they were not in place, then significant costs would be incurred for their training and recruitment. Trikon Technologies outlined the approach used to value this asset as follows:

> The assembled workforce value was determined based on an appraisal utilizing a cost valuation methodology. To arrive at the estimate of the fair value of the assembled workforce, the replacement cost was estimated based on the costs to recruit and interview candidates, and to train new employees in their positions. Search, interview, and training costs per employee were totaled to arrive at an indication of total acqui-

Exhibit 12.3. Previously Off-Balance-Sheet Assets Recorded in Purchase Acquisitions

Company	Acquired Intangible Assets
Access Worldwide Communictions, Inc. (1998)	Assembled workforce
A.C. Nielsen Corp. (1998)	Customer lists
Adaptive Solutions, Inc. (1997)	
Service contracts	
All American Food Group, Inc. (1997)	Kosher certification
	Favorable lease agreement
American Educational Products, Inc. (1998)	Copyrights
Bradley Pharmaceuticals, Inc. (1998)	Marketing data
	Registrations
	Marketing rights
Dentsply International, Inc. (1998)	Product manufacturing rights
Elite Information Group, Inc. (1998)	Maintenance contracts
Micrel, Inc. (1998)	Customer relationships
Premiere Technologies, Inc. (1998)	Developed technology
Rational Software Corp. (1997)	Customer base
SSE Telecom, Inc. (1998)	Distributor relationships
Stocker & Yale, Inc. (1998)	Developed patented technology
Tanner's Restaurant Group, Inc. (1998)	Recipes

Sources: Companies' annual reports. The year following each company name designates the annual report from which each example is drawn.

sition costs per employee, and then multiplied by the number of employees being acquired to arrive at a total cost.[25]

For the outside analyst, obtaining the data to make an estimate of the replacement cost of an in-place workforce is probably not feasible. The workforce is not an asset that could be sold separately from the entity itself. The emergence of this asset as part of the acquisitions accounting process may simply highlight a deficiency in the current accounting treatment being applied to recruitment and training costs. The difficulty of developing this cost in the typical case, and the prospect that it would not be very material, probably rules out its inclusion in a formal adjusted-balance-sheet analysis. However, the emergence in company disclosures of an in-place workforce does highlight the value of the workforce, and some portion of the potential costs that would be incurred if there were a significant defection of employees subsequent to an acquisition.

A. C. Nielsen Corporation: Customer Lists

The second of the quotes that open this chapter stresses the importance of customer lists and their status as assets: ". . . customer lists are among Unistar's most important assets." These lists share most of the characteristics of an in-place work-force. However, unlike an in-place workforce, the customer lists are assets that might have value separate from the firm itself, although estimation of the value of such lists by the outside analyst is probably not feasible.

Adaptive Solutions, Inc. and Elite Information Group, Inc.: Service and Maintenance Contracts

As with customer lists, there might be some prospect of transferring service contracts separately from the firm itself. The costs of acquiring these contracts were probably written off by the acquired firm as they were incurred. The assignment of value to these contracts as part of accounting for the acquisition is consistent with their being a valuable asset, even though not on the balance sheet of the selling firm. A case could be made for making some effort to approximate the value of these contracts for inclusion in an adjusted-balance-sheet analysis. These could be very significant items in the case of companies in the computer and computer software businesses.

All-American Food Group, Inc.: Kosher Certification and Favorable Lease Agreements

Kosher certification in this case was not a material balance and would not be included in an adjusted-balance-sheet analysis. However, its presence is clearly critical to the value of a firm that produces kosher products.

The favorable lease agreements, if material, would be a candidate for inclusion in adjusted-balance-sheet analysis. The value of a favorable lease agreement is something that might be realized separately for the firm itself. In the past, this has taken the form of subleasing or being bought out by the lessor. Where material, an effort to recognize this asset in adjusted-balance-sheet analysis would be in order.

American Educational Products, Inc.: Copyrights

Copyrights could clearly represent substantial unrecognized value, in the form of valuation differences, for publishers and related firms. They are typically on the books of the original owner of the copyright at relatively small amounts. Where they are likely to be very material, efforts to incorporate their unrecognized value, either qualitatively or quantitatively, into adjusted-balance-sheet analysis may be worthwhile.

Bradley Pharmaceuticals, Inc. and Dentsply International, Inc.: Marketing Data, Registrations, Marketing, and Manufacturing Rights

Although it is difficult to know exactly what underlies the preceding terminology, an effort to include any of these in adjusted-balance-sheet analysis will turn in large measure on the ability of an analyst to develop reasonable value estimates on a cost-beneficial basis, as well as the likely materiality of the amounts. The likelihood that some of these items could be transferred separately would favor their inclusion in adjusted-balance-sheet analysis.

Micrel, Inc., Rational Software, and SSE Telecom, Inc.: Customer Relationships, Customer Base, and Distributor Relationships

All of these relationships are clearly of value to a firm. This value should be reflected in the purchase price of a firm. As with many of the other examples, they are not items that can easily be sold separately from the firm. Inclusion in adjusted-balance-sheet analysis may not be appropriate.

Premiere Technologies, Inc. and Stocker & Yale, Inc.: Developed and Patented Technology

Both developed and patented technology can presumably be sold separately. Where significant, a valuation aimed at inclusion in adjusted-balance-sheet analysis should be considered. A stronger case can no doubt be made for inclusion of the technology that is both developed and patented.

Tanner's Restaurant Group, Inc.: Recipes

The recipes of a restaurant could no doubt be of value. However, an analyst would probably find it difficult to estimate their value. Moreover, there is the issue of whether their value is the appropriate objective or the cost to develop replacement recipes, much like the cost of replacing an in-place workforce in the discussion above the assembled workforce of Access Worldwide Communications, Inc. Inclusion in an adjusted-balance-sheet analysis is problematic.

A Recap

The items included in Exhibit 12.3 were almost all valued as part of the process of accounting for purchase accounted acquisitions. They supplement in an important way the valuation differences and off-balance-sheet items in the discussions centered on Exhibits 12.1 and 12.2. Exhibit 12.2 disclosures provide quantitative data for existing companies that can be used in adjusted-balance-sheet analysis. They are provided as examples of unrecognized value found in existing companies that might be incorporated in adjusted-balance-sheet analysis.

Items in Exhibit 12.3, which were suggested for inclusion in adjusted-balance-sheet analysis, typically had one or more of the following characteristics: (a) they had value that could be evaluated separately from the firm itself; (b) they could be transferred to another party as a separate asset; (c) they had a separate legal status; and (d) reasonable estimates could be made of their values by outside analysts.

Off-balance-sheet items and valuation differences that fail to satisfy the above criteria should, of course, not be ignored in the analysis of a firm's financial strength or prospective financial performance. Not everything that affects the financial status or performance of the firm lends itself to easy or reliable quantification.[26] However, such items should still be included in commentary included with the analysis of financial statements and associated disclosures. In this sense, all of the items included in Exhibit 12.3 are potentially relevant and should be incorporated in either quantitative or qualitative analysis of firms.

A relevant observation on the role of quantitative and qualitative information in financial analysis is provided below from Standard & Poor's Corporation's:

> In determining a rating, both quantitative and qualitative analyses are employed. The judgment is qualitative in nature and the role of the quantitative analysis is to help make the best possible overall qualitative judgment, because, ultimately, a rating is an opinion.[27]

With the conclusion of this discussion of individual off-balance-sheet items and valuation differences, the chapter now turns to examples of more comprehensive adjusted-balance-sheet analysis.

COMPREHENSIVE REVISED-BALANCE-SHEET ANALYSIS

The term *comprehensive* is used here with qualification. As the preceding discussion has shown, there are off-balance-sheet items and valuation differences that bear on the strength of financial position that are very difficult for outside analysts to quantify. The following adjusted-balance-sheet analysis is confined to those items for which company disclosures are sufficient to make adjustments. Therefore, they are comprehensive only in the sense that they include all disclosed off-balance-sheet assets and liabilities and valuation differences.

Philip Morris Companies, Inc.: Revised-Balance-Sheet Analysis

The 1998 annual report of the Philip Morris Companies, Inc. discloses several valuation differences, but no obvious off-balance-sheet items.[28] Five potential valuation differences are listed below:

1. A $1.1 billion inventory valuation difference due to use of the LIFO inventory method
2. Cumulative foreign currency translation adjustment of $1,081,000,000
3. A net deferred tax liability position of $3,638,000,000

4. Unrecognized pension overfunding of $1,449,000,000

5. An unrecognized other postretirement-benefits obligation of $105 million

Other items that might be considered, but that are not incorporated in this revised-balance-sheet analysis, include the following:

• R&D expense over the 1996 through 1998 period of $1,554,000,000
• Contingent obligations due to tobacco-related litigation
• Litigation related to Italian valued-added taxes

Exhibit 12.4 provides the liabilities and shareholders' equity information of Philip Morris, and Exhibit 12.5 provides selected disclosure information on items one to five above.

LIFO Inventory Valuation Difference

The $1.1 billion inventory valuation difference is a clear candidate for inclusion in adjusted-balance-sheet analysis. As discussed in Chapter Four, it is common to see these balances added to shareholders' equity, on an after-tax basis, in analyses designed to produce more realistic measures of financial leverage.

Foreign Currency Translation Adjustments

The foreign currency translation adjustment of $1,081,000,000 is listed as a possible adjustment item. This cumulative reduction in total shareholders' equity did not entail a cash outflow. Moreover, it may be reversed by subsequent appreciation in foreign currencies and, in any event, may never become a realized item. In fact, Philip Morris reports that federal income taxes have not been provided on $3.4 billion of accumulated earnings of foreign subsidiaries "that are expected be permanently reinvested."[29]

Financial covenants in credit agreements sometimes exclude translation adjustments from measures of shareholders' equity used to measure limit or control financial leverage. This is based on the view that translation adjustments, whether producing either increases or decreases in shareholders' equity, do not have a significant effect on the debt-service capacity of the firm.

Net Deferred Tax Liability

Philip Morris Companies, Inc. has a net deferred tax liability of $3,638,000,000 at the end of 1998. The overall net deferred tax liability position is principally due to the leasing activities of its financial services operations. From an economic perspective, this net deferred tax liability is overstated because it is not measured

Exhibit 12.4. Partial Balance Sheet: Philip Morris Companies, Inc., December 31, 1997 and 1998 (Millions of Dollars)

	1997	1998
Liabilities		
Consumer products		
Short-term borrowings	$157	$225
Current portion of long-term debt	1,516	1,822
Accounts payable	3,318	3,359
Accrued liabilities:		
Marketing	2,149	2,637
Taxes, except income taxes	1,234	1,408
Employment taxes	1,083	968
Settlement charges	886	1,135
Other	2,894	2,608
Income taxes	862	1,144
Dividends payable	972	1,073
Total current liabilities	15,071	16,379
Long-term debt	11,585	11,906
Deferred income taxes	889	709
Accrued postretirement health care costs	3,432	2,543
Other liabilities	6,281	7,019
Total consumer products liabilities	36,195	38,776
Financial services		
Long-term debt	845	709
Deferred income taxes	3,877	4,151
Other liabilities	110	87
Total financial services liabilities	4,832	4,947
Total liabilities	41,027	43,723
Contingencies (Note 16)		
Stockholders' Equity		
Common stock, par value $0.33 1/3 per share		
(2,805,961,317 shares issued)	935	935
Earnings reinvested in the business	24,924	26,261
Accumulated other comprehensive earnings (including		
currency translation of $1,109 and $1,081)	(1,109)	(1,106)
Cost of repurchased stock (380,474,028 and 375,426,742 shares)	(9,830)	(9,893)
Total stockholders' equity	14,920	16,197
Total liabilities and stockholders' equity	$55,947	$59,920

Source: Philip Morris Companies, Inc., annual report, December 1998, p. 39.

Exhibit 12.5. Miscellaneous Disclosures Bearing on Adjusted-Balance-Sheet Analysis: Philip Morris Companies, Inc., Years Ended December 31, 1997–1998 (Millions of Dollars)

Note 5. Inventories
The cost of approximately 50% of inventories in 1997 and 1998 was determined using the LIFO method. The stated LIFO values of inventories were approximately $1.0 billion and $1.1 billion lower than the current cost of inventories at December 31, 1997 and 1998, respectively.

Note 11. Pre-Tax Earnings and Provision for Income Taxes (key summarized data only)

	1997	1998
Consumer Product's net deferred tax asset positions	$495	$513
Financial Service's net deferred tax liability positions	(3,877)	(4,151)
Net Philip Morris deferred tax liability positions	$3,382	$3,638

Note 13. Benefit Plans (key summarized data only)

Pensions plans:	1997	1998
Fair value of plans assets	$10,274	$10,951
Benefit obligations	8,224	9,421
Excess of plan assets over benefit obligations	2,050	1,530
Net prepaid pension asset	293	81
Postretirement Benefit Plans:		
Accumulated postretirement-benefit obligation	$2,627	$2,771
Accrued postretirement health care costs obligation	2,563	2,666
Unrecognized obligation	64	105

Note 14. Additional Information (key summarized data only)

	1996	1997	1998
Research and development expense	$515	$533	$506

Source: Philip Morris Companies, Inc., annual report, December 1998, pp. 45, 48, 51, 52.

at present value. Therefore, there is clearly a valuation difference that, arguably, could be added back to shareholders' equity.

It is important to bear in mind that the net deferred tax liability of $3,638,000,000 has reduced net income by the same amount.[30] Therefore, if the liability is overstated, it follows that shareholders' equity also understated.

It is not uncommon to hear deferred tax liabilities referred to as *quasi-equity.* Companies will on occasion ask lenders to add deferred tax liabilities back to shareholders' equity in assessing their compliance with leverage covenants in credit agreements. Moreover, in many countries deferred tax liabilities are recorded only in part or not at all. Consider the following accounting policy statements of a British and Mexican firm, respectively:

- **Cadbury Schweppes.** Deferred taxation: Under UK GAAP, no provision is made for deferred taxation if there is reasonable evidence that such deferred taxation will not be payable in the foreseeable future.

- **Bufete Industrial, SA.** Deferred income tax: Income tax is recorded in accordance with MEX-GAAP following interperiod allocation procedures under the partial liability method. Deferred income taxes are provided only for identifiable, nonrecurring timing differences that are expected to be realized in a foreseeable period of time.[31]

In countries where the "partial" tax allocation method—described in Bufete Industrial above—is used, the unrecorded tax liability is typically disclosed as a contingent liability.

If it is reasonable to expect Philip Morris to at least maintain or even grow its leasing business, then the deferred tax liability would seem to fit the characterizations above as not being payable within the foreseeable future. Further, the liability is clearly overstated because under current U.S. GAAP it is not measured and recorded at present value. There is a valuation difference represented by an excess of the recorded amount over the present value of the net deferred tax liability. At least part of the Philip Morris deferred tax liability could be added back to shareholders' equity in an adjusted-balance-sheet analysis. That is, it is a form of "*quasi-equity*."

Unrecognized Pension Overfunding

A benefit from the overfunded status of the Philip Morris pension plans is being registered in shareholders' equity each year. Because of the overfunded position, Philip Morris reported net pension income in 1996 and 1997 on its U.S. pension plans of $54 million and $77 million, respectively. Moreover, pension income would have resulted in 1998 for the U.S. plans if nonrecurring termination, settlement, and curtailment charges of $251 million were excluded from the net pension cost of $189 million. The result would be 1998 pension income of $62 million.

Even though each year's income statement is benefiting from the overfunding of its plans, there remains an unrecognized valuation difference of $1,449,000,000 at the end of 1998. Some or all of this difference could also be included in an adjusted-balance-sheet analysis.

Unrecognized Postretirement Benefit Obligation

As outlined in Chapter Eleven, unrecognized net postretirement-benefit obligations can emerge because a firm elects to amortize the initial unrecognized obligation over future years or because of deferred actuarial losses and prior service cost. In the Philip Morris case, unrecognized actuarial losses of $201 million, offset by $96 million of postservice costs "benefits," explain the unrecognized obligation of $105 million at the end of 1998.

There is a valuation difference of $105 million that represents the excess of the accumulated other postretirement obligation over the amount recognized on the books of Philip Morris. This amount, either before or after tax, could be deducted from shareholders' equity in order to have a more realistic measure of shareholders' equity.

Other Potentially Relevant Items

The 1996 through 1998 R&D expenses of $1,554,000,000 would suggest that there is some resulting unrecognized value. Estimating the value of this off-balance-sheet value is beyond the scope of this book. However, work by Lev provides some direction. Consider the following approach outlined by Lev to "build up" a firm's R&D capital in cost terms:

> For example, based on a straight-line 15% annual amortization assumption, a firm's R&D capital at the end of a given year would be equal to 85% of its R&D expenditure in that year, plus 70% of R&D in the prior year, plus 55% of R&D expenditure in the year before that, and so on until a fully amortized R&D layer is reached.[32]

An example of the estimation of the R&D capital of a specific firm, Merck & Co., is found in other work by Lev and Sougiannis.[33] While the industries of Merck & Co. and Philip Morris are very different, it is interesting to note that across the period 1987 to 1991, their annual estimates of Merck's R&D capital (asset) averaged about 2.6 times R&D expenditure (i.e., expense) in each year. This might at least represent a starting point in developing an estimate for Philip Morris Companies. Lev and Sougiannis also provide data on amortization rates, which are the key to developing estimates of R&D capital, for some other industries.[34]

Litigation-Related Contingent Obligations

Tobacco-related litigation represents a key contingent obligation. The other litigation is related to tax disputes in Italy. The tobacco-related litigation is obviously an area in which special expertise would need to be consulted. It may or may not lend itself to quantification, but it clearly must be considered in an evaluation the financial strength of Philip Morris Companies, Inc.

Summarizing the Effects of the Valuation Differences and Off-Balance-Sheet Items

The goal of this section is to distill, along the lines of the sustainable earnings analysis of Chapter Three, the potential balance sheet adjustments into a single summary statistic. For simplicity, a simple leverage ratio computed as total lia-

Exhibit 12.6. Summarizing the Effects of the Valuation Differences and Off-Balance-Sheet Items: Philip Morris Companies, Inc., December 31, 1998 (Amounts in Millions, Except Ratios)

	As Reported	Adjusted No. 1[a]		Adjusted No. 2[b]	
		Pretax	After Tax	Pretax	After Tax
Liabilities	$43,723	$43,828	$43,786	$42,009	$42,964
Shareholders' equity	$16,197	$18,641	$17,726	$21,000	$20,022
Liabilities-to-equity ratio	2.70	2.35	2.47	2.00	2.15

[a]Adjustments include the LIFO valuation difference, the unrecognized pension overfunding, and the unrecognized other postretirement obligation. A 40% rate is used for tax adjustments and the offset to the shareholders' equity increase or decrease is an addition to or deduction from the net tax liability, respectively.

[b]Adjustments include all those included in revision one plus one-half of the deferred tax liability is added back to equity and deducted from as-reported liabilities. In addition, one-half of the translation adjustment is added to shareholders' equity. No tax adjustment is made to the translation adjustment in the after-tax revision.

Source: Philip Morris Companies, Inc., annual report, December 1998, various pages.

bilities divided by total shareholders' equity is used. Because of the clear judgmental issues involved with some potential adjustments, several different adjusted ratios are presented in Exhibit 12.6.

The baseline for considering the effects of balance sheet adjustments is the liabilities-to-equity ratio computed from the as-reported balance sheet of Philip Morris Companies, Inc. Each of the two adjusted ratios is developed both with and without income tax adjustments. In some cases, tax adjustments would seem to clearly be in order. The picture is less clear with some other items.

The first adjusted ratio in Exhibit 12.6, with no tax adjustments, is developed by adding the LIFO valuation difference and the unrecognized pension overfunding to shareholders' equity: $1.1 billion + $1,449,000,000. In addition, the unrecognized other postretirement-benefits obligation of $105 million is deducted from shareholders' equity and added to as-reported liabilities. These significant net additions to shareholders' equity result in a decline, that is, improvement in the liabilities-to-equity ratio from 2.70/1 to 2.35/1.

With the tax-adjusted version of adjustment one, the improvement in the liabilities-to-equity ratio is more modest because the pretax increase in shareholders' equity is reduced by tax charges. These tax adjustments use an assumed combined tax rate of 40 percent and are applied to each of the adjustment items. In the case of the LIFO valuation difference and the unrecognized pension overfunding, the pretax increases in shareholders' equity are reduced to 60 percent of their pretax values—to $660 million for inventory and $869 million for pensions. The associated taxes of $440 million and $580 million for inventory and pensions, respectively, are also added to total liabilities. With the unrecognized other post-

Exhibit 12.7. Adjustment Items in Revised Leverage Ratios: Philip Morris Companies, Inc., December 31, 1998

Adjustment Items	Adjusted Liability-to-Equity Ratios	
	Set One	Set Two
Inventory undervaluation	X	X
Unrecognized pension overfunding	X	X
Unrecognized other postretirement-benefits obligation	X	X
One-half of the net deferred tax liabilities		X
One-half of the accumulated translation adjustment		X

retirement benefits obligation of $105 million, an after-tax amount of $63 million is deducted from shareholders' equity and $42 million is also added to total liabilities.

The first set of adjusted ratios, both with and without tax adustments, would probably appeal to most analysts. The second set of ratios in Exhibit 12.6 is a bit more judgmental and involves some ad hoc adjustments. The adjustments made in both sets of ratios are summarized in Exhibit 12.7.

The case for treating some or all of the net deferred tax liabilities as "*quasi-equity*" has been made in the income tax chapter (Chapter Five) as well in earlier discussions in this chapter. The keys are (1) its overstatement by virtue of not being measured at present value, and (2) its tendency to simply remain on the balance sheet and grow, in some cases for decades. The addition of one-half of the net deferred tax liabilities to as-reported shareholders' equity is simply an ad hoc method of treating a portion of the amount as equity.

The similar ad hoc adjustment of one-half of the accumulated translation adjustment, in the second set of adjusted ratios, is also designed to restore a portion of this unrealized loss to shareholders' equity. This loss is noncash in nature and would only become realized upon the disposition in whole or in part of the foreign subsidiaries. The Philip Morris tax disclosures include the following statement in explaining why taxes have not been accumulated on the retained profits of some of its foreign subsidiaries:

> At December 31, 1998, applicable United States federal income taxes and foreign withholding taxes have not been provided on approximately $3.4 billion of accumulated earnings of foreign subsidiaries that are expected to be permanently reinvested.[35]

No tax adjustment is made for the translation adjustment in the after-tax adjusted ratios. The translation adjustment is essentially treated as a permanent difference.

The second set of adjusted ratios of liabilities to equity show a further reduction in leverage. This is to be expected because the two additional adjustments for the deferred tax liabilities and the cumulative translation adjustment both involved making additions to as-reported shareholders' equity. On an after-tax basis, the ratios are as-reported, 2.70/1; first adjusted ratio, 2.47/1; and the second adjusted ratio, 2.15/1.

Recap of the Philip Morris Companies, Inc. Adjusted-Balance-Sheet Analysis

The statements and notes of the Philip Morris Companies, Inc. reveal a number of items that are included in the revised financial ratios. Because the Company had significant unrecognized value, the revised ratios show a somewhat less highly leveraged firm than the same ratios based on as-reported numbers. The revised ratios present what should be seen as being more realistic representations of the leverage position of Philip Morris.

Some of the adjustments made in arriving at the revised ratios clearly involve the exercise of judgment and the application in some cases of somewhat ad hoc methods. However, the exercise of judgment is always part of the process of forming impressions about the financial performance and financial position of firms. If the day comes when such judgments are no longer a part of financial analysis, then the current and prospective employment prospects of those engaged in financial analysis will be sharply reduced.

Delta Air Lines, Inc.: Revised-Balance-Sheet Analysis

The financial statements of Delta Air Lines, Inc. provide a further opportunity to consider the adjustment of as-reported information in financial analysis. The Delta statements include several adjustment items not found in the statements of the Philip Morris Companies, Inc. The potential adjustment items, at June 30, 1999, are listed below:

- A valuation difference of about $1.19 billion on 18.6 million warrants to purchase Priceline.com common shares for $.93 per share
- A valuation difference of about $325 million on the excess of market over carrying value of shares in an associated (equity-accounted) company[36]
- Off-balance-sheet operating lease commitments of $14.53 billion
- Net deferred tax liabilities of $417 million
- Unrecognized pension overfunding of $513 million
- A favorable valuation difference on another postemployment-benefits obligation (i.e., the recognized obligation exceeds the accumulated benefit obligation by $353 million)
- Deferred sale and leaseback gains of $642 million

Exhibit 12.8.   Summarizing the Effects of the Valuation Differences and Off-Balance-Sheet Items: Delta Air Lines, Inc., Year Ended June 30, 1999 (Amounts in Millions, Except Ratios)

	As Reported	Adjusted Ratios*	
		Pretax	After Tax
Liabilities	$12,096	$17,893	$19,122
Shareholders' equity	$4,448	$7,729	$6,500
Liabilities-to-equity ratio	2.72/1	2.32/1	2.94/1

*Includes the following items: The valuation difference on priceline.com warrants; the valuation difference on equity-accounted investments; the present value of off-balance-sheet operating lease commitments; one-half of the net deferred tax liability; a valuation difference due to unrecognized pension overfunding; a favorable valuation difference on an other postretirement-benefits obligation; and all of the deferred sale and leaseback gains.

Source: Delta Air Lines, Inc., annual report, June 1999, various pages.

Adjusted ratios of liabilities-to-shareholders' equity for Delta Air Lines, Inc. are presented in Exhibit 12.8. All of the preceding items are included in the revised ratios and, unlike the case of Philip Morris Companies, Inc., only a single set of revised ratios is produced.

The first two adjustments from the previous listing each involve the recognition of the undervaluation of investments. These investments are accounted for in accordance with GAAP. However, in the case of the equity-accounted investments, GAAP does not permit them to be carried at market value. Rather, they are carried at original cost, which is increased for the investor's share of profits and decreased by the amount of dividends received. The current undervaluation of the Priceline.com stock-purchase warrants will apparently be eliminated in whole or part as Delta Air Lines, Inc. has reported that:

> We are currently evaluating which portion of the warrants will become readily available within the next year. Upon completion of this evaluation during the first quarter of fiscal 2000, we will record the estimated fair value of these warrants on our Consolidated Balance Sheet.[37]

Moreover, the current ownership of the warrants is probably not the full economic equivalent of owning the Priceline.com shares. Delta's disclosures point out that, "These warrants, and the shares issuable when the warrants are exercised, are not registered under the Securities Act of 1933."[38] However, all of the unrecognized value of both the shares of the associated companies and the common stock that underlies the Priceline.com warrants is included in the adjusted shareholders' equity. Some "haircut" on the valuation of the Priceline.com warrants could probably be justified.

The adjustment for the operating lease commitments is standard in financial analysis based on adjusted-balance-sheet information. The commitments of

$14.53 billion were converted to a liability amount by finding their present value using the "direct present value" method illustrated in Chapter Ten. A discount rate of 10 percent was used. This rate approximated the rate present in Delta's capital leases and is reasonably consistent with their long-term debt rates. This resulted in an addition to total liabilities of $7,513,000,000.

Just as in the Philip Morris example, half of the Delta Air Lines' net deferred tax liability was added back to shareholders' equity and also removed from total liabilities.

Favorable valuation differences, in the case of both pensions and other post-retirement benefits, were added back to shareholders equity and also deducted from total liabilities.

The deferred sale and leaseback gain was added back to shareholders' equity. These assets were sold, cash was received, and title to the assets was no doubt transferred. This is a balance that fits into the "*quasi-equity*" classification. It is common for analysts to add this balance to shareholders' equity in doing adjusted-balance-sheet analysis.

For the tax-adjusted ratio, tax adjustments were made for all of the adjustment items with the exception of the operating leases and the adjustment for one-half of the net deferred tax liability. Tax adjustments are not made on tax balances. With the operating leases, the objective of the adjustment is simply to include the present value of these commitments among the liabilities so that a more realistic measure of the degree of financial leverage can be developed. Because there is no earnings effect, there is no need for a tax adjustment.[39] As with the case of Philip Morris Companies, Inc., a flat 40 percent tax rate was used in the adjustments.

The adjusted Delta ratios of liabilities-to-shareholders' equity decrease from 2.72/1 on an as-reported basis to 2.32/1 on an adjusted pretax basis. But they increase again to 2.95/2 when tax adjustments are applied. The significant growth in equity from the recognition of undervalued investments is reduced by 40 percent when taxes are deducted from the pretax growth in shareholders' equity. However, in each of the adjusted ratios, pretax and after-tax, the sharp increase in liabilities from the operating leases remains the same in each computation. However, in the absence of the recognition of substantial positive valuation differences (i.e., valuation differences that increase shareholders' equity), the increase in the liabilities-to-equity ratios would have been far more substantial.

In the cases of both Philip Morris and Delta Air Lines, the objective was to incorporate off-balance-sheet assets and liabilities as well as valuation differences into revised measures of financial leverage. These revised financial statistics are more value-based and should do a better job of representing the basic financial strength of companies.

SUMMARY

The focus of this chapter has been to illustrate how valuation differences and off-balance-sheet items can be incorporated into adjusted-balance-sheet analysis. The following are key points for the reader to consider:

- All of the major topical areas covered in this book have the potential to produce valuation differences and off-balance-sheet assets and liabilities. While developments in GAAP over the past several decades have narrowed somewhat the range of these items, many still exist.

- The comprehensive analysis of valuation differences and off-balance-sheet items can benefit from a summarization technique similar to the sustainable earnings series that is used to consolidate information on nonrecurring items for earning analysis. This chapter has illustrated such a summarization procedure that makes adjustments for valuation differences and off-balance-sheet items and summarizes their effect in a revised measure of financial leverage.

- The illustrated procedure is not a strictly mechanical exercise. As with many facets of financial analysis, there are frequent occasions when it is necessary to make judgments and to sometimes employ ad hoc techniques in the effort to produce more realistic and more reliable financial information.

- The range of valuation differences and off-balance-sheet items is substantial. Additional examples were provided that were developed from an analysis of information associated with the implementation of the purchase method of accounting for acquisitions. These included such things as in-place workforce, customer lists, favorable lease agreements, recipes, and so on. This information is designed to provide examples of unrecognized items that in some cases might be quantified and incorporated into adjusted-balance-sheet analysis.

- The opening quotes of this chapter speak both of the occasional downside of balance sheets with "all that glitters is not gold" and of the unrecognized value represented by the declaration that "customer lists are among Unistar's most important assets." Whereas our examples have probably included far more unrecognized value than overstated assets or understated liabilities, the careful analyst/prospector also needs to be on the lookout for "fool's gold."

GLOSSARY

Adjusted-balance-sheet analysis   The incorporation of off-balance-sheet assets and liabilities as well as valuation differences in the assessment of balance sheet strength.

Developed technology   As distinguished from in-process research and development, developed technology represents completed research that has yielded a finished product. Unlike in-process research, developed technology acquired in a purchase transaction is recorded as an asset on the books of the acquiring firm and not written off immediately as in the case of in-process research and development.

Financial leverage   The degree to which borrowed funds (i.e., debt) are employed in financing the firm in relationship to shareholders' equity. The ratio of debt to equity is a common measure, on an industry by industry basis, of the degree of financial leverage.

Negative goodwill   The excess of the fair value of net assets acquired over their purchase price, after all noncurrent assets, with the exception of marketable securities, have been reduced to zero.

Off-balance-sheet assets   Something with value, however uncertain, from the perspective of the firm, its shareholders, creditors, or other stakeholders, which is not recorded on the balance sheet.

Off-balance-sheet liability   An obligation of the firm to pay cash or to provide goods or services in the future which is not recorded on the balance sheet. Operating lease commitments are the most common off-balance-sheet liability; research and development is an example of an off-balance-sheet asset.

Partial tax allocation   A method of accounting for deferred taxes that only records those deferred tax obligations that are expected to become payable within the foreseeable future.

Purchased in-process research and development   The value assigned, in an acquisition transaction accounted for using the purchase method, "to research and development projects of the acquired business that were commenced but not yet completed at the date of acquisition, for which technological feasibility has not been established and which have no alternative future use in research and development activities or otherwise."[40]

Quasi-equity   Items usually classified as liabilities on the balance sheet that might be considered to be shareholders' equity, for example, portions of net deferred tax liabilities and deferred gains on sale and leaseback transactions.

Strong balance sheet   Typically used to indicate a conservative debt position and the presence of undervalued or off-balance-sheet assets.

Valuation difference   A difference, either positive or negative, between the carrying value of an asset or liability and its market or liquidation value. Partially recorded pension and other postretirement-benefit obligations are examples of liability valuation difference; under- or overvalued equity-accounted investments are an example of an asset valuation difference.

NOTES

1. From Shakespeare, *The Merchant of Venice.*

2. J. Weil, "Unistar Financial Service Trading is Stopped Once Again, but CEO is Mum on Any Big News," *The Wall Street Journal* (July 22, 1999), p. C2. Quotation is from a progress report by Unistar Financial Service.

3. SFAS No. 2, "Accounting for Research and Development Costs" (Stamford, CT: Financial Accounting Standards Board, October 1974).

4. B. Lev and T. Sougiannis, "The Capitalization, Amortization and Value-Relevance of R&D," *Journal of Accounting and Economics* (February 1996), pp. 107–138. For more discussion, also see B. Lev, "R&D and Capital Markets," *Journal of Applied Corporate Finance* (Winter 1999), pp. 22–35. This paper includes an extensive bibliography of research on the valuation implications of R&D and its accounting treatment.

5. T. Sougiannis, "The Accounting Based Valuation of Corporate R&D," *The Accounting Review* (January 1994), pp. 65–66.

6. C. Reither, "What are the Best and Worst Accounting Standards?" *Accounting Horizons* (September 1998), pp. 283–292.

7. SFAS No. 5, "Accounting for Contingencies" (Stamford, CT: Financial Accounting Standards Board, May 1975).

8. SFAS No. 13, "Accounting for Leases" (Stamford, CT: Financial Accounting Standards Board, November 1976).

9. SFAS No. 87, "Employers' Accounting for Pensions" (Stamford, CT: Financial Accounting Standards Board, December 1985); and SFAS No. 106, "Employers' Accounting for Postretirement Benefits Other than Pensions" (Norwalk, CT: Financial Accounting Standards Board, December 1990).

10. SFAS No. 94, "Consolidation of All Majority-Owned Subsidiaries" (Stamford, CT: Financial Accounting Standards Board, October 1987).

11. C. Reither, "What are the Best and Worst Accounting Standards?" *Accounting Horizons* (September 1998), pp. 283–292.

12. For example, on pension liabilities, see D. Dhaliwal, "Measurement of Financial Leverage in the Presence of Unfunded Pension Obligations," *The Accounting Review* (October 1986), pp. 651–661; on leases, see A. Abdel-khalik, Principal Researcher, *The Economic Effects on Lessees of FASB Statement No. 13, Accounting for Leases* (Stamford, CT: Financial Accounting Standards Board, June 1981), Chapters Six and Seven; and on unconsolidated subsidiaries, see E. Comiskey, R. McEwen, and C. Mulford, "A Test of Pro Forma Consolidation of Finance Subsidiaries," *Financial Management* (Autumn 1987), pp. 45–50.

13. SFAS No. 109, "Accounting for Income Taxes" (Norwalk, CT: Financial Accounting Standards Board, February 1992).

14. SFAS No. 115, "Accounting for Certain Investments in Debt and Equity Securities" (Norwalk, CT: Financial Accounting Standards Board, May 1993).

15. SFAS No. 121, "Accounting for the Impairment of Long-Lived Assets" (Norwalk, CT: Financial Accounting Standards Board, March 1995).

16. M. Barth, "Fair Value Accounting: Evidence from Investment Securities and the Market Valuation of Banks," *The Accounting Review* (January 1994), p. 23.

17. SFAS No. 133, "Accounting for Derivative Instruments and Hedging Activities" (Norwalk, CT: Financial Accounting Standards Board, June 1998).

18. Chiquita Brands International, Inc., annual report, December 1998, p. 45. In 1997, Chiquita Brands disclosed a $6.2 million fair value, an asset balance, for a foreign currency swap contract that was not carried on the balance sheet at all. This is an instance of an off-balance-sheet item as opposed to a valuation difference.

19. Relevant GAAP are provided in Accounting Principles Board (APB) Opinion No. 18, "The Equity Method of Accounting for Investments in Common Stock" (New York: American Institute of Certified Public Accountants, March 1971); and SFAS No. 115.

20. *SEC Handbook* (Chicago: CCH Incorporated, November 1995), para. 35, 451.

21. Delta Air Lines, Inc., Form 10-K annual report to the Securities and Exchange Commission (June 1999), p. 42.

22. It is common for analysts to include deferred gains on sale and leaseback transactions in an adjusted shareholders' equity balance. The logic is that the gains have usually be backed by cash and title to the assets sold has been passed.

23. Admittedly, the dates associated with these data are not all the same. However, the objective is simply to identify some valuation differences that would need to be incorporated into a comprehensive analysis of the real balance sheet strength of Delta Air Lines.

24. A bargain purchase transaction occurs if the fair value of the net assets acquired exceeds the purchase price. In this case, such excess is first assigned to reduce the carrying value of noncurrent assets, with the exception of marketable securities, to zero. If a balance still remains, then it is assigned to negative goodwill.

25. Trikon Technologies, Inc., annual report, December 1998. Information obtained from Disclosure, Inc. *Compact D/SEC: Corporate Information on Public Companies Filing with the SEC* (Bethesda, MD: Disclosure, Inc., June 1999).

26. Examples might include the quality of a firms management, competitive conditions in the marketplace, the regulatory climate, etc.

27. *S&P's Corporate Finance Criteria* (New York: Standard and Poor's Corporation, 1991), from unnumbered introductory material.

28. Philip Morris Companies, Inc., annual report, December 1998.

29. *Ibid.,* p. 48.

30. To the extent that the net deferred tax liability includes the effects of items included in other comprehensive income, then comprehensive income and not net earnings would be affected.

31. Cadbury Schweppes, PLC, annual report, December 1998, and Bufete Industrial, SA, annual report, December 1997. Information obtained from Disclosure, Inc. *Compact D/SEC: Corporate Information on Public Companies Filing with the SEC* (Bethesda, MD: Disclosure, Inc., June 1999.

32. B. Lev, "R&D and Capital Markets," *Journal of Applied Corporate Finance* (Winter 1999), p. 27.

33. See B. Lev and T. Sougiannis, "The Capitalization, Amortization, and Value-Relevance of R&D," *Journal of Accounting and Economics* (February 1996), pp. 134–137.

34. *Ibid.,* p. 121.

35. Philip Morris Companies, Inc., annual report, December 1998, p. 48.

36. This value is arrived at by deduction. The unrealized gains on the collective Delta Air Lines' investments in marketable securities, including its interest in Comair Holdings, Inc., are reported to be $568 million at June 30, 1999 (p. 34 of the fiscal 1999 annual report). Elsewhere, $243 million of unrealized gains were attributed to holdings in Singapore Airlines Ltd., SairGroup, and SkyWest, Inc. (p. 43 of the fiscal 1999 annual report). The difference between the total unrealized gains of $568 and the $243 associated with the three preceding investments, is assumed to be the unrealized gain on Comair Holdings. As an equity-accounted investment, the unrealized gain of Comair would not have been recognized in its carrying value.

37. Delta Air Lines, Inc., annual report, June 1999, p. 43.

38. *Ibid.,* p. 31.

39. If the goal were to produce results that parallel those under the capital-lease treatment, then an earnings effect and associated tax adjustment would have been required.

40. E. I. DuPont de Nemours and Company, annual report, December 1998, p. 48.

Chapter 13

Identifying Sustainable Sources of Cash Flow

> For the full fiscal year, the Company generated more than $1 million in net income and more than $3 million in Earnings Before Interest, Taxes, Depreciation and Amortization (EBITDA), which is frequently used as a measure of operating cash flow.[1]

> Funds From Operations ("FFO") . . . is considered to be a meaningful and useful measure of real estate operating performance. The Corporation's presentation of "Cash Flow from Operations" is consistent with . . . FFO.[2]

This book uses an organizing theme to help equity investors and creditors effectively process the flood of information found in financial reports. That organizing theme—assessing financial quality—is focused on evaluating corporate earning power, which is defined as the ability to generate a sustainable stream of earnings that provide cash flow. Ultimately, both equity investors and creditors are interested in a company's ability to generate cash flow. To equity holders, cash flow is important for reinvestment to produce capital gains, for dividends, and for stock buybacks. For credit holders, cash provides for the payment of interest and principal on loans.

If our objective is to evaluate whether a firm is able to generate a sustainable stream of earnings and cash flow, it would seem that all we need to do is locate profitable companies that are generating positive cash. Unfortunately, it is not that simple. Some profitable companies may be generating profits from nonrecurring sources. Losses will likely be forthcoming. Other nonprofitable companies may be losing money because of nonrecurring losses. Positive earnings are likely in the near term. Earlier chapters looked carefully at the components of earnings with the objective of finding sustainable sources. This chapter focuses on the cash flow component of those earnings and the implications when those cash flows are negative.

Much as careful analysis is required to determine whether earnings are generated by recurring sources, the analysis of cash flow must also be performed in a careful and concerted manner. The existence of positive cash flow does not necessarily indicate that it will be recurring. Cash flow can be generated in the short run through asset liquidation and the expansion of liabilities. In the absence of a renewable source, such cash flow will ultimately cease. In other cases, such as with growing companies, the consumption of cash may be an expected and healthy circumstance. Positive cash flow may be the next step as growth slows from an earlier, more torrid pace.

Interestingly, although one might think that cash is a known commodity, as the opening quotes to this chapter attest, there is a disagreement on what constitutes cash flow. In addition to the standard cash provided by operating activities, such financial metrics as earnings before interest, taxes, depreciation, and amortization (EBITDA) and funds from operations (FFO) are often used to measure "cash flow" performance.

The purpose of this chapter is to strengthen the financial statement reader's ability to analyze cash flow. The chapter provides clarification on selected definitions of cash flow used in financial reports and equips equity analysts and credit analysts to identify recurring cash flow sources.

IMPORTANCE OF CASH FLOW INFORMATION

It is hard to overstate the importance to investors and creditors of cash flow information. Acknowledging this importance, early in its development of a set of concepts to provide a foundation for financial reporting standards, the Financial Accounting Standards Board (FASB) stated:

> Financial reporting should provide information to help present and potential investors and creditors and other users in assessing the amounts, timing, and uncertainty of prospective cash receipts from dividends or interest and the proceeds from the sale, redemption, or maturity of securities or loans.[3]

The FASB did go on to note that although investors and creditors need information on cash flow, accrual-based earnings information was more useful in assessing a firm's ability to generate future cash flows than simply historical cash flow information. The FASB noted:

> The primary focus of financial reporting is information about an enterprise's performance provided by measures of earnings and its components. Investors, creditors, and others who are concerned with assessing the prospects for enterprise net cash inflows are especially interested in that information. Their interest in an enterprise's future cash flows and its ability to generate favorable cash flows leads primarily to an interest in information about its earnings rather than information directly about its cash flows. Financial statements that show only cash receipts and payments . . . cannot adequately indicate whether or not an enterprise's performance is successful.[4]

The FASB's position that the interests of investors and creditors in cash flow are best served by providing accrual-based earnings information is consistent with the definition of earning power used throughout this book. *Earning power* has been defined as the ability to generate a sustainable stream of earnings that provides cash flow. That definition puts the focus first on the ability to generate accrual-based earnings. However, ultimately, only earnings that are backed by cash flow, either currently or in future periods, will have value.

Several research studies have looked at the relative value to investors of accrual-based earnings and cash flow information. Generally, the research has found value relevance for both accrual-based earnings and cash flow information. For example, Rayburn found that both operating cash flow and accounting accrual data, defined as the difference between earnings and operating cash flow, explained security returns that varied from returns expected as a result of general market movements.[5] Neither item outperformed the other. Wilson looked at power of operating cash flow, earnings, and their difference, which he termed total accruals, to explain share price movements.[6] He found that operating cash flow and total accruals have incremental explanatory power beyond earnings themselves. He did find, however, that the total accruals variable had incremental explanatory power over operating cash flow. Cheng, Liu, and Schaefer looked at the value to investment analysis of cash flow disclosures versus estimates of cash flow information that investors might derive from other available financial statements.[7] The authors studied contemporaneous associations between cash flow disclosures and stock price changes after controlling for earnings information. They found that cash flow disclosures were relevant to investment decisions. They also found that the value of corporate cash flow disclosures exceeded estimates of such cash flow information that investors might make using other noncash financial statement disclosures.

WHAT IS CASH FLOW?

Although there is agreement as to the value of cash flow information, a general disagreement exists as to what constitutes cash flow. That such a disagreement exists is clear from the quotes opening this chapter. As described in the opening quotes, EBITDA and FFO would not appear to be spendable cash; however, the companies that use these metrics clearly refer to them as a form of cash flow. Do these measures constitute cash flow?

The FASB's Definition of Cash

The cash flow metric in Statement of Financial Accounting Standards (SFAS) No. 95, "Statement of Cash Flows," is cash and cash equivalents. Cash includes currency on hand and demand deposits.[8] Cash equivalents are highly liquid debt instruments with original maturities of three months or less that can be viewed as essentially the same as cash. An example cash flow statement for Prab, Inc. is provided in Exhibit 13.1.

As can be seen in Exhibit 13.1, the cash flow statement for Prab, Inc. focuses on the change in *cash*. The company's statement separates changes in cash into three major categories: operating cash flow, investing cash flow, and financing

Exhibit 13.1. Consolidated Statement of Cash Flows, Indirect Method: Prab, Inc., Year Ending October 31, 1998

	1998
Cash flows from operating activities:	
Net income	$921,040
Adjustments to reconcile net income to net cash from operating activities:	
Depreciation and amortization	182,679
Amortization of discounts on subordinated notes	1,740
Bad debt expense	31,558
Deferred taxes	452,361
Loss on retirement of subordinated debt	117,443
(Increase) decrease in assets:	
Accounts receivable	(34,703)
Inventories	(45,615)
Other current and noncurrent assets	74,583
Increase (decrease) in liabilities:	
Accounts payable	(126,939)
Customer deposits	(103,615)
Accrued expenses	85,757
Deferred compensation	1,144
Net cash provided by operating activities	1,557,433
Cash flows from investing activities:	
Purchase of equipment	(222,797)
Cash flows from financing activities:	
Repayment of short-term debt	(250,000)
Payments on long-term debt	(1,040,000)
Payment of dividends	(19,250)
Net cash used in financing activities	(1,309,250)
Net increase (decrease) in cash	25,386
Cash—beginning of year	26,235
Cash—end of year	$51,621

Source: Prab, Inc., annual report, October 1998, p. 14. Note that Prab does not report the existence of cash equivalents.

cash flow. The sum of these three subtotals equals the actual change in cash reported on the balance sheet for the year.

Cash Flows from Operating Activities

Cash provided by operating activities or operating cash flow consists of the cash effects of transactions that enter into the determination of net income, such as cash receipts from sales of goods and services and cash payments to suppliers and employees for acquisitions of inventory and operating expenses and to lenders for interest expense. With only limited exceptions, operating cash flow can be considered to be the cash flow counterpart of net income from continuing operations measured on the accrual basis. One exception is gains and losses from the sale of investments and property, plant, and equipment. Such gains and losses are included in net income from continuing operations, but proceeds from their sale are excluded from operating cash flow and reported with investing cash flow. Similarly, in Exhibit 13.1, Prab reports a Loss on retirement of subordinated debt. Amounts paid to retire debt are considered a financing activity. By adding the loss on debt retirement back to net income, Prab is removing its effects from operating cash flow. The total amount paid to retire the debt is reported in the financing section as payments on long-term debt.

Another exception is the operating component of discontinued operations. Although that item is excluded from net income from continuing operations, any accompanying cash flow is reported with cash provided by operating activities. Also, all income taxes paid are included with operating activities, even though on an accrual basis; those tax effects may have been allocated to such nonoperating items as discontinued operations, extraordinary items, and the cumulative effect of changes in accounting principle.

Indirect-Method Format

The operating section of the Prab, Inc. cash flow statement (Exhibit 13.1) does not report actual cash inflows and outflows. Rather, cash provided by operating activities is calculated by adjusting net income for noncash expenses, such as depreciation and amortization, bad-debt expense, and deferred tax expense, and for changes in operating-related asset and liability accounts, such as accounts receivable, inventories, and accounts payable. Because operating cash flow is derived or calculated from net income in this way, the format presented is termed the indirect-method format. It derives operating cash flow indirectly, from net income. An alternative format, though one that is infrequently used, is a direct-method format. Here, operating cash flow is calculated directly, by combining operating inflows and outflows of cash. Operating cash flow under the two alternative formats—the indirect- and direct-method formats—will be the same amount. More is said about the direct-method format below.

Two cash flow items that are not apparent in the operating section of an indirect-method cash flow statement are interest paid and income taxes paid. Be-

Exhibit 13.2. *Pro Forma* Consolidated Statement of Cash Flows, Operating
Section, Direct Method: Prab, Inc., Year Ending October 31, 1998

	1998
Cash flows from operating activities:	
Cash received from customers	$18,234,228
Cash paid to suppliers and employees	(16,546,245)
Interest received	7,214
Interest paid	(119,886)
Income taxes paid	(17,878)
Net cash provided by operating activities	$1,557,433

Note that the amount of cash provided by operating activities, $1,557,433, is the same as the indirect
format presented in Exhibit 13.1.

Source: Prepared to approximate what a direct-method cash flow statement would look like from data
contained in the Prab, Inc., annual report, October 1998.

cause of the importance of these items to equity analysts and credit analysts and
other users of financial statements, generally accepted accounting principles
(GAAP) dictate that the amount of interest and income taxes paid during a reporting period must be disclosed in the financial statements. This is typically done
either at the bottom of the cash flow statement or, as in the case of Prab, in a
footnote.

Direct-Method Format

In a direct-method format cash flow statement, the operating section presents
actual cash receipts and cash payments. Operating receipts include cash received
from customers and interest and dividends received. Cash payments include cash
paid to suppliers and employees, interest paid, and income taxes paid. The sum
of these inflows and outflows will equal cash provided by operating activities. A
pro forma presentation of the operating section of the cash flow statement for
Prab, Inc. in the direct-method format is presented in Exhibit 13.2.

When using the direct-method format, a company must also provide a reconciliation of net income to cash provided by operating activities. This reconciliation is essentially an indirect-method cash flow statement. The reconciliation
can be provided as a continuation of the cash flow statement or in a footnote.

SFAS No. 95 recommends that companies provide a direct-method cash flow
statement. In the view of the FASB, a direct-method statement is more useful
because it provides information on actual operating cash collections and payments
and a supplementary reconciliation of net income to cash provided by operating
activities. However, aware that accounting systems may not capture cash flow
information in the manner needed for a direct-method format statement, SFAS
No. 95 does give reporting companies the option of preparing their cash flow
statements in the indirect-method format.

Exhibit 13.3. Method of Reporting Cash Flows from Operating Activities

	1994	1995	1996	1997
Indirect method	586	585	589	590
Direct method	14	15	11	10
Total companies	600	600	600	600

Source: Accounting Trends and Techniques: Annual Survey of Accounting Practices Followed in 600 Stockholders' Reports, 52nd ed. (New York: American Institute of Certified Public Accountants, 1998), p. 485.

As seen in Exhibit 13.3, most companies provide indirect-method cash flow statements. Presumably, this is because the statement requires less accounting data and is not as onerous to prepare. Moreover, the number of companies providing direct-method cash flow statements is declining.

Cash Flow from Investing Activities

Cash provided or used from investing activities consist of changes in cash and cash equivalents from making and collecting loans, from acquiring and disposing of debt or equity instruments and property, plant, and equipment or other productive assets. Whereas cash expended to invest in assets is reported in the investing section of the cash flow statement, cash income from those investments is reported in the operating section. Thus, an investment in bonds or common stock is reported in the investing section. The cash interest or dividend income generated by those investments is reported in the operating section.

Whether the operating section of the cash flow statement is an indirect- or direct-method format, the investing section of the cash flow statement is presented in a direct format. That is, it presents actual cash receipts, such as proceeds from the sale of property, plant, and equipment, and cash payments, such as capital expenditures or purchases of property, plant, and equipment.

Cash Flow from Financing Activities

Financing cash flows consist of changes in cash and cash equivalents by obtaining resources from owners and providing them with a return on, and a return of, their investment, from borrowing money and repaying amounts borrowed, and from obtaining and paying for other resources obtained from creditors on long-term credit. Cash raised from stock issues and borrowed money are financing activities. Dividends paid on equity are also a financing activity. However, interest paid on borrowed money is reported in the operating activities section. This discrepancy from the treatment of dividends paid is needed to maintain symmetry between operating cash flow and net income. Net income is defined as amounts available for shareholders after senior claims, including those of debt holders, have been covered. Thus, interest—a claim of debt holders—is subtracted in computing net income. Dividends, however, are a payment to shareholders—a distribution of profits available for them—and are not subtracted in measuring net income. In this way, net income consists of earnings available for all shareholders, common and preferred. Similarly, cash provided by operating activities consists of cash flow available for all shareholders after interest claims of debt holders have been covered.

Like the investing section, the financing section of the cash flow statement is presented in a direct format. It presents actual cash receipts, such as proceeds from borrowings and cash payments, such as repayments of long-term debt.

Noncash Investing and Financing Activities

Although not resulting in cash flows per se, certain transactions have cash flow implications for which SFAS No. 95 requires disclosure. Such transactions are referred to as noncash investing and financing activities. SFAS No. 95 defines them as ". . . investing and financing activities of an enterprise during a period that affect recognized assets or liabilities but that do not result in cash receipts or cash payments."[9] Examples include conversions of debt to equity, asset acquisitions by assuming related liabilities, and acquisitions through the issuance of stock. Disclosure can be as part of the statement of cash flows or in a footnote. In a footnote to its annual report, Prab indicated, "There were no significant noncash financing or investing activities during 1998 and 1997."[10]

Alternative Definitions of Cash Flow

SFAS No. 95 is very clear on its definition of cash and cash equivalents. In establishing cash and cash equivalents as the cash flow measure of choice, the FASB wanted to get away from what had been a long-accepted practice of using "funds"or working capital as a liquidity metric. Also driving the FASB in its quest to replace funds or working capital with cash was a distrust by investors and creditors in working capital as a liquidity metric that had developed at the time SFAS No. 95 was approved.

Funds, or working capital, is calculated as current assets less current liabilities. Working capital provided by operations is calculated generally as net income from continuing operations adjusted for nonoperating gains and losses and revenue and expenses that affect noncurrent assets and liabilities and thus do not provide or consume working capital. For example, in calculating working capital from operations, depreciation expense on property, plant, and equipment is added back to net income, as is deferred tax expense related to a noncurrent deferred tax liability. However, as it reduces a current-asset account and thus reduces working capital, the amortization of a current deferred tax asset would not be added back to net income in calculating working capital provided by operations.

Working capital provided by operations differs from cash provided by operations by the amount of changes in all noncash working capital accounts. Thus, a company can generate working capital from operations as working capital accounts, such as accounts receivable, inventories, and current deferred tax assets increase, without generating any cash. The company would be generating liquidity, but would not be able to pay its bills.

A noteworthy business failure that was unanticipated by many and helped focus attention on the need for detailed cash flow information was W. T. Grant Co., Inc. For a decade leading to the mid-1970s, Grant was profitable and generating ample amounts of working capital from operations. During much of that period, however, the company was consuming cash from operations. The difference was a buildup in current asset accounts. Later, when these accounts proved to be unrealizable and were written down, the company reported significant losses and ultimately failed.[11]

Citing examples like W. T. Grant, and prodded by the FASB, the analysis pendulum swung solidly toward analyzing cash flows and away from working capital in the 1980s and 1990s. Since cash flow was the ultimate objective of investors and creditors, it was logical for them to focus carefully on the analysis of cash flow.

However, since the mid-1990s, we have noticed a decided interest once again in the analysis of working capital. Moreover, it is an interest we have seen not only with specific industries—for example, real estate investment trusts and cable TV—but with industries across the business spectrum and by both equity analysts and credit analysts. It is not a wholesale movement away from cash flow analysis. Yet, the new found interest in working capital, after its apparent demise years earlier, is noteworthy.

We are unclear as to the cause of this shift in focus. We do note that companies are able to generate more liquidity and appear more financially healthy on a working capital than on a cash flow basis. It is possible that the historically high financial asset prices being experienced in the late 1990s has led some analysts to prefer more liberal analytical tools. However, this is only conjecture.

To demonstrate how working capital generated by operations can give a more positive signal than cash generated by operations, consider the summarized financial information for Bindley Western Industries presented in Exhibit 13.4.

As can be seen in Exhibit 13.4, with revenues and net income up 37 percent and 32 percent, respectively, on an earnings basis, Bindley Western had an excellent year in 1997. In terms of working capital from operations, the company also did well, adding to its liquidity. Working capital provided by operations is calculated by removing from net income the effects of any nonoperating gains and losses and any revenue and expenses that affect noncurrent assets and liabilities. From Exhibit 13.4, depreciation of $7,431,000 and other noncash items of $2,532,000 are added to net income while deferred income taxes of $3,834,000 and a gain on sale of fixed assets of $103,000 are subtracted from net income. The result is working capital provided by operations of $29,772,000.

However, during 1997, on a cash flow basis, the company's performance was not as healthy. To calculate cash provided by operations in 1997, the $29,772,000

Exhibit 13.4.   Summary of Selected Financial Statement Information: Bindley Western Industries, Inc., Year Ended December 31, 1996 and 1997 (Thousands of Dollars)

Selected Income Statement Information	1996	1997
Revenues	$5,318,933	$7,311,804
Selected expenses:		
Depreciation and amortization	6,719	7,431
Interest expense	12,992	15,907
Provision for income taxes	12,865	15,806
Net income[a]	$18,006	$23,746

Consolidated Statements of Cash Flows–Operating Activities Section	1996	1997
Net income	$18,006	$23,746
Adjustments to reconcile net income to net cash provided (used) by operating activities:		
Depreciation and amortization	6,719	7,431
Deferred income taxes[b]	(2,031)	(3,834)
Gain on sale of fixed assets	(58)	(103)
Other noncash items[b]		2,532
Net working capital provided by operating activities[b]	$22,636	$29,772
Change in assets and liabilities, net of acquisitions:		
Accounts receivable	51,826	(229,518)
Finished goods inventory	(99,713)	(63,401)
Accounts payable	63,106	151,302
Other current assets and liabilities	6,097	4,724
Net cash provided (used) by operating activities	$43,952	$(107,121)

[a]Net earnings cannot be calculated by subtracting reported expenses from revenues because not all expenses are reported here.

[b]The company did not disclose net working capital provided by operating activities on its cash flow statement. The subtotal was added here to demonstrate its calculation. The deferred income taxes and other noncash items are assumed to be noncurrent.

Source: Bindley Western Industries, Inc., annual report, December 1997. Information obtained from Disclosure, Inc., *Compact D/SEC: Corporate Information on Public Companies Filing with the SEC* (Bethesda, MD: Disclosure, Inc., March 1999).

working capital provided is adjusted for changes in noncash working capital accounts.[12] As seen in Exhibit 13.4, noncash working capital accounts consist of increases in accounts receivable and finished goods inventory of $229,518,000 and $63,401,000, respectively, which are subtracted from working capital provided by operations in computing operating cash flow, and an increase in accounts payable of $151,302,000 and changes in other current assets and liabilities of $4,724,000, which are added. Measured on a cash flow basis, during 1997, the company consumed $107,121,000 in cash from operating activities.

The more liberal interpretation of liquidity afforded working capital over cash can lead to misleading interpretations of financial performance. Analysts using working capital provided by operations and not cash to evaluate performance must remember that working capital other than cash cannot be spent. While working capital does provide a measure of liquidity and a potential source of cash, realizability of the accounts involved must be considered.

In the case of Bindley Western, the accounts appear to be sound and working capital provides a valid measure of liquidity. With W. T. Grant, that was not the case. The different measures of "cash flow" mentioned in the introductory section of this chapter—EBITDA and FFO—are not measures of cash flow as defined by the FASB. Rather, they are variations on the working capital theme. A closer look at these and other alternative measures of "cash flow" are provided in subsequent sections.

Before proceeding, one additional point should be made. Even when a company focuses on alternatives to the FASB-defined cash provided by operating activities in measuring operating liquidity, that company's general purpose financial statements will include a cash flow statement prepared in accordance with FASB-provided guidelines. Those guidelines are part of generally accepted accounting principles and must be followed by reporting companies. Companies and analysts that draw attention to alternative measures of cash flow are doing so because they believe that the alternative measures provide more meaningful information. It must be remembered that the alternative information provided is supplementary to, and does not replace that provided in accordance with generally accepted accounting principles.

Research Results and Working Capital versus Cash Flow

Several studies have looked at the relative value for security analysis of earnings, cash flow from operations, and working capital from operations. The results of two representative studies are provided here. The findings are mixed.

In their paper, Bowen, Burgstahler, and Dale looked at the role played by earnings, working capital from operations, and operating cash flow in an explanatory model of security prices.[13] After controlling for the information contained in earnings, they found that operating cash flow had incremental power for explaining the movement of security prices. However, in a similar design, working capital provided by operations did not have such incremental explanatory power. The implication of this finding is that operating cash flow has information for security pricing over and above that contained in earnings, but working capital provided by operations does not have such incremental information value.

In a follow-up study, Ali also looked at the valuation role played by earnings, working capital from operations, and operating cash flow.[14] Under the premise that the relationship between these variables and security prices may not be linear, the author employed a nonlinear model. In this setting, operating cash flow did not outperform working capital from operations in explaining the movement of security prices.

EBITDA

In the opening quote to this chapter, Ambi, Inc. states that EBITDA is "frequently used as a measure of operating cash flow." As we noted earlier, cash provided by operating activities is the cash flow counterpart of net income. It is actual cash flow. Like net income, it is after interest expense and after income taxes. EBITDA is a more liberal interpretation of performance than even working capital provided by operations which is after interest and taxes. EBITDA is loosely referred to as cash flow because it entails adding back to earnings a significant, often the most significant component of noncash expense, depreciation, and amortization. If there are no changes in working capital accounts other than cash—a very restrictive and unreasonable assumption—then EBITDA will approximate cash generated by operations before interest and taxes.

Interest on debt is serviced out of earnings before interest expense and taxes. Thus, to the extent that working capital accounts other than cash are realizable, for example, accounts receivable are collectable and the inventory can be sold, EBITDA is a valid measure of a company's ability to service interest on debt. For this reason, creditors can use EBITDA in evaluating a borrower's ability to service interest.

However, in some instances, EBITDA is also used by equity holders to evaluate performance. EBITDA is not a measure of earnings available for equity holders. Theoretically, these holders are determining whether a company can, at a minimum, service outstanding debt and avoid default. For example, in a leveraged buyout, equity holders can use EBITDA in determining whether the leveraged firm can handle its new and higher debt load. Unfortunately, the opportunity exists for some equity investors to lose sight of what EBITDA truly represents and begin thinking of the metric as a more traditional measure of income. This is done possibly because the companies in which they are interested are not generating income measured in the traditional manner. Whatever the reason for using it, we think that a long-term focus on EBITDA by equity holders can have a disappointing outcome.

Funds from Operations and Net Income plus Depreciation

FFO is another working capital–based measure of performance that is used broadly by real estate investment trusts (REITs). One such company that focuses strongly on the measure is BRE Properties, Inc. The company provides the following description of this performance metric in its annual report.

> Management considers Funds from Operations ("FFO") to be an appropriate supplemental measure of the performance of an equity REIT because it is predicated on cash flow analyses which facilitate an understanding of the operating performances of the Company's properties without giving effect to non-cash items such as depreciation. FFO is defined by the National Association of Real Estate Investment Trusts as net income or loss (computed in accordance with generally accepted accounting principles) excluding gains or losses from debt restructuring and sales of property, plus depreciation and amortization of real estate assets.[15]

Funds from operations is roughly net income plus depreciation. Though before adding back depreciation, net income is adjusted to remove gains and losses from property sales, which are considered to be an investing as opposed to an operating activity, and gains and losses from debt restructuring, which are considered to be a financing activity. Included with depreciation would be any non-cash amortization expense, for example, amortization of debt discount or premium and goodwill and other intangibles.

Unlike EBITDA, funds from operations is after interest expense and after taxes. That fact, combined with the adjustment to remove nonoperating gains and losses, makes funds from operations much closer to the FASB-defined cash provided by operating activities. Again, however, FFO does not include adjustments for changes in noncash working capital accounts and accordingly, will not equal operating cash flow. If working capital is increasing, funds from operations will be greater than operating cash flow. That has been the case at BRE Properties, where for the five years ended December 31, 1997, funds from operations have exceeded operating cash flow by a cumulative $10,550,000. During that time frame, funds from operations totaled $204,507,000, versus $193,957,000 in cash provided by operating activities.

Drawing a distinction between FFO and cash provided by operating activities, BRE Properties made the following observation:

> FFO does not represent cash generated from operating activities in accordance with generally accepted accounting principles, and therefore should not be considered a substitute for net income as a measure of results of operations or for cash flow from operations as a measure of liquidity.[16]

Sometimes, equity analysts and credit analysts refer to net income plus depreciation as cash flow or as traditional cash flow. For example, the Value Line Investment Survey refers to "cash flow" as net income plus depreciation.[17] By now, it should be clear that this is not actual cash flow. It will differ from cash flow by the amount of other noncash expenses and changes in operating-related working capital accounts. Aware of the difference between net income plus depreciation and actual cash flow, Value Line puts the term "cash flow" in quotes.

Cash Earnings per Share

As an additional example of how varied the definition of the term cash can be, equity analysts have recently begun providing a second performance measure for selected Internet companies in addition to traditionally measured earnings per share (EPS). That new performance measure is called cash flow earnings per share, or cash EPS, and will be reported by First Call Corporation, a research company that tracks analysts' estimates of corporate earnings. Though referred to as a cash flow measure, the new figure is not a cash flow amount. It is defined as earnings plus goodwill amortization. Because Internet companies are spending such large sums on acquisitions that result in significant amounts of goodwill and amortization expense, it was felt that an alternative measure of performance was needed. For example, First Call estimates that MindSpring Enterprises, Inc., an Internet service provider, will report a 93-cent loss in regular EPS for its 1999 fiscal year. For that same period, cash EPS is estimated to be a positive 94-cent profit.[18]

While the title of the new performance measure suggests that it is a form of cash flow, it certainly is not cash flow. Cash EPS does not take into account noncash expenses other than goodwill amortization. Moreover, it does not factor in changes in working capital accounts. We suspect the new measure is an attempt to put a more positive spin on the performance results of Internet companies.

Interestingly, the reference to net income plus goodwill amortization as a measure of cash flow is not limited to the Internet companies. ConAgra, Inc. is a case in point. In its annual report, the Company uses the term "cash earnings," described as follows:

> ConAgra is committed to major financial performance objectives that drive how we manage our company and serve our mission to increase stockholders' wealth. We incorporate in our financial objectives a concept called "cash earnings"—net earnings plus goodwill amortization. Businesses run on cash. The principal source of internally generated cash is net earnings before depreciation of fixed assets and amortization of goodwill. Cash from depreciation is generally needed for replenishment to help maintain a going concern. On the other hand, goodwill represents valuable non-depreciating brands and distribution systems. We invest and incur expense throughout the year to maintain and enhance the value of these brands and distribution systems. Consequently, goodwill amortization typically is not a true economic cash cost. It, along with net earnings, is a source of "decision cash"—cash available to invest in ConAgra's growth and pay dividends. It is this decision cash that we call cash earnings. We believe the cash earnings concept is an appropriate way to manage and measure our businesses. We use the cash earnings concept in our financial objectives for return on common equity and dividend growth.[19]

In the view of ConAgra, because goodwill (amounts paid for brands and distribution systems) does not depreciate, its amortization is not an expense per se. Moreover, because amortization does not entail an ongoing cash outlay, cash earnings can be calculated as net income plus goodwill amortization.

We take exception to the view that goodwill does not depreciate or decline in value. Brand loyalties and modes of distribution change. Also, acquiring companies are not immune from overpaying for an acquisition as part of a heated bidding war. We offer the company's views as another example of how varied the definition of cash flow can be.

Free Cash Flow

Free cash flow is a true cash flow measure and is more conservatively defined than the FASB's cash provided by operating activities. Because cash provided by operating activities is before depreciation expense, it contains no provision for replacement of productive capacity consumed in operations. Free cash flow incorporates replacement of consumed productive capacity and is calculated by subtracting replacement capital expenditures from cash provided by operating activities. It is designed to measure cash available to the firm for discretionary uses after all required cash payments have been made.

Many equity valuation models in finance use free cash flow as an input. As a discretionary cash flow measure, it is cash available for reinvestment, dividends, and stock buybacks. Essentially, it is cash available for shareholders.

Estimating replacement capital expenditures can be a problem. Depreciation provides one useful estimate provided an appropriate depreciation rate is used and historical cost approximates replacement cost. Rather than estimating replacement capital expenditures, some advocates of free cash flow use total capital expenditures instead of the replacement amount. The use of total capital expenditures is appropriate when a growth component for capital equipment is desired.

Some users of free cash flow would also subtract from cash provided by operating activities any required principal payments on debt. In our view, required principal payments should not be subtracted in the same way that borrowings are not added. Consider a firm that purchases capital equipment using installment debt. The capital expenditure is subtracted from cash provided by operating activities in computing free cash flow. Subtracting the required principal payment on the debt would double count this disbursement.

For creditors, a free cash flow measure computed before interest would be more relevant. It is this amount of cash flow that is available for debt service.

IDENTIFYING SUSTAINABLE SOURCES OF CASH FLOW

Although it would appear that cash generated from any source would be of interest to equity and credit holders, the fact is that not all cash flow is the same. Corporate earning power requires a sustainable source of cash flow. Cash from all sources is not sustainable.

As noted earlier, a loss company can generate cash flow through liquidation of assets or expansion of liabilities. However, without earnings, such cash flow will ultimately cease. Assets available for liquidation run short and sources of credit dry up. The company is shrinking in size and gradually going out of business. Claimants dependent on cash flow generated by such a company will ultimately be disappointed.

Eastern Airlines, Inc. provides a case in point. Over several years leading up to its ultimate demise over a decade ago, Eastern reported operating losses. However, the company was able to generate cash from operations through significant noncash expenses, such as depreciation expense, and by reducing the cash component of certain cash-type expenses, such as wages. The company was successful in issuing a special form of preferred stock to employees in order to reduce its use of cash. Although the company was able to generate positive operating cash flow during these difficult times, that cash flow was not sustainable and eventually led to failure.

Earnings provide an engine for cash flow generation—a renewable source of recurring cash flow. Through its profits, a company produces new assets to liquidate and, in the process, generates a long-term source of cash flow to support equity and credit holders.

At the time of its public offering in 1984, Coca-Cola Enterprises, Inc., a collection of Coca-Cola bottling companies, was touted not for its earnings but for its ability to generate cash flow. At the time, analysts described its performance not in terms of earnings per share but in terms of cash flow per share. Although the company reported positive earnings, those earnings were depressed by significant charges for depreciation of property, plant, and equipment and amortization of goodwill arising from acquisitions. Because these were noncash expenses, they did not reduce the company's reported cash flow. In those early years, the company did not have a strong earnings component to its operating cash flow. Accordingly, its stock price languished near the initial offering price for an extended period. It was not until many years later when the company began to report earnings increases that its stock price began to respond in a positive way.

Microsoft Corporation is an excellent example of a company that is generating ample amounts of cash flow that are supported by a sustainable earnings base. For the eight-year period ending June 30, 1998, the company's net income has grown by a compound annual rate of over 41 percent. During that same time frame, due especially to increases in unearned revenue, operating cash flow has grown by a compound annual rate of over 49 percent.[20] Investors, acknowledging the company's unquestionable earning power, have bid the company's share price up significantly.

There are, of course, many examples of profitable companies that are consuming cash from operations. Growth companies may report positive earnings for many years without producing any cash. This happens as earnings generated are reinvested in such operating accounts as accounts receivable and inventory.

For the five years ended December 31, 1997, net income at Insight Enterprises, Inc., a marketer of computer hardware and software to small and medium-sized enterprises, has grown at a compound annual rate of over 60 percent. Over that same time frame, the company has consistently consumed cash from operations. In fact, over the years, the more profits the company has reported, the more negative its operating cash flow has become. For the year ended December 31, 1997, Insight reported net income of $13,218,000. During that same year, the company consumed $39,896,000 in operating cash flow.[21] The biggest reasons for the use of cash were increases in accounts receivable and inventory of $38,999,000 and $46.1 million, respectively, offset by only marginal changes in such operating-related liabilities as accounts payable and accrued expenses payable.

To stay in business, Insight Enterprises must be supported by cash infusions from investors and creditors. Over the five years ended December 31, 1997, the company has raised nearly $70 million from equity offerings and nearly $30 million in net new debt. Such cash infusions will continue to be forthcoming only if participants remain convinced that the company's cashflow shortfalls will run for only a finite period of time. Then, the shortfalls will be replaced with positive cash flow as growth and the level of reinvestment in operating accounts slow.

Some companies are both losing money and consuming cash. On the surface, given this total lack of positive prospects, it would appear that such firms would have trouble attracting capital. Sensible reasoning would suggest that investors and creditors would see the lack of earnings and cash flow as a true negative performance indicator and pursue opportunities elsewhere. Though as this book is written, Internet-related companies are completing successful initial public offerings at a frenzied pace. Share prices of such recent offerings as Claimsnet.com, Inc., iTurf, Inc., and Usinternetworking, Inc. have doubled and more on their first day of trading. This is happening even though the prospects for profits and cash flow for these companies are quite distant. David Menlow, president of IPO Financial Network, noted that internet IPO mania "is going to stop somewhere, but for right now investor demand is adjusting itself upward such that it does not take into serious consideration the revenue or profit streams of these companies."[22]

For the years ended December 31, 1994, 1995, 1996, and 1997, Amazon.com, Inc., an internet retailer of books, music, and video, lost $52,000, $303,000, $15,900,000, and $23,937,000. Moreover, the company consumed $24,000 in operating cash flow in 1994, $232,000 in 1995, and $1,735,000 in 1996. In the year ended December 31, 1997, the company reported positive operating cash flow of $3,522,000. If it were not for an increase in operating-related liabilities, primarily accounts payable, of over $30 million, the company would have again consumed cash from operations.[23] Yet, over this same time period, the company's share price has doubled several times.

Although the interest of many investors in a company like Amazon.com is focused on selling acquired shares in a short-term flip to new investors, there are those that take a long-term view and expect ultimate profits and cash flow. They see short-term losses and spending as investments designed to build market share

Exhibit 13.5. A Company's Life Cycle

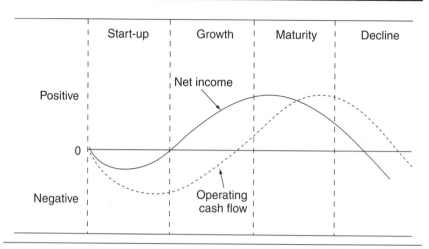

Sources: E. Comiskey and C. Mulford, "Anticipating Trends in Operating Profits and Cash Flows," *Commercial Lending Review* (Spring 1993), p. 42; and E. Comiskey and C. Mulford, *Financial Warnings* (New York: John Wiley & Sons, 1996), p. 337.

and produce future returns. Without such expectations of future earnings and cash flow, the company would not be able to attract the financing it needs to pursue its business plan. Whether these long-term investors are ultimately disappointed remains to be seen.

A Company's Life Cycle

An important first step in identifying sustainable sources of cash flow is determining the stage at which a company currently operates within its life cycle. Net income and operating cash flow have certain characteristic relationships as a company progresses through the normal four stages of its life cycle: start-up, growth, maturity, and decline. For example, a firm in the early stages of the growth phase of its life cycle may be profitable but typically consumes cash from operations due to significant increases in accounts receivable and inventory. Negative operating cash flow is to be expected until the company becomes a more established growth company. Or, for example, during the decline phase, a company may generate ample amounts of cash as assets accumulated over prior growth years are liquidated.

Considering a company's stage in its life cycle, we can form an opinion as to what relationship between net income and cash flow to expect. If a company diverges significantly from its expected characteristic relationship, there is reason to investigate further. For example, while it is not unusual for an early-stage growth firm to consume cash from operations, it is unusual for a mature firm to do so. A careful understanding of the reasons behind the development is needed. One explanation would be that the company is having difficulty collecting receivables or selling inventory.

Knowing a company's stage in its life cycle is also helpful in anticipating future cash flow developments. Losses and negative operating cash flow are to be expected in the start-up phase and should be followed first by profits and then by positive cash flow as the firm becomes more established. However, losses and negative operating cash flow in the decline phase leave little in the way of future prospects.

The life cycle of a company, consisting of the start-up, growth, maturity, and decline stages, is presented in Exhibit 13.5. A graph of net income and operating cash flow is drawn through each of these stages.

As seen in Exhibit 13.5, both net income and operating cash flow are negative through the start-up segment. With the beginning of the growth stage, net losses turn to income. It is not until later in the growth segment that operating cash flow turns positive. Both net income and operating cash flow remain positive through the latter part of the growth stage and throughout maturity, turning negative again only in the late stages of decline. A more detailed description of each of the four stages is presented below.

Start-Up

In the start-up stage, net income and operating cash flow are negative amounts. The company is losing money and consuming cash in the process. Through at least 1997, Amazon.com would be an example of a company in this stage of its life cycle. The company is losing money and consuming cash from operations. Although it did generate a meager amount of positive cash flow in 1997, as noted, that was due primarily to a buildup in accounts payable.

Because of its significant rate of growth in sales, some would describe Amazon.com as a growth company. We would reserve that characterization for a company that has left its start-up losses behind and has demonstrated an ability to generate sustainable profits.

Growth

As the start-up becomes more established, revenues increase sufficiently to offset operating expenses and the company begins to report a profit. During the earlier stages of growth, however, as the company experiences increases in such operating-related items as accounts receivable and inventory, operating cash flows remain negative. It is not until later in the company's growth segment, as growth slows a bit from an earlier, more torrid pace, that operating uses of cash turn into operating sources. The timing of this conversion of operating uses to operating sources of cash varies by company and is a function of many factors, including the rate of growth being experienced at the time, its profit margins, and the length of time that cash is tied up in operations. More is said about these factors in subsequent paragraphs of this chapter.

Companies mentioned earlier that fit the growth-stage characterization include Insight Enterprises, Inc. and Microsoft Corporation. Insight Enterprises is profitable and consuming cash from operations. It is classified as an early-stage growth company. Given its significant rate of growth and ability to generate ample amounts of cash flow, Microsoft is classified later in the growth segment. Interestingly, while many late-stage growth firms generate positive operating cash flow, it is more typical for these companies, due to continued significant rates of growth in operating-related current asset accounts, to report higher net income than operating cash flow. This was not the case with Microsoft, where in recent years, operating cash flow has exceeded net income. As indicated earlier, the buildup in unearned revenue is an important factor behind the company's cash flow performance.

Maturity

In the maturity segment of a company's life cycle, revenue and net income will continue to grow, but at much slower rates than can be sustained for extended periods. Identifying when a company leaves the growth stage and enters maturity is not a precise science. However, since the characteristic relationship between net income and operating cash flow is no different for the two, an exact specification is not needed. One useful way of determining when a growth company moves into the maturity segment of its life cycle is when its rate of growth in revenue slows to a rate commensurate with the rate of nominal growth in the overall economy.

In early maturity, net income may exceed operating cash flow. But later, as revenue growth slows considerably and begins to decline and net income begins an extended drop, operating cash flow may move above net income as current assets such as accounts receivable and inventory are liquidated. The late maturity segment of the company's life cycle is the mirror image of the growth segment.

A decade ago, we would have classified Coca-Cola Enterprises as a mature firm. Revenue was growing slowly, the company was generating a consistent, though somewhat flat stream of net income, and operating cash flow was consistently positive and exceeded net income. However, changes at the company have instilled new growth, and the company would now be classified more appropriately as a growth firm.

Campbell Soup Company can be classified as a mature firm. Revenue and net income from continuing operations for the company's fiscal year ended August 2, 1998, were $6,696,000,000 and $689,000,000, respectively, barely changed from amounts reported five years earlier. Operating cash flow, excluding discontinued operations, was higher than net income, reaching $902 million in 1998, down slightly from the amount reported five years earlier.

Decline

During the decline stage, declines in revenue that began in late maturity continue and may accelerate. Net income continues to decline, though is likely exceeded by operating cash flow. At some point in the decline, management may become aware that amounts invested in assets such as accounts receivable, inventory, property, plant and equipment, and goodwill may not be realized. Write-downs become necessary. Steps to restructure operations may also take place. The write-downs and restructuring steps are likely to necessitate special charges that are taken to income. Losses ensue. Ultimately, even operating cash flow turns negative as the business continues to sour.

In its last few years, Eastern Airlines, Inc. fit the definition of a company in decline. As revenue waned, expenses mounted and losses ensued. Operating cash flow declined. The final chapter was a bankruptcy filing and liquidation of the company.

A more recent example of a declining firm is Bradlees, Inc., a chain of discount department stores. Bradlees has been operating in the decline phase of its life cycle for several years. Over the five years ended May 30, 1998, revenue has declined at a compound annual rate of nearly 9 percent. After nominal profits in 1994 and 1995, the company reported net losses of $207,413,000, $218,759,000, and $22,557,000, respectively, in 1996, 1997, and 1998. Contributing significantly to the losses in 1996 and 1997 were special charges of $164,361,000 and $110,574,000, respectively, recorded to write down impaired long-lived assets and to restructure operations. The company reported positive operating cash flow in 1994, 1995, and 1996. In 1997, however, the company began to consume cash from operations and reported a use of operating cash flow of $53,149,000 and $9,124,000, respectively, in 1997 and 1998. Attesting to the company's ongoing problems, its auditors have noted substantial doubt about its going-concern status.

Cash Flow Analysis

Although the life-cycle stage at which a company operates is helpful in understanding the firm's ability to generate sustainable cash flow, it is only a starting point. An identification of the company-specific determinants of cash flow surpluses or shortages is needed. Identifying those determinants—growth, changes in operating profitability, and changes in operating efficiency—will help the equity analyst or credit analyst assess whether observed cash flow surpluses or shortages will continue. The analyst will then be better equipped to determine whether the company in question has the ability to generate a sustainable stream of cash flow.

Growth

Growth in revenue has a pervasive effect on all aspects of operating cash flow. While increases in revenue provide cash flow, increases in associated expenses

Exhibit 13.6. The Effect of Revenue Growth on Operating Cash Flow

Cash Flow Determinant Affected by Revenue Growth	Cash Flow Effect*
Gross profit	Positive
Selling, general and administrative expenses	Negative
Accounts receivable	Negative
Inventory	Negative
Accounts payable	Positive

*Positive and negative cash flow effects indicate the impact on operating cash flow. Positive effects refer to increases in operating cash flow while negative effects refer to decreases in operating cash flow. The impact of a decline in revenue would produce exactly opposite effects.

Source: E. Comiskey and C. Mulford, *Financial Warnings* (New York: John Wiley & Sons, 1996), p. 348.

(e.g., the variable components of cost of goods sold and selling, general and administrative expense) consume cash. For a company with a positive operating profit margin (revenue less cost of goods sold, selling, general and administrative expense, and research and development, all as a percent of revenue), the net effect of revenue growth should be an increase in operating cash flow.

However, growth also affects key balance sheet accounts that affect cash flow. With increases in revenue, there is typically the need for increases in accounts receivable and inventory, which consume cash. Offsetting the cash needs of increases in these asset accounts is the funding provided by growth-related additions to accounts payable.

Thus, growth may or may not result in a use of cash. For most companies, growth does consume cash. It is, however, a function of the rate of growth, the firm's operating profit margin, and its accounts receivable, inventory, and accounts payable requirements. A summary of the effect of revenue growth on key components of operating cash flow is provided in Exhibit 13.6.

Changes in Operating Profitability

Unlike growth, which does not have an unambiguous effect on operating cash flow, changes in operating profitability have very direct cash flow implications. Specifically, decreases in operating profit margin, whether from decreases in gross profit margin (revenue less cost of goods sold, as a percentage of revenue) or increases in selling, general and administrative expense as a percentage of revenue (henceforth SGA%), or research and development (R&D) as a percentage of revenue, will negatively affect operating cash flow. A decline in gross margin indicates that a greater percentage of revenue is being consumed by the cost of producing inventory. An increase in SGA% indicates that more revenue dollars are being spent on the company's operations. On the other side of the equation, increases in operating profit margin will improve operating cash flow.

Changes in Operating Efficiency

As with changes in operating profitability, changes in operating efficiency also have very direct implications for operating cash flow. The areas of operating efficiency about which we are most interested focus on three key accounts: accounts receivable, inventory, and accounts payable.

We measure efficiency using three popular ratios. For accounts receivable, we use accounts receivable days (A/R days). A/R days measure the average collection period for accounts receivable. Viewed another way, it measures the length of time it takes to collect outstanding accounts receivable. The higher the measure, the longer it takes to collect outstanding accounts receivable. An increase in A/R days is a use of cash. A/R days are calculated by dividing trade accounts receivable by sales per day, and thus represents the number of days' sales carried in accounts receivable. Sales per day are calculated by dividing total sales by 365.

For inventory, we use inventory days to measure efficiency. Inventory days measure the average period over which inventory is carried before it is sold. The higher the measure, the longer it takes to sell inventory. An increase in inventory days is a use of cash. Inventory days are calculated by dividing inventory by cost of goods sold per day, where cost of goods sold per day is calculated by dividing cost of goods sold by 365. Cost of goods sold is used instead of sales because cost of goods sold, like inventory, excludes a markup. Days inventory thus represents the number of day's cost of goods sold activity carried in inventory.

We use accounts payable days (A/P days) to measure accounts payable efficiency. Accounts payable days measures the average period taken before accounts payable are settled. The higher the measure, the longer is the period taken to pay accounts payable. An increase in accounts payable days is a source of cash. Thus, in terms of accounts payable, efficiency and operating cash flow are improved by taking longer payment terms. Accounts payable days are calculated by dividing accounts payable by cost of goods sold per day.

Exhibit 13.7 summarizes the effects of changes in operating profitability and operating efficiency on cash flow.

Cash Cycle

The cash cycle measures the total number of days over which cash is tied up in operating assets. For a merchandising firm, cash is first tied up in inventory, both during the manufacturing process, if there is one, and then while inventory is carried as finished goods. Once it is sold, cash is still not collected because it is tied up in accounts receivable. The combination of inventory days plus A/R days is referred to as a firm's *operating cycle*. A service company that carries little or no inventory, or a retail firm that carries small accounts receivable balances will have a shorter operating cycle than a firm with both inventory and accounts receivable.

The cash cycle is calculated by subtracting A/P days from the operating cycle. More simply, it is inventory days plus A/R days, less A/P days. While the firm

Exhibit 13.7. The Effect of Changes in Operating Profitability and Efficiency on Operating Cash Flow

Cash Flow Determinant Affected by Changes in Profitability and Efficiency	Cash Flow Effect*
Increase in gross margin	Positive
Decrease in gross margin	Negative
Increase in SGA%	Negative
Decrease in SGA%	Positive
Increase in A/R days	Negative
Decrease in A/R days	Positive
Increase in inventory days	Negative
Decrease in inventory days	Positive
Increase in A/P days	Positive
Decrease in A/P days	Negative

*Positive and negative cash flow effects indicate the impact on operating cash flow. Positive effects refer to increases in operating cash flow, while negative effects refer to decreases in operating cash flow. Due to its very discretionary nature and its limitation to technology firms, research and development spending has been excluded from the exhibit.

Source: E. Comiskey and C. Mulford, *Financial Warnings* (New York: John Wiley & Sons, 1996), p. 349.

ties up cash as it is carried in inventory and accounts receivable, a portion of that cash, as represented by accounts payable, is not its own. Thus, the cash cycle measures the total number of days over which a company's own cash is tied up in operating assets. The shorter the cash cycle, the easier it is for a company to generate operating cash flow. Such a reduction can be achieved by reducing inventory days and A/R days, or by increasing A/P days.

It is to be expected that the cash cycle will differ by industry. These differences are due to inherent differences in operating cycles—service firms carry little or no inventory, retailers carry low accounts receivable. For example, we collected data on the cash cycles for several industries within three major industry groups: manufacturing, retailing, and service. Representative data from our survey are provided in Exhibit 13.8.

As can be seen in Exhibit 13.8, there are dramatic differences in cash cycles across industries and industry groups. Firms within the manufacturing group carry both inventory and accounts receivable. However, the short shelf life of dairy products necessitates a shorter period over which inventory can be carried. The special nature of jewelry and precious metals and the need for an aging process for wines and distilled liquor result in longer inventory periods.

Due to the extensive use of cash and credit card sales, the retailers carry very small accounts receivable balances. In fact, with no accounts receivable, and a longer A/P days period than inventory days, the drinking places (alcoholic) in-

Exhibit 13.8.   Cash Cycles for Selected Industries

	Inventory Days	A/R Days	A/P Days	Cash Cycle
Manufacturing:				
Bottled and canned soft drinks	24	28	25	27
Dairy products	20	26	23	23
Drugs and medicine	107	52	46	113
Jewelry and precious metals	135	56	34	157
Laboratory analytical instruments	146	61	42	165
Wines, distilled liquor, and liqueurs	365	37	47	355
Retailing:				
Autos—new and used	63	5	2	66
Boat dealers	159	4	6	157
Drinking places (alcoholic)	19	0	23	(4)
Groceries and meats	23	2	14	11
Jewelry	261	11	66	206
Vending machine operators	32	3	29	6
Service:				
Accounting, auditing, and bookkeeping	—	62	—	62
Amusement parks—outdoor	—	1	—	1
Auto repair—general	—	11	—	11
Consulting services—management	—	59	—	59
Chiropractors	—	4	—	4
Refuse systems	—	41	—	41

Source: Robert Morris Associates, *Annual Statement Studies: 1998–1999* (Philadelphia: Robert Morris Associates, 1998).

dustry enjoys a *negative* cash cycle. In essence, vendors finance the working capital needs of these companies. Even though the retailers carry low balances of accounts receivable, the inventory needs for some of these industries can be substantial. The specialized nature and extended selling period for boat dealers and jewelry stores result in long inventory days periods and accompanying cash cycles.

Companies in the service industry generally carry accounts receivable. However, firms dealing on a retail basis with the public, such as amusement parks and chiropractors, have very low A/R days figures. Cost of goods sold, inventory days, and A/P days are undefined for pure service firms, because they do not carry inventory.

In addition to differences in cash cycles across industries, cash cycles will also differ within industries. These company-specific differences in the cash cycle due to differences in efficiency in managing inventory, accounts receivable, and accounts payable directly affect a firm's ability to generate operating cash flow.

Exhibit 13.9. Cash Cycles for Two Computer Makers

Company	1994	1995	1996	1997
Compaq Computer Corp.				
Inventory days	89.9	64.0	31.1	32.1
A/R days	+ 76.8	+ 68.8	+ 67.8	+ 42.9
Operating cycle	166.7	132.8	98.9	75.0
A/P days	− 39.8	− 41.0	− 51.5	− 58.1
Cash cycle	126.9	91.8	47.4	16.9
Operating cash flow/sales	(1.4%)	6.2%	17.8%	15.0%
Dell Computer Corp.				
Inventory days	39.1	37.0	15.0	8.9
A/R days	+ 56.5	+ 50.0	+ 42.5	+ 44.0
Operating cycle	95.6	87.0	57.5	52.9
A/P days	− 53.7	− 40.2	− 62.3	− 62.4
Cash cycle	41.9	46.8	(4.8)	(9.5)
Operating cash flow/sales	0.7%	0.3%	17.6%	12.9%

Note: The fiscal years for Compaq Computer Corp. are the calendar years ending December 31. The fiscal years for Dell Computer Corp. are the 52 and 53 week periods ending on the Sunday nearest January 31. In the exhibit, fiscal 1997 for Dell is the period ending February 1, 1998. A similar dating scheme is used for the years 1994–1996.

Source: Disclosure, Inc. *Compact D/SEC: Corporate Information on Public Companies Filing with the SEC* (Bethesda, MD: Disclosure, Inc. March 1999).

Exhibit 13.9 contrasts the cash cycles and cash-generating capability for two computer makers: Compaq Computer Corporation and Dell Computer Corporation.

Exhibit 13.9 indicates that both Dell and Compaq have been successful in recent years in reducing their cash cycles. Dell's business model is very focused on carrying little inventory. The company's success in this regard is apparent from the decline in inventory days from 39.1 in 1994 to 8.9 in 1997. That reduction in inventory days accompanied by an increase in A/P days has resulted in a negative cash cycle for both 1996 and 1997.

Compaq's cash cycle is longer than Dell's. But the company has reduced it dramatically from 126.9 days in 1994 to 16.9 days in 1997. Compaq's success in this regard can be attributed to reductions in inventory days and A/R days, and an increase in A/P days.

Improvements in the cash cycle at both Compaq and Dell have resulted in an enhanced ability at both firms to generate operating cash flow. At Compaq, operating cash flow divided by sales has improved from a negative 1.4 percent in

Exhibit 13.10. Operating Profit Margins for Two Computer Makers

Company	1994	1995	1996	1997
Compaq Computer Corp.				
Gross profit margin	25.1%	26.3%	25.8%	27.5%
SGA%*	−11.4%	−13.1%	−12.5%	−12.0%
Operating profit margin	13.7%	13.2%	13.3%	15.5%
Dell Computer Corp.				
Gross profit margin	21.2%	20.1%	21.5%	22.1%
SGA%*	−12.2%	−11.2%	−10.6%	−9.8%
Operating profit margin	9.0%	8.9%	10.9%	12.3%

*Excludes research and development expense.

Note: The fiscal years for Compaq Computer Corp. are the calendar years ending December 31. The fiscal years for Dell Computer Corp. are the 52 and 53 week periods ending on the Sunday nearest January 31. In the exhibit, fiscal 1997 for Dell is the period ending February 1, 1998. A similar dating scheme is used for the years 1994–1996.

Source: Disclosure, Inc. *Compact D/SEC: Corporate Information on Public Companies Filing with the SEC* (Bethesda, MD: Disclosure, Inc. March 1999).

1994 to 15.0 percent in 1997. At Dell, operating cash flow divided by sales has improved from .7 percent to 12.9 percent over that same time frame.

Exhibit 13.9 incorporates only the operating efficiency component of each company's ability to generate cash flow. It does not reflect operating profitability or the effects on operating cash flow of other factors such as the amount of noncash expenses, including depreciation, amortization, and deferred tax expense, or changes in other operating assets and liabilities. In contrasting Compaq and Dell, it is Compaq's higher operating profit margin that explains the company's ability to translate a higher percentage of sales into operating cash flow even with a longer cash cycle. Exhibit 13.10 contrasts the operating profit margins for the two companies.

As can be seen in Exhibit 13.10, Compaq enjoys a higher operating profit margin than Dell. Compaq's operating profit margin increased from 13.7 percent to 15.5 percent between 1994 and 1997. At Dell, the operating profit margin has also increased, but from a much lower level. Dell's operating profit margin increased from 9.0 percent in 1994 to 12.3 percent in 1997.

A third computer maker, Gateway 2000, Inc., will serve as the subject for a closer analysis of cash flow and application of the tools discussed in this section. Gateway competes directly with Dell and Compaq in sales of computers or "boxes" to individuals. Like its competitors, the company has in recent years enjoyed strong growth in sales, earnings, and cash flow. For the five years ended December 31, 1998, Gateway's sales and net income have grown at compound annual rates of 23.5 and 37.8 percent, respectively. Over that same time period, the company's operating cash flow has remained positive and has grown at a remarkable compound annual rate of 45.6 percent. Moreover, in the year ended December 31, 1998, operating cash flow increased to $907,651,000 from $442,797,000 in 1997, an increase of 105 percent. This exceptional increase in operating cash flow was achieved on an 18.7 percent increase in sales and 56.2 percent increase in net income.[24]

Given its sales and earnings growth, and ability to generate positive operating cash flow, Gateway would clearly be classified as an established growth company. Barring any unforeseen changes in fundamentals, a continued ability to generate operating cash flow should be expected. The question to be raised here is: How was the company able to generate such a significant increase in operating cash flow in 1998? The answer is important because it will directly affect expectations regarding cash flow generation in future years.

To answer the question, we will identify the key factors or drivers behind the company's cash flow surplus. In particular, we will identify the effects on operating cash flow of growth, changes in operating profitability and changes in operating efficiency. Exhibit 13.11 presents selected financial information for Gateway for the years ended December 31, 1997 and 1998.

In reviewing Exhibit 13.11, it can be seen that the company's sales increased by $1,174,245,000, or 18.7 percent, to $7,467,925,000 in 1998 from $6,293,680,000 in 1997. It was noted earlier that growth affects operating cash flow in different ways. For a company like Gateway, with a positive operating profit margin, an increase in sales will result in higher operating profits, which will increase cash flow. However, the cash requirements of growth for increases in accounts receivable and inventory, offset with cash provisions from growth-related increases in accounts payable, will likely decrease cash flow.

Exhibit 13.12 summarizes the cash effects of growth for Gateway 2000. In calculating the cash effects of growth in 1998, the company's gross margin, SGA%, and A/R days, inventory days, and A/P days are assumed unchanged from levels experienced in 1997. In so doing, the cash effects of growth in sales on gross profit, selling, general and administrative expense, accounts receivable, inventory, and accounts payable can be isolated. For example, to measure the cash effects of growth on gross profit and selling, general and administrative expense, 1997's gross profit percent and SGA% are multiplied by the increase in sales during 1998. To measure the cash effects of growth on accounts receivable, A/R days in 1997 is multiplied by the increase in sales per day during 1998. Finally, to measure the cash effects of growth on inventory and accounts payable, inventory days and A/P days in 1997, respectively, are multiplied by the increase in cost of goods sold per day during 1998.

In reviewing Exhibit 13.12, it can be seen that due to its growth during 1998, Gateway consumed operating cash flow in the amount of $8,778,000. Had the company not grown during 1998, it would have generated $8,778,000 *more* in

Exhibit 13.11. Selected Financial Information: Gateway 2000, Inc., Years Ended December 31, 1997 and 1998 (Thousands of Dollars)

	1997	1998	Increase (Decrease)
Operating cash flow	$442,797	$907,651	$464,854
Sales	$6,293,680	$7,467,925	$1,174,245
Cost of goods sold	5,217,239	5,921,651	704,412
Gross profit	$1,076,441	$1,546,274	$469,833
Sales per day[a]	$17,242.959	$20,460,068	$3,217,109
Cost of goods sold per day[a]	$14,293.805	$16,223.701	$1,929.896
Gross margin	17.104%	20.706%	3.602%
Selling, general and administrative expenses	$786,168	$1,052,047	$265,879
SGA%	12.491%	14.088%	1.597%
Accounts receivable	$510,679	$558,851	$48,172
A/R days[b]	29.617	27.314	(2.303)
Inventory	$249,224	$167,924	($81,300)
Inventory days[c]	17.436	10.351	(7.085)
Accounts payable	$488,717	$718,071	$229,354
A/P days[c]	34.191	44.261	10.070

[a]Calculated as sales and cost of goods sold, respectively, divided by 365.

[b]Calculated as accounts receivable divided by sales per day.

[c]Calculated as inventory and accounts payable, respectively divided by cost of goods sold per day.

Note: Ratios are carried out to three places to lessen rounding effects on cash flow calculations.

Source: Gateway 2000, Inc., Form 10K annual report to the Securities and Exchange Commission (December 1998), pp. 20–22.

cash flow than it did. Certainly growth was not the reason the company generated such a cash flow surplus during 1998.

Gateway's profile of fundamentals in 1997, that is, its mix of gross margin, SGA%, A/R days, inventory days, and A/P days, was such that the level of growth experienced in 1998 was sufficient to result in the company consuming cash flow due to growth. The likely culprit was not the company's cash cycle, which at 12.8 days (1997 inventory days of 17.4 + A/R days of 29.6 − A/P days of 34.2) was quite short. Rather, its operating profit margin of 4.6 percent (gross margin percent of 17.1 − SGA% of 12.5) was sufficiently tight to cause the company to consume cash as it grew.

Gateway's ability to generate cash flow in 1998 can be attributed to changes during the year in the company's operating profit margin and cash cycle. The cash effects of these changes are summarized in Exhibit 13.13.

During 1998, Gateway improved its operating profit margin by 2 percentage points. A 3.6 percent point improvement in gross margin increased operating cash

Exhibit 13.12.   The Cash Effects of Growth: Gateway 2000, Inc., Year Ended December 31, 1998 (Thousands of Dollars)

Cash Flow Determinant Affected by Sales Growth	Computations Increase (Decrease)	Cash Flow Effect Source (Use)
Increase in sales impact on gross profit	$1,174,245 x 17.104%[a]	$200,843
Increase in sales impact on selling, general and administrative expense	$1,174,245 x 12.491%[b]	($146,675)
Increase in sales per day impact on accounts receivable	$3,217.109 x 29.617[c]	($95,281)
Increase in cost of goods sold per day impact on inventory	$1,929.896 x 17.436[d]	($33,650)
Increase in cost of goods sold per day impact on accounts payable	$1,929.896 x 34.191[e]	$65,985
Total cash flow effects of growth		($8,778)

[a] 1997 gross margin times the 1998 increase in sales.

[b] 1997 SGA% times the 1998 increase in sales.

[c] 1997 A/R days times the 1998 increase in sales per day.

[d] 1997 inventory days times the 1998 increase in cost of goods sold per day.

[e] 1997 A/P days times the 1998 increase in cost of goods sold per day.

flow by $268,995,000, but was offset by a $119,263,000 use of cash due to a 1.6 percentage point increase in selling, general and administrative expense. The company also reduced its cash cycle during 1998 to *negative* 6.6 days in 1998 (10.4 inventory days + 27.3 A/R days − 44.3 A/P days) from 12.8 days in 1997 (17.4 inventory days + 29.6 A/R days − 34.2 A/P days). This decline in the cash cycle added $325,438,000 to operating cash flow during 1998, consisting of $47,120,000 from the decline in A/R days, $114,945,000 from the decline in inventory days, and $163,373,000 from the increase in A/P days. Combined, the improvement in operating profit margin and the decline in the cash cycle added $475,170,000 to Gateway's operating cash flow during 1998.

Gateway generated $907,651,000 in operating cash flow during 1998, up from $442,797,000 in 1997. Had the company not improved its operating profit margin and cash cycle during 1998, operating cash flow that year would have been lower by $475,170,000, and more in line with cash flow generated during 1997.

Going forward, for the company to continue generating levels of operating cash flow in line with amounts generated in 1998, the company will need to hold its operating profit margin and cash cycle at the new, improved levels. Continued improvements in operating cash flow will require additional improvements in the

Exhibit 13.13.   The Cash Effects of Changes in Operating Profitability and Efficiency: Gateway 2000, Inc., Year Ended December 31, 1998, (Thousands of Dollars)

Cash Flow Determinant Affected by Changes in Profitability and Efficiency	Computations Increase (Decrease)	Cash Flow Effect Source (Use)
Increase in gross margin impact on gross profit	3.602% x $7,467,925[a]	$268,995
Increase in SGA% impact on selling, general and administrative expenses	1.597% x $7,467,925[b]	($119,263)
Decrease in A/R days impact on accounts receivable	(2.303) x $20,460.068[c]	$47,120
Decrease in inventory days impact on inventory	(7.085) x $16,223.701[d]	$114,945
Increase in A/P days impact on accounts payable	10.070 x $16,223.701[e]	$163,373
Cash flow effects of changes in operating profitability and efficiency		$475,170

[a]Change in gross margin between 1997 and 1998 times 1998's sales.

[b]Change in SGA% between 1997 and 1998 times 1998's sales.

[c]Change in A/R days between 1997 and 1998 times 1998's sales per day.

[d]Change in inventory days between 1997 and 1998 times 1998's cost of goods sold per day.

[e]Change in A/P days between 1997 and 1998 times 1998's cost of goods sold per day.

company's operating profit margin and cash cycle. There are clearly limits as to how far these performance measures can be driven. There remains room for the company to improve its operating profit margin from the 6.6 percent level experienced in 1998 (gross margin of 20.7 percent − SGA% of 14.1). Compaq and Dell are enjoying much higher operating profit margins. However, counting on significant reductions in the company's cash cycle from the negative 6.6 days experienced in 1998 would appear to be questionable, though Dell does enjoy a marginally lower cash cycle.

The approach to cash flow analysis employed here focuses on the effects of growth and changes in operating profitability and efficiency on operating cash flow. Exhibit 13.14 demonstrates how the cash flow calculations can be used to explain changes during 1998 in the affected income statement and balance sheet accounts.

SUMMARY

The organizing theme of this book—assessing financial quality—focuses on corporate earning power to help equity investors and creditors use financial statements

Exhibit 14.14. Reconciling Cash Effects of Growth and Changes in Profitability and Efficiency to Changes in Selected Income Statement and Balance Sheet Items: Gateway 2000, Inc., Year Ended December 31, 1998, (Thousands of Dollars)

Income Statement Item	Change During 1998
Gross profit, 1997	$1,076,441
Cash effect of growth	+200,843
Cash effect of change in gross margin	+268,995
Rounding differences	−5
Gross profit, 1998	$1,546,274
Selling, general and administrative expense, 1997	$786,168
Cash effect of growth	+146,675
Cash effect of change in SGA%	+119,263
Rounding differences	−59
Selling, general and administrative expense, 1998	$1,052,047

Balance Sheet Item	Change during 1998
Accounts receivable, 1997	$510,679
Cash effect of growth	+95,281
Cash effect of change in A/R days	−47,120
Rounding differences	+11
Accounts receivable, 1998	$558,851
Inventory, 1997	$249,224
Cash effect of growth	+33,650
Cash effect of change in inventory days	−114,945
Rounding differences	−5
Inventory, 1998	$167,924
Accounts payable, 1997	$488,717
Cash effect of growth	+65,985
Cash effect of change in A/P days	+163,373
Rounding differences	−4
Accounts payable, 1998	$718,071

effectively. Corporate earning power is defined as the ability to generate a sustainable stream of earnings that provide cash flow. Given the importance of cash flow to evaluating earning power, it is important to devote a chapter to identifying sustainable sources of cash flow. A summary of key points raised in this chapter follows:

- Popular usage of the term *cash flow* has resulted in many different definitions of cash. The FASB uses cash and cash equivalents, which is spendable cash. Other definitions, such as funds, working capital, EBITDA, funds from operations, and net income plus depreciation are not true cash flow measures.
- Funds or working capital is a more liberal definition of liquidity. A firm that is able to generate funds or working capital from operations is not necessarily able to generate cash flow from operations.
- Publicly reporting firms are required to provide a statement of cash flows as part of their general-purpose financial statements. The statement of cash flows uses the FASB definition of cash.
- The statement of cash flows divides the change in cash and cash equivalents into three categories: operating activities, investing activities, and financing activities.
- Transactions resulting in changes in assets and liabilities that do not result in cash receipts or cash payments are referred to as noncash investing and financing activities. These transactions must also be disclosed on a statement of cash flows or in an accompanying footnote.
- The life of a company can be separated into four main segments: start-up, growth, maturity, and decline. Each segment has different implications for the firm's ability to generate current and future cash flows.
- Cash flow analysis is a search for the reasons behind cash flow surpluses and shortages. Key factors behind a firm's cash flow performance are growth, changes in operating profitability, and changes in operating efficiency.

GLOSSARY

Accounts payable days (A/P days) The average period taken before accounts payable are settled. Calculated by dividing accounts payable by cost of goods sold per day.

Accounts receivable days (A/R days) The average collection period for accounts receivable. Calculated by dividing trade accounts receivable by sales per day.

Cash Coins and currency on hand, undeposited checks, and demand deposits.

Cash cycle The total number of days over which cash is tied up in operating assets. Calculated as inventory days plus A/R days less A/P days.

Cash equivalents   Highly liquid debt instruments with original maturities of three months or less that can be viewed as essentially the same as cash.

Cash flow earnings per share (Cash EPS)   Earnings plus goodwill amortization.

Cash provided by operating activities   The cash effects of transactions that enter into the determination of net income, such as cash receipts from sales of goods and services and cash payments to suppliers and employees for acquisitions of inventory and operating expenses and to lenders for interest expense.

Cash provided or used from financing activities   Changes in cash and cash equivalents from obtaining resources from owners and providing them with a return on, and a return of, their investment, from borrowing money and repaying amounts borrowed, and from obtaining and paying for other resources obtained from creditors on long-term credit.

Cash provided or used from investing activities   Changes in cash and cash equivalents from making and collecting loans, from acquiring and disposing of debt or equity instruments and property, plant, and equipment or other productive assets.

Cost of goods sold per day   The average cost of goods sold expense per day. Calculated by dividing cost of goods sold by 365.

Direct-method format cash flow statement   A format for the operating section of the cash flow statement that presents actual cash receipts and cash payments.

EBITDA   Earnings before interest, taxes, depreciation, and amortization.

Free cash flow   Cash provided by operating activities less replacement capital expenditures. It is designed to measure cash available to the firm for discretionary uses after all required cash payments have been made.

Funds   Working capital.

Funds from operations (FFO)   Defined by the National Association of Real Estate Investment Trusts as net income or loss excluding gains or losses from debt restructuring and sales of property, plus depreciation and amortization of real estate assets.

Gross profit margin   The percentage of each revenue dollar remaining after all direct and indirect costs of producing a company's product or service have been covered. Calculated as gross profit divided by revenue.

Indirect-method format cash flow statement   A format for the operating section of the cash flow statement that presents the derivation of cash flow provided by operating activities from net income. The format starts with net income and adjusts for all noncash expenses and changes in working capital accounts.

Inventory days   The average period over which inventory is carried before it is sold. Calculated by dividing inventory by cost of goods sold per day.

Life cycle   A series of stages over which a company progresses during its lifetime. Net income and operating cash flow have certain characteristic relationships as a company progresses through the normal four stages of its life cycle: start-up, growth, maturity, and decline.

Noncash investing and financing activities Investing and financing activities of an enterprise during a period that affect recognized assets or liabilities but that do not result in cash receipts or cash payments.

Operating cycle The total number of days over which inventory is carried plus the number of days required to convert resulting accounts receivable to cash.

Operating efficiency A measure of a company's effectiveness in managing its current assets, in particular, its accounts receivable, inventory, and accounts payable.

Operating profit margin The percentage of each sales dollar remaining after all normal operating costs, such as cost of goods sold, research and development, and selling, general and administrative expenses, have been covered. Calculated as gross profit margin less SGA% and less research and development as a percent of revenue.

Sales per day The average dollar amount of sales per day. Calculated by dividing total sales by 365.

Selling, general and administrative expense percentage (SGA%) The percentage of each revenue dollar consumed by selling, general and administrative expenses. Calculated as selling, general and administrative expense divided by revenue.

Working capital Current assets less current liabilities

Working capital provided by operations Increases in working capital as a result of operating as opposed to investing or financing activities. Calculated as net income less the effects of any nonoperating gains and losses and any revenue and expenses that affect noncurrent assets and liabilities.

NOTES

1. Ambi, Inc., annual report, June 1998. Information obtained from Disclosure, Inc. *Compact D/SEC: Corporate Information on Public Companies Filing with the SEC* (Bethesda, MD: Disclosure, Inc. March 1999).

2. Trizec Hahn Holdings, Ltd., annual report December 1997. Information obtained from Disclosure, Inc. *Compact D/SEC: Corporate Information on Public Companies Filing with the SEC* (Bethesda, MD: Disclosure, Inc. March 1999).

3. Statement of Financial Accounting Concepts (SFAS) No. 1, "Objectives of Financial Reporting by Business Enterprises" (Stamford, CT: Financial Accounting Standards Board, November 1978), para. 37.

4. *Ibid.,* para. 43.

5. J. Rayburn, "The Association of Operating Cash Flow and Accruals with Security Returns," *Journal of Accounting Research* (Supplement 1986), pp. 112–133. Note that accruals are the accounting adjustments that result in differences between earnings and operating cash flow. Thus, earnings can be viewed as consisting of two components, operating cash flow and accounting adjustments.

6. G. Wilson, "The Relative Information Content of Accruals and Cash Flows: Combined Evidence at the Earnings Announcement and Annual Report Release Date," *Journal of Accounting Research* (Supplement 1986), pp. 165–200.

7. C. Cheng, C. Liu, and T. Schaefer, "The Value-Relevance of SFAS No. 95 Cash Flows from Operations as Assessed by Security Market Effects," *Accounting Horizons* (September 1997), pp. 1–15.

8. SFAS No. 95, "Statement of Cash Flows" (Stamford, CT: Financial Accounting Standards Board, November 1987).

9. *Ibid.,* para. 32.

10. Prab, Inc., annual report, October 1998, p. 22.

11. Refer to J. Largay and C. Stickney, "Cash Flows, Ratio Analysis, and the W. T. Grant Company Bankruptcy," *Financial Analysts' Journal* (July/August 1980), pp. 51–54.

12. Technically, adjustments are made for operating-related working capital accounts only. Thus, an increase in a short-term investment or a decrease in a short-term borrowing would not be subtracted from working capital provided by operating activities in computing cash provided by operating activities.

13. R. Bowen, D. Burgstahler, and L. Daley, "The Incremental Information Content of Accrual Versus Cash Flows," *The Accounting Review* (October 1987), pp. 723–747.

14. A. Ali, "The Incremental Information Content of Earnings, Working Capital from Operations, and Cash Flows," *Journal of Accounting Research* (Spring 1994), pp. 61–74.

15. BRE Properties, Inc., annual report, December 1997, p. 14.

16. *Ibid.*

17. *The Value Line Investment Survey,* "Ratings and Reports" (New York, NY: Value Line Publishing, Inc., April 1999).

18. *The Wall Street Journal* (April 14, 1999), p. A4.

19. ConAgra, Inc., annual report, May 1998, p. 3.

20. Microsoft Corporation, annual report, June 1998. Information obtained from Disclosure, Inc. *Compact D/SEC: Corporate Information on Public Companies Filing with the SEC* (Bethesda, MD: Disclosure, Inc., March 1999).

21. Insight Enterprises, Inc., annual report, December 1997. Information obtained from Disclosure, Inc. *Compact D/SEC: Corporate Information on Public Companies Filing with the SEC* (Bethesda, MD: Disclosure, Inc., March 1999).

22. *The Wall Street Journal* (April 12, 1999), p. C20.

23. Amazon.com, Inc., annual report, December 1997. Information obtained from Disclosure, Inc. *Compact D/SEC: Corporate Information on Public Companies Filing with the SEC* (Bethesda, MD: Disclosure, Inc., March 1999).

24. Gateway 2000, Inc., Form 10K Annual Report to the Securities and Exchange Commission (December 1998), pp. 20–22. Net income growth for 1998 was calculated after removing the effects of nonrecurring expenses from the results for 1997.

Company Index

General Electric Company, 1–3, 71, 489, 492, 493, 508–511, 548, 551
General Electric Company Specialty Insurance, 413
General Electric Credit Corporation, 2
General Motors Acceptance Corporation, 4
General Motors Corporation, 3–4, 45, 401–402, 527–529
Georgia Gulf Corporation, 270, 272–273
Gerber Scientific, Inc., 187, 188, 194, 212, 223–224
Giant Cement Holdings, Inc., 531
Gibson Greetings, Inc., 43, 254
Gleason Corporation, 46, 114, 116, 148, 187
Global Internet.Com, 391
Global Internet Software Group, 391
Gloucester County Bankshares, Inc., 383–384
Golden Books Family Entertainment, Inc., 145
Goodyear Tire and Rubber Company, 293, 295–296, 309
The Gorman-Rupp Company, 148
Gottschalks, Inc., 188
Go-Video, Inc., 439
GPA Group, PLC, 453, 455
Graco, Inc., 148, 493
Granite Construction, Inc., 129
Granite Construction Company, 128
Great Lakes Aviation, Ltd., 470
Green Street Financial Corporation, 355
Greyhound Lines, Inc., 471
Gull Laboratories, Inc., 463
Gundle Environmental Systems, Inc., 124, 126
Gundle SLT Environmental, Inc., 127
Guy F. Atkinson Company, 128, 129

H

H. B. Fuller Company, 531
H. J. Heinz Company, 42, 187, 309, 320–324
Halliburton Company, 128, 129
Handy and Harman, 56–58, 148
Hasbro, Inc., 118, 531
Hawaiian Airlines, Inc., 120, 439
Healthdyne Technologies, Inc., 393
Henry Schein, Inc., 326
Hercules, Inc., 89, 103, 109
Herman Miller, Inc., 36, 38–40
The Hertz Corporation, 211
Holly Corporation, 188
Homestake Mining Company, 57, 64–65, 70
Horizon CMS Healthcare Corporation, 41
Hovnanian Enterprises, Inc., 164
Hudson's Grill of America, Inc., 463

Hughes Christensen, 95
Huntway Refining Company, 158

I

IBM Corporation, *See* International Business Machines Corporation
IBM Credit Corporation, 457–461
Illinois Tool Works, Inc., 117, 118, 463, 528–530, 548, 552
Imperial Holly Corporation, 43
Importer, Inc., 293–294, 304–306
Infinium Software, Inc., 116
Insight Enterprises, Inc., 587, 590
Integrated Circuit Systems, Inc., 42
Intel Corporation, 7, 344
Interlake Corporation, 7, 43–45, 49–50
Interlinq Software Corporation, 42
International Business Machines Corporation (IBM), 3, 4, 457, 463
International Lease Finance Corporation, 453, 455
International Thunderbird Gaming Corporation, 43
Intime Systems International, Inc., 471
IPO Financial Network, 587
ITC DeltaCom, Inc., 415, 417
ITC Holding, Inc., 415, 417
iTurf, Inc., 587
IVC Industries, Inc., 470
IVI Publishing, Inc., 42

J

J&L Specialty Steel, Inc., 7–8
Johns Manville Corporation, 187
Johnson and Johnson, 309
Johnson Controls, Inc., 128, 129
Johnston Industries, Inc., 116

K

Kaman Corporation, 124
Kasler Holding Company, 128
Kasler Holdings Company, 129
Kaye Group, Inc., 337, 346
Kellwood Company, 41, 220, 221
KeyCorp., 48
Keystone Consolidated Industries, Inc., 512, 523
Kroger, 136
Kronos, Inc., 463
KTM Process Equipment, Inc., 92

Subject Index